Texts in Computer Science

Series Editors

Orit Hazzan (iD), Faculty of Education in Technology and Science, Technion—Israel Institute of Technology, Haifa, Israel

Frank Maurer, Department of Computer Science, University of Calgary, Calgary, Canada

Titles in this series now included in the Thomson Reuters Book Citation Index!

'Texts in Computer Science' (TCS) delivers high-quality instructional content for undergraduates and graduates in all areas of computing and information science, including core theoretical/foundational as well as advanced applied topics. TCS books should be reasonably self-contained and aim to provide students with modern and clear accounts of topics ranging across the computing curriculum. As a result, the books are ideal for semester courses or for individual self-study in cases where people need to expand their knowledge. All texts are authored by established experts in their fields, reviewed internally and by the series editors, and provide numerous examples, problems, and other pedagogical tools; many contain fully worked solutions.

The TCS series is comprised of high-quality, self-contained books that have broad and comprehensive coverage and are generally in hardback format and sometimes contain color. For undergraduate textbooks that are likely to be more brief and modular in their approach, Springer offers the flexibly designed *Undergraduate Topics in Computer Science* series, to which we refer potential authors.

Adis Alihodžić

Exploring Computational Geometry

Theory and Python Implementations

 Springer

Adis Alihodžić (iD)
Department of Mathematics and Computer
Science
University of Sarajevo
Sarajevo, Bosnia and Herzegovina

ISSN 1868-0941   ISSN 1868-095X (electronic)
Texts in Computer Science
ISBN 978-3-032-06392-2   ISBN 978-3-032-06393-9 (eBook)
https://doi.org/10.1007/978-3-032-06393-9

This Springer imprint is published by the registered company Springer Nature Switzerland AG
The registered company address is: Gewerbestrasse 11, 6330 Cham, Switzerland

If disposing of this product, please recycle the paper.

Contents

Preface

Computational Geometry emerged in the late 1970s as a distinct field within algorithm design and analysis, and today it stands as a pivotal research area in theoretical computing and applied sciences. A solid understanding of computational geometry is essential for efficiently solving geometric problems across various application domains. Its significance is underscored by numerous scientific journals, conferences, and an active research community. Beyond the mathematical elegance of its problems and the efficiency of algorithmic solutions, the rapid advancement of this field has been driven by its broad applicability in modern technologies. Geometric algorithms now play a crucial role in computer graphics, shape recognition, optimization and neural networks, generative artificial intelligence, geographic information systems (GIS), robotics, and autonomous systems like drones. They are also integral to medical image analysis, computer vision, bioinformatics, 3D modeling, simulations of physical phenomena, and the optimization of complex networks and systems. Furthermore, computational geometry finds extensive application in various transportation sectors, enabling efficient planning and analysis of object movements in space. In road transportation, it is used for route optimization considering obstacles, traffic flows, and terrain topography. In air transportation, it ensures precise monitoring of aircraft and drone flights, optimization of air corridors, and collision avoidance through real-time data processing algorithms. Similarly, in maritime transportation, it aids in tracking ships on the open sea, analyzing optimal routes considering weather conditions and ocean currents, and detecting potential collisions. These problems often involve methods such as Voronoi diagrams, shortest path algorithms, and geometric overlap, making computational geometry a key tool for enhancing safety and efficiency in transportation systems.

Initially, solutions to many geometric problems were too complex or inefficient for practical application, but recent algorithmic approaches have significantly improved and simplified previous methods. This textbook aims to bring contemporary solutions from computational geometry to a broader audience, providing a clear and systematic introduction to fundamental concepts and algorithms. While primarily written as a textbook for a university course in computational geometry, it can also serve as a valuable resource for self-study and research.

This textbook is the result of years of lectures and exercises conducted by the author for third- and fourth-year students at the Department of Mathematics and Computer Science, Faculty of Natural Sciences and Mathematics, University of Sarajevo. It is primarily intended for students of the Faculty of Natural Sciences and Mathematics and the Faculty of Electrical Engineering, as well as students from other faculties who wish to learn more about geometric algorithms and their applications, and for anyone interested in the topics covered. The structure of the textbook comprises twelve chapters, each (except the first) beginning with a problem arising from an application of computational geometry. This problem is then transformed into a purely geometric one and solved using computational geometry techniques. Each chapter from the third onward presents several smaller projects, most of which are thoroughly explained and implemented. For many geometric problems addressed, multiple different approaches are presented. Furthermore, for most problems, after their description, complete Python implementations are provided. At the end of each chapter, readers are offered a set of exercises for independent work. The textbook covers techniques such as divide and conquer, plane sweep methodology, and randomized algorithms. The goal of the textbook is to spark interest not only among researchers in the field of algorithms but also among professionals from various disciplines, especially in artificial intelligence, as computational geometry and artificial intelligence are complementary fields whose advancements often contribute to innovations in both areas.

The first chapter lays the foundation for understanding and implementing geometric and algorithmic concepts by introducing a comprehensive set of core programming structures and algorithms in Python. It begins by exploring the principles of object-oriented design, including object creation, method invocation, and operator overloading, followed by an overview of Python's module organization, indentation rules, and use of the main function for structuring programs. Additionally, essential design patterns and idiomatic Python constructs are presented to support clean and reusable code development. A critical part of the chapter addresses computational complexity, beginning with a discussion of how computer architecture and memory hierarchy affect algorithm performance. This is followed by an introduction to asymptotic analysis, including time complexity notations and their practical interpretation in the context of Python list operations and algorithmic execution. The second half of the chapter delves into fundamental data structures and recursive programming techniques. The concept of recursion is thoroughly examined through the lens of memory management, with special emphasis on the interaction between the call stack and the heap. Several recursive examples illustrate how Python handles function scopes and recursive calls, including visualizations of call stacks and the role of state during execution. The chapter proceeds to cover ordered and associative collections, including lists, stacks, queues, sets, and hash maps, alongside their associated algorithms such as sorting, memoization, and dynamic lookup. Both one-dimensional and two-dimensional linked structures are introduced to model more complex data representations. The final sections are dedicated to tree-based data structures, starting from binary search trees and progressing to balanced trees, with a particular focus on AVL trees and their role in maintaining search efficiency. Throughout the chapter, numerous examples and Python implementations are provided to demonstrate the practical use and performance of each structure. These implementations are designed not only to clarify the theoretical content but also to serve as robust components for advanced algorithmic solutions developed in later chapters.

The second chapter of the textbook deals with geometric objects, their representations in the plane and space, and basic techniques for their processing. For each geometric object, an appropriate Python class is implemented, equipped with methods that enable efficient management and manipulation of these objects. Within these classes, methods utilizing robust algorithms for working with key geometric entities, including vectors, points, vertices, segments, polygons, and triangles, are developed. Special attention is given to operations such as intersection testing between objects, as well as analyses and transformations in two-dimensional and three-dimensional space. To aid understanding, concrete examples illustrating the practical application of classes and their methods are presented. This chapter lays the foundation for working with geometric objects in computational geometry and provides a crucial basis for advanced techniques covered in later chapters. At the end of the chapter, exercises for independent work help readers gain practical experience through the implementation and testing of the presented concepts.

The third chapter addresses topics related to the intersection and union of geometric objects, forming the foundation of computational geometry. Various problems associated with the intersection of geometric objects, including segments, rectangles, and polygons, are considered, along with efficient algorithms that provide precise and rapid solutions. The analysis begins with the problem of segment intersection, starting from a simple yet inefficient naive approach, gradually progressing to more advanced algorithms that significantly enhance performance. Furthermore, more complex problems, such as the intersection of segments with rectangles, clipping of convex and concave polygons, as well as intersections of convex polygons and half-planes, are examined. Additionally, special attention is given to the problem of the union of rectangles, which has broad applications in various domains, including graphical modeling, geometric data processing, and computing. For each of the considered problems, robust algorithms ensuring efficient solutions are presented, accompanied by concrete examples that facilitate understanding of the methods and their applications. To ensure the mathematical validity of the approaches, necessary definitions are introduced, and certain lemmas are formulated and proven for each geometric problem, providing a solid mathematical foundation. All algorithms are implemented in Python, enabling their practical application and experimentation on concrete data. The chapter concludes with exercises for independent work, offering readers the opportunity to test their acquired knowledge through the implementation and analysis of algorithms.

The fourth chapter of the textbook focuses on algorithms for determining the convex hull, which play a crucial role in computational geometry, particularly in space optimization and working with geometric objects. Various algorithms enabling the computation of the convex hull for a set of points in two-dimensional and three-dimensional space are considered, with particular attention to their efficiency and practical application. These algorithms find wide application in areas such as computing, robotics, and geographic information systems. Before implementing the algorithms, the necessary mathematical theory, including definitions, lemmas, and theorems, is introduced, ensuring a solid foundation for each described algorithm. The analysis begins with the two-dimensional case, starting from simple polygons, then progressing to algorithms for determining the convex hull in 2D space. Various methods are considered, from basic approaches to more advanced and efficient algorithms, including Graham's algorithm, Andrew's algorithm, incremental algorithm, Quickhull algorithm, Mergehull algorithm, Chan's algorithm, as well as the Akl-Toussaint heuristic. In addition to detailed descriptions of each algorithm, their advantages, disadvantages, and specific challenges, such as execution time optimization and handling degenerate cases encountered in practice, are analyzed. After addressing the two-dimensional case, the theory extends to determining the convex hull in three-dimensional space. Initially, Platonic solids are presented as basic geometric objects in space, followed by a transition to algorithms for determining the 3D convex hull. The introduction of an additional dimension significantly increases complexity compared to the 2D version of the problem, requiring more sophisticated algorithms and efficient optimization techniques. Each algorithm is thoroughly analyzed in terms of implementation, efficiency, and application in real scenarios, with particular emphasis on optimization for working in 3D space. All algorithms are implemented in Python, enabling practical testing and experimentation with different data sets. Implementations not only facilitate understanding of the presented techniques but also allow their direct application, especially in the analysis of complex 3D structures. The chapter concludes with exercises for independent work.

The fifth chapter is dedicated to the triangulation of simple polygons in the plane, one of the key topics in computational geometry with numerous applications in graphical modeling, data analysis, robotics, and other fields. The chapter is structured into several sections covering various methods and algorithms for triangulation, with particular emphasis on the specific challenges of working with monotone polygons. The introductory part examines the basic properties of simple polygons, followed by an analysis of different algorithms for their triangulation. Special attention is given to the naive algorithm, the ear clipping algorithm, the recursive approach, and the efficient plane sweep method. These algorithms provide fast and precise solutions for triangulation problems in practical scenarios. In addition to the fundamental methods, specific problems such as the art gallery problem are also explored, with particular attention given to Steve Fisk's proof that establishes the minimal upper bound for triangulation. To provide readers with a deeper understanding, the necessary mathematical theory is introduced before the algorithm implementations, including definitions, lemmas, and theorems, thereby ensuring a solid theoretical foundation for each described algorithm. All algorithms are implemented in Python, allowing readers to practically observe and test their results. At the end of the chapter, exercises for independent study offer an opportunity for deeper exploration and application of the techniques learned.

The sixth chapter focuses on Delaunay triangulation, one of the key techniques in computational geometry, especially for generating triangulations in spaces with dense point sets and complex structures. This triangulation has wide applications in data analysis, robotics, geographic information systems, and many other fields. The chapter is structured into several sections covering both theoretical foundations and practical applications of Delaunay triangulation. It starts with the triangulation of planar point sets and continues with angle-optimal triangulations, including methods based on edge flipping. Special attention is given to the properties of Delaunay triangulation and its efficient computation through various algorithms, such as the edge-flipping algorithm and the incremental algorithm. These algorithms are implemented in Python, enabling immediate practical application and experimentation. Before the implementations, the necessary mathematical theory is introduced to ensure a solid theoretical basis for each algorithm. In addition to the theoretical overview, the chapter includes exercises for independent study, offering readers the chance to explore and implement Delaunay triangulation in practice.

The seventh chapter is dedicated to the study of Voronoi diagrams, a fundamental tool in computational geometry with applications in robotics, geographic information systems, data analysis, simulations, and many other domains. These diagrams provide an efficient way to partition space into regions, each corresponding to the nearest point in a given set. The chapter is organized into several sections that cover the basic definitions and properties of Voronoi diagrams, as well as algorithms for their construction. Various approaches are examined, including the naive algorithm, the recursive algorithm, the incremental algorithm, and the plane sweep algorithm, along with an analysis of the corresponding data structures that facilitate their efficient implementation. The naive algorithm is presented with a Python implementation, while Fortune's algorithm is described in detail, supplemented by a simulation of its execution. Special attention is given to the connection between Voronoi diagrams and Delaunay triangulation, as well as their relationship to the 3D convex hull. The chapter concludes by discussing the practical application of Voronoi diagrams in UAV path planning. In addition to the theoretical and practical overview, the chapter includes exercises for independent study, providing readers with an opportunity to explore Voronoi diagrams, their inverses, and a wide range of applications.

The chapter eight focuses on algorithms for visualizing 3D objects, which play a key role in their representation and processing in computer graphics. These algorithms enable efficient rendering of objects in space, including transformations, perspective projections, shading, and various methods for constructing and managing scenes. The chapter covers a broad range of visualization techniques, from basic transformation matrices to advanced methods such as the Z-buffer algorithm and modified painter's algorithms. Furthermore, BSP trees are discussed in detail, both in two-dimensional and three-dimensional spaces, as efficient data structures for optimizing the visualization of complex scenes. The core algorithms for constructing and applying BSP trees in computer graphics are presented. All algorithms are implemented in Python, allowing readers to observe the outcomes of their execution in practice. At the end of the chapter, exercises for independent study offer an opportunity for deeper exploration and a better understanding of the material.

The ninth chapter focuses on algorithmic techniques for spatial data exploration and geometric range searching, addressing both theoretical foundations and practical implementations across one, two, and higher-dimensional spaces. It begins with one-dimensional range queries and systematically extends to two-dimensional and multidimensional spatial searches. A series of six core algorithms are presented and implemented in Python, including a naive method, the projection method, the grid-based method, and several approaches based on binary trees and their generalizations. These methods are thoroughly analyzed, with particular attention given to their design, performance characteristics, and adaptability to complex spatial structures. The chapter also explores the inherent challenges of high-dimensional search, such as the curse of dimensionality, and introduces heuristic strategies like adaptive splitting to improve efficiency. For each algorithm, graphical visualizations are provided to illustrate how spatial queries are processed and to enhance intuitive understanding. Furthermore, a detailed comparative analysis is conducted, measuring algorithm performance in relation to the number of data points and execution time. This empirical evaluation offers valuable insight into the scalability and practical applicability of each method. The chapter concludes with a set of exercises designed to deepen the reader's understanding and encourage hands-on experimentation with the presented algorithms.

The tenth chapter explores the application of quadtree data structures in geometric modeling, mesh generation, and real-time spatial analysis. It begins with a conceptual overview of quadrant trees, emphasizing their hierarchical structure and utility in adaptive spatial decomposition. A key focus is placed on geometric modeling and finite element analysis (FEA) of thermal behavior in printed circuit boards (PCBs), demonstrating how uniform and non-uniform meshes can be effectively generated using quadtree-based subdivision. The chapter details the construction of quadtree structures, followed by a step-by-step implementation of corresponding algorithms in Python. A significant part of the chapter is devoted to a real-world application: real-time collision detection in drone swarms. Drones are modeled as point entities navigating in a 2D plane, and a quadtree-based algorithm is introduced to efficiently detect and prevent collisions during their movement. The Python implementation of this system is accompanied by a real-time simulation, visually demonstrating how the algorithm dynamically updates and identifies potential collisions. Additionally, multiple algorithms for quadtree construction and collision detection are implemented and analyzed. Their performance is compared in terms of execution time and data scale, providing a comprehensive understanding of their practical efficiency. The chapter concludes with a series of exercises, allowing readers to experiment with quadtree algorithms, implement their own variants, and explore further applications in computational geometry and spatial analysis.

The eleventh chapter focuses on one of the central topics in computational geometry and robotics—robot motion planning. It introduces the foundational concept of configuration spaces, which provides a formal framework for modeling the movement of robots through environments with obstacles. The initial sections develop the theoretical basis by analyzing motion planning for a point robot, followed by the formulation of the shortest path problem. To bridge theory and implementation, the chapter presents a naive algorithm for finding shortest paths with cubic time complexity, which serves as a stepping stone for understanding algorithmic limitations and motivates the need for more sophisticated methods. This is followed by an in-depth treatment of robot motion planning for polygonal robots, including a rigorous derivation of the Minkowski sum technique for transforming obstacles into configuration space obstacles. The chapter includes formal mathematical proofs that underpin the correctness and efficiency of the presented algorithms. In addition, complete Python implementations are provided to demonstrate practical aspects of robot path planning in both point and polygonal models. Through these implementations, readers gain hands-on experience in translating geometric reasoning into algorithmic procedures. To consolidate understanding, the chapter concludes with a set of exercises aimed at reinforcing both the theoretical and practical components, enabling readers to explore and extend robot motion planning techniques in computational environments.

The twelfth and final chapter explores the intersection of artificial intelligence (AI) and computational geometry, showcasing how intelligent methods can enhance geometric reasoning across diverse domains. The chapter is structured into several thematic sections, each focusing on specific application areas where

AI techniques integrate with geometric algorithms to address real-world challenges. The opening section is devoted to coverage optimization, examining problems such as camera and sensor placement in polygonal environments and leveraging swarm intelligence for optimizing geometric triangulations. Additionally, coverage path planning is presented as a practical solution for systematic exploration of spatial domains. In the field of image processing, the chapter discusses advanced techniques such as fractal compression, shape-based object detection, and morphological operations—each of which relies on the geometric properties of structuring elements and spatial relationships within images. The section on geographic information systems (GIS) highlights AI-driven solutions to spatial problems, including crop mapping, spatial clustering, polygonal map generalization, and terrain modeling, all of which benefit from geometric abstraction and efficient representation. In the domain of bioinformatics, the chapter illustrates how geometric modeling supports critical tasks such as molecular docking, protein surface representation, and sequence alignment, bridging the gap between spatial geometry and biological function. The final section addresses core AI topics in geometric contexts, including motion planning, pathfinding, and obstacle avoidance, as well as learning-based geometric reconstruction and classification algorithms for geometric objects. These subsections emphasize the synergy between traditional geometry and modern machine learning techniques. Through a carefully curated set of illustrative figures and an extensive collection of relevant references, the chapter highlights how AI techniques can be harnessed to address complex geometric problems in adaptive, data-driven, and scalable ways—emphasizing the increasing importance of artificial intelligence in the advancement of computational geometry.

Code Availability. All Python source codes developed for this book are organized by chapters and are publicly available on GitHub at: https://github.com/adis-alihodzic/exploring-computational-geometry.

Finally, I extend my sincere gratitude to all those who contributed in any way to bringing this textbook to life and making it available to students and other readers. I am particularly grateful to the reviewers, who thoroughly and thoughtfully reviewed the manuscript, providing numerous valuable comments, suggestions, and recommendations, significantly enhancing the clarity, precision, and completeness of specific sections of the text. Lastly, I owe my deepest gratitude to my family for their unwavering support, patience, and endless understanding throughout the long process of writing this textbook.

2025.

Author

List of Symbols

$d(A)$	depth of node A in a binary tree
$h(A)$	height of node A in a binary tree
$T(n)$	time complexity of an algorithm for an input of size n
$S(n)$	space complexity of an algorithm for an input of size n
$\mathcal{O}(1)$	constant time complexity of an algorithm
$\mathcal{O}(f(n))$	asymptotic upper bound (worst-case scenario)
$\Omega(f(n))$	asymptotic lower bound (best-case scenario)
$\Theta(f(n))$	tight asymptotic complexity (both upper and lower bounds)
$\emptyset$	empty set
$\mathbb{N}$	set of natural numbers $\{1, 2, 3, \dots\}$
$\mathbb{R}$	set of real numbers
$\mathbb{R}^+$	set of positive real numbers
$\mathbb{C}$	set of complex numbers
$A \subseteq B$	set A is a subset of set B
$A = B$	set A is equal to set B
$A \cup B$	union of sets A and B
$A \cap B$	intersection of sets A and B
$A \setminus B$	difference of sets A and B
$A \times B$	Cartesian product of sets A and B
A^n	n-th Cartesian power of set A
$\mathbb{R}^n$	n-dimensional real vector space
S_n	set of all permutations of the set $\{1, 2, \dots, n\}$
$\binom{n}{k}$	binomial coefficient
$\lvert x \rvert$	absolute value of the number $x \in \mathbb{R}$ or $x \in \mathbb{C}$
$\lceil x \rceil$	smallest integer greater than or equal to x
$n_1 \ll n_2$	n_1 is strictly less than n_2
$\lfloor x \rfloor$	largest integer less than or equal to x
$a \in A$	element a belongs to the set A
(a, b)	open interval of real numbers $x \in \mathbb{R}$ such that $a < x < b$
$[a, b]$	set of real numbers between a and b, including both a and b
$\tau(p)$	truth value of the proposition p

$\forall$	universal quantifier
$\forall(x)P(x)$	statement: "For all x, property P holds"
$\exists$	existential quantifier
$\exists(x)P(x)$	statement: "There exists an x such that P holds"
$\neg$	negation of a proposition ($\neg p$ is the negation of p)
$\wedge$	conjunction of propositions ($p \wedge q$ is the conjunction of p and q)
$\vee$	disjunction of propositions ($p \vee q$ is the disjunction of p and q)
$\Rightarrow$	implication of propositions ($p \Rightarrow q$ means p implies q)
$\Leftrightarrow$	equivalence of propositions p and q, i.e., $p \Leftrightarrow q$
$O_1 \leftarrow O_2$	object O_2 is assigned the object O_1
C_n	the n-th Catalan number, representing the total number of triangulations of a convex polygon
$\sum_{i=1}^{n} a_i$	sum of the elements in a finite series
$f : A \mapsto B$	function f from set A to set B
$f_1 \circ f_2$	composition of the function f_1 with the function f_2
$M_1 \circ M_2$	composition of matrices M_1 and M_2
$M_{x,\alpha}$	rotation matrix M by angle α around the x-axis
$M_{y,\beta}$	rotation matrix M by angle β around the y-axis
$M_{z,\gamma}$	rotation matrix M by angle γ around the z-axis
M_p	view matrix that transforms world coordinates into camera coordinates
$\vec{i}, \vec{j}, \vec{k}$	unit orthonormal vectors in $\mathbb{R}^3$
$\overrightarrow{OA}$	position vector from point O to point A
$\vec{0}$	zero vector
$\angle(\vec{a}, \vec{b})$	angle between vectors $\vec{a}$ and $\vec{b}$
$\vec{a} \cdot \vec{b}$	dot product of vectors $\vec{a}$ and $\vec{b}$
$\vec{a} \times \vec{b}$	cross product of vectors $\vec{a}$ and $\vec{b}$
$(\vec{a} \times \vec{b}) \cdot \vec{c}$	scalar triple product of vectors $\vec{a}$, $\vec{b}$, and $\vec{c}$
$\vec{a} \perp \vec{b}$	vector $\vec{a}$ is orthogonal to vector $\vec{b}$, i.e., $\vec{a} \cdot \vec{b} = 0$
$\|\cdot\|_2$	L^2-norm, i.e., standard Euclidean norm
$\|\vec{a}\|_2$	L^2-norm of vector $\vec{a}$
$G = (V, E)$	graph G consisting of a set of vertices V and a set of edges E
$F(G)$	set of faces (regions) of graph $G = (V, E)$
$d(v)$	degree of vertex v in graph $G = (V, E)$
V_-	adjacent vertex of vertex V obtained by traversing the polygon in the clockwise direction
V_+	adjacent vertex of vertex V obtained by traversing the polygon in the counterclockwise direction
$dist(P_1, P_2)$	Euclidean distance between points P_1 and P_2
$P_1 = P_2$	points $P_1(x_1, y_1)$ and $P_2(x_2, y_2)$ coincide, i.e., $x_1 = x_2 \wedge y_1 = y_2$
$\overline{P_1 P_2}$	line segment defined by points P_1 and P_2, where P_1 is the starting point and P_2 is the ending point
$B(P_1, P_2)$	bisector (axis of symmetry) of the segment $\overline{P_1 P_2}$
$H(P_1, P_2)$	open half-plane containing point P_1 but excluding point P_2
(P_1, P_2)	ordered pair (P_1, P_2) representing a directed segment, with P_1 and P_2 as endpoints
$\{P_1, P_2\}$	undirected segment defined by points P_1 and P_2, which are its endpoints
$|P_1 P_2|$	length of the segment $\overline{P_1 P_2}$ between points P_1 and P_2

$\overrightarrow{P_1P_2}$	vector from point P_1 to point P_2
$l(t)$	parametric equation of the line l passing through points P_1 and P_2
$p_1 \parallel p_2$	lines p_1 and p_2 are parallel
$d_1 \cong d_2$	segment d_1 is congruent to segment d_2
$p_1 = p_2$	lines p_1 and p_2 are coincident
$p_1 \cap p_2$	set of points belonging to both lines p_1 and p_2
$p_1 \cap p_2 = \emptyset$	lines p_1 and p_2 do not intersect
$p_1 \cap p_2 = \{Q\}$	lines p_1 and p_2 intersect at point Q
$\triangle P_1P_2P_3$	triangle with vertices P_1, P_2, and P_3
$\pi(\mathbb{T})$	plane π defined by triangle $\mathbb{T}$
$I(\mathbb{T})$	triangulation indicator
$P(\triangle P_1P_2P_3)$	area of the triangle $\mathscr{A}(\triangle P_1P_2P_3)$
$P_4 \in \triangle P_1P_2P_3$	point P_4 lies on the sides or inside the triangle $\triangle P_1P_2P_3$
$\mathbb{T}_1 \sim \mathbb{T}_2$	similarity relation between triangles $\mathbb{T}_1$ and $\mathbb{T}_2$
$\mathbb{T}_1 \cong \mathbb{T}_2$	congruence of triangles $\mathbb{T}_1$ and $\mathbb{T}_2$
$k_1 \cong k_2$	congruence of circles k_1 and k_2
k_t	circle over a segment whose endpoints are defined by a parametric equation in terms of t
$\mathscr{C}(A,B)$	family of circles passing through points A and B
$\square P_1P_2P_3P_4$	quadrilateral with vertices P_1, P_2, P_3, P_4
$\triangleright P_1P_2P_3P_4$	tetrahedron with vertices P_1, P_2, P_3, P_4
$\mathscr{P}$	set of points $\{P_1, P_2, P_3, \dots\}$ in the plane or space
$\|\mathscr{P}\|$	number of points in set $\mathscr{P}$, i.e., its cardinality
$\mathscr{A}(\mathscr{P})$	area of a simple polygon $\mathscr{P}$
$\partial\mathscr{P}$	polygonal chain (or closed path) of polygon $\mathscr{P}$
$\oint_{\mathscr{C}}$	line integral along a simple closed curve $\mathscr{C}$
$\iint_D$	double integral over the region $\mathscr{D}$ bounded by curve $\mathscr{C}$
$P \in \mathscr{P}$	point P lies on the sides or inside polygon $\mathscr{P}$
$P \notin \mathscr{P}$	point P does not lie on the sides or inside polygon $\mathscr{P}$
$\mathscr{P} \cap \mathscr{Q}$	intersection of polygons $\mathscr{P}$ and $\mathscr{Q}$
$\mathscr{P} \cup \mathscr{Q}$	union of polygons $\mathscr{P}$ and $\mathscr{Q}$
$\mathscr{P} \subseteq \mathscr{Q}$	polygon $\mathscr{P}$ is a subset of polygon $\mathscr{Q}$
$CH(\mathscr{P})$	convex hull of the set $\mathscr{P}$
$\mathscr{H}_i$	convex hull constructed in the i-th step
$\mathscr{P}_i$	polygon obtained by decomposing the previous polygon $\mathscr{P}_{i-1}$
$Vor(\mathscr{P})$	Voronoi diagram of the set $\mathscr{P}$
$V(P_k)$	Voronoi cell of site P_k
l^-	half-plane containing Voronoi sites located on the right side of the sweep line l
I_A	intensity of ambiently reflected light from an object
I_D	intensity of diffuse reflection
I_S	intensity of specular reflection from an object (according to the Phong model)
h^+	positive half-space in d-dimensional space
h^-	negative half-space in d-dimensional space

List of Algorithms

List of Implementations

List of Figures

List of Tables

About the Author

Adis Alihodžić is a Full Professor at the Department of Mathematics and Computer Science, Faculty of Natural Sciences and Mathematics, University of Sarajevo, where he teaches courses in computational geometry, image processing, neural networks, machine learning, databases, programming, and computer systems. He earned his Bachelor's degree in 2006 with a thesis on *"Fortune's Algorithm for Voronoi Diagram Construction"*, his Master's degree in 2011 with a thesis on *"Reconstruction of Multidimensional Images from Projections Using Integral Transforms with Applications in Medicine"*, and his PhD in Computer Science in 2016 with a dissertation on *"Improving the Bat Algorithm Metaheuristic for Constrained Optimization Problems"*.

Throughout his career, he has taught at all levels of study and has served as a lecturer and mentor in doctoral programs. He is the author and co-author of several textbooks, covering topics such as dynamic web systems, computability theory, statistics, computational geometry, machine learning, and databases.

His research interests include artificial intelligence, machine learning, optimization problems, metaheuristics, computational geometry, digital image processing, object recognition, algorithms, and data structures. He has published over 70 scientific papers in international journals and conference proceedings, including publications in the *Lecture Notes in Computer Science*, *Studies in Computational Intelligence*, and IEEE conference series.

He is a member of editorial boards and serves as a reviewer for several international scientific journals. He actively participates in international projects (COST Actions) and has supervised numerous Master's and PhD theses. His digital skills cover a wide range of programming languages, tools, algorithms, and information technologies.

More information is available at: https://osoblje.pmf.unsa.ba/alihodzic-adis/

1. Core Structures and Algorithms

In computational problem solving, operations on abstract object types are defined by *abstract data types* (ADTs), while their concrete representations in memory are realized through *data structures*. For instance, a list exemplifies an ADT that supports operations such as access, insertion, and deletion, independent of how these elements are physically stored. In Python, a high-level programming language, this separation is formalized through built-in structures such as lists, sets, dictionaries, stacks, and queues. These structures abstract away low-level concerns such as memory management and reference manipulation, thereby allowing developers to focus on algorithmic design and modularity. This chapter uses Python to introduce and implement foundational data structures and algorithms that serve as the basis for solving a wide range of geometric problems. Beginning with the fundamental principles of object behavior and program structure, progressing through recursion, computational complexity, and ordered collections, the chapter culminates in advanced topics such as hash tables, balanced search trees (e.g., AVL trees), and their applications in computational geometry—most notably in constructing geometric structures like Voronoi diagrams. Understanding the design and application of ADTs in Python enables a high-level, modular perspective on algorithms, while maintaining the flexibility to adapt implementations for specific problem domains. Conceptually, a data structure is defined by three interrelated components:

- abstract operations that manipulate data objects,
- storage mechanisms for representing those objects in memory,
- concrete implementations of each operation tailored to the chosen storage model.

This distinction between abstract specification and physical implementation—known as *data abstraction*—is essential in algorithm design. By focusing on the behavior of operations rather than low-level details, modular, reusable, and maintainable solutions are achieved. Moreover, the choice of data structure directly influences an algorithm's efficiency, scalability, and clarity. As this book demonstrates, mastery of these structures is essential for implementing robust solutions in computational geometry and beyond.

1.1 Object Behavior and Program Structure in Python

To understand how Python programs are organized and how objects behave within them, it is essential to revisit core principles of programming structure and object-oriented design. This chapter introduces key syntactic and semantic elements of Python, including object creation, method invocation, operator overloading, modularization, and code block structuring through indentation. Python's simplicity and dynamic nature make it well suited for modeling object behavior, while its module system and indentation

A. Alihodžić, *Exploring Computational Geometry*, Texts in Computer Science,
https://doi.org/10.1007/978-3-032-06393-9_1

rules support clean and maintainable program architecture. Throughout this chapter, examples illustrate how these foundational concepts contribute to writing robust, reusable, and readable code.

1.1.1 Creating Objects

Python is an object-oriented language in which all data elements are objects. Each object is defined by its type, or *class*, with the terms *type* and *class* being used interchangeably. Built-in types such as int, float, str, list, and dict serve as fundamental building blocks for data representation. Objects can be created either via *literal values* or by invoking a type constructor on existing data. For instance, writing x = 6 creates an int object with value 6 and assigns it to the reference x. Similarly, calling int('6') or float('3.2') constructs numeric objects from string representations. Literals such as 42, 3.14, "hello", [], or 'a': 1 provide concise syntax for common values. Non-literal creation enables transformation and composition, e.g., converting strings to numbers or decomposing strings into lists. This mechanism generalizes as variable = type(existing_data). Understanding how objects are instantiated—either from literals or through constructors—is essential for working effectively with Python's data model.

1.1.2 Invoking Methods on Objects

In Python, objects encapsulate both data and behavior. Methods define how an object responds to operations and are classified as either *accessor* or *mutator* methods. Accessor methods retrieve information without modifying the object, while mutator methods alter the object's internal state. Consider the following example of an accessor method:

```
temperature = "cold"
forecast = temperature.replace("cold", "warm")
print(forecast)   # Output: warm
```

The original string remains unchanged, demonstrating immutability. In contrast, mutator methods modify objects in place:

```
numbers = [30, 10, 20]
numbers.sort()
print(numbers)   # Output: [10, 20, 30]
```

Here, *sort*() alters the state of the list object directly. Immutable types such as str, int, and float support only accessors, while mutable types like list and dict offer both kinds of methods. Object-oriented programming centers around defining *classes*—templates that encapsulate attributes and behaviors. Each class includes a constructor method __init__() used to initialize object instances. Consider the following class:

```
class Book:
    def __init__(self, title, author):
        self.title = title
        self.author = author
    def info(self):
        return f"{self.title} by {self.author}"
    def rename(self, new_title):
        self.title = new_title
```

Creating and interacting with instances:

```
b1 = Book("Geometry for Programmers", "Adis Alihodzic")
print(b1.info()) # Accessor
b1.rename("Geometric Algorithms")   # Mutator
print(b1.info())
```

The keyword `self` refers to the current instance and must appear as the first parameter of every instance method. Python automatically passes this reference when methods are invoked. Understanding how to design and invoke methods is fundamental for modeling data-rich systems and building modular, reusable code.

Table 1.1: Common special methods for operator overloading in Python

Method Definition	Operator	Description
`__add__(self, y)`	`x + y`	Adds two objects; the type of x determines the method invoked.
`__sub__(self, y)`	`x - y`	Computes the difference between two objects.
`__mul__(self, y)`	`x * y`	Returns the product of two objects.
`__mod__(self, y)`	`x % y`	Computes the remainder of x divided by y.
`__eq__(self, y)`	`x == y`	Returns True if x and y are equal.
`__ne__(self, y)`	`x != y`	Returns True if x and y are not equal.
`__lt__(self, y)`	`x < y`	Returns True if x is less than y.
`__le__(self, y)`	`x <= y`	Returns True if x is less than or equal to y.
`__gt__(self, y)`	`x > y`	Returns True if x is greater than y.
`__ge__(self, y)`	`x >= y`	Returns True if x is greater than or equal to y.
`__contains__(self, y)`	`y in x`	Tests whether y is an element of collection x.
`__getitem__(self, y)`	`x[y]`	Retrieves the element at index y from x.
`__setitem__(self, i, y)`	`x[i] = y`	Sets the element at index i in x to y.
`__len__(self)`	`len(x)`	Returns the number of elements in x.
`__iter__(self)`	`for v in x`	Returns an iterator over x.
`__int__(self)`	`int(x)`	Converts x to an integer.
`__hash__(self)`	`hash(x)`	Returns a hash value for x.
`__neg__(self)`	`-x`	Returns the unary negation of x.
`__repr__(self)`	`repr(x)`	Returns a developer-friendly string representation of x.
`__str__(self)`	`str(x)`	Returns a user-friendly string representation of x.

1.1.3 Overloading of Operators

Operator overloading in Python enables custom classes to support standard operators (e.g., $+, -, ==$) in a natural and intuitive way. This is achieved by implementing special methods—often called *magic methods*—whose names begin and end with double underscores. For instance, the + operator is mapped to the `__add__()` method. By defining this method in a user-defined class, objects of that class can be combined using + syntax. Consider the following example:

```python
class Book:
    def __init__(self, title, pages):
        self.title = title
        self.pages = pages
    def __add__(self, other):
        return Book(f"{self.title} & {other.title}", self.pages + other.pages)
    def __str__(self):
        return f"'{self.title}' ({self.pages} pages)"
```

Now we can combine books in a meaningful way:

```python
b1=Book("Geometry", 120)
b2=Book("Topology", 100)
b3=b1+b2
print(b3)   # Output: 'Geometry & Topology' (220 pages)
```

This mechanism extends to operators like `__eq__`, `__lt__`, and `__str__`, enabling intuitive comparisons and representations. While `__str__` provides user-friendly output, `__repr__` yields an unambiguous, evaluable string. Table 1.1 lists essential special methods that support operator overloading and enhance integration with Python's native syntax.

1.1.4   Program Structure: Modules, Indentation, Main Function

Python promotes modular design by allowing code to be organized into reusable components called modules. To access external functionality, one imports a module using either the selective or fully qualified syntax. For example:

```python
import math
area=math.pi * (2 ** 2)
```

This approach maintains namespace isolation, ensuring that local identifiers do not conflict with those from imported modules. Alternatively, importing all names into the global namespace `from math import *` can lead to name collisions and is generally discouraged in larger applications. Indentation in Python is not stylistic—it defines block structure. Consistent indentation delineates the body of control statements and functions:

```python
def greet(name):
    if name: print("Hello,", name)
```

All statements with the same indentation level belong to the same logical block. Misaligned indentation results in a syntax error. Most modern IDEs support block-based indentation editing to ease this process. Python programs often begin execution in a designated entry point—a `main()` function—called conditionally via:

```python
def main():
    print("Running core logic...")
    if name == "main": main()
```

This idiom ensures that the main logic executes only when the file is run directly, not when imported as a module. It promotes reusable design and separates program execution from module definition.

1.1.5   Design Patterns and Practical Extensions in Python

A container class encapsulates a collection of objects and provides controlled access to them. Instead of using a built-in list, we may define a class that mimics list behavior while offering domain-specific enhancements. For instance:

```python
class CommandList:
    def __init__(self):
        self._commands = []

    def add(self, command):
        self._commands.append(command)

    def __iter__(self):
        return iter(self._commands)
```

This design allows structured accumulation and iteration of command objects, such as drawing operations or transformations. Polymorphism allows objects of different types to be treated uniformly through shared interfaces. Consider multiple drawing commands, each implementing a render() method:

```
1 class DrawLine:
2     def render(self, canvas):
3         canvas.draw_line()
4
5 class DrawCircle:
6     def render(self, canvas):
7         canvas.draw_circle()
```

The client code can invoke command.render(canvas) regardless of the specific command type, improving extensibility and modularity. This pattern initializes a variable before a loop and updates it iteratively. It is often used for aggregation. Such idioms promote code clarity and are central to many data-processing routines. For example, summing the areas of multiple shapes:

```
1 total_area = 0
2 for shape in shapes:
3     total_area += shape.area()
```

Graphical interfaces in Python are commonly implemented using the tkinter module. GUI applications are event-driven, reacting to user input via buttons, menus, or mouse events. The example below initializes a simple window with a label and a button:

```
1 import tkinter as tk
2
3 def greet():
4     print("Hello world!")
5
6 root = tk.Tk()
7 tk.Label(root, text="Welcome").pack()
8 tk.Button(root, text="Greet", command=greet).pack()
9 root.mainloop()
```

Widgets are arranged using layout managers such as pack(), grid(), or place(), while user interactions are handled through event-driven callbacks. In more sophisticated applications, developers often extend the Frame class to encapsulate interface logic and compose multiple interactive components. This modular design paradigm—combining custom containers, polymorphism, programming idioms, and graphical interfaces—highlights the expressive capacity of Python for constructing both algorithmic solutions and responsive user-driven systems.

1.2 Computational Complexity

Key principles of computational efficiency are introduced in this section. Fundamental aspects of computer architecture are examined to provide an understanding of the cost of basic operations. With this knowledge, algorithmic performance can be assessed, runtime behavior can be estimated, and informed design choices can be made when writing performance-sensitive code.

1.2.1 Computer Architecture and Memory Access

A computer consists of a Central Processing Unit (CPU), memory (RAM), and I/O devices such as a keyboard, screen, and disk. When a program is run, it is loaded from a storage device into RAM, while the CPU executes instructions by reading data from RAM, performing operations (e.g., addition or comparison), and writing results back to RAM. The CPU itself has limited internal memory (registers) for temporary values. For example, when computing a sum:

```
1 a = 5
2 b = 3
3 c = a + b
```

the values a and b are loaded into registers, the addition is performed, and the result is stored in RAM. It is important to highlight here that unlike a post office where finding a box takes time, RAM allows constant-time access: retrieving a value at any memory address takes the same time regardless of position. An analogy: if each memory location is a person listening for their name, the CPU can call a name and instantly receive the corresponding value. Modern computers use word-based access: on a 64-bit system, a word is 8 bytes, enabling efficient bulk memory operations.

1.2.2 Accessing Elements in Python Lists

Python lists are implemented as arrays of contiguous memory locations. Accessing or modifying an element at any index is a constant-time operation, independent of list size. This hypothesis can be tested using a simple experiment:

```
1 import random, time
2 size=10**9
3 L=[0]*size
4 start=time.perf_counter()
5 for _ in range(10000):
6     idx = random.randint(0, size-1)
7     L[idx]=random.randint(0, 100)
8 end=time.perf_counter()
9 print("Average access time:", (end - start)/10000) # 1.0870099999010564e-06
```

Results confirm that access time remains stable across different list positions and sizes, supporting the constant-time model of memory access.

1.2.3 Time Complexity Notation

In computer science, we analyze how algorithms behave as input size n grows. For example, accessing an element in a Python list—implemented as a contiguous array—takes constant time, regardless of n. This property, called *constant-time access*, is denoted by the Big-Oh notation $\mathcal{O}(1)$. More formally, a function $f(n)$ is said to be $O(g(n))$ if there exist constants $d > 0$ and $n_0 \geq 0$ such that:

$$0 \leq f(n) \leq d \cdot g(n) \quad \text{for all} \quad n \geq n_0.$$

For example, if list access time never exceeds $100\mu s$, we can write $f(n) = \mathcal{O}(1)$. Let's illustrate this with a Python experiment that confirms list access time is independent of position:

```
1 import time
2 pixels = [0] * 10**9 # Simulate an image with 10^9 black pixels (0)
3 # Measure time to update 10,000 specific pixel positions
4 indices = [i * 100 for i in range(10000000)]  # Predefined positions
5 start = time.perf_counter()
6 for idx in indices:
7     pixels[idx] = 255  # Change pixel color to white
8 end = time.perf_counter()
9 print("Average update time:", (end-start)/len(indices)) #5.136648999759927e-08
```

This example simulates updating pixel colors in a list (representing an image), a common task in graphics applications. The use of fixed indices, rather than fully random values, emphasizes that neither the order nor the size of the list affects the average access time—access to any element remains $\mathcal{O}(1)$. While many operations, such as arithmetic (+, -,*, /) and comparisons, are $\mathcal{O}(1)$, others depend on n. For instance, naive sorting algorithms like Bubble Sort exhibit quadratic growth, $\mathcal{O}(n^2)$, while more efficient approaches, like Merge Sort, achieve $\mathcal{O}(n\log n)$ complexity. In practical terms, inefficient code can lead to severe performance issues. Consider a file system scanner that reads directory entries: using an $\mathcal{O}(n^2)$ algorithm, scanning 100,000 files could take hours. Optimizing the algorithm to $\mathcal{O}(n\log n)$ might reduce this to seconds. When designing algorithms, we aim for the lowest possible complexity, balancing theoretical bounds with practical performance. The table 1.2 summarizes common complexities. Understanding complexity is essential for efficient algorithm design, especially when working with large datasets. In the next sections, we will explore how Python optimizes certain operations, such as the list append method, achieving $O(1)$ amortized performance.

Table 1.2: Common Complexity Classes

Complexity	Example
$\mathcal{O}(1)$	Accessing an element in a list
$\mathcal{O}(\log n)$	Binary search in a sorted list
$\mathcal{O}(n)$	Linear search, summing a list
$\mathcal{O}(n\log n)$	Merge Sort, efficient sorting
$\mathcal{O}(n^2)$	Bubble Sort, naive comparisons
$\mathcal{O}(c^n)$	Exhaustive search in combinatorial problems

1.2.4 Asymptotic Analysis and Notation

To evaluate the efficiency of algorithms, we use asymptotic notation—a formal framework for describing growth rates as input size n increases. These relationships are illustrated in Fig. 1.1, where the growth of common complexity classes is depicted. Constant-time operations are shown as flat curves, while exponential-time operations exhibit rapid growth. Three key notations are used:

- **Big-Oh** ($\mathcal{O}$): An *upper bound* on growth. For instance, accessing an element in a list is $O(1)$.
- **Omega** (Ω): A *lower bound*. For example, checking if a point lies inside a convex polygon requires at least $\Omega(\log n)$ operations if the polygon is convex (see Chapter 4).
- **Theta** (Θ): A *tight bound*, when both upper and lower bounds match. For instance, computing the convex hull of n points has $\Theta(n\log n)$ complexity, as is the case when using the Graham Scan algorithm (see Chapter 4).

Formally, the corresponding complexity classes are defined as follows:

$$\mathcal{O}(g(n)) = \{f(n)\,|\,\exists d > 0, n_0 \geq 0,\ \text{s.t.}\ f(n) \leq d \cdot g(n)\ \text{for all}\ n \geq n_0\}$$
$$\Omega(g(n)) = \{f(n)\,|\,\exists c > 0, n_0 \geq 0,\ \text{s.t.}\ f(n) \geq c \cdot g(n)\ \text{for all}\ n \geq n_0\}$$
$$\Theta(g(n)) = \{f(n)\,|\,\exists c, d > 0, n_0 \geq 0,\ \text{s.t.}\ cg(n) \leq f(n) \leq dg(n)\ \text{for all}\ n \geq n_0\}$$

Amortized complexity is an analytical framework used to describe the *average* cost per operation over a sequence of operations, particularly in cases where occasional operations are more expensive but the majority are cheaper. This approach enables a more precise understanding of performance in scenarios where individual operations may vary in cost, yet the overall cost is evenly distributed across the entire sequence. Some operations, like appending to a list, exhibit *amortized* $\mathcal{O}(1)$ time. For example:

```
L = []
for i in range(10**6):
    L.append(i)  # Amortized O(1) per append
```

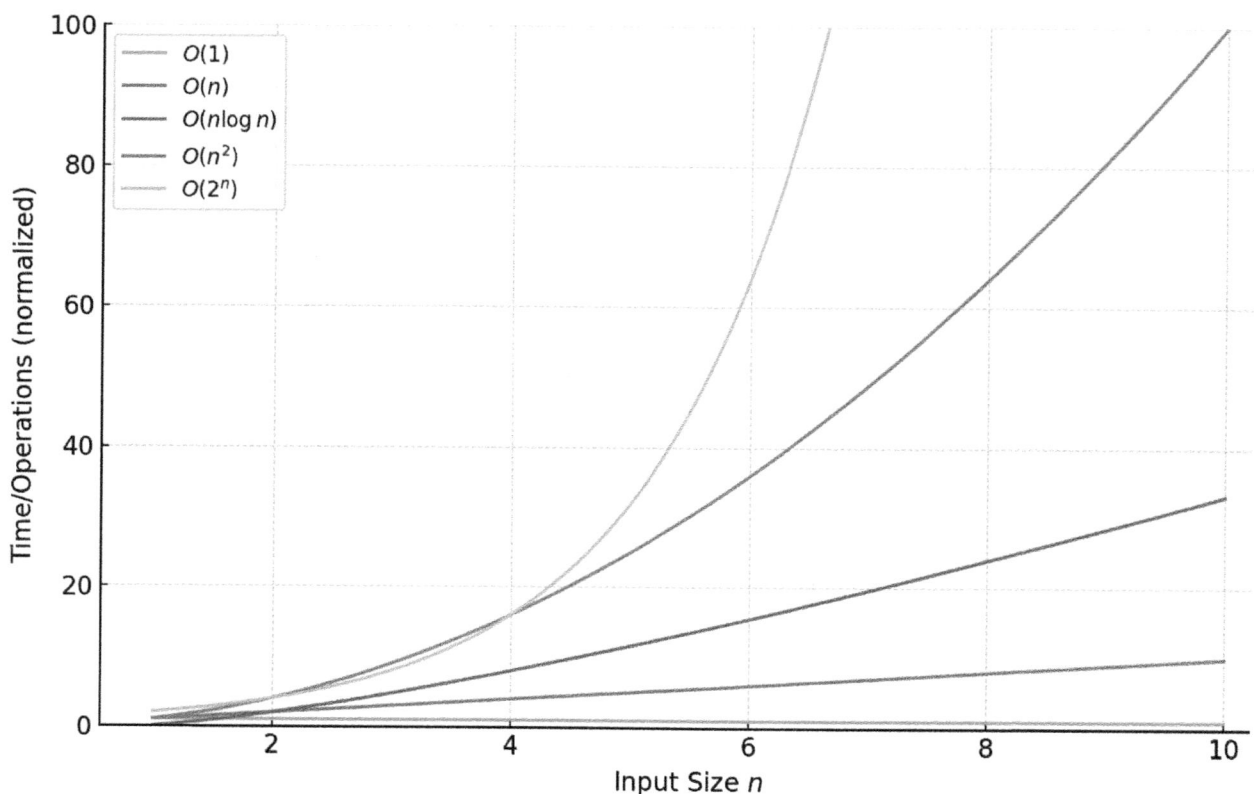

Figure 1.1: Asymptotic growth of common complexity classes.

Though occasional resizings occur (with $\mathcal{O}(n)$ cost), the average time per append remains constant, achieved via doubling the underlying array size. While in some cases it would be possible to use either Big-Oh ($\mathcal{O}$) or Omega (Ω) notation, the table below employs Theta (Θ) notation for clarity and precision, as the exact asymptotic bounds (both upper and lower) are known for the listed examples.

Table 1.3: Common Complexity Classes and Examples

Complexity	Example
$\Theta(1)$	Accessing an element in a list
$\Theta(\log n)$	Binary search in a sorted array
$\Theta(n)$	Linear search or point-in-polygon test (Brute force)
$\Theta(n \log n)$	Convex hull computation (e.g., Graham Scan)
$\Theta(n^2)$	Checking all segment pairs for intersection
$\Theta(2^n)$	Enumerating all subsets of a set

A deep understanding of these notations is essential for designing algorithms that are both correct and efficient in the context of computational geometry and beyond.

1.3 Recursive Function Calls and Scopes in Python

Recursion is a fundamental concept in functional programming, where a function is defined in terms of itself. Unlike imperative programming, which relies on loops and mutable state, recursion provides a declarative approach to problem-solving by expressing solutions in terms of simpler subproblems. For instance, consider the computation of a factorial:

```
1 def factorial(n):
2     if n==0: return 1
3     return n*factorial(n-1)
```

Here, the *factorial* function calls itself with a smaller argument until a base case is reached. Recursion eliminates the need for explicit for or while loops, promoting a more abstract style of reasoning.

1.3.1 Scopes and Memory Management

Understanding recursion requires a solid grasp of *scope* and memory management in Python. Scope defines the region of a program where an identifier is accessible, while memory management determines how data is stored and retrieved during program execution. In Python, the resolution of identifiers follows a well-defined, hierarchical system known as the **LEGB rule**:

- **Local Scope**: The innermost scope, created within a function or method, where variables are defined as local to that specific call.
- **Enclosing Scope**: The scope of the immediately enclosing function, relevant in the context of nested functions.
- **Global Scope**: The module-level scope, where variables defined outside any function are stored.
- **Built-in Scope**: The outermost scope, containing Python's predefined identifiers and functions such as int, len, and sum.

When an identifier is referenced, Python resolves it by searching through scopes in the following order: **Local → Enclosing → Global → Built-in**. This hierarchical lookup ensures that the innermost and most relevant definition is selected. The code snippet below demonstrates this scope resolution mechanism in the context of nested functions:

```
1 PI = 3.14   # Global Scope
2 def area(radius):   # Enclosing Scope
3     def square(x):   # Local Scope within square
4         return x * x
5     return PI*square(radius)
6
7 print(area(5)) # Local scope of 'radius' within area
```

In the example above, the call to square searches for x in the local scope of square, for radius in the enclosing scope of area, and for PI in the global scope. The square function is an example of a closure that captures variables from its enclosing environment. This layered approach allows for clear modularization but also introduces potential pitfalls. For example, a variable defined in a local scope may shadow a variable with the same name from an enclosing or global scope, leading to unintended behavior. The following code snippet demonstrates exactly that:

```
1 value = 10   # Global
2 def outer():
3     value = 5   # Enclosing
4     def inner():
5         value = 2   # Local
6         return value
7     return inner()
8
9 print(outer())   # Outputs 2
10 print(value)     # Outputs 10
```

A deep understanding of the **LEGB** model is crucial for writing correct recursive functions and for managing variables in complex programs. When writing recursive algorithms, careful use of scope avoids name conflicts, unintended shadowing, and subtle bugs. When an identifier is referenced, Python resolves it by searching the scopes in the LEGB order. For instance, if we call square within area, Python first looks in the local scope of square, then in the enclosing scope of area, and so on. Careful management of variable names is crucial. If a variable is redefined in a local scope, it may shadow variables from outer scopes, potentially leading to errors. For example:

```
1 x = 10   # Global
2 def foo():
3     x = 5   # Local (shadows global x)
4     return x
5
6 print(foo())   # 5
7 print(x)       # 10
```

Understanding recursion and scope is essential for writing clear and correct Python programs, especially in computational geometry, where recursive algorithms—such as the incremental algorithm for Delaunay triangulation (see Chapter 6)—play a fundamental role within the divide-and-conquer paradigm.

1.3.2 The Role of the Stack and Heap in Recursive Algorithms

Understanding memory management is essential for mastering recursion and function calls in Python. The Python runtime environment organizes memory into two key regions (see Fig. 1.2 (a)):

- **Run-Time Stack**: Manages function calls. Each time a function is invoked, an *activation record* (or stack frame) is pushed onto the stack, storing the function's local variables and parameters. When the function returns, its activation record is popped from the stack.

- **Heap**: A dynamically allocated memory area that stores objects such as lists, dictionaries, and user-defined instances. The stack holds references to these objects, but the actual data resides in the heap.

The separation of memory into distinct regions enables efficient function execution and dynamic data management. Consider the following recursive function for computing the factorial of a number:

```
1 def factorial(n):
2     if n==0: return 1
3     return n*factorial(n-1)
4
5 result=factorial(4)   # The stack grows with each recursive call
```

During the execution of factorial(4), the stack holds activation records for each call—factorial(4), factorial(3), factorial(2), and so on. Each record stores its own local variable n, which is removed (popped) from the stack once the function returns, freeing memory. Objects created during function calls, such as lists or custom objects, are stored in the heap. The stack holds references to these objects, but the actual data resides in the heap. The following code snippet demonstrates this:

```
1 def build_list(n):
2     L = [i for i in range(n)]   # L is a reference; the list is in the heap
3     return L
4
5 data = build_list(1000)
```

Here, L is a local variable stored in the stack, while the actual list of 1000 elements is stored in the heap. Once build_list returns, the reference L is removed, but the list remains in memory, accessible via data.

This interaction between the run-time stack and the heap is fundamental to recursive calls: each recursion level generates a new activation record in the stack, while objects (e.g., lists or geometric structures) are stored in the heap. Figure 1.2 (a) visually illustrates this relationship, showing how activation records on the stack point to objects in the heap. A clear understanding of this model is crucial for writing efficient recursive programs. In the next section, we explore recursive function design, emphasizing the importance of base cases, termination conditions, and recursive problem-solving patterns.

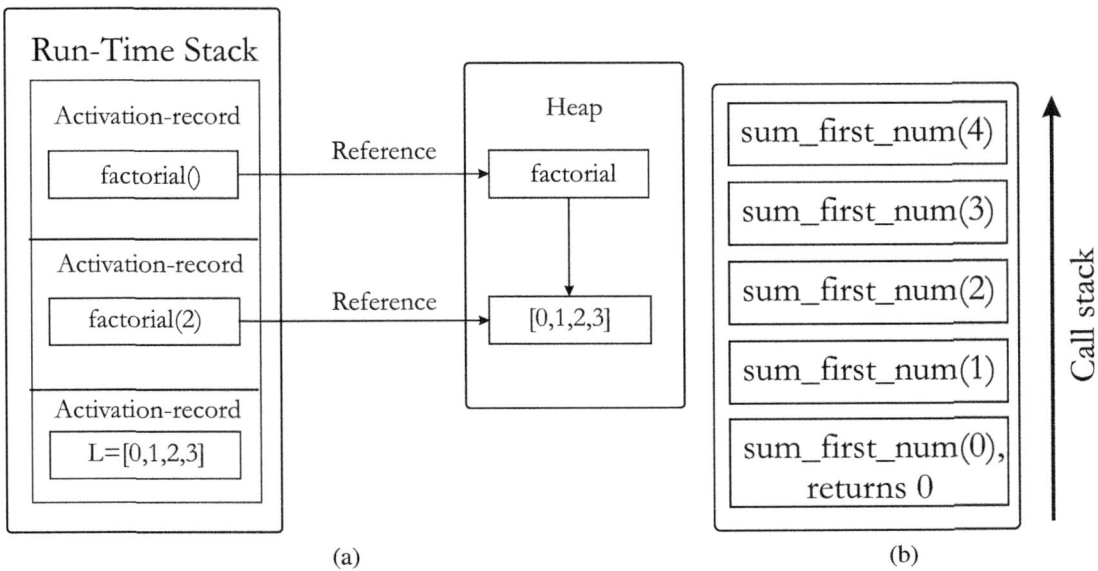

(a)   (b)

Figure 1.2: (a) Run-time stack and heap interaction in Python: Activation records store references; objects reside in the heap. (b) Growth and shrinking of the recursive call stack for sum_first_n(4).

1.3.3 Understanding Recursive Call Stacks

As previously noted, a thorough understanding of recursive call stacks is fundamental to comprehending both their structure and execution flow. Each recursive call generates a new *activation record* on the run-time stack, which stores local variables and parameters specific to that call. As recursion unwinds, activation records are systematically removed (popped) from the stack, enabling correct memory management and ensuring that resources are released appropriately. Consider the following recursive function that computes the sum of the first *n* natural numbers:

```python
def sum_first_n(n):
    if n==0: return 0
    return n+sum_first_n(n-1)

result=sum_first_n(4)   # Recursive calls: n=4,3,2,1,0
```

The execution proceeds as follows:

- sum_first_n(4) calls sum_first_n(3),
- sum_first_n(3) calls sum_first_n(2),
- sum_first_n(2) calls sum_first_n(1),
- sum_first_n(1) calls sum_first_n(0), which hits the base case and returns 0.

Each call has its own copy of n, stored in the corresponding activation record on the stack. As functions return, activation records are removed, and results propagate back up the call chain, culminating in `result = 10`. A visual representation of this process is provided in Fig. 1.2 (b), illustrating the growth and shrinking of the stack during recursion, while objects such as lists and intermediate results reside in the heap. Each activation record corresponds to a distinct function invocation, holding its own local variables. As recursion unwinds, the stack shrinks, returning results back to previous calls.

Recursive functions elegantly handle problems like reversing lists or strings by breaking them into smaller subproblems. In each call, a new activation record is pushed onto the run-time stack, while the list object remains in the heap. For strings, a similar recursive approach can be applied by modifying the base case and the concatenation operation. This recursive approach is particularly important in solving complex problems, such as computing the minimum-weight triangulation of a set of points, which belongs to the class of NP-hard problems. The following code snippet demonstrates how recursive list reversal can be easily implemented:

```python
def reverse_list(lst):
    if not lst: return []
    return [lst[-1]]+reverse_list(lst[:-1])

print(reverse_list([1,2,3,4])) # Output: [4,3,2,1]
```

Recursive algorithms extend beyond simple examples and are crucial for designing efficient solutions especially in computational geometry. Each recursive call creates a distinct scope with its own local variables, while the depth of recursion depends on the problem size and the base case. The run-time stack manages control flow and local variables, while the heap holds persistent objects like lists, strings, and user-defined instances. Python's *type reflection* further enhances recursive solutions by enabling generic handling of multiple data types. For instance, the following example illustrates how a single recursive function can reverse both lists and strings by checking the type of the input:

```python
def reverse(seq):
    if not seq: return seq
    if isinstance(seq, str): return seq[-1] + reverse(seq[:-1])
    else: return [seq[-1]] + reverse(seq[:-1])

print(reverse([1, 2, 3]))   # Output: [3, 2, 1]
print(reverse("abc"))       # Output: "cba"
```

The function *reverse*(·) can be elegantly rewritten without an explicit calling of the function *is_instance*(·,·) by leveraging type reflection and dynamically creating an empty element of the same type:

```python
def reverse(seq):
    if not seq: return seq
    return seq[-1:] + reverse(seq[:-1])
```

A solid understanding of recursion, scope, and memory management is essential for writing correct and efficient algorithms, especially in computational geometry, where divide-and-conquer strategies like Convex hull computation (see Chapter 4) and Delaunay triangulation (see Chapter 6) heavily rely on recursion.

1.4 **Ordered Collections**

Large volumes of information are efficiently processed by computers through repetitive application of operations to similar data. To manage such tasks effectively, data must be organized into structured collections that allow systematic traversal and manipulation. In this section, various techniques for structuring data into ordered collections enabling controlled access and modification—are presented. Intuitive manipulation of sequences is facilitated by Python's operator overloading capabilities, while the chosen organizational structure directly affects the computational complexity of operations. Fundamental *abstract data types* (ADTs), including lists, stacks, queues, and linked structures, are introduced, laying the groundwork for advanced data management strategies.

1.4.1 **Lists and Their Operations**

Lists are fundamental structures in Python, implemented internally as dynamically sized arrays, akin to C-style arrays. This array-based representation allows for *random access* to elements in constant time, $\mathscr{O}(1)$, because the memory layout guarantees that each element occupies a fixed-size slot, and its address can be computed directly by an offset from the base address. Consequently, operations like retrieving or setting an element by index are efficient and predictable, regardless of list size. However, some operations on lists, such as insertion or deletion at arbitrary positions, require shifting elements to maintain the contiguous layout of the array. For example, inserting an element at the start of the list requires moving all subsequent elements one position to the right, resulting in $\mathscr{O}(n)$ complexity in the worst case, where n is the number of elements after the insertion point. This trade-off highlights the importance of understanding both the *underlying representation* of data structures and the *asymptotic behavior* of their operations.

Python's list operations are intuitive and expressive, primarily due to operator overloading and a rich set of built-in methods. The time complexity of these operations is summarized as follows:

- Accessing an element in the list L by index 5: `L[5]` $\rightarrow \mathscr{O}(1)$.
- Modifying an element of the list L by index 2: `L[2] = 7` $\rightarrow \mathscr{O}(1)$.
- Appending an element at the end of the list L: `L.append(5)` $\rightarrow$ amortized $\mathscr{O}(1)$.
- Inserting the element 3 at an arbitrary position in the list L: `L.insert(3, 'x')` $\rightarrow \mathscr{O}(n)$.
- Deleting an element: `del L[4]` or `L.pop(4)` $\rightarrow \mathscr{O}(n)$.
- Iterating through the list L: `for x in L` $\rightarrow \mathscr{O}(n)$.

The following code snippet demonstrates the creation and manipulation of a list representing student grades:

```
grades = [85, 90, 78, 92]
grades.append(88) # Append new grade: O(1)
grades[2] = 80 # Update grade: O(1)
grades.insert(1, 95) # Insert grade at position 1: O(n)
print(grades) # Output: [85, 95, 90, 80, 92, 88]
```

A solid understanding of the time complexity of list operations is considered fundamental for the design of efficient algorithms, particularly in domains such as computational geometry, artificial intelligence, and machine learning. Lists in Python are implemented as dynamic arrays, which accounts for the fact that certain operations, such as appending elements at the end, exhibit an amortized time complexity of $\mathscr{O}(1)$, while inserting elements at arbitrary positions typically incurs a time complexity of $\mathscr{O}(n)$. Awareness of these trade-offs is regarded as crucial when working with large datasets or designing algorithms that depend on list manipulations. In the following sections, a custom `MyList` class is developed to demonstrate how internal design choices impact performance, memory usage, and algorithmic efficiency (see Listing

1.1). The MyList class serves as a simplified model of Python's built-in list, showcasing fundamental list operations and their associated time complexities.

Listing 1.1: Definition of the class **MyList**

```python
class MyList:
    def __init__(self,  contents=None, size=10):
        self.items = [None] * size # internal array
        self.num_items = 0 # the current number of elements stored
        self.size = size # the total allocated capacity of the array
        if contents:
            for item in contents: self.append(item)

    def __resize(self):
        new_size = self.size + max(1, self.size // 4)
        new_items = [None] * new_size
        for i in range(self.num_items): new_items[i] = self.items[i]
        self.items = new_items
        self.size = new_size

    def append(self, item):
        if self.num_items == self.size:
            self.__resize # Resize the internal array if full
        self.items[self.num_items] = item
        self.num_items += 1

    def insert(self, index, item):
        if self.num_items == self.size: self.__resize()
        if index<self.num_items:
            for i in range(self.num_items-1, index-1, -1):
                self.items[i+1]=self.items[i]
            self.items[index]=item
            self.num_items+=1
        else: self.append(item)

    def __delitem__(self, index):
        if index<self.num_items:
            for i in range(index, self.num_items-1):self.items[i]=self.items[i+1]
            self.num_items-=1
        else: raise IndexError("Index out of range")

    def __iter__(self): # linear search via the iterator
        for i in range(self.num_items): yield self.items[i]

    def __contains__(self, item): # binary search O(log n) if a list is sorted
        left, right = 0, self.num_items-1
        while left <= right:
            mid=(left+right)//2
            if self.items[mid]==item: return True
            elif self.items[mid]<item: left=mid+1
            else: right=mid-1
        return False

    def __add__(self, other):
        result = MyList(size=self.num_items + other.num_items)
        for i in range(self.num_items): result.append(self.items[i])
        for i in range(other.num_items): result.append(other.items[i])
        return result
```

```
54
55    def __eq__(self, other):
56        if type(other)!=type(self) or self.num_items!=other.num_items:return False
57        for i in range(self.num_items):
58            if self.items[i]!=other.items[i]: return False
59        return True
60
61    def __getitem__(self, index):
62        if 0 <= index < self.num_items: return self.items[index]
63        raise IndexError("Index out of range")
64
65    def __setitem__(self, index, value):
66        if 0 <= index < self.num_items: self.items[index] = value
67        else: raise IndexError("Index out of range")
68
69    def __len__(self): return self.num_items
70
71    def __repr__(self): # string representation
72        return f"MyList: ({[self.items[i] for i in range(self.num_items)]})"
```

The following code snippet demonstrates the usage of the `MyList` class:

```
1 list1 = MyList(['a', 'b', 'c', 'd', 'e', 'f'])
2 print("The length of list: ",len(list1))
3 list1.insert(5,'g')# ['a','b','c','d','e','g','f']
4 del list1[5]
5 list2 = MyList(['a1','b1','c1','d1','e1','f1'])
6 my_list=list1+list2
7 print(my_list.items) #['a','b','c','d','e','f','a1','b1','c1','d1','e1','f1']
8 print(my_list) # MyList: ['a','b','c','d','e','f','a1','b1','c1','d1','e1','f1']
```

Table 1.4: Time Complexities and Usage of `MyList` Methods

Operation	Complexity	Usage	Method
List creation	$\mathcal{O}(n)$ or $O(1)$	x = MyList(y)	__init__(y)
Indexed get	$\mathcal{O}(1)$	a = x[i]	x.__getitem__(i)
Indexed set	$\mathcal{O}(1)$	x[i] = a	x.__setitem(i,a)__
Concatenate	$\mathcal{O}(n)$	z = x+y	z=x.__add__(y)
Append	$\mathcal{O}(1)$ amortized	x.append(a)	x.append(a)
Insert	$\mathcal{O}(n)$	x.insert(i,e)	x.insert(i,e)
Delete	$\mathcal{O}(n)$	del x[i]	x.__delitem(i)__
Equality	$\mathcal{O}(n)$	x == y	x.__eq__(y)
Iterate	$\mathcal{O}(n)$	for a in x:	x.__iter__()
Length	$\mathcal{O}(1)$	len(x)	x.__len__()
Membership	$\mathcal{O}(n)$	a in x	x.__contains__(a)
Sort	$\mathcal{O}(n\log n)$	x.sort()	x.sort() (not implemented)

Based on the contents of Listing 1.1, Table 1.4 summarizes the time complexities, operation names, and corresponding method usage for the `MyList` class. Listing 1.1 demonstrates a simplified implementation of a dynamic array, mirroring the behavior of Python's built-in lists, which are implemented in C. The private method `__resize()` ensures that capacity is expanded by a proportional factor (typically 25%) when the array becomes full, thereby maintaining efficient performance for subsequent append operations. While an individual append may incur an $\mathcal{O}(n)$ cost due to resizing, the amortized complexity across a sequence of operations remains $\mathcal{O}(1)$, ensuring scalability under repeated insertions. Accessing or modifying an element by index is performed directly through the internal array, leveraging its random-access property and achieving $\mathcal{O}(1)$ complexity. In contrast, inserting or deleting an element at an arbitrary position requires shifting subsequent elements to preserve the contiguous structure, resulting in a worst-case time complexity of $\mathcal{O}(n)$. Concatenation involves constructing a new array containing elements from both lists, while equality testing compares corresponding elements in linear time. A solid understanding of these principles is critical when designing algorithms that rely on list manipulations, particularly in performance-sensitive applications such as sorting, searching, and implementing abstract data types like stacks, queues, and priority queues. The MyList implementation provides valuable insights into the internal mechanisms and trade-offs of dynamic array design, reinforcing the importance of algorithmic efficiency and data structure awareness.

1.4.2 Algorithms for Sorting Collections

Sorting algorithms are fundamental in computer science, providing a basis for efficient data organization and retrieval. Among the earliest and simplest methods is *Selection Sort*, which operates by repeatedly finding the minimum element in the unsorted portion of the list and placing it in its correct position. Although conceptually straightforward, Selection Sort has a time complexity of $\mathcal{O}(n^2)$, making it inefficient for large datasets. The core of Selection Sort is the select function:

```
def select(seq, start):
    min_index = start
    for j in range(start+1, len(seq)):
        if seq[j]<seq[min_index]: min_index = j
    return min_index
```

The sorting procedure swaps the selected minimum element into place:

```
def selection_sort(seq):
    for i in range(len(seq)-1):
        min_index=select(seq,i)
        seq[i],seq[min_index]=seq[min_index],seq[i]
```

While Selection Sort serves as a useful pedagogical example, it is not practical for real-world applications. More efficient algorithms like *Merge Sort* and *Quicksort* achieve $\mathcal{O}(n \log n)$ complexity by employing divide-and-conquer strategies. For instance, Merge Sort recursively divides the sequence, sorts each part, and then merges them:

```
def merge_sort(seq):
    if len(seq) > 1:
        mid = len(seq) // 2
        L, R = seq[:mid], seq[mid:]
        merge_sort(L); merge_sort(R)
        i = j = k = 0
        while i < len(L) and j < len(R):
            seq[k] = L[i] if L[i] < R[j] else R[j]
            if L[i] < R[j]: seq[k] = L[i]; i += 1
            else: seq[k] = R[j]; j += 1
            k += 1;
        seq[k:] = L[i:] + R[j:] # Merge L and R
```

Quicksort, the algorithm behind Python's `list.sort()` method, partitions the list around a pivot, recursively sorting the sublists. This method is favored in practice for its speed and in-place sorting:

```python
def quick_sort(seq):
    if len(seq) <= 1: return seq
    pivot = seq[0]
    less = [x for x in seq[1:] if x <= pivot]
    greater = [x for x in seq[1:] if x > pivot]
    return quick_sort(less) + [pivot] + quick_sort(greater)
```

The following code snippet illustrates how elements are sorted using the previously described algorithm:

```python
list1 = [100, -100, 0, 2, -4, 5, 10]
selection_sort(list1)
print(list1) #[-100, -4, 0, 2, 5, 10, 100]
list2 = ['a', 'A', 'c', 'D', 'd', 'e']
merge_sort(list2)
print(list2) # ['A', 'D', 'a', 'c', 'd', 'e']
list3= [100, 50, 40, 30, 20, 10, 5, 2, 1]
quick_sort(list3)
print(list3) # [1, 2, 5, 10, 20, 30, 40, 50, 100]
```

It is important to emphasize that the implemented sorting functions—*selection_sort*($\cdot$), *merge_sort*($\cdot$), and *quick_sort*($\cdot$)—can be used to sort elements of a custom list class, such as MyList. However, if the instances of this class store complex objects (e.g., instances of built-in or user-defined classes like MyObject), it is essential to define a comparison criterion by overloading or implementing the `__lt__` method. The following code snippet demonstrates this approach:

```python
class MyObject:
    def __init__(self, value): self.value = value
    def __lt__(self, other): return self.value < other.value
    def __repr__(self): return f"MyObject({self.value})"

list1 = MyList([MyObject(0), MyObject(2), MyObject(-3), MyObject(-10)])
selection_sort(list1)
print(list1) #[MyObject(-10), MyObject(-3), MyObject(0), MyObject(2)]
```

A solid understanding of the aforementioned algorithms, their time complexities, and their appropriate use cases is essential for writing efficient code across diverse domains, including computational geometry, artificial intelligence, and data science.

1.4.3 Linked Lists and Two-Dimensional Arrays

Efficient data structures play a pivotal role in representing and manipulating complex data in scientific computing. This section explores *linked lists*—a dynamic structure enabling efficient insertions and deletions—and *two-dimensional arrays*, a versatile format for storing matrix-like data. These foundational concepts are integral to a wide range of applications, including computational geometry, artificial intelligence, and data analysis.

Unlike lists, which are implemented as dynamic arrays, *linked lists* are linear data structures composed of nodes that store data elements and references (pointers) to other nodes in the sequence. A *singly linked list* maintains a reference only to the next node, supporting efficient insertions and deletions at the head of the list in $\mathcal{O}(1)$ time. In contrast, a *doubly linked list* maintains references to both the next and the previous nodes, enabling more flexible traversal and efficient insertions and deletions at both ends of the list (see

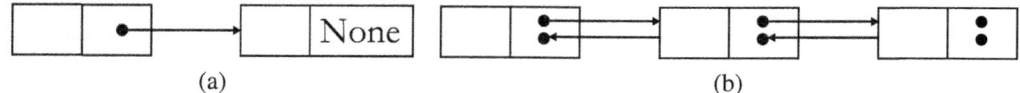

Figure 1.3: (a) Singly Linked List. (b) Doubly Linked List.

Fig. 1.3 (b)). However, both singly and doubly linked lists lack random access capabilities; operations such as indexed retrieval, concatenation, and membership testing remain linear ($\mathcal{O}(n)$) due to the need for sequential traversal. This trade-off highlights the importance of choosing the appropriate data structure based on problem requirements: arrays (lists) are preferred for random access and indexed operations, while linked lists are better suited for scenarios requiring frequent insertions and deletions. Listing 1.2 presents a simple implementation of a singly linked list, whose graphical illustration is given in Fig. 1.3 (a).

Listing 1.2: Definition of the class **SingleLinkedList**

```
1 class Node:
2       def __init__(self, item, next=None):
3           self.item = item
4           self.next = next
5
6 class SingleLinkedList:
7     def __init__(self):
8         self.head = Node(None) # dummy node
9         self.tail = self.head
10        self.size = 0
11
12    def append(self, item):
13        node = Node(item)
14        self.tail.next = node
15        self.tail = node
16        self.size += 1
17
18    def __getitem__(self, index):
19        if index < 0 or index >= self.size: raise IndexError("Index out of range")
20        cursor = self.head.next
21        for _ in range(index): cursor = cursor.next
22        return cursor.item
```

The following code snippet showcases the usage of a singly linked list in action:

```
1 s_lst= SingleLinkedList() # Create a new linked list
2 # Append several elements as instances of the class MyObject.
3 s_lst.append(MyObject(0)); s_lst.append(MyObject(1)); s_lst.append(MyObject(2))
4 # Access elements by index
5 print("First element:", s_lst[0])# Output:  MyObject(0)
6 print("Second element:", s_lst[1])# Output:  MyObject(1)
7 print("Third element:", s_lst[2]) # Output:  MyObject(2)
8 # Attempting to access an invalid index will raise an error
9 try:
10    print(s_lst[10])  # Out of range
11 except IndexError as e:
12    print("Error:", e)
```

Two-dimensional collections, such as matrices, are commonly represented in Python as lists of lists, stored in a row-major format. This structure allows intuitive indexing using matrix[row][col], where each row is a sublist. Such representations are indispensable in numerous applications, including board games like Tic-Tac-Toe. A dedicated Board class can encapsulate a grid of objects (e.g., Dummy, X, or O), supporting essential operations such as state evaluation, rendering, and resetting the game state. For instance, a Board class tailored for a Tic-Tac-Toe game may be structured as follows:

```python
class Board:
    def __init__(self, contents=None):
        self.items = [[None for _ in range(3)] for _ in range(3)]
        if contents:
            for i in range(3):
                for j in range(3):
                    self.items[i][j]=contents[i][j]

    def __getitem__(self, index):
        return self.items[index]

    def reset(self):
        for i in range(3):
            for j in range(3):
                self.items[i][j] = None
```

1.4.4 Stacks and Queues

A *stack* is an essential linear data structure characterized by the Last-In-First-Out (**LIFO**) principle: the most recently added element is the first to be removed. Core stack operations include push (inserting an element), pop (removing the top element), and top (accessing the top element without removal). Stacks play a pivotal role in various algorithms and applications, such as expression evaluation, the convex hull problem (e.g., Graham's Scan algorithm), balanced parentheses checking, string reversal, and managing function calls in recursion. Listing 1.3 provides a simple Python implementation of the MyStack class.

Listing 1.3: Definition of the simple class **MyStack**

```python
class MyStack:
    def __init__(self):
        self.items = [] # the list of itmes
    def push(self, item):
        self.items.append(item)
    def pop(self):
        if not self.items: raise RuntimeError("Empty stack")
        return self.items.pop() # the pop() here operates on the self.items list
    def top(self):
        if not self.items: raise RuntimeError("Empty stack")
        return self.items[-1]
    def is_empty(self):
        return len(self.items) == 0
```

A *queue* is a fundamental linear data structure that operates under the First-In-First-Out (**FIFO**) principle: the element enqueued first is the first to be dequeued. Core operations include enqueue (inserting an element at the end) and dequeue (removing an element from the front). Queues play a crucial role in scheduling algorithms, breadth-first search (BFS), constructing Voronoi diagrams, and task management systems. A basic implementation of a queue in Python is presented in Listing 1.4.

Listing 1.4: Definition of the simple class **MyQueue**

```python
class MyQueue:
    def __init__(self):
        self.items = []
        self.front_id = 0
    def enqueue(self, item): #append an item
        self.items.append(item)
    def __compress(self): # Amortized removal of elements
        self.items = self.items[self.front_id:]
        self.front_id = 0
    def dequeue(self): # read and remove an item
        if self.front_id >= len(self.items):raise RuntimeError("Empty queue")
        item = self.items[self.front_id]
        self.front_id += 1
        if self.front_id*2>len(self.items): self.__compress()
        return item
    def is_empty(self):# test if the queue contains no elements
        return self.front_id >= len(self.items)
    def front(self): # read the first element
        if self.is_empty():raise RuntimeError("Empty queue")
        return self.items[self.front_id]
```

The following code snippet demonstrates the usage of the **MyStack** and **MyQueue** classes:

```python
s = MyStack() #create object s
for i in range(5): s.push(i)
print("Top element:", s.top())   # Output 4
while not s.is_empty():print("Popped:", s.pop())

q = MyQueue() # create object q
# Enqueue elements 0 through 4
for i in range(5): q.enqueue(i)
print("Front element:", q.front()) #Output: 0
while not q.is_empty(): print("Dequeued:", q.dequeue())
```

Table 1.5 summarizes the operations and complexities of the **MyStack** and **MyQueue** classes described above. It is important to note that in the **MyQueue** class, the dequeue() method internally invokes the private __compress() method. This mechanism periodically removes elements from the underlying list self.items when self.front exceeds half of the list's length, thereby preventing memory leaks and ensuring efficient performance over time.

1.5   Hash Tables, Sets, Maps, and the Role of Memoization

In the previous section, sequences were discussed as data structures that permit duplicate elements, such as lists of integers containing repeated values. In contrast, this section focuses on two fundamental data structures—*sets* and *maps*—which enforce different constraints and support distinct operations. Sets, implemented as hash tables in Python, store collections of unique elements, while maps (also referred to as dictionaries or hash tables) associate unique keys with corresponding values, enabling constant-time ($\mathscr{O}(1)$) membership tests and key-based retrieval in the average case. The technique of *hashing* is emphasized as a central concept for achieving such efficiency, with algorithms for locating elements in sets extended to

Table 1.5: Complexity of Stack and Queue Operations

Operation	Complexity	Usage	Description
Stack Creation	$\mathcal{O}(1)$	`s = MyStack()`	Calls the constructor for a stack.
Queue Creation	$\mathcal{O}(1)$	`q = MyQueue()`	Calls the constructor for a queue.
`push` (Stack)	$\mathcal{O}(1)$	`s.push(a)`	Pushes the item a onto the stack s.
`enqueue` (Queue)	$\mathcal{O}(1)$	`q.enqueue(a)`	Enqueues the item a onto the queue q.
`pop` (Stack)	$\mathcal{O}(1)$	`a = s.pop()`	Removes and returns the last item from s.
`dequeue` (Queue)	$\mathcal{O}(1)$	`a = q.dequeue()`	Returns the first item enqueued in q.
`top` (Stack)	$\mathcal{O}(1)$	`a = s.top()`	Read the top item from s.
`front` (Queue)	$\mathcal{O}(1)$	`a = q.front()`	Read the front item from q.
`isEmpty` (Stack)	$\mathcal{O}(1)$	`s.isEmpty()`	Returns True if s has no elements.
`isEmpty` (Queue)	$\mathcal{O}(1)$	`q.isEmpty()`	Returns True if q has no elements.

the construction of maps. Additionally, *memoization* is introduced as a powerful optimization method that leverages hashing to cache intermediate results, significantly improving the efficiency of algorithms, particularly in computationally intensive problems such as the NP-hard Minimum Weight Triangulation (**MWT**) in computational geometry. The interplay between hash tables, sets, maps, and memoization highlights the importance of efficient data access patterns in algorithm design, which will be demonstrated through Python examples in the subsequent sections.

1.5.1 Hash Tables

A *hash table* is a fundamental data structure that facilitates efficient key-based access by computing a hash value for each key and mapping it to an index within a contiguous array. In Python, hash tables form the core implementation mechanism for both *sets* and *maps* (dictionaries). To resolve collisions—cases where multiple keys produce the same index—Python employs an open-addressing scheme with probing, akin to linear probing. The hash value of an object is determined by the built-in *hash()* function, which must return an integer. As a result, only immutable and hashable objects (such as integers, strings, and tuples) can be used as keys in Python hash tables, since mutable objects may change their hash value during execution, potentially leading to inconsistencies. The design of hash tables enables constant-time average-case complexity ($\mathcal{O}(1)$) for fundamental operations such as insertion, lookup, and deletion. To maintain efficiency and reduce the likelihood of collisions, Python hash tables dynamically resize based on the current load factor, typically maintaining it below 0.66.

1.5.2 Sets

A *set* is an unordered collection of distinct elements, explicitly disallowing duplicates. Sets can store heterogeneous data types, including integers, strings, and custom objects, and support a variety of operations such as union, intersection, and difference. In Python, sets are implemented as hash tables, enabling constant-time ($\mathcal{O}(1)$) membership tests and efficient set manipulations, as summarized in Table 1.6. Sets serve as a fundamental building block in numerous algorithms, including hash-based data structures such as dictionaries and advanced techniques like memoization, which will be discussed in subsequent sections. The uniqueness constraint of sets makes them ideal for modeling collections where duplicate elements are semantically invalid or unnecessary.

Python provides support for both mutable and immutable sets, through the `set` and `frozenset` classes, respectively. While `set` objects allow elements to be added and removed, `frozenset` objects are immutable, ensuring that their contents remain unchanged after creation. Python also introduces infix operators as syntactic shortcuts for common set operations: `s|t` represents the union of sets s and t, `s&t` denotes their intersection, and `s-t` computes the difference. These operators improve code readability but should be used with care to maintain clarity in complex expressions.

Table 1.6: Common Set Operations and Their Complexities

Operation	Complexity	Description
set([iterable])	$\mathcal{O}(n)$	Creates a set from an iterable.
len(s)	$\mathcal{O}(1)$	Returns the number of elements in s.
e in s	$\mathcal{O}(1)$	Checks membership of e in s.
s.union(t)	$\mathcal{O}(n)$	Returns a set containing elements from s and t.
s.intersection(t)	$\mathcal{O}(n)$	Returns a set with elements common to s and t.
s.difference(t)	$\mathcal{O}(n)$	Returns a set with elements in s but not in t.
s.add(e)	$\mathcal{O}(1)$	Adds element e to s.
s.remove(e)	$\mathcal{O}(1)$	Removes e from s; raises an error if e is not found.

■ **Example 1.1** Consider the following Python code, which demonstrates basic set operations:

```python
A = set([4, 1, 3, 2]); A.add(6)
B = set([5, 4, 3]); B.add(7)
print("Union:", A | B)  # {1, 2, 3, 4, 5, 6, 7}
print("Intersection:", A & B)  # {3, 4}
print("Union:", A | B)  # {1, 2, 6}
B.remove(7); print("B: ",B)  # {3, 4, 5}
print("Is 2 in A?", 2 in A)  # True
```

■

1.5.3 Maps

A *map* or a *dictionary* is a data structure that associates unique keys with corresponding values, enabling efficient key-based retrieval. Mathematically, a map is a function that assigns each key in a domain to a value in a range. In Python, maps or dictionaries (*dict*) are implemented as hash tables, supporting constant-time average-case complexity ($\mathcal{O}(1)$) for insertion, lookup, and deletion operations. Keys in a dictionary must be hashable, typically immutable objects such as integers, strings, or tuples. Maps extend the concept of sets by associating each unique key with a value, allowing key-based access and manipulation. As in sets, hashing is used to compute the storage location of keys, ensuring fast membership tests and updates. Python offers a rich set of methods and operators for efficient manipulation of dictionaries, as summarized in Table 1.7.

Table 1.7: Common Dictionary Operations in Python

Operation	Complexity	Usage
Create	$\mathcal{O}(1)$ / $\mathcal{O}(n)$	d = dict([iterable])
Size	$\mathcal{O}(1)$	len(d)
Membership	$\mathcal{O}(1)$	k in d, k not in d
Add/Update	$\mathcal{O}(1)$	d[k] = v
Lookup	$\mathcal{O}(1)$	d[k], d.get(k,default)
Remove	$\mathcal{O}(1)$	del d[k], d.pop(k), d.popitem()
Views	$\mathcal{O}(1)$	d.items(), d.keys(), d.values()
Set Default	$\mathcal{O}(1)$	d.setdefault(k,default)
Update	$\mathcal{O}(n)$	d.update(e)
Clear	$\mathcal{O}(1)$	d.clear()
Copy	$\mathcal{O}(n)$	d.copy()

It is important to note that creating an empty dictionary requires constant time ($\mathcal{O}(1)$), whereas creating a dictionary from an iterable of size n has a time complexity of $\mathscr{O}(n)$, as each key-value pair must be inserted individually.

■ **Example 1.2** Basic usage of dictionaries in Python:

```
1 D = {'name': 'Adis', 'age': 30} #create a dictionary D
2 D['location'] = 'Sarajevo'
3 print(D['name']) # Adis
4 print('age' in D) # True
5 D['age'] = 31 # Update value
6 del D['location'] # Remove key-value pair
7 print(D.keys()) # dict_keys(['name', 'age'])
```

■

While the underlying implementation of maps and sets relies on hashing, their usage patterns differ: sets model collections of distinct elements, while maps model associations between keys and values. Understanding the properties and performance characteristics of hash-based data structures is essential for designing efficient algorithms and applications.

1.5.4 Memoization

Building upon the structures discussed above, the concept of *memoization* is introduced as a powerful optimization technique that leverages hashing to cache and reuse intermediate results in computational problems. The relationship between hash tables, sets, and maps highlights the importance of efficient data access patterns in algorithm design. The following example demonstrates how memoization, implemented via a dictionary, enables an exponential-time problem, such as computing Fibonacci numbers, to be solved efficiently. The performance improvements can be observed in the results presented in Table 1.8.

■ **Example 1.3** Basic usage of memoization for efficiently computing Fibonacci numbers in Python:

```
1  import sys
2  sys.setrecursionlimit(1000000)
3
4  def fib_naive(n):# Non-memoized version
5      if n <= 2: return 1
6      return fib_naive(n-1) + fib_naive(n-2)
7
8  memo = {}  # Initialize an empty dictionary for caching results
9  def fib_memo(n):  # Recursive Fibonacci function with memoization
10     if n in memo: return memo[n]  # Reuse cached result if available
11     if n <= 2: result = 1
12     else: result = fib_memo(n-1) + fib_memo(n-2)
13     memo[n] = result  # Store computed result in memo
14     return result
```

■

1.6 Trees

A tree is a nonlinear hierarchical data structure consisting of nodes connected by edges, where each node may have multiple children but at most one parent (except the root). Trees model parent-child relationships, making them suitable for representing hierarchical data. In computer science, trees are typically visualized with the root node at the top and leaves at the bottom. A *Binary Tree* (BT) is a special case where each node has at most two children: a left and a right subtree. Each node, except the root, has exactly one parent. The left subtree contains nodes with values less than the parent, while the right subtree contains

Table 1.8: Execution time comparison for the functions *fib_naive*(·) and *fib_memo*(·)

n	fib_memo (n)	fib_naive (n)	Result
30	0.0	0.096820	832040
35	0.0	1.057348	9227465
40	0.0	11.615583	102334155
45	0.0	128.905846	1134903170
50	0.0	1429.440840	12586269025
100	0.0	?	354224848179261915075
1000	0.0	?	BN
10000	0.005983	?	BN
20000	0.015957	?	BN

The symbol BN indicates a very large number, while the symbol ? denotes that the Fibonacci number could not be computed within a reasonable time frame.

nodes with values greater than or equal to the parent. Nodes are classified as either *internal* (storing data) or *external* (empty placeholders). The size of a binary tree is defined by the number of internal nodes. If a node A has a child B, then A is the *parent* and B the *descendant*. Two nodes are *siblings* if they share the same parent. A *unique path* connects a parent to a descendant, and its length is measured by the number of edges. The *depth* of a node A, denoted by $d(A)$, is the number of edges from the root to A:

$$d(A) = \begin{cases} 0, & \text{if } A \text{ is the root,} \\ 1 + d(\text{parent}(A)), & \text{otherwise.} \end{cases}$$

The *height* of a node A, denoted by $h(A)$, is the length of the longest path from A to a leaf:

$$h(A) = \begin{cases} 0, & \text{if } A \text{ is a leaf,} \\ 1 + \max(h(\text{left}(A)), h(\text{right}(A))), & \text{otherwise.} \end{cases}$$

One of the important applications of trees is the *Abstract Syntax Tree* (AST), which represents the syntactic structure of expressions or programs during parsing and evaluation. For instance, the arithmetic expression $(5+4) \cdot 6 + 3$ can be represented as an AST, where the root node is the operator $+$, and operands and subexpressions are organized within the subtrees. In Python, ASTs are automatically generated when executing code.

An example of constructing an AST in Python for arithmetic expressions is given below:

```python
class PlusNode:
    def __init__(self, l, r): self.left, self.right = l, r
    def eval(self): return self.left.eval() + self.right.eval()

class TimesNode:
    def __init__(self, l, r): self.left, self.right = l, r
    def eval(self): return self.left.eval() * self.right.eval()

class NumNode:
    def __init__(self, n): self.num = n
    def eval(self): return self.num

expr = PlusNode(TimesNode(PlusNode(NumNode(5), NumNode(4)), NumNode(6)), NumNode(3)
    )
print(expr.eval())  # Output: 57
```

Nodes in a tree can be traversed in various ways:

- **Inorder** (Left-Node-Right): visits the left subtree, then the node, then the right subtree;
- **Postorder** (Left-Right-Node): visits the left subtree, then the right subtree, then the node;
- **Preorder** (Node-Left-Right): visits the node, then the left subtree, then the right subtree.

Trees are essential for expression parsing, data organization, and the implementation of various algorithms in computer science.

1.6.1 Binary Search Trees

A *Binary Search Tree* (BST) is a hierarchical data structure where each node has at most two children: a left and a right subtree. The tree satisfies the binary search property: all values in the left subtree of a node A are strictly less than the value at A, while all values in the right subtree are strictly greater than or equal to the value at A. Both subtrees must themselves be binary search trees. This property enables efficient search, insertion, and deletion operations with an average-case time complexity of $\mathcal{O}(\log n)$. However, in the worst case—such as when inserting already sorted data—the tree degenerates into a linear structure (see the last tree in Fig. 1.4), and the complexity deteriorates to $\mathcal{O}(n)$. It is important to note that the same set of elements can produce different BST structures depending on the order of insertion. For instance, the elements $1, 2, 3, 4, 5$ can form various valid BSTs, as illustrated in Fig. 1.4.

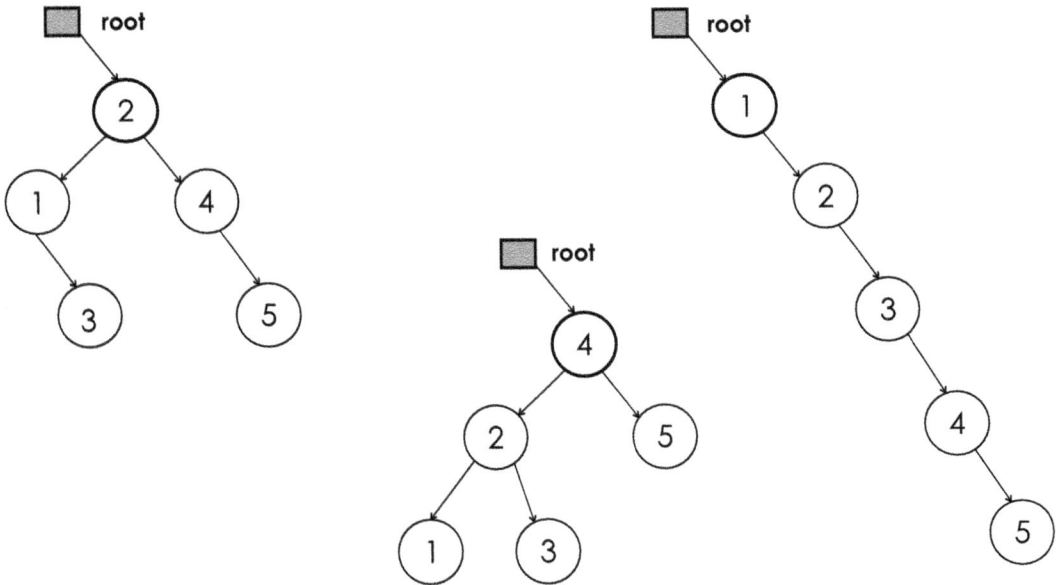

Figure 1.4: Three ways of representing elements within a binary tree.

It is also important to note that since a linear ordering exists among the items (i.e., the data stored in the nodes of a binary tree), these items can be compared. For example, if the nodes contain numbers, standard comparison operators such as less than (<), equal to (=), or greater than (>) can be used. If the nodes contain character strings, they can be compared lexicographically. Furthermore, if the nodes store more complex geometric objects (e.g., line segments), comparisons are made according to a predefined *comparison criterion*. In general, searching for *items* in a binary search tree is based on a *comparison function*, which is a user-defined rule for comparing elements. This function returns values from the set $\{-1, 0, 1\}$ according to the following logic:

a) If the first item (a data value or a variable) is smaller than the second item, the comparison function returns -1.

b) If the first item is equal to the second item, the function returns 0.

c) If the first item is greater than the second item, the function returns 1.

Listing 1.5 provides a simple Python implementation of the **BinarySearchTree** class with insertion and in-order traversal.

Listing 1.5: Definition of the simple class **BinarySearchTree**

```
1 class BinarySearchTree:
2     class Node:
3         def __init__(self,val,left=None,right=None):#the constructor for class
              Node
4             self.val, self.left, self.right = val, left, right
5         def __iter__(self): # In-order travesal
6             if self.left: yield from self.left
7             yield self.val
8             if self.right: yield from self.right
9     def __init__(self): self.root = None #the constructor of the class BST
10    def insert(self, val):
11        def _insert(node, val):
12            if node is None: return self.Node(val)
13            if val < node.val: node.left = _insert(node.left, val)
14            else: node.right = _insert(node.right, val)
15            return node
16        self.root = _insert(self.root, val)
17    def __iter__(self): # calls __iter__ of the class Node if root is not None
18        return iter(self.root) if self.root else iter([])
```

The following code snippet demonstrates the usage of the BinarySearchTree class for inserting numeric elements (3, 1, 2, 5, 4) and string elements ("delta", "alpha", "beta"). The resulting sorted order of these elements is verified through an in-order traversal, which is invoked when printing the instance of the BinarySearchTree class.

```
1 bst = BinarySearchTree()# Create an empty binary search tree
2 for value in [3,1,2,5,4]: #Insert elements into the BST
3     bst.insert(value)
4 print("In-order traversal:")
5 for elem in bst:#print elements in ascending order
6     print(elem, end=' ') # Output: 1 3 5 7 8 9 10
7 bst.insert(5)
8 print("\nIn-order traversal after inserting duplicate 5:")
9 for elem in bst: print(elem, end=' ') # Output: 1 3 5 5 7 8 9 10
10 # Insert string values to demonstrate lexicographic ordering
11 bst_str = BinarySearchTree()
12 for value in ["delta","alpha","beta"]: bst_str.insert(value)
13 print("\nIn-order traversal of strings:")
14 for elem in bst_str: print(elem, end=' ')# Output: alpha beta delta
```

BSTs are conceptually important but may not be optimal in practice; self-balancing trees (e.g., AVL trees and Red-Black trees) provide guaranteed logarithmic complexity and are studied in subsequent sections.

1.6.2 Balanced Binary Search Trees

In the previous section, it was noted that the main limitation of **binary search trees** (BSTs) lies in their tendency to become unbalanced, particularly when inserting already sorted data. This imbalance can lead to a degradation in performance, with search, insertion, and deletion operations requiring linear time complexity, $\mathscr{O}(n)$. To address this issue, *balanced binary search trees* introduced by Adelson-Velskii and Landis in 1962, ensure that the height difference between the left and right subtrees of any node does not exceed one. This balance property guarantees logarithmic time complexity, $\mathscr{O}(\log n)$, for fundamental operations such as search, insert, and delete. Balanced search trees find widespread applications in computer science, notably in scenarios where maintaining a dynamically sorted dataset is critical. They are particularly valuable in computational geometry, where balanced BSTs are integral to algorithms for constructing structures such as *Voronoi diagrams*. By enabling efficient event handling and dynamic updates during the plane sweep algorithm, balanced BSTs support robust and scalable geometric computations. While hash tables (HashSet, HashMap) and heaps provide efficient insert and delete operations, they do not preserve ordering. Balanced BSTs are a preferred choice when maintaining a sorted sequence is essential.

1.6.3 AVL Trees

AVL trees are a class of self-balancing binary search trees, introduced by Adelson-Velskii and Landis in 1962, representing a significant advancement in maintaining balance within binary search trees. An AVL tree guarantees that for any node A, the *balance factor*, defined as $\text{balance}(A) = \text{height}(A.\text{right}) - \text{height}(A.\text{left})$, satisfies the invariant $\text{balance}(A) \in \{-1, 0, +1\}$. This property ensures that basic operations such as search, insertion, and deletion are performed in logarithmic time, $\Theta(\log n)$. The robustness and efficiency of AVL trees make them a preferred data structure in applications requiring frequent dynamic updates and ordered traversals, including database indexing, caching systems, and geometric algorithms such as the construction of Voronoi diagrams.

Maintaining the balance property in AVL trees requires rebalancing the structure after insertions or deletions. This is accomplished through local transformations known as *single* and *double rotations*, guided by the balance factor. These operations act only on small portions of the tree, allowing for efficient rebalancing without reconstructing the entire structure. By preserving the height of the tree within $\Theta(\log n)$, rotations ensure that search, insertion, and deletion operations maintain logarithmic time complexity. A *single rotation* (either left or right) resolves imbalances that create a linear, skewed structure, where nodes are aligned entirely to one side. In contrast, a *double rotation* (a sequence of left and right rotations) is required when the imbalance forms a "zig-zag" pattern—where the imbalance shifts direction between a node and its child. These rotations restore the AVL balance invariant, ensuring efficient operations and maintaining the tree's optimal height.

Left Rotation

A *left rotation* is applied when the right subtree of a node becomes "heavier" (i.e., has greater height) compared to its left subtree. This operation proceeds as follows:

- Let node z be unbalanced, such that its right subtree y has greater height.
- Node y becomes the new root of the subtree.
- Node z becomes the left child of y.
- The former left subtree of y becomes the right subtree of z.

After the rotation, the heights of nodes z and y are updated to reflect the new values.

Right Rotation

The right rotation is a symmetric operation to the left rotation and is applied when the left subtree of a node becomes "heavier" (i.e., has greater height) than the right. The procedure is as follows:

- Let node z be unbalanced, with its left subtree y having a greater height.
- Node y becomes the new root of the subtree.
- Node z becomes the right child of y.
- The previous right subtree of y becomes the left subtree of z.

As in the case of a left rotation, the heights of nodes z and y are updated after the rotation.

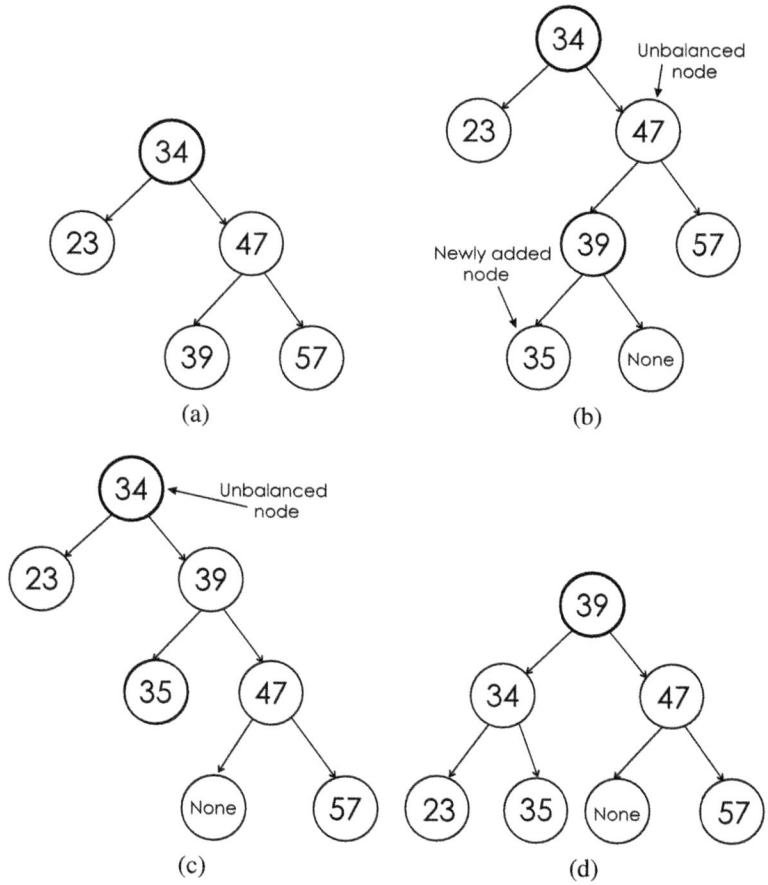

Figure 1.5: (a) Balanced tree. (b) Unbalanced tree due to the added node 35. (c) Right rotation of the tree. (d) Left rotation of the tree.

In Fig. 1.5 (a), a balanced binary search tree is shown. Upon inserting the element 35, the tree becomes unbalanced, as illustrated in Fig. 1.5 (b). This insertion causes node $z = 47$ to become unbalanced, with its left subtree y being taller than the right. To restore balance, a right rotation is performed at node z, as depicted in Fig. 1.5 (c). However, the tree remains unbalanced, since node $z = 34$ now exhibits an imbalance, where its right subtree y has greater height. Consequently, a left rotation at node z is required, resulting in the balanced tree shown in Fig. 1.5 (d). Listing 1.6 provides a simple Python implementation of the **AVLTree** class with insertion and in-order traversal.

Listing 1.6: Definition of the simple class AVLTree

```python
class AVLNode:
    def __init__(self, key):
        self.key=key; self.height=1# Height of node (for balance factor).
        self.left=None; self.right=None
class AVLTree:
    def get_height(self, node):
        if not node: return 0
        return node.height

    def get_balance(self, node):
        if not node: return 0
        return self.get_height(node.left) - self.get_height(node.right)

    def inorder_traversal(self, root):
        if not root: return []
        return (self.inorder_traversal(root.left)+[root.key]+self.
            inorder_traversal(root.right))

    def insert(self, root, key):
        if not root: return AVLNode(key)#normal BST insertion
        elif key<root.key: root.left=self.insert(root.left, key)
        else: root.right=self.insert(root.right, key)
        # Update the height of the ancestor node
        root.height=1+max(self.get_height(root.left),self.get_height(root.right))
        balance = self.get_balance(root)# Calculate the balance factor
        # Balance the tree
        if balance>1 and key<root.left.key: #Case 1: Left Left (LL)
            return self.right_rotate(root)
        if balance<-1 and key>root.right.key: #Case 2: Right Right (RR)
            return self.left_rotate(root)
        if balance>1 and key>root.left.key: #Case 3: Left Right (LR)
            root.left=self.left_rotate(root.left)
            return self.right_rotate(root)
        if balance < -1 and key < root.right.key: # Case 4: Right Left (RL)
            root.right = self.right_rotate(root.right)
            return self.left_rotate(root)
        return root

    def left_rotate(self, z):
        y=z.right; w=y.left
        y.left=z; z.right=w # Perform rotation
        # Update heights
        z.height=1+max(self.get_height(z.left),self.get_height(z.right))
        y.height=1+max(self.get_height(y.left),self.get_height(y.right))
        return y# Return the new root

    def right_rotate(self, z):
        y=z.left; w=y.right
        y.right=z; z.left=w # Perform rotation
        # Update heights
        z.height=1+max(self.get_height(z.left),self.get_height(z.right))
        y.height=1+max(self.get_height(y.left),self.get_height(y.right))
        return y # Return the new root
```

Based on the explanation of left and right rotations, the implementation of the *left_rotate*(·) and *right_rotate*(·)

methods becomes straightforward, as demonstrated in Listing 1.6. Unlike the *insert*(·) method in the **BinarySearchTree** class, the *insert*(·) method in the **AVLTree** class is designed to maintain balance and height invariants. After each insertion, the tree is traversed back up the recursive stack, and the heights of nodes and their balance factors are updated accordingly. If an imbalance is detected—i.e., a balance factor of +2 or -2—appropriate rotations (single or double) are applied to restore the AVL property. This rebalancing mechanism ensures that the AVL tree maintains logarithmic height, guaranteeing that subsequent search, insertion, and deletion operations remain efficient within $\Theta(\log n)$ time complexity. Example usage of the **AVLTree** class is provided below:

```
1 root=None; avl_tree=AVLTree()# Initialize the AVL Tree
2 for e in [10,20,30,40,50,25]: # Insert elements
3     root=avl_tree.insert(root, e)
4 # Perform in-order traversal
5 print("In-order traversal of the AVL tree:",avl_tree.inorder_traversal(root))
```

At the end of this section, a brief overview of the **SortedDict** class is provided, which is based on *AVL trees*. Specifically, SortedDict is designed as an advanced data structure that extends the functionality of Python's built-in dict by maintaining the keys in sorted order. Unlike standard dictionaries, which are implemented using hash tables and do not preserve order, SortedDict is built on top of self-balancing binary search trees—typically *AVL trees* or *Red-Black trees*. This approach ensures that keys remain sorted, while search, insertion, and deletion operations can be performed in logarithmic time, $\mathcal{O}(\log n)$. The SortedDict class is particularly suited for use cases where efficient lookups and ordered traversals are required. Common scenarios include:

- efficient retrieval of the minimum or maximum key;
- iteration over keys in sorted order;
- identification of the smallest key greater than or equal to a given value using bisect;
- execution of range queries on key intervals.

Key methods available in SortedDict include:

- insert(key, value) — a new key-value pair is inserted;
- delete(key) — a key-value pair is removed by key;
- get(key) — the value associated with a key is retrieved;
- popitem(index=-1) — the last (or first) key-value pair is removed and returned;
- bisect(key) — the position of a key in the sorted order is found;
- keys(), values(), items() — keys, values, and key-value pairs are accessed.

The following examples illustrate how SortedDict is typically used:

```
1 from sortedcontainers import SortedDict
2 grades = SortedDict()
3 grades['Alice'] = 90
4 grades['Bob'] = 85
5 grades['Charlie'] = 92
6 for name in grades: print(name, grades[name])
7 #The first key >= 'B' is located
8 index = grades.bisect('B')
9 print("First key >= 'B':", grades.iloc[index])
```

The SortedDict class, by leveraging self-balancing trees, provides an efficient and reliable solution for scenarios that demand both quick key-based access and ordered data structures, such as database indexing, ranking systems, and algorithms for interval and geometric data handling.

2. Geometric Objects in Python

In this chapter, the most important geometric objects used in solving highly complex geometric problems are presented [71]. Geometric objects will be implemented using an object-oriented approach in the Python programming language [116, 197]. This approach includes class interfaces and method implementations for manipulating two-dimensional (2D) and three-dimensional (3D) objects, as geometric problems predominantly pertain to such spaces [112]. In the two-dimensional case, the operations and methods supported by the mentioned classes will include subdividing polygons into smaller parts, computing intersection points of segments, and classifying a point relative to the position of segments, planes, triangles, and polygons [172]. In the three-dimensional case, the developed classes will contain methods that enable point classification concerning a plane, as well as determining the intersection point of a segment and a triangle in space, which has far-reaching implications for solving a wide range of problems in computer graphics [73, 134].

2.1 Vectors in the Plane

It is well known that an ordered pair (x,y) can be interpreted as a complex number $z = x + iy$, a point in the plane $A = (x,y)$, or a radius vector $\overrightarrow{OA}$ with coordinates (x,y). Since this chapter focuses on studying geometric objects without loss of generality, the ordered pair (x,y) can be regarded as a directed vector (the radius vector $\overrightarrow{OA}$) that starts at the point $O(0,0)$ and ends at the point $A(x,y)$. The coordinate origin $O(0,0)$ is called the **zero vector** and will be denoted as $\vec{0}$ in the following text. Primitive vector operations, such as addition, subtraction, magnitude computation, dot product, and cross product, will not be examined here, as they are well-known from the introductory course in linear algebra. A triangle $\triangle P_1 P_2 P_3$ formed by the points P_1, P_2, and P_3 is said to be **positively oriented** if the vertex P_3 is located to the *left* of the segment $\overline{P_1 P_2}$, as shown in Fig. 2.1 (a). The points P_1, P_2, and P_3 are oriented in the **counterclockwise direction**. Conversely, the triangle $\triangle P_1 P_2 P_3$ is said to be **negatively oriented** if the vertex P_3 is located to the *right* of the segment $\overline{P_1 P_2}$, as illustrated in Fig. 2.1 (b). The points P_1, P_2, and P_3 are oriented in the **clockwise direction**. In the context of vectors, if we define $\vec{a} = \overrightarrow{P_1 P_2}$, $\vec{b} = \overrightarrow{P_1 P_3}$, and denote by $\theta = \angle(\vec{a}, \vec{b})$ the angle between vectors $\vec{a}$ and $\vec{b}$ oriented in the counterclockwise direction, then the triangle $\triangle P_1 P_2 P_3$ is said to be *positively oriented* if $\theta \in (0, 180)$ or *negatively oriented* if $\theta \in (180, 360)$. In order to implement this in the context of a method, the following section provides a procedure for determining the orientation of the triangle $\triangle P_1 P_2 P_3$ based on the angle θ.

Let α and β represent the angles between the positive part of the x-axis and the vectors $\vec{a}$ and $\vec{b}$, respectively.

© The Author(s), under exclusive license to Springer Nature Switzerland AG 2026
A. Alihodžić, *Exploring Computational Geometry*, Texts in Computer Science,
https://doi.org/10.1007/978-3-032-06393-9_2

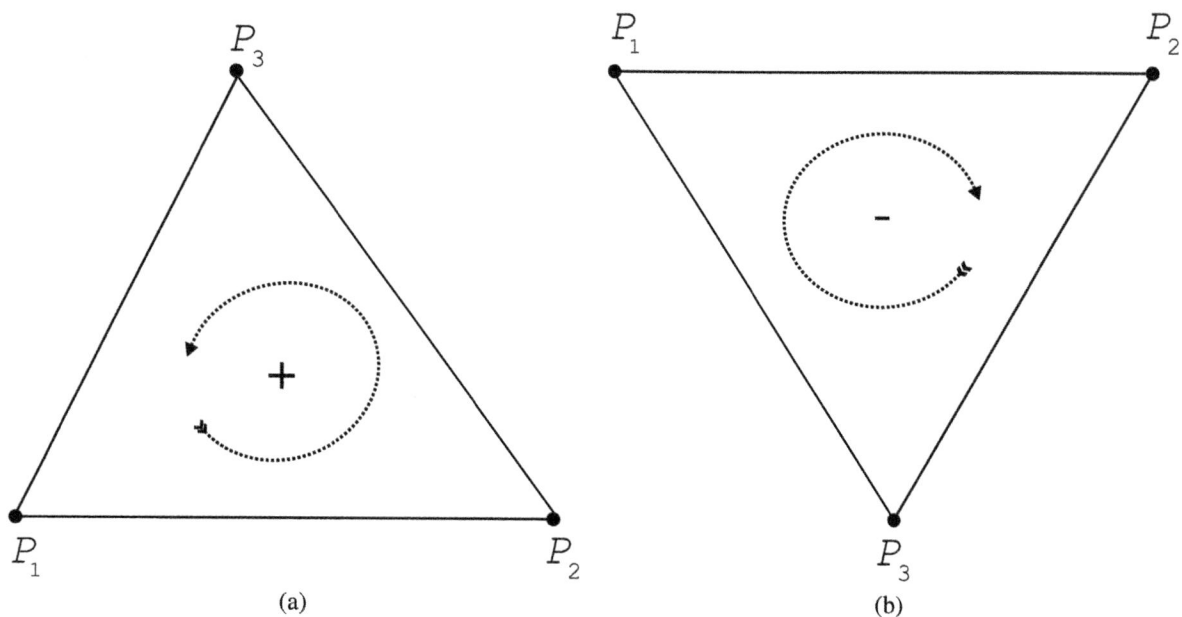

(a)   (b)

Figure 2.1: (a) Positive orientation of the triangle $\triangle P_1 P_2 P_3$. (b) Negative orientation of the triangle $\triangle P_1 P_2 P_3$.

Then, it follows that $\theta = \beta - \alpha$, leading to four possible cases, as shown in Fig. 2.2.

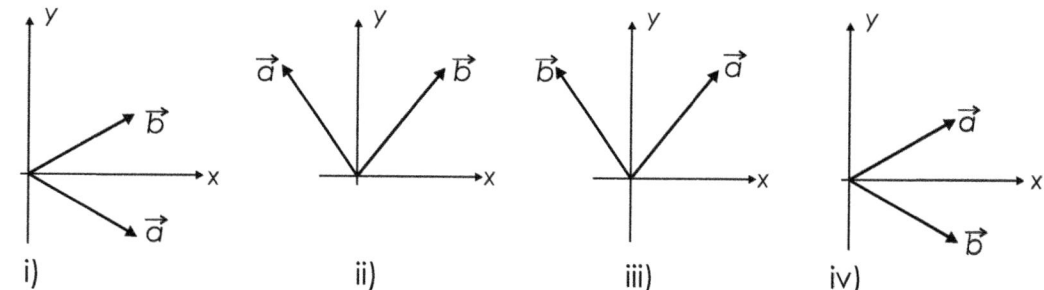

Figure 2.2: Four positions of the angle θ for determining the triangle's orientation $\triangle P_1 P_2 P_3$.

These cases describe the relationship that can be established between the *orientation of the triangle* $\triangle P_1 P_2 P_3$ represented by the vectors $\vec{a}$ and $\vec{b}$, the *angle* θ, and the *sine of the angle* θ $(\sin \theta)$, as shown in Table 2.1. Based on the data shown in Table 2.1, the orientation of the triangle $\triangle P_1 P_2 P_3$ is determined by

Table 2.1: Orientation of the triangle $\triangle P_1 P_2 P_3$ based on the position of the angle θ.

Scenario	Angle $\theta = \beta - \alpha$	Orientation $\triangle P_1 P_2 P_3$	Sine of the Angle θ
i)	$\theta \in (-360, -180)$	Positive	$\sin \theta > 0$
ii)	$\theta \in (-180, 0)$	Negative	$\sin \theta < 0$
iii)	$\theta \in (0, 180)$	Positive	$\sin \theta > 0$
iv)	$\theta \in (180, 360)$	Negative	$\sin \theta < 0$

calculating $\sin \theta$. Based on the **Addition Formulas**, we obtain

$$\sin \theta = \sin \beta \cos \alpha - \sin \alpha \cos \beta. \tag{2.1}$$

Since the vectors $\vec{a} = \overrightarrow{P_1 P_2}$ and $\vec{b} = \overrightarrow{P_1 P_3}$ in the plane are represented by the coordinates (x_a, y_a) and (x_b, y_b), it directly follows that holds:

- $\sin \alpha = \frac{y_a}{\|a\|}$;
- $\sin \beta = \frac{y_b}{\|b\|}$;
- $\cos \alpha = \frac{x_a}{\|a\|}$;
- $\cos \beta = \frac{x_b}{\|b\|}$.

By substituting these trigonometric representations into Eq. 2.1, a convenient expression for examining the triangle's orientation is obtained:

$$\sin \theta = \frac{1}{\|a\| \, \|b\|} (x_a y_b - x_b y_a). \tag{2.2}$$

Taking into account that the vectors $\vec{a}$ and $\vec{b}$ are nonzero, it follows that $\|a\| \, \|b\| > 0$. Based on Eq. 2.2, the triangle's orientation is positive or negative if the expression $(x_a y_b - x_b y_a)$ is greater or less than zero, respectively. From this, it follows that to determine the orientation of the triangle, it is sufficient to check the sign of the expression $(x_a y_b - x_b y_a)$, even though initially it seemed necessary to compute angles using computationally demanding trigonometric functions such as sine and cosine. The procedure for determining the triangle's orientation will be incorporated into the method for examining the triangle's orientation. Thus, to check the triangle's orientation, only three primitive arithmetic operations are required: *two multiplications and one subtraction*. From a geometric point of view, the expression $(x_a y_b - x_b y_a)$ represents the sign of the area of the parallelogram spanned by the vectors $\vec{a}$ and $\vec{b}$, with vertices expressed through the following four vectors: $\vec{0}, \vec{a}, \vec{b}. \overrightarrow{a+b}$.

2.2 Points in the Plane

In this section, the class **Point2D** will be defined and implemented to represent points in the plane. It is well known that a point in the plane is stored in a computer's memory as an ordered pair of Cartesian coordinates. In some cases, it is more convenient to represent a point in the plane $A = (x, y)$ as a vector or a 2×1 matrix whose elements are x and y. During the design and implementation of the **Point2D** class, explanations of parts related to more straightforward member functions will be omitted due to its simplicity. Short methods will be implemented within the class body. In contrast, more complex methods such as *classification($\cdot$)*, *orientation($\cdot$,$\cdot$)*, *classification_m($\cdot$,$\cdot$)*, *polar_angle()*, and *distance($\cdot$)*, although formally remaining within the class, will be implemented later. The interface of the **Point2D** class is given in Listing 2.1.

Listing 2.1: Definition of the class **Point2D**

```python
import math
import copy
class Point2D:
    def __init__(self,x=0.0,y=0.0,id=0):
        self.__x = x
        self.__y = y
        self.__id = id
    def __eq__(self,p):
        return self.is_equal(self.__x,p.__x) and self.is_equal(self.__y,p.__y)
    def __ne__(self,p):
        return not self.__eq__(p)
    def __lt__(self,p):
```

```
13      return self.__x<p.__x or (self.is_equal(self.__x,p.__x) and self.__y<p.__y
            )
14  def __gt__(self,p):
15      return self.__x>p.__x or (self.is_equal(self.__x,p.__x) and self.__y>p.__y
            )
16  def __add__(self,p):
17      return Point2D(self.__x+p.__x,self.__y+p.__y)
18  def __sub__(self,p):
19      return Point2D(self.__x-p.__x,self.__y-p.__y)
20  def __getitem__(self,idx):
21      return self.__x if idx==0 else self.__y
22  def __setitem__(self,idx,value):
23      if idx==0:
24          self.__x=value
25      else: self.__y=value
26  def __mul__(self,p):
27      if isinstance(p,Point2D):return self.__x*p.__x+self.__y*p.__y
28  def get_id(self):
29      return self.__id
30  def magnitude(self):
31      return math.sqrt(self.__x**2+self.__y**2)
32  def is_on_segment(self, s)-> bool:
33      p1, p2=s[1]-s[0], self-s[1]
34      return (p1[0]*p2[1]-p1[1]*p2[0])>=0
```

In the following, the first four methods will be implemented first, while the last member function will be postponed until the discussion on objects representing line segments in the plane. The method *orientation*$(\cdot,\cdot)$ is used to determine on which side of the segment $\overline{P_1P_2}$ the point P_3 is located. This method, depending on the sign of the expression $(x_a y_b - x_b y_a)$, returns:

- +1, if the orientation of the triangle $\triangle P_1P_2P_3$ is positive;
- -1, if the orientation of the triangle $\triangle P_1P_2P_3$ is negative;
- 0, if the vertices of the triangle $\triangle P_1P_2P_3$ are collinear points, i.e., they lie on the same line.

Therefore, the implementation of this method can be written as follows:

```
1 def orientation(self,p1,p2):
2     vA=p2-p1 #vector A
3     vB=self-p1 #vector B
4     sTeta=vA[0]*vB[1]-vB[0]*vA[1]  # sine of the angle
5     if sTeta>0:return 1   # positive orientation
6     elif sTeta<0:return -1   # negative orientation
7     return 0   # points self, t1, and t2 are collinear
```

The next method to be implemented is *classification*$(\cdot,\cdot)$. This method aims to classify the point P_3 in relation to the vector $\overrightarrow{P_1P_2}$ or the segment $\overline{P_1P_2}$. Before implementing this method, it is necessary to consider all possible positions of point P_3 about segment $\overline{P_1P_2}$. In Fig. 2.3 (a), it can be seen that there are seven possible position classifications of point P_3 about segment $\overline{P_1P_2}$. Thus, point P_3 is located:

1. to the *left* of the segment $\overline{P_1P_2}$;
2. to the *right* of the segment $\overline{P_1P_2}$;
3. *in front of* the segment $\overline{P_1P_2}$;
4. *behind* the segment $\overline{P_1P_2}$;
5. *between* the start and end of the segment $\overline{P_1P_2}$;

6. at the *start* of the segment $\overrightarrow{P_1P_2}$;

7. at the *end* of the segment $\overline{P_1P_2}$.

In the sixth or seventh scenario, point P_3 coincides with the start or the end of the segment $\overline{P_1P_2}$, i.e., point P_3 coincides with points P_1 or P_2, respectively. Therefore, to check whether point P_3 is at the start or the end of the segment $\overline{P_1P_2}$, it is sufficient to use the already implemented __eq__ operator function. Detection of whether point P_3 is in front of the segment $\overline{P_1P_2}$ is performed using the implemented member function *magnitude*() on an object of type **Point2D**, which is initialized as the difference between the vectors $\vec{a} = \overrightarrow{P_1P_2}$ and $\vec{b} = \overrightarrow{P_1P_3}$. Point P_3 is behind the segment $\overline{P_1P_2}$ only if the vectors $\vec{a}$ and $\vec{b}$ have the same direction but opposite orientation. Finally, if point P_3 does not fall into any of the previously mentioned classifications, it is located between the segment's start and end. For easier tracking, the classification of point P_3 is stored as an enumerated type **TypeP2**:

```
from enum import Enum
class TypeP2(Enum):
    LEFT = 1
    RIGHT = 2
    IN_FRONT = 3
    BEHIND = 4
    BETWEEN = 5
    START = 6
    END = 7
```

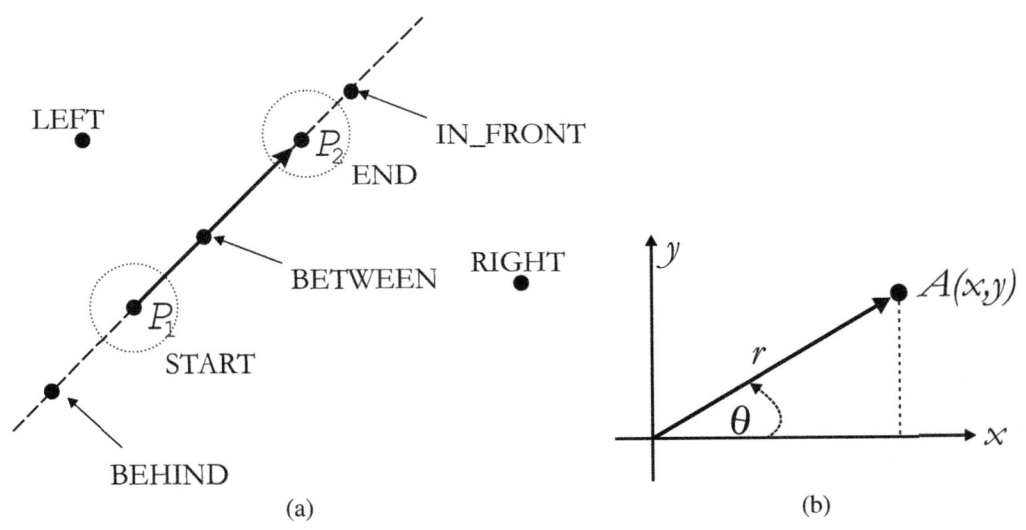

Figure 2.3: (a) Seven classifications of the point P_3. (b) Polar coordinates θ and r of the point A.

The implementation of the method *classification*($\cdot$,$\cdot$) looks as follows:

```
from TypeP2 import TypeP2
def classification(self,p1,p2):
    p3=Point2D(self.__x, self.__y)
    vA=p2-p1#vector A
    vB =p3-p1#vector B
    if p3.orientation(p1,p2)>0:return TypeP2.LEFT
    elif p3.orientation(p1,p2)<0:return TypeP2.RIGHT
    elif (vA[0]*vB[0]<0) or (vA[1]*vB[1]<0):return TypeP2.BEHIND
    elif vA.magnitude()<vB.magnitude():return TypeP2.IN_FRONT
```

```
10      elif p3==p1:return TypeP2.START
11      elif p3==p2:return TypeP2.END
12      return TypeP2.BETWEEN
```

In the implementation of scenario 4, the fact that the vectors $\vec{a} = (x_a, y_a)$ and $\vec{b} = (x_b, y_b)$ are oppositely oriented is utilized *iff* $x_a x_b < 0$ or $y_a y_b < 0$. Additionally, for the realization of scenario 3, the *magnitude*() method is exploited, which internally calls the CPU-intensive built-in function **sqrt**. The resolution of this scenario can be replaced with that of scenario five by implementing a method *between*($\cdot, \cdot$), whose task is to determine whether point P_3 is located between points P_1 and P_2. The implementation of this method is highly efficient since it performs primitive operations such as inequality comparisons and basic logical operations. The implementation of the mentioned method can be written as follows:

```
1 def between(self,p1,p2):
2      p3=Point2D(self.__x,self.__y)
3      if(min(p1[0],p2[0])<p3[0]<max(p1[0],p2[0]))or(min(p1[1],p2[1])<p3[1]<max(p1
         [1],p2[1])):return True
4      return False
```

A faster version for classifying points in the plane can be written using the method *between*($\cdot, \cdot$). Therefore, in addition to the method *classification*($\cdot, \cdot$), a modified version *classification_m*($\cdot, \cdot$) will be written, which is fundamentally more efficient:

```
1 def classification_m(self,p1,p2):
2      p3=Point2D(self.__x,self.__y)
3      vA=p2-p1#vector A
4      vB=p3-p1#vector B
5      if p3.orientation(p1,p2)>0:return TypeP2.LEFT
6      elif p3.orientation(p1,p2)<0:return TypeP2.RIGHT
7      elif (vA[0]*vB[0]<0) or (vA[1]*vB[1]<0):return TypeP2.BEHIND
8      elif p3.between(p1,p2):return TypeP2.BETWEEN
9      elif p3==p1:return TypeP2.START
10     elif p3==p2:return TypeP2.END
11     return TypeP2.IN_FRONT
```

The remaining task is implementing the method *polar_angle*(). Before its implementation, it is necessary to determine the angle θ between the positive part of the x-axis and the point $A(x, y)$. To achieve this, the Cartesian coordinates x and y are expressed in terms of the polar coordinates θ and r (see Fig. 2.3 (b)):

$$x = r\cos\theta, \quad y = r\sin\theta, \quad \theta \in [0, 2\pi], \quad r = \sqrt{x^2 + y^2}. \tag{2.3}$$

Since $\tan\theta = \frac{\sin\theta}{\cos\theta} = \frac{y}{x}$, it follows that the angle θ can be expressed as $\theta = \arctan\frac{y}{x}$, where $x \neq 0$. If, during implementation, it happens that $x = y = 0$, then this case should be handled separately. Additionally, special cases where $x = 0, y \neq 0$ are considered separately. Since the built-in Python function **atan**(y/x) for $x \neq 0, y \neq 0$ returns angles in the interval $[-\frac{\pi}{2}, \frac{\pi}{2}]$, cases such as $x > 0, y > 0$, $x > 0, y < 0$, and $x < 0$ need to be considered separately. The implementation of the *polar_angle*() method using the built-in function **atan**(y/x) is as follows:

```
1 def polar_angle(self):
2      if self.__x==0 and self.__y==0: return 0
3      elif self.__x==0: return 90 if self.__y>0 else 270
4      theta=math.atan(self.__y/self.__x)# Angle in radians
5      theta*=360/(2*math.pi)# Convert angle to degrees
```

```
6      if self.__x>0:return theta if self.__y >=0 else 360 + theta #I, IV quadrants
7      return 180 + theta #II, III quadrants
```

Besides the built-in Python function **atan**($\cdot$), there is another variant called **atan2**(y,x), which was introduced into the Python core language to handle some of the previously considered cases automatically. However, it should be noted that this function returns angles in the interval $[-\pi, \pi]$. In this way, the previous implementation of the *polar_angle*() method can be modified, resulting in a more concise version:

```
1 def polar_angle_m(self):
2      theta=math.atan2(self.__y,self.__x) # Angle in radians
3      theta*=360/(2*math.pi) # Convert angle to degrees
4      return theta if self.__y >= 0 else 360 + theta
```

2.3 Line Segments in the Plane

During the work with geometric algorithms, segments (edges or line segments) are almost always involved, making the definition of segments as geometric primitives essential. It is well known that an edge or line segment $\overline{P_1P_2}$ can be represented as a convex combination of points P_1 and P_2, i.e., $\lambda P_1 + (1 - \lambda)P_2$, where $\lambda \in [0, 1]$. If the order of points P_1 and P_2 is important, then the segment is considered directed, denoted as the vector $\overrightarrow{P_1P_2}$. When discussing geometric objects such as a polygon, segments are understood as directed line segments or directed vectors, ensuring that the polygon's interior remains on the right side of the vectors forming the polygon. Listing 2.2 partially implements the interface of the **Segment2D** class. Within it, implementing five methods such as *rotation*(), *line_intersection*($\cdot$,$\cdot$), *intersection_segments*($\cdot$,$\cdot$), *is_inside_polygon*($\cdot$), *intersect_polygon*($\cdot$) is left for later, as they are more complex than the others implemented in place.

Listing 2.2: Definition of the class **Segment2D**

```
1 from Point2D import Point2D
2 from TypeP2 import TypeP2
3 from TypeS2 import TypeS2
4
5 class Segment2D:
6      def __init__(self, s=None, e=None):
7          self.s = s if s is not None else Point2D(0, 0) # s is start of segment
8          self.e = e if e is not None else Point2D(1, 0) # e is end of segment
9      def __getitem__(self,i):return self.s if i == 0 else self.e
10     def __setitem__(self, i, value):
11         if i==0: self.s = value
12         else: self.e = value
13     def flip(self): return self.rotate().rotate()
14     def is_vertical(self): return self.s[0] == self.e[0]
15     def slope(self):
16         if self.s[0] != self.e[0]:
17             return (self.e[1] - self.s[1]) / (self.e[0] - self.s[0])
18         return 1E10
19     def y_coord(self, x): return self.slope()*(x-self.s[0])+self.s[1]
20     def point_at(self, t):return self.s+t*(self.e-self.s)
21     def __eq__(self, s):
22         return (self.s == s[0] and self.e == s[1]) or
23                (self.s == s[1] and self.e == s[0])
24     def __ne__(self, s): return not self.__eq__(s)
```

```
25    def scalar_product(self, v1, v2): return v1[0] * v2[0] + v1[1] * v2[1]
26    def disjoint_ends(self, s):
27        return not (self.s==s[0] or self.s==s[1] or self.e==s[0] or self.e==s[1])
```

In the following, the *rotation*() method will be implemented first. The purpose of this method is to rotate the segment $\overline{P_1P_2}$, i.e., the vector $\overrightarrow{P_1P_2}$, in the clockwise direction around its midpoint M by an angle of $\frac{\pi}{2}$ (see Fig. 2.4 (a)). Since the point M is the midpoint of the segment $\overline{P_1P_2}$, it follows that it is given by $M = (P_1 + P_2)/2$, while $\vec{n}$ represents the normal vector of the segment $\overline{P_1P_2}$. Given that the ordered pairs (x_1, y_1) and (x_2, y_2) correspond to the coordinates of the points P_1 and P_2, respectively, it follows that the coordinates of the direction vector of the line containing the segment $\overline{P_1P_2}$ are $(x_2 - x_1, y_2 - y_1)$. Furthermore, the coordinates of the normal vector $\vec{n}$ are given as the ordered pair $(y_2 - y_1, -(x_2 - x_1))$, while the coordinates of the midpoint M are given by $\left(\frac{x_1+x_2}{2}, \frac{y_1+y_2}{2}\right)$.

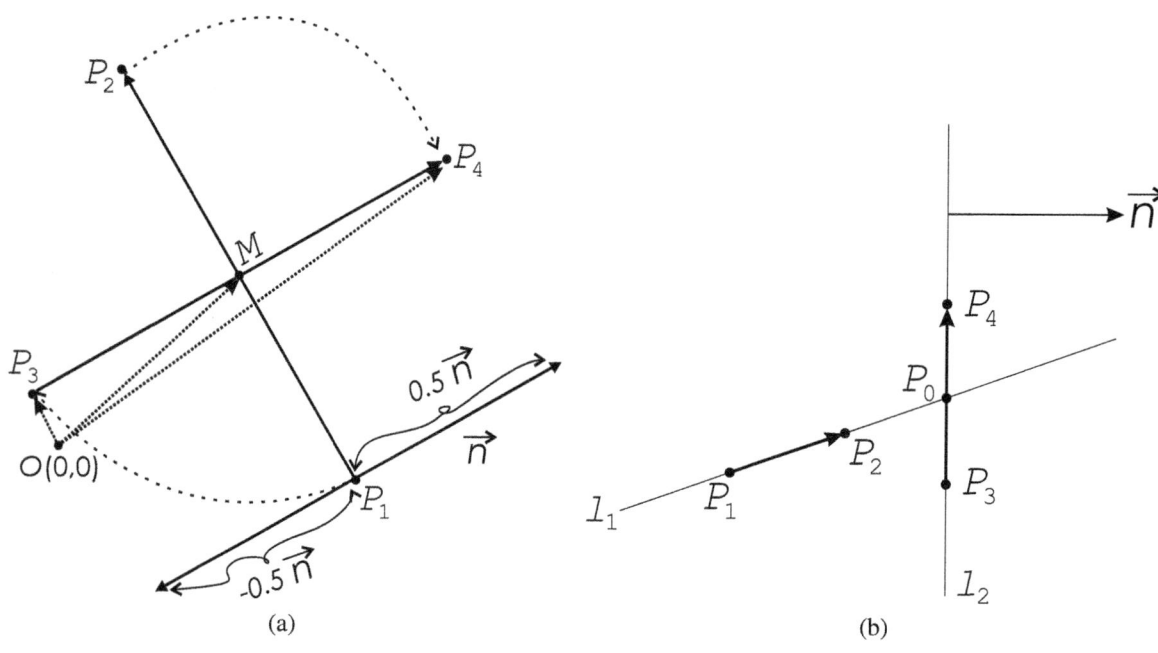

Figure 2.4: (a) Rotation of the segment $\overline{P_1P_2}$ around the midpoint M by an angle of $\frac{\pi}{2}$. (b) Intersection of the lines l_1 and l_2.

The coordinates of points P_3 and P_4 are obtained by rotating points P_1 and P_2 around point M by an angle of $90°$. The coordinates of these points will be determined vectorially in the following discussion. The vector $\overrightarrow{OP_3}$ is computed as $\overrightarrow{OP_3} = \overrightarrow{OM} + \overrightarrow{MP_3} = \overrightarrow{OM} - \overrightarrow{P_3M}$ (Fig. 2.4 (a)). Since the vectors $\overrightarrow{MP_3}$ and $-0.5\vec{n}$ are collinear, we obtain $\overrightarrow{OP_3} = \overrightarrow{OM} - 0.5\vec{n}$. Based on this, the coordinates of point P_3 are directly derived as $\left(\frac{x_1+x_2}{2}, \frac{y_1+y_2}{2}\right) - \left(\frac{y_2-y_1}{2}, \frac{x_1-x_2}{2}\right) = \left(\frac{x_2+x_1-(y_2-y_1)}{2}, \frac{x_2-x_1+y_2+y_1}{2}\right)$. Similarly, we obtain $\overrightarrow{OP_4} = \overrightarrow{OM} + 0.5\vec{n}$, so the coordinates of point P_4 are $\left(\frac{x_2+x_1+y_2-y_1}{2}, \frac{x_1-x_2+y_1+y_2}{2}\right)$. Based on the above analysis, the implementation of the *rotation*() method can be derived, which returns the segment $\overline{P_3P_4}$ obtained by rotating the segment $\overline{P_1P_2}$ by $90°$ in the clockwise direction. It is important to note that the implementation of the method *rotation*() below is written within the **Segment2D** class.

```
1 def rotate(self):
2     m = (self.s + self.e) * 0.5  # Midpoint of the segment
```

```
3      a = self.e - self.s  # Direction vector of the segment
4      n = Point2D(a[1], -a[0]) * 0.5  # Normal vector, scaled to half its length
5      self.s = m + n  # New start point of the segment
6      self.e = m - n  # New end point of the segment (clockwise rotation)
7      return self  # Return the modified segment
```

It is important to note that the *rotation()* method will not create a new segment; instead, it will modify the coordinates of the initial points of the existing segment on which it is invoked. This method returns an *l*-value, meaning it does not return a copy of the object but rather the object by reference. Such an object can later be used in chain operations, as with the *flipping()* method, where it applied the rotation operation twice to the initial segment. Further, the implementations of the methods *intersection_segments($\cdot,\cdot$)* and *Intersection_lines($\cdot,\cdot$)* of the **Segment2D** class are provided, where the first method deals with segment intersections. Before writing the implementations, several useful properties of the dot product will be presented, as it serves as an auxiliary routine for finding line intersections. In the **Segment2D** class, the implementation of the *scalar_product($\cdot,\cdot$)* method is provided, which returns the value $x_1 x_2 + y_1 y_2$ when the points $P_1(x_1, y_1)$ and $P_2(x_2, y_2)$ are passed as formal parameters. It is entirely justified since points in the plane can be viewed as their radius vectors. Some properties of the dot product $\vec{a} \cdot \vec{b} = \|\vec{a}\| \|\vec{b}\| \cos\theta$, where $\theta = \angle(\vec{a}, \vec{b})$, are:

- $\vec{a} \cdot \vec{b} > 0 \iff \theta < 90°$;
- $\vec{a} \cdot \vec{b} < 0 \iff \theta > 90°$;
- $\vec{a} \cdot \vec{b} = 0 \iff \theta = 90°$;
- if $\vec{a} = \vec{0}$, then $\vec{a} \cdot \vec{a} = 0$, otherwise, $\vec{a} \cdot \vec{a} > 0$;
- $\|\vec{a}\|^2 = \vec{a} \cdot \vec{a}$;
- If s is a scalar (a number), then the following holds: $(s\vec{a}) \cdot \vec{b} = s(\vec{a} \cdot \vec{b}) = \vec{a} \cdot (s\vec{b})$.

Also, for vectors, the commutative and associative laws hold. The first step in finding the intersection of the lines l_1 and l_2 that contain the segments $\overline{P_1 P_2}$ i $\overline{P_3 P_4}$ is their representation in parametric form:

$$l_1 : L_1(t) = P_1 + t(P_2 - P_1), \ l_2 : L_2(t) = P_3 + t(P_4 - P_3),$$

where $t \in \mathbb{R}$ is a parameter, and the points $L_1(t)$ and $L_2(t)$ "walk" along the segments $\overline{P_1 P_2}$ and $\overline{P_3 P_4}$ whenever the parameter t "walks" through the closed interval $[0, 1]$. If the lines l_1 and l_2 are neither parallel nor coincident, then there exists a number $t_0 \in \mathbb{R}$ $P_0 = L_1(t_0)$ is the intersection point of the lines l_1 and l_2 (Fig. 2.4 (b)). The figure denotes the vector normal to the line l_2 by $\vec{n}$. From the figure, it is observed that the vectors $\vec{n}$ and $\overrightarrow{P_3 P_0}$ are orthogonal, so the equation $\vec{n} \cdot \overrightarrow{P_3 P_0} = 0$ holds. By directly substituting the point $P_0 = P_1 + t_0(P_2 - P_1)$ into the scalar product $\vec{n} \cdot \overrightarrow{P_3 P_0} = 0$, and after a few elementary transformations, the expression for calculating the parameter t_0 is obtained:

$$t_0 = \frac{\vec{n} \cdot (P_1 - P_3)}{\vec{n} \cdot (P_1 - P_2)} \ (P_1 \neq P_2). \tag{2.4}$$

It is important to note that the relation 2.4 is used if the lines l_1 and l_2 are steep or slanted, i.e., when there is precisely one intersection point. If the lines are parallel or coincident, then their direction vectors $\overrightarrow{P_1 P_2}$ and $\overrightarrow{P_3 P_4}$ are parallel, so in that case, the scalar product is equal to zero. In order to encompass all cases, it is necessary to introduce a new enumerated data type **TypeS2**:

```
1 from enum import Enum
2 class TypeS2(Enum):
3     COINCIDE = 1
4     PARALLEL = 2
```

```
5    INTERSECT = 3
6    INTERSECT_SEG= 4
7    NON_INTERSECT_SEG = 5
```

After explaining the procedure for finding the intersection point of parametrically defined lines, the implementation of the method *intersection_lines*(·,·) is as follows:

```
1 def intersection_lines(self, s, p):
2     # Parameter p passed by reference
3     p1 = self.s; p2 = self.e
4     p3 = s[0]; p4 = s[1]
5     # Normal vector n of the segment
6     n = Point2D(p4[1]-p3[1],p3[0]-p4[0])
7     # Denominator in the intersection formula
8     denominator = self.scalar_product(n, p2-p1)
9     if math.isclose(denominator, 0.0, rel_tol=1e-9, abs_tol=1e-12):
10        s_type = p1.classification(s[0],s[1])
11        if s_type == TypeP2.LEFT or s_type == TypeP2.RIGHT:
12            return TypeS2.PARALLEL #COINCIDE = 1, PARALLEL = 2
13        return TypeS2.COINCIDE  # Same line
14    #Return value by reference using list t
15    p[0] = -self.scalar_product(n, p1-p3) / denominator
16    return TypeS2.INTERSECT  # Lines intersect
```

It is not difficult to notice that the member function *intersection_lines*(·,·) is necessary but insufficient for finding the segments' intersection. However, if we use the fact that two segments intersect *if and only if* their endpoints lie on opposite sides, it appears that the mentioned method can be used for segment intersection. Namely, we first check whether the corresponding lines intersect and then verify whether the endpoints of the segments lie on opposite sides. Unfortunately, this is insufficient, as the segments may coincide or lie on the same line but do not overlap. In both cases, the expected results are not obtained, i.e., it is impossible to determine on which side the endpoints of the segments lie or whether their intersection forms a new sub-segment. Therefore, additional entries have been added to the enumerated data type TypeS2 to handle the mentioned cases, such as INTERSECT_SEG and NON_INTERSECT_SEG. Now it is possible to use the method *intersection_lines*(·,·) as an auxiliary function to implement the method *intersection_segments*(·,·), which has been done in the code snippet below:

```
1 def intersection_segments(self,s,p):
2     """Determines the type of intersection between two segments."""
3     intersection_type=s.intersection_lines(self, p)
4     if intersection_type in (TypeS2.COINCIDE, TypeS2.PARALLEL):return
          intersection_type
5     if p[0]<0 or p[0]>1: return TypeS2.NON_INTERSECT_SEG
6     self.intersection_lines(s,p)# Determine the exact intersection of segments
7     if (p[0]>=0 and p[0]<=1): return TypeS2.INTERSECT_SEG
8     return TypeS2.NON_INTERSECT_SEG
```

2.3.1 Segment-Segment Intersection Test

In this section, we demonstrate how to create instances of the **Segment2D** class and how to test the relationships between two segments. The most common types of relationships encountered are:

1. The segments do not intersect:

```
1 s1=Segment2D(Point2D(0,0),Point2D(5,0)) # First segment
```

```
2 s2=Segment2D(Point2D(-1,-5),Point2D(-1,5)) # Second segment
3 p=[0] # Prepare a placeholder for the intersection point
4 print(s1.intersection_segments(s2,p)) # Expected: TypeS2.NON_INTERSECT_SEG
```

2. The segments intersect:

```
1 s1=Segment2D(Point2D(0,0),Point2D(5,0)) # First segment
2 s2=Segment2D(Point2D(2,-5),Point2D(2,5)) # Second segment
3 p=[0] # Prepare a placeholder for the intersection point
4 print(s1.intersection_segments(s2,p)) # Expected: TypeS2.INTERSECT_SEG
5 p_of_i=s1.point_at(p[0]) # Determine the point of intersection
6 print(p_of_i)#Expected: Point2D(2.0, 0.0)
```

3. The segments are parallel:

```
1 s1=Segment2D(Point2D(0,0),Point2D(5,0)) # First segment
2 s2=Segment2D(Point2D(-1,-1),Point2D(1,-1)) # Second segment
3 p=[0] # Prepare a placeholder for the intersection point
4 print(s1.intersection_segments(s2,p)) # Expected: TypeS2.PARALLEL
```

4. The segments lie on the same line:

```
1 s1=Segment2D(Point2D(4,0),Point2D(5,0)) # First segment
2 s2=Segment2D(Point2D(6,0),Point2D(10,0)) # Second segment
3 p=[0] # Prepare a placeholder for the intersection point
4 print(s1.intersection_segments(s2,p)) # Expected: TypeS2.COINCIDE
```

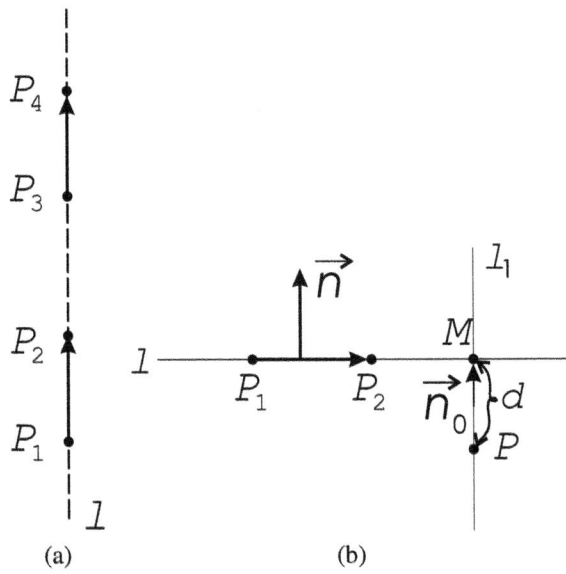

(a)   (b)

Figure 2.5: (a) Relationship between segments. (b) Distance of point P from line l.

If the segments $\overline{P_1P_2}$ and $\overline{P_3P_4}$ lie on the same line l (see Fig. 2.5 (a)), then the possible relationships between them are:

a) the segment $\overline{P_1P_2}$ is located behind the segment $\overline{P_3P_4}$;

b) the segment $\overline{P_1P_2}$ is located within the segment $\overline{P_3P_4}$;

c) the segment $\overline{P_1P_2}$ is located in front of the segment $\overline{P_3P_4}$;

 d) the segment $\overline{P_1P_2}$ strictly contains the segment $\overline{P_3P_4}$;

 e) the segment $\overline{P_1P_2}$ coincides with the segment $\overline{P_3P_4}$;

 f) the segment $\overline{P_1P_2}$ touches the segment $\overline{P_3P_4}$ at the point $P_2 = P_3$ or at the point $P_1 = P_4$;

 g) the segment $\overline{P_1P_2}$ overlaps with the segment $\overline{P_3P_4}$, resulting in new sub-segments $\overline{P_3P_2}$ and $\overline{P_1P_4}$, respectively.

■ **Example 2.1** Implement the method *classify*$(\cdot,\cdot)$ of the **Segment2D** class, which covers the cases from a) to g). This method should return the relationship between the two segments, as well as the overlapping segment by reference, if one exists.   ■

It remains to implement the method *distance*$(\cdot)$ of the **Point2D** class. From analytic geometry, it is known that the distance, denoted by d, from the point $P_0(x_0, y_0)$ to the line l given in implicit form $l : Ax + By + C = 0$ is calculated as follows:

$$d = \frac{|Ax_0 + By_0 + C|}{\sqrt{A^2 + B^2}}. \tag{2.5}$$

However, for implementation purposes, the distance d from point P to line l is computed slightly differently for the sake of efficiency (see Fig. 2.5 (b)). The procedure for calculating the distance d consists of four steps. In the first step, the normal vector $\vec{n}$ of the line l is determined, which is uniquely defined by the points P_1 and P_2. The normal vector $\vec{n}$ can be determined as in the case of line intersection, although it can also be calculated differently by rotating the line l by $90°$ in the clockwise direction (by calling the *rotation*() method on the segment s contained by the line l), whereby the normal vector $\vec{n}$ is obtained from the direction vector of the rotated line. In this step, the unit normal vector $\vec{n_0}$ is also computed as $\vec{n_0} = \frac{\vec{n}}{\|\vec{n}\|}$. In the second step, the line l_1 is determined, which is perpendicular to line l and passes through point P. To define this line, it is sufficient to determine a segment it contains, i.e., a segment with starting point P and ending point P'. The point P' is obtained by translating point P along the unit normal vector $\vec{n_0}$. In the third step, the intersection point M of the lines l and l_1 is found. In the final step, the distance between points P and M is calculated, which actually represents the distance from point P to the line l, uniquely defined by the segment $s = \overline{P_1P_2}$. Following this procedure for computing the distance, the implementation of the *distance*$(\cdot)$ method is as follows:

```python
def distance(self, s):
    from Segment2D import Segment2D #lazy import
    s1 =copy.copy(s) # Make a copy of the segment and rotate it
    s1.rotate()
    n = s1[0] - s1[1] # Compute normal vector
    n = (1.0 / n.magnitude()) * n # n is a unit vector
    s1 = Segment2D(self, self + n) # Construct segment s1 from self to self + n
    t = [0.0]
    s.intersection_lines(s1, t)    # Find intersection of lines
    n = s.point_at(t[0]) - self # Compute distance vector and return its magnitude
    return n.magnitude()
}
```

It is not difficult to observe that the parameter t within the member function *distance*$(\cdot)$ can be used to determine on which side of the line l the point P lies. For example, if $t > 0$, then the point P is located on the right side of the segment $\overline{P_1P_2}$, i.e., the vector $\overrightarrow{P_1P_2}$, whereas if $t < 0$, it is located on its left side. Otherwise, the points P_1, P_2, and P are collinear.

2.4 Vertices and Their Role in Geometric Structures

Due to the need to store information about the vertices of a polygon, the class **Vertex** will be defined and implemented in the following sections. This class multiple inherits both **Point2D** and **Node** classes. Objects of the **Vertex** class will behave as points in the plane on the one hand, while on the other hand, they will act as nodes in a doubly linked circular list. The purpose of the **Vertex** class is to inherit the attributes prev_node and next_node from the **Node** class, as well as the attributes x and y from the **Point2D** class. At this point, a convention is adopted whereby the attributes next_node and prev_node respectively denote the *next adjacent vertex* and the *previous adjacent vertex* when traversing the doubly linked circular list in the clockwise and counterclockwise directions, respectively. Due to the simplicity of the methods in the **Vertex** class, Listing 2.3 provides the class definition and the implementation of all methods.

Listing 2.3: Definition of the class **Vertex**

```python
from Point2D import Point2D
from Node import Node

class Vertex(Point2D, Node):
    def __init__(self, x=0.0, y=0.0):
        # Explicitly initialize both parent classes
        Point2D.__init__(self, x, y) # Initialize Point2D class
        Node.__init__(self)  # Initialize Node class
    def clockwise(self):return self.next_node
    def counter_clockwise(self):return self.previous_node
    def neighbor(self, orientation):# Neighboring point based on orientation
        return self.clockwise() if orientation<0 else self.counter_clockwise()
    # Return the vertex point as a new instance of Point2D
    def vertex_point(self):return Point2D.Point2D(self.__x, self.__y)
    # Insert a new vertex into the Node structure
    def insert(self, v):return Node.insert(self, v)
    # Remove the vertex from the Node structure
    def remove(self): return Node.remove(self)
    # Connect the vertex with another vertex
    def connect(self, v): Node.connect(self,v)
    def is_convex(self)->bool:
        u=self.counter_clockwise(); w=self.clockwise()
        c = w.classification_m(u.vertex_point(), self.vertex_point())
        return (c ==TypeP2.BEHIND or c == TypeP2.RIGHT)
    def split(self, v):
        # Insert a new Vertex at v's counter-clockwise position
        v1 = v.counter_clockwise().insert(Vertex(v.vertex_point()))
        self.insert(Vertex(self.vertex_point())) # Insert the current vertex
        self.connect(v1) # Connect the current vertex with the new vertex v1
        return v1
```

2.5 Polygons: Structure and Representation

This section describes working with polygons, introduces fundamental definitions and concepts, and designs and implements the necessary classes for their modeling. A polygon denoted by $\mathcal{P}$ is a *closed curve* in the plane composed of segments (edges) called the *polygon edges*. The endpoints of the segments are the vertices of the polygon where adjacent segments meet. The number of vertices in a polygon determines its size. A polygon $\mathcal{P}$ is said to be a *simple polygon* if it does not intersect itself. A simple polygon divides the plane into two parts: the *interior of the polygon* and the *exterior of the polygon*. The *exterior* and *interior* of the polygon lie to the left and right, respectively, of a walker moving along the polygon edges in the clockwise direction. Polygon edges form the boundary between the interior and exterior, and are usually referred to as the *polygon boundary*. An arbitrary point A belongs to the polygon $\mathscr{P}$ if it lies on its boundary or strictly inside it. The vertices of the polygon are cyclically ordered with respect to the polygon's boundary. A neighboring vertex V_2 of vertex V_1 is called a *successor* if it lies in the clockwise direction relative to V_1. Conversely, the vertex V_2 is called a *predecessor* if it lies in the counterclockwise direction relative to V_1. *Polygon traversal* implies a circular traversal of the polygon's vertices in either the clockwise or counterclockwise direction. Each vertex of a polygon can be classified as either a *convex vertex* or a *reflex vertex*. A vertex is convex if its interior angle is less than $180°$, while a vertex is reflex if its interior angle is greater than $180°$. However, if the interior angle is exactly $180°$, the vertex is neither convex nor reflex; such a vertex is degenerate, since three consecutive points lie on the same line and do not form an angle of the polygon. If all vertices of polygon $\mathscr{P}$ are convex, then the polygon $\mathscr{P}$ is called a *convex polygon*. This provides one way to verify the convexity of a polygon. Another way to verify the convexity of a polygon $\mathscr{P} = \{V_0, V_1, \cdots, V_{n-1}\}$ composed of n vertices $V_0, V_1, \cdots, V_{n-1}$ is to check the orientations of the triangles: $\triangle V_0 V_1 V_2$, $\triangle V_1 V_2 V_3$, $\cdots$, $\triangle V_{n-2} V_{n-1} V_0$. If all triangle orientations have the same sign (either all positive or all negative), then the polygon $\mathscr{P}$ is convex; otherwise, it is not. A segment connecting any two non-adjacent vertices is called a *polygon diagonal*. A diagonal is *interior* if it lies entirely within the polygon (which is the case for convex polygons), or *exterior* if it lies outside the interior of the polygon (which can happen in concave polygons). From a mathematical perspective, a polygon $\mathscr{P}$ is said to be convex if, for any two points P and Q within $\mathscr{P}$, the segment $\overline{PQ}$ lies entirely within the polygon $\mathscr{P}$. Due to this nice property of convexity, it is easy to show that the intersection of any two convex polygons is again a convex polygon. In Listing 2.4, the definition of the **Polygon** class is proposed, including **inline** implementations of basic class methods. From the content of the listing, it can be seen that several methods have been inline implemented, such as:

- *from_points* – used to create a polygon from a given list of points;
- *from_vertex* – used to create a polygon starting from a vertex;
- copy - makes a deep copy of the polygon;
- __del__ – destructor used to release resources such as memory;
- __eq__ – operator for checking the equality of polygons;
- *current_vertex* – returns the active (currently marked) vertex of the polygon;
- *size* – returns the number of vertices of the polygon;
- *point_of_current* – returns the point corresponding to the current vertex;
- *current_edge* – returns the segment (current edge of the polygon) incident to the current vertex and its neighbour;
- *cw_neighbor* – returns the neighbour of the current vertex oriented in the clockwise direction (negative orientation);
- *ccw_neighbor* – returns the neighbour of the current vertex oriented in the counterclockwise direction (positive orientation);
- *neighbour* – returns the neighbour of the current vertex depending on the orientation;
- *update_current* – sets the current vertex and then returns it;
- *move_current* – moves the current vertex in the clockwise direction and then returns it;
- *insert* – adds a point to the polygon via a vertex passed as a formal parameter, which is then returned from the method;
- *remove* – deletes the currently marked vertex (current) from the polygon and redirects the pointer to the previous vertex;
- *change_orientation* – changes the orientation of the current polygon so that the vertices are oriented in the clockwise direction;

- *decrease_count* – decreases the number of vertices in the polygon by one.

The **Polygon** class is intrinsically linked to the Vertex class, as the vertices of a polygon—represented as attributes of the Polygon class—are maintained as instances of the **Vertex** class.

Listing 2.4: Definition of the class Polygon

```python
from Segment2D import Segment2D
from Vertex import Vertex
from Point2D import Point2D

class Polygon:
    @classmethod
    def from_points(cls, points):
        polygon = cls()
        for pt in points: polygon.insert(pt)
        return polygon
    @classmethod
    def from_vertex(cls, v):
        p=cls(); p.current=v; p.update_count(); return p
    def copy(self):
        return Polygon(self) #Returns a deep copy of the polygon
    def __eq__(self, other):
        if not isinstance(other,Polygon) or self.count!=other.count:return False
        v1 = self.current
        v2 = other.current
        for _ in range(self.count):
            if v1.vertex_point()!=v2.vertex_point():return False
            v1 = v1.clockwise()
            v2 = v2.clockwise()
        return True
    def current_vertex(self): return self.current
    def size(self): return self.count
    def point_of_current(self): return self.current.vertex_point()
    def current_edge(self):
        return Segment2D(self.point_of_current(),self.current.clockwise().
            vertex_point())
    def cw_neighbor(self): return self.current.clockwise()
    def ccw_neighbor(self): return self.current.counter_clockwise()
    def neighbor(self, orientation): return self.current.neighbor(orientation)
    def update_current(self, v):
        self.current = v
        return self.current
    def move_current(self, direction):
        self.current = self.current.neighbor(direction)
        return self.current
    def insert(self, point):
        vertex = Vertex(point[0], point[1]) if isinstance(point, (tuple, list))
            else Vertex(point.__getitem__(0), point.__getitem__(1))
        if self.count == 0: self.current = vertex
        else: self.current.counter_clockwise().insert(vertex)
        self.count += 1
        return self.current
    def remove(self):
        if self.count == 0: return
        elif self.count == 1:
            del self.current
            self.current = None
```

```
50      else:
51          self.current = self.current.counter_clockwise()
52          self.current.clockwise().remove()
53      self.count -= 1
54  def decrease_count(self): self.count -= 1
55  def change_orientation(self):
56      temp = []
57      for _ in range(self.count):
58          temp.append(self.point_of_current())
59          self.move_current(1)
60      for _ in range(self.count): self.remove()
61      for i in range(len(temp)): self.insert(temp[len(temp) - i - 1])
62  def __del__(self):
63      if self.current:
64          v = self.current.clockwise()
65          while v != self.current:
66              temp = v.clockwise()
67              v.remove()
68              v = temp
69          del self.current
```

The following provides the implementation of both the default constructor and the copy constructor together. In addition, several other utility methods are implemented to facilitate convenient usage of the **Polygon** class.

```
1  def __init__(self, other=None):
2      self.current = None
3      self.count = 0
4      if isinstance(other, Polygon):
5          self.count = other.size()
6          if self.count == 0: return
7          p_c = other.point_of_current()
8          v_new= self.current = Vertex(p_c[0], p_c[1])
9          for _ in range(1, self.count):
10             other.move_current(-1)
11             p_c= other.point_of_current()
12             v_new = v_new.insert(Vertex(p_c[0], p_c[1]))
13         other.move_current(-1)
14         self.current = v_new.clockwise() # close the polygon
```

To enable object duplication, the copy() method creates and returns a new, independent instance of the **Polygon** class, as demonstrated below:

```
1  def __copy__(self):
2      new_poly = Polygon()
3      new_poly.count = self.count
4      if self.count == 0: return new_poly
5      original = self.current
6      p_c = self.point_of_current()
7      new_poly.current = Vertex(p_c[0], p_c[1])
8      v_new = new_poly.current
9      for _ in range(1, self.count):
10         self.move_current(-1) # clockwise direction
11         p_c = self.point_of_current()
12         v_new = v_new.insert(Vertex(p_c[0], p_c[1]))
13     self.update_current(original)
```

```
14    new_poly.current = v_new.clockwise()
15    return new_poly
```

The next method of the **Polygon** class is the *split*(·) method, whose task is to divide the polygon into two sub-polygons, $\mathscr{P}_1$ and $\mathscr{P}_2$, depending on the vertex passed to it as a formal parameter. After the split is performed, i.e., after invoking the mentioned method on an instance of the **Polygon** class, the current polygon $\mathscr{P}$ becomes $\mathscr{P}_1$, while the second polygon $\mathscr{P}_2$ generated by the split is returned from the method. The implementation of the *split*(·) method is shown in the code snippet below:

```
1 def split(self, v):
2     #Divides the polygon with respect to the current vertex and the vertex v
3     v1 = self.current.split(v)
4     self.update_count()
5     return Polygon.from_vertex(v1)
```

The method *update_count*() is called during the division of a polygon into two sub-polygons in order to subsequently calculate the number of vertices in one of the newly created sub-polygons. Its purpose is to count how many vertices are currently present in the list. The implementation is given below:

```
1 def update_count(self):
2     if not self.current: self.count = 0
3     else:
4         v = self.current.clockwise()
5         self.count = 1
6         while v != self.current:
7             self.count += 1
8             v = v.clockwise()
```

The procedure for testing polygon convexity was previously described, and its implementation is provided below:

```
1 def is_convex(self):
2     if self.count<3: return False
3     prev_p=self.neighbor(1).vertex_point()# Previous point for orientation check
4     # Determine the initial orientation type using classification_m
5     o=prev_p.classification_m(self.neighbor(-1).vertex_point(), self.
          point_of_current())
6     for _ in range(1, self.count):# Iterate through all vertices of polygon
7         self.move_current(1)
8         prev_p=self.neighbor(1).vertex_point()
9         c_o=prev_p.classification_m(self.neighbor(-1).vertex_point(),self.
              point_of_current())
10        if c_o!= o: return False
11    return True
```

The implementation of the following method of the **Polygon** class concerns testing whether a polygon is simple or not. An exhaustive search is required to check whether any pair of non-adjacent edges intersect. Clearly, this search requires quadratic time, which can be time-consuming for a large number of points. Although a more intelligent approach for testing polygon simplicity exists with complexity $\Theta(n\log n)$, it will not be considered here. Instead, a quadratic-time version of the method, with $\mathscr{O}(n^2)$ complexity, will be implemented. The implementation of the mentioned quadratic method is given below:

```
1  def is_simple(self):
2      # Extract all vertices into a list, including the wraparound to the first
3      vertices = []
4      start = self.current
5      for _ in range(self.count):
6          vertices.append(self.point_of_current())
7          self.move_current(1)
8      vertices.append(vertices[0])  # Close the polygon
9      # Compare all pairs of non-adjacent segments
10     for i in range(self.count):
11         s1 = Segment2D(vertices[i], vertices[i + 1])
12         for j in range(i + 2, self.count -(1 if i == 0 else 0)):
13             s2 = Segment2D(vertices[j], vertices[j + 1])
14             p = [0.0]  # Dummy variable to capture intersection parameter
15             if s1.intersection_segments(s2,p)==TypeS2.INTERSECT_SEG: return False
16     return True
```

The implementation of the next method in the **Polygon** class concerns determining the orientation of a polygon. For certain algorithms, it is essential to verify whether all vertices are provided in a clockwise order or not. Therefore, it is necessary to implement a method that, depending on how the polygon vertices are given, returns a negative value (for clockwise orientation) or a positive value (for counter-clockwise orientation). It is clear that in the case of a convex polygon, by examining the orientation of any triplet of consecutive vertices (e.g., the first three vertices (P_1, P_2, P_3)), the orientation of the polygon can be determined in constant time. The situation becomes slightly more complex when the polygon is not convex. In the case of a concave polygon, its orientation matches the orientation of three consecutive vertices P_{i-1}, P_i, P_{i+1} *if and only if* the vertex P_i is convex. If the vertex P_i is reflex, then the orientation of the polygon differs from the orientation formed by the neighboring vertices P_{i-1}, P_i, P_{i+1}. Thus, it is sufficient to find one convex vertex of the polygon—specifically, a vertex whose interior angle is less than a straight angle. Such a vertex can be found in $\mathcal{O}(n)$ time. One such candidate is the vertex with the smallest x-coordinate; if there are multiple with the same x-coordinate, then the one with the smallest y-coordinate is selected. Without loss of generality, let this be vertex P_i. The polygon is said to be positively (negatively) oriented if the neighboring vertices P_{i-1}, P_i, P_{i+1} form a positively (negatively) oriented triplet, i.e., if the point P_{i+1} lies to the left (right) of the segment $\overline{P_{i-1}P_i}$. If the points P_{i-1}, P_i, P_{i+1} are collinear, then the orientation of the polygon is neutral. Accordingly, the implementation of the *orientation()* method can be written as follows:

```
1  def orientation(self):
2      min_vertex = self.current
3      min_point = self.point_of_current()
4      for _ in range(1, self.count):# Move through the pol. to find the min. vertex
5          self.move_current(-1)
6          if self.point_of_current() < min_point:
7              min_vertex = self.current
8              min_point = self.point_of_current()
9      self.update_current(min_vertex)# Update current to the min. vertex
10     curr_p=self.point_of_current() # Get current
11     prev_p=self.neighbor(-1).vertex_point() # Get previous around current
12     next_p=self.neighbor(1).vertex_point() # Get next around current
13     classification = next_p.classification_m(prev_p,curr_p)
14     if classification == TypeP2.RIGHT: return 1
15     elif classification == TypeP2.LEFT: return -1
16     return 0
```

The implementation of the next method concerns calculating the area of a polygon. Let the polygon $\mathscr{P}$ consist of n vertices $P_0(x_0, y_0)$, $P_1(x_1, y_1)$, $\cdots$, $P_{n-1}(x_{n-1}, y_{n-1})$. Then, the area of the polygon is computed using the following formula:

$$A(\mathscr{P}) = \frac{1}{2} \sum_{i=0}^{n-1} (x_{i+1} + x_i)(y_{i+1} - y_i). \tag{2.6}$$

In equation 2.6, the point $P_n(x_n, y_n)$ coincides with the point $P_0(x_0, y_0)$. The proof of correctness of the mentioned formula will be presented in the following chapters, when polygon triangulation is discussed. Based on the stated formula, the implementation of the *area*() method becomes straightforward:

```python
def area(self):
    total = 0.0
    for _ in range(self.count):
        t = self.point_of_current()
        s = self.neighbor(1).vertex_point()
        total += (t[0] + s[0]) * (s[1] - t[1])
        self.move_current(1)
    return 0.5 * total
```

The following section presents the implementations of the methods *contains_point*($\cdot$), *get_vertex*($\cdot$), and *is_subset*($\cdot$). In the case of the method *contains_point*($\cdot$), the implementation will focus on testing whether a point A belongs to a convex polygon $\mathscr{P}$. If the polygon $\mathscr{P}$ is not convex, then the membership test for point A is reduced to checking the number of intersections between the polygon's edges and a ray q originating at A and extending in the direction parallel to the positive x-axis. If the number of such intersections is *odd*, then point A lies inside the polygon $\mathscr{P}$. Otherwise, point A lies outside the polygon $\mathscr{P}$. The implementation of this method is given below:

```python
def contains_point(self, p: Point2D):
    if self.is_convex(): # convex case
        left=right=False
        c_v = self.current_vertex() #current vertex
        for i in range(0, self.size()):#curent edge
            c_e = self.current_edge()
            cl=p.classification_m(c_e[0], c_e[1])
            if (cl==TypeP2.LEFT): left = True
            elif (cl==TypeP2.RIGHT): right = True
            if left and right: self.update_current(c_v); return False
            self.move_current(-1)
        if ((left and not right) or (right and not left)): return True
        return False
    else:  # non-convex case: ray-casting algorithm
        i_count = 0 # intersection count
        far_point = Point2D(p[0] + 1e3, p[1])  # point far to the right
        ray = Segment2D(p, far_point)
        p0 = [0.0]
        for _ in range(self.count):
            s=self.current_edge()
            if s.intersection_segments(ray,p0)==TypeS2.INTERSECT_SEG: i_count+=1
            self.move_current(-1)
        return i_count % 2 == 1
```

It is not difficult to conclude from the above implementation that the time required to check whether a point lies inside a convex polygon is of order $\mathscr{O}(n)$ in the worst case.

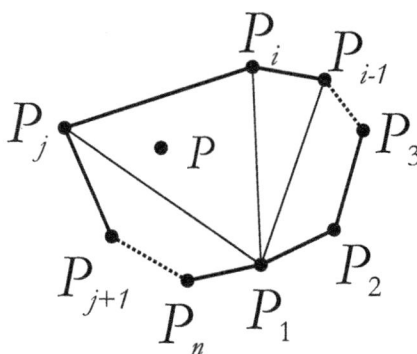

Figure 2.6: Locating a point P inside a convex polygon in $\mathcal{O}(\log n)$ time.

At this point, we describe a procedure that guarantees the membership of a point in a convex polygon can be verified in logarithmic time. Without loss of generality, let the point P be given inside a convex polygon consisting of n vertices (see Fig. 2.6). Since the polygon is convex, checking whether the point belongs to it essentially reduces to testing whether it lies inside one of its angles. The point P lies within the angle $\angle P_i P P_j$ *if and only if* the points P_j and P lie on the same side (left or right) of the segment $\overline{P_1 P_i}$, and the points P_i and P also lie on the same side of the segment $\overline{P_1 P_j}$. For example, the point $P \in \angle P_i P P_j$ *if and only if* the points P_j and P lie on the left (or right) side of the segment $\overline{P_1 P_i}$, while the points P_i and P lie on the right (or left) side of the segment $\overline{P_1 P_j}$. An $\mathcal{O}(\log n)$ time complexity algorithm for determining whether a point P lies inside a convex polygon $\mathscr{P}$ with n vertices can be formulated as follows. First, check whether the point P lies within the angle $\angle P_n P P_1$. If not, the algorithm terminates because in that case, the point P cannot lie inside the convex polygon $\mathscr{P}$. If it does, the interval $[1, n]$ is split into two subintervals, $[1, m]$ and $[m+1, n]$, where m is the integer part of $(n+2)/2$, i.e., the midpoint of the interval. Next, it is checked whether the point P lies inside the angle $\angle P_m P_1 P_2$. If it does, the interval $[1, m]$ is further divided into two subintervals, and the procedure continues recursively on them. Otherwise, the point P lies within the angle $\angle P_n P_1 P_m$, and the second interval $[m+1, n]$ is split into two new subintervals, to which the previously described angle-membership testing procedure is recursively applied. The algorithm stops as soon as the polygon vertices P_i and P_j become adjacent. Immediately before that, it is necessary to verify whether the point P lies inside the triangle $\triangle P_i P P_j$. If it does, then P lies inside the convex polygon; otherwise, it does not. The entire membership test procedure is completed after exactly $\mathcal{O}(\log n)$ recursive calls. Based on the description above, it is not difficult to implement the algorithm, which is left to the reader as an exercise.

In the following section, the methods *is_subset*($\cdot$) and *find_vertex*($\cdot$) of the **Polygon** class will be implemented, as well as the method *intersects_polygon*($\cdot$) of the **Segment2D** class. The remaining methods *is_inside_polygon*($\cdot$), *tangent*($\cdot$,$\cdot$), *tangent_points*($\cdot$,$\cdot$), *merge*($\cdot$), *get_convex_vertex*(), *nearest_vertex*($\cdot$), *farthest_vertex*($\cdot$,$\cdot$), *is_monotone*(), *triangulate_eca*(), *triangulate_recursive*($\cdot$), *triangulate_monotone*($\cdot$), and *triangulate_merge*() of the **Polygon** class will be implemented in the following chapters of the book. The *intersects_polygon*($\cdot$) method of the **Segment2D** class will be implemented first, since it is later called within the *is_subset*($\cdot$) method. The *intersects_polygon*($\cdot$) method returns **False** if there is no intersection between the segment and the polygon sides. Otherwise, it returns **True** as an indicator that an intersection has occurred. Its implementation is given as follows:

```python
def intersects_polygon(self, polygon):
    s = Segment2D(self.s, self.e)  # Copy of this segment
    start_point = polygon.point_of_current()
    c_vertex = polygon.current_vertex()
    while True:
        s_vertex = c_vertex.neighbor(-1)  # clockwise neighbor
```

```
7      s1= Segment2D(c_vertex.vertex_point(), s_vertex.vertex_point())
8      p = [0.0]
9      if (s.disjoint_ends(s1) and s.intersection_segments(s1, p) == TypeS2.
           INTERSECT_SEG): return True
10     c_vertex = s_vertex
11     if c_vertex.vertex_point() == start_point: break
12  return False
```

The purpose of the method *is_subset*(·) is to verify whether polygon *A* is a subset of polygon *B*. Its implementation is given below:

```
1 def is_subset(self, B):
2     A = self.copy() # Copy of the current polygon
3     vertices = [] # The vertices of polygon A
4     for _ in range(A.size()):
5         if not B.contains_point(A.point_of_current()):return False
6         vertices.append(A.point_of_current())
7         A.move_current(1)
8     vertices.append(vertices[0])  # Close the polygon A
9     # Test the intersection between sides of polygon A with polgon B
10    for i in range(len(vertices)-1):
11        s = Segment2D(vertices[i], vertices[i+1])
12        if s.intersects_polygon(B): return False
13    return True
```

The last method of the **Polygon** class returns a vertex that satisfies a given comparison criterion, which is passed as a function argument. Depending on the definition of the comparison function (see Example 2.3), this method can return the rightmost vertex, the leftmost vertex, or any other vertex based on the specified condition. The implementation is provided below:

```
1 def find_vertex(self, comparator):
2     c_vertex = self.current # current_vertex
3     for _ in range(1, self.count):
4         self.move_current(-1) # clockwise
5         if comparator(self.current, c_vertex) < 0: c_vertex = self.current
6     self.update_current(c_vertex)
7     return c_vertex
```

2.5.1 Examples of Using the Polygon Class

This section presents different ways of creating instances of the **Polygon** class and demonstrates how to invoke its methods. Special attention is given to the methods used for checking point membership in the polygon and for determining the leftmost and rightmost vertices. Other methods of the **Polygon** class are called in a similar manner, depending on their specific purpose.

■ **Example 2.2** Let a polygon $\mathscr{P}$ be given in the plane by the points $P_0 = (1,1)$, $P_1 = (3,0.5)$, $P_2 = (4,1)$, $P_3 = (5,3)$, $P_4 = (3,2)$, and $P_5 = (3,4.5)$. Determine whether the point $P = (2,2)$ lies inside the polygon.
■

```
1 p = Polygon()
2 p.insert(Point2D(1, 1)); p.insert(Point2D(3, 0.5)); p.insert(Point2D(4, 1))
3 p.insert(Point2D(5, 3)); p.insert(Point2D(3, 2)); p.insert(Point2D(3, 4.5))
4 print(p.contains_point(Point2D(2, 2))) #True
5 print(p.contains_point(Point2D(2, 4.5))) #False
```

▪ **Example 2.3** Implement two criterion functions *leftmost_vertex*(·,·) and *rightmost_vertex*(·,·), which, when passed as function arguments to the method *find_vertex*(·) of the **Polygon** class, cause the mentioned method to return the leftmost or rightmost vertex of the polygon, respectively.   ▪

The first criterion function, *leftmost_vertex*(·,·), is used to find the leftmost vertex of a polygon, that is, the vertex whose point has the smallest *x*-coordinate. Its main purpose is to compare vertex points using the "less than" relation, which is implemented through the special method `__lt__` in the **Point2D** class. The implementation of the mentioned function is given below:

```
def leftmost_vertex(a, b):
    if a < b: return -1
    elif a > b: return 1
    return 0
```

In a similar manner, the criterion function *rightmost_vertex*(·,·) is implemented:

```
def rightmost_vertex(a, b):
    return leftmost\_vertex (b, a)
```

The usage of the above-defined criterion functions is given below:

```
p=Polygon.from_points([Point2D(1, 5), Point2D(6, 6), Point2D(7, 3), Point2D(2, 1)])
print(p.find_vertex(leftmost_vertex).vertex_point()) # Point2D(1, 5)
print(p.find_vertex(rightmost_vertex).vertex_point()) # Point2D(7, 3)
```

2.6 Triangles: Basic Building Blocks of Geometry

Triangle is one of the key concepts in computational geometry. It is defined by three points *A*, *B*, and *C*, which are referred to as the vertices of the triangle. The triangle determined by these points consists of the set of three segments $\overline{AB}$, $\overline{BC}$, and $\overline{CA}$, which are known as its *sides*. A triangle is often described as a portion of the plane bounded by these segments. Since a triangle is a special case of a polygon (a polygon with three vertices), its implementation is not provided here, but will instead be handled through the **Polygon** class. An example of defining a triangle using the Polygon class is shown below:

```
triangle= Polygon.from_points([Point2D(0, 0),Point2D(10, 0),Point2D(5, 5)])
```

2.7 Points in Three-Dimensional Space

This section introduces the definition and implementation of the **Point3D** class, which serves to model points in three-dimensional space. Similar to the **Point2D** class, **Point3D** provides a collection of methods essential for performing various operations with points and vectors in 3D space. The interface of this class is presented in Listing 2.5.

Listing 2.5: Definition of the **Point3D** class with the implementation of basic methods

```
from math import sqrt, fabs
from TypeP3 import TypeP3

class Point3D:
    def __init__(self,x=0.0,y=0.0, z=0.0,id=0):
        self.__x=x; self.__y=y
```

```
7        self.__z=z; self.__id=id
8    def __copy__(self): #Copy constructor
9        return Point3D(self.__x,self.__y,self.__z,self.__id)
10   def get_id(self):return self.__id
11   def set_id(self, id):self.__id=id
12   def _equal(self,x,y,eps=1e-12):return fabs(x-y)<=eps*(fabs(x)+fabs(y))
13   def __eq__(self, p):
14       return self._equal(self.__x,p.__x) and self._equal(self.__y,p.__y) and
             self._equal(self.__z,p.__z)
15   def __ne__(self,p): return not self.__eq__(p)
16   def __lt__(self,p):
17       if self.__x<p.__x:return True
18       elif self._equal(self.__x,p.__x) and self.__y<p.__y:return True
19       elif self._equal(self.__x,p.__x) and self._equal(self.__y,p.__y) and self.
             __z<p.__z:return True
20       else:return False
21   def __gt__(self,p):return not self<p and self!=p
22   def __add__(self,p):return Point3D(self.__x+p.__x,self.__y+p.__y,self.__z+p.
         __z)
23   def __sub__(self,p):return Point3D(self.__x-p.__x,self.__y-p.__y,self.__z-p.
         __z)
24   def __getitem__(self, i):
25       if i not in (0,1,2): raise IndexError("Index out of range")
26       return [self.__x,self.__y,self.__z][i]
27   def __setitem__(self, i, value):
28       if i == 0: self.__x = value
29       elif i == 1: self.__y = value
30       elif i == 2: self.__z = value
31       else: raise IndexError("Index out of range")
32   def __mul__(self,p):#dot product
33       if isinstance(p,Point3D):#if p is Point3D, compute dot product
34           return self.__x*p.__x+self.__y*p.__y+self.__z*p.__z
35       else:# Scalar multiplication
36           return Point3D(self.__x*p,self.__y*p,self.__z*p)
37   def __rmul__(self,p): return self.__mul__(p)
38   def __mod__(self,p):# Cross product
39       return Point3D(
40           self.__y*p.__z-self.__z*p.__y,
41           self.__z*p.__x-self.__x*p.__z,
42           self.__x*p.__y-self.__y*p.__x
43       )
44   def norm(self):return sqrt(self.__x**2+self.__y**2+self.__z**2)
45   def _sign(self, x): return 1 if x>0 else -1 if x<0 else 0
46   def same_sign(self, p):
47       for i in range(3):
48           if self._sign(self[i])!=self._sign(p[i]): return False
49       return True
50   def __repr__(self):
51       return f"Point3D({self.__x}, {self.__y}, {self.__z})"
52   def classify(self, tr:'Triangle3D')->TypeP3: #Placeholder for point
         classification relative to a triangle
53       raise NotImplementedError
54   def distance(self, object):# Placeholder for distance to line or plane
55       raise NotImplementedError
```

The methods *classify*(·) and *distance*(·) will be implemented later when modeling segments and triangles in three-dimensional space. Since a point in space can assume four positions (LEFT, RIGHT, ON_TRIANGLE,

IN_PLANE) relative to a triangle contained in a plane, a new enumeration type **TypeP3** will be introduced:

```
1 from enum import Enum
2 class TypeP3(Enum):
3     LEFT = 0
4     RIGHT = 1
5     ON_TRIANGLE = 2
6     IN_PLANE = 3
```

2.8 Triangles as Fundamental Units in 3D Geometry

This section proposes the definition and implementation of a class that models a triangle in three-dimensional space. Before presenting the interface of the **Triangle3D** class, it is essential to highlight key aspects related to the representation of triangles in 3D space. For working with triangles in space, it is useful to introduce the following elements:

- the **bounding box** of the triangle;
- the **normal vector** of the triangle;
- the **information** about the triangle's vertices.

The bounding box of a geometric object (e.g., a triangle) is the smallest box that fully encloses the object, with sides parallel to the coordinate axes. In the plane, the bounding box reduces to the smallest rectangle containing the given object (see Fig. 2.7, parts (a) and (b)).

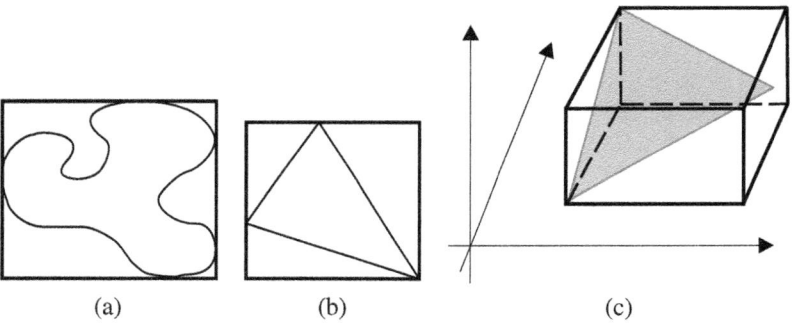

(a)   (b)   (c)

Figure 2.7: (a) Bounding box for a 2D curve. (b) Bounding box for a triangle in the plane. (c) Bounding box for a triangle in space.

In analytic geometry, a vector orthogonal to a plane is referred to as the *normal vector*. Given three coplanar points P_0, P_1, and P_2 in a plane π, the normal vector $\vec{n}$ is defined as the cross product of vectors $\vec{a}$ and $\vec{b}$, that is, $\vec{n} = \vec{a} \times \vec{b}$, where $\vec{a} = (a.x, a.y, a.z)$ and $\vec{b} = (b.x, b.y, b.z)$ are constructed as follows: $\vec{a} = \overrightarrow{P_0P_1} = \overrightarrow{OP_1} - \overrightarrow{OP_0}$, and $\vec{b} = \overrightarrow{P_0P_2} = \overrightarrow{OP_2} - \overrightarrow{OP_0}$. The vectors $\vec{n}$ and $-(\vec{a} \times \vec{b})$ share the same line of action but opposite orientation, thus having equal magnitudes. Furthermore, when the vectors $\vec{a}$ and $\vec{b}$ lie in the *xy*-plane, their *z*-components are zero, and the magnitude of $\vec{n}$ simplifies to $|a.x\,b.y - a.y\,b.x|$. After outlining these fundamental properties of 3D vector representation via points in space, the definition of the **Triangle3D** class is provided in Listing 2.6.

Listing 2.6: Definition of the **Triangle3D** class supported by the implementation of basic methods

```
1 class Triangle3D:
2     def __init__(self, p1=None, p2=None, p3=None, id=0):
```

```
3        self.vertices=[p1,p2,p3];self.__marked=False;self.__id=id
4        if p1 and p2 and p3:
5            self.__box = [
6                [min(p1[0],p2[0],p3[0]),min(p1[1],p2[1],p3[1]),min(p1[2],p2[2],p3
                    [2])],
7                [max(p1[0],p2[0],p3[0]),max(p1[1],p2[1],p3[1]),max(p1[2],p2[2],p3
                    [2])]
8            ]
9            n=(p2-p1)%(p3-p1)
10           self.__normal=n*(1.0/n.norm()) if n.norm()!=0 else n
11       else:self.__normal=None; self.__box=None
12   def __getitem__(self, idx):
13       if idx not in (0,1,2): raise IndexError("Index out of range")
14       return self.vertices[idx]
15   def __setitem__(self, index, value): self.vertices[index] = value
16   def get_box(self): return self.__box
17   def get_normal(self):return self.__normal
18   def get_id(self): return self.__id
19   def get_mark(self): return self.__marked
20   def set_mark(self, mark):self.__marked = mark
21   def contains_point(self,p):
22       return self.position(p) and abs(self.__normal*(p-self.vertices[0]))<=1e-9
23   def orientation(self):
24       vAC=self.vertices[2]-self.vertices[0]
25       vBC=self.vertices[2]-self.vertices[1]
26       return 1 if (self.__normal * (vAC % vBC)) > 1 else -1
27   def assign(self, t):#operator =
28       self.__normal=t.__normal; self.__box=t.__box
29       self.__id=t.__id; self.__marked=t.__marked
30       self.vertices=[v for v in t.vertices]
31       return self
32
33   def tetrahedron_volume(self, p):#Placeholder for volume of tetrahedron
34       raise NotImplementedError("Position test not implemented.")
35   def position(self, p): #Placeholder for proper point-in-triangle test in 3D
36       raise NotImplementedError("Position test not implemented.")
37   def overlaps(self, other, mode):# Placeholder: needs specific implementation
38       raise NotImplementedError("Overlap test not implemented.")
39   def projection(self, axis1, axis2):# Placeholder for projecting onto a plane
40       raise NotImplementedError("Projection not implemented.")
41   def occludes(self, other):# Placeholder for occlusion test
42       raise NotImplementedError("Occlusion test not implemented.")
43   def intersect(self, other):# Placeholder for 3D triangle intersection
44       raise NotImplementedError("Intersection not implemented.")
45
46   def __repr__(self):
47       return f"Triangle3D(A={self.vertices[0]},B={self.vertices[1]},C={self.
           vertices[2]})"
```

According to the content of Listing 2.6, it is evident that six public methods must be implemented. As shown in the listing, the purpose of the constructor is to assign the following properties to each created instance of the **Triangle3D** class:

a) a unique identifier (ID);

b) a label (mark);

c) a bounding box (a rectangle in the plane, or a polyhedron in 3D space).

The bounding box is stored using two extreme points that define the endpoints of a segment s in space.

This segment is oriented from the first extreme point toward the second. Typically, the first extreme point is the one with the smallest x, y, and z-coordinates among the triangle's vertices, while the second extreme point is the one with the largest coordinate values. A segment defined in this manner represents the diagonal of the polygon in the plane or the diagonal of the polyhedron in 3D space (see Fig. 2.7 (c)). From the constructor's implementation, it is clear that for each created triangle (i.e., instance of the **Triangle3D** class), the constructor first assigns a unique ID, then labels it with the value 0, and finally constructs the bounding box. The next method to implement is *tetrahedron_volume*($\cdot$). From analytic geometry, it is known that the volume of a tetrahedron $\triangleright ABCD$, defined by the points $A = (A.x, A.y, A.z)$, $B = (B.x, B.y, B.z)$, $C = (C.x, C.y, C.z)$, and $D = (D.x, D.y, D.z)$, is computed using the scalar triple product:

$$V = \frac{1}{6}|(\overrightarrow{AB} \times \overrightarrow{AC}) \cdot \overrightarrow{AD}| = \frac{1}{6}\begin{vmatrix} B.x - A.x & B.y - A.y & B.z - A.z \\ C.x - A.x & C.y - A.y & C.z - A.z \\ D.x - A.x & D.y - A.y & D.z - A.z \end{vmatrix} \tag{2.7}$$

The implementation of the public method *tetrahedron_volume*($\cdot$) can be realized as follows:

```
def tetrahedron_volume(self, p):
    ab=self.vertices[1]-self.vertices[0]
    ac=self.vertices[2]-self.vertices[0]
    ad=p-self.vertices[0]
    return abs(((ab%ac)*ad)/6.0)
```

In situations where it is necessary to determine on which side of a 3D triangle a given point lies, the aforementioned method is written without the absolute value. This will be discussed in detail in Chapter 4 of this book, where the problem of computing the convex hull in three-dimensional space is addressed. The next public method to be implemented is the member function *position*($\cdot$), which is invoked within the method *contains_point*($\cdot$). Purpose of the method *contains_point*($\cdot$) is to determine whether an instance of the **Triangle3D** class contains the point passed via a formal parameter. In other words, the mentioned method should answer whether a given point lies inside the triangle, assuming both the point and the triangle are specified in 3D space. This question can be addressed similarly to the case when both the point and the triangle are defined in a plane. It is well known that a point P in a plane lies within a triangle $\triangle ABC$ *if and only if* it is located on the same side (either left or right) of all sides (edges or segments) of the triangle. That is, all ordered triples of points A-B-P, B-C-P, and C-A-P, or equivalently A-C-P, C-B-P, and B-A-P, have the same orientation—either counterclockwise or clockwise. It is straightforward to observe that if these triples have the same orientation, then the normal vectors $\vec{n}_1 = \overrightarrow{AB} \times \overrightarrow{AP}$, $\vec{n}_2 = \overrightarrow{BC} \times \overrightarrow{BP}$, and $\vec{n}_3 = \overrightarrow{CA} \times \overrightarrow{CP}$ are aligned in the same direction. Therefore, when the normal vectors are aligned, their dot products are non-negative, i.e., the following conditions hold: $\vec{n}_1 \cdot \vec{n}_2 \geq 0$, $\vec{n}_1 \cdot \vec{n}_3 \geq 0$, and $\vec{n}_2 \cdot \vec{n}_3 \geq 0$. This property will be utilized in the implementation of the *position*($\cdot$) method, as shown in the following code snippet:

```
def position(self, p:Point3D) -> bool:
    n1= (self.vertices[1]-self.vertices[0]) % (p-self.vertices[0])
    n2= (self.vertices[2]-self.vertices[1]) % (p-self.vertices[1])
    n3= (self.vertices[0]-self.vertices[2]) % (p-self.vertices[2])
    return ((n1*n2)>=0 and (n1*n3)>=0 and (n2*n3)>=0)
```

The next public method of the **Point3D** class to be implemented is *classify*($\cdot$), while the public method *distance*($\cdot$) of the same class will be implemented later, in the section on modeling segments in 3D space. To implement the *classify*($\cdot$) method, it is necessary to define the concepts of the positive and negative half-spaces in space. In plane, it is well known that a line divides the plane into two half-planes: all points located to the left (or right) of the line belong to the positive (or negative) half-plane. Similarly, in three-dimensional space, a plane π, uniquely determined by points A, B, and C (the vertices of a triangle), divides the space into two half-spaces. The half-space in which all points lie on the same side of the plane as a point D, such that the volume of the tetrahedron formed by vectors $\overrightarrow{AB}$, $\overrightarrow{AC}$, and $\overrightarrow{AD}$ is positive, is called the *positive half-space*. Points that do not belong to the positive half-space are classified as points of the *negative half-space*. When observing the triangle $\triangle ABC$ from the positive half-space, point C is located to the left of segment $\overline{AB}$. Conversely, point C is located to the right of segment $\overline{AB}$ when observed from the negative half-space. It is also possible for a point to lie in the plane separating the half-spaces, analogous to the case in the plane where a point lies on the line dividing the half-planes. Such cases will be treated separately. Based on this reasoning, the previously implemented method *tetrahedron_volume($\cdot$)* can be utilized for the implementation of the *classify($\cdot$)* method by omitting the **abs** function from the *tetrahedron_volume($\cdot$)* method. The implementation of the public method *classify($\cdot$)* of **Point3D** class, which determines in which half-space a point lies relative to the triangle passed as a formal parameter, is provided below:

```
1  def classify(self, tr:'Triangle3D')->TypeP3:
2      vecAD = self-tr.vertices[0]
3      if vecAD.norm() == 0: return TypeP3.ON_TRIANGLE
4      vecAD = vecAD * (1.0 / vecAD.norm())   # Normalize the vector
5      scalar_product = vecAD* tr.get_normal())
6      if scalar_product > 1e-12: return TypeP3.LEFT
7      elif scalar_product < -1e-12: return TypeP3.RIGHT
8      else: return TypeP3.ON_TRIANGLE
```

In the implementation of the method above, the properties of the dot product are utilized. Specifically, when the angle $\alpha = \angle(\vec{a}, \vec{b})$ lies within the intervals $[0, \frac{\pi}{2}) \cup (\frac{3\pi}{2}, 2\pi]$, the dot product $\vec{a} \cdot \vec{b}$ is positive, as $\cos\alpha > 0$. Conversely, the dot product is negative when the angle α belongs to the interval $(\frac{\pi}{2}, \frac{3\pi}{2})$. When the dot product is positive, the face of the triangle is considered *visible* from the viewpoint. Otherwise, it is not visible. A point lies in the plane defined by the triangle *if and only if* the dot product satisfies $\vec{a} \cdot \vec{b} = 0$, which corresponds to $\alpha = \frac{\pi}{2}$ or $\alpha = \frac{3\pi}{2}$. In the implementation of the *classify($\cdot$)* method, the viewpoint is represented by the reference self. The following code snippet demonstrates the use of this method:

```
1  tr=Triangle3D(Point3D(0,-1,0),Point3D(3,3,0),Point3D(-1,3,0),1)
2  Point3D(0,0,4).classify(tr) # Output: TypeP3.LEFT
3  Point3D(0,0,-4).classify(tr) # Output: TypeP3.RIGHT
4  Point3D(0,0,0).classify(tr) # Output: TypeP3.ON_TRIANGLE
```

The dot product property described above has significant applications in computer graphics. Specifically, when the dot product is negative, the face of the triangle is not visible from the viewpoint, and therefore it should not be rendered on the screen. This directly impacts the rendering efficiency of the entire scene or its components, which are often approximated by a large number of triangles in three-dimensional space. The following section presents the implementation of the previously introduced methods. The first method is *overlaps($\cdot$, $\cdot$)*, which determines whether two triangles indirectly overlap along the i-th axis. Since the triangles are represented by their bounding boxes, i.e., 3D segments, the problem of triangle overlap reduces to checking whether their corresponding segments overlap. This, in turn, can be further reduced to verifying whether their projections onto a particular coordinate axis intersect. Formally, the implementation is based on examining whether two intervals $I_1 = (a, b)$ and $I_2 = (c, d)$ on the real axis intersect at any point. These intervals overlap *if and only if* either the starting point a or the endpoint b of the first interval I_1 lies within I_2, or the starting point c or the endpoint d of the second interval I_2 lies within I_1. Based on this reasoning, the implementation of the *overlaps($\cdot$, $\cdot$)* method is as follows:

```
1 def overlaps(self, other: 'Triangle3D', i: int) -> bool:
2     from Segment3D import Segment3D
3     box1 = Segment3D(self.get_box())
4     box2 = Segment3D(other.get_box())
5     a, b = box1[0][i], box1[1][i]
6     c, d = box2[0][i], box2[1][i]
7     return ((c<=a<=d) or (c<=b<=d) or (a<=c<=b) or (a<=d<=b))
```

The next method to be implemented is *occludes*($\cdot$). Before its implementation, it is necessary to define what it means for a triangle $\mathbb{T}_j$ to occlude a triangle $\mathbb{T}_k$. Specifically, $\mathbb{T}_j$ does not occlude $\mathbb{T}_k$ *if and only if* at least one of the following predicates is false:

P1. The projections of the spatial segments defining the bounding boxes of triangles $\mathbb{T}_j$ and $\mathbb{T}_k$ overlap along the x-axis.

P2. The projections of the spatial segments overlap along the y-axis;

P3. The triangle $\mathbb{T}_j$ does not lie entirely behind $\mathbb{T}_k$, nor does it lie in the plane defined by $\mathbb{T}_k$;

P4. The triangle $\mathbb{T}_k$ does not lie entirely in front of $\mathbb{T}_j$, nor does it lie in the plane defined by $\mathbb{T}_j$;

P5. The projections of the triangles $\mathbb{T}_j$ and $\mathbb{T}_k$ overlap.

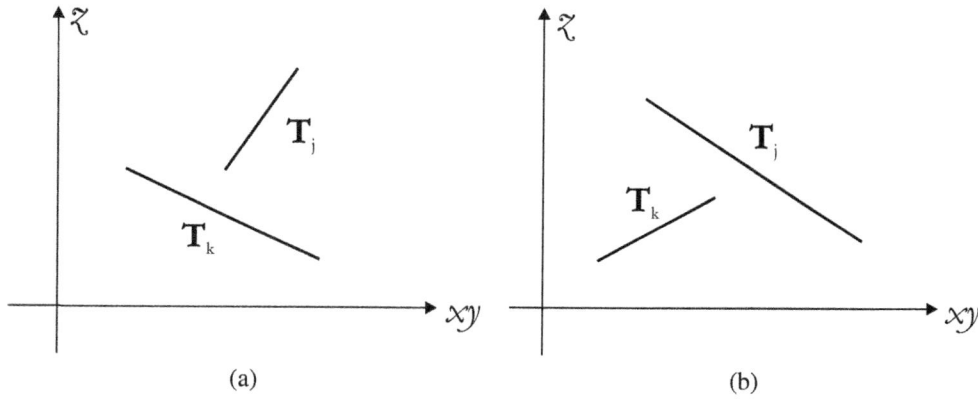

(a)   (b)

Figure 2.8: (a) Triangle $\mathbb{T}_j$ lies behind triangle $\mathbb{T}_k$. (b) Triangle $\mathbb{T}_k$ lies in front of triangle $\mathbb{T}_j$.

If predicate P1 is false, that is, if $\tau(P_1) = \perp$, the projections do not overlap along the x-axis, and triangle $\mathbb{T}_j$ does not occlude triangle $\mathbb{T}_k$. Conversely, if the projections do overlap, the triangle $\mathbb{T}_j$ may potentially occlude $\mathbb{T}_k$. When all the aforementioned predicates are true (none is false), it implies that triangle $\mathbb{T}_j$ occludes triangle $\mathbb{T}_k$. For example, if predicate P3 is false, i.e., $\tau(P_3) = \perp$, triangle $\mathbb{T}_j$ lies entirely behind triangle $\mathbb{T}_k$ or within the plane defined by $\mathbb{T}_k$, indicating that $\mathbb{T}_j$ does not occlude $\mathbb{T}_k$ (see Fig. 2.8 (a)). The interpretation of predicate P4 is analogous to P3, as illustrated in Fig. 2.8 (b). It remains to clarify the meaning of predicate P5. To evaluate this predicate, it is necessary to verify whether the projections $\mathbb{T}'_j$ and $\mathbb{T}'_k$ of triangles $\mathbb{T}_j$ and $\mathbb{T}_k$ onto the xy-plane intersect. The intersection of these projections is determined by the member function *intersect*($\cdot, \cdot$). It is straightforward to observe that the planar triangles (the projections $\mathbb{T}'_j$ and $\mathbb{T}'_k$) intersect *if and only if* at least one of the following predicates holds:

Q1. A vertex of triangle $\mathbb{T}'_j$ lies inside triangle $\mathbb{T}'_k$;

Q2. A vertex of triangle $\mathbb{T}'_k$ lies inside triangle $\mathbb{T}'_j$;

Q3. An edge of triangle $\mathbb{T}'_j$ intersects an edge of triangle $\mathbb{T}'_k$.

Hence, if all the above predicates are false, the projections $\mathbb{T}'_j$ and $\mathbb{T}'_k$ do not intersect, implying that the original triangles $\mathbb{T}_j$ and $\mathbb{T}_k$ do not intersect either. Based on these considerations, the implementations of the methods *projection*$(\cdot,\cdot)$, *occludes*$(\cdot)$ and the static method *intersection*$(\cdot,\cdot)$ become clear, as demonstrated in the code below:

```python
def projection(self, u: int, v: int) -> Polygon:
    points_2d = [] # Project 3D triangle onto uv-plane
    for i in range(3): points_2d.append(Point2D(self[i][u], self[i][v]))
    pol = Polygon()
    for i in range(2): pol.insert(points_2d[i])
    # Insert the third point depending on the position relative to the first two
    if points_2d[2].classification_m(points_2d[0], points_2d[1])==TypeP2.LEFT:
        pol.move_current(-1)
    pol.insert(points_2d[2])
    return pol
```

```python
@staticmethod
def intersection(tj: Polygon , tk: Polygon ) -> bool : # Intersection of tj and tk
    for _ in range(3):# Check if any vertex of tj is inside tk
        if tk.contains_point(tj.point_of_current()): return True
        tj.move_current(-1)
    for _ in range(3):# Check if any vertex of tk is inside tj
        if tj.contains_point(tk.point_of_current()):return True
        tk.move_current(-1)
    # Check if any edge of tj intersects any edge of tk
    for _ in range(3):
        e=tj.current_edge()
        for _ in range(3):
            s=tk.current_edge(); p = [0.0]
            if s.intersection_segments(e,p)==TypeS2.INTERSECT_SEG: return True
            tk.move_current(-1)
        tj.move_current(-1)
    return False
```

```python
def occludes(self, tr) -> bool:
    if self.overlaps(tr, 0) or not self.overlaps(tr, 1):return False
    # Check if any vertex of self is classified as RIGHT with respect to tr
    if all(v.classify(tr) != TypeP3.RIGHT for v in self.vertices):return False
    # Check if any vertex of tr is classified as LEFT with respect to self
    if all(v.classify(self) != TypeP3.LEFT for v in tr.vertices):return False
    # Check 2D projection intersection
    if not Triangle3D.intersection(self.projection(0,1), tr.projection(0,1)):
        return False
    return True
```

The final public method to implement is *intersect*$(\cdot)$, which determines whether there is an intersection between triangles $\mathbb{T}_k$ and $\mathbb{T}_j$ in three-dimensional space. This method takes as its first formal parameter the triangle $\mathbb{T}_j$, which defines the plane used to cut triangle $\mathbb{T}_k$. In fact, this parameter corresponds to the self reference. The method returns by reference the resulting parts, i.e., the triangles created during the splitting of triangle $\mathbb{T}_k$. Additionally, it returns by value the number of parts generated by the division of $\mathbb{T}_k$ by $\mathbb{T}_j$. The algorithm used in this member function consists of two phases. In the first phase, the intersection points between the plane π, defined by triangle $\mathbb{T}_j$, and the edges (or lines containing the

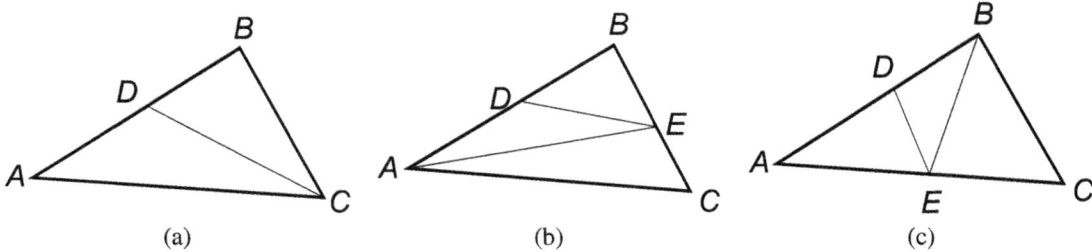

Figure 2.9: Division of triangle $\triangle ABC$ into two parts in case (a), and into three parts in cases (b) and (c).

edges) of triangle $\mathbb{T}_k$ are determined. It is evident that this plane can intersect the edges of $\mathbb{T}_k$ in at most two points, given that adjacent vertices of the triangle must not lie in the same half-space; in other words, they must lie in different half-spaces. If adjacent vertices lie in the same half-space, then the plane π does not intersect triangle $\mathbb{T}_k$, and in such a case, the number of resulting parts is one—meaning no division occurs. In the second phase of the algorithm, the resulting parts (triangles) created by the interaction of plane π with triangle $\mathbb{T}_k$ are determined. Specifically, if A, B, and C are the vertices of triangle $\mathbb{T}_k$, then the plane π intersects $\mathbb{T}_k$ in at most one point D, assuming it contains vertex C (see Fig. 2.9 (a)). In this case, points A and C, as well as points B and C, lie in the same half-space, while points A and B lie in different half-spaces. Conversely, if the plane π intersects triangle $\mathbb{T}_k$ at points D and E, as shown in Figs. 2.9 (b) and 2.9 (c), points A and B, as well as points B and C, lie in different half-spaces (Fig. 2.9 (b)), while points A and C lie in the same half-space. A similar situation is illustrated in Fig. 2.9 (c). Therefore, when the plane π contains vertex C of triangle $\mathbb{T}_k$ and intersects it, the splitting results in triangles $\triangle DBC$ and $\triangle ADC$. If the plane π does not contain any vertex of $\mathbb{T}_k$ but intersects it, the resulting triangles are $\triangle DBE$, $\triangle ADE$, and $\triangle AEC$, or alternatively, $\triangle ADE$, $\triangle BED$, and $\triangle CEB$, as shown in Fig. 2.9 (b) and (c), respectively. Based on this description, the implementation of the method *intersect*($\cdot$) can be carried out as follows:

```python
def intersect(self, tj: Triangle3D):
    intersection_points = [None, None]
    side = [0, 0, 0]; id_edges = [0, 0]; num_triangles = 0
    # First phase: classify vertices and find intersection points
    for i in range(3): side[i] = self[i].classify(tj)
    for i in range(3):
        s1, s2 = side[i], side[(i+1)%3]
        if (s1 == TypeP3.LEFT and s2 == TypeP3.RIGHT) or (s1 == TypeP3.RIGHT and
            s2 == TypeP3.LEFT):
            e = Segment3D(self[i], self[(i+1)%3]); p=[0.0]
            _, p= e.intersects_plane(tj)  # Compute intersection parameter p
            intersection_points[num_triangles] = e.point_at(p)
            id_edges[num_triangles] = i
            num_triangles += 1
    if num_triangles == 0: return 1 # No splitting
    # Second phase: create new triangles
    a=self[id_edges[0]]; b=self[(id_edges[0]+1)%3]
    c=self[(id_edges[0]+2)%3]
    if num_triangles == 1: # The plane pi contains one vertex of triangle t_k
        d = intersection_points[0]
        tk1 = Triangle3D(d, b, c, self.id)
        tk2 = Triangle3D(a, d, c, self.id)
        return num_triangles+1, tk1, tk2
    else: # The plane pi does not contain a vertex of triangle t_k
```

```
24        d, e = intersection_points
25        if id_edges[1]==(id_edges[0] + 1) % 3:# Case b)
26            tk1 = Triangle3D(d, b, e, self.id)
27            tk2 = Triangle3D(a, d, e, self.id)
28            tk3 = Triangle3D(a, e, c, self.id)
29        else: # Case c)
30            tk1 = Triangle3D(a, d, e, self.id)
31            tk2 = Triangle3D(b, e, d, self.id)
32            tk3 = Triangle3D(c, e, b, self.id)
33        return num_triangles+1,tk1,tk2,tk3
```

2.9 Line Segments in 3D

Analogous to the two-dimensional case, a segment in three-dimensional space is defined as a portion of a line bounded by two points. A segment may be considered either *directed* or *undirected*, depending on whether a distinction is made between the starting and ending points, or whether these points are regarded merely as boundaries of the segment, without an explicit orientation. The line that contains the segment, or the line on which the segment lies, is referred to as the *support of the segment*. Formally, a segment in three-dimensional space is represented as an ordered pair (for directed segments) or an unordered pair (for undirected segments) of points, which define the segment's boundaries. For example, the ordered pair (A, B) denotes a directed segment, while the unordered pair $\{A, B\}$ represents an undirected segment, where points A and B are the endpoints. As in the planar case, a directed segment (A, B) is often treated as the vector $\overrightarrow{AB}$, although it is important to note that the concept of a vector has a much broader meaning in the context of linear algebra and analytic geometry. Listing 2.7 presents a partial implementation of the **Segment3D** class interface. The implementations of the public methods *intersects_plane*($\cdot$), *intersects_triangle*($\cdot$) *intersects_line*($\cdot$), *intersects*($\cdot$) are left for further development. The remaining methods, given their relative simplicity, are defined and implemented directly within the class.

Listing 2.7: Definition of the class **Segment3D**

```
1  from Point2D import Point2D
2  from Point3D import Point3D
3  from TypeP2 import TypeP2
4  from TypeS2 import TypeS2
5  from TypeP3 import TypeP3
6  class Segment3D:
7      def __init__(self, s=None, e=None): self.s=s; self.e=e
8      def __getitem__(self,i):return self.s if i == 0 else self.e
9      def __setitem__(self, i, value):
10         if i==0: self.s = value
11         else: self.e = value
12     def point_at(self, t):return self.s+t*(self.e-self.s)
13     def contains_point(self, p: Point3D, eps=1e-9): #robust method
14         v=self.e-self.s; vp=p-self.s; dot=v*vp
15         if dot<-eps or dot>v*v + eps:return False
16         cross = v % vp
17         return cross.norm()<eps
18     def __hash__(self):
19         return hash((min(self.s, self.e), max(self.s, self.e)))
20     def __eq__(self, p):
21         if not isinstance(p, Segment3D): return NotImplemented
22         return (self.s==p.s and self.e==p.e) or (self.s==p.e and self.e==p.s)
23     def __repr__(self):
```

```
24    return f"Segment3D({self.s}, {self.e})"
25
26    def intersects_plane(self, tr: 'Triangle3D'):
27        # Placeholder for intersection between segment3d and plane
28        raise NotImplementedError("Not implemented.")
29    def intersects_triangle(self, tr: 'Triangle3D'):
30        # Placeholder for intersection between segment3d and triangle 3d
31        raise NotImplementedError("Not implemented.")
32    def intersects_line(self, l2:'Segment3D'):
33        # Placeholder for intersection between lines in the space
34        raise NotImplementedError("Not implemented.")
35    def intersects(self, s:'Segment3D'):
36        # Placeholder for intersection between segments in the space
37        raise NotImplementedError("Not implemented.")
```

The following section presents the implementation of the *intersects_plane*($\cdot$) method, which determines the geometric relationship between a plane (represented by an instance of the **Triangle3D** class) and a line (represented by an instance of the **Segment3D** class). In addition to identifying the relationship between the line and the plane, the method also returns the intersection parameter t in parametric form, provided that an intersection exists. If no intersection is detected, the method returns zero. In three-dimensional space, a line and a plane can be in one of three possible configurations: they may COINCIDE, they may INTERSECT, or they may be PARALLEL. To formally capture these cases, as well as to classify the relative positions of lines and segments in three-dimensional space, the enumerated type **TypeS3** is introduced in the following section.

```
1 from enum import Enum
2 class TypeS3(Enum):
3     COINCIDE = 0
4     PARALLEL = 1
5     INTERSECT = 2
6     NON_INTERSECT=3
7     SKEW=4
8     INTERSECT_SEG = 5
9     NON_INTERSECT_SEG = 6
```

The implementation of this method can be expressed in the following form:

```
1 def intersects_plane(self, tr: 'Triangle3D'):#plane defined by 3d triangle
2     n = tr.get_normal()
3     denom = n *(self.e-self.s)
4     if abs(denom) < 1e-9:
5         cl=self.s.classify(tr)
6         if cl in [TypeP3.LEFT, TypeP3.RIGHT]: return (TypeS3.PARALLEL, 0)
7         else: return (TypeS3.COINCIDE, 0)
8     t=-(n*(self.s-tr[0]))/denom
9     return (TypeS3.INTERSECT, t)
```

The following code excerpt illustrates the application of the method implemented above:

```
1 A=Point3D(1, 0, 0); B=Point3D(0, 0, 0); C=Point3D(0, 1, 0)
2 s1=Segment3D(Point3D(1,0,1), Point3D(0,1,1)); s2=Segment3D(A, C)
3 s3=Segment3D(Point3D(10,10,-2), Point3D(10,10,2)); tr=Triangle3D(A,B,C)
4 cl1, t1=s1.intersects_plane(tr) # Output: PARALEL, 0
5 cl2, t2=s2.intersects_plane(tr) # Output: COINCIDE, 0
6 cl3, t3=s3.intersects_plane(tr) # Output: INTERSECT, 0.5
```

It is important to emphasize that the method *intersects_plane*(·) can be effectively utilized for determining the intersection between a triangle and a line in three-dimensional space. As illustrated by the previous example, the intersection point between the line (defined by segment s_3) and the plane (defined by triangle *tr*) does not necessarily lie within the bounds of the triangle *tr*. Consequently, the implementation of the *intersects_triangle*(·) method can build upon the *intersects_plane*(·) method. Specifically, the procedure first identifies the intersection point between the plane and the line, and subsequently verifies whether this point lies within the boundaries of the triangle. The implementation of the *intersects_triangle*(·) method for detecting intersections between a triangle and a line in space is provided in the following code snippet:

```python
def intersects_triangle(self, tr: 'Triangle3D'):
    # Verify whether the line defined by self intersects the triangle
    cl,res=self.intersects_plane(tr)
    if cl in [TypeS3.COINCIDE, TypeS3.PARALLEL]: return (cl,0)
    pt=self.point_at(res)
    if res<0 or res>1: return (TypeS3.NON_INTERSECT,0)
    if tr.contains_point(pt) (TypeS3.INTERSECT,res)
    return (TypeS3.NON_INTERSECT,0)
```

Similarly, the problem of determining the intersection between a triangle and a segment in three-dimensional space can be reduced to computing the intersection between the triangle and the line containing the segment, which is performed by invoking the method *intersects_triangle*(·). Subsequently, it is necessary to verify whether the intersection point lies within the boundaries of the segment. If this condition is satisfied, the intersection point is confirmed as the point of intersection between the triangle and the segment in space. This process is demonstrated in the following example:

```python
A=Point3D(1,0,0); B=Point3D(0,0,0); C=Point3D(0,1,0); tr=Triangle3D(A,B,C)
s=Segment3D(Point3D(0.1,0.1,-1), Point3D(0.1,0.1,1))
cl,r=s.intersects_triangle(tr)
if cl==TypeS3.INTERSECT:
    pt=s.point_at(r) # intersection point
    if s.contains_point(pt): print("Intersection point lies on the segment.")
    else: print("The segment does not intersect the triangle.")
else: print("No intersection exists.")
```

The following section presents the implementations of methods for computing the intersection of lines and segments in three-dimensional space. Before introducing the method for determining the intersection of two lines, a mathematical model for the problem is outlined. It is well known that two lines l_1 and l_2 in space can exhibit four distinct configurations: they may be parallel, coincident (overlapping), intersecting, or skew (non-intersecting and non-coplanar). Lines in three-dimensional space are parallel, coincident, or intersecting *if and only if* they are *coplanar*, that is, if there exists a unique plane containing both lines. If two lines are not coplanar, they are referred to as *skew lines*. Let the lines l_1 and l_2 be defined by direction vectors $\vec{p}$ and $\vec{q}$ and points $P \in l_1$ and $Q \in l_2$, respectively. It is straightforward to observe that the lines are either coincident or parallel *if and only if* their direction vectors $\vec{p}$ and $\vec{q}$ are collinear. More precisely, the lines are *coincident if and only if* the vectors $\overrightarrow{PQ}$, $\vec{p}$, and $\vec{q}$ are mutually collinear, while they are *parallel if and only if* the direction vectors $\vec{p}$ and $\vec{q}$ are collinear, but not collinear with the vector $\overrightarrow{PQ}$.

For implementation purposes, the collinearity of vectors $\vec{p} = (p_x, p_y, p_z)$ and $\vec{q} = (q_x, q_y, q_z)$ is verified by checking whether their cross product $\vec{p} \times \vec{q}$ is the zero vector. In other words, if the norm of the vector $\vec{p} \times \vec{q}$ is zero, the vectors $\vec{p}$ and $\vec{q}$ are collinear. It is well known from analytic geometry that if two vectors are collinear, they are linearly dependent, meaning one can be expressed in terms of the other. Consequently, the matrix formed by their components exhibits linear dependence among its rows,

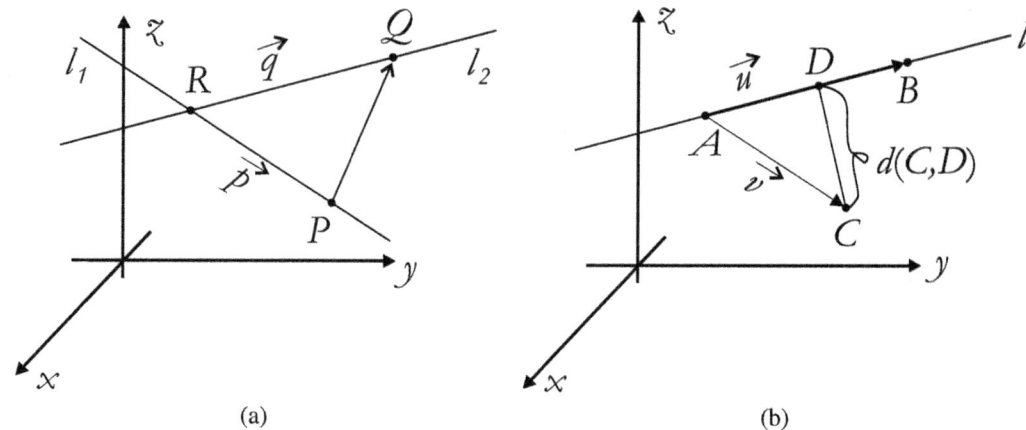

(a)   (b)

Figure 2.10: (a) Intersection of lines in three-dimensional space. (b) Distance from point C to the line l.

resulting in a determinant of zero. It directly implies that the magnitude of the cross product is zero, as all scalar coefficients accompanying the unit vectors $\vec{i}$, $\vec{j}$, and $\vec{k}$ are zero. For example, the vectors $\vec{p} = (1,1,1)$ and $\vec{q} = (-2,-2,-2)$ are collinear, since there exists a scalar $\lambda = -2$ such that $\vec{q} = \lambda\vec{p}$. Therefore, $\vec{p} \times \vec{q} = \vec{i}(-2+2) - \vec{j}(-2+2) + \vec{k}(-2+2) = \vec{0}$, and the norm of the cross product $\vec{p} \times \vec{q}$ is zero. Moreover, if two lines either intersect or are skew, their direction vectors are not collinear. More precisely, two lines l_1 and l_2 intersect *if and only if* the vectors $\vec{p}$ and $\vec{q}$ are not collinear and the vectors $\vec{p}$, $\vec{q}$, and $\overrightarrow{PQ}$ are coplanar. Conversely, the lines l_1 and l_2 are skew *if and only if* the vectors $\vec{p}$, $\vec{q}$, and $\overrightarrow{PQ}$ are not coplanar. The condition for coplanarity of the vectors $\vec{p}$, $\vec{q}$, and $\overrightarrow{PQ}$, or equivalently their linear dependence, is verified by computing the scalar triple product $(\vec{p} \times \vec{q}) \cdot \overrightarrow{PQ}$. If the scalar triple product equals zero, the vectors are coplanar; conversely, if the scalar triple product is nonzero, the vectors are not coplanar. Before proceeding to the implementation of the *intersects_line($\cdot$)* method, the mathematical procedure for determining the intersection point R between lines l_1 and l_2 will be described (see Fig. 2.10 (a)). The intersection point $R = (R.x, R.y, R.z)$, expressed in parametric form is given as follows

$$R(t) = P \pm t\vec{p}, \tag{2.8}$$

where the parameter $t \in \mathbb{R}^+$ is determined as

$$t = \frac{\left\| \vec{q} \times \overrightarrow{PQ} \right\|}{\left\| \vec{q} \times \vec{p} \right\|}. \tag{2.9}$$

In equation 2.8, the positive sign for the parameter t is used if the vectors $\vec{q} \times \overrightarrow{PQ}$ and $\vec{q} \times \vec{p}$ are oriented in the same direction. Otherwise, the negative sign is applied. Two vectors $\vec{a} = (a_0, a_1, a_2)$ and $\vec{b} = (b_0, b_1, b_2)$ are considered to have the same orientation *if and only if* all their corresponding components have the same sign, that is, $sign(a_i) = sign(b_i)$ for all $i \in \{0,1,2\}$. The following example illustrates the process of determining the intersection point R of the lines l_1 and l_2.

■ **Example 2.4** Determine the intersection of lines l_1 and l_2, which are defined by the direction vectors $\vec{p} = (6,7,0)$ and $\vec{q} = (6,7,4)$, respectively, and points $P = (6,8,4) \in l_1$ and $Q = (6,8,2) \in l_2$.

Solution. First, it is necessary to determine the relative position of the lines. Since the cross product $\vec{p} \times \vec{q}$ equals $(28,-24,0)$, it follows that it is not the zero vector, indicating that the lines are neither coincident nor parallel. Since the vector $\overrightarrow{PQ}$ is $(0,0,-2)$, the scalar triple product $(\vec{p} \times \vec{q}) \cdot \overrightarrow{PQ}$ equals zero, implying that the vectors $\vec{p}$, $\vec{q}$, and $\overrightarrow{PQ}$ are coplanar. Consequently, the lines l_1 and l_2 intersect. To determine the intersection point, the cross products $\vec{a} = \vec{q} \times \overrightarrow{PQ}$ and $\vec{b} = \vec{q} \times \vec{p}$ are computed, yielding $\vec{a} = (-14, 12, 0)$ and $\vec{b} = (-28, 24, 0)$. Since the vectors $\vec{a}$ and $\vec{b}$ have components of the same sign, they are oriented in the same direction. Therefore, the positive sign is taken in front of the parameter t. The value of the parameter t is straightforwardly computed as $\frac{340}{680} = \frac{1}{2}$. The intersection point R then has coordinates $(9, \frac{23}{2}, 4)$. ∎

After outlining the mathematical procedure for determining the intersection of lines in three-dimensional space, the implementation of the *intersects_line*($\cdot$) method is as follows:

```python
def intersects_line(self, l2:'Segment3D'):
    vec_p=self.e-self.s # Line l1 is defined by self
    vec_q = l2.e-l2.s; vec_pq = l2.s-self.s
    cross = vec_q % vec_p
    if cross.norm() < 1e-9: # The lines are parallel or coincide
        a=vec_pq % vec_p; b = vec_pq % vec_q
        if a.norm() < 1e-9 or b.norm() < 1e-9: return (TypeS3.COINCIDE, 0)
        return (TypeS3.PARALLEL, 0)
    if abs(-(cross*vec_pq))<1e-9: # The lines are intersecting
        cross1=vec_q % vec_pq
        t=cross1.norm()/cross.norm()
        if not cross1.same_sign(cross): t*=-1
        return (TypeS3.INTERSECT, t)
    return (TypeS3.SKEW, 0) # The lines are skew
```

The following code snippet demonstrates the usage of the method presented above:

```python
l1 = Segment3D(Point3D(6,8,4), Point3D(12,15,4))
l2 = Segment3D(Point3D(6,8,2), Point3D(12,15,6))
cl, t = l1.intersects_line(l2)
print("Intersection of l1 and l2:", cl, t) # Output: INTERSECT, 0.5
print("Intersection point:", l1.point_at(t)) # Output: Point3D(9,11.5,4)
```

The final method, *intersects*($\cdot$), within the **Segment3D** class, addresses the problem of determining the intersection of segments in three-dimensional space. A necessary condition for two segments to intersect is that the lines containing them intersect in space. However, this condition alone is not sufficient, as the lines may intersect, while the segments lying on these lines may not share a common point. A sufficient condition for the intersection of segments is that the intersection point of the lines lies within both segments. If the lines are parallel or skew, the corresponding segments do not intersect. Conversely, when the lines coincide, the segments may relate in various ways: they may be nested within one another, overlap partially, touch at a single point, or not intersect at all. For the purposes of this implementation, all such cases are collectively classified as segment overlaps, without further differentiation. Accordingly, the existing enumerated type TypeS3 is extended with additional items: OVERLAP and NON_OVERLAP. Based on these rules, the implementation of the *intersects*($\cdot$) method can be structured as follows:

```python
def intersects(self, s:'Segment3D'):
    cl,t=self.intersects_line(s)
    if cl in [TypeS3.PARALLEL, TypeS3.SKEW]: return (cl,0)
    elif cl==TypeS3.COINCIDE:
        conditions = [
            self.contains_point(s[0]) and self.contains_point(s[1]),
            s.contains_point(self[0]) and s.contains_point(self[1]),
            self.contains_point(s[0]) or self.contains_point(s[1]),
            s.contains_point(self[0]) or s.contains_point(self[1])
        ]
        return (TypeS3.OVERLAP,0) if any(conditions) else (TypeS3.NON_OVERLAP,0)
```

```
12    else:
13        i_p= self.point_at(t) #intersection point
14        return (TypeS3.INTERSECT_SEG,t) if self.contains_point(i_p) and s.
            contains_point(i_p) else (TypeS3.NON_INTERSECT_SEG,0)
```

Given that the necessary methods for determining the distance from a point to a line and a plane in three-dimensional space have already been developed, their implementations will now be presented. The first implementation concerns the method of the **Point3D** class that computes the distance from a point to a line, followed by the method for computing the distance from a point to a plane. To implement the first method, named *distance*($\cdot$), the mathematical model for calculating the distance between a point $C = (C.x, C.y, C.z)$ and a line l defined by the segment $\overline{AB}$ (or, equivalently, by the direction vector $\vec{u} = \overrightarrow{AB}$) is first explained. Here, points A and B are given by their coordinates, $A = (A.x, A.y, A.z)$ and $B = (B.x, B.y, B.z)$ (see Fig. 2.10 (b)). The orthogonal projection of the point C onto the line l, denoted as D, is computed as follows:

$$D = A + \frac{\vec{u} \cdot \vec{v}}{\|\vec{u}\|^2} \vec{u}, \tag{2.10}$$

where $\vec{v} = \overrightarrow{AC}$. It is evident that the vector $\overrightarrow{OD}$ can be expressed as the sum of the vectors $\overrightarrow{OA}$ and $\overrightarrow{AD}$, where the vector $\overrightarrow{AD}$ can be written in the form $\left(\frac{\vec{u} \cdot \vec{v}}{\|\vec{u}\|^2}\right) \cdot \vec{u}$. Once the point D is determined, the distance between the point C and the line l, denoted as $d(C, D)$, is computed as $\left\|\overrightarrow{CD}\right\|$. Based on this formulation, the implementation of the *distance*($\cdot$) method is as follows:

```
1 def distance(self, s:'Segment3D'):
2     u=s[1]-s[0]; v=self-s[0]
3     l=(u*v)/(u*u)
4     ad=l*u; d=s[0]+ad; cd=d-self
5     return cd.norm()
```

From analytic geometry, it is known that the distance from a point $P = (x_0, y_0, z_0)$ to a plane $\pi : ax + by + cz + d = 0$ is computed as follows:

$$d(P, \pi) = \frac{|ax_0 + by_0 + cz_0 + d|}{\sqrt{a^2 + b^2 + c^2}}. \tag{2.11}$$

For implementation purposes, the aforementioned distance will be formulated in vector form, where the plane is defined by the vertices of a triangle. Accordingly, the implementation of the *distance*($\cdot$) method, which computes the distance from a point $P(x_0, y_0, z_0)$ to the plane π, can be structured as follows:

```
1 def distance(self, tr:'Triangle3D'):
2     from Segment3D import Segment3D
3     n=tr.get_normal(); s=Segment3D(self,self+n)
4     cl,t=s.intersects_plane(tr)
5     i_p=s.point_at(t) #intersection point
6     return (self-i_p).norm()
```

2.10 **Exercises**

Exercise 2.1 Write a method named *is_reflex()* in the **Vertex** class that determines whether the vertex on which it is called is reflex or not.

Exercise 2.2 Write a function *f* that takes two triangles in 3D space as formal parameters and returns information on whether they intersect or not.

Exercise 2.3 Explain why the copy constructor of the **Polygon** class performs deep copying.

Exercise 2.4 Discuss the advantages and disadvantages of implementing a **Segment** class to represent different types of lines: *infinite lines*, *line segments*, *rays*, etc.

Exercise 2.5 Design a data structure for representing a convex polygon composed of n points, which allows testing whether a point lies inside the polygon in $\mathcal{O}(\log n)$ time.

Exercise 2.6 Write a function that checks whether the segment connecting two vertices of a polygon is an internal diagonal.

Exercise 2.7 Write a function *g* that takes a polygon as a formal parameter and returns information on whether the polygon is simple or not. The algorithm used by the function should have a time complexity of $\Theta(n \log n)$.

Exercise 2.8 Write a new method named *intersection*($\cdot$) in the **Polygon** class that, in $\mathcal{O}(n \log n)$ time, checks whether the polygon on which the method is called intersects with another polygon passed as a formal parameter. Let n denote the total number of vertices of the polygons tested for intersection.

Exercise 2.9 Write a function that takes two convex polygons as formal parameters and returns information about their intersection. The intersection test algorithm should have a time complexity of $\mathcal{O}(n)$, where n is the total number of vertices of the polygons.

Exercise 2.10 Write a function that finds the intersection point between a line and a triangle in 3D space. The function should directly compute the intersection point, without relying on projecting the triangle onto a plane.

3. Algorithms for Geometric Objects

This chapter describes and implements a wide range of algorithms for computing intersections and unions of various geometric objects, including: intersection among n segments, between a segment and a triangle, a segment and a rectangle, a segment and a convex polygon, a rectangle and a concave polygon, between convex polygons, half-planes, and unions of rectangles [21, 133]. Intersections of geometric objects have significant practical applications, particularly in Geographic Information Systems [126, 156]. *Geographic Information Systems* (**GIS**) store data about vegetation, elevation, precipitation, and other environmental features, which are displayed on maps in the form of *layers*. Sometimes only one layer is used, but more often multiple layers are displayed and analyzed simultaneously. In such cases, it is necessary to extract data from multiple layers to determine intersections or unions of regions of different types. For example, one can identify low-altitude areas covered by coniferous forests or locate regions where allergy-inducing plants are present. If these regions are modeled as simple polygons, the mentioned operations reduce to finding their intersections. Intersections of geometric shapes also find application in commercial software such as CorelDraw and AutoCAD [27]. Moreover, intersections are crucial in the design of electrical circuits on printed circuit boards, where it is essential to avoid intersections between conductors to prevent short circuits, with the number of segments potentially reaching several million. In computer games, intersections are fundamental to *collision detection*, where it is checked whether objects have collided with one another [24, 134]. In computer graphics, the visibility problem of objects from a specific viewpoint is often reduced to analyzing intersections of projections of objects onto a plane that is typically perpendicular to the viewing direction. Increasingly, the computation of intersections between geometric objects is also observed in other scientific disciplines, such as artificial intelligence and physics, where atomic collisions are modeled by testing the intersection of extremely small segments.

3.1 Intersection of Segments

The segment intersection problem is frequently encountered in practice. Computer scientists face this problem when designing video games, while its variations are also confronted by biologists and wildlife conservationists in the Kenai National Wildlife Refuge. The issue arises due to the intersection of the refuge with a road used by motor vehicles, leading to unpleasant encounters between humans and wild animals, resulting in traffic accidents and, worse, the death of these already endangered species. This problem also occurs in cartography during regional mapping, transportation systems, and many other domains. At first glance, finding intersections among segments may not appear to be a significant

© The Author(s), under exclusive license to Springer Nature Switzerland AG 2026
A. Alihodžić, *Exploring Computational Geometry*, Texts in Computer Science,
https://doi.org/10.1007/978-3-032-06393-9_3

challenge. Namely, for a set of n segments, one could check for intersections between each pair and, if an intersection exists, return the corresponding intersection points. However, it is easy to observe that this naive algorithm requires $\frac{n(n-1)}{2}$ checks, which results in a runtime proportional to $\mathcal{O}(n^2)$. This approach cannot be improved in the worst-case scenario where all segments intersect with each other (the so-called "all-against-all" principle). However, in practice, not all segments intersect; on the contrary, only a small number typically do, making the total number of intersections significantly lower than quadratic. In such cases, it becomes necessary to find a more efficient algorithm, especially when the number of segments reaches several million. For instance, if atoms are modeled as extremely short segments, it is crucial to quickly detect their collisions—that is, to find their intersections. In other words, what is needed is an algorithm whose runtime depends not only on the number of segments but also on the number of intersection points. Such an algorithm is called an *output-sensitive algorithm*, i.e., an algorithm whose execution time depends on the size of the output, or the solution itself [47, 110].

3.1.1 Visualization of Geometric Algorithms in Python

Visualization plays a crucial role in understanding the behavior and correctness of geometric algorithms. By visualizing key steps such as the creation of geometric objects, their transformation, and interaction (e.g., intersections), readers gain better intuition and insight into how algorithms work in practice. For improved testing and easier understanding of the algorithms presented in this book, a simple graphical user interface (**GUI**) developed using the standard Python library `tkinter` will be used. Each interactive demonstration of an algorithm will be executed through this GUI, whose basic form is shown in Listing 3.1.

Listing 3.1: Minimalist Graphical Interface for Algorithm Visualization

```python
import tkinter as tk

class GeometricVisualizer:
    def __init__(self, master):
        self.master = master
        self.master.title("Simple GUI for Algorithm Visualization")

        self.main_frame = tk.Frame(master)
        self.main_frame.pack(fill=tk.BOTH, expand=True)

        self.canvas = tk.Canvas(self.main_frame, width=800, height=600, bg="white")
        self.canvas.pack(side=tk.LEFT, padx=10, pady=10)

        self.control_frame = tk.Frame(self.main_frame)
        self.control_frame.pack(side=tk.RIGHT, padx=10, pady=10, fill=tk.Y)

        self.label = tk.Label(self.control_frame, text="Number of objects:")
        self.label.pack(pady=5)

        self.entry = tk.Entry(self.control_frame)
        self.entry.pack(pady=5)

        self.generate_button = tk.Button(self.control_frame, text="Generate Objects
            ", command=self.generate_objects)
        self.generate_button.pack(pady=5)

        self.execute_button = tk.Button(self.control_frame, text="Execute Algorithm
            ", command=self.execute_algorithm)
        self.execute_button.pack(pady=5)

```

```
29    def generate_objects(self):
30        print("Write the code for generating of geometric objects.")
31
32    def execute_algorithm(self):
33        print("The code for executing the specific algorithm goes here.")
34
35 if __name__ == '__main__':
36    root = tk.Tk()
37    app = GeometricVisualizer(root)
38    root.mainloop()
```

From Listing 3.1, it can be observed that the graphical interface includes the following key components:

- a text input field for specifying the number of geometric objects (e.g., number of points or segments),
- a button for generating random or user-defined objects,
- a button for executing a selected geometric algorithm (such as segments intersection, convex hull construction, polygon triangulation, etc.),
- and a drawing canvas for the visual representation of the generated objects and algorithm results.

This GUI structure offers a clean and intuitive interface for interacting with algorithms, making it easier to visualize both the initial setup and the step-by-step progression of each solution. Built upon this foundation, a unified framework is established to support the visual demonstration of all subsequent algorithms. The minimalist GUI skeleton is purposefully designed for flexibility and scalability, enabling seamless extensions and adaptations for the visualization of every algorithm explored in the following chapters of the book. Figure 3.1 illustrates the appearance of the GUI created based on the code from Listing 3.1.

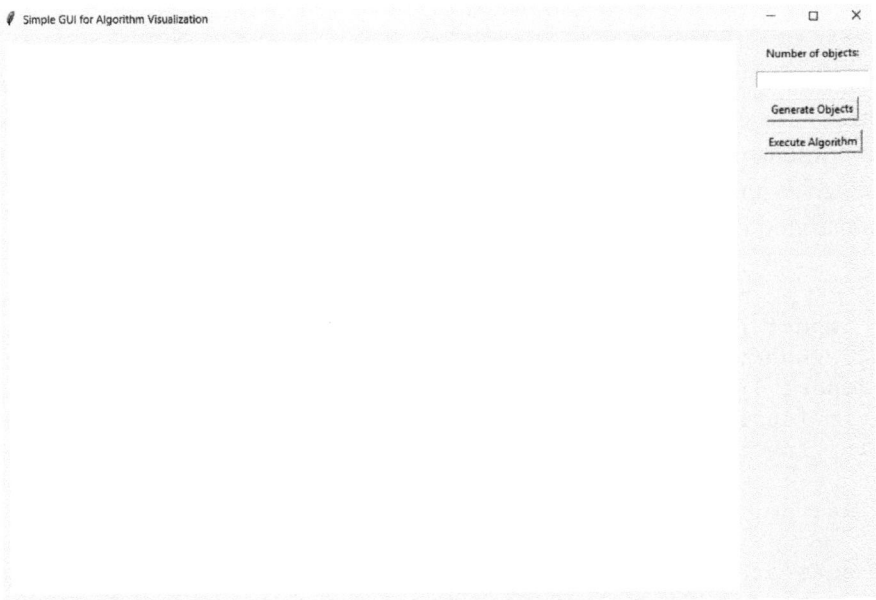

Figure 3.1: Minimalist Graphical Interface for Algorithm Visualization.

3.1.2 Exhaustive Search Approach

In this section, the *Exhaustive Search* (ES) method will be briefly described for naively detecting intersections among segments in a set $\mathscr{S}$ of cardinality n. In certain situations, it is sufficient to simply determine whether any segments intersect, while in other cases, it is necessary to find all intersection points among them. For both purposes, two straightforward functions can be implemented. For example, the function *do_intersect*(·,·) checks and returns information about the existence of an intersection, whereas the function *segments_intersections*(·,·) finds and returns all intersection points among segments. In the implementation of the *do_intersect*(·,·) function, all pairs of segments are tested, and the verification process stops as soon as the first intersection is found. Its implementation is given below:

```
def do_intersect(s):
    p = [0.0]
    for i in range(len(s)):
        for j in range(i+1,len(s)):
            if s[i].intersection_segments(s[j],p)==TypeS2.INTERSECT_SEG:
                return True
    return False
```

It is not difficult to observe that the execution time of the mentioned function can, in the best case, be constant if a pair of intersecting segments is immediately found, or in the worst case, it is of order $\mathcal{O}(n^2)$, if no intersection between segments is found . On the other hand, within the body of the function *segments_intersections*(·,·), it is necessary to perform $\mathcal{O}(n^2)$ operations in order to find all intersections and store them in a list, as shown below:

```
def segments_intersections(s):
    intersections = []  # List to store intersection points
    p = [0.0]
    for i in range(len(s)):
        for j in range(i+1,len(s)):
            if s[i].intersection_segments(s[j],p)==TypeS2.INTERSECT_SEG:
                intersections.append(s[i].point_at(p[0]))
    return intersections
```

A graphical interface for computing segment intersections using the naive approach can be obtained by extending the contents of Listing 3.1 with the following methods: *generate_segments*() and *visualise_naive_intersections*(). In addition, minor modifications are made within the listing to invoke these methods, as demonstrated in the code snippet below:

```
import random # new added to listing
from Point2D import Point2D # new added to listing
from Segment2D import Segment2D # new added to listing
from TypeS2 import TypeS2 # new added to listing
class GeometricVisualizer:
    def __init__(self, master):
        #----------------- same as in original ------------------------
        self.master.title("Naive Approach for Segments Intersection") #update
        #----------------- same as in original ------------------------
        self.generate_button = tk.Button(self.control_frame,text="Generate
            Segments",command=self.generate_segments) #update
        #----------------- same as in original ------------------------
        self.execute_button = tk.Button(self.control_frame,text="Naive Algorithm",
            command=self.visualise_naive_intersections) #update
        #----------------- same as in original ------------------------
        self.segments = [] # new added to listing
    def generate_segments(self): # new added to listing
        try:
            num_segments = int(self.entry.get())
            for _ in range(num_segments):
```

```
19        x1,y1=random.randint(0, 750), random.randint(0, 550)
20        len=random.randint(20, 50)
21        x2=x1+int(len*random.choice([-1,1])*random.uniform(0.5,1.0)*1.5)
22        y2=y1+int(len*random.choice([-1,1])*random.uniform(0.5,1.0)*1.5)
23        self.segments.append(Segment2D(Point2D(x1, y1), Point2D(x2, y2)))
24        self.canvas.create_line(x1, y1, x2, y2, fill='black')
25      except ValueError: print("Please enter a valid number.")
26  def segments_intersections(self,s): # new added to listing
27      intersections = []   # List to store intersection points
28      p = [0.0]
29      for i in range(len(s)):
30          for j in range(i+1,len(s)):
31              if s[i].intersection_segments(s[j],p)==TypeS2.INTERSECT_SEG:
32                  intersections.append(s[i].point_at(p[0]))
33      return intersections
34  def visualise_naive_intersections(self): #new added to listing
35      intersections = self.segments_intersections(self.segments)
36      for pt in intersections:
37          self.canvas.create_oval(pt[0]-2,pt[1]-2,pt[0]+2,pt[1]+2,fill='blue')
38 #------------------- same as in original ----------------------------
```

Figure 3.2 shows the process of detecting intersections among randomly generated segments in the plane.

Figure 3.2: Naive method applied to one hundred randomly generated segments.

3.1.3 Efficient Method

In this section, an efficient algorithm for detecting intersections among segments is proposed, based on the *Sweep Line Algorithm* [21]. This algorithm finds intersections with a time complexity proportional to $\Theta((n+r)\log n)$, where n is the total number of segments and r is the number of their intersection points. As previously stated, the exhaustive method for a set of n segments requires a time complexity of $\mathscr{O}(n^2)$. For instance, when $n = 10^9$, this results in as many as 10^{18} operations, which demands a tremendous amount of CPU time. Fortunately, in practical applications, it is known that not all segments intersect with each other, which motivates the development of algorithms that avoid checking all possible pairs of segments. Instead, only those segments that are sufficiently close to each other to potentially intersect are considered. The segments $\overline{A_1B_1}, \overline{A_2B_2}, \cdots, \overline{A_nB_n}$ can be represented by the coordinates of their endpoints: $A_1 = (x_a^1, y_a^1)$, $B_1 = (x_b^1, y_b^1)$, $\cdots$, $A_n = (x_a^n, y_a^n)$, $B_n = (x_b^n, y_b^n)$. By projecting these segments onto the x-axis and y-axis, arrays of intervals are obtained. Based on these projections, pairs of segments that certainly do not intersect can be eliminated — if their intervals do not overlap, then they cannot intersect. However, projections alone are not precise enough for a final decision, since segments may project onto the same interval without actually intersecting. Therefore, projections are only used to exclude impossible pairs, which reduces the number of necessary checks. This technique was a key motivation for introducing the sweep line algorithm, which is *sensitive to the number of intersection points*. Thanks to this feature, the algorithm is highly efficient in cases where the number of segments is large but the number of intersections is relatively small ($r \ll n(n+1)/2$). Conversely, the exhaustive method may be more suitable when the number of segments is small, e.g., $n = 100$, or when nearly all segments intersect with each other. Figure 3.3 illustrates six segments (s_1 through s_6), all intersecting each other, which results in a total of $r = \frac{6\cdot5}{2} = 15$ intersection points.

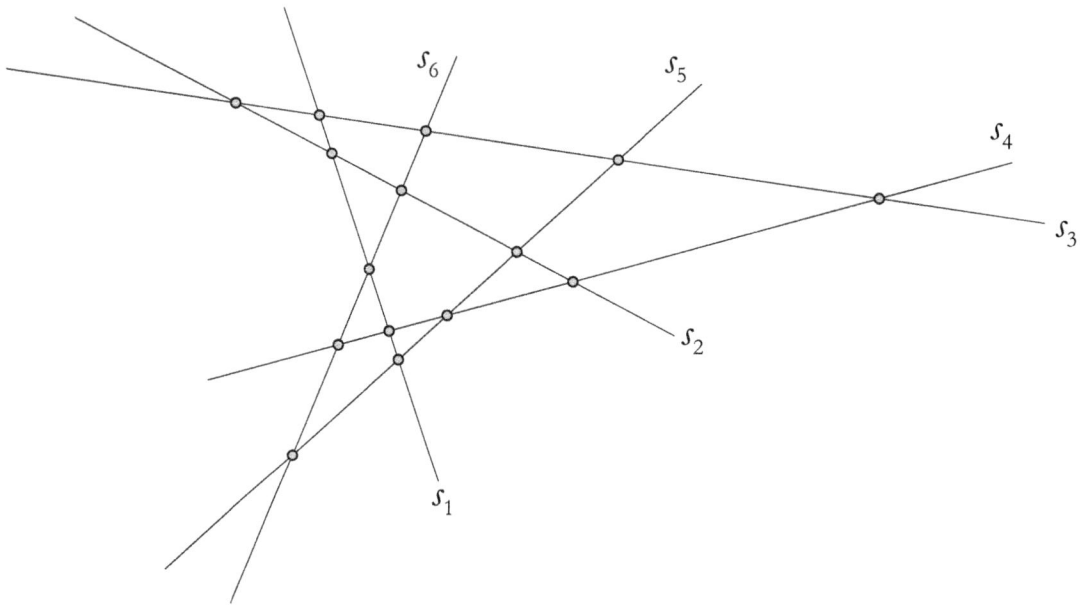

Figure 3.3: Order of six mutually intersecting segments.

As previously mentioned, the *Sweep Line Algorithm* is based on the principle of moving an imaginary line l. Without loss of generality, this chapter assumes that the imaginary line l moves from left to right. Within this algorithm, the *sweep line status* is defined as the set of segments that intersect the line. As the line moves, its status does not change continuously, but only at specific *event points* . Event points mark the moments when the algorithm performs certain operations, such as checking for intersections. For detecting segment intersections, the event points considered in the sweep line algorithm are: *start of segment*, *end of segment*, and *intersection of segments*. The details of what occurs at each of these event points will be explained below. When the sweep line moves from left to right and "hits" the start of a segment, that segment is inserted into an appropriate data structure (which will be described in detail later). Then, this segment is checked for intersections with the segments already intersecting the sweep line l. However, in many cases, there are numerous segments that are far from the current one and clearly do not intersect it. Horizontal segments are a classic example of such cases. To resolve this and ensure that the algorithm maintains a time complexity of $\Theta(n \log n)$, additional steps are required. Specifically, all segments intersecting the sweep line, including the current one, are sorted in ascending order by the y-coordinates of their intersection points with the sweep line l. After sorting, the intersection test between the current segment and others is reduced to checking only its closest vertical neighbors. In other words, for some current segment c, it is sufficient to examine only its two vertically closest neighboring segments a and b, as illustrated in Fig. 3.4 (a). This procedure significantly reduces the number of potential candidates for intersection with the current segment c.

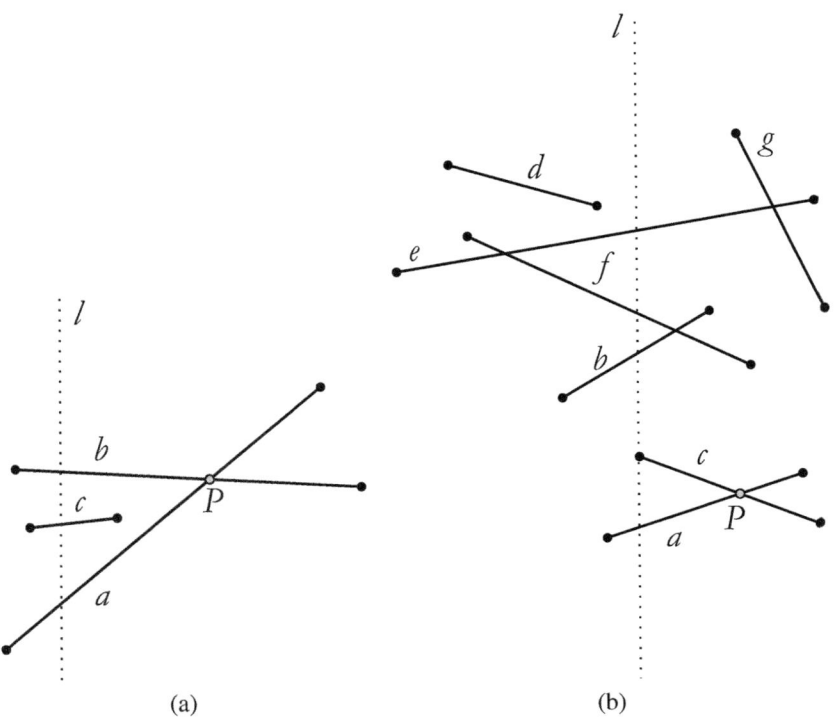

(a)   (b)

Figure 3.4: (a) Segments a and b are not vertical neighbors; rather, the vertical neighbors are segments a and c, and c and b. (b) Detection of the intersection point P during the "collision" of the sweep line l with segment c.

However, it is necessary to justify this approach, because if it is incorrect—that is, if it does not cover all segments that may intersect with the current segment—some intersection points might remain undetected. The following lemma provides a proof of the correctness of this approach.

Lemma 3.1.1 Let segments a and b intersect at point P, which lies to the right of the sweep line l. If P is the first event point that the sweep line encounters, then segments a and b are vertical neighbors with respect to the sweep line l.

Proof. Let segments a and b intersect at point P, which lies to the right of the sweep line l. Suppose that P is the first event point that the sweep line l will encounter, i.e., there is no segment endpoint or any other intersection point between the right side of the sweep line l and point P. It needs to be shown that segments a and b are vertical neighbors with respect to line l. Assume this is not the case, i.e., segments a and b are not vertically adjacent. Then, there must exist a segment c that intersects the sweep line l and lies between segments a and b, as illustrated in Fig. 3.4 (a). Moreover, it can be assumed that segment c intersects segment a or b at point Q, which lies between line l and point P. If this is the case, by moving the sweep line l from left to right, we reach the following conclusion: the sweep line l will first encounter the endpoint of segment c (if c does not intersect a or b), or it will reach the intersection point Q. In either case, this contradicts the initial assumption that line l first reaches point P. Therefore, the assumption that segments a and b are not vertical neighbors leads to a contradiction, and must be rejected. This concludes the proof of the lemma. ∎

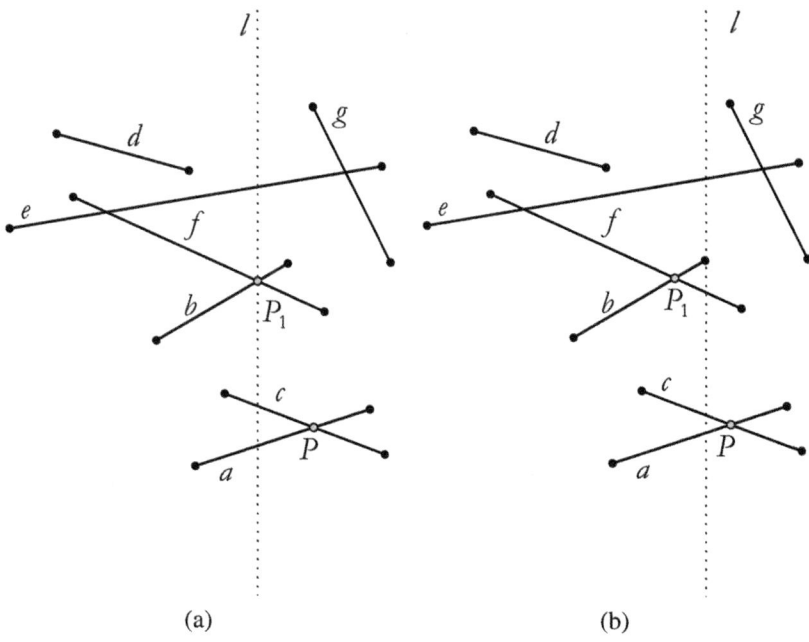

Figure 3.5: Illustration of the sweep line ℓ passing through the event points P_1 and the endpoint of segment b in steps (a) and (b).

In the following, we consider what happens when the event point is the *start of a segment*. Let the sweep line l "hit" a segment c during its left-to-right traversal (see Fig. 3.4 (b)). Based on Lemma 3.1.1, it is sufficient to check whether segment c intersects its vertical neighbors. Prior to the sweep line l reaching the start of segment c (see Fig. 3.4 (b)), it is evident that segments a and b were vertically adjacent. Therefore, since the start of segment c lies between segments a and b, it suffices to check whether segment c intersects its closest vertical neighbors, a and b. Figure 3.4 (b) shows that segment c intersects segment a at point P, which constitutes a newly detected event point. It is important to note that during sweep line status handling, only essential event points located to the right of the sweep line play a role, while the event points on the left side have already been processed. Event points to the right of the sweep line are associated with *dormant segments* (i.e., segments whose endpoints are both located to the right of the sweep line), while those on the left side are associated with *dead segments* (segments whose endpoints lie entirely to the left of the sweep line). This is illustrated in Fig. 3.4 (b), where segment g is dormant, and segment d is dead. In addition to dormant and dead segments, there are also *active segments*, which have endpoints on opposite sides of the sweep line l. Examples of active segments in Fig. 3.4 (b) include segments a, b, c, e, and f. Just before the sweep line l touches the start of segment c, this segment is considered dormant; upon contact, it is promoted to an active segment. Once the start of segment c is processed, the algorithm continues to the next event point. In Fig. 3.5 (a), the intersection point P_1 between segments b and f represents the next event point the sweep line hits. In this case, since segments f and b intersect, their vertical neighbors are updated: segment f becomes a vertical neighbor of segment c, instead of segment d, while segment b becomes vertically adjacent to segment d, instead of c as it was prior to the sweep line reaching intersection point P_1. In this way, segments f and b obtain new neighbors, which are then checked for intersections. As before, only event points on the right side of the sweep line are relevant for further processing. Newly detected intersection points in this step are also treated as event points and are added to the corresponding data structure. It can be observed that some event points have already been detected as intersections between other segments. For example, the intersection between segments e and f had already been detected as an event point, while future intersections between segments *a* and *c*, as well as between *e* and *g*, will be identified in subsequent steps. By moving the sweep line *l* to the right, it strikes the endpoint of segment *b* (see Fig. 3.5 (b)), which is treated as a new event, i.e., as an event point. At that moment, segment *b* no longer intersects the sweep line *l*, which signals that it should be removed from the data structure in which it had previously been stored, thereby acquiring the status of a dead segment. Additionally, as part of this event, the immediate neighbors of the removed segment *b* must be tested for intersections. In Fig. 3.5 (b), segments *e* and *f* are the immediate neighbors of the removed segment *b*, and they become direct neighbors after its deletion. As previously mentioned, these segments should be tested for intersection. If they do intersect and the intersection lies to the right of the sweep line, it becomes a new event point. It is possible that the intersection between these segments was previously detected, as is the case with segments *e* and *f*. These segments have the status of active segments and therefore cannot yet be removed from the structure. The algorithm terminates when the sweep line reaches the final endpoint event, at which point all intersection points of the segments have been found. These will be located exclusively to the left of the sweep line, while all segments will have acquired the status of dead segments. This concludes the conceptual description of the sweep line algorithm.

The following section describes the data structures used for the implementation of the sweep line algorithm for detecting intersections among *n* segments given in the plane. The implementation relies on a set as the primary structure for maintaining the *active segments*—segments that currently intersect the sweep line as it moves from left to right. In other words, active segments represent the status of the sweep line as it progresses, stopping only at predefined *event points*. This implementation considers only two types of events (START_OF_SEGMENT and END_OF_SEGMENT). Due to the use of the set data structure, it does not support operations such as local comparison of neighboring segments or efficient retrieval of a segment's predecessor and successor. These capabilities are essential features in the original Bentley-Ottmann algorithm for detecting segment intersections, as previously discussed. For each input segment s_i, where $i = 1, \ldots, n$, two events are added to the *event list* Ω:

- START_OF_SEGMENT – an event triggered when the sweep line encounters the starting point of a segment.
- END_OF_SEGMENT – an event triggered when the sweep line passes the endpoint of a segment.

In the implementation, all events are stored in the list events as tuples of the form $(x, \text{type}, \text{segment})$, and are sorted by their *x*-coordinates to simulate the left-to-right sweep of the sweep line. In case of identical *x*-coordinates, the END_OF_SEGMENT event is given priority to prevent redundant intersection detections. The set of active segments is managed through a dynamic structure denoted by Γ, which maintains all segments currently intersected by the sweep line. This structure is dynamic in the sense that newly encountered segments are added when they begin intersecting the sweep line *l*, while segments that no longer intersect the line (i.e., are considered dead) are removed. In Python, the structure Γ is implemented using the set type, which internally relies on a hash table. This ensures that the fundamental operations of lookup, insertion, and deletion all have an expected constant time complexity, i.e., $\mathcal{O}(1)$. When the sweep line reaches the starting point of a segment (i.e., a START_OF_SEGMENT event), the segment is inserted into the set active_segments using the *add*(·) method. At this point, the new segment is checked for intersections with all other segments already present in active_segments, and any found intersection points are appended to the intersections list. If the set active_segments contains *k* elements, the intersection checking step requires $\mathcal{O}(k)$ time, which from a theoretical perspective is suboptimal. However, in practice, this linear scan performs efficiently because the number of simultaneously active segments is usually much smaller than the total number of input segments. When the sweep line reaches a segment's endpoint, the segment is removed from the active_segments set via the *discard*(·) method. Having described the data structures Ω (event list) and Γ (active segments), the full segment intersection detection procedure is formalized in the pseudocode shown in Algorithm 1.

Algorithm 1: Pseudocode of an efficient sweep line algorithm for segment intersections.

Step 1: Initialize the event list Ω by adding the endpoints of the segments.

Step 2: Sort all events $\omega \in \Omega$ based on their x-coordinates. Then, create an empty set Γ to store active segments, and initialize an empty list of intersections.

Step 3: For each event ω in the event list Ω, **do**

    a) If P is the event point of $\omega \in \Omega$ of type START_OF_SEGMENT, insert the segment s associated with the event into the active segment set Γ, and iterate through Γ to detect all intersections between s and the existing segments. Append all detected intersection points to the intersection list.

    b) If P is the event point of $\omega \in \Omega$ of type END_OF_SEGMENT, remove the segment s of the event ω from the set Γ.

In the pseudocode of Algorithm 1, it is necessary to elaborate further on the procedures related to the mentioned steps of the algorithm. First, steps 1 and 2 will be explained in detail, followed by step 3. In Step 1, the initialization of the event list Ω is performed as follows:

```
events=[] # list of events
for s in segments:
    p1,p2=(s[1],s[0]) if s[1]<s[0] else (s[0],s[1])# Order endpoints left to right
    events.append((p1[0],'START_OF_SEGMENT',s))# Add START event
    events.append((p2[0],'END_OF_SEGMENT',s)) # Add END event
```

Step 2 can be implemented as follows:

```
events.sort(key=lambda e:(e[0],e[1]=='END_OF_SEGMENT'))#Sort by x;end before start
active_segments = set() # Structure Gamma (active segments)
intersections = [] # List of segment intersections
```

From the implementation, it is evident that the *sort*($\cdot$) method orders the list of events primarily by the x-coordinate of the event point e (i.e., e[0]). In the case where multiple events share the same x-coordinate, priority is given to END_OF_SEGMENT events over START_OF_SEGMENT ones. This ordering ensures that segments terminating at a given point are removed from the active set before inserting any new segments that begin at the same location, effectively preventing the detection of incorrect or redundant intersections. The implementation of the final step of Algorithm 1 is carried out as follows:

```
for event in events:
    _, type_event, s1 = event
    if type_event == 'START_OF_SEGMENT':
        for s2 in active_segments:
            p = [0.0]
            if s1.intersection_segments(s2, p)==TypeS2.INTERSECT_SEG:
                p_i=s1.point_at(p[0]) # point of intersection
                intersections.append((p_i[0], p_i[1]))
        active_segments.add(s1)
    elif type_event == 'END_OF_SEGMENT': active_segments.discard(s1)
```

With the implementation of this final step, the sweep line algorithm for detecting intersections among a set of segments in the plane is completed. For the purpose of visualizing the sweep line algorithm (see Fig. 3.6), the aforementioned steps of Algorithm 1 are integrated into the function *sweep_line_intersections*($\cdot$),

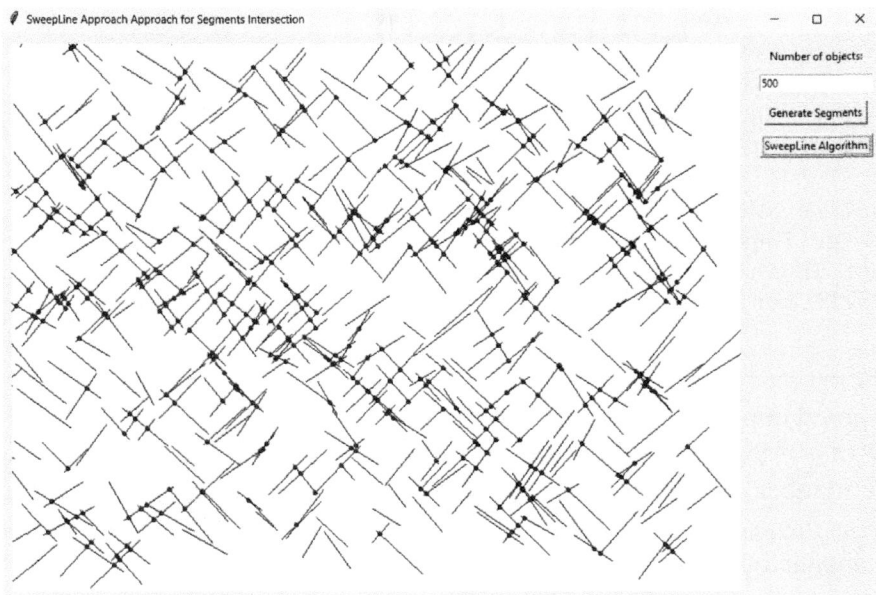

Figure 3.6: Result of computing intersections among five hundred randomly generated segments.

which, similarly to the function *segments_intersections*(·), is incorporated into the framework of Listing 3.1. Accordingly, the modified content of the listing is presented below:

```python
# --------------- same as in naive approach ----------------------------
class GeometricVisualizer:
    def __init__(self, master):
        #--------------- same as in original ----------------------------
        self.master.title("SweepLine Approach for Segments Intersection") #update
        #--------------- same as in original ----------------------------
        self.generate_button = tk.Button(self.control_frame,text="Generate
            Segments",command=self.generate_segments) #update
        #--------------- same as in original ----------------------------
        self.execute_button = tk.Button(self.control_frame,text="SweepLine
            Algorithm",command=self.visualise_sweep_line_intersections) #update
        #--------------- same as in original ----------------------------
        self.segments = [] # new added to listing
    def generate_segments(self): # new added to listing
        #--------------- same as in naive approach ---------------------
    def sweep_line_intersections(self,segments): #new added to listing
        events=[] # list of events
        for s in segments:
            p1,p2=(s[1],s[0]) if s[1]<s[0] else (s[0],s[1])# Order endpoints
            events.append((p1[0],'START_OF_SEGMENT',s))# Add START event
            events.append((p2[0],'END_OF_SEGMENT',s)) # Add END event

        events.sort(key=lambda e:(e[0],e[1]=='END_OF_SEGMENT')) # Sort by x
        active_segments = set() # Structure for active segments
        intersections = [] # List of segment intersections

        for event in events:
            _, type_event, s1 = event
            if type_event == 'START_OF_SEGMENT':
                for s2 in active_segments:
                    p = [0.0]
                    if s1.intersection_segments(s2, p)==TypeS2.INTERSECT_SEG:
```

```
31                          p_i=s1.point_at(p[0]) # point of intersection
32                          intersections.append((p_i[0], p_i[1]))
33                  active_segments.add(s1)
34              elif type_event == 'END_OF_SEGMENT': active_segments.discard(s1)
35              return intersections
36
37      def visualise_sweep_line_intersections(self): #new added to listing
38          intersections = self.sweep_line_intersections(self.segments)
39          for pt in intersections:
40              self.canvas.create_oval(pt[0]-2,pt[1]-2,pt[0]+2,pt[1]+2,fill='blue')
41      #---------------- same as in original ------------------------------
```

Although the proposed implementation of the sweep line algorithm does not achieve the theoretical time complexity of $\Theta((n+r)\log n)$, it has proven to be highly efficient in practice, especially in scenarios involving a large number of segments with relatively few intersections. The table below provides a comparison between the performance of this implementation and the naive method for various input sizes. The results were obtained through empirical testing conducted by the author.

Table 3.1: Sweep line vs. brute-force algorithm on randomly generated segments.

No. of segments	No. of intersections	Sweep Line Time (sec.)	Naive Time (sec.)
100	15	0.01	**0**
1000	1715	0.012	**0.006**
10000	166878	**0.098**	0.538
40000	2707900	**1.305**	8.652
70000	8329982	**4.207**	26.501
100000	16940605	**9.25**	54.479
200000	67800941	**39.419**	221.353

Table 3.1 clearly demonstrates the performance advantage of the sweep line algorithm, implemented through the function *sweep_line_intersections*($\cdot$), over the naive approach (*segments_intersections*($\cdot$)) when processing randomly generated segments. Although both algorithms exhibit acceptable performance for small datasets (e.g., 100 or 1000 segments), the performance gap widens dramatically as the number of segments increases. For instance, when processing 10,000 segments, the sweep line algorithm completes in just under 0.1 seconds, whereas the naive method requires over half a second—making the sweep line method approximately 5.5 times faster. As the dataset grows further, this difference becomes even more pronounced. At 100,000 segments, the sweep line method runs nearly 6 times faster (9.25s vs. 54.48s), and at 200,000 segments, the difference increases to a factor of around 6 as well. These results confirm the theoretical advantages of the sweep line paradigm. While the naive algorithm operates in $\mathcal{O}(n^2)$ time, checking every pair of segments, the sweep line algorithm—although not optimized to reach its ideal complexity of $\mathcal{O}((n+r)\log n)$—still achieves significantly improved runtime performance in practice. This makes it highly suitable for applications involving large numbers of segments, particularly when the number of intersections remains relatively sparse in comparison to the total number of possible segment pairs.

3.2 Clipping a Segment with a Rectangle

In this section, a highly efficient algorithm known as the Cohen–Sutherland algorithm is proposed for detecting the intersection between a rectangle and a segment. This algorithm was originally developed by Daniel Cohen and Ivan Sutherland in 1967, and was later improved by Jiang and Han [95]. The problem of segment–rectangle intersection can be reduced to the more general segment–segment intersection problem, since the sides of a rectangle are themselves segments. However, the emphasis here is on an algorithm whose primitive operations are executed significantly faster compared to the algorithm described in the previous section. The main motivation for solving the segment–rectangle intersection problem arises from commercial applications. In certain commercial software packages (e.g., Corel Draw, AutoCAD), after determining the intersection points of objects under intersection testing, one of the objects can be extracted or clipped. For instance, the portion of a segment inside the rectangle can be isolated, which in turn allows for further operations on it, such as coloring, adjusting thickness, etc. Since many such clipping operations may occur while creating a single drawing, it is desirable that intersection detection, and consequently clipping, be performed as efficiently as possible. *Clipping* is defined as the process of removing a geometric object from any bounded region. What follows is a description of an algorithm that renders only the portion of a segment—or the entire segment—that lies inside a given rectangle. If the segment lies completely outside the rectangle, no clipping is performed and the segment is discarded. Let a segment $s = \overline{AB}$ and a rectangle $\square V_1V_2V_3V_4$ be given, defined by the intersection of the lines $x = x_{min}$, $x = x_{max}$, $y = y_{min}$, and $y = y_{max}$ (see Fig. 3.7 (a)). From the figure, it is evident that the segment s does not lie entirely within the rectangle $\square V_1V_2V_3V_4$, and intersects it only at point A''. Since point B lies above the line $y = y_{max}$, the y-coordinate of A'' is given by $y = y_{max}$. To determine the x-coordinate of this point, the similarity of triangles $\triangle AA'A''$ and $\triangle AB'B$ is used. From the relation $\triangle AA'A'' \sim \triangle AB'B$, we obtain:

$$\frac{\overline{AB'}}{\overline{AA'}} = \frac{\overline{BB'}}{\overline{A''A'}} \tag{3.1}$$

If the x-coordinates of points A, A', A'', B, and B' are denoted by x_a, x_t, x_t, x_b, and x_b, respectively, and the y-coordinates of points A and B are denoted by y_a and y_b, then the relation 3.1 takes the following form:

$$\frac{x_b - x_a}{x_t - x_a} = \frac{y_b - y_a}{y_{max} - y_a}. \tag{3.2}$$

Based on relation 3.2, the x-coordinate x_t of the intersection point A'' between the segment s and the edge of the rectangle $\square V_1V_2V_3V_4$ can be easily determined. Namely, since the values x_a, x_b, y_a, and y_b are known in advance, the coordinate x_t is computed as follows:

$$x_t = x_a + \frac{(x_b - x_a)(y_{max} - y_a)}{y_b - y_a}.$$

After computing the x-coordinate x_t of the intersection point A'', it becomes straightforward to draw the subsegment $s' \subset s$, which is marked in Fig. 3.7 (a) with a bold black edge and bounded by endpoints A and A''. The procedure described above does not represent a general clipping method for line segments, as it only determines the intersection between a segment and one of the polygon sides. For instance, if point B lies far to the right of the line $x = x_{max}$, it cannot be immediately concluded that the intersection point A'' lies on one of the lines $y = y_{max}$, $y = y_{min}$, or $x = x_{max}$. Therefore, in the following, the Cohen-Sutherland algorithm is proposed, which, as a general method, takes into account all possible scenarios. In this algorithm, the lines $x = x_{min}$, $x = x_{max}$, $y = y_{min}$, and $y = y_{max}$ divide the plane into nine distinct regions (see Fig. 3.7 (b)). Each region is assigned a binary code $b_3b_2b_1b_0$, which uniquely identifies that region. The correspondence between an arbitrary point in the plane $P = P(x,y)$ and its binary representation $b_3b_2b_1b_0$ is defined as follows:

$$b_3 = 1 \Leftrightarrow x < x_{min}, \; b_2 = 1 \Leftrightarrow x > x_{max}, \; b_1 = 1 \Leftrightarrow y < y_{min}, \; b_0 = 1 \Leftrightarrow y > y_{max}.$$

Based on the aforementioned condition, a point P lies inside the rectangle *if and only if* its binary representation has the form 0000. Consequently, the segment $s = \overline{AB}$ lies entirely within the rectangle if and only if both endpoints A and B have zero-valued binary representations. However, if neither

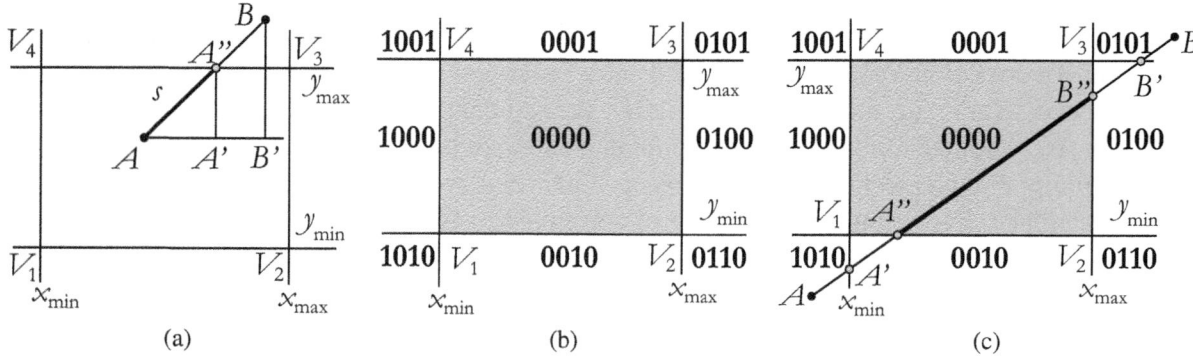

Figure 3.7: (a) Intersection of segment s with rectangle $V_1V_2V_3V_4$. (b) Binary representation of rectangle $V_1V_2V_3V_4$. (c) Clipping in the binary representation.

endpoint lies inside the rectangle (see Fig. 3.7 (c)), the algorithm iteratively replaces the endpoints A and B with the intersection points of the segment s and the boundary lines $x = x_{min}$, $x = x_{max}$, $y = y_{min}$, and $y = y_{max}$. This replacement continues until a segment (or subsegment) is found whose endpoints both have a zero binary representation, indicating that the algorithm has finished. Moreover, if at the beginning the binary representations of points A and B are $b_3b_2b_1b_0$ and $c_3c_2c_1c_0$ respectively, and there exists some $j \in \{0,1,2,3\}$ such that $b_j = c_j = 1$, then the segment s lies entirely outside the rectangle. In this case, the algorithm terminates immediately, since no clipping occurs between the segment and the rectangle. This general principle will now be applied to the clipping of a segment s against the rectangle $\square V_1V_2V_3V_4$ (see Fig. 3.7 (c)). Since the endpoints of segment s do not have zero-valued binary representations, and there is no index j such that $b_j = c_j$, the algorithm replaces point A with point A' because A lies to the left of the line $x = x_{min}$. The algorithm then proceeds with processing the segment $s' = \overline{A'B}$, as the new point A' and point B still do not have zero-valued binary representations. Since A' lies below the line $y = y_{min}$, it is replaced by a new point A''. The replacement is based on triangle similarity, performed using relation 3.2. As point A'' now has a zero binary representation, it becomes one endpoint of the final clipped segment. A similar procedure is applied to point B. Since B lies above the line $y = y_{max}$ and to the left of it, it is replaced with point B'. The algorithm then processes the segment $\overline{A''B'}$. As B' lies to the right of the line $x = x_{max}$ and still does not have a zero binary representation, it is replaced by $\overline{B''}$. Since B'' has a zero binary representation, the algorithm terminates. Finally, the resulting segment $\overline{A''B''}$ is clipped against the rectangle $\square V_1V_2V_3V_4$ (see Fig. 3.7 (c)). After explaining the Cohen–Sutherland algorithm for clipping a segment against a rectangle, its implementation is provided within the function $clip\_segment\_with\_rectangle(\cdot, \cdot, \cdot)$. The first formal parameter of this function represents the segment to be clipped, while the second and third parameters define the clipping rectangle, uniquely specified by its bottom-left and top-right vertices.

```
def clip_segment_with_rectangle(s: Segment2D, A: Point2D, B: Point2D):
    #Rectangle R is defined by bottom-left(A) and top-right corner(B)
    xA, yA = s[0][0], s[0][1]
    xB, yB = s[1][0], s[1][1]

    xMin, yMin = A[0], A[1]
    xMax, yMax = B[0], B[1]

    b0 = bin_rep(s[0], A, B)
    b1 = bin_rep(s[1], A, B)
```

```
12      if (b0|b1)==0: return True, s  # The endpoints of segment s have zero
           representation.
13
14      while (b0|b1):
15          if(b0&b1)!=0: return False, None  # No clipping is performed because
16          # The endpoints of segment s lie on the same side.
17          dx,dy = xB - xA, yB - yA
18          if b0:  # The first endpoint of segment s is updated.
19              if b0 & 8:    yA += (xMin - xA) * dy / dx; xA = xMin
20              elif b0 & 4:  yA += (xMax - xA) * dy / dx; xA = xMax
21              elif b0 & 2:  xA += (yMin - yA) * dx / dy; yA = yMin
22              elif b0 & 1:  xA += (yMax - yA) * dx / dy; yA = yMax
23              b0 = bin_rep(Point2D(xA, yA), A, B)
24          else:  # The second endpoint of segment s is updated.
25              if b1 & 8:    yB+= (xMin - xB) * dy / dx; xB = xMin
26              elif b1 & 4:  yB+= (xMax - xB) * dy / dx; xB = xMax
27              elif b1 & 2:  xB+= (yMin - yB) * dx / dy; yB = yMin
28              elif b1 & 1:  xB+= (yMax - yB) * dx / dy; yB = yMax
29              b1 = bin_rep(Point2D(xB, yB), A, B)
30      return True, Segment2D(Point2D(xA, yA), Point2D(xB, yB))
```

The main function *clip_segment_with_rectangle*($\cdot,\cdot,\cdot$) is highly efficient, as the operations frequently executed within it are performed using binary logic, i.e., bitwise operations. This approach is significantly faster compared to using other arithmetic types such as **integer** (*int*) or **floating-point** (*double*). Moreover, within the **while** loop, only a constant number of conditions are checked each time, and the loop terminates as soon as the binary representations of the segment endpoints become zero, i.e., when the condition b0|b1 becomes zero. In addition, the main function invokes a helper function *bin_rep*($\cdot,\cdot,\cdot$), whose purpose is to assign a binary representation of the form $b_3b_2b_1b_0$ to a given point $P = P(x,y)$. Its implementation is provided below:

```
1 def bin_rep(p: Point2D, a: Point2D, b: Point2D):
2     return (8 if p[0]<a[0] else 0)|(4 if p[0]>b[0] else 0)|(2 if p[1]<a[1] else 0)
          |(1 if p[1]>b[1] else 0)
```

Based on the implementation of the Cohen-Sutherland algorithm, it can be observed that the bitwise operations **AND** (&) and **OR** (|) are heavily utilized. Due to their efficiency, these operations can significantly speed up program execution, in some cases by several times. It is not difficult to observe that the Cohen-Sutherland algorithm can be generalized for clipping a convex polygon and a segment. To visualize the clipping of a segment against a rectangle, the basic GUI previously used for segment intersection visualization must be modified. Specifically, the rectangle is drawn by initiating a left mouse click on the canvas (which defines the starting point of the diagonal) and dragging the cursor along the diagonal. Releasing the mouse button sets the opposite corner of the diagonal, thus completing the rectangle. Similarly, the segment is drawn with a second mouse click: after releasing the mouse button, the segment is rendered, and the clipping operation is automatically triggered by invoking the method *clip_segment_with_rectangle*($\cdot, \cdot, \cdot$). The clipped portion is then highlighted using a bold stroke. Accordingly, it is necessary to define the following mouse events: <ButtonPress-1>, <B1-Motion>, and <ButtonRelease-1>, as well as implement interaction logic to distinguish between drawing a rectangle and drawing a segment. The following listing provides the modified code that enables interactive visualization of segment clipping with rectangle.

Listing 3.2: GUI for Visualizing Segment Clipping with a Rectangle

```python
import tkinter as tk
from Point2D import Point2D
from Segment2D import Segment2D
from ch3_helper_functions import clip_segment_with_rectangle

class ClippingApp:
    def __init__(self, master):
        self.master = master
        self.canvas = tk.Canvas(master, width=800, height=600, bg='white')
        self.canvas.pack()

        self.s_p = None # start point
        self.r= None # rectangle
        self.s = None # segment
        self.p= 'draw_rectangle'  # or 'draw_segment' phase
        self.t_s = None # temp shape

        self.canvas.bind("<ButtonPress-1>", self.on_mouse_press)
        self.canvas.bind("<B1-Motion>", self.on_mouse_drag)
        self.canvas.bind("<ButtonRelease-1>", self.on_mouse_release)

    def on_mouse_press(self, event): self.s_p = Point2D(event.x, event.y)

    def on_mouse_drag(self, event):
        if self.t_s: self.canvas.delete(self.t_s)
        e_p = Point2D(event.x, event.y) # end point
        if self.p == 'draw_rectangle':
            self.t_s=self.canvas.create_rectangle(self.s_p[0],self.s_p[1],e_p[0],
                e_p[1],outline='blue')
        elif self.p == 'draw_segment':
            self.t_s=self.canvas.create_line(self.s_p[0],self.s_p[1],e_p[0],e_p
                [1],fill='black',dash=(2,2))

    def on_mouse_release(self, event):
        e_p= Point2D(event.x, event.y) #end point
        if self.p == 'draw_rectangle':
            self.r = [self.s_p, e_p]
            self.canvas.create_rectangle(self.s_p[0],self.s_p[1],e_p[0],e_p[1],
                outline='blue')
            self.p = 'draw_segment'
        elif self.p== 'draw_segment':
            self.s = Segment2D(self.s_p, e_p)
            self.canvas.create_line(self.s_p[0],self.s_p[1],e_p[0],e_p[1],fill='
                black')
            self.p = 'done'
            self.clip_and_draw()
            self.t_s=None

    def clip_and_draw(self):
        if self.r and self.s: # both objects were drawn
            if(self.r[0][0]>self.r[1][0]): self.r[0],self.r[1]=self.r[1],self.r[0]
            R,C=clip_segment_with_rectangle(self.s,self.r[0],self.r[1])
            if C: # clipped segment
                a, b = C[0], C[1]
                self.canvas.create_line(a[0],a[1],b[0],b[1], fill='gray',width=3)
```

```
53 if __name__ == "__main__":
54     root = tk.Tk()
55     root.title("Clipping Segment With Rectangle")
56     app = ClippingApp(root)
57     root.mainloop()
```

The graphical interface for the Cohen–Sutherland algorithm used to clip a segment against a rectangle, implemented based on Listing 3.2, is illustrated in Fig. 3.8.

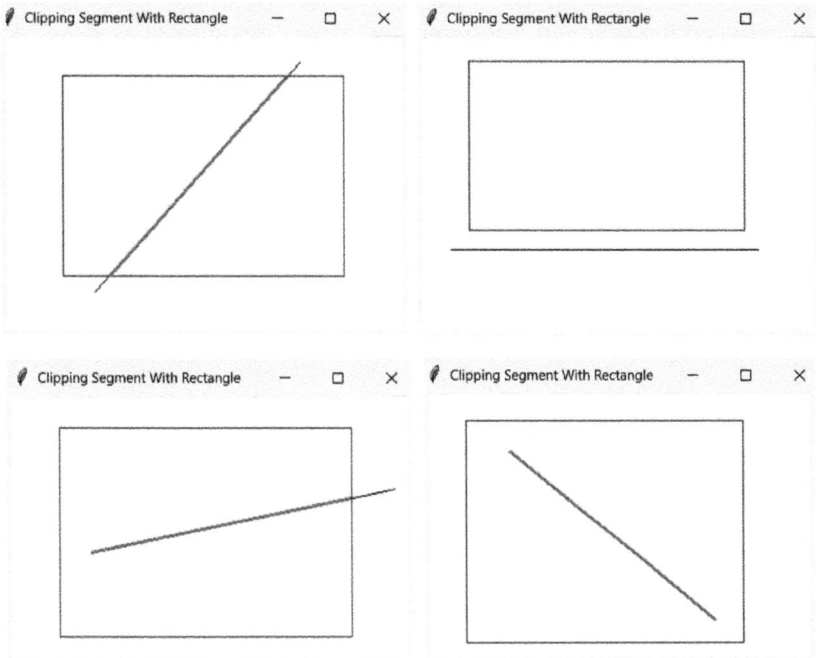

Figure 3.8: Visualization of different cases of segment and rectangle clipping, where the result of the clipping is a thickened segment colored in gray.

3.3 Clipping a Convex Polygon and a Segment

This section describes the **Cyrus-Beck** algorithm for clipping a convex polygon and a segment. The algorithm was developed by John Cyrus and Bruce Beck in 1978. It generalizes the Cohen-Sutherland and Liang-Barsky algorithms, providing an efficient method for clipping line segments within convex regions. The approach is based on the parametric representation of the segment and scalar products between the normal vectors of the polygon's edges and the segment's direction vector. An enhancement of this algorithm was proposed by Skala in 1997 [168]. Let the algorithm take as input two geometric objects: a segment $s = \overline{AB}$ and a convex polygon $\mathscr{P}$ consisting of n vertices, i.e., $\mathscr{P} = \{P_0, P_1, \cdots, P_{n-1}\}$. The algorithm first associates the segment s with a line q, and each edge $e_i = \overline{P_i P_{i+1}}$ (for $i = \overline{0, n-1}$) with a corresponding line r_i. The polygon vertices are assumed to be given in a clockwise circular order. The goal of the algorithm is to determine whether the segment can be clipped by the polygon. If clipping is possible, the clipped portion is extracted; otherwise, the original segment remains unchanged. It is evident that the line q intersects the polygon edges r_i in at most two points. The core idea of the Cyrus-Beck algorithm is to classify intersection points of the segment s and the polygon edges as either *entering* or *exiting* points. Entering points are denoted by P_i, and exiting points by P_o. If the segment lies entirely inside the polygon, the endpoints of s are classified as $P_i = A$ and $P_o = B$. However, more complex situations arise when the segment is partially or completely outside the polygon $\mathscr{P}$. If the segment lies entirely outside the polygon, the intersection is empty, and the algorithm terminates without performing any clipping—this trivial case is not of interest here. Thus, we focus on the scenario where some portion of the segment lies within the polygon. Suppose the lines q and r_j intersect at a point C, as shown in Fig. 3.9 (a). The point C is classified as a *potential entering point* if the line q pierces the polygon edge s_j from the left side to the right side. If the intersection between s and s_j is non-empty, the point C is confirmed as an entering intersection point P_i. Conversely, if the line q crosses s_j from the right to the left side, the intersection point C is classified as an exiting point P_o (Fig. 3.9 (b)). In this case, the clipped portion of the segment lies beyond point C inside the polygon $\mathscr{P}$, as illustrated by the shaded area in the same figure. Following this classification, the points of intersection between the segment s and polygon $\mathscr{P}$ are designated as P_i and P_o, respectively. The next step is to determine these points precisely. Let $\vec{n}$ be the inward-pointing normal vector of the polygon edge s_j. A point C is classified as an entering point P_i *if and only if* the angle $\alpha = \angle(\vec{n}, \overrightarrow{AB})$ between the normal vector $\vec{n}$ and the segment direction vector $\overrightarrow{AB}$ is less than $90°$ (Fig. 3.10 (a)). Conversely, the point C is an exiting point P_o *if and only if* $\alpha > 90°$ (Fig. 3.10 (b)). Using the properties of the dot product and the facts that $\cos\alpha < 0 \Leftrightarrow \alpha \in (90°, 270°)$ and $\cos\alpha > 0 \Leftrightarrow \alpha \in [0°, 90°) \cup (270°, 360°]$, the point C is an entering point P_i iff $\vec{n} \cdot \overrightarrow{AB} > 0$, and an exiting point P_o iff $\vec{n} \cdot \overrightarrow{AB} < 0$. Based on these principles, the implementation of the Cyrus-Beck algorithm for clipping a segment s against a convex polygon $\mathscr{P}$ is presented below.

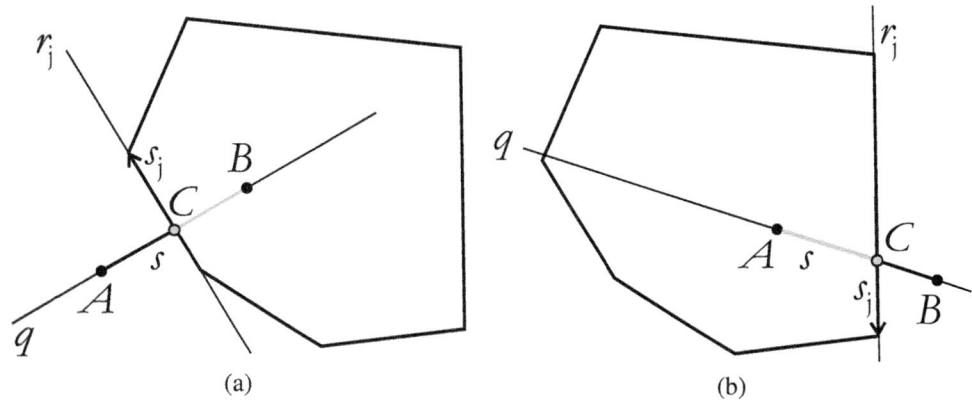

(a)   (b)

Figure 3.9: (a) Determining the entering point P_i. (b) Determining the exiting point P_o.

```
1  def do_polygon_segment_clip(s: Segment2D, p: Polygon, cS: Segment2D) -> bool:
2      p_i = 0.0   # lower bound for the clipped segment
3      p_o = 1.0   # upper bound for the clipped segment
4      p0 = [0.0]
5      v_s = s[1] - s[0]   # direction vector of segment s = AB
6      if p.area()>0: p.change_orientation() # ensure clockwise orientation
7      if p.contains_point(s[0]) and p.contains_point(s[1]):
8          cS.s = s.point_at(0.0); cS.e = s.point_at(1.0)
9          return True
10     for _ in range(p.size()):
11         sj = p.current_edge()   # segment of the polygon
12         if s.intersection_segments(sj, p0) == TypeS2.INTERSECT_SEG:
13             temp= Segment2D(sj[0], sj[1]).rotate()
14             n =temp[1]-temp[0] # normal vector to sj
15             dot = n[0] * v_s[0] + n[1] * v_s[1]
16             if dot > 0.0 and p0[0] > p_i: p_i = p0[0]   # update entering point
```

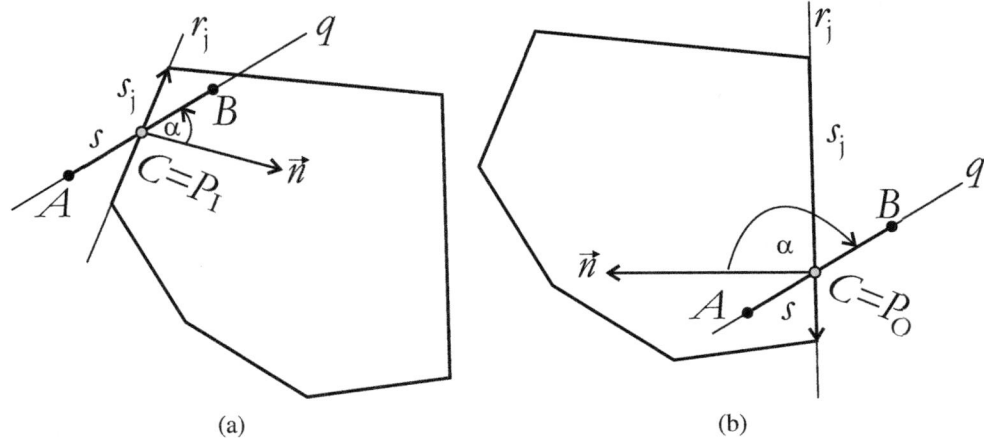

Figure 3.10: (a) Exact computation of the entering point P_i. (b) Exact determination of the exiting point P_o.

```
17          elif p0[0] < p_o: p_o = p0[0]  # update exiting point
18      p.move_current(1)
19  if p_i <= p_o:
20      if p_i==0 and p_o==1: return False # segment lies outside polygon
21      cS.s = s.point_at(p_i); cS.e = s.point_at(p_o)
22      return True  # segment is clipped
23  return False  # segment lies outside the polygon
```

The Cyrus-Beck algorithm can also be used for clipping a segment against a rectangle, since a rectangle is a special case of a convex polygon. However, the Cohen-Sutherland algorithm is significantly faster in terms of primitive operation execution, even though, from an asymptotic point of view, it is not faster than the Cyrus-Beck algorithm. At the end of this section, it is worth noting that the Cyrus-Beck algorithm, with certain modifications, can be adapted for computing the intersection between a rectangle and a concave polygon, which will be the topic of the next section. The visualization of the clipping process between a convex polygon and a segment is realized by first drawing the polygon on the canvas, followed by the segment. The polygon is drawn by specifying its vertices through left mouse clicks, and the drawing process is completed with a right mouse click. The segment is drawn in the same manner as in the case of clipping with a rectangle. Consequently, it was necessary to significantly modify Listing 3.2, and for the sake of clarity, a new version of the listing is provided (see Listing 3.3).

Listing 3.3: GUI for Visualizing Segment Clipping with a Convex Polygon

```
1 import tkinter as tk
2 from Point2D import Point2D
3 from Segment2D import Segment2D
4 from Polygon import Polygon
5 from ch3_helper_functions import do_polygon_segment_clip
6
7 class ClippingApp:
8     def __init__(self, master):
9         self.master = master
10        self.canvas = tk.Canvas(master, width=800, height=600, bg='white')
11        self.canvas.pack()
12
```

```python
13        self.v_p: List[Point2D] = [] # vertices of polygon
14        self.A= None # segment start
15        self.seg = None # segment
16        self.phase = 'draw_polygon' # phases: draw_polygon, draw_segment, done
17        self.temp_line = None
18
19        self.canvas.bind("<ButtonPress-1>", self.on_left_click)
20        self.canvas.bind("<ButtonPress-3>", self.on_right_click) # finish polygon
21        self.canvas.bind("<B1-Motion>", self.on_mouse_drag)
22        self.canvas.bind("<ButtonRelease-1>", self.on_mouse_release)
23
24    def on_left_click(self, e):
25        if self.phase == 'draw_polygon':
26            pt = Point2D(e.x,e.y)
27            self.v_p.append(pt)
28            if len(self.v_p) > 1:
29                l=self.v_p[-2]
30                self.canvas.create_line(l[0], l[1], pt[0], pt[1], fill='blue')
31        elif self.phase == 'draw_segment': self.A= Point2D(e.x,e.y)
32
33    def on_right_click(self, e):
34        if self.phase == 'draw_polygon' and len(self.v_p) >= 3:
35            F= self.v_p[0] #first vertex
36            L= self.v_p[-1] # last vertex
37            self.canvas.create_line(L[0],L[1],F[0],F[1],fill='blue')
38            self.phase = 'draw_segment'
39
40    def on_mouse_drag(self, e):
41        if self.phase == 'draw_segment' and self.A:
42            if self.temp_line: self.canvas.delete(self.temp_line)
43            self.temp_line=self.canvas.create_line(self.A[0],self.A[1],e.x,e.y,
                fill='black', dash=(2, 2))
44
45    def on_mouse_release(self, e):
46        if self.phase == 'draw_segment' and self.A:
47            B = Point2D(e.x,e.y) # B is end point
48            self.seg = Segment2D(self.A, B)
49            self.canvas.create_line(self.A[0],self.A[1],B[0],B[1],fill='black')
50            self.phase = 'done'
51            self.clip_and_draw()
52            self.temp_line = None
53
54    def clip_and_draw(self):
55        if self.seg:
56            c_s=Segment2D() # clipped_segment
57            if do_polygon_segment_clip(self.seg,Polygon.from_points(self.v_p),c_s)
                :
58                a, b = c_s.s, c_s.e
59                self.canvas.create_line(a[0], a[1], b[0], b[1], fill='gray', width
                    =3)
60
61 root = tk.Tk()
62 root.title("Clipping Segment With Convex Polygon")
63 app = ClippingApp(root)
64 root.mainloop()
```

The graphical interface of the Cyrus-Beck algorithm for computing the intersection between a convex polygon and a segment implemented based on Listing 3.3, is illustrated in Fig. 3.11.

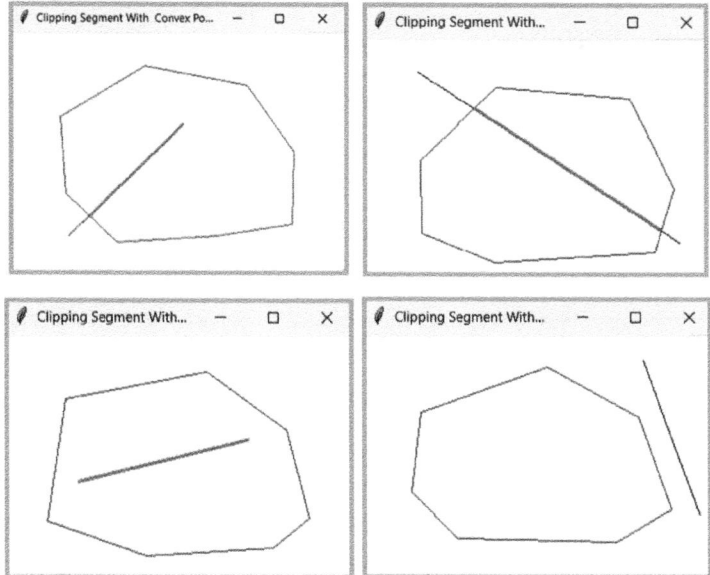

Figure 3.11: Visualization of different cases of segment and convex polygon clipping, where the result of the clipping is a thickened segment colored in gray.

3.4 Clipping of a Rectangle and a Concave Polygon

In this section, the **Sutherland-Hodgman** algorithm is described and implemented. It was developed by Ivan Sutherland and Gary Hodgman in 1974. This algorithm is used for clipping convex and concave polygons within a rectangular window or another convex region by applying successive clipping against each edge of the clipping polygon [174]. In the remainder of this section, we describe how this algorithm is used for clipping a rectangle $\square ABCD$ and a concave polygon $\mathscr{P}$. In this type of clipping, the resulting polygon can generally have more vertices than the original polygon. For example, Fig. 3.12 (a) shows the clipping of a concave polygon $\mathscr{P} = \{P_0, P_1, \cdots, P_8\}$ and a rectangle $\square ABCD$, where the resulting polygon $\mathscr{Q} = \{P_0, U_0, U_1, P_2, U_2, U_3, P_5, U_4, U_5, P_7, U_6, U_7\}$ has three more vertices compared to the initial polygon $\mathscr{P}$. The working principle of the Sutherland-Hodgman algorithm is based on clipping the edges of the rectangle with the polygon sides. For example, one starts by selecting an arbitrary edge of the rectangle $\square ABCD$ (e.g., edge $\overline{AB}$) and performs clipping with all polygon sides $\mathscr{P}$. As a result, a new polygon $\mathscr{P}_1$ is obtained. This process continues between polygon $\mathscr{P}_1$ and the remaining edges of the rectangle, such as edge $\overline{BC}$, resulting in polygon $\mathscr{P}_2$. Analogously, polygons $\mathscr{P}_3$ and $\mathscr{P}_4$ are formed when considering edges $\overline{CD}$ and $\overline{DA}$, respectively. The final polygon $\mathscr{P}_4$ represents the clipped polygon $\mathscr{Q}$, as shown in Fig. 3.12 (a). At first glance, it may seem that the Cyrus-Beck algorithm could be used for clipping between the edges of the rectangle and the polygon sides, as was done in the previous section. Unfortunately, this is not possible here, since this section deals with concave polygons.

Accordingly, the following section describes the procedure for clipping a segment (a side of the rectangle) against the edges of a concave polygon. Let $p = \overline{P_i P_j}$ be an arbitrary edge of the polygon (without loss of generality, it can be the first edge, i.e., $\overline{P_0 P_1}$), and let $s = \overline{AB}$ be the segment, i.e., a side of the rectangle used for clipping the polygon. Then, the segment p can intersect the segment s in four possible ways, which are illustrated in Fig. 3.13. Scenario i) occurs when the segment $p = \overline{P_0 P_1}$ lies entirely to the right of segment s, meaning both endpoints P_0 and P_1 of segment p lie to the right of segment s. In this case, the point P_1 is added to the resulting polygon. Scenario ii) arises when segment p intersects segment s such

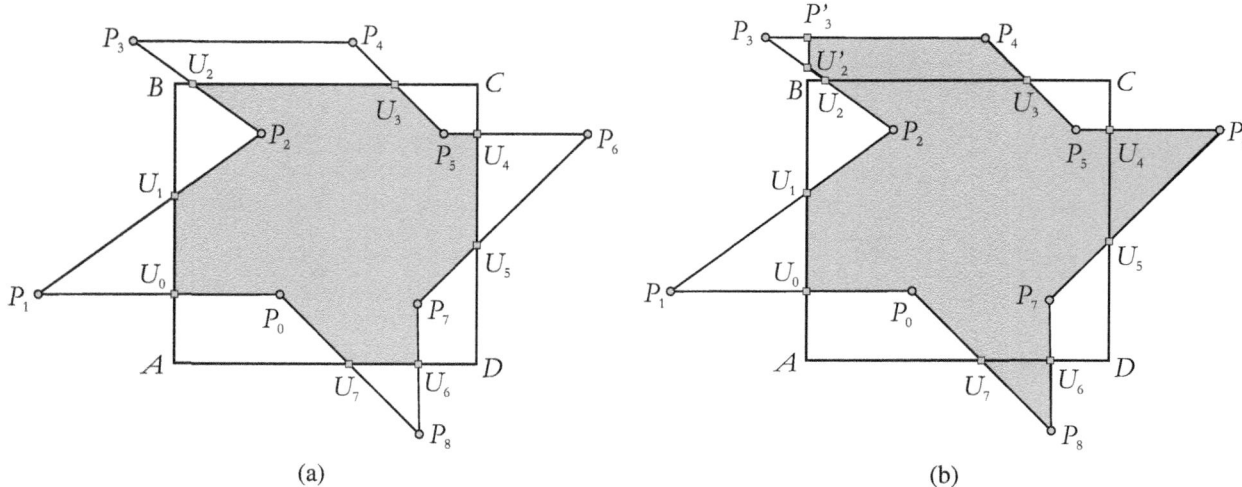

(a)   (b)

Figure 3.12: (a) Clipping of rectangle $ABCD$ and polygon $\mathscr{P}$. (b) Result of clipping polygon $\mathscr{P}$ with segment $\overline{AB}$.

that point P_0 lies to the right of s and point P_1 lies to its left. In this case, the intersection point P is added to the resulting polygon.

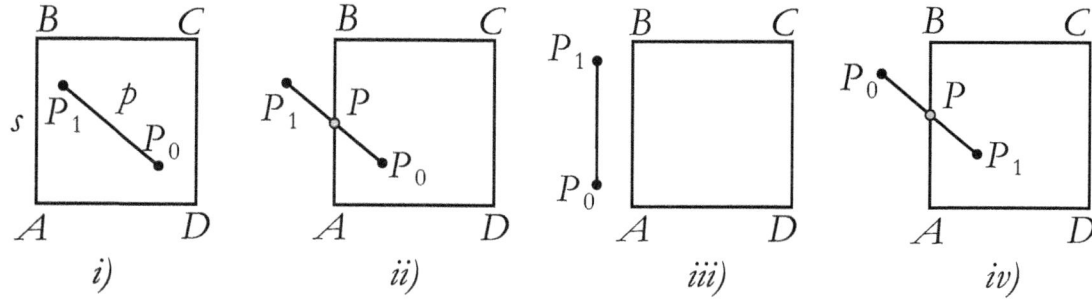

$i)$ $ii)$ $iii)$ $iv)$

Figure 3.13: Four possible scenarios involving the segments $\overline{P_0 P_1}$ and $\overline{AB}$, illustrated in steps (i) through (iv).

Scenario iii) occurs when the segment p lies entirely to the left of the segment s. In this case, nothing is added to the resulting polygon. Scenario iv) arises when the segment p intersects the segment s such that the point P_0 lies to the left of s and the point P_1 lies to the right of it. In this situation, the intersection point P and the endpoint P_1 of the segment p are added to the polygon. The idea of clipping the segment s of the rectangle $\square ABCD$ against the segment p of the polygon $\mathscr{P}$ is implemented within the function $clip\_polygon\_with\_segment(\cdot,\cdot)$, whose purpose is to return the resulting polygon produced by clipping an arbitrary concave polygon against an arbitrary segment. This function returns the polygon $\mathscr{P}_1 = \{P_0, U_0, U_1, P_2, U_2, U_2', P_3', P_4, P_5, P_6, P_7, P_8\}$ when it is called with the concave polygon $\mathscr{P}$ and the segment $\overline{AB}$ as formal parameters, as illustrated in Fig. 3.12 (b). That is, the original polygon $\mathscr{P}$ is divided into two parts, and the subpolygon located on the right-hand side of the segment $\overline{AB}$ is returned.

```
1 from Point2D import Point2D
2 from Segment2D import Segment2D
3 from Polygon import Polygon
4 from TypeS2 import TypeS2
5 from TypeP2 import TypeP2
```

```
 6
 7 def clip_polygon_with_segment(cP: Polygon, s: Segment2D) -> Polygon | None:
 8     pol= Polygon()  # Resulting polygon may be concave
 9     for _ in range(cP.size()):
10         p0 = cP.point_of_current()
11         p1 = cP.ccw_neighbor().vertex_point()
12         c0 = p0.classification_m(s[0], s[1])
13         c1 = p1.classification_m(s[0], s[1])
14         p_i = None # intersection point
15         if c0 != c1:
16             p = [0.0]
17             s.intersection_lines(Segment2D(p0, p1), p)
18             p_i = s.point_at(p[0])   # Intersection point
19         if c0==TypeP2.RIGHT and c1==TypeP2.RIGHT: pol.insert(p1) # i)
20         elif c0==TypeP2.RIGHT and c1==TypeP2.LEFT and p0!=p_i:pol.insert(p_i)# ii)
21         elif c0==TypeP2.LEFT and c1==TypeP2.LEFT: pass # iii), nothing added
22         else:
23             pol.insert(p_i) # iv)
24             if p1 != p_i: pol.insert(p1)
25         cP.move_current(1)
26     return pol if pol.size() > 0 else None
```

After implementing the auxiliary function *clip_polygon_with_segment*($\cdot$, $\cdot$), it becomes straightforward to write the main function *do_polygon_rectangle_clip*($\cdot$,$\cdot$), which internally calls *clip_polygon_with_segment* multiple times to perform clipping of all rectangle edges against the edges of a concave polygon. Therefore, its implementation is simple, as shown below:

```
 1 def do_polygon_rectangle_clip(cP: Polygon, rP: Polygon) -> Polygon | None:
 2     q = cP.copy()  # Initial polygon to be clipped
 3     for _ in range(rP.size()):
 4         rP.move_current(-1)  # Move to previous vertex (clockwise)
 5         s = rP.current_edge()  # Current edge as segment
 6         res = clip_polygon_with_segment(q, s)
 7         if res is not None: q = res  # Update q with clipped polygon
 8         else: return None  # No clipping result - the clipped polygon is empty
 9     return q
```

Given that the visualization of clipping a rectangle with a polygon requires only a minor adjustment of Listing 3.3, the reader is encouraged to implement the graphical interface for the Sutherland-Hodgman algorithm independently. An example implementation is illustrated in Fig. 3.14. Within this GUI, the polygon is first drawn by specifying its vertices, followed by the drawing of a rectangle. After that, the function *do_polygon_rectangle_clip*($\cdot$, $\cdot$) is automatically called to determine the clipped polygon.

3.5 Intersection of Convex Polygons

In this section, we describe an efficient method for determining the intersection between two convex polygons $\mathscr{P}$ and $\mathscr{Q}$ in $\mathcal{O}(m+n)$ time, where m and n denote the number of vertices of polygons $\mathscr{P}$ and $\mathscr{Q}$, respectively [142]. It is evident that the Sutherland–Hodgman algorithm could be used to find the intersection, but its time complexity is $\Theta(nm)$. Likewise, the sweep line algorithm for computing intersections among a set of segments could be applied, with an overall complexity of $\Theta((n+m+r)\log(n+m))$. Readers interested in implementing these approaches are encouraged to do so on their own. In the remainder, we focus on a method whose runtime is proportional to $\mathcal{O}(m+n)$. During the intersection process, we assume that no degenerate cases occur (i.e., two edges of $\mathscr{P}$ and $\mathscr{Q}$ coincide or intersect

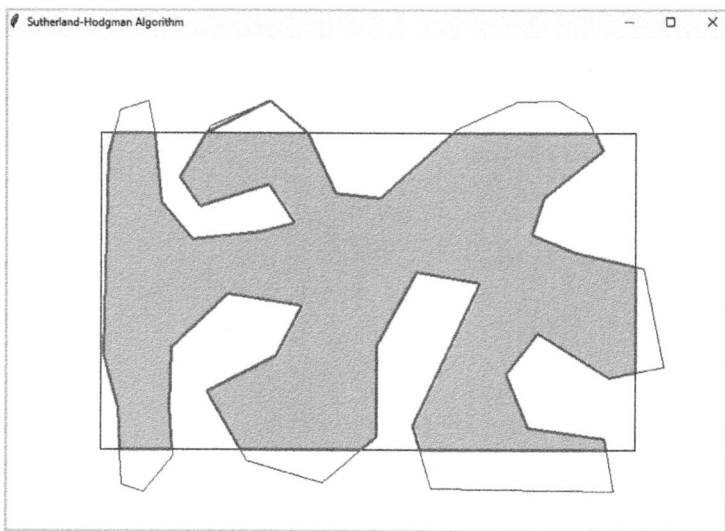

Figure 3.14: Graphical illustration of the clipping between a rectangle and a concave polygon.

in infinitely many points, or meet exactly at their vertices). Although these degenerate situations can be handled relatively easily, they are not considered here for clarity. Excluding degenerate cases, the intersection $\mathscr{P} \cap \mathscr{Q}$ consists of alternating chains A_1A_2, A_2A_3, A_3A_4, A_4A_1 that sequentially follow the vertices of polygon $\mathscr{Q}$, then polygon $\mathscr{P}$, then again $\mathscr{Q}$, and so on (see Fig. 3.15). In general, a *chain of vertices* refers to an open polyline that connects the vertices and does not self-intersect. From Fig. 3.15, it can be observed that the grey-shaded region represents the intersection $\mathscr{P} \cap \mathscr{Q}$, which consists of the following alternating chains: $\overline{A_1A_2} \in \mathscr{Q}$, $\overline{A_2P_6}, \overline{P_6A_3} \in \mathscr{P}$, $\overline{A_3Q_5}, \overline{Q_5A_4} \in \mathscr{Q}$, $\overline{A_4P_2}, \overline{P_2P_3}, \overline{P_3A_1} \in \mathscr{P}$. These chains alternate between the two polygons $\mathscr{P}$ and $\mathscr{Q}$. Furthermore, it is apparent that by removing the polygonal regions $A_1 - P_4 - P_5 - A_2 - A_1$, $A_2 - Q_3 - Q_4 - A_3 - P_6 - A_2$, $A_3 - P_7 - P_0 - P_1 - A_4 - Q_5 - A_3$, and $A_4 - Q_0 - Q_1 - Q_2 - A_1 - P_3 - P_2 - A_4$, the resulting figure corresponds to the desired intersection $\mathscr{P} \cap \mathscr{Q}$. The shape of these polygons resembles a *sickle* . In such polygons, the alternating chains terminate at intersection points of polygons $\mathscr{P}$ and $\mathscr{Q}$. For instance, the hatched sickle $A_4 - P_2 - P_3 - A_1 - Q_2 - Q_1 - Q_0 - A_4$ ends at the intersection points A_1 and A_4, which are obtained, respectively, as the intersections of segments $\overline{Q_2Q_3}$ and $\overline{P_3P_4}$, and segments $\overline{Q_5Q_0}$ and $\overline{P_1P_2}$. The remaining sickles are created in a completely analogous manner. It is easy to conclude that the intersection $\mathscr{P} \cap \mathscr{Q}$ is bounded by an even number of sickles, and that the interior chains of this intersection always alternate between polygons $\mathscr{P}$ and $\mathscr{Q}$, as already mentioned. Based on the above, the algorithm for computing the intersection of convex polygons consists of two phases.

First phase of the algorithm

In the first phase of the algorithm, the polygons $\mathscr{P}$ and $\mathscr{Q}$ are assigned their corresponding windows p and q, respectively. A window is a rectangle that bounds or "slides" along the sides of a polygon (see Fig. 3.15). The windows p and q are moved in the clockwise direction until they are positioned over the sides of the polygons that belong to the same sickle. Initially, the windows are arbitrarily placed (bounding randomly chosen sides of $\mathscr{P}$ and $\mathscr{Q}$), so their initial configuration is irrelevant. It is not difficult to show that, regardless of how the windows are initially positioned over the polygon sides, in the worst-case scenario, each window needs to slide over at most two full traversals of its polygon to reach the sides belonging to the same sickle. This claim will be formally proved later. It is important to note that moving a window implies its shift—or "slide"—from one polygon side to the next.

Second phase of the algorithm

In the second phase of the algorithm, the windows p and q continue to move in the clockwise direction,

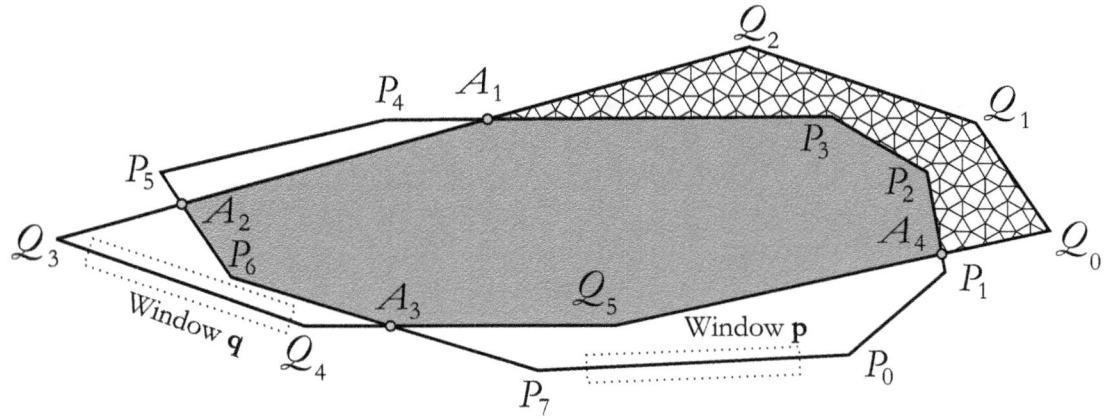

Figure 3.15: Intersection of polygons $\mathscr{P}$ and $\mathscr{Q}$ generated through alternating chains.

now transitioning from the current to the neighboring sickle. Before both windows leave the current sickle and enter the next adjacent one, they must pass through the intersection point of the polygon sides, i.e., the point where the sickles meet. For example, if window p is currently positioned on the side $\overline{P_6P_5}$ of polygon $\mathscr{P}$ and window q is on side $\overline{Q_3Q_2}$ of polygon $\mathscr{Q}$, then they pass through the intersection point A_2 when leaving the second sickle $S_2 : A_2 - Q_3 - Q_4 - A_3 - P_6 - A_2$. In this case, the first sickle $S_1 : A_1 - P_4 - P_5 - A_2 - A_1$ and the second sickle S_2 meet at the intersection point A_2. In this manner, the sides of the desired intersection $\mathscr{P} \cap \mathscr{Q}$ are directly constructed, meaning the intersection begins to grow. It is easy to observe that each time a window continues to traverse polygon $\mathscr{P}$ in a clockwise direction, the endpoint of that window is included as a vertex of the intersection $\mathscr{P} \cap \mathscr{Q}$ only if the side along which the window slides belongs to the inner chain of the current sickle. For instance, if window p contains the side $\overline{P_4P_3}$, then the vertex P_3 becomes a vertex of the intersection $\mathscr{P} \cap \mathscr{Q}$ since the segment $\overline{P_4P_3}$ is part of the inner chain of the sickle S_4 ($A_4 - Q_0 - Q_1 - Q_2 - A_1 - P_3 - P_2 - A_4$). The same applies to window q. In this way, almost all the vertices of the desired intersection are generated. By including the intersection points where the windows p and q intersect, the complete set of vertices of the intersection $\mathscr{P} \cap \mathscr{Q}$ is obtained. The theoretical framework presented so far provides a general description of the procedure for determining the intersection between convex polygons $\mathscr{P}$ and $\mathscr{Q}$, which is not yet sufficient for implementing the algorithm. Therefore, it is necessary to introduce several additional details in the form of specific rules. For instance, one must define a rule that determines which of the two windows should move forward first. Before introducing this rule, we need to define what it means for a vector $\vec{a}$ to be directed towards another vector $\vec{b}$ (see Fig. 3.16).

Definition 3.5.1 A vector $\vec{a}$ is said to be *directed toward* a vector $\vec{b}$ if the line l containing vector $\vec{b}$ lies in front of vector $\vec{a}$.

From Fig. 3.16, it can be seen that the line l is not in front of vectors $\vec{a}_3$, $\vec{a}_4$, $\vec{a}_5$, and $\vec{a}_6$, while it is in front of the other vectors. The direction of vector $\vec{a}$ toward vector $\vec{b}$ can be verified using the vector product $\vec{a} \times \vec{b}$.

Definition 3.5.2 A vector $\vec{a}$ is said to be *directed toward* a vector $\vec{b}$ *if and only if* any of the following conditions holds:

- $\vec{a} \times \vec{b} \geq \vec{0}$ and the endpoint of vector $\vec{a}$ does not lie to the right of vector $\vec{b}$;
- $\vec{a} \times \vec{b} < \vec{0}$ and the endpoint of vector $\vec{a}$ does not lie to the left of vector $\vec{b}$.

It is known that the vector product $\vec{a} \times \vec{b}$ can be expressed using a determinant in the following form:

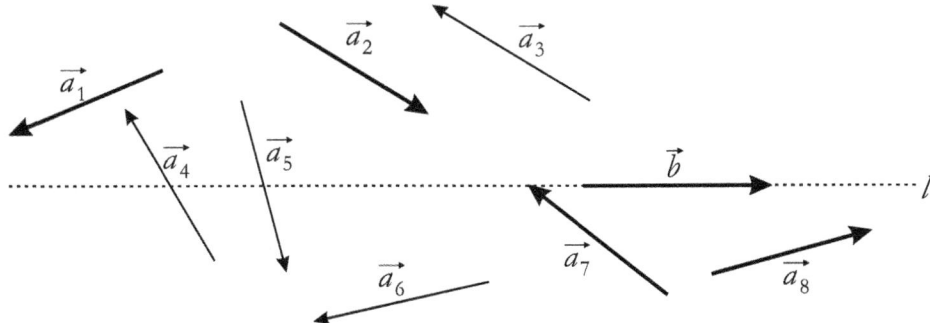

Figure 3.16: The vectors $\vec{a}_1$, $\vec{a}_2$, $\vec{a}_7$, and $\vec{a}_8$ are directed toward the vector $\vec{b}$.

$$\vec{a} \times \vec{b} = \begin{vmatrix} \vec{i} & \vec{j} & \vec{k} \\ a_x & a_y & 0 \\ b_x & b_y & 0 \end{vmatrix} = \vec{k}(a_x \cdot b_y - b_x \cdot a_y). \tag{3.3}$$

Therefore, the condition $\vec{a} \times \vec{b} \geq \vec{0}$ is verified by checking whether the inequality $a_x \cdot b_y \geq b_x \cdot a_y$ holds, since $\vec{k} = (0,0,1)$ is the unit orthonormal vector. To test whether the vector $\vec{a}$ is directed toward vector $\vec{b}$, it is sufficient to implement only the above condition. For any two arbitrarily chosen but fixed windows p and q, four cases can occur in which they participate (see Fig. 3.17):

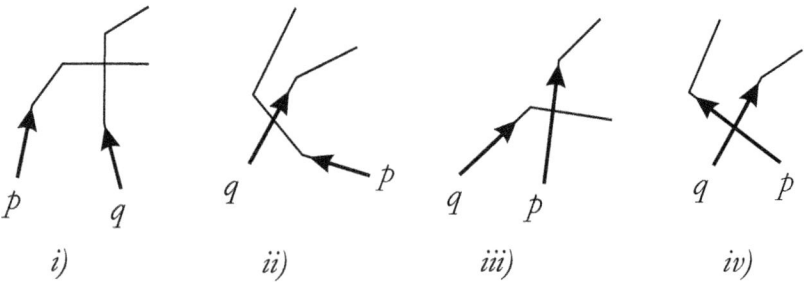

Figure 3.17: Four possible scenarios in which the windows p and q may occur, illustrated in steps (i) through (iv).

i) The windows p and q are directed towards each other. In this case, the window located outside the other is advanced. In Fig. 3.17 (i), this is window p, because window q lies inside window p, specifically on its right side. The intersection point between windows p and q cannot lie on the side of polygon $\mathscr{P}$ along which window p slides, since window p is located outside the intersection $\mathscr{P} \cap \mathscr{Q}$;

ii) Window p is directed toward window q, while window q is not directed toward window p (see Fig. 3.17 (ii)). In this case, the endpoint of window p is stored, provided that window p is not outside of window q. If it is, window p is advanced. In Fig. 3.17 (ii), window p does not contain the next intersection point, although in general it may contain an intersection point if it lies inside window q;

iii) Window q is directed toward window p, while window p is not directed toward window q (see Fig. 3.17 (iii)). In this case, if window q is not outside of window p, the endpoint of window q is stored, and the traversal continues from window q. In Fig. 3.17 (iii), this is not the case, as window q is located outside of window p;

iv) Windows p and q are not directed toward each other (see Fig. 3.17 (iv)). In this case, the window over the polygon side that lies outside the other window is advanced. In Fig. 3.17 (iv), window p is advanced along the next side of polygon $\mathscr{P}$, since that side lies outside window q.

These four scenarios will be implemented within the function *convex_polygon_intersection*$(\cdot,\cdot)$, which is used to determine the intersection of convex polygons $\mathscr{P}$ and $\mathscr{Q}$. The relationship between the windows p and q is tracked using the enumerated values UNKNOWN, INSIDEP, and INSIDEQ of the enumerated type **TypeI2**:

```
1 from enum import Enum
2 class TypeI2(Enum):
3     UNKNOWN = 1
4     INSIDEP = 2
5     INSIDEQ = 3
```

The implementation of the function *convex_polygon_intersection*$(\cdot,\cdot)$ is carried out as follows:

```
1 def convex_polygon_intersection(P: Polygon, Q: Polygon) -> Optional[Polygon]:
2     result = Polygon(); i = j = 0; flag = TypeI2.UNKNOWN; first_point = False
3     while ((i<P.size() or j<Q.size()) and (i<2*P.size() and j<2*Q.size())):
4         p = P.current_edge() # current window of P
5         q = Q.current_edge() # current window of Q
6         p_side = p[1].classification_m(q[0], q[1])
7         q_side = q[1].classification_m(p[0], p[1])
8         p0 = [0.0]
9         intersection_type = p.intersection_segments(q, p0)
10        if intersection_type == TypeS2.INTERSECT_SEG:
11            i_p = p.point_at(p0[0]) # a point of intersection segments
12            if not first_point and flag==TypeI2.UNKNOWN: i=j=0; first_point=True
13            result.insert(i_p)
14            if p_side == TypeP2.LEFT: flag = TypeI2.INSIDEP
15            elif q_side == TypeP2.LEFT: flag = TypeI2.INSIDEQ
16
17        vA = p[1] - p[0]; vB = q[1] - q[0]
18        direction = vA[0] * vB[1] - vB[0] * vA[1]
19
20        if direction==0 and p_side==TypeP2.RIGHT and q_side==TypeP2.RIGHT:
21            return None
22        elif direction == 0 and p_side.value > 2 and q_side.value > 2:
23            if flag == TypeI2.INSIDEP: Q.move_current(-1); j += 1
24            else: P.move_current(-1); i += 1
25        elif direction >= 0:
26            if q_side == TypeP2.LEFT:
27                P.move_current(-1); i += 1
28                if flag == TypeI2.INSIDEP: result.insert(P.point_of_current())
29            else:
30                Q.move_current(-1); j += 1
31                if flag == TypeI2.INSIDEQ: result.insert(Q.point_of_current())
32        else:
33            if p_side == TypeP2.LEFT:
34                Q.move_current(-1); j += 1
35                if flag == TypeI2.INSIDEQ: result.insert(Q.point_of_current())
36            else:
37                P.move_current(-1); i += 1
38                if flag == TypeI2.INSIDEP: result.insert(P.point_of_current())
39    if result.size() > 0: return result
40    else:
41        if Q.contains_point(P.point_of_current()): return P
```

```
42          elif P.contains_point(Q.point_of_current()): return Q
43          return None
```

The correctness of the algorithm underlying the implementation of the function *convex_polygon_intersection*($\cdot,\cdot$) will be discussed below. As can be observed from the code of the mentioned function, the algorithm iterates at most $2(|\mathscr{P}|+|\mathscr{Q}|)$ times. If no intersection point is found within this limit, the algorithm terminates and returns None as an indicator that no intersection exists between the polygons. Additionally, the method *contains_point*($\cdot$) from the **Polygon** class is used to determine whether $\mathscr{P} \subset \mathscr{Q}$, $\mathscr{Q} \subset \mathscr{P}$, or $\mathscr{P} \cap \mathscr{Q} \neq \emptyset$. The correctness of the algorithm follows directly from the following lemma.

> **Lemma 3.5.1** Prove the following:
>
> a) If the windows p and q belong to the same sickle, then their intersection point—where the sickle ends—will be found as the next intersection point of the mentioned windows;
>
> b) If the polygons $\mathscr{P}$ and $\mathscr{Q}$ intersect, then the windows p and q will intersect at some point in no more than $2(|\mathscr{P}|+|\mathscr{Q}|)$ iterations.

Proof. Case b) guarantees that the algorithm will find an intersection point if one exists, while claim (a) states that the remaining intersection points will be discovered in order, provided that the windows p and q intersect and belong to the same sickle. To prove case a), suppose that windows p and q belong to the same sickle such that window q reaches the intersection point earlier than window p (as shown in Fig. 3.15, window $q = \overline{Q_0Q_5}$ reaches the intersection point A_4 before window $p = \overline{P_3P_2}$). In this case, window q remains fixed (i.e., does not move), while window p continues to advance until it reaches the intersection point. To demonstrate this behavior, it is necessary to consider two distinct cases.

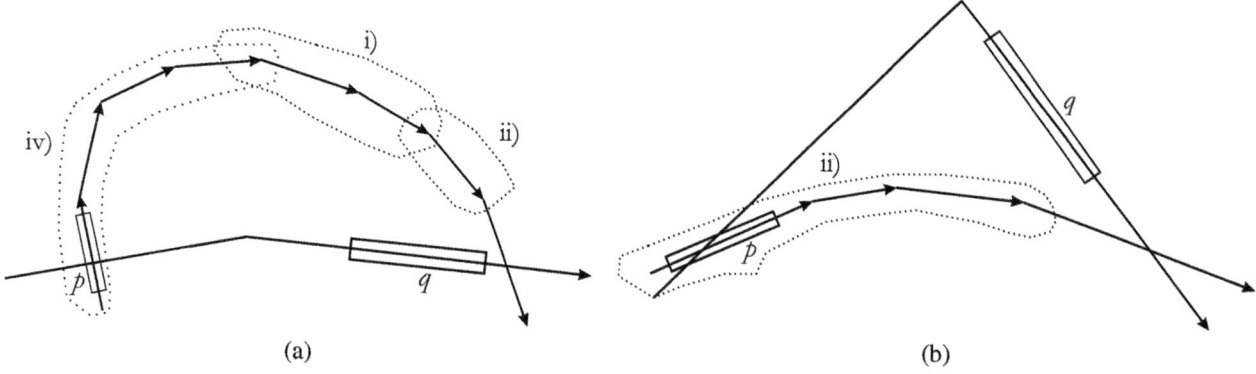

(a)   (b)

Figure 3.18: (a) The window p is outside the window q. (b) The window p is inside the window q.

In the first case, the polygon containing window p lies outside the polygon containing window q (see Fig. 3.18 (a)). In this case, window q remains fixed, and based on scenario iv), window p moves one or more times as long as condition iv) is satisfied. In Fig. 3.18 (a), window p moves three times according to rule iv). Then, according to rule i), p moves twice, and based on rule ii), p moves exactly once. In the second case, the polygon containing window p lies inside the polygon containing window q (see Fig. 3.18 (b)). Analogous to the first case, window q remains fixed, while window p moves forward according to rule ii). If it happens that window p reaches the intersection point before window q, then window p becomes fixed, while q advances using rule iii) instead of rule ii), with everything else remaining the same by simply swapping the roles of windows p and q. This completes the proof of Case a).

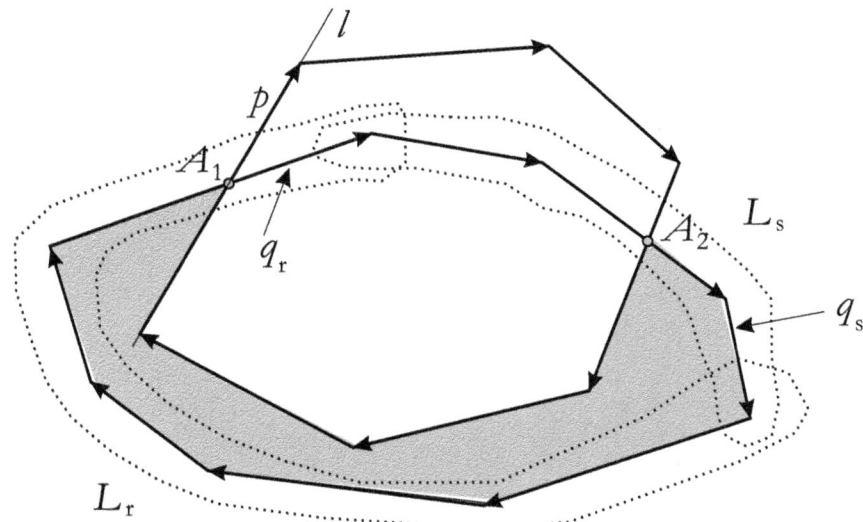

Figure 3.19: Intersection of polygons $\mathscr{P}$ and $\mathscr{Q}$.

To prove claim b), let us assume that polygons $\mathscr{P}$ and $\mathscr{Q}$ intersect as shown in Fig. 3.19. It is evident that after $|\mathscr{P}|+|\mathscr{Q}|$ iterations, either window p or window q will have traversed all the sides of one of the polygons. Without loss of generality, assume that window p traverses all sides of polygon $\mathscr{P}$ after the aforementioned number of iterations. At some point, window p will be positioned such that it contains an intersection point between polygons $\mathscr{P}$ and $\mathscr{Q}$, where polygon $\mathscr{Q}$ is being traversed from the outside toward the interior of polygon $\mathscr{P}$ (In Fig. 3.19, A_1 is the intersection point). Next, the boundary of polygon $\mathscr{Q}$ is divided into two chains, L_r and L_s. The first chain L_r ends at the endpoint of the polygon side q_r (this side intersects a side of polygon $\mathscr{P}$ at point A_1), while the second chain L_s ends at side q_s, such that its endpoint lies to the right of the line l that contains segment p, and it is the farthest from line l. Now, two scenarios can occur depending on whether side q belongs to chain L_r or to chain L_s:

1) If side q belongs to chain L_r: window p remains fixed, while window q is advanced one or more times using the following rules in sequence: iii), iv), i), and finally iii). At the last application of rule iii), the intersection point A_1 is reached.

2) If side q belongs to chain L_s: window q remains fixed, and window p is advanced one or more times using rule ii), followed by rule iv), then rule i), and finally rule ii), at which point window p lies inside window q. After that, windows p and q are advanced a certain number of times, during which window q cannot be moved beyond the next intersection point (in Fig. 3.19, this is point A_2) until window p first reaches the previous intersection point (in Fig. 3.19, this is point A_1). After this, windows p and q end up in the same sickle (e.g., the gray-shaded region in Fig. 3.19), and based on case a), it follows that windows p and q will intersect at the terminal point of the sickle (in Fig. 3.19, this is point A_1).

To demonstrate why at most $2(|\mathscr{P}|+|\mathscr{Q}|)$ iterations are sufficient to find the intersection point of windows p and q, one should observe that the initial positions of windows p and q (where window p is aligned with line l, and window q can begin on any side of polygon $\mathscr{Q}$) meet after a number of steps that does not exceed $|\mathscr{P}|+|\mathscr{Q}|$ iterations. The same number of iterations is necessary if the roles of windows p and q are swapped, since the situation is symmetric. In such cases, since neither p nor q traverse a full loop around their respective polygons before reaching the first intersection point, it follows that no more than $|\mathscr{P}|+|\mathscr{Q}|$ iterations are needed. Therefore, in any case, the total number of iterations is less than or equal to $2(|\mathscr{P}|+|\mathscr{Q}|)$, which completes the proof. This concludes the proof of the lemma. ∎

Graphical implementation of the linear-time algorithm for determining the intersection of convex polygons was developed in the Python programming language using the Tkinter graphical environment. It is illustrated in Fig. 3.20.

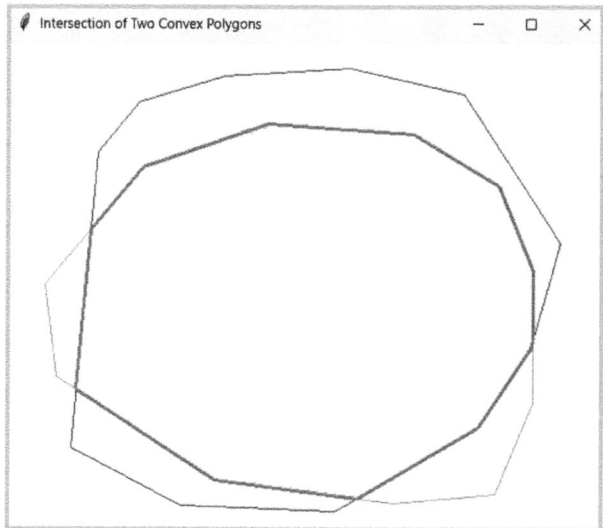

Figure 3.20: Graphical illustration of the intersection of convex polygons.

3.6   Intersection of Half-Planes

In this section, we describe the procedure for determining the intersection of half-planes. It is known that an arbitrary line p divides the plane into two half-planes H_1 and H_2, such that the first half-plane H_1 lies to the left of line p, and the second half-plane H_2 to its right. Although half-planes are generally classified as the simplest convex regions, by combining them through intersection and union operations, one can obtain an arbitrary convex polygon in the plane. The focus is now placed on the intersection of half-planes. Let $\mathcal{H}$ denote a collection of half-planes, and let $\mathcal{I}$ be their intersection. It is not difficult to show that the set $\mathcal{I}$ is convex, since it is obtained as the intersection of convex regions. A proof of this statement can be found in Chapter 7, when Voronoi diagrams are discussed. Figure 3.21 shows two convex regions formed by the intersection of half-planes, where each half-plane is determined by a segment. In Fig. 3.21 (a), the convex region is bounded, while this is not the case in Fig. 3.21 (b). During implementation, the intersection of half-planes generates a bounded convex region, since the segments are drawn on a canvas that is limited—usually by the screen dimensions or slightly smaller due to other UI elements placed outside the canvas. The brute-force algorithm for a set of n half-planes finds their intersection in quadratic time, i.e., in $\Theta(n^2)$ time. As with the intersection of segments or lines, all intersections between pairs of half-planes are checked. Fortunately, a faster recursive algorithm exists for computing such intersections, based on the *divide and conquer* paradigm . This approach is possible because the operation of intersecting convex regions is associative and commutative, meaning the order of intersection does not matter. In other words, if three convex (bounded or unbounded) regions $\mathcal{A}_1$, $\mathcal{A}_2$, and $\mathcal{A}_3$ are given, then any of the following intersections $(\mathcal{A}_1 \cap \mathcal{A}_2) \cap \mathcal{A}_3$, $(\mathcal{A}_1 \cap \mathcal{A}_3) \cap \mathcal{A}_2$, $\mathcal{A}_1 \cap (\mathcal{A}_2 \cap \mathcal{A}_3)$ results in the same convex region.

Also, due to commutativity, we have $\mathcal{A}_1 \cap \mathcal{A}_2 = \mathcal{A}_2 \cap \mathcal{A}_1$. Therefore, the mentioned paradigm divides an arbitrary collection of half-planes $\mathcal{H}$ into two non-empty subsets $\mathcal{H}_1$ and $\mathcal{H}_2$ of approximately equal size. If these subsets are unit-sized (i.e., contain only one element), the recursion terminates and returns their intersection $\mathcal{I}$, i.e., $\mathcal{I} = \mathcal{H}_1 \cap \mathcal{H}_2$. Otherwise, the recursion continues, and the mentioned subsets are further divided into smaller subsets, and their intersections are computed recursively. If the collection $\mathcal{H}$

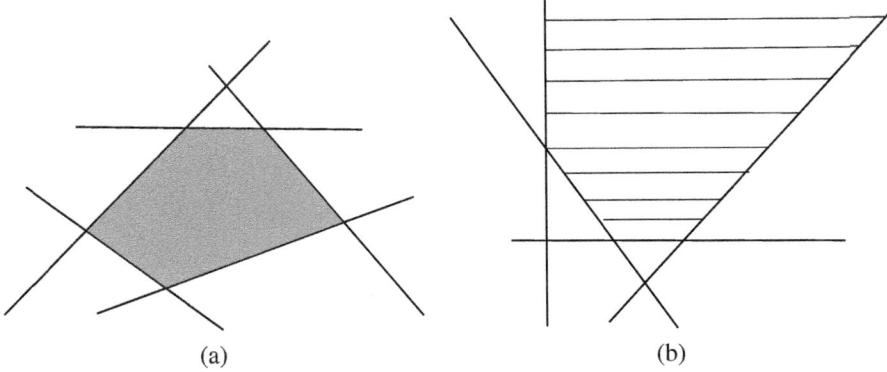

(a) (b)

Figure 3.21: (a) Bounded convex region. (b) Unbounded convex region.

initially contains only one element ($n = 1$), then it is returned as the final result. For the implementation of this recursive algorithm, all half-planes, as well as the intermediate intersections computed during execution, will be clipped by a *bounding box*, ensuring that the resulting convex region is bounded by a closed simple curve. Based on the above, the implementation of the recursive algorithm for computing the intersection of n half-planes generated by n line segments is given in the function *half_plane_intersection*($\cdot$, $\cdot$, $\cdot$). This function takes as formal parameters the array (A) containing n line segments in the plane, the number of segments (n), and a bounding box (b_box) passed as the third parameter. It returns a convex polygon as the result. Since the function *clip_polygon_with_segment*($\cdot$, $\cdot$) generates a half-plane located to the right of the segment passed as its second parameter, it follows that all half-planes involved in the intersections lie to the right of the segments from which they are defined. Furthermore, each of these half-planes is bounded by the bounding box. The implementation of the function *half_plane_intersection*($\cdot$, $\cdot$, $\cdot$) is given below:

```
1 from typing import Optional, List
2 from geometry import Point2D, Segment2D, Polygon, TypeI2, TypeP2, TypeS2
3 from ch3_helper_functions import convex_polygon_intersection
4 def half_plane_intersection(S: List[Segment2D], n: int, b_box: Polygon) ->
    Optional[Polygon]:
5     if n == 1: return clip_polygon_with_segment(b_box.copy(), S[0])
6     else:
7         m = n // 2
8         p1 = half_plane_intersection(S[:m], m, b_box)
9         p2 = half_plane_intersection(S[m:], n - m, b_box)
10        if p1 is None or p2 is None: return None
11        result = convex_polygon_intersection(p1, p2)
12        return result
```

The time complexity of this recursive algorithm is measured by the recurrence relation

$$T(n) = \begin{cases} 2T\left(\frac{n}{2}\right) + an, & \text{for } n > 1 \\ b, & \text{otherwise} \end{cases},$$

where the term an indicates the amount of time needed by the function *convex_polygon_intersection*($\cdot$,$\cdot$) to compute the intersection of two convex polygons. By solving the recurrence $T(n)$, we obtain that the total runtime of the algorithm is proportional to $\mathcal{O}(n \log n)$. It is not difficult to show that this is indeed the optimal time, since the intersection of half-planes can be reduced to the intersection of segments, for which it was previously proven that this is the best achievable complexity. A graphical interface of the recursive algorithm for computing the intersection of half-planes is illustrated in Fig. 3.22. The graphical interface was developed in the Python programming language using the Tkinter graphical environment.

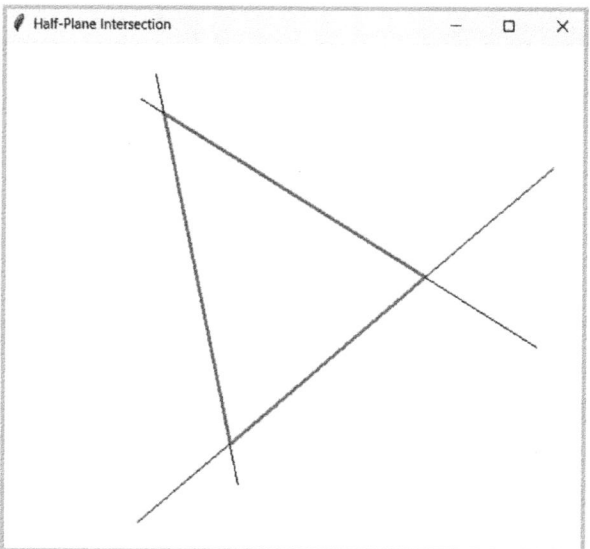

Figure 3.22: Graphical illustration of the intersection of half-planes induced by three segments.

3.7   Union of Rectangles

In this section, several approaches dealing with the problem of unioning a collection of rectangles given in the plane will be presented. For instance, one approach may focus on computing the total area covered by the given rectangles, such that the intersected regions are counted only once. In Fig. 3.23 (a), the rectangle $\square ABCD$ is not included in the total area, as it represents the intersection of a horizontal and a vertical rectangle. Another approach may concern the determination of the outer contour of the rectangles whose sides are aligned with the coordinate axes (see Fig. 3.23 (b)). This approach is most commonly used in *Design of Integrated Circuits* (IC). Figure 3.23 (c) shows the design of such a contour. In what follows, the solution to the first approach will be described first, followed by an efficient solution to the second approach based on the use of a sweep line. The first approach can be implemented both naively and efficiently. A naive computation of the area (formed by the union of n rectangles) can be done in quadratic time. Specifically, suppose we are given n rectangles $\mathscr{R}_1, \mathscr{R}_2, \cdots, \mathscr{R}_n$. Initially, all rectangles that are strict subsets of other rectangles are removed, resulting in a new set of m rectangles ($m \leq n$). Next, the intersection of the first rectangle $\mathscr{R}_1$ with all remaining rectangles $\mathscr{R}_j$ ($j > 1$) is computed, and those intersections are stored in a list $\mathscr{L}$. Then, the process continues by determining the intersection of rectangle $\mathscr{R}_2$ with all rectangles $\mathscr{R}_k$ ($k > 2$), which are also added to the list $\mathscr{L}$. This process continues until the intersection between $\mathscr{R}_{m-1}$ and $\mathscr{R}_m$ is computed.

After that, all intersections from the list $\mathscr{L}$ that are subsets of other intersections are removed. Finally, the total area is computed as the difference between the sum of the areas of the m processed rectangles at the beginning and the sum of the areas of the rectangles stored in the list $\mathscr{L}$. This approach requires quadratic time for preprocessing and postprocessing, and constant time for checking the intersection of two rectangles. Therefore, the total complexity of the naive algorithm is of order $\mathscr{O}(n^2)$. The implementation of the naive approach is realized within the function *union_of_rectangles*($\cdot$), as shown below:

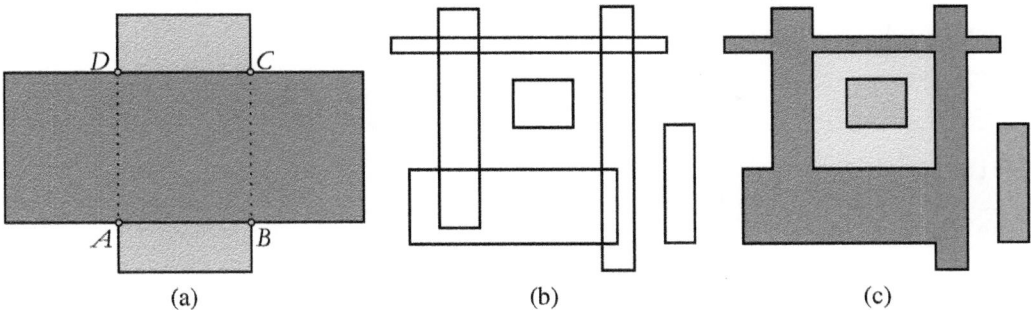

Figure 3.23: (a) Computing the area of a group of rectangles. (b) Determining the common contour. (c) Generating a contour from the union of six rectangles.

```python
from typing import Optional, List
from geometry import Point2D, Segment2D, Polygon
from ch3_helper_functions import do_polygon_rectangle_clip

def union_of_rectangles(polygons: List[Polygon]) -> float:
    proc_polygons = process_polygons(polygons)  # Remove subsets
    intersections: List[Polygon] = []
    L = list(proc_polygons); n = len(L)
    # Compute pairwise intersections
    for i in range(n):
        for j in range(i + 1, n):
            intersection = do_polygon_rectangle_clip(L[i], L[j])
            if intersection: intersections.append(intersection)
    # Process intersections to remove redundant ones
    processed_intersections = process_polygons(intersections)
    # Compute total area of original minus area of intersections
    total_area = sum(p.area() for p in L)
    intersection_area = sum(p.area() for p in processed_intersections)
    return total_area - intersection_area
```

The implementation of the auxiliary function *process_polygons*(·) is provided below. This function is responsible for removing rectangles that are subsets of other rectangles. Within it, the method *is_subset*(·) from the **Polygon** class is invoked, which checks whether one convex polygon $\mathscr{P}$ is a subset of another polygon $\mathscr{Q}$, i.e., whether the condition $\mathscr{P} \subseteq \mathscr{Q}$ holds.

```python
def process_polygons(polygons: List[Polygon]) -> List[Polygon]:
    processed = []
    for i, pi in enumerate(polygons):
        is_subset = False
        for j, pj in enumerate(polygons):
            if i != j and pi.is_subset(pj): is_subset = True; break
        if not is_subset: processed.append(pi)
    return processed
```

The graphical visualization of the union of rectangles is performed by first specifying the number of rectangles to be drawn via a text input field. After that, the rectangles are drawn on the canvas, and by clicking the **Compute Area** button, the area of their union is calculated (see Fig. 3.24). The function *union_of_rectangles*($\cdot$) can be implemented more elegantly by using the class **Rectangle**, whose definition is given in Listing 3.4.

Listing 3.4: Definition of class Rectangle

```python
class Rectangle:
    def __init__(self, sw=None, ne=None, rect_id=0):
        self.sw = sw  # sw: southwest corner for lower-left corner
        self.ne = ne  # ne: northeast corner for upper-right corner
        self._id = rect_id
    def __getitem__(self, i): return self.sw if i == 0 else self.ne
    def __setitem__(self, i, value):
        if i == 0: self.sw = value
        else: self.ne = value
    def get_id(self): return self._id
    def set_id(self, rect_id): self._id = rect_id
    def contains_point(self, t):
        return (self.sw[0]<=t[0]<=self.ne[0]) and (self.sw[1]<=t[1]<=self.ne[1])
    def intersects(self, o):
        u0 = ((self.sw[0]<=o[0][0]<=self.ne[0]) or (o[0][0]<=self.sw[0]<=o[1][0]))
        u1 = ((self.sw[1]<=o[0][1]<=self.ne[1]) or (o[0][1]<=self.sw[1]<=o[1][1]))
        return u0 and u1
    def __repr__(self):
        return f"Rectangle(ID={self._id},SW={self.sw},NE={self.ne})"
```

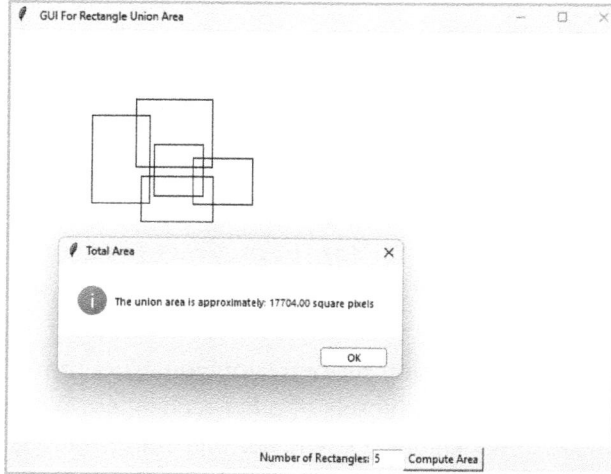

Figure 3.24: Graphical illustration of determining the area of the union of five given rectangles.

An efficient method for determining the area of a region obtained by the union of a set of rectangles can be performed using a sweep line. In what follows, we describe an efficient sweep line-based algorithm for finding the common contour of a set of rectangles whose sides are parallel to the coordinate axes. Let a set of n rectangles be given. Then there are $2n$ horizontal segments as well as $2n$ vertical segments. The idea of the algorithm is to move a sweep line from left to right across the n rectangles while performing the following:

a) At each position of the sweep line, all horizontal sides of the rectangles are detected (revealed) if they lie to the left of the line. Moreover, if for these sides (segments parallel to the x-axis) both endpoints do not lie to the left of the sweep line, then they do not yet have the status of revealed sides. They acquire the revealed status as soon as the sweep line hits their right endpoint.

b) During the sweep line movement, it first processes vertical segments, then horizontal, then vertical again, and so on. Vertical segments or rectangle sides (left and right) are classified as *Event Points*.

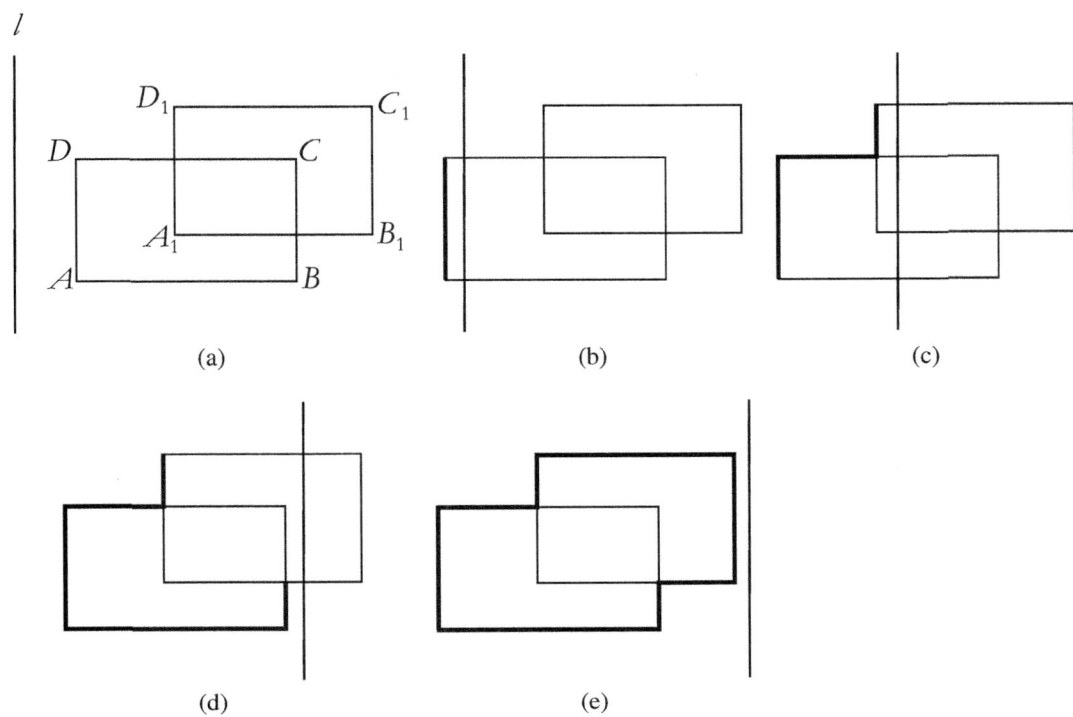

Figure 3.25: Detection of the contour during the sweep line movement, illustrated in steps (a) through (e).

In Figure 3.25, steps from (a) to (e) illustrate the process of detecting the common contour of rectangles $\square ABCD$ and $\square A_1B_1C_1D_1$. From the figure, it can be observed that moving the sweep line to the right gradually reveals the sides of the common contour, which are marked in bold. A detailed description of the contour detection will be provided later. Since the sweep line processes the sides of rectangles by translating to the right, we first present the definition of the class **AxisAlignedEdge** in Listing 3.5. As the name of the class suggests, it will be used together with its methods to process the $2n$ horizontal and vertical segments (which form the group of rectangles) for the purpose of determining the common contour.

Listing 3.5: Definition of class **AxisAlignedEdge**

```python
from geometry import Segment2D, Point2D, Rectangle

class AxisAlignedEdge:
    def __init__(self, rectangle: Rectangle, edge_type: int):
        self.rect = rectangle # the rectangle which contain the edge
        self.edge_type = edge_type  # 0-left, 1-right, 2-bottom, 3-top
        self.count = 0 # to count active edges
        self.m = -1.0e5 # uses for update position of sweep line

    def set_count(self, val): self.count = val
    def get_count(self): return self.count
    def get_type(self): return self.edge_type
    def update_position(self, m): self.m = m
```

```
14      def get_rectangle(self): return self.rect
15
16      def position(self):
17          if self.edge_type == 0: return self.rect[0][0]
18          elif self.edge_type == 1: return self.rect[1][0]
19          elif self.edge_type == 2: return self.rect[0][1]
20          else: return self.rect[1][1]
21
22      def __eq__(self, b):
23          if not isinstance(b, AxisAlignedEdge):return NotImplemented
24          return (self.position(),self.edge_type,self.rect.get_id())==(b.position(),
                    b.edge_type,b.rect.get_id())
25
26      def __lt__(self, b):
27          if not isinstance(b, AxisAlignedEdge):return NotImplemented
28          if self.position() != b.position(): return self.position() < b.position()
29          if self.edge_type!= b.edge_type: return self.edge_type < b.edge_type
30          return self.rect.get_id() < b.rect.get_id()
31
32      def __hash__(self):
33          return hash((self.position(), self.edge_type, self.rect.get_id()))
34
35      def min_val(self):
36          if self.m > -1.0e5: return self.m
37          if self.edge_type in [0, 1]: return self.rect[0][1]
38          return self.rect[0][0]
39
40      def max_val(self):
41          if self.edge_type in [0, 1]: return self.rect[1][1]
42          return self.rect[1][0]
43
44      def __repr__(self):
45          return f"AxisAlignedEdge(type={self.get_type()}, position={self.position()
                    }, rect_id={self.rect.get_id()})"
```

The *position*() method returns the coordinate of the line containing the given segment, which represents a side of a rectangle. If the segment is vertical—meaning it lies along a line perpendicular to the x-axis—the method returns its x-coordinate. Conversely, if the segment is horizontal—aligned with a line perpendicular to the y-axis—the method returns its y-coordinate. The *min_val*() method computes the smaller of the two endpoint coordinates based on the segment's orientation. For vertical segments (i.e., left or right sides of a rectangle), it returns the smaller y-coordinate. For instance, for the segment defined by the points (1,2) and (1,4), the method yields 2. In the case of horizontal segments (i.e., top or bottom sides), it returns the smaller x-coordinate—for example, 1 for the segment from (1,2) to (5,2). The *max_val*() method behaves similarly but returns the larger of the two coordinates. The functions *process_left_edge*($\cdot,\cdot,\cdot$) and *process_right_edge*($\cdot,\cdot,\cdot$), which are invoked within the main function *find_contour*($\cdot$), will be implemented below. The task of the main function *find_contour*($\cdot$) is to determine the contour using the sweep line algorithm based on the list of rectangles (passed as a formal parameter), ensuring that the overall time complexity is, in the best case, $\Theta(n \log n)$. At the beginning, this function performs preprocessing of the vertical segments (there are $2n$ of them as sides of n rectangles) by sorting them in increasing order with respect to the x-coordinate of the line containing them, which is perpendicular to the x-axis. After that, a dictionary named *sweepline* is created and initialized with a large rectangle R (intended to encompass all n rectangles). The mentioned dictionary will store the active horizontal segments that the sweep line intersects during its transition from left to right. Depending on the type of the vertical segment (left or right), the function invokes either the *process_left_edge*($\cdot,\cdot,\cdot$) or the *process_right_edge*($\cdot,\cdot,\cdot$) method to determine the segments participating in the formation of the desired contour. Finally, the computed contour is stored in a list of segments that were previously found during the transitions of the sweep line, more precisely through calls to the methods *process_left_edge*(·,·,·) and *process_right_edge*(·,·,·). Based on the above, the implementation of the *find_contour*(·) function is given as follows:

```
from typing import Optional, List,Tuple
from geometry import Point2D, Rectangle, AxisAlignedEdge
from sortedcontainers import SortedDict

def find_contour(rectangles: List[Rectangle]):
    edges = sort_vertical_edges(rectangles)
    segments = []
    sweep = SortedDict() # dictionary for storing active segments
    large_rect = Rectangle(Point2D(-1.0e5, -1.0e5), Point2D(1.0e5, 1.0e5), -1)
    base_edge = AxisAlignedEdge(large_rect, 2)
    sweep[base_edge] = base_edge
    for edge in edges:
        if edge.get_type()==0: process_left_edge(edge,sweep, segments)
        elif edge.get_type()==1: process_right_edge(edge,sweep, segments)
    return segments
```

The function *sort_vertical_edges*(·) is used for preprocessing in order to form the event points, i.e., vertical segments, which are known in advance. Based on the given rectangles, it creates a list of $2n$ elements by alternately storing the left and then the right sides of the rectangles. After that, the elements of the list (vertical sides) are sorted according to the criterion function *compare_edges*(·,·), which will be described and implemented in more detail later. Upon completion of the sorting, the function returns the list of sorted segments. Its implementation is given below:

```
from functools import cmp_to_key
def sort_vertical_edges(rects: List[Rectangle])->List[AxisAlignedEdge]:
    edges = []
    for rect in rects:
        edges.append(AxisAlignedEdge(rect, 0)) # 0 - left vertical edge
        edges.append(AxisAlignedEdge(rect, 1)) # 1 - right vertical edge
        edges.sort(key=cmp_to_key(compare_edges)) # the using of custom comparator
    return edges
```

Within the body of the function *sort_vertical_edges*(·), the generic function *sort*(·,·) is invoked to sort the segments. It is known that this function uses the Timsort algorithm, which was first proposed for Python version 2.3 in 2002. This algorithm has a time complexity of $\mathcal{O}(n\log n)$ in both the average and worst cases. Therefore, the complexity of the *sort_vertical_edges*(·) function is of the same order, given that the *compare_edges*(·,·) function operates in constant time. This function compares instances of the **AxisAlignedEdge** class based on the x-coordinates of vertical segments. If those coordinates are equal, the comparison continues based on the edge type, where a left edge is considered smaller than a right edge. Consequently, if a left vertical edge s of the rectangle $\square ABCD$ has the same x-coordinate as the right vertical edge s_1 of the rectangle $\square A_1B_1C_1D_1$, the edge s will be processed before the edge s_1. If the edge types are the same, the identifiers of the rectangles to which the segments belong are compared. Since the *compare_edges*(·,·) function can also be used for horizontal segments, these are compared in the same manner, except that y-coordinates are considered instead of x-coordinates, and bottom and top edges are considered instead of left and right ones. In this case, a bottom edge is considered smaller than a top edge. The implementation of the aforementioned function is as follows:

```
1 def compare_edges(a: AxisAlignedEdge, b: AxisAlignedEdge):
2     if a.position()!=b.position(): return -1 if a.position()<b.position() else 1
3     if a.get_type()!=b.get_type(): return -1 if a.get_type()<b.get_type() else 1
4     if a.get_rectangle().get_id()!=b.get_rectangle().get_id():
5         return -1 if a.get_rectangle().get_id()<b.get_rectangle().get_id() else 1
6     return 0
```

It should be noted that the *compare_edges*($\cdot,\cdot$) function is also used as the comparator function for the **SortedDict** structure in the sweepline algorithm. At this point, it is important to explain what happens when the sweep line encounters or starts to contain a vertical segment, as different cases are treated depending on whether the sweep line hits a left or a right vertical segment. When the sweep line reaches a left vertical segment, it is said that it enters a rectangle, while when it reaches a right vertical segment, it is said to leave a rectangle. In both cases, it is necessary to keep track of the number of active horizontal segments. This number can be defined as the number of rectangles intersected by the sweep line when considering the current segment and the next one located directly above it. For instance, in Fig. 3.26 (a), the segment $\overline{A_1B_1}$ is counted exactly once, because on the stretch from this segment (point P_1) to its next segment $\overline{C_1D_1}$ directly above it (point Q_1), there is exactly one rectangle $\square A_1B_1C_1D_1$. Therefore, the active horizontal segment $\overline{A_1B_1}$ is counted once. On the other hand, the segment $\overline{C_1D_1}$ is not counted at all, since there are no rectangles between point Q_1 and point P_2. Similarly, the horizontal segments (rectangle sides) $\overline{A_2B_2}, \overline{A_3B_3}, \overline{C_2D_2}$, and $\overline{C_3D_3}$ appear 1, 2, 1, and 0 times, respectively (see Fig. 3.26 (a)). Clearly, the segments $\overline{A_4B_4}$ and $\overline{C_4D_4}$ are not considered at all, as they are not active horizontal segments yet — the sweep line does not intersect them. The number of occurrences of horizontal segments changes as the sweep line moves to the right, as seen in Fig. 3.26 (b). Specifically, the count for all segments increases by one, except for segment $\overline{C_4D_4}$, whose count remains zero. In this scenario, a contour is formed that includes part of the vertical segment $\overline{A_4D_4}$ and parts of horizontal segments $\overline{A_1B_1}, \overline{C_1D_1}, \overline{A_2B_2}$, and $\overline{C_3D_3}$. Next, we describe what happens when the sweep line "hits" an event point corresponding to a left vertical segment, such as segment $\overline{A_4D_4}$ in Fig. 3.26 (a). Indeed, let the sweep line l hit the vertical segment $\overline{A_4D_4}$. Then, the horizontal segments $\overline{A_4B_4}$ and $\overline{C_4D_4}$ are inserted into the "sweepline" dictionary. Afterwards, using dictionary operations (methods), active horizontal segments are traversed starting from segment $\overline{A_4B_4}$ up to segment $\overline{C_4D_4}$. During this traversal, three types of contour segments are identified. These are the segments that participate in forming the final contour. The first type includes horizontal contour segments along the bottom edges of rectangles whose counter is equal to one (these are the segments $\overline{A_1B_1}$ and $\overline{A_2B_2}$ in Fig. 3.26 (a)). The second type consists of horizontal segments along the top edges of rectangles whose counter is equal to zero (In Fig. 3.26 (a), these are the segments $\overline{C_1D_1}$ and $\overline{C_3D_3}$). The final type includes vertical segments whose endpoints are incident to:

a) *bottom sides* of rectangles, whose counter is equal to one (the bold vertical segment between segments $\overline{A_4B_4}$ and $\overline{A_1B_1}$);

b) *top sides* of rectangles, whose counter is equal to zero (the bold vertical segment between segments $\overline{C_3D_3}$ and $\overline{C_4D_4}$);

c) *both bottom and top sides* simultaneously, such that the bottom sides have counter equal to one, and the top sides have counter equal to zero (the bold vertical segment between segments $\overline{C_1D_1}$ and $\overline{A_2B_2}$).

It is also important to emphasize that updates to the counters associated with active horizontal segments (instances of the class **AxisAlignedEdge**) must be performed. For example, in Fig. 3.26 (a), the counters of all active horizontal segments lying between the segments $\overline{A_4B_4}$ and $\overline{C_4D_4}$ are incremented. Then, the counters of these segments are initialized based on the counters of the active horizontal segments located immediately below them. Based on the above description of what happens when the sweep line "reaches" the left vertical edge (an instance of the class **AxisAlignedEdge** for which edge_type=0) of a rectangle,

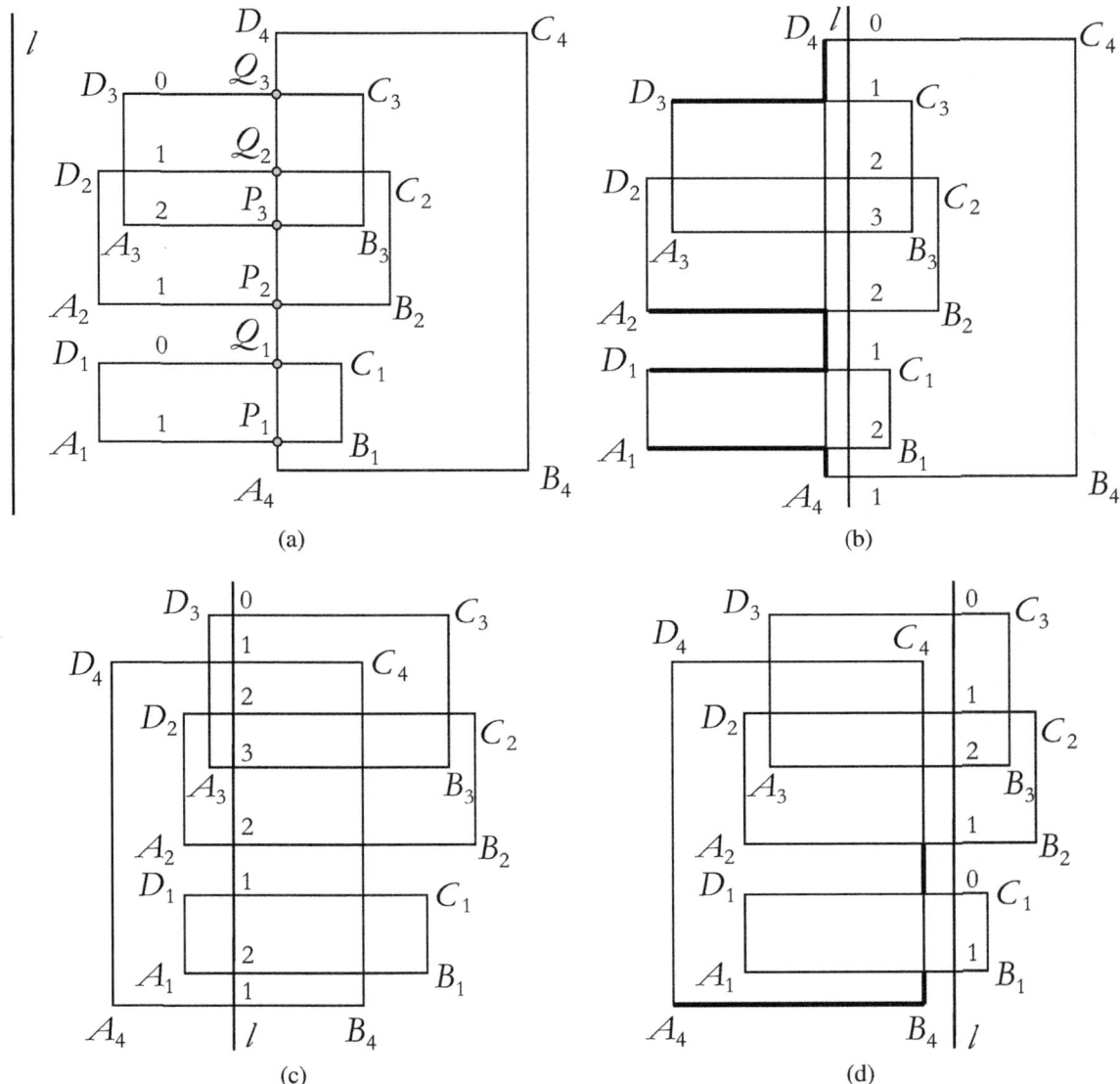

Figure 3.26: Processing events by assigning counters indicating their occurrences, illustrated in steps (a) through (d).

the implementation of the method *process_left_edge*($\cdot$,$\cdot$,$\cdot$) is given below:

```
1 def process_left_edge(edge:AxisAlignedEdge,sweep:SortedDict,segments:List[
      Segment2D])->None:
2     top = AxisAlignedEdge(edge.rect, 3) # 3 is top horizontal edge
3     bottom = AxisAlignedEdge(edge.rect, 2) # 2 is bottom  horizontal edge
4     sweep[bottom] = bottom; sweep[top] = top
5     keys = list(sweep.keys()); i=keys.index(bottom) # i is idx of bottom
6     previous = keys[i-1]; bottom.count=previous.count + 1
7     pos_sl = edge.position()#position of sweep line
8     p = keys[i]; i+=1; l = keys[i] # l is lower edge
9     while l!=top:
10        if l.get_type() == 2:
11            if l.count == 1:
12                segments.append(Segment2D(Point2D(pos_sl,l.position()),Point2D(
```

```
                 pos_sl,l.position()))))
13             segments.append(Segment2D(Point2D(l.min_val(),l.position()),
                 Point2D(pos_sl,l.position()))))
14         l.count += 1
15     elif l.get_type() == 3:
16         if l.count == 0:
17             segments.append(Segment2D(Point2D(l.min_val(),l.position()),
                 Point2D(pos_sl,l.position()))))
18         l.count += 1
19     i+=1; p = l; l=keys[i]
20
21     l.count = p.count - 1
22     if l.count == 0:
23         segments.append(Segment2D(Point2D(pos_sl,p.position()),Point2D(pos_sl,l.
             position()))))
```

What remains is to implement the function *process_right_edge*($\cdot,\cdot,\cdot$), which handles the case when the sweep line exits a rectangle. Consider the layout of rectangles as shown in Fig. 3.26 (c), where the sweep line l has not yet exited the rectangle $\square A_4B_4C_4D_4$. As before, due to the arrangement of rectangles, the bottom and top edges are assigned counters. To implement the aforementioned function, it is necessary to describe what happens when the sweep line reaches the right vertical edge of the rectangle $\square A_4B_4C_4D_4$, i.e., when it exits the rectangle. In Fig. 3.26 (d), the sweep line l exits the rectangle $\square A_4B_4C_4D_4$. At that point, its horizontal edges are considered first. In Fig. 3.26 (c), these are the segments $\overline{A_4B_4}$ and $\overline{C_4D_4}$. Then, all active horizontal segments between $\overline{A_4B_4}$ and $\overline{C_4D_4}$ are traversed, during which two types of contour segments are detected. The first type refers to the horizontal segments of the rectangle $\square A_4B_4C_4D_4$, i.e., its bottom and top edges. For instance, the bottom edge of the rectangle is a contour segment if its counter equals one (In Fig. 3.26 (c), this is the segment $\overline{A_4B_4}$). The top edge of the rectangle is also considered a contour segment if its counter equals zero (In Fig. 3.26 (c), the segment $\overline{C_4D_4}$ is not a contour segment).The second type of contour segments are vertical segments connecting any top horizontal edge whose count is one to a bottom horizontal edge whose count is two. In Fig. 3.26 (c), such vertical segments are located between the horizontal segments $\overline{A_4B_4}$ and $\overline{A_1B_1}$, and between $\overline{C_1D_1}$ and $\overline{A_2B_2}$. After the sweep line l exits the rectangle $\square A_4B_4C_4D_4$, the counters on the visited edges are decremented by one, as shown in Fig. 3.26 (d). Following the decrementing, it is necessary to update the sweep line position for the top horizontal edges where the counter is reduced to zero, as well as for the bottom horizontal edges where the counter is set to one. Finally, after the rectangle $\square A_4B_4C_4D_4$ has been processed, its horizontal edges must be removed from the sweep line structure. After this description, the implementation of the function *process_right_edge*($\cdot,\cdot,\cdot$) is given below:

```
1 def process_right_edge(edge:AxisAlignedEdge,sweep:SortedDict,segments:List[
      Segment2D])->None:
2     top_key = AxisAlignedEdge(edge.rect, 3)
3     bottom_key = AxisAlignedEdge(edge.rect, 2)
4     top = sweep[top_key]; bottom = sweep[bottom_key]
5     pos_sl = edge.position()
6     if bottom.count == 1:
7         segments.append(Segment2D(Point2D(bottom.min_val(), bottom.position()),
              Point2D(pos_sl, bottom.position())))
8     if top.count == 0:
9         segments.append(Segment2D(Point2D(top.min_val(), top.position()), Point2D(
              pos_sl, top.position())))
10    keys = list(sweep.keys()); i=keys.index(bottom_key) # i is idx of bottom
11    p=keys[i]; i+=1; l=keys[i] #p is previous edge, and l is lower edge in sweep
12
```

```
13    while l!=top_key:
14        if l.get_type() == 2:
15            l.count -= 1
16            if l.count == 1:
17                segments.append(Segment2D(Point2D(pos_sl,p.position()),Point2D(
                      pos_sl,l.position())))
18                l.m = pos_sl
19        elif l.get_type() == 3:
20            l.count -= 1
21            if l.count == 0: l.m = pos_sl
22        i += 1; p = l; l = keys[i]
23
24    if l.count == 0:
25        segments.append(Segment2D(Point2D(pos_sl,p.position()),Point2D(pos_sl,l.
              position())))
26
27    del sweep[top_key]; del sweep[bottom_key]
```

Finally, it remains to analyze the time complexity of the sweep line-based algorithm. Let n denote the number of input rectangles, and let R be a large bounding rectangle that encompasses all of them. The transitions are handled using a sweep line structure, which typically requires $\Theta(\log n)$ time per operation, in addition to time proportional to the number of active horizontal segments between the lower and upper edge of rectangle R. In the worst case, there can be up to $\mathcal{O}(n)$ such segments active at once, which directly affects the overall runtime. Therefore, a single transition in the worst case may take up to $\mathcal{O}(n)$ time. Since there are $2n$ vertical edges to process (each corresponding to a transition), the total worst-case time complexity of the algorithm is $\mathcal{O}(n^2)$. However, in practice, the number of active horizontal segments is generally much smaller—typically on the order of $\mathcal{O}(\log n)$. Consequently, the average-case time complexity of the algorithm becomes $\mathcal{O}(n \log n)$. Based on experimental analysis conducted by the author, the presented algorithm consistently produces contour results significantly faster than the naive approach, which always operates in $\mathcal{O}(n^2)$ time. One example of a graphical interface for determining the common contour of five randomly given rectangles is shown in Fig. 3.27.

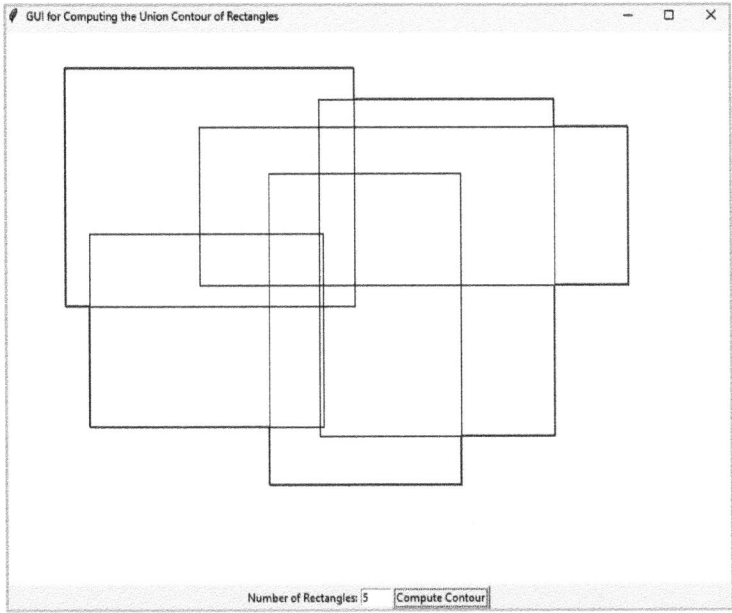

Figure 3.27: Graphical illustration of contour determination for five randomly given rectangles.

3.8 Exercises

Exercise 3.1 Given two convex polygons $\mathscr{A}$ and $\mathscr{B}$ with m and n vertices respectively, implement an algorithm with time complexity $\mathcal{O}(m+n)$ for merging (union of) the given polygons using the "rotating calipers" method.

Exercise 3.2 Given n points in the plane, implement an algorithm with time complexity $\mathcal{O}(n)$ that finds the smallest enclosing circle C.

Exercise 3.3 Given n points in the plane and a fixed diameter r, implement an algorithm with time complexity $\mathcal{O}(n^2 \log n)$ that finds at least one circle C of diameter r that contains the maximum number of points.

Exercise 3.4 Given n circles in the plane, implement an algorithm with time complexity $\mathcal{O}((n + k) \log n)$ to determine their intersections using the sweep line algorithm, where k denotes the number of intersection points.

Exercise 3.5 Given n triangles in the plane, implement an algorithm with time complexity $\mathcal{O}(n \log n)$ for computing their intersection using the sweep line algorithm.

Exercise 3.6 Given n disjoint triangles in the plane, implement an algorithm with time complexity $\mathcal{O}(n \log n)$ that finds $n - 1$ segments in the plane connecting the triangles such that any triangle can be reached from any other triangle. The segments must not intersect triangles, may not intersect each other, nor lie inside triangles. Segments may only touch or be tangent to triangle edges.

Exercise 3.7 Given n axis-aligned rectangles in the plane, implement an efficient algorithm for computing their intersection. The algorithm's running time should be subquadratic.

Exercise 3.8 Given n points in the plane contained within a rectangle R, implement an efficient algorithm to find the largest-area rectangle $\square ABCD$ that does not contain any point and lies entirely within R.

Exercise 3.9 Given n parabolas in the plane, implement an efficient algorithm for computing their intersection such that the overall time complexity is subquadratic.

Exercise 3.10 Given a set of n horizontal and vertical segments in the plane, find all their intersections in time $\mathcal{O}(n \log n + r)$, where r is the total number of intersections.

Exercise 3.11 Given n disjoint triangles in the plane, where some triangles may be fully contained within others, implement an algorithm with time complexity $\mathcal{O}(n \log n)$ that identifies only the points (among n given) that lie outside all triangles.

Exercise 3.12 Given n disjoint segments in the plane and a point P that does not lie on any of them, implement an algorithm with complexity $\mathcal{O}(n \log n)$ that detects only the segments visible from point P.

4. Convex Hull Algorithms

In this chapter, we present and implement geometric algorithms for computing the convex hull in two and three dimensions [21, 50]. These algorithms illustrate the key techniques used for convex hull construction. The problem of finding the convex hull is one of the fundamental problems in computational geometry, with applications in the plane, space, and higher dimensions. In the two-dimensional space, convex hull computation has wide applications in robotics, shape recognition, image processing, statistics, and geographic information systems. The following sections describe specific examples of problems that are successfully solved using the convex hull. The first example in the plane concerns finding the shortest polygonal line that encloses a given set of objects using the convex hull. The second example deals with determining the shortest path between points A and B in the plane, when a direct path between them is not available. In this case, the optimal path follows the boundary of the convex hull of the given polygon. If the polygon is not convex, it can be decomposed into a set of convex polygons, enabling the same strategy to be applied. The third example relates to fast collision detection of objects in the plane using the convex hull. Here, each object is enclosed by its convex hull, and it is checked whether the hulls intersect. If they do not intersect, then the objects themselves are not in contact. However, if the convex hulls intersect, an additional check must be performed to determine the actual collision between objects. Besides these applications, convex hulls are frequently used to model the habitat zones of animals and plants, track the spread of epidemics, analyze radiation, and solve other similar problems in various scientific fields.

Determining the convex hull in three-dimensional space has wide applications, particularly in collision detection of objects in video games and animations. In order to determine whether a collision occurs, it is necessary to test for contact between objects in space. The accuracy of this test is significantly improved when the objects are approximated by their three-dimensional convex hulls rather than using spheres for rough representation. Although spheres provide a simple method for collision testing, their use often results in inaccurate outcomes, where the test may indicate a collision even when there is none in reality. For example, suppose two objects (such as persons) are approximated by spheres, and each object is strictly located vertically within its respective sphere. In that case, the objects are considered to collide if their mutual distance equals the sum of the radii of the spheres, $r_1 + r_2$, where r_1 and r_2 are the radii of the first and second sphere, respectively. However, such a test frequently yields incorrect results, as it does not take into account the actual shape and spatial arrangement of the objects. Besides applications in computer graphics, the three-dimensional convex hull finds extensive use in other fields as well, including computer vision, statistics, combinatorial optimization, economics, geometric modeling, ethology, quantum physics, and many other disciplines. The remainder of this chapter will present algorithms for computing the

A. Alihodžić, *Exploring Computational Geometry*, Texts in Computer Science,
https://doi.org/10.1007/978-3-032-06393-9_4

convex hull in both two-dimensional and three-dimensional spaces.

4.1   Algorithms in the Two-Dimensional Case

This section is dedicated to the fundamental concepts related to determining a simple polygon and the convex hull for a given set of points in the plane. It begins with a description of the method for constructing a simple polygon, followed by the presentation of several algorithms for computing the convex hull in the plane.

4.1.1   Simple Polygon

Before proposing an algorithm for determining a simple polygon, that is, a simple closed path, it is necessary to precisely define the concept of a simple polygon formed from a set of points in the plane [158].

> **Definition 4.1.1** Let $\mathscr{P} = \{P_1, P_2, \cdots, P_n\}$ be a given set of points in the plane. The elements of the set $\mathscr{P}$ form a *simple polygon* if the path composed of them does not intersect itself.

Based on Definition 4.1.1, a direct method for finding a simple polygon is not immediately apparent, and therefore it will be described in more detail below. Let $\mathscr{P} = \{P_1, P_2, \cdots, P_n\}$ be a set of n points given in the plane, for which it is necessary to construct a simple polygon. These points are typically stored in a sequential or dynamic data structure, such as arrays, vectors, or lists. Without loss of generality, it can be assumed that the elements of the set $\mathscr{P}$ are stored in an array A. Initially, the array is renumbered by finding the point with the smallest y-coordinate, and in the case of multiple such points, the one with the largest x-coordinate is selected. Let this point be denoted as P_j ($j \in \{1, 2, \cdots, n\}$). It is called the *anchor point*, and it swaps positions with the point P_1 in the array A, forming a new renumbered array A'. After renumbering, the angles α_i between the anchor point and the remaining points in the array A' are computed, i.e., $\alpha_i = \angle(P_1, P_i)$, for $i = 2, 3, \cdots, n$. The elements of the array A' are then sorted in ascending order according to the computed angles, and in the case of equal angles, they are additionally sorted by their distance from the anchor point. Upon completion of the sorting, a new array A'' is obtained, whose elements form the vertices of a simple polygon. Any known sorting algorithm with a guaranteed time complexity of $\Theta(n \log n)$ can be applied for this operation, such as *Merge Sort* or *Heap Sort*. Alternatively, hybrid algorithms like *Tim Sort* may be used; although it has a worst-case time complexity of $\mathcal{O}(n \log n)$, it performs in $\Theta(n)$ time on nearly sorted data. Since the renumbering of the array requires at most $\mathcal{O}(n)$ operations in the worst case, the total time complexity of the algorithm is $\Theta(n \log n)$. The implementation of this algorithm is realized within the function *simple_polygon*($\cdot$), as shown in Listing 4.1.

Listing 4.1: Implementation of the algorithm for finding a simple polygon.

```
def simple_polygon(points: list[Point2D]) -> Polygon:
    anchor, idx = anchor_point(points)
    points[0],points[idx]=anchor,points[0] # swap elements
    sorted_points=[points[0]]+sorted(points[1:],key=lambda p:((p-anchor).
        polar_angle_m(),(p-anchor).norm()))
    p = Polygon()
    for pt in sorted_points: p.insert(pt)
    return p
```

The function *simple_polygon*($\cdot$) uses the auxiliary function *anchor_point*($\cdot$) to determine the anchor point. Its implementation is given below:

```
1 def anchor_point(A: list[Point2D]) -> tuple[Point2D, int]:
2     j = 0
3     for i in range(1,len(A)):
4         if (A[i][1]<A[j][1]) or (A[i][1]==A[j][1] and A[i][0]>A[j][0]):j=i
5     return A[j], j
```

Since the same GUI will be used for all algorithms in this chapter, Listing 4.2 provides the code for the graphical visualization of constructing a simple polygon based on a randomly generated set of points on the canvas (see Fig. 4.1).

Listing 4.2: Minimalist Graphical Interface for Algorithm Visualization

```
1 import tkinter as tk
2 import random
3 from geometry import Point2D, Segment2D, Polygon
4 from ch4_helper_functions import simple_polygon
5
6 class GeometricVisualizer:
7     def __init__(self, master):
8         self.master = master
9         self.master.title("Simple Polygon Determination GUI")
10        self.main_frame = tk.Frame(master)
11        self.main_frame.pack(fill=tk.BOTH,expand=True)
12        self.canvas = tk.Canvas(self.main_frame,width=800,height=600,bg="white")
13        self.canvas.pack(side=tk.LEFT,padx=10,pady=10)
14        self.control_frame = tk.Frame(self.main_frame)
15        self.control_frame.pack(side=tk.RIGHT,padx=10,pady=10,fill=tk.Y)
16        self.label = tk.Label(self.control_frame,text="Number of points:")
17        self.label.pack(pady=5)
18        self.entry_var = tk.StringVar(value="10")
19        self.entry = tk.Entry(self.control_frame, textvariable=self.entry_var)
20        self.entry.pack(pady=5)
21        self.generate_button = tk.Button(self.control_frame,text="Generate Points"
               ,command=self.generate_points)
22        self.generate_button.pack(pady=5)
23        self.sim_pol_button = tk.Button(self.control_frame,text="Simple Polygon",
               command=self.visualise_simple_polygon)
24        self.sim_pol_button.pack(pady=5)
25        self.points = []
26
27     def generate_points(self):
28         try:
29             num_points = int(self.entry.get())
30             for _ in range(num_points):
31                 x, y = random.randint(10, 700), random.randint(10, 500)
32                 self.points.append(Point2D(x, y))
33                 self.canvas.create_oval(x - 2, y - 2, x + 2, y + 2, fill='black')
34         except ValueError: print("Please enter a valid number.")
35
36     def visualise_simple_polygon(self):
37         polygon = simple_polygon(self.points)
38         if not polygon or polygon.size() < 2:return
39         for _ in range(polygon.size()):
40             seg = polygon.current_edge()
41             x1,y1=seg[0][0],seg[0][1]; x2,y2=seg[1][0],seg[1][1]
42             self.canvas.create_line(x1, y1, x2, y2, fill='blue', width=2)
```

```
43              polygon.move_current(1)
44
45 if __name__ == '__main__':
46 root = tk.Tk()
47 app = GeometricVisualizer(root)
48 root.mainloop()
```

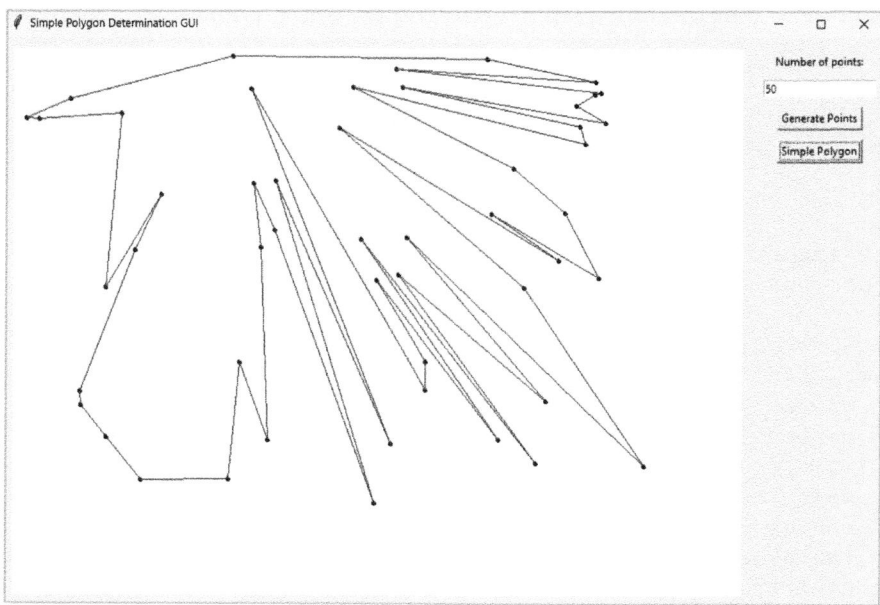

Figure 4.1: Result of constructing a simple polygon for 50 randomly selected points.

■ **Example 4.1** Let an arbitrary set of points in the plane be given. Prove or disprove the existence of a unique simple polygon.

Solution. There does not exist a unique simple polygon for an arbitrarily given set of points, as illustrated in Fig. 4.2. Specifically, for the set of points $\mathscr{P} = \{P_1, P_2, P_3, P_4\}$, it can be observed that there exist two distinct simple polygons.

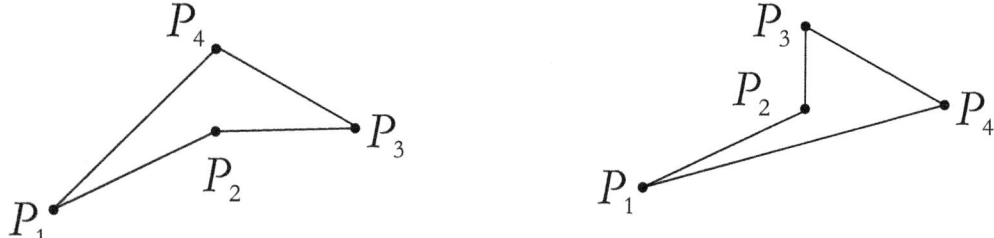

Figure 4.2: Non-uniqueness of the simple polygon.

■

4.1.2 Convex Hull

In this section, after introducing the preliminary concepts, we will present and implement in detail the geometric algorithms necessary for computing the convex hull of a planar set of points.

Definition 4.1.2 The segment denoted by $\overline{PQ}$ represents the set of points $\alpha P + \beta Q$, where $\alpha, \beta \in \mathbb{R}^+$ and $\alpha + \beta = 1$.

Definition 4.1.3 A convex combination of the points $P_1, P_2, \cdots, P_k$ is defined as the sum $\sum_{i=1}^{k} \alpha_i P_i$, such that $\sum_{i=1}^{k} \alpha_i = 1$ and $\alpha_i \in \mathbb{R}^+$ for every i.

Observation 4.1.1 The line segment $\overline{PQ}$ is a convex combination of its endpoints P and Q, while the triangle $\triangle ABC$ is a convex combination of its vertices A, B, and C.

Definition 4.1.4 A set of points $\mathscr{P}$ given in the plane is called a *convex set* if, for any two points $Q_1, Q_2 \in \mathscr{P}$, the segment $\overline{Q_1 Q_2}$ is also contained in $\mathscr{P}$.

Definition 4.1.5 A polygon $\mathscr{P}$ composed of points P_i ($i = \overline{1,n}$) is called a *convex polygon* if, for any two points Q_1 and Q_2 within the region bounded by polygon $\mathscr{P}$, the segment $\overline{Q_1 Q_2}$ lies entirely within that region.

Definition 4.1.6 The smallest convex polygon, denoted by $H(\mathscr{P})$, that contains or encloses all the points of the set $\mathscr{P} = \{P_1, P_2, \cdots, P_n\}$ is called the *convex hull*.

Observation 4.1.2 The convex hull $H(\mathscr{P})$ of the point set $\mathscr{P}$ can be expressed as the union of triangles defined over the points in the set $\mathscr{P}$.

Definition 4.1.7 Any point $P_i \in \mathscr{P}$ ($i = \overline{1,n}$) is called an *extreme point* if its interior angle is smaller than a straight angle.

Definition 4.1.8 An edge e is called an *extreme edge* if all the points of the set $\mathscr{P}$ lie on the line or on one side of the line that contains this edge.

Observation 4.1.3 A point is considered extreme if there exists a line passing through that point such that all other points lie strictly on one side of that line. Moreover, if points lie on an edge (segment, side) of the convex hull, they are also considered extreme points.

The following section presents algorithms for finding the convex hull. Before that, it is necessary to make a brief digression about extreme points. Let a set of points in the plane be given, arranged in an arbitrary order. It is easy to observe that the points with the smallest and largest x-coordinates, as well as the points with the smallest and largest y-coordinates, are four fundamental extreme points. In addition to these, points with the highest y-coordinate that have different x-coordinates also represent extreme points. Similarly, the leftmost, rightmost, and lowest points are considered extreme points. If lines parallel to the x-axis or y-axis are drawn through each of them, it can be seen that they do not intersect the convex hull.

Lemma 4.1.1 Let a set of points $\mathscr{P} = \{P_1, P_2, \ldots, P_n\}$ be given in the plane. The convex hull of the set $\mathscr{P}$ is the set of all convex combinations of the points in $\mathscr{P}$.

Proof. Let the set $\mathscr{M} = \{\lambda_1 P_1 + \lambda_2 P_2 + \cdots + \lambda_n P_n : \sum_{i=1}^{n} \lambda_i = 1, \ \lambda_i \geq 0 \ (\forall i)\}$ represent the set of all convex combinations of the points in $\mathscr{P}$. It is required to prove that $H(\mathscr{P}) = \mathscr{M}$. To establish this, it is sufficient to show both $H(\mathscr{P}) \subseteq \mathscr{M}$ and $\mathscr{M} \subseteq H(\mathscr{P})$.

$\Rightarrow$) First, we prove that $H(\mathscr{P}) \subseteq \mathscr{M}$. From the definition of the set $\mathscr{M}$, it is easy to verify that it contains the set $\mathscr{P}$. Therefore, it remains to show that $\mathscr{M}$ is a convex set, since $H(\mathscr{P})$ is by definition the smallest such set. Thus, it is necessary to prove that the segment $\overline{AB} \in \mathscr{M}$ for any two elements A and B from $\mathscr{M}$.

The segment $\overline{AB}$ belongs to the set $\mathcal{M}$ if every point C on the segment $\overline{AB}$ lies in $\mathcal{M}$. Hence, let C be an arbitrary but fixed point on the segment $\overline{AB}$. This means that there exist α and β such that $C = \alpha A + \beta B$, with $\alpha + \beta = 1$ and $\alpha \geq 0$, $\beta \geq 0$. Since the points A and B belong to $\mathcal{M}$, it follows that there exist $\lambda_i, \lambda_i' \in [0,1]$ such that $A = \sum_{i=1}^n \lambda_i P_i$ and $B = \sum_{i=1}^n \lambda_i' P_i$, with $\sum_{i=1}^n \lambda_i = 1$, $\sum_{i=1}^n \lambda_i' = 1$, and $\lambda_i, \lambda_i' \geq 0$ for all $i = \overline{1,n}$. Substituting this into the expression for C, we get $C = \sum_{i=1}^n (\alpha \lambda_i + \beta \lambda_i') P_i$. If we can show that $\sum_{i=1}^n (\alpha \lambda_i + \beta \lambda_i') = 1$ and $\alpha \lambda_i + \beta \lambda_i' \geq 0$ for all i, then it automatically follows that the set $\mathcal{M}$ is convex. Based on the assumptions for $\lambda_i, \lambda_i', \alpha$, and β, we have that hold $\alpha \lambda_i + \beta \lambda_i' \geq 0$ for all i, as well $\sum_{i=1}^n (\alpha \lambda_i + \beta \lambda_i') = \alpha \sum_{i=1}^n \lambda_i + \beta \sum_{i=1}^n \lambda_i' = \alpha + \beta = 1$.

$\Leftarrow$) Using the principle of mathematical induction, we will prove that $\mathcal{M} \subseteq H(\mathcal{P})$. Let P be an arbitrary point in the set $\mathcal{M}$. We need to show that $P \in H(\mathcal{P})$. Since $P \in \mathcal{M}$, it follows that $P = \lambda_1 P_1 + \lambda_2 P_2 + \cdots + \lambda_n P_n$. For $n = 1$, we have $\mathcal{P} = \{P_1\}$, and thus $P = P_1$, and $H(\mathcal{P}) = P_1$, so clearly $P \in H(\mathcal{P})$. Similarly, for $n = 2$, we have $\mathcal{P} = \{P_1, P_2\}$, which implies $P = \lambda_1 P_1 + (1 - \lambda_1) P_2$. This means that P is an arbitrary point on the segment $\overline{P_1 P_2}$. Since the convex hull of $\mathcal{P}$ is exactly the segment $\overline{P_1 P_2}$, it follows that $P \in H(\mathcal{P})$. Assume that the statement holds for the set of points $\mathcal{M}' = \lambda_1' P_1 + \lambda_2' P_2 + \cdots + \lambda_k' P_k \subseteq H(\mathcal{P}')$, where $|\mathcal{P}'| = n - 1$, $k = n - 1$, $\sum_{i=1}^n \lambda_i' = 1$, and $\lambda_i' \geq 0$ for all $i = \overline{1,k}$. We now prove that the statement holds for $k = n$, i.e., that $\mathcal{M} \subseteq H(\mathcal{P})$, where $|\mathcal{P}| = n$. Since $\mathcal{P}' \subset \mathcal{P}$, by the convexity property it follows that $H(\mathcal{P}') \subseteq H(\mathcal{P})$, and therefore by the inductive hypothesis we obtain $\mathcal{M}' \subseteq H(\mathcal{P})$. Let $P' \in \mathcal{M}'$ be an arbitrary fixed element. Set $\lambda_i' = \frac{\lambda_i}{1 - \lambda_n}$ for $i = \overline{1, n-1}$. Then $\sum_{i=1}^{n-1} \lambda_i' = 1$, because $\sum_{i=1}^n \lambda_i = 1$. Since $P' \in \mathcal{M}' \subseteq H(\mathcal{P})$ and $P_n \in H(\mathcal{P})$, the convexity property implies that the segment $\overline{P' P_n} \in H(\mathcal{P})$, and therefore any point of the form $(1 - \lambda_n) P' + \lambda_n P_n \in H(\mathcal{P})$ for $\lambda_n \in [0,1]$. This implies that $P \in H(\mathcal{P})$, since $(1 - \lambda_n) P' + \lambda_n P_n = (1 - \lambda_n) \sum_{i=1}^{n-1} \lambda_i' P_i + \lambda_n P_n = (1 - \lambda_n) \sum_{i=1}^{n-1} \frac{\lambda_i}{1 - \lambda_n} P_i + \lambda_n P_n = P$. Finally, since P was chosen arbitrarily, it follows that $\mathcal{M} \subseteq H(\mathcal{P})$. This completes the proof of the lemma. ∎

The first two naive algorithms for finding the convex hull are closely related to identifying extreme points and edges. In other words, determining the convex hull indirectly depends on identifying points that are not extreme. The following lemma provides a characterization of the extremity of a point.

> **Lemma 4.1.2** Let $\mathcal{S}$ be a given set of points in the plane. A point $A \in \mathcal{S}$ is not extreme *if and only if* it lies strictly in the interior of some triangle defined over the set $\mathcal{S}$.

Proof. During the proof, the convex hull of the set $\mathcal{S}$ is taken to be the union of all triangles defined over $\mathcal{S}$.

$\Leftarrow$) Suppose that the point A lies strictly in the interior of some triangle defined over the set of points $\mathcal{S}$. It is necessary to show that the point A is not extreme. Assume the contrary, i.e., that the point A is extreme. Then, there exists a line l such that $A \in l$ and all other points of the set $\mathcal{S}$ lie strictly on one side of it (for example, on the left side). However, this contradicts the assumption about the location of point A, since it lies strictly inside the triangle, which further implies that there is at least one point lying on the opposite (right) side of the line l, i.e., there are points of $\mathcal{S}$ on both sides of l. Hence, the assumption that point A is extreme is false and must be rejected.

$\Rightarrow$) Suppose that the point A is not extreme. It must be proven that it lies strictly inside some triangle defined over the set $\mathcal{S}$. Assume the contrary — that the point A does not lie strictly in the interior of any triangle defined over $\mathcal{S}$. Consequently, point A does not lie strictly inside a triangle whose one side corresponds to an edge of the convex hull. This further implies that point A may be coincident with a vertex of the triangle, lie on one of its sides, or be located outside the hull. In all such cases, point A is classified as extreme, which is a contradiction. Therefore, the assumption must be rejected. ∎

Based on Lemma 4.1.2, the pseudocode of Algorithm 2 is obtained, which computes the convex hull for a set of n points with a time complexity of $\mathcal{O}(n^4)$.

Algorithm 2: Pseudocode with time complexity $\mathcal{O}(n^4)$ for computing the convex hull.

for $i=1\!:\!n$ **do**
    for $j=i+1\!:\!n$ **do**
        for $k=j+1\!:\!n$ **do**
            for $l=k+1\!:\!n$ **do**
                if $P_l \in \triangle P_i P_j P_k$ **then**
                    | The point P_l is not extreme.
                end
            end
        end
    end
end

In the pseudocode of Algorithm 2, the expression $P_l \in \triangle P_i P_j P_k$ refers to testing whether the point P_l lies strictly in the interior of the triangle. A point lies strictly in the interior of a triangle if it is not coincident with any of its vertices and does not lie on any of its sides.

Using the definition of an extreme edge, an algorithm with time complexity $\mathcal{O}(n^3)$ for computing the convex hull can be proposed, as shown in the pseudocode of Algorithm 3.

Algorithm 3: Pseudocode with time complexity $\mathcal{O}(n^3)$ for computing the convex hull.

for $i=1\!:\!n$ **do**
    for $j=i+1\!:\!n$ **do**
        for $k=j+1\!:\!n$ **do**
            if P_k *lies on the line l* $(\overline{P_i P_j} \subset l)$ *or is located strictly on one of its sides* **then**
                | the edge $\overline{P_i P_j}$ is extreme.
            end
        end
    end
end

Based on Observation 4.1.3, an algorithm with quadratic complexity for computing the convex hull can be proposed. Namely, the process of finding extreme points can be indirectly performed by identifying lines that contain those points such that all other points lie strictly on one side of those lines. Since the process of identifying such lines is carried out analogously for all points, the following description focuses on how to identify one such line. The search begins with a line l defined by a given point from the input set (e.g., the point $P_0(x_0, y_0)$) and a direction vector parallel to the x-axis. This line is then rotated by an angle θ, while simultaneously checking whether all remaining points P_i lie on one side of the rotated line. If they do, the point P_0 is an extreme point. To accelerate the execution of the algorithm, some preprocessing must be done at the beginning. Since the canonical form of a line is given by $y = kx + n$, where $k = \tan(\alpha)$ and $\alpha \in \{0, 1, \ldots, 360\}$, in the worst-case scenario, checks need to be performed for 360 distinct angles. The tangent values of these angles can be precomputed and stored in an auxiliary array, e.g., tangentAngles. After that, for the point P_0, the y-intercept n is computed as $n = y_0 - $ tangentAngles$[\alpha] \cdot x_0$, and the line l is defined as $y = $ tangentAngles$[\alpha] \cdot x + n$. For this line, it is then checked whether the remaining $n - 1$ points P_i (for $i = 1, 2, \ldots, n - 1$) lie strictly on one side. If they do, then the point $P_0(x_0, y_0)$ is an extreme point, and the procedure continues for the remaining points P_i ($i > 0$). Otherwise, the angle α is incremented by one degree, and the procedure for computing the intercept n and checking point positions is repeated for the new rotation of the line. Finally, the identified extreme points are stored in a new array. The time complexity of this algorithm in the general case is proportional to $\mathcal{O}(n^2)$, since the line is rotated by one degree in each iteration, resulting in a total of $360n(n-1)$ checks.

4.1.3 Gift Wrapping

This section demonstrates how a small variation in the concept of an extreme edge reduces the time complexity of the algorithm from $\mathcal{O}(n^3)$ to $\mathcal{O}(n^2)$. To achieve this, the extreme edge must be exploited as an anchor for determining the next extreme edge. This is possible because extreme edges are interconnected and form the boundary of the convex hull. It is easy to show that the convex polygon of a set consisting of n points can contain at most n extreme edges. Therefore, the number of candidates for extreme edges is bounded from above by $\mathcal{O}(n)$. It is not difficult to observe that the first extreme edge can be found in linear time. Moreover, each subsequent extreme edge is determined starting from the previously found extreme edge. In the worst case, finding each new extreme edge requires $\mathcal{O}(n)$ time. Since there are at most n extreme edges, the overall worst-case complexity of the algorithm is $\mathcal{O}(n^2)$. The process of identifying extreme edges closely resembles the *selection sort algorithm*. From a geometric point of view, the described method for finding the convex hull based on extreme edges is very similar to the *gift wrapping* algorithm (also known as *gift wrapping*). In the literature, this algorithm is also known as the *Jarvis algorithm* or the *Jarvis March algorithm*, invented by R. A. Jarvis in 1973 [94, 148]. Historically, the authors D. R. Chand and S. S. Kapur published in 1970 a more robust algorithm for computing the convex hull in n-dimensions. Since the Jarvis algorithm in two dimensions ($n = 2$) is a special case of the algorithm proposed by these authors, their method is often referred to in the literature as the *Chand-Kapur algorithm* for convex hull computation. Due to the complexity of this general algorithm, we describe here its simpler version, namely the Jarvis algorithm. The idea of this algorithm is to first find an anchor point P_1. Then, a vector orthogonal to the x-axis is drawn from P_1, which is subsequently rotated around that point in a clockwise direction until it hits the next point. Let this point be P_2. Then the extreme edge $\overline{P_1 P_2}$ of the convex hull has been found. The process continues from point P_2 and terminates when all points are processed and the algorithm returns to the starting point P_1. The entire process of computing the convex hull is illustrated in Fig. 4.4 through steps (a), (b), (c), (d), (e), and (f). To implement this process, the planar points are initially stored in an array A. Let the size of this array be n. The anchor point P_1 is located and placed as the first element of the array. This involves a renumbering of the array A, similar to the case of finding a simple polygon. Then, a line l is introduced, containing the point P_1 and parallel to the x-axis, and the counter is set to two, i.e., $i = 2$. The following procedure is then repeated until all points of the convex hull are found:

a) The point P_i is obtained by requiring that the line defined by the points P_{i-1} and P_i forms the smallest angle with the line l. Alternatively, the point P_i can be found by requiring that all remaining points P_j lie to the left of the segment $\overline{P_{i-1} P_i}$;

b) The point P_i is added as the i-th element of the array A, i.e., in this case as well, the array A is renumbered, meaning that a swapping operation is performed;

c) The counter i is incremented by one, i.e., $i \leftarrow i + 1$.

It is not difficult to observe, based on the above description of Jarvis's algorithm, that its worst-case time complexity is quadratic, i.e., proportional to $\mathcal{O}(n^2)$. If the worst-case scenario is excluded, the time complexity of Jarvis's algorithm is of the order $\mathcal{O}(nh)$, where h denotes the number of extreme points, i.e., the number of points in the solution. In the worst-case scenario, the number of extreme points h equals n, which occurs when all the given points lie on the convex hull. In practice, this case is very rare, and thus $h \ll n$. The implementation of this algorithm is provided in Listing 4.3.

Listing 4.3: Implementation of Jarvis's algorithm for computing the convex hull.

```
1
2 def gift_wrapping(points: list[Point2D]) -> Polygon | None:
```

```
3     n = len(points)
4     if n < 3: return None
5     points.append(points[0])
6     p = Polygon(); j = 0
7     for i in range(1, n):
8           if points[i] < points[j]:j = i
9     points[n] = points[j]; i=0   # The anchor point is appended at the end
10    while i < n:
11          points[i], points[j] = points[j], points[i] # swap points
12          p.insert(points[i]); j = i + 1
13          for k in range(i + 2, n + 1): # Includes the anchor point at the end
14              l = points[k].classification_m(points[i], points[j])
15              if l == TypeP2.LEFT or l == TypeP2.BEHIND: j = k
16          if j == n: return p  # The anchor point has been reached again
17          i += 1
18    return None
```

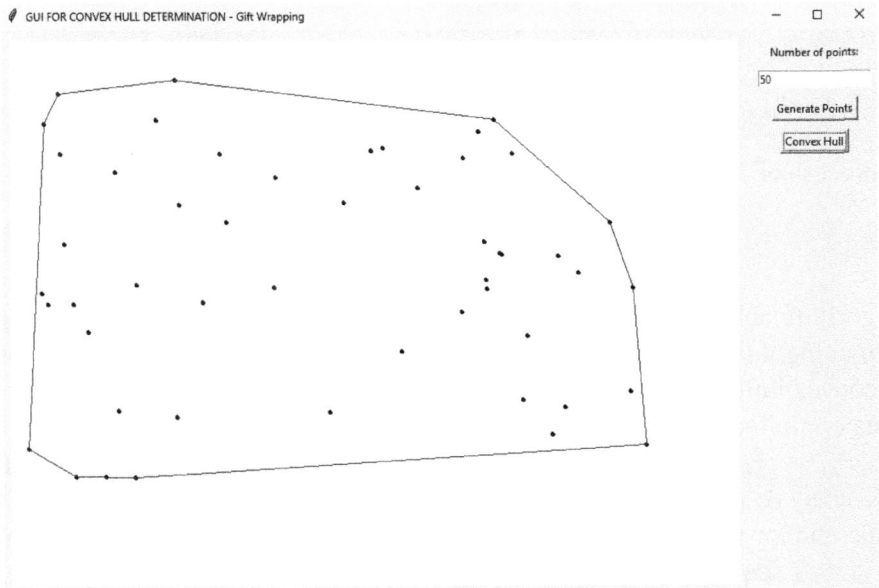

Figure 4.3: Application of Jarvis's algorithm to 50 random points.

An alternative version of Jarvis's algorithm can also be implemented using angles, although it tends to be slightly slower due to repeated calls to the built-in **atan2**($\cdot,\cdot$) function. A graphical visualization of the convex hull algorithm developed in the Python programming language is shown in Fig. 4.3.

4.1.4 Graham Scan Algorithm

In the previous section, it was noted that the *Jarvis March algorithm* becomes efficient when the number of points on the convex hull is very small, i.e., when $h \ll n$. However, if the number of extreme points h equals the total number of points n, then its time complexity becomes quadratic, making the algorithm inefficient for very large point sets, for example $n = 10^6$, which is not uncommon in practice. Statistically, it has been shown that if points are randomly distributed within a circular region, the expected number of points on the convex hull grows proportionally to $\Theta(n^{\frac{1}{3}})$, which is certainly greater than $\Theta(\log n)$. In this case, the time complexity of the *Jarvis March algorithm* becomes $\Theta(n^{\frac{4}{3}})$, which is less favorable than $\Theta(n \log n)$. This created a need for algorithms with time complexity $\Theta(n \log n)$. Thus, in 1972, *Ronald Graham* proposed the *Graham's Scan Algorithm*, often referred to in the literature simply as *Graham scan*

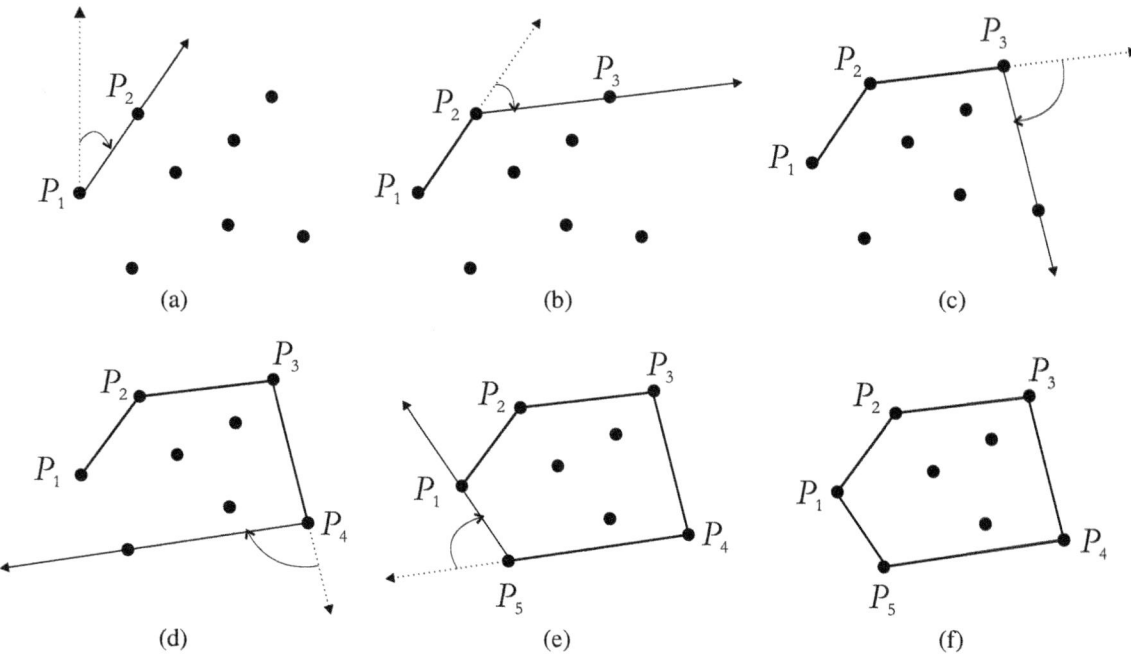

Figure 4.4: The process of computing the convex hull for a set of eight given planar points, shown in steps (a)–(f).

[12, 74]. This algorithm achieves a time complexity of $\Theta(n \log n)$, regardless of the number of points on the convex hull, making it more efficient than the *Jarvis March algorithm* whenever the expected number of points on the convex hull exceeds $\log n$. The main idea behind Graham's algorithm is very simple and similar to the idea exploited in constructing a simple polygon. Let a sequence of points in the plane be given as $A = \{P_1, P_2, \cdots, P_n\}$. The algorithm consists of two phases. In the first phase, the anchor point P_k is found in the array A, and then it is swapped with the first point P_1, so that the first element of the array becomes the anchor point. Next, the elements of the array are sorted around the point P_1. This results in a new sorted sequence of points $B = \{P_1', P_2', \cdots, P_n'\}$. In the second phase of the algorithm, the sorted points are either pushed onto or popped from the stack depending on the mutual position of three points: the current point (P_i'), the penultimate point (P_j'), and the last point (P_k'). Specifically, the algorithm checks on which side of the segment $\overline{P_j' P_k'}$ the point P_i' lies. In other words, the sorted points are pushed or popped from the stack based on the positive/negative orientation of the triangle $\triangle P_i' P_j' P_k'$. To better understand this process, it is illustratively shown in Fig. 4.5 for a given sorted sequence of points $B = \{P_1', P_2', P_3', P_4', P_5', P_6', P_7', P_8', P_9'\}$. As can be seen from the figure, all the points are sorted around the anchor point P_1' according to their polar angle. The extreme points used to construct the convex hull are maintained on a stack, so the entire management of points is carried out using the stack.

Initially, the first two points of the sorted list, P_1' and P_2', are pushed onto the stack S, so that the state of the stack becomes $S = \{P_2', P_1'\}$, where P_2' is at the top of the stack. Since point P_3' lies to the left of the segment $\overline{P_1' P_2'}$ (left turn at point P_2' in Fig. 4.5 (b)), it is added to the top of the stack S, resulting in $S = \{P_3', P_2', P_1'\}$. The next point considered is P_4'. Since it lies to the right of segment $\overline{P_2' P_3'}$ (right turn at P_3' in Fig. 4.5 (c)), point P_3' is popped from the stack, updating its state to $S = \{P_2', P_1'\}$. The popping of the element is illustrated graphically with a dashed line (see Fig. 4.5 (c)). Then, point P_4' is added to the stack, as it lies to the left of segment $\overline{P_1' P_2'}$. The new stack state is $S = \{P_4', P_2', P_1'\}$. Continuing this process, points P_5', P_6', and P_7' are pushed onto the stack, so the stack after these insertions becomes

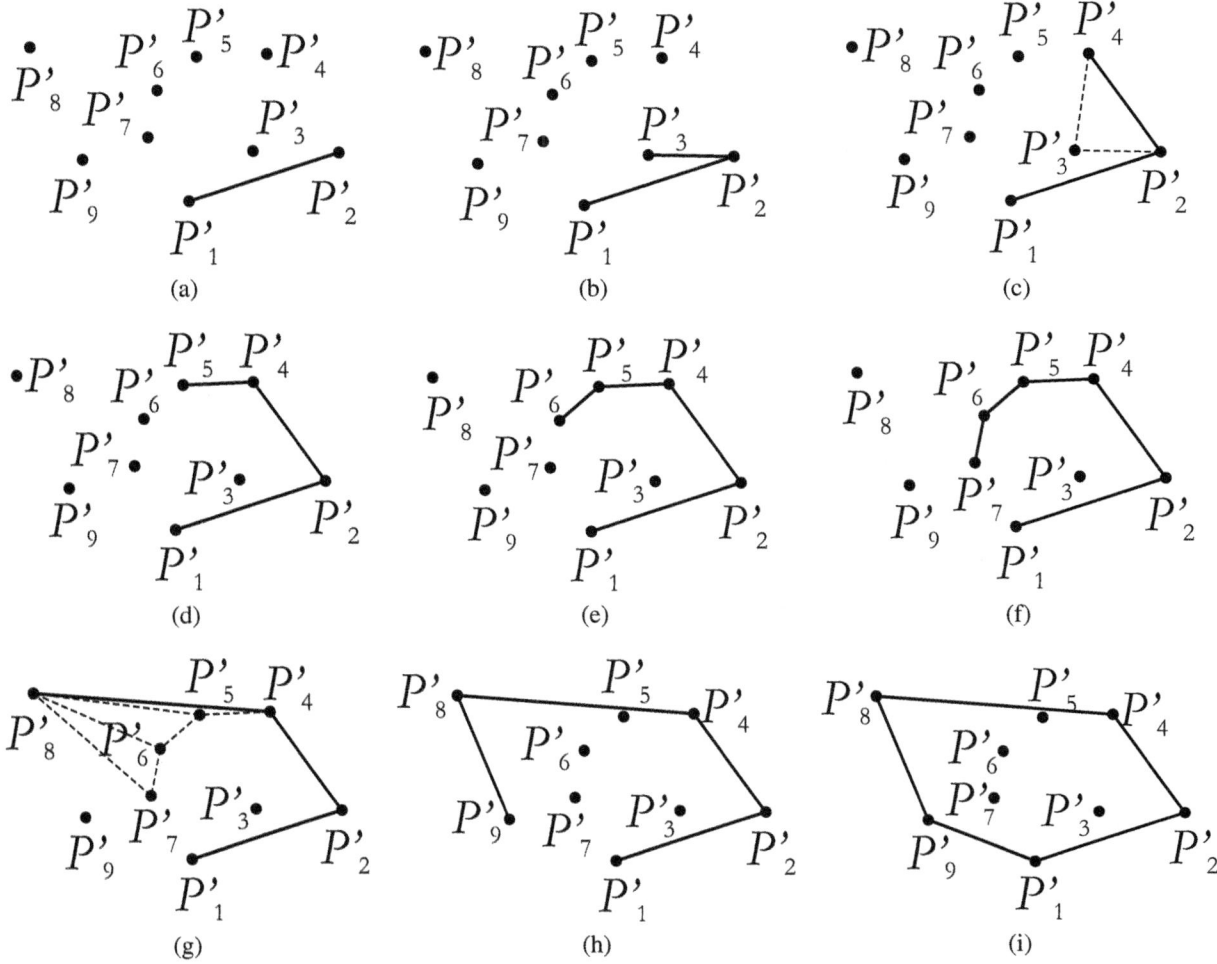

Figure 4.5: Gradual construction of the convex hull using Graham's algorithm from (a) to (i).

$S = \{P_7', P_6', P_5', P_4', P_2', P_1'\}$. Considering point P_8' in Fig. 4.5 (g), the stack is emptied due to three right turns at points P_7', P_6', and P_5', respectively. The popping of elements from the stack is illustrated with dashed lines. After popping, point P_8' is added since it lies to the left of segment $\overline{P_2'P_4'}$. Therefore, the current stack state becomes $S = \{P_8', P_4', P_2', P_1'\}$. After processing the remaining points, the final stack state is $S = \{P_1', P_9', P_8', P_4', P_2', P_1'\}$. Thus, the stack contains the extreme points that form the convex hull, and by popping these points from the stack, the convex hull is created, which is graphically illustrated in Fig. 4.5 (i). The time complexity of this approach in the worst case is proportional to $\Theta(n \log n)$ when considering the operations performed in both phases of the algorithm. In the first phase, finding the anchor point and sorting the points together require $\Theta(n \log n)$ in the worst case. In the second phase, for all points except the first two, it is necessary to check whether they form a left or right turn, which is done with a very small number of checks—precisely one check if the point is pushed onto the stack, or a few if the point is popped. Altogether, the second phase does not take more than $\mathcal{O}(n)$ time in the worst case. In total, both phases of the algorithm are executed in $\Theta(n \log n)$ time. Based on the description, it is clear that once the points are sorted, the algorithm operates in linear time. According to the outlined logic of Graham's algorithm, its implementation is provided in Listing 4.4.

```
1  def graham_scan(points: List[Point2D]) -> Polygon:
2      n = len(points)
3      if n < 3: return None
4      anchor, idx = anchor_point(points)
5      points[0], points[idx] = anchor, points[0] #swap elements
6      shifted = [p - anchor for p in points]
7      sorted_shifted = [shifted[0]] + sorted(shifted[1:], key=lambda p: (p.
           polar_angle_m(), p.norm()))
8
9      stack = [sorted_shifted[0], sorted_shifted[1]] #realization of a stack by list
10     for i in range(2, n):
11         while len(stack)>=2 and sorted_shifted[i].classification_m(stack[-2],stack
               [-1])!=TypeP2.LEFT: stack.pop()
12         stack.append(sorted_shifted[i])
13
14     hull = Polygon()
15     for p in reversed(stack): hull.insert(p + anchor)
16     return hull
17  }
```

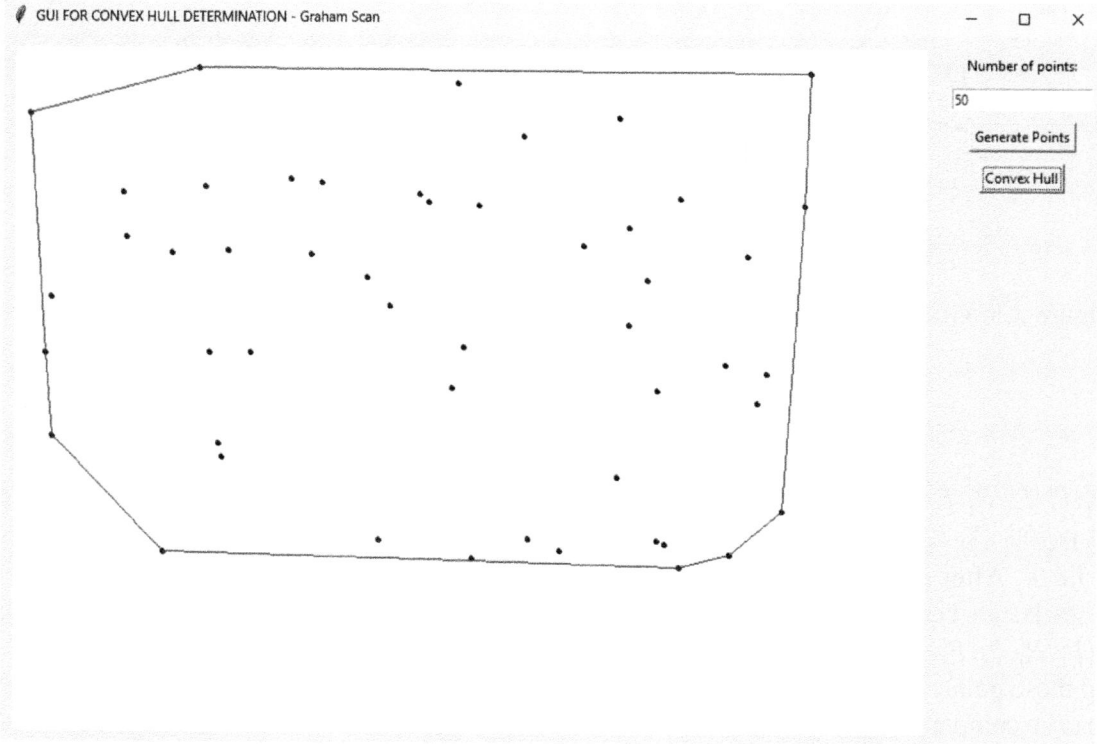

Figure 4.6: Determining the convex hull using Graham's algorithm for 50 randomly generated points.

Based on the previous discussion, the main advantage of Graham's algorithm over other convex hull algorithms, such as Jarvis's algorithm, is that each point is processed exactly once. Specifically, once it is determined that a point cannot be a vertex of the convex hull, it is no longer considered — which is not the case with the gift wrapping algorithm. From an algorithmic standpoint, Graham's algorithm is an example of an algorithm based on backtracking . These algorithms follow the paradigm: "Try something and keep going until you encounter a problem; when a problem arises, backtrack one step and try a different approach; if that also fails, backtrack another step and try again," and so on. In Graham's algorithm, this is precisely what happens: new points are added until a problem with their addition is detected. Once this occurs, the algorithm steps back, removes points, and continues processing the remaining points. The visualization of the convex hull obtained using the Graham Scan algorithm, implemented in the Python programming language, is shown in Fig. 4.6.

■ **Example 4.2** Let a set of n points in the plane be given, denoted as $\mathscr{A} = \{A_1, A_2, \cdots, A_n\}$, which are cyclically ordered with respect to a circle whose center lies within the convex hull $\mathscr{H}(\mathscr{A})$. Modify Graham's algorithm so that it can operate on the given point set without requiring initial sorting.   ■

■ **Example 4.3** Demonstrate using Graham's algorithm that from a given set of n points in the plane, it is possible to successively discard r points for some sufficiently large value of r.

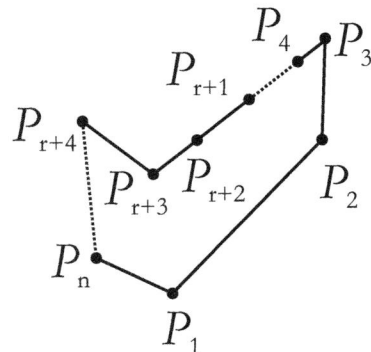

Figure 4.7: Successive discarding of r points using Graham's algorithm.

Solution. Let n planar points P_i be given for $i = \overline{1, n}$, as illustrated in Fig. 4.7. It is clear that such an arrangement of points is not unique—that is, the specification of points can be carried out in arbitrarily many ways such that each of them allows Graham's algorithm to successively discard r points for a sufficiently large r. From the figure, it can be observed that the segment $\overline{P_3 P_{r+3}}$ contains $r + 1$ points out of the total n given. Based on the description of how Graham's algorithm operates, during the construction of the convex hull, the r points $P_4, P_5, \ldots, P_{r+3}$ will be eliminated, since the final convex hull consists only of the points $P_1, P_2, P_3, P_{r+4}, P_n$.   ■

■ **Example 4.4** Show that the Graham's algorithm can be implemented in such a way that the second phase of the algorithm is carried out without using any collection that supports appending to the end, as was the case with a stack.   ■

■ **Example 4.5** Let a set of n points in the plane be given. Propose an algorithm with time complexity $\Theta(n \log n)$ for finding the two farthest points.

Solution. An algorithm with time complexity $\Theta(n \log n)$ for determining the farthest pair of points consists of two phases. Since the two farthest points must lie on the convex hull, the first phase of the algorithm applies the Graham Scan algorithm to the initial set of points. The Graham's algorithm generates the convex hull (a polygon) composed of m vertices in $\Theta(n \log n)$ time, where $m \le n$. In the second phase, among the m convex hull points, the two farthest points are identified in linear time using the *Rotating Calipers* algorithm. This method was first proposed by Michael Shamos in 1978. Shamos demonstrated that the diameter of a convex polygon formed by n points can be found in $\mathscr{O}(n)$ time. It has been shown that the rotating calipers technique solves the following geometric problems in linear time: *determining the minimum-area rectangle that encloses a simple polygon, finding the maximum distance between two simple polygons, computing the Minkowski sum of two polygons*, and *merging convex polygons*. Of course, the method based on the idea of rotating calipers has far wider application beyond the four mentioned problems, but for the sake of brevity, this section focuses on its use in locating the farthest pair of points. Thus, the rotating calipers algorithm seeks the farthest pair of points in $\mathcal{O}(m)$ time. Without loss of generality, the principle of the rotating calipers algorithm is explained through an example of a convex polygon composed of seven points ($m = 7$), as shown in Fig. 4.8. To identify the farthest pair of convex hull points, one must determine their indices p_1 and p_2. Let the ends of the calipers be denoted by i and j. Initially, set $i = 1$ and $j = 2$. The value of j should be updated so that point P_j is the farthest point from the segment $\overline{P_{m-1}P_0}$. In the case of the polygon shown in Fig. 4.8, j is increased by two, since the area of triangle $\triangle P_6 P_0 P_3$ is greater than the areas of triangles $\triangle P_6 P_0 P_1$ and $\triangle P_6 P_0 P_2$. Thus, only two iterations were needed to find the farthest point from segment $\overline{P_6 P_0}$. Next, the antipodal pairs p_1 and p_2 are identified. Initially, set $p_1 \leftarrow i - 1$, $p_2 \leftarrow j$, and let the maximum distance be $d = dist(CH[p_1], CH[p_2])$, where the array CH contains the vertices of the convex hull. The second caliper end j is incremented as long as $j < m$, and the area of triangle $\triangle ABC$ is greater than the area of triangle $\triangle ABC'$, where $A = CH[i-1]$, $B = CH[i]$, $C = CH[j+1]$, and $C' = CH[j]$. In this case, the current maximum distance d is updated to $dist(CH[i-1], CH[j])$ if it is greater than the previous value, and the antipodal pairs p_1 and p_2 are updated accordingly. The algorithm iterates while $i \leq k$ and $j \leq m$, where k is initialized to the value of the second caliper end found at the beginning (in the case of the simple polygon in Fig. 4.8, this is four, i.e., $k = 4$). Moreover, each time i is incremented—moving the first caliper end to a new convex hull vertex—it must be checked whether the current distance d is less than $dist(CH[i-1], CH[j])$. If so, it is updated, along with the antipodal pairs as before. Following the outlined description of the algorithm based on the rotating calipers technique, it is concluded that points P_3 and P_6 form the farthest pair of the convex hull (see Fig. 4.8).

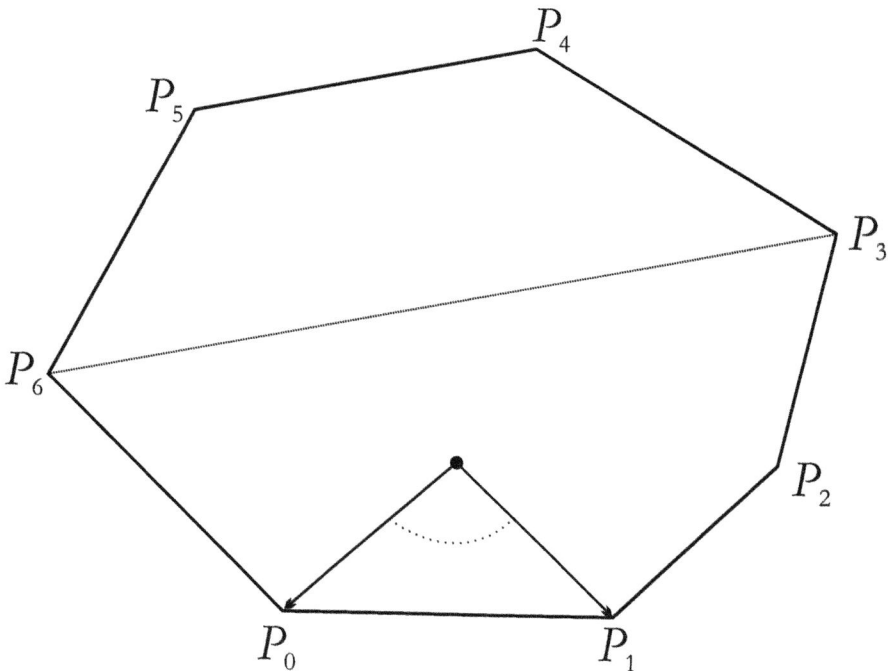

Figure 4.8: Optimal search for the two farthest points using the Rotating Calipers Method.

■ **Example 4.6** Implement a two-phase algorithm based on Graham's algorithm and the rotating calipers method for determining the two farthest points.

Solution. After explaining the principle of the rotating calipers method in the previous example, Listing 4.5 presents an efficient two-phase algorithm which, in $\Theta(n \log n)$ time, identifies the two farthest points from the set $\mathscr{A}$ consisting of n planar points.

Listing 4.5: Two-Phase Algorithm for Finding the Two Farthest Points

```python
from geometry import Point2D, Segment2D, Polygon
from ch4_helper_functions import graham_scan

def farthest_pair(points: list[Point2D]) -> Tuple[Point2D, Point2D]:
    polygon = graham_scan(points) # First phase: Graham Scan to get convex hull
    if not polygon or polygon.size() < 2: return None
    cH=[] # Extract points from polygon into a list cH
    for _ in range(polygon.size()):
        cH.append(polygon.point_of_current()); polygon.move_current(-1)
    cH.append(cH[0]); m = len(cH)-1; # Closing the polygon
    s=Segment2D(cH[m-1],cH[0]); k=2; # Second phase: Rotating Calipers
    while k<m and cH[k].distance(s)>cH[k-1].distance(s): k+=1
    j=k; max_distance = 0.0; p1 = p2 = 0;
    for i in range(1,k+1):
        d=(cH[i-1]-cH[j]).norm()
        if d > max_distance: max_distance = d; p1, p2=i-1, j
        s=Segment2D(cH[i-1],cH[i])
        while j<m and cH[j+1].distance(s)>cH[j].distance(s):
            j += 1; d=(cH[i-1]-cH[j]).norm();
            if d > max_distance: max_distance=d; p1, p2=i-1, j
    return cH[p1], cH[p2] # Return two farthest points
```

■

4.1.5 Andrew's Algorithm

For a planar set of points $\mathscr{A} = \{A_1, A_2, \cdots, A_n\}$, the following question is posed: "Can the second phase of Graham's algorithm be used to compute the convex hull if the points of set $\mathscr{A}$ are not sorted by polar angle but instead lexicographically by their coordinates?" The answer to this question is affirmative and represents a modification of Graham's algorithm proposed by A. M. Andrew in 1979 [13]. This modification is referred to in the literature as the *Andrew's Monotone Chain Algorithm*. In the first phase of Andrew's algorithm, the points of set $\mathscr{A}$ are sorted lexicographically, for example, in increasing order of their x-coordinates. After sorting, the first point in the sorted set $\mathscr{A}$ is the point A_{min} with the smallest x-coordinate (the leftmost point), while the last point in the set is A_{max}, the point with the largest x-coordinate (the rightmost point). The line passing through the leftmost and rightmost points divides the set $\mathscr{A}$ into two subsets $\mathscr{A}_1$ and $\mathscr{A}_2$, where the set $\mathscr{A}_1$ contains points located to the left of the segment $\overline{A_{min}A_{max}}$, while $\mathscr{A}_2$ includes the remaining points located to the right of the aforementioned segment. Additionally, let both subsets $\mathscr{A}_1$ and $\mathscr{A}_2$ include the points A_{min} and A_{max}. Before applying the second phase of Graham's algorithm, a point $(x_{max}, y_{max} + 100)$ is added at the end of the set $\mathscr{A}_1$, and a point $(x_{max}, y_{max} - 100)$ is added at the end of the set $\mathscr{A}_2$. Applying the core procedure of Graham's algorithm to the sets $\mathscr{A}_1$ and $\mathscr{A}_2$ yields the upper and lower hulls, respectively. Merging the upper and lower hulls results in the desired convex hull. The implementation of Andrew's algorithm is provided within the function *andrew_algorithm*($\cdot$) in Listing 4.6, where it is evident that the convex hull is obtained as the union of the upper and lower hulls of the point set. The graphical interface showcasing Andrew's algorithm for computing the convex hull has been developed using the Python programming language. Its functionality and visualization capabilities are illustrated in Fig. 4.9.

Listing 4.6: Implementation of Andrew's Algorithm for Construction of Convex Hull.

```python
from geometry import Point2D, Polygon, TypeP2
from typing import List

```

```
4 def andrew_algorithm(points: List[Point2D]) -> Polygon:
5     n = len(points)
6     if n<3: return None
7     s_points=sorted(points,key=lambda p:(p[0],p[1])) #Lexicographic sorted points
8     u_hull=[]; # First phase: Upper hull
9     Amax=Point2D(s_points[-1][0],s_points[-1][1]-100)
10    u_hull.append(Amax); u_hull.append(s_points[-1])
11    for i in range(n-2,-1,-1):
12        if s_points[i].orientation(s_points[0],s_points[-1])<0:continue
13        while len(u_hull)>=2 and s_points[i].classification_m(u_hull[-2],u_hull
              [-1])!=TypeP2.LEFT: u_hull.pop()
14        u_hull.append(s_points[i])
15    l_hull = [] # Second phase: Lower hull
16    Amax = Point2D(s_points[0][0],s_points[0][1]+100)
17    l_hull.append(Amax); l_hull.append(s_points[0])
18    for i in range(1, n):
19        if s_points[i].orientation(s_points[0],s_points[-1])>0:continue
20        while len(l_hull) >= 2 and s_points[i].classification_m(l_hull[-2],l_hull
              [-1])!=TypeP2.LEFT: l_hull.pop()
21        l_hull.append(s_points[i])
22    convex_hull = Polygon() # Merging upper and lower hulls into a convex hull
23    for i in range(1,len(u_hull)): convex_hull.insert(u_hull[i])
24    for i in range(1,len(l_hull)): convex_hull.insert(l_hull[i])
25    return convex_hull
```

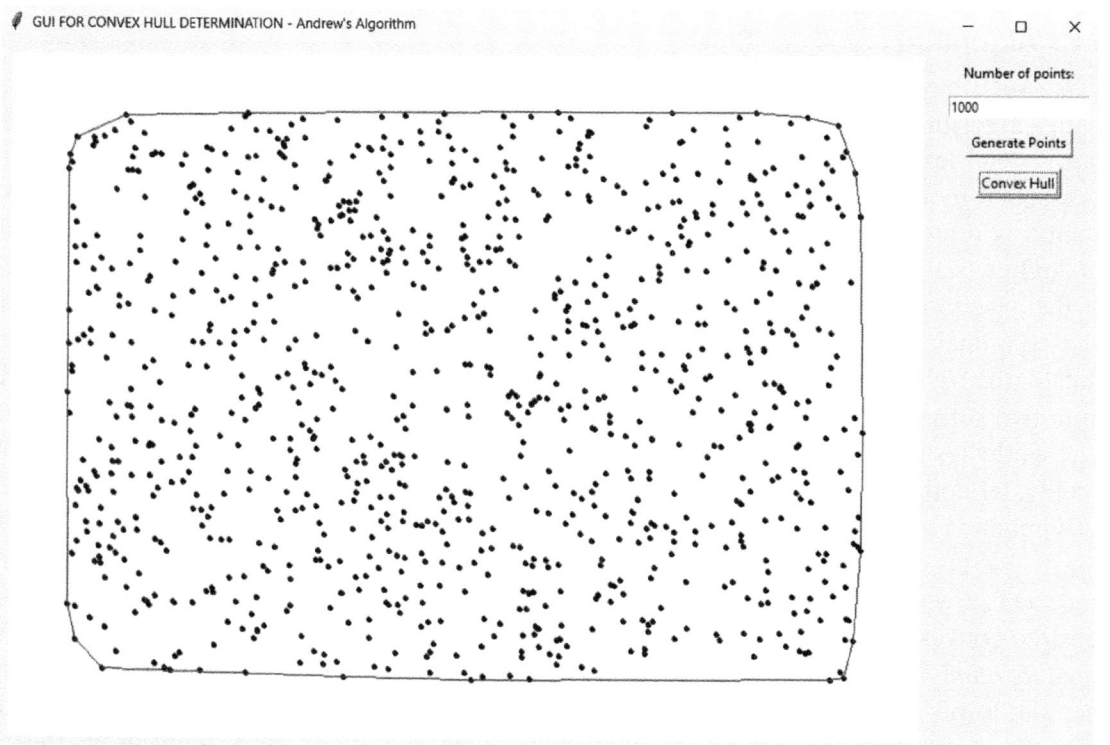

Figure 4.9: Convex hull via Andrew's algorithm for one thousand randomly generated points.

In the following section, the advantages and limitations of Andrew's algorithm compared to Graham's algorithm will be discussed. The primary advantage of Andrew's algorithm lies in its use of lexicographic sorting, which requires significantly fewer arithmetic-logical operations than sorting based on polar angle comparisons. It is well known that polar comparison, implemented via the *polar_angle()* function, involves computing the arctangent, a trigonometric function that introduces a non-negligible runtime overhead in practice—even though, from a theoretical standpoint, its time complexity is constant, i.e., $\mathscr{O}(1)$. Consequently, the point-sorting phase in Andrew's algorithm tends to be slightly faster (by a constant factor) than in Graham's algorithm. Furthermore, if the input set of points is already lexicographically sorted, Andrew's algorithm becomes linear. On the downside, Andrew's algorithm typically requires more memory, as it necessitates either two separate collections (e.g., two stacks) or a single collection with enough capacity to store twice as many elements compared to Graham's algorithm. Thus, its spatial complexity is somewhat higher compared to the Graham's algorithm.

■ **Example 4.7** Show that Andrew's algorithm can be executed in such a way that the second phase of the algorithm is carried out without using any collection that supports appending elements to the end, such as lists or stacks. ■

4.1.6 Incremental Algorithm

In the previous sections, it was shown that the introduction of Graham's algorithm, as well as its modifications, requires asymptotic time which, in the worst case, is of the order $\Theta(n\log n)$. Due to the sorting step used in these algorithms, a shorter execution time for computing the convex hull does not exist. Since this time complexity is the most optimal for convex hull construction in two dimensions, it is entirely sufficient to exploit Graham's algorithm for building the convex hull. However, as it is very difficult—if not impossible—to extend Graham's algorithm to higher dimensions, there arises a need for introducing alternative algorithms that can be more easily generalized and applied for computing convex hulls in higher-dimensional spaces. In 1984, M. Kallay proposed an algorithm that allows such an extension to dimensions higher than two. Moreover, if implemented efficiently, this algorithm can achieve an execution time proportional to $\Theta(n\log n)$. This algorithm is known as the *Incremental Algorithm* [103]. It is also referred to in the literature as the *Inductive Algorithm*. What follows is a description of this algorithm. Let a planar point set be given, $\mathscr{P} = \{P_1, P_2, \cdots, P_n\}$, with cardinality greater than three. By selecting any three non-collinear points from the set, a convex hull can be constructed, which in this case forms a triangle. Without loss of generality, let these points be P_1, P_2, and P_3, and let $\mathscr{H}_3$ denote their convex hull. The core idea of the algorithm is that, in an arbitrary i-th step ($i \geq 4$), the convex hull $\mathscr{H}_i$ is constructed by merging the previous convex hull $\mathscr{H}_{i-1}$ with the point P_i. As a result of this update, two cases may occur:

- the point P_i belongs to the previous convex hull $\mathscr{H}_{i-1}$, i.e., $P_i \in \mathscr{H}_{i-1}$;

- the point P_i lies outside the convex hull $\mathscr{H}_{i-1}$, i.e., $P_i \notin \mathscr{H}_{i-1}$.

If the first case occurs, then the point P_i is discarded and not further considered. Likewise, the point P_i is not processed if it lies on the boundary of the previous hull $\mathscr{H}_{i-1}$. However, if the second case takes place, then two tangents are drawn from the point P_i to the previous hull $\mathscr{H}_{i-1}$, and based on them, the hull $\mathscr{H}_{i-1}$ is modified to form the new convex hull $\mathscr{H}_i$. To better understand the process of constructing the convex hull, consider, without loss of generality, a set consisting of 13 points (see Fig. 4.10). From the figure, it is evident that the convex hull $\mathscr{H}_6$ consists of the extreme points P_1, P_2, P_3, P_4, P_5, and P_6. This hull contains six points, so the only remaining point outside the hull is P_7. Although the steps of constructing $\mathscr{H}_3$, $\mathscr{H}_4$, $\mathscr{H}_5$, and $\mathscr{H}_6$ are omitted at this stage, all of them—except for $\mathscr{H}_3$—are built analogously to the construction of $\mathscr{H}_7$, which will be described in the sequel. Clearly, the hull $\mathscr{H}_3$ forms the triangle $\triangle P_1 P_2 P_3$, and thus its construction is straightforward. From the point P_7, it is necessary to determine two tangents to the hull $\mathscr{H}_6$. In the figure, these are the tangents t_1 and t_2, defined by the segments $\overline{P_7 P_3}$ and $\overline{P_7 P_6}$, respectively. The question arises as to how to determine these tangents, specifically how to identify the points P_3 and P_6. In order to find the point P_6, one starts from the point closest to P_7—in the figure, this is the point P_5.

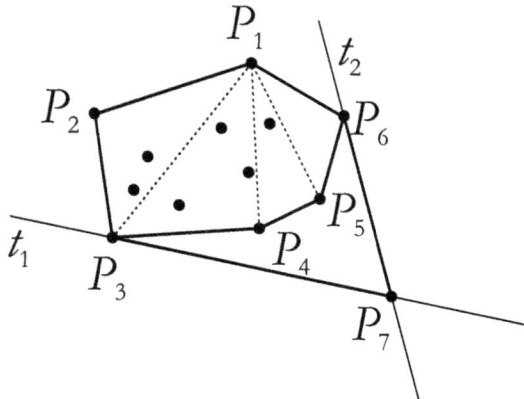

Figure 4.10: Illustration of the Incremental Algorithm for Constructing the Convex Hull.

The method for finding the nearest point, as well as the computational cost of this operation in terms of time, will be explained later. Once the point P_5 has been located, the search for the upper tangent t_2—i.e., the segment $\overline{P_7P_6}$—begins from the segment $\overline{P_7P_5}$ by verifying whether all points of the current hull $\mathcal{H}_6$ lie to the left of it. If this condition is satisfied, then P_5 is the tangent point, and the segment $\overline{P_7P_5}$ uniquely determines the upper tangent t_2. If the condition is not met, the process continues by traversing the current hull in a counterclockwise direction, checking the next point. Specifically, in the figure, this is the point P_6, which is indeed the tangent point, as all hull points lie to the left of the segment $\overline{P_7P_6}$. The lower tangent t_1, defined by the segment $\overline{P_7P_3}$, is found analogously. However, in this case, the current hull is traversed in a clockwise direction, and it is required that all hull points lie to the right of the desired tangent. Based on this, the implementation of the public method *tangent*($\cdot$, $\cdot$) of the **Polygon** class is given as follows:

```
def tangent(self, p: Point2D, side):
    orien= -1 if side == TypeP2.LEFT else 1 # determine orientation
    a=self.current; b=self.neighbor(orien)
    c=b.classification_m(p, a.vertex_point())
    while c == side or c == TypeP2.BEHIND or c == TypeP2.BETWEEN:
        self.move_current(orien);a = self.current
        b = self.neighbor(orien);c = b.classification_m(p, a.vertex_point())
```

By locating the upper and lower tangents, the current hull is divided into two chains (Fig. 4.10):

- **near chain** – this chain encompasses the closer vertices or points, such as P_4 and P_5;

- **far chain** – this chain encompasses the more distant vertices or points, such as P_1 and P_2.

The vertices of the near chain are removed from the current hull, and the current vertex or point P_7 is inserted in their place. In this way, a new hull is formed, $\mathcal{H}_7 = \{P_1, P_2, P_3, P_7, P_6\}$. The search for the remaining hulls $\mathcal{H}_i$ ($i > 7$) is performed incrementally with respect to the counter i.

The implementation of the incremental algorithm is carried out within the function *incremental_algorithm*($\cdot$), as shown in Listing 4.7.

Listing 4.7: Implementation of the Incremental Algorithm for Convex Hull Construction.

```
def incremental_algorithm(points: list[Point2D]) -> Polygon:
    n = len(points); p = Polygon()
    p.insert(points[0]); p.insert(points[1])
    for i in range(2, n):
        if p.contains_point(points[i]): continue
```

```
6      c = points[i]
7      nV = p.find_vertex(lambda a, b: -1 if (c - a).norm() < (c - b).norm()
8          else 1 if (c - a).norm() > (c - b).norm() else 0) #Lambda phrases
9      p.tangent(c, TypeP2.LEFT) # Compute lower tangent
10     v=p.current_vertex()
11     p.update_current(nV)
12     p.tangent(c, TypeP2.RIGHT)# Compute upper tangent
13     p.split(v) # Remove closer portion of the hull
14     p.insert(c) # Insert new point
15  return p
```

The time complexity of the incremental algorithm is proportional to $\mathcal{O}(nh)$, where h is the number of points on the convex hull and n is the total number of given planar points. Specifically, the method *contains_point*($\cdot$) of class **Polygon** requires, in the worst case, h passes, which is of order $\mathcal{O}(h)$. However, this method can be improved to achieve logarithmic time for testing point membership in the convex hull. The method *find_vertex*($\cdot$) is, in the worst case, also proportional to $\mathcal{O}(h)$. The last method, *tangent*($\cdot,\cdot$), in the worst case requires logarithmic time, i.e., it is of order $\mathcal{O}(\log h)$. Summarizing, the mentioned methods consume $\mathcal{O}(h)$ time. Since it is necessary to process $n-3$ vertices, the overall complexity of this algorithm is $\mathcal{O}(nh)$. If initially all points lie on the convex hull, then the incremental algorithm has quadratic time complexity. Fortunately, this time complexity can be improved to $\Theta(n\log n)$ by lexicographically sorting all planar points, e.g., with respect to the x-coordinate, and then processing the points in sorted order, as done in the case of the modified Graham's algorithm. In this way, each new point always lies outside the convex hull of the previously processed points. Moreover, after lexicographic sorting, the methods *contains_point*($\cdot$) and *find_vertex*($\cdot$) can be completely omitted. The method *tangent*($\cdot,\cdot$) can, for each point outside the convex hull, find two tangents to the current hull in $\mathcal{O}(\log n)$ time. Therefore, the time complexity of finding the tangents for all points, in the worst case, is $\Theta(n\log n)$, and thus the total running time of the algorithm is of order $\Theta(n\log n)$. Figure 4.11 illustrates the graphical interface, developed in the Python programming language, which was used to implement the incremental algorithm.

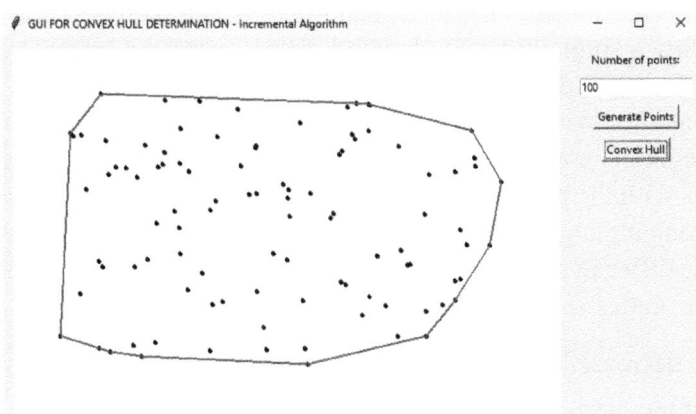

Figure 4.11: Convex Hull via Incremental Algorithm for 100 Random Points.

■ **Example 4.8** Let $\mathscr{P} = \{P_1, P_2, \cdots, P_n\}$ be an arbitrarily chosen convex polygon in the plane, and let $P \notin \mathscr{P}$ be a point. Show that two tangents from the point P to the polygon $\mathscr{P}$ can be constructed in $\Theta(\log n)$ time.

Solution. As shown in Fig. 4.12, two tangents t_1 and t_2 are drawn from the point P to the convex polygon $\mathscr{P}$ so that they form, respectively, the largest and the smallest angles with the positive part of the x-axis. In what follows, these tangents will be found, more precisely, the points P_i and P_j will be located in logarithmic time. Let each vertex P_k ($k = \overline{1, n}$) of the convex hull be associated with an

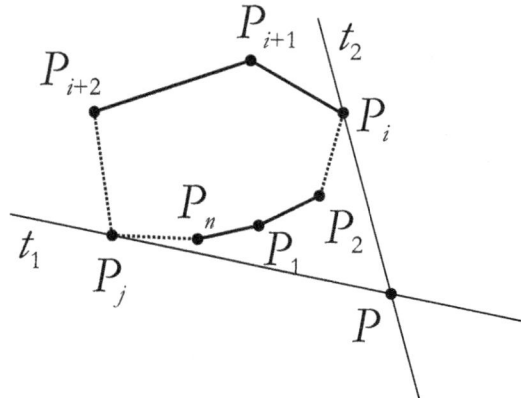

Figure 4.12: Construction of tangents from the point P to the convex polygon $\mathscr{P}$.

angle $\alpha_k = \angle(\overrightarrow{PP_1}, \overrightarrow{PP_k})$, representing the angle between the vectors (oriented segments) $\overrightarrow{PP_1}$ and $\overrightarrow{PP_k}$, respectively. The angles α_k can be positive or negative, and depending on that, different scenarios may occur. To begin with, suppose all angles are positive. This will happen only if the vertices P_i and P_1 form equal angles with the positive part of the x-axis. In that case, the vertex P_j corresponds to the largest angle among all the angles. To find the point P_j, or more precisely the index j, it is not necessary to search through all n indices; instead, it suffices to perform a binary search over $\log n$ indices. Namely, as the index k increases, the angles α_k initially increase up to $k = j$, and then they begin to decrease. Since binary search will be used, the midpoint $m = \lfloor \frac{n+2}{2} \rfloor$ is first determined for the search interval $[2, n]$. Then, the angles α_m and α_{m+1} are compared, leading to two possible cases:

a) $\alpha_{m+1} > \alpha_m$: in this case, the index k corresponding to the largest angle lies in the interval $[m+1, n]$;

b) $\alpha_{m+1} < \alpha_m$: the index k lies in the interval $[2, m]$.

In both cases, the search is narrowed to the identified interval, and the interval is repeatedly halved until an interval containing only a single index is obtained, that is, until the interval width becomes two (for example, the interval $[3, 5]$ has width 2 and contains the index 4). As soon as an interval of width two is obtained, the index k contained within it is the desired index j corresponding to the largest angle α_j. An entirely analogous procedure is applied when all angles are negative, which occurs when the vertices P_j and P_1 form equal angles with the positive part of the x-axis. In this case, the vertex P_i corresponds to the most negative angle among all angles, that is, the largest angle in absolute value. It remains to consider the case when the angles differ in sign. It is clear that there are two symmetric possibilities in which, as the index k increases, the angles α_k:

i) first increase, then decrease, and then increase again;

ii) first decrease, then increase, and then decrease again.

In the first case, the vertices are traversed in the clockwise direction, while in the second case, they are traversed in the counterclockwise direction. In both cases, binary search is used to find two adjacent vertices corresponding to angles of opposite signs. These two vertices divide the index interval into two subintervals, such that all positive angles are contained in one subinterval and all negative angles in the other. Using the previously described method, the vertex P_i is found from one of these subintervals, and the vertex P_j from the other. It is important to emphasize at this point that, instead of explicitly calculating the angles α_k, one can use the method *classification_m*$(\cdot, \cdot)$ from the **Point2D** class, similarly to the implementation of the *gift_wrapping*$(\cdot, \cdot)$ function used for realizing Jarvis's algorithm.

■

The new implementation of the incremental algorithm with time complexity $\Theta(n \log n)$ is provided in Listing 4.8. Based on the content of the mentioned listing, it can be seen that the initial sorting requires, in the worst case, $\Theta(n \log n)$ time, while the methods *split*($\cdot$) and *insert*($\cdot$) take constant time $\mathcal{O}(1)$, precisely because the points of the hull are stored in a doubly linked circular list. Finally, the time required to find all the tangents for $n - 2$ points amounts to $\Theta(n \log n)$. Therefore, the overall time complexity of the mentioned approach is $\Theta(n \log n)$.

Listing 4.8: Fast Incremental Algorithm for Convex Hull Construction.

```python
def fast_incremental_algorithm(points: list[Point2D]) -> Polygon:
    n = len(points);
    if n<3: return None
    s_points=sorted(points,key=lambda p:(p[0],p[1]))
    p = Polygon(); p.insert(s_points[0]); p.insert(s_points[1])
    for i in range(2, n):
        if s_points[i]==s_points[i-1]: continue
        p.tangent(s_points[i], TypeP2.LEFT) # Compute lower tangent
        v=p.current_vertex()
        p.tangent(s_points[i], TypeP2.RIGHT)# Compute upper tangent
        p.split(v)
        p.insert(s_points[i]); p.update_current(p.current_vertex().clockwise())
    return p
```

4.1.7 QuickHull Algorithm

In this section, a recursive algorithm for finding the convex hull is introduced for the first time, which bears significant similarity to the Quicksort algorithm used for sorting numbers. Inspired by the Quicksort algorithm, A. Bykat and W. Eddy were the first to propose the recursive Quickhull algorithm for determining the convex hull in 1978 [16]. It is well known that after computing the convex hull of a given set of points, in most cases, nearly 90% of the points located inside the hull can be discarded. In the context of the Quickhull algorithm, this means that it is crucial to focus on the points near the edges of the convex hull, while the remaining points can be ignored. To achieve this, the first phase of the Quickhull algorithm begins by sorting the set of points $\mathscr{P}$. Without loss of generality, let the points be sorted by their x-coordinates in ascending order (see Fig. 4.13). After sorting, the first and the last points from $\mathscr{P}$, denoted as A and B, represent the extreme points of the hull. The line containing the segment $\overline{AB}$ divides the set $\mathscr{P}$ into two subsets. The points above this line (i.e., to the left of the segment $\overline{AB}$) form the upper hull, while the points below the line (i.e., to the right of the segment $\overline{AB}$) form the lower hull. The entire convex hull is obtained as the union of these two hulls. The procedure for determining the upper and lower convex hulls is described in detail below. To determine the upper convex hull, the first step is to find the farthest vertex of the polygon that lies to the left of the segment $\overline{AB}$, that is, to the left of the vector $\overrightarrow{AB}$. The distance of that vertex is measured relative to the segment $\overline{AB}$. The search for this vertex, performed in $\mathcal{O}(n)$ time, is implemented within the method *farthest_vertex*($\cdot,\cdot$) of class **Polygon**, whose implementation is given below:

```python
def farthest_vertex(self,s: Segment2D, direc: int) -> Optional[Vertex]:
    if s[0]==self.neighbor(1).vertex_point(): return None
    else:
        max_dist=-1; v=v1=None # v1 is the most distant vertex
        while True:
            v = self.move_current(1)
            if v.vertex_point() == s[0]: break
```

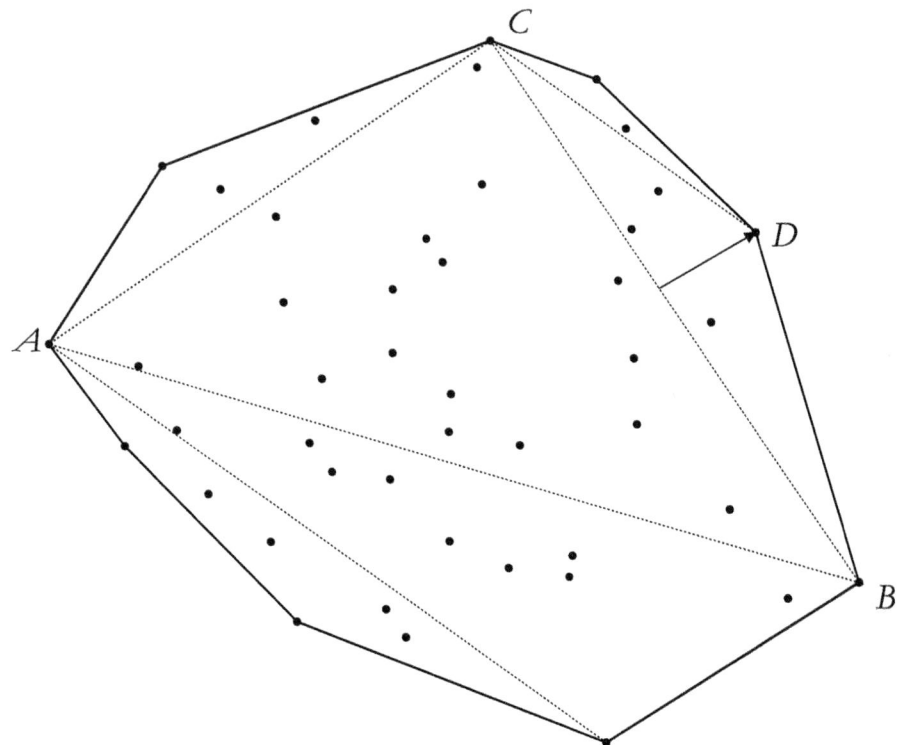

Figure 4.13: The arrangement of the points of the set $\mathscr{P}$ after sorting.

```
8        d=(v.vertex_point()).distance(s)
9        orien=(v.vertex_point()).orientation(s[0],s[1])
10       if (direc==TypeP2.LEFT and orien> 0 and d>max_dist): max_dist=d; v1=v
11       elif (direc==TypeP2.RIGHT and orien<0 and d>max_dist): max_dist=d;v1=v
12    return v1
```

By invoking the above method, the farthest vertex of the polygon relative to the segment passed as a formal parameter is determined. In Fig. 4.13, this vertex is marked as C relative to the segment $\overline{AB}$. After identifying vertex C, all points inside the triangle $\triangle ABC$ are discarded and no longer considered. Instead, the algorithm is recursively applied to the remaining points located to the left of the vectors $\overrightarrow{AC}$ and $\overrightarrow{CB}$. To enable the recursive search for points situated to the left of a given vector, it is necessary to implement an appropriate procedure. The implementation of the function $q\_hull(\cdot,\cdot,\cdot,\cdot,\cdot)$, whose working principle fully corresponds to the described process, is provided below:

```
1 def q_hull(pol: Polygon, hull: Polygon, a: Vertex, b: Vertex, direc: int):
2     s = Segment2D(a.vertex_point(), b.vertex_point())
3     c = pol.farthest_vertex(s, direc)
4     if c is None:
5         if direc == TypeP2.LEFT: hull.insert(a.vertex_point())
6         else: hull.insert(b.vertex_point())
7     else:
8         if direc == TypeP2.LEFT:
9             pol.update_current(b); q_hull(pol, hull, c, b, direc)
10            pol.update_current(c); q_hull(pol, hull, a, c, direc)
11        else:  # direction == TypeP2.RIGHT
12            pol.update_current(a); q_hull(pol, hull, a, c, direc)
13            pol.update_current(c); q_hull(pol, hull, c, b, direc)
```

From the function $q\_hull(\cdot,\cdot,\cdot,\cdot,\cdot)$, it is clear that if there are no points to the left of a given vector, the recursion terminates, and the extreme point is returned as a vertex of the convex hull. In Fig. 4.13, since there are no points to the left of the vector $\overrightarrow{DB}$, the algorithm returns the point D, thereby signaling the end of the corresponding recursive branch. When all extreme points are identified through this procedure, connecting them forms the upper convex hull. The lower convex hull is constructed analogously, with the only difference being that in this case, the points located to the right of the vector are considered. The implementation of the function $convex\_hull\_qh(\cdot)$ is provided below:

```python
def convex_hull_qh(points: list[Point2D]) -> Polygon:
    n = len(points)
    if n < 3: return None
    sorted_points = sorted(points, key=lambda p: (p[0], p[1]))
    p = Polygon(); q = Polygon() # create initial polygon p and hull q
    for pt in sorted_points: p.insert(pt)
    b = p.current_vertex(); a = p.neighbor(-1)
    q_hull(p, q, a, b, TypeP2.LEFT)   # upper hull
    p.update_current(b)
    q_hull(p, q, a, b, TypeP2.RIGHT) # lower hull
    return q
```

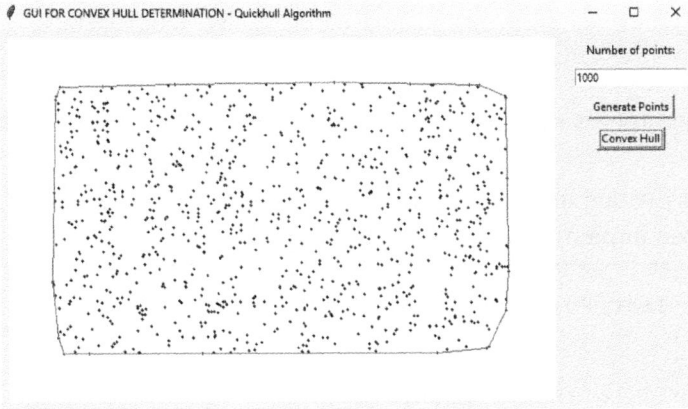

Figure 4.14: Application of the QuickHull algorithm for finding the convex hull of 1000 random points.

Based on the previously defined functions, it can be easily shown that the complexity of finding the convex hull, in the best case, is $\mathcal{O}(n\log n)$. In general, the time complexity of the QuickHull algorithm consists of the time required for sorting the points, along with an additional pseudo-linear factor nh, where $h \ll n$. This algorithm can be generalized to determine the convex hull of points in higher-dimensional spaces, which will be described in more detail below. Figure 4.14 shows the graphical interface of the QuickHull algorithm for computing the convex hull, implemented in the Python programming language.

4.1.8 Mergehull Algorithm

Researchers F. P. Preparata and S. J. Hong proposed the recursive Mergehull algorithm for finding the convex hull in 1977 [147]. This algorithm is fundamentally based on the work of the well-known recursive Mergesort algorithm for sorting numbers. It is known that the Mergesort algorithm uses the **divide and conquer** strategy, which has proven to be very effective in solving difficult problems in computer science. As is well known, the principle of this technique is based on dividing a problem into two subproblems of approximately equal size, solving each of them recursively, and then combining their solutions to form a complete solution. The Mergehull algorithm for finding the convex hull of a set of n given planar points is described below. Without loss of generality, it is initially assumed that there are no degenerate cases, such as point collinearity or all points lying on a vertical line. This algorithm can be described in four steps. In the first step, the points are sorted by their x-coordinate. In the second step, the sorted points are divided into two sets, $\mathscr{A}$ and $\mathscr{B}$, such that the left set $\mathscr{A}$ contains the first $\lceil \frac{n}{2} \rceil$ points, while the right set $\mathscr{B}$ contains the remaining $\lfloor \frac{n}{2} \rfloor$ points. In the third step, the convex hulls of sets A and B are computed recursively. In the final step, the convex hull of the original set is determined by merging the recursively computed hulls in $\mathcal{O}(n)$ time. Steps two, three, and four are repeated as long as the number of points in the sets is greater than one. During the merging process, the right chain is removed from the left set $\mathscr{A}$, and the left chain is removed from the right set $\mathscr{B}$, as illustrated in Fig. 4.15. Afterward, the two sets are merged using the upper and lower tangents, which are guaranteed to exist, since the sets $\mathscr{A}$ and $\mathscr{B}$ are mutually disjoint due to the sorting performed in the first step.

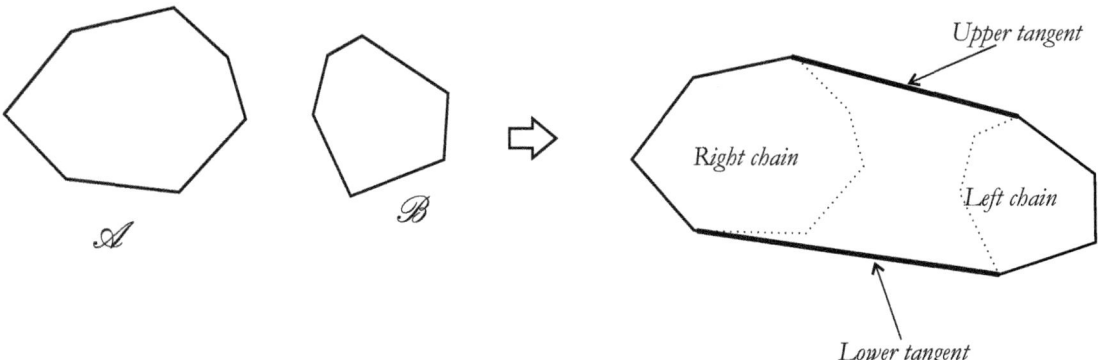

Figure 4.15: The process of merging the left and right hulls in the Mergehull algorithm.

The initial set of points is divided into two approximately equal subsets, $\mathscr{A}$ and $\mathscr{B}$, by calling the recursive function *m_hull* ($\cdot$), whose implementation is provided below:

```
def m_hull(points: list[Point2D]) -> Polygon:
    n = len(points)
    if n==1 or n==2:
        q = Polygon(); q.insert(points[0])
        if n==2: q.insert(points[1])
        return copy.deepcopy(q)
    else:
        m = n // 2
        A = m_hull(points[:m]); B = m_hull(points[m:])
        return copy.deepcopy(A.merge(B)) #join polygon A with polygon B
```

As shown in the previous function, the member function *merge*($\cdot$) of the **Polygon** class is used to merge the recursively computed hulls, and its implementation can be carried out in the following way:

```
def merge(self, B: 'Polygon') -> 'Polygon':
    vA=self.find_vertex(lambda b,a:-1 if a<b else (1 if a>b else 0))#rightmost pt.
    vB=B.find_vertex(lambda a,b:-1 if a<b else (1 if a>b else 0)) #leftmost pt.
    self.tangent_points(B, False) #upper tangent
    a1 = self.current; b1 = B.current
    self.update_current(vA); B.update_current(vB)
    self.tangent_points(B, True) #lower tangent
    a2 = self.current; b2 = B.current
    # Split and connect
    self.update_current(a1); p1=self.split(b1)
```

```
11      B.update_current(b2); p2 = B.split(a2)
12      return B # Finally, connect both parts
```

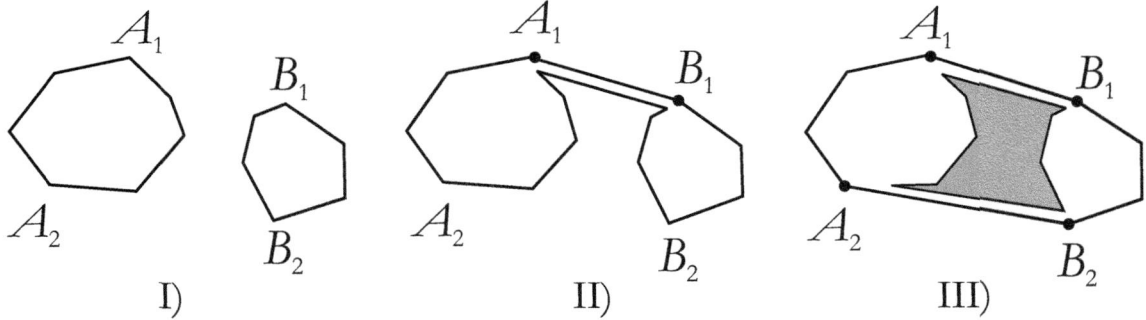

A_1 B_1 A_1 B_1 A_1 B_1

A_2 A_2 A_2

B_2 B_2 B_2

I)   II)   III)

Figure 4.16: The process of determining the tangent points in the Mergehull algorithm.

In the implemented *merge*(·) method, the method *tangent_points*(·,·) of the **Polygon** class is called, which is used to determine the endpoints of the upper and lower tangents drawn to the recursively computed convex hulls $\mathscr{A}$ and $\mathscr{B}$. Once the tangent points for the upper and lower tangents are identified, the chains are removed and the hulls are merged. This process is graphically illustrated in Fig. 4.16. As can be seen in step II), the upper tangent partially connects the left and right subpolygons (hulls), while in step III), after the lower tangent is found, the left and right subpolygons, that is, the hulls, are merged. During this merging, the part of the polygon shaded in gray is eliminated from the hull. Therefore, the implementation of the *tangent_points*(·,·) method is as follows:

```
1 def tangent_points(self, B: 'Polygon', upper: bool) -> tuple:
2     t = 0 if not upper else 1 # t denotes the type of a tangent
3     orientation = [TypeP2.LEFT, TypeP2.RIGHT]
4     while True:
5         vA = self.current_vertex(); vB = B.current_vertex()
6         self.tangent(B.point_of_current(), orientation[1 - t])
7         B.tangent(self.point_of_current(), orientation[t])
8         if vA == self.current_vertex() and vB == B.current_vertex(): break
```

The implementation of the *convex_hull_mh*(·) function used to compute the convex hull is provided below:

```
1 def convex_hull_mh(points: list[Point2D]) -> Polygon:
2     s_points = sorted(points, key=lambda p: (p[0], p[1]))  # lexicographic sorting
3     return m_hull(s_points)
```

In conclusion, it is necessary to determine the time complexity $T(n)$ required to find the convex hull for a set consisting of n points. Since merging the subsets, that is, the convex hulls $\mathscr{A}$ and $\mathscr{B}$, requires $\Theta(n)$ time in the worst case, the total time needed to compute the entire convex hull can be obtained by solving the following recurrence relation:

$$T(n) = 2T\left(\frac{n}{2}\right) + an, \quad n > 3, \tag{4.1}$$

where a is a constant. Solving this recurrence shows that the total running time of the algorithm is $\Theta(n \log n)$. It is also important to note that Preparata and Hong extended the Mergehull algorithm to handle the case of points given in higher-dimensional spaces. The graphical interface of the Mergehull algorithm for computing the convex hull, implemented within the Python environment, is illustrated in Fig. 4.17.

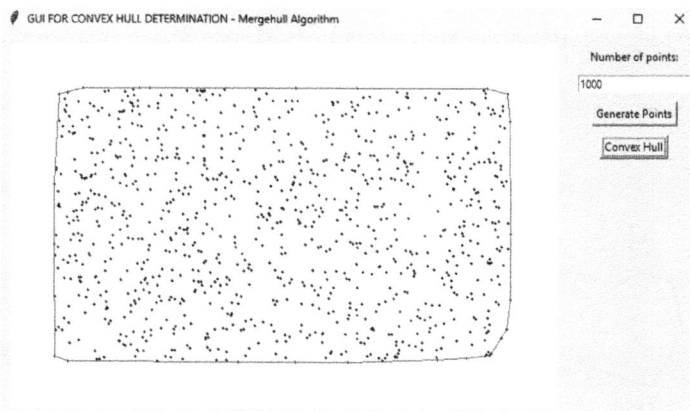

Figure 4.17: The convex hull found using the Mergehull algorithm for 1000 random points.

4.1.9　Chan's Algorithm

In 1993, Timothy M. Chan developed a highly efficient algorithm for finding the convex hull, which he named the **Chan's Algorithm** [36]. This algorithm represents a combination of Jarvis's algorithm, Graham's algorithm, and the binary search algorithm. Chan's algorithm invokes both of these algorithms as subroutines over certain subsets of points with the goal of achieving a running time of order $\Theta(n \log h)$, where h is the number of points lying on the convex hull. The algorithm consists of two phases. Before describing these phases, it is necessary to first find an extreme point (for example, the leftmost point among all points) from the initial set of points P_l $(l = 1, 2, \cdots, n)$, which is then inserted into the desired hull C_H. Let this point be P_i, so that the current state of the convex hull becomes $C_H = \{P_i\}$. Following this, the first phase of the algorithm begins, in which the input set of points is divided into $K = \left\lceil \frac{n}{m} \right\rceil$ groups Q_k $(k = 1, 2, \cdots, K)$ such that each group Q_k contains at most m points. Thus, if the number n is divisible by m, then $K = \frac{n}{m}$; otherwise, $K = \frac{n}{m} + 1$. For each group Q_k, the convex hull C_k is computed using Graham's algorithm in $\Theta(m \log m)$ time. Since there are K groups, the complexity of this phase is of order $\Theta(K \cdot (m \log m)) = \Theta(n \log m)$. In the second phase, Jarvis's algorithm is applied to the computed convex hulls C_k $(k = 1, 2, \cdots, K)$ to find the convex hull of the original set of points. Following a procedure similar to Jarvis's algorithm, among the K groups, the point P_j is found such that all points of the original set lie to the right of the segment $\overline{P_i P_j}$. To find the point P_j in $\Theta(K \log m)$ time, it is necessary to find tangents from it to the K convex hulls C_k and select the one that maximizes the angle $\angle(P_{i-1}, P_i, P_j)$. Typically, at the beginning, for the previous point P_{i-1} of the leftmost point P_i, the point $(P_i.x, -10^5)$ is used. Once the point P_j is found, the state of the desired convex hull becomes $C_H = \{P_i, P_j\}$. A graphical illustration of this procedure is shown in Fig. 4.18, where it is assumed that two convex hull points P_{i_1} and P_{i_2} have already been found, and the next convex hull point P_{i_3} is being sought.

Using binary search from the point P_{i_2}, all tangents are found relative to the computed groups of convex hulls (In Fig. 4.18, four groups ($K = 4$) of convex hulls are shown, where $m = 5$ and $n = 19$). Among them, the tangent that maximizes the angle $\alpha = \angle(P_{i_1}, P_{i_2}, P_{i_3})$ is selected, where P_{i_3} is a vertex of some convex hull C_k through which the tangent passes. It is important to note that binary search can be applied to the convex hulls C_k, since they are obtained using Graham's algorithm, and thus all vertices of C_k are oriented either in the counterclockwise or clockwise direction, depending on the implementation of Graham's algorithm. Since the number of groups is K, and each group contains at most m elements, and given that a tangent can be constructed from an arbitrary point in logarithmic time, it follows that the complexity of finding the next convex hull point, that is, the point P_j, is proportional to $\Theta(K \log m)$. Analogous to Jarvis's algorithm, starting from the point P_j, the next point of the convex hull is found in the same manner as the previous point P_j. It is known that Jarvis's algorithm completes after at most h steps by finding the convex hull. Therefore, the complexity of the second phase is of order $\Theta(hK \log m)$,

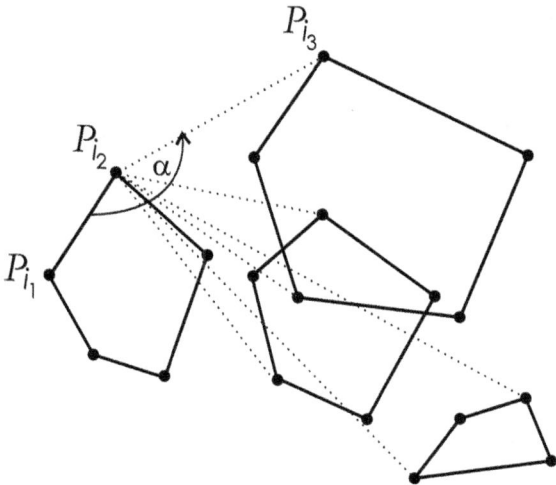

Figure 4.18: The process of finding tangents in Chan's algorithm.

since finding a single vertex of the convex hull requires $\Theta(K \log m)$, and the total number of convex hull vertices is h. Thus, the time complexity $\Theta(hK \log m)$ is equivalent to $\Theta(n \log m)$ if the number m is chosen to be very close to h. If the number h were known in advance, it would be possible to set $m = h$, and in that case, the complexity of Chan's algorithm would be of order $\Theta(n \log h)$. However, since the number h is not known at the beginning, it is necessary to find a strategy for selecting m such that the overall complexity remains proportional to $\Theta(n \log m)$. If the number m is chosen randomly, then for $m < h$, the algorithm would fail to find all the convex hull points — that is, the hull would not be successfully found, even though $\Theta(n \log m)$ time would be consumed. To preserve the algorithm's complexity, it is shown that the *quadratic strategy* is the appropriate approach for selecting the number m. Initially (iteration $t = 0$), the number m is set to two, and then in each t-th iteration, the number m is chosen as follows:

$$m = \min(n, 2^{2^t}).$$

With the number m chosen in this way, at most $\Theta(\log \log h)$ iterations are performed. In other words, the algorithm terminates as soon as the number of passes, that is, the number of iterations t, becomes greater than or equal to $\log \log h$. This directly follows from the following inequality:

$$m = 2^{2^t} \geq h \Leftrightarrow \log 2^{2^t} \geq \log h \Leftrightarrow 2^t \geq \log h \Leftrightarrow \log 2^t \geq \log \log h \Leftrightarrow t \geq \log \log h.$$

The last inequality indicates that the first phase of the algorithm must be executed at least $\lceil \log \log h \rceil$ times in order to find the convex hull of the entire set. Since the time complexity of the first part of the algorithm is of order $\Theta(n \log m)$, and the number m is chosen as $m = \min(n, 2^{2^t})$, it follows that the total time complexity of the first part can be calculated as follows:

$$\Theta\left(\sum_{t=0}^{\lceil \log \log h \rceil} n \log 2^{2^t}\right) = \Theta\left(n \sum_{t=0}^{\lceil \log \log h \rceil} 2^t\right) = \Theta(n(2^{\lceil \log \log h \rceil + 1} - 1)).$$

Taking into account that for every real number r the inequality $\lceil r \rceil \leq r + 1$ holds, it is easy to show that holds:

$$2^{\lceil \log \log h \rceil + 1} - 1 \leq \log h + 1.$$

Based on the last inequality, it directly follows that $\Theta(n(2^{\lceil \log \log h \rceil + 1} - 1)) = \Theta(n \log h)$, that is, the time complexity of the first part is of order $\Theta(n \log h)$. Similarly, it can be shown that the second part of the algorithm has the same complexity as the first part, and therefore, the total complexity of the entire algorithm is proportional to $\Theta(n \log h)$. In the implementation of this algorithm, based on the operating principle of Jarvis's algorithm, Chan's algorithm terminates if, during the second phase, while processing the vertices of the convex hull (i.e., finding the maximal tangents), it returns to the first vertex (the leftmost point) of the convex hull, which was added at the very beginning just before the first phase of the algorithm. If the first element P_i of the convex hull is not reached, the value of m is updated, and the algorithm restarts from the first phase. Chan's algorithm can also be generalized for finding the convex hull in space, with the difference that, in the first phase, instead of using Graham's algorithm, the recursive Mergehull algorithm with time complexity $\Theta(n \log n)$ should be used. In this way, an algorithm of order $\Theta(n \log h)$ is obtained for finding the convex hull in space.

4.1.10 Akl–Toussaint Heuristic

The Akl–Toussaint heuristic was developed in 1978 by researchers S. G. Akl and G. G. Toussaint. It is used for preprocessing in the process of determining the convex hull. In the literature, it is known as the *Interior Elimination Method* [1]. Unlike other techniques, this heuristic does not directly find the convex hull for a given set of n points; instead, it efficiently eliminates points that do not participate in forming the convex hull. The time complexity of this heuristic is $\mathcal{O}(n)$. After eliminating points from the initial set, experimental results have shown that, on average, the number of remaining points is proportional to $\mathcal{O}(\sqrt{n})$, meaning that even a quadratic method for finding the convex hull would then have a time complexity of $\mathcal{O}(n)$. Thus, the average time complexity of a quadratic method using this heuristic for preprocessing is linear with respect to the number of points n in the initial set. If instead of a quadratic method, an algorithm such as Graham's algorithm or, even better, Chan's algorithm is used, then in combination with the mentioned heuristic, the expected running time in most cases is $\mathcal{O}(n)$, that is, linear. Of course, this does not hold for all cases: if the initial points are such that (lying on the convex hull) no points can be eliminated after applying the heuristic, then the total running time remains $\Theta(n \log h)$ when Chan's algorithm is used for finding the convex hull.

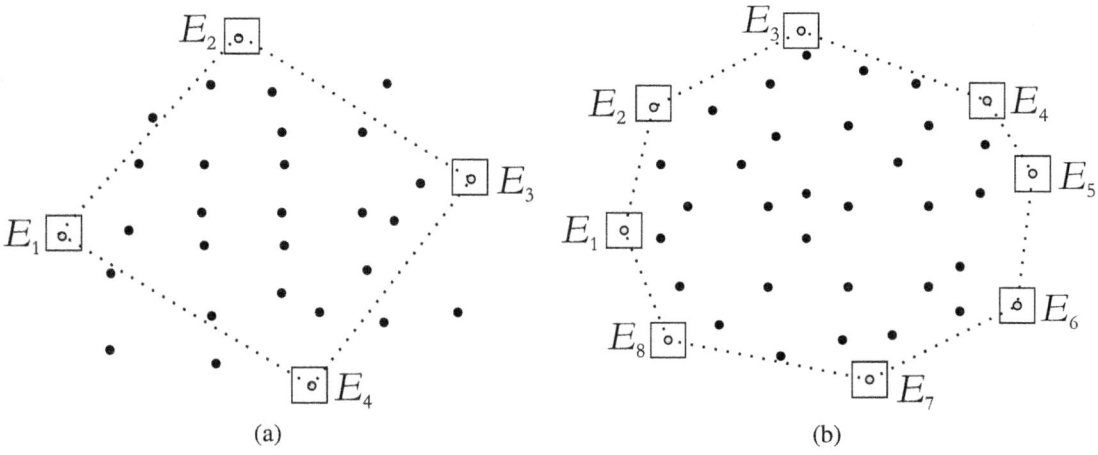

Figure 4.19: Finding four or eight extreme points.

The main idea of the aforementioned heuristic is based on identifying extreme points. It is already known that there are four such points E_1, E_2, E_3, and E_4, i.e., the points with the smallest and largest x-coordinates or y-coordinates, as shown in Fig. 4.19 (a). It is not difficult to observe that there are four additional such points (in Fig. 4.19 (b) these are the points E_2, E_4, E_6, and E_8) that form an angle of $\pm\frac{\pi}{4}$ with the x-axis. The first eight extreme points E_j $(j = 1, 2, \cdots, 8)$ can be determined from the initial set of points

P_i $(i = 1, 2, \cdots, n)$ by checking whether the following condition is satisfied

$$\alpha_k \cdot P_i[0] + \beta_k P_i[1] < \alpha_k \cdot E_k[0] + \beta_k E_k[1] \quad (\forall i \in \{1, 2, \cdots, n\})(\forall k \in \{1, 2, \cdots, 8\}),$$

where the coefficients α_k and β_k take values from the sets $A = \{1, 1, 0, -1, -1, -1, 0, 1\}$ and $B = \{0, 1, 1, 1, 0, -1, -1, -1\}$, respectively. Initially, all elements of the array E are initialized with the first element P_0 of the input set of points. Then, in $\mathcal{O}(n)$ time, all extreme points are found using the above condition, as implemented within the body of the function *eight_extreme_points*(·):

```
from typing import List
def eight_extreme_points(points: List['Point2D']) -> List['Point2D']:
    a = [1, 1, 0, -1, -1, -1, 0, 1]
    b = [0, 1, 1, 1, 0, -1, -1, -1]
    E = [points[0] for _ in range(8)]
    for k in range(8):
        for i in range(1, len(points)):
            if a[k]*points[i][0] + b[k]*points[i][1] < a[k]*E[k][0] + b[k]*E[k
                ][1]:E[k] = points[i]
    return E
```

It is not difficult to observe from the body of the function *eight_extreme_points*(·) that, for example, the leftmost point is determined when $k = 0$, that is, the entire input set of points is traversed, and the point with the smallest x-coordinate is assigned to E_0. Similarly, the rightmost point is found for $k = 4$. The lowest point is found for $k = 2$, while the highest point is found for $k = 6$. For the remaining values of k (1, 3, 5, 7), the other four extreme points are determined. Once the extreme points are found, the remaining $n - 8$ points located inside the convex polygon formed by the 8 extreme points can be eliminated in $\mathcal{O}(n)$ time. That is, for each of the $n - 8$ points, in the worst case, it is necessary to perform 8 checks to verify whether the given point lies on the same side of the polygon's sides. This process can be further accelerated by using binary search, in which case only 3 checks are required per point. Therefore, the total number of checks will be either $8 \cdot (n - 8)$ or $3 \cdot (n - 8)$, both of which are of order $\mathcal{O}(n)$. By invoking the function *eight_extreme_points*(·), a new set of points can be created from the original set, consisting only of points lying outside the convex hull formed by the extreme points. As previously mentioned, this resulting set is significantly smaller compared to the original set. The following function demonstrates the above principle:

```
def transform_points(points: List['Point2D']) -> List['Point2D']:
    extreme_points=eight_extreme_points(points)
    extreme_hull=Polygon()
    for i in range(0,8): extreme_hull.insert(extreme_points[i])
    remaining_points = [p for p in points if not extreme_hull.contains_point(p)]
    for i in range(0,8): remaining_points.append(extreme_points[i])
    return remaining_points
```

4.1.11 Performance Evaluation of Convex Hull Algorithms

In computational geometry, the efficiency of an algorithm is commonly assessed through its theoretical complexity. However, practical performance may be influenced by various factors such as implementation details, memory access patterns, and the structure of input data. Consequently, an empirical evaluation is deemed essential to observe how convex hull algorithms perform under varying input sizes and configurations. In this section, a comparative analysis is conducted for several classical convex hull algorithms, whose theoretical aspects have already been addressed in detail. Each algorithm has been previously implemented, and for some, illustrative examples demonstrating their behavior on specific datasets have been provided. To ensure fair benchmarking, a single randomly generated dataset of a given size is used for all algorithms, and their execution times are measured on that identical dataset in seconds.

Table 4.1: Execution time (in seconds) for different convex hull algorithms based on input size.

Algorithm	100 pts	1,000 pts	10,000 pts	100,000 pts	1,000,000 pts
Gift Wrapping	0.0043	0.0524	0.6116	6.9300	53.2322
Graham Scan	0.0012	0.0059	0.0634	0.7136	9.2863
Andrew's Algorithm	0.0013	0.0075	0.0887	0.9505	10.1940
Incremental	0.0106	0.1299	1.0373	10.7481	105.7080
QuickHull	0.0261	0.3252	2.4422	9.4663	56.2185
MergeHull	0.0092	0.0802	0.7749	7.1469	54.0548

The performance analysis presented in Table 4.1 highlights substantial differences in the efficiency of six convex hull algorithms, depending on the size of the input point set. Among the evaluated methods, *Graham Scan* and *Andrew's Algorithm* consistently exhibited the best performance. Even for input sizes of up to 1,000,000 points, their execution times remained below 11 seconds, validating their theoretical time complexity of $\mathcal{O}(n\log n)$. Notably, *Graham Scan* achieved the lowest execution time across nearly all input sizes. In contrast, the *Gift Wrapping* algorithm displayed significantly slower growth, consistent with its $\mathcal{O}(nh)$ complexity. For example, with 1,000,000 input points, its runtime reached 53.2 seconds—several times higher than that of Graham Scan. The *Incremental* algorithm demonstrated moderate efficiency on smaller inputs but revealed scalability issues as input size increased. While its performance for 100,000 points was acceptable (10.7 seconds), the execution time increased dramatically to 105.7 seconds for 1,000,000 points, suggesting a practical time complexity between $\mathcal{O}(n\log n)$ and $\mathcal{O}(n^2)$. *QuickHull* delivered reasonable results for small and mid-sized datasets but was ultimately outperformed by *Graham Scan* and *Andrew's Algorithm* on larger inputs. A similar trend is observed for *MergeHull*, which performed efficiently up to 10,000 points, but its runtime increased notably with input size, reaching over 54 seconds for 1,000,000 points. Figure 4.20 presents a graph based on the tabular data, illustrating the comparative performance analysis of the aforementioned algorithms.

It is important to emphasize that when the Akl–Toussaint heuristic (ATH) is applied as a preprocessing step—particularly in combination with the *QuickHull* and *MergeHull* algorithms—the execution time is nearly halved. This improvement is especially evident in the case of 1,000,000 input points, where the *QuickHull+ATH* algorithm completes in 33.9445 seconds, and the *MergeHull+ATH* algorithm requires only 34.4812 seconds.

4.2   Algorithms in the Three-Dimensional Case

This section introduces and implements algorithms for computing the convex hull in three-dimensional space. Since a convex hull in 3D is, by definition, a convex polyhedron—i.e., a geometric solid determined by a set of points in space—it is necessary to define the following concepts: *polyhedron*, *faces of a polyhedron*, *edges of a polyhedron*, and *diagonal of a polyhedron*. These definitions apply strictly to finite polyhedra, as infinite polyhedra are not considered in this textbook.

Definition 4.2.1 A *polyhedron* is a geometric solid bounded by a finite number of polygons, which are referred to as the *faces of the polyhedron*. The line segments where two adjacent faces meet are called the *edges of the polyhedron*, while the points where adjacent edges intersect are known as the *vertices of the polyhedron*. A line segment connecting two vertices of the polyhedron that does not lie on any of its faces is called a *diagonal of the polyhedron*.

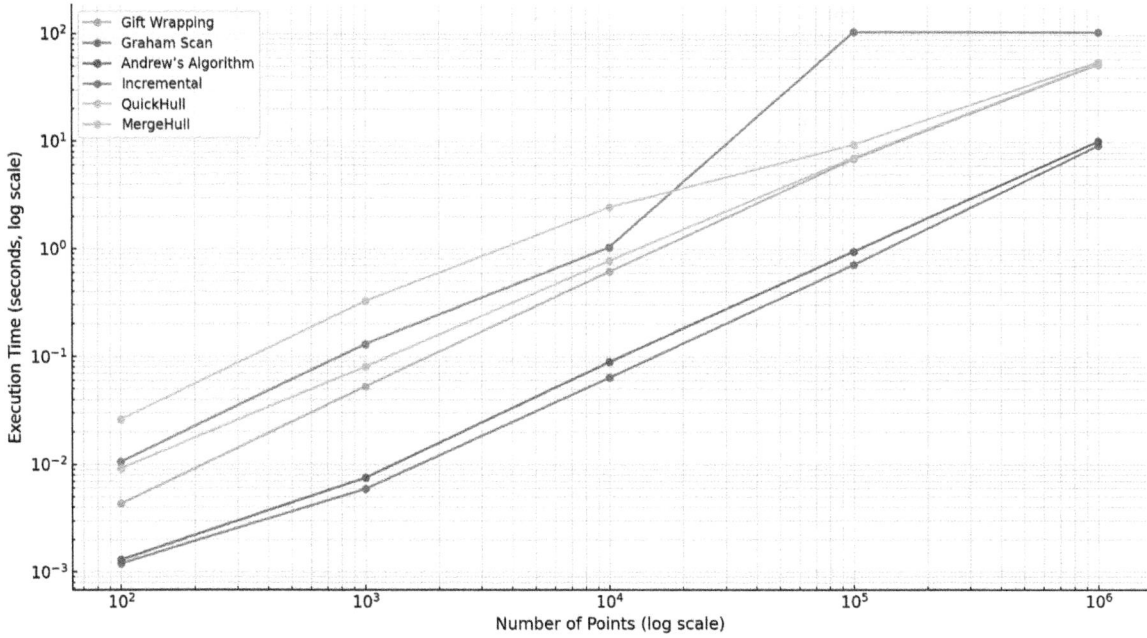

Figure 4.20: Execution Time of Convex Hull Algorithms.

A polyhedron is visualized as a region of space whose boundary consists of a finite number of polygonal faces, where any two faces are either disjoint or share a common edge or vertex. Polyhedra can be either convex or concave [143, 147]. In convex polyhedra, all diagonals lie entirely within the solid itself, whereas this is not the case for concave polyhedra (see Fig. 4.21 (b)).

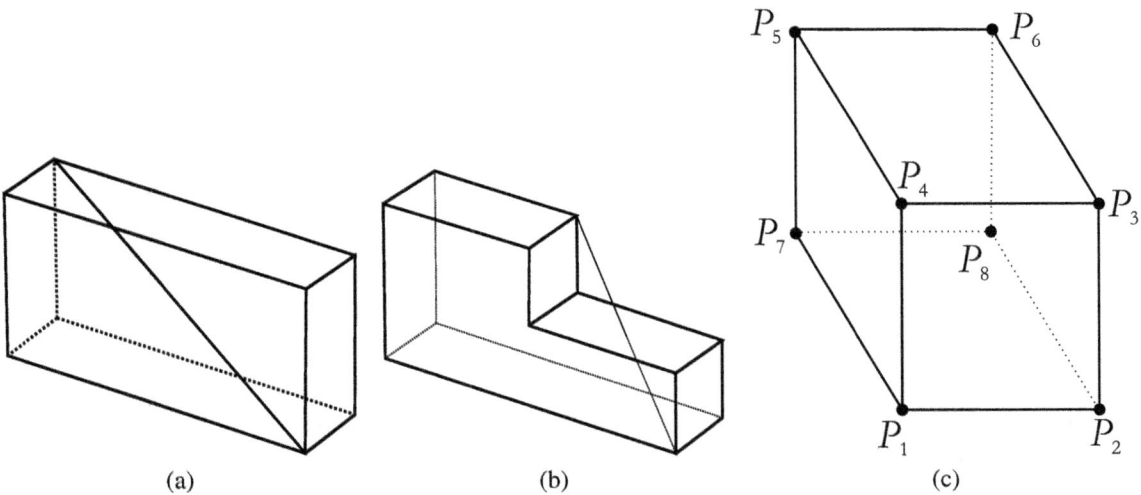

Figure 4.21: (a) Convex polyhedron. (b) Concave polyhedron. (c) Wireframe model of a cube.

Polyhedra are fundamental geometric objects that are widely used for modeling spatial structures, analogous to how polygons are exploited for approximating shapes in the plane. Like polygons, polyhedra also have vertices (i.e., points in space). However, unlike polygons, a polyhedron cannot be described simply by an ordered list of vertices in which each vertex has exactly two neighbors (a previous and a next vertex). In polyhedra, a single vertex may be adjacent to many others, making it impossible to represent the connectivity of the structure using only a linear ordering of vertices. Therefore, more complex data structures than a simple vertex list are required to describe polyhedra. In particular, additional information is needed to specify how the vertices are connected. The approach to modeling a polyhedron largely depends on how it is to be visualized in two dimensions—i.e., what exactly is intended to be displayed on the screen or paper as the result of the visualization process. The simplest models used for this purpose are known as *wireframe models*, which represent a polyhedron as a set of edges. According to this model, the polyhedron is defined solely by its edges, while its faces are considered transparent, meaning that they do not obscure the view of other elements. As a result, all edges are assumed to be visible, with no hidden lines. Visualizing wireframe models is relatively straightforward. All that is required is to transform each edge from three-dimensional (3D) space into two-dimensional (2D) space using projection techniques (the transformation of an edge effectively reduces to transforming its endpoints), and then draw the resulting line segments. Since projection produces logical coordinates in the 2D plane, these coordinates must be further converted into physical coordinates corresponding to the output medium (e.g., a screen) before actual rendering takes place. Figure 4.21 (c) shows a wireframe model of a cube, visualized using orthogonal projection. In general, planar geometric projections are employed when it is necessary to map higher-dimensional coordinates (e.g., from 3D space) into lower-dimensional representations (e.g., the 2D plane). Planar geometric projections are essentially performed by casting projection rays that originate from a designated *center of projection* **COP**), pass through all points of the object, and intersect the *view plane*, thereby forming a new projected shape within that plane. The two fundamental classes of planar projections are: *perspective projection* and *parallel projection*.

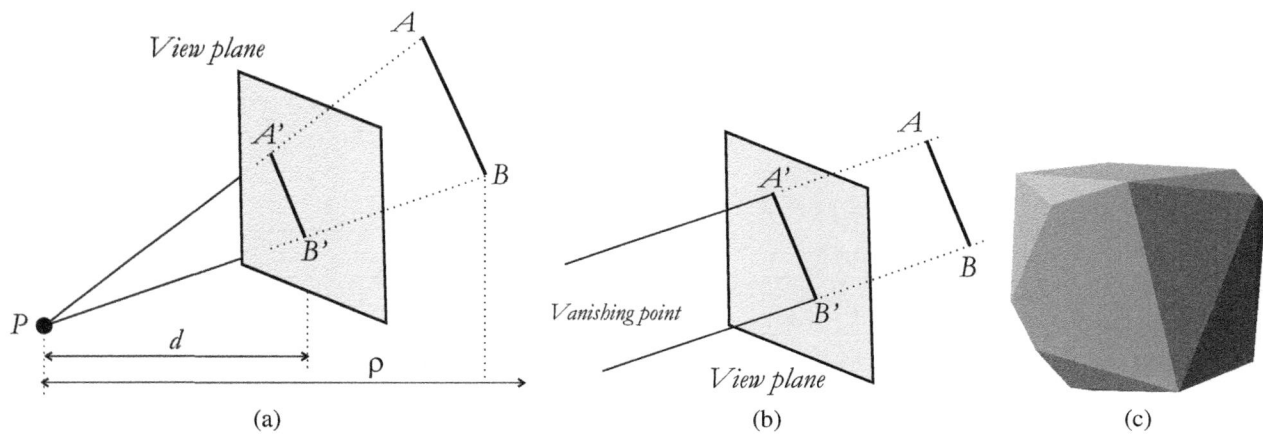

Figure 4.22: (a) Perspective projection of the segment $\overline{AB}$. (b) Parallel projection of the segment $\overline{AB}$. (c) 3D Convex hull.

In perspective projection, the *center of projection*, also referred to as the *view point*, and the *view plane* are located at a finite distance d (see Fig. 4.22(a)). In contrast, in parallel projection, the center of projection is assumed to be at infinity relative to the view plane (see Fig. 4.22(b)). Furthermore, the distance ρ between the view point P and the object being visualized (In Fig. 4.22(a), it is the segment $\overline{AB}$ in space) plays an important role. When the view point is positioned closer to the object, the projection appears more prominent and visually pronounced. On the other hand, if the view point is located far away from the object, the resulting perspective projection behaves similarly to a parallel projection (see Fig. 4.22 (b)). Additionally, the distance d from the view point to the view plane affects the relative scale of the projected image compared to the actual size of the object. If k denotes the relative scaling factor—$k > 1$ for magnification and $k < 1$ for reduction—then the distance d should be chosen as $d = k\rho$, where ρ is the approximate distance between the view point P and the object being visualized. A more detailed discussion on the analytical representation of projections and their application in convex hull algorithms in three-dimensional space will follow. The focus in the remainder of this chapter will be exclusively on convex polyhedra, which constitute a special case of convex polytopes in three-dimensional space. To precisely describe their properties and the algorithms for their construction, it is necessary to introduce foundational concepts from polytope theory, including: the *polytope* in d-dimensional space, the *face* of a polytope, and the *facet* of a polytope.

Definition 4.2.2 A *polytope* in d-dimensional space is a geometric object composed of a finite number of faces of various dimensions, such that each of its faces is itself a polytope of lower dimension. A *face of a polytope* is a maximal subset of coplanar points on its boundary. A *facet of a polytope* in d-dimensional space is a face of dimension $d - 1$.

Without loss of generality, only convex faces will be considered, since any concave face can be decomposed into multiple convex components. This is a well-known problem in computational geometry, often addressed through polygon triangulation, with the added requirement that adjacent faces remain coplanar. Figure 4.22 (c) shows a convex hull in 3D space constructed from 50 randomly distributed points on the surface of a sphere. The resulting hull consists of 144 edges and 96 faces, indicating that the number of vertices is significantly smaller than the number of edges. Unlike the planar case—where the number of edges for n points does not exceed n—in higher dimensions the relationships between vertices, edges, and faces are more complex. According to Euler's formula for polyhedra, $f + n = m + 2$, where n is the number of vertices, m the number of edges, and f the number of faces. For $n = 50$ and $m = 144$, this yields $f = 96$. Later, it will be shown that for arbitrary convex polyhedra, both the number of faces and edges grow linearly with the number of vertices n, leading to the following inequality:

$$m \leq 3n - 6, f \leq 2n - 4, \tag{4.2}$$

where equality holding in the case of convex polyhedra. Specifically, for a 3D convex hull composed of 758 vertices, we have $m = 3 \cdot 50 - 6 = 144$ and $f = 2 \cdot 50 - 4 = 96$. The following lemma provides a characterization of both the number of faces and the number of edges for a set of n given points in space.

Lemma 4.2.1 Let $\mathscr{P}$ be a polytope consisting of n vertices. Then the number of edges of the polytope is bounded above by $3n - 6$, and the number of faces is bounded above by $2n - 4$.

Proof. The proof of the lemma relies on Euler's formula, which holds for connected planar graphs consisting of n vertices. It is given by $f + n = m + 2$, where m is the number of edges in the graph and f is the number of simple closed contours in the graph. Since a polytope can be mapped onto the plane, its boundary can be interpreted as a planar graph (see Fig. 4.23). Therefore, Euler's formula can also be applied to polytopes. Interestingly, Euler's formula was originally formulated for polytopes and only later extended to planar graphs. In the general case—whether the polytope is convex or not—the following inequality holds: $2m \geq 3f$, because each contour (i.e., face of the polytope) must consist of at least three edges, and each edge in the graph is incident to exactly two faces. This inequality becomes an equality for polytopes in which every face is a triangle. An example of such a polytope is a tetrahedron (see Fig. 4.24 (a)), which has 6 edges and 4 faces, so $2 \cdot 6 = 3 \cdot 4$. From Euler's formula it follows that $f + n - 2 \geq \frac{3}{2}f$, which further implies $f \leq 2n - 4$. Analogously, one can show that $m \leq 3n - 6$. Indeed, from $f = m - n + 2 \leq 2n - 4$, it follows directly that $m \leq 3n - 6$. This completes the proof of the lemma. ∎

Based on Lemma 4.2.1, it follows that there exists a linear relationship between the number of vertices (n) of the polytope $\mathscr{P}$ and its number of edges (m) and faces (f). In other words, both the number of edges and the number of faces are of order $\mathscr{O}(n)$.

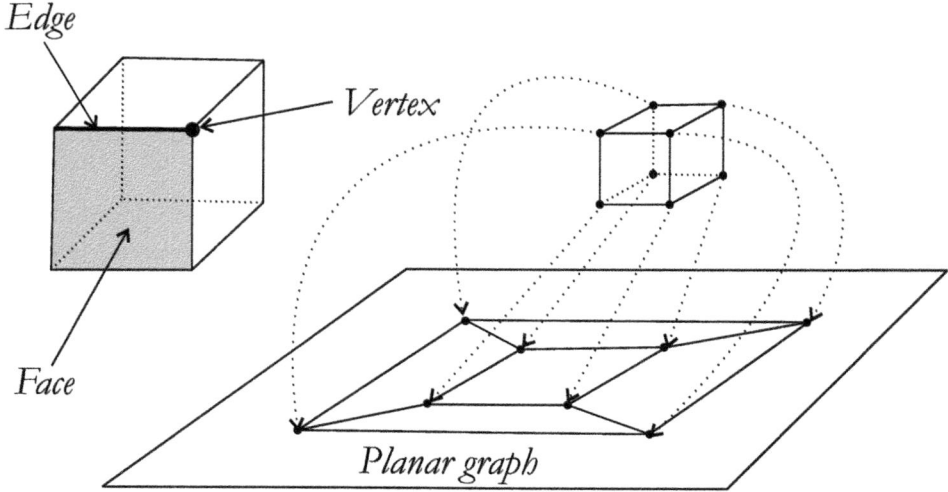

Figure 4.23: Projection of a convex polytope onto a planar graph.

4.2.1 Platonic Solids

This section introduces a special class of convex regular polyhedra, commonly known in the literature as *Platonic solids*. These solids are characterized by perfect regularity—all of their faces are congruent regular polygons, and all vertices are equivalent, meaning that the same configuration of faces and angles surrounds each vertex. It has been proven that exactly five such solids exist: the *tetrahedron*, *hexahedron*, *octahedron*, *dodecahedron*, and *icosahedron*. Their graphical representations, along with their corresponding planar realizations, are shown in Fig. 4.24, in parts (a) through (e), respectively. Before proceeding further, it is necessary to define the fundamental concepts of *regular polygons* and *regular polyhedra*, and to establish their connection to the Platonic solids [131].

Definition 4.2.3 A *regular polygon* is a convex geometric shape in which all sides have equal length and all interior angles are equal. A *regular polyhedron* is a convex polyhedron whose faces are congruent regular polygons. Moreover, each of its vertices has the same configuration of faces and dihedral angles, meaning that all vertices are equivalent.

Examples of regular polygons include the *equilateral triangle*, *square*, *regular pentagon*, and *regular hexagon*. Moreover, there are infinitely many regular polygons, as for every number of sides $n \geq 3$, there exists exactly one regular n-gon.

Definition 4.2.4 The *tetrahedron* is the first and simplest Platonic solid, as well as the simplest regular polytope. All of its faces are regular polygons—specifically, equilateral triangles—and each vertex is incident to exactly three faces. The tetrahedron has a total of four vertices, six edges, and four faces.

Definition 4.2.5 The *hexahedron* is the second Platonic solid. It has 8 vertices, 12 edges, and 6 faces, with each vertex being incident to 3 faces. Each face is a square. The hexahedron is also commonly known as the cube.

Definition 4.2.6 The *octahedron* is the third Platonic solid, consisting of 6 vertices, 12 edges, and 8 faces. Each vertex is incident to 4 faces, and each face has 3 sides.

Definition 4.2.7 The *dodecahedron* is the fourth Platonic solid. It has 20 vertices, 30 edges, and 12 faces, with each vertex being incident to 3 faces. Each face is a regular pentagon.

Definition 4.2.8 The *icosahedron* is the fifth Platonic solid, consisting of 12 vertices, 30 edges, and 20 faces. Each vertex is incident to 5 faces, and each face has 3 sides.

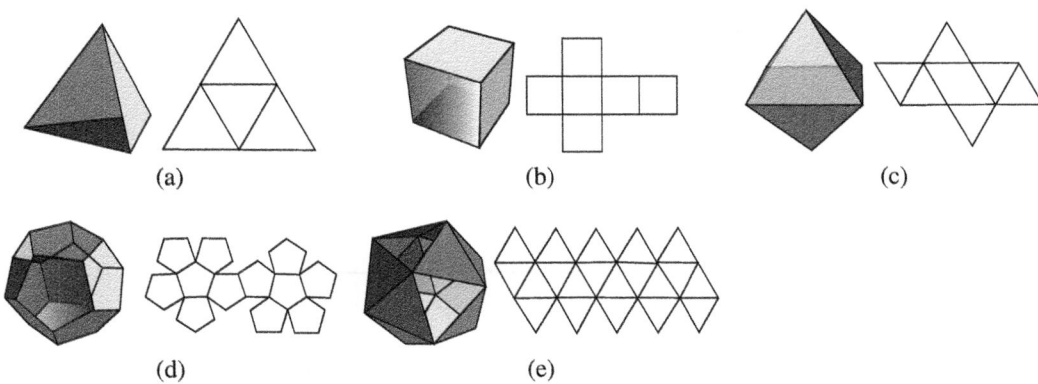

Figure 4.24: (a) Tetrahedron. (b) Hexahedron. (c) Octahedron. (d) Dodecahedron. (e) Icosahedron.

The following sections describe four well-known algorithms for computing the convex hull in three-dimensional space:

- **Naive Algorithm** – time complexity is of order $\mathcal{O}(n^4)$;
- **Gift Wrapping** – time complexity is proportional to $\mathcal{O}(n^2)$;
- **Incremental Algorithm** – time complexity is quadratic in the worst case;
- **Recursive Algorithm** – time complexity is proportional to $\Theta(n \log n)$.

In general, the time complexity of computing the convex hull in d dimensions is of order $\Omega(n^{\lfloor \frac{d}{2} \rfloor})$.

4.2.2 Naive Algorithm for 3D Convex Hull Construction

The naive algorithm for determining the convex hull in 3D space is based on the same idea as its planar counterpart, where the convex hull is constructed by identifying supporting planes, analogous to detecting extreme edges in the two-dimensional case. Let $\{P_1, P_2, \ldots, P_n\}$ be a set of n points in space, with the assumption that no four points are coplanar, i.e., no four of them lie in the same plane. Coplanarity of four points can be easily checked using the scalar triple product: it is sufficient to examine the sign of the volume of the tetrahedron defined by the corresponding position vectors. If the volume is zero, then the points lie in the same plane and are therefore coplanar. Moreover, every such triplet of non-coplanar points uniquely defines a plane. To compute the 3D convex hull, it is necessary to examine every ordered triplet of points (P_i, P_j, P_k) (with distinct indices i, j, and k) to determine whether the plane defined by those points is a supporting plane.

Definition 4.2.9 A plane π, defined by the points (P_i, P_j, P_k), is called a *supporting plane* if all remaining points P_l, for $l \notin \{i, j, k\}$, that do not lie on the plane π, are located on the same side of that plane.

It is well known that the sign of the area of a triangle is used to determine whether an edge in the plane is extreme—i.e., whether all points of the input set lie strictly on one side of that edge. A similar approach is applied in three-dimensional space, except that instead of considering the sign of a triangle's area, one examines the sign of the volume of a tetrahedron spanned by the non-coplanar vectors $\overrightarrow{P_iP_j}$, $\overrightarrow{P_iP_k}$, and $\overrightarrow{P_iP_l}$ (see Fig. 4.25). It is known that the volume of a tetrahedron is one-sixth the volume of the parallelepiped $\mathcal{V}$ formed by the vectors $\overrightarrow{P_iP_j}$, $\overrightarrow{P_iP_k}$, and $\overrightarrow{P_iP_l}$ as follows

$$V = \frac{1}{6} |(\overrightarrow{P_iP_j} \times \overrightarrow{P_iP_k}) \cdot \overrightarrow{P_iP_l}|. \tag{4.3}$$

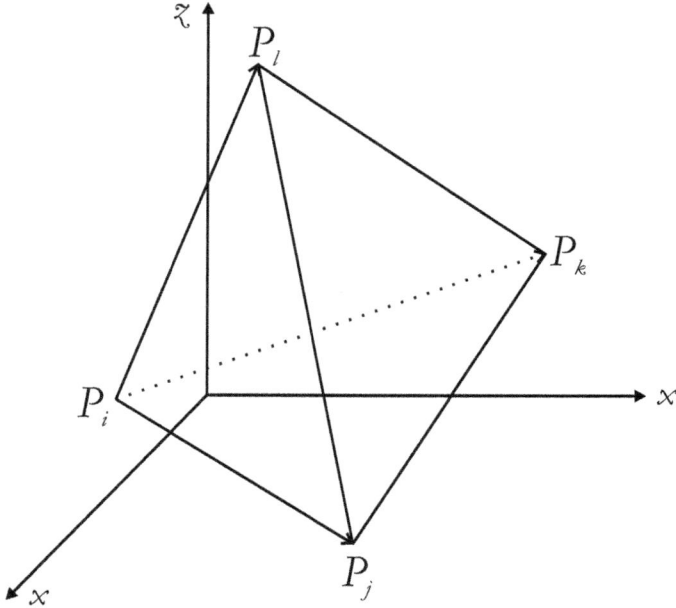

Figure 4.25: Illustration of the scalar triple product.

Based on the above, a plane π, defined by points P_i, P_j, and P_k, is considered a supporting plane if all remaining points P_l form parallelepipeds whose volumes share the same sign. In that case, the plane π is added to the list of supporting planes that participate in the construction of the convex hull. However, if for some plane α it turns out that certain points lie on its right side while others lie on its left side, then the plane is not considered supporting and is discarded—i.e., it is not added to the list of supporting planes. Following this principle, the pseudocode of Algorithm 4 is derived, which computes the 3D convex hull for a set of n points in space and has a time complexity of $\mathcal{O}(n^4)$.

Algorithm 4: Pseudocode of Naive Algorithm for Computing 3D Convex Hull.

---

for $i=1$:n **do**
    for $j=i+1$:n **do**
        for $k=j+1$:n **do**
            for $l=k+1$:n **do**
                if *for all points the volume V of the tetrahedron has the same nonzero sign* **then**
                    the plane π defined by points P_i, P_j, and P_k is a supporting plane and is added
                    to the list.
                end
            end
        end
    end
end

In the pseudocode of Algorithm 4, the points P_i, P_j, and P_k are coplanar, i.e., they lie on the same plane, while the point P_l must not lie on that plane. Moreover, instead of planes, triangles are added to the list, since they uniquely define the corresponding supporting plane.

In the following section, a naive algorithm for computing the 3D convex hull will be implemented using the geometric objects defined in the second chapter of this book. A fundamental aspect of this algorithm, as well as of all algorithms for computing the 3D convex hull, lies in the identification and construction of faces. Consequently, based on the pseudocode of Algorithm 4, the function *create_faces*($\cdot$) will be implemented as shown in the following code snippet:

```
1  def create_faces(points: List[Point3D])->List[Triangle3D]:
2      n=len(points); faces = []
3      for i in range(n):
4          for j in range(i+1, n):
5              for k in range(j+1, n):
6                  tr = Triangle3D(points[i], points[j], points[k], 0)
7                  s1 = s2 = False; is_face = True
8                  for idx, pt in enumerate(points):
9                      if idx in [i, j, k]:continue
10                     cl=pt.classify(tr)
11                     if tr.tetrahedron_volume(pt) < 1e-5:continue
12                     if cl==TypeP3.LEFT or cl==TypeP3.ON_TRIANGLE: s1 = True
13                     else: s2 = True
14                     if s1 and s2: is_face = False;break
15                 if is_face:faces.append(tr)
16     return faces
```

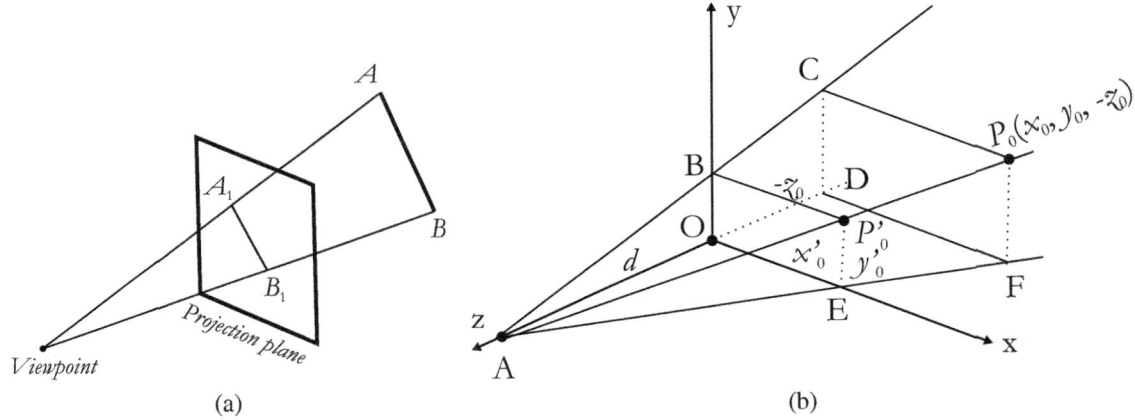

(a)   (b)

Figure 4.26: (a) Perspective projection of the segment $\overline{AB}$. (b) Perspective projection model.

Before implementing the function *visualize_hull()*, which is used to visualize the 3D convex hull on a screen, it is essential to establish the underlying mathematical foundations. Since the screen is inherently a two-dimensional medium, it is necessary to project three-dimensional objects onto a two-dimensional plane. This projection allows the user to perceive spatial relationships between objects, despite the constraints of a 2D surface. For projecting 3D points onto the screen, *perspective projection* is employed. This type of projection creates a sense of depth by making objects closer to the viewpoint appear larger, while those farther away appear smaller.

The perspective projection is mathematically modeled using the concept of similar triangles. Specifically, for projecting a point $P_0(x_0, y_0, z_0)$ onto the xOy-plane, the following formula is used:

$$x_0' = \frac{dx_0}{d - z_0}, \quad y_0' = \frac{dy_0}{d - z_0}, \tag{4.4}$$

where d denotes the distance between the projection plane and the center of projection (viewpoint), while x_0' and y_0' represent the coordinates of the projected point within the plane. This principle is illustrated in Fig. 4.26 (b), where point A serves as the center of projection, and the xOy-plane defines the projection

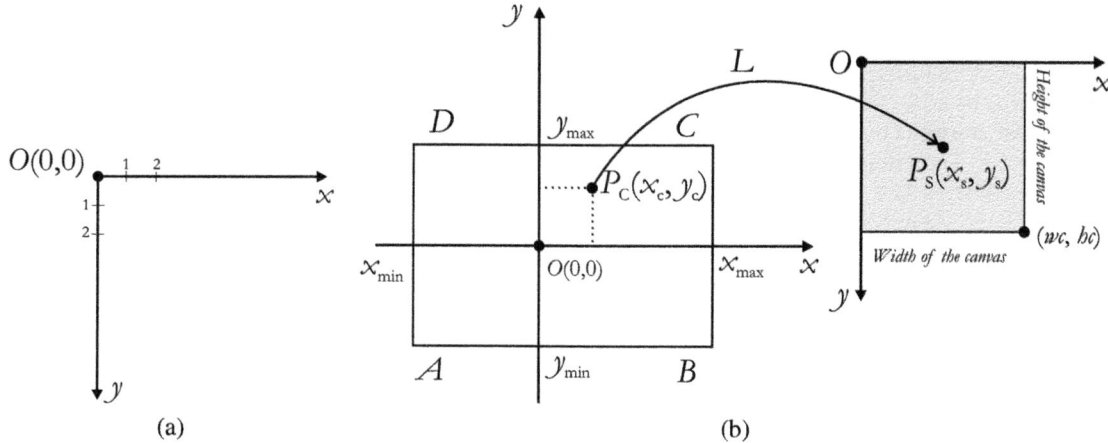

Figure 4.27: (a) Screen coordinate system. (b) Mapping from the Cartesian to the Screen coordinate system.

plane. Once the projection is performed into the Cartesian coordinate system, it becomes necessary to transform the projected points into the screen coordinate system (see Fig. 4.27 (a)). This transformation is accomplished through a linear mapping L, which projects an arbitrary point P_C from the Cartesian coordinate system into the point P_S of the screen coordinate system, according to the following relations (see Fig. 4.27 (b))

$$x_e = a_x x_c + b_x, \quad y_e = a_y y_c + b_y,$$ (4.5)

where a_x, b_x, a_y, b_y are real coefficients determined based on the boundaries of the logical and physical systems. Specifically, using the known minimum and maximum values of the x and y-coordinates in the Cartesian system (within the rectangle $\square ABCD$) and the dimensions of the drawing canvas $wc \times hc$, the following relations are obtained:

$$a_x = \frac{wc}{x_{max} - x_{min}}, \quad b_x = -a_x x_{min}, \quad a_y = \frac{hc}{y_{min} - y_{max}}, \quad b_y = -a_y y_{max}.$$ (4.6)

For interactive rotation of the object around the coordinate axes x, y, and z, a composition of rotations defined by the matrices $M_{x,\alpha}$, $M_{y,\beta}$, and $M_{z,\gamma}$ is used. These matrices specify rotation about the corresponding axes by angles α, β, and γ. Applying these transformations to each point of the object enables the visualization of the object from different perspectives. Following the theoretical description of projecting points from three-dimensional space onto a plane, the implementation of the method *visualize_hull()* from the **GeometricVisualizer** class is provided. It utilizes the `Matplotlib` library for projection and rendering of the object:

```
1  def visualize_hull(self):
2      self.ax.clear()
3      if not self.points: self.canvas.draw(); return
4      self.faces = create_faces(self.points); hull_vertices = set()
5      for face in self.faces:
6          for v in face.vertices:
7              hull_vertices.add((v[0], v[1], v[2]))
8      xs_hull, ys_hull, zs_hull = [], [], []
9      xs_inner, ys_inner, zs_inner = [], [], []
10     for p in self.points:
11         if (p[0], p[1], p[2]) in hull_vertices:
```

```
12        xs_hull.append(p[0]); ys_hull.append(p[1]); zs_hull.append(p[2])
13      else:
14        xs_inner.append(p[0]); ys_inner.append(p[1]); zs_inner.append(p[2])
15   self.ax.scatter(xs_hull, ys_hull, zs_hull, color='red', s=50, label="Convex
       Hull Vertices")
16   self.ax.scatter(xs_inner, ys_inner, zs_inner, color='black', s=5, label="
       Interior Points")
17   for face in self.faces:
18     verts = [[(v[0], v[1], v[2]) for v in face.vertices]]
19     poly_visible = Poly3DCollection(verts, alpha=0.5, facecolor='yellow',
          edgecolor='black', linestyle='solid')
20     self.ax.add_collection3d(poly_visible)
21   self.ax.set_box_aspect([1, 1,1])
22   self.ax.legend(loc='upper right')
23   self.canvas.draw()
```

The Matplotlib library employs the concept of a virtual camera and projection matrices to transform the 3D coordinates of objects into 2D coordinates on the screen. It enables the rendering of points (using the scatter method) and polygon edges (via the Poly3DCollection class). Based on these principles, the following listing presents the implementation used to create the graphical interface for determining the convex hull in 3D space (see Fig. 4.28):

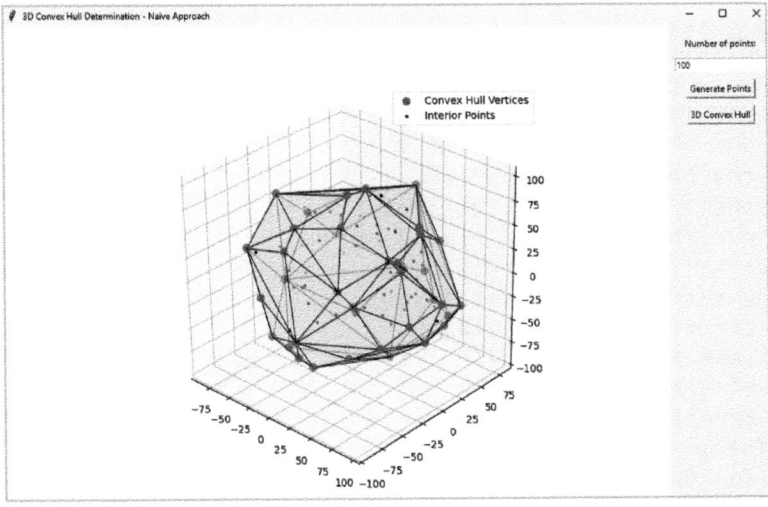

Figure 4.28: Creating a 3D convex hull using the naive algorithm for 100 randomly generated points.

Listing 4.9: Graphical Interface for 3D Convex Hull Visualization

```
1 import tkinter as tk
2 import random
3 import numpy as np
4 import time
5 from matplotlib.backends.backend_tkagg import FigureCanvasTkAgg
6 from matplotlib.figure import Figure
7 from mpl_toolkits.mplot3d.art3d import Poly3DCollection
8 from geometry import Point3D, Triangle3D
9 from ch4_helper_functions import create_faces
10
11 class GeometricVisualizer:
12     def __init__(self, master):
```

```
13          self.master = master
14          self.master.title("3D Convex Hull Determination - Naive Approach")
15          self.main_frame = tk.Frame(master)
16          self.main_frame.pack(fill=tk.BOTH, expand=True)
17          self.fig = Figure(figsize=(7, 5))
18          self.ax = self.fig.add_subplot(111, projection='3d')
19          self.canvas = FigureCanvasTkAgg(self.fig, master=self.main_frame)
20          self.canvas.get_tk_widget().pack(side=tk.LEFT, fill=tk.BOTH, expand=True)
21          self.control_frame = tk.Frame(self.main_frame)
22          self.control_frame.pack(side=tk.RIGHT, padx=10, pady=10, fill=tk.Y)
23          tk.Label(self.control_frame, text="Number of points:").pack(pady=5)
24          self.entry_var = tk.StringVar(value="10")
25          self.entry = tk.Entry(self.control_frame, textvariable=self.entry_var)
26          self.entry.pack(pady=5)
27          self.generate_button = tk.Button(self.control_frame, text="Generate Points
               ", command=self.generate_points)
28          self.generate_button.pack(pady=5)
29          self.hull_button = tk.Button(self.control_frame, text="3D Convex Hull",
               command=self.visualize_hull)
30          self.hull_button.pack(pady=5)
31          self.points = []; self.faces = []
32      def generate_points(self):
33          try:
34              num_points = int(self.entry.get())
35              seed = int(time.time() * 1000)
36              rng = np.random.default_rng(seed)
37              r_min, r_max = 50, 100
38              for _ in range(num_points):
39                  phi = rng.uniform(0, 2 * np.pi)
40                  costheta = rng.uniform(-1, 1)
41                  theta = np.arccos(costheta)
42                  r = rng.uniform(r_min, r_max)
43                  x = r * np.sin(theta) * np.cos(phi)
44                  y = r * np.sin(theta) * np.sin(phi)
45                  z = r * np.cos(theta)
46                  self.points.append(Point3D(x, y, z))
47          self.ax.clear()
48          xs, ys, zs = [p[0] for p in self.points], [p[1] for p in self.points], [p
               [2] for p in self.points]
49          self.ax.scatter(xs, ys, zs, color='black', s=10, label="Generated Points")
50          self.ax.set_box_aspect([1, 1, 1])
51          self.ax.legend(loc='upper right')
52          self.canvas.draw()
53      except ValueError: print("Invalid input for number of points.")
54
55 if __name__ == '__main__':
56 root = tk.Tk()
57 app = GeometricVisualizer(root)
58 root.mainloop()
```

4.2.3 Jarvis's Algorithm for 3D Convex Hull Construction

This section describes the Jarvis March algorithm for computing the convex hull in 3D space. The 3D version of Jarvis's algorithm is a direct extension of its 2D counterpart, applied to a set of n given points in space. Similar to the 2D case, the algorithm begins by identifying an extreme plane α, i.e., a plane such that all points lie strictly on one side of it—e.g., on the right-hand side. Typically, an extreme plane is represented as a face defined by a 3D triangle. Starting from this initial extreme face, the remaining extreme faces are found analogously to the 2D case, ensuring that all points lie on the right-hand side of each face. Let the set of n points in space be denoted by $P_1, P_2, \cdots, P_n$. Without loss of generality, let the first three points P_1, P_2, and P_3 define the initial extreme plane or face F_1 of the 3D convex hull. This face F_1 can be found by sorting the input points in descending order with respect to their z-coordinates. The top three points from the sorted set define the initial extreme face. Hence, F_1 can be found in $\Theta(n \log n)$ time. The next face F_2 is found by considering all combinations involving the edges $\overline{P_1 P_2}$, $\overline{P_1 P_3}$, and $\overline{P_2 P_3}$ of face F_1. In general, for each face, all its bounding edges need to be processed. For example, to process face F_1, one starts with edge $\overline{P_1 P_2}$ and checks whether the points P_1, P_2, and P_i $(i > 3)$ form a face. If they do, then a new face F_2 is found, which shares the edge $\overline{P_1 P_2}$ with F_1. Face F_2 introduces two new edges, $\overline{P_1 P_i}$ and $\overline{P_2 P_i}$, which must also be processed. Before that, the remaining two edges $\overline{P_1 P_3}$ and $\overline{P_2 P_3}$ of F_1 are processed in a completely analogous manner. Continuing this process, it becomes evident that once all edges are processed—which, according to Lemma 4.2.1, are linearly proportional to n—the algorithm terminates and generates a set of connected convex faces, i.e., a polytope. Clearly, the time complexity of this algorithm is proportional to $\mathcal{O}(nf)$, or $\mathcal{O}(n^2)$ in the worst case, where f is the total number of faces. This verbal description can be formalized through the pseudocode given in Algorithm 5. Curious readers are encouraged to implement this algorithm as an exercise, which will contribute to a deeper understanding of its behavior.

Algorithm 5: Pseudocode of the Jarvis's algorithm for 3D convex hull construction

Input: A set $\mathscr{P} = \{P_1, P_2, \ldots, P_n\}$ of n points in 3D space.

Output: A list of triangular faces defining the convex hull.

Step 1. Sort points in descending order by their z-coordinate. Select the top three points to form the initial face F_1. Add F_1 to the list $\mathscr{L}$ of convex hull faces.;

Step 2. Initialize a queue $\mathscr{Q}$ with the edges of F_1.;

Step 3. while *there are unprocessed edges in the queue $\mathscr{Q}$* **do**

    a) Extract the next edge $e = \overline{P_i P_j}$ from the queue $\mathscr{Q}$;

    b) **for** *each remaining point P_k not in e* **do**

        if *triangle $\triangle P_i P_j P_k$ forms a valid face (all other points lie on the same side)* **then**

            c) add face $\triangle P_i P_j P_k$ to the list $\mathscr{L}$;

            d) add new edges $\overline{P_i P_k}$ and $\overline{P_j P_k}$ to the queue $\mathscr{Q}$ if not already processed;

            e) break the loop for this edge;

return *List $\mathscr{L}$ of all discovered convex hull faces.*

4.2.4 Incremental Algorithm for 3D Convex Hull Construction

This section describes the incremental algorithm for computing the convex hull in 3D space. The time complexity of the algorithm is proportional to $\Theta(nf)$, where f is the number of faces in the convex hull. Although this algorithm is not the theoretically fastest method for determining the 3D convex hull, it has proven to be highly efficient in practice. The paradigm of this algorithm is similar to its planar counterpart. Let $\mathscr{Q} = \mathscr{H}_{i-1}$ be the convex hull obtained after the $(i-1)^{\text{th}}$ iteration. Then, in the ith iteration, the algorithm incrementally constructs a new hull $\mathscr{Q} \cup P_i$ by adding the new point P_i to the current hull $\mathscr{Q}$. Analogous to the planar case, when adding the point P_i, it is necessary to check whether the point lies inside the current hull, i.e., inside the convex polytope $\mathscr{Q}$. If it does, the point is discarded and not considered further. Otherwise, it participates in the construction of the new convex hull $\mathscr{H}_i = \mathscr{H}_{i-1} \cup P_i$. To determine whether a point belongs to the interior of a polytope (i.e., the current hull $\mathscr{Q}$), it is necessary to check whether the point lies on the same side of all faces that constitute the current hull. This verification is entirely analogous to the planar case, where a point is considered to be inside a polygon if and only if it lies on the same side of all its edges. Traditionally, this is verified by checking whether the point lies on the left side of each polygon edge. The same paradigm is applied in 3D, except that instead of edges, planes (i.e., faces defined by triangles) are considered. In this context, we adopt the convention that if the volume of the tetrahedron is positive, then the point lies on the left side of the face. Otherwise, the point lies on the right side of the face. Let the point P_i lie outside the convex hull (polytope), as illustrated in Fig. 4.29 (a). In the planar version of the incremental algorithm, two tangents were drawn from the point P_i to the current hull. In three-dimensional space, instead of tangents, tangential planes are drawn, which bound a cone whose apex is the point P_i, and whose base consists of the horizon and the polygonal chain formed by the edges of the visible faces of the hull $\mathcal{Q}$. In Fig. 4.29 (a), the horizon is shown—it lies between the visible faces (colored white) and the non-visible faces (colored gray). Thus, the horizon represents the boundary of the visible region. The faces of the cone can be determined based on the horizon, i.e., from the edges of those faces that are visible from the apex P_i.

Algorithm 6: Pseudocode of the incremental algorithm for computing the 3D convex hull.

Let $\mathcal{P}$ be a set of n points in space, i.e., $\mathcal{P} = \{P_0, P_1, P_2, \cdots, P_{n-1}\}$. Select any four non-coplanar points, for example P_0, P_1, P_2, and P_3, and use them to form a tetrahedron $\mathcal{H}_3$.

for $i=4{:}n{\text-}1$ **do**

    for $\forall f \in \mathcal{H}_{i-1}$ **do**

        Compute the volume V of the tetrahedron defined by the face f and the point P_i.

        if $V < 0$ **then**

            The face f is added to the set $\mathcal{S}$ of visible faces.

        end

    end

    if *the number of elements in the set $\mathcal{S}$ is greater than zero* **then**

        Based on the edges of the faces in the set $\mathcal{S}$, the horizon is identified, and a cone is formed from the point P_i toward the horizon. Then, the visible faces in $\mathcal{S}$ are removed from both the set $\mathcal{S}$ and the current hull $\mathcal{H}_{i-1}$, and the faces of the cone are unified with the remaining faces of $\mathcal{H}_{i-1}$ to form the new hull $\mathcal{H}_i$.

    end

end

Formally, a face f is said to be *visible* from a point P_i *if and only if* any interior point X of the face is visible from P_i, i.e., if the line l containing the segment $\overline{P_i X}$ intersects the face only at the point X. It follows that if only one edge of a face is visible, the face itself is considered not visible. In Fig. 4.29 (b), the face f is visible from point P_i, but not from point P_1, since only one edge of the face f is visible from that point. To test whether a face f (triangle $\triangle ABC$) is visible from a point D, it is sufficient to compute the volume of the corresponding tetrahedron. If the volume is negative, the face is visible. Effectively, this visibility test can be computed using the following determinant:

$$V = \begin{vmatrix} A.x & A.y & A.z & 1 \\ B.x & B.y & B.z & 1 \\ C.x & C.y & C.z & 1 \\ D.x & D.y & D.z & 1 \end{vmatrix}. \tag{4.7}$$

The pseudocode of the incremental algorithm for computing the convex hull in 3D space is given in Algorithm 6. From the pseudocode, it can be seen that the time complexity of the algorithm is proportional to $\mathcal{O}(nf)$. According to Lemma 4.2.1, the number of faces f grows linearly with n, making this algorithm quadratic in nature. Fortunately, the algorithm can be accelerated to achieve a time complexity of $\Theta(n \log n)$. The key optimization lies in initially sorting all points of the input set in descending order with respect to their z-coordinate. This eliminates the need to check whether the point P_i lies inside the current convex hull $\mathcal{H}_{i-1}$, which significantly improves efficiency. The implementation of this algorithm is left to the reader as a valuable exercise for gaining deeper insight into the topic and algorithmic techniques.

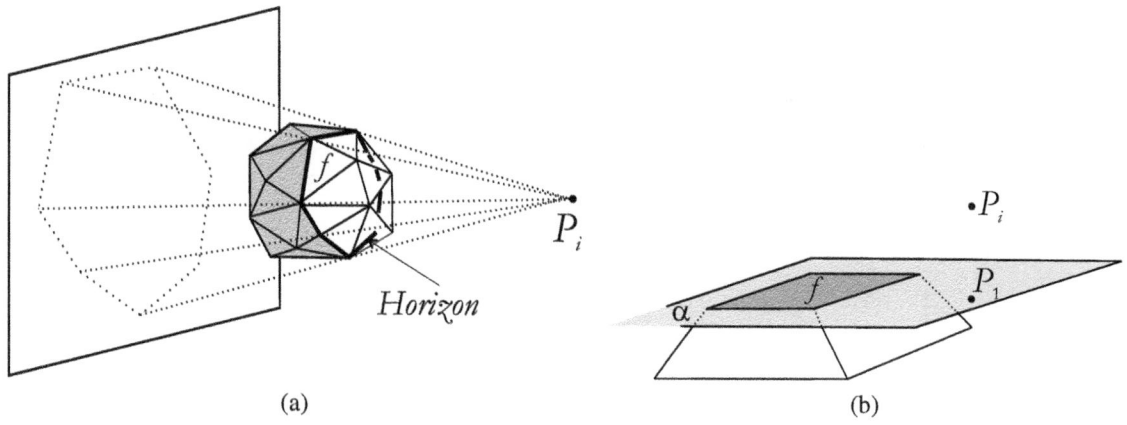

Figure 4.29: Visibility of a face from point P_i .

4.2.5 Recursive Algorithm for 3D Convex Hull Construction

In the final part of this chapter, we consider a recursive algorithm for computing the convex hull in 3D space, which follows the same paradigm as in the 2D case. In the first step, the points are sorted according to their x-coordinate. If multiple points share the same x-coordinate, they are further sorted by their y-coordinate. If ties still exist, the points are finally sorted by their z-coordinate. This sorting step has a time complexity of $\Theta(n \log n)$. In the second step, the sorted points are divided into two sets: a left set $\mathscr{A}$ containing the first $\lceil \frac{n}{2} \rceil$ points, and a right set $\mathscr{B}$ containing the remaining $\lfloor \frac{n}{2} \rfloor$ points. In the third step, convex hulls are recursively computed for the sets $\mathscr{A}$ and $\mathscr{B}$. Finally, in the fourth step, the convex hull of the entire point set $\mathscr{S}$ is constructed by merging the previously computed hulls, which takes $\mathscr{O}(n)$ time. These steps (splitting, recursive computation, and merging) are repeated until the number of points in a set becomes less than or equal to one. In the third step of the algorithm, based on the sorted points, two polytopes are constructed—one for each of the sets $\mathscr{A}$ and $\mathscr{B}$—as illustrated in Fig. 4.30. The merging of polytopes $\mathscr{A}$ and $\mathscr{B}$ is carried out by determining a connecting strip composed of a number of linking faces that bridge these polytopes (see Fig. 4.31 (a)). The number of such linking faces is linear in the sizes of polytopes $\mathscr{A}$ and $\mathscr{B}$. Specifically, each linking face is incident to at least one edge of polytope $\mathscr{A}$ or $\mathscr{B}$, so the total number of linking faces does not exceed the total number of edges of both polytopes. Therefore, the merging of polytopes can be performed in linear time, provided that each face is added in constant time.

Let π be a connecting plane that joins the polytopes $\mathscr{A}$ and $\mathscr{B}$ from below, such that polytope $\mathscr{A}$ touches it at point P_0 and polytope $\mathscr{B}$ at point P_1. Without loss of generality, assume that P_0 and P_1 are the only contact points between the plane π and the polytopes $\mathscr{A}$ and $\mathscr{B}$, respectively. Then, the plane π contains the line p defined by the segment $\overline{P_0 P_1}$ (see Fig.4.31 (b)). Now suppose that the plane π is "folded" along the line p and one of its halves is rotated until it strikes one of the two polytopes. If the first point it hits is a point P_2 of polytope $\mathscr{A}$, then the segment $\overline{P_0 P_2}$ represents an edge of $\mathscr{A}$. In other words, the first point P_2 struck by the plane π is adjacent to either P_0 or P_1. Thus, once point P_2 is found, the triangle $\triangle P_0 P_1 P_2$ forms one face of the connecting strip. This process continues around the line passing through P_1 and P_2, since P_2 lies on polytope $\mathscr{A}$. The procedure terminates when the rotating plane "closes" on itself. After the wrapping around the identified polytopes is complete, it is necessary to remove the faces that are covered by the connecting strip. Although the wrapping process does not explicitly identify which faces of $\mathscr{A}$ are visible from $\mathscr{B}$ (and vice versa), it does reveal the edges of $\mathscr{A}$ and $\mathscr{B}$ that are incident to one of the wrapped faces. Even though this algorithm theoretically guarantees an asymptotic complexity of $\mathscr{O}(n \log n)$, its implementation is highly challenging due to the need for appropriate data

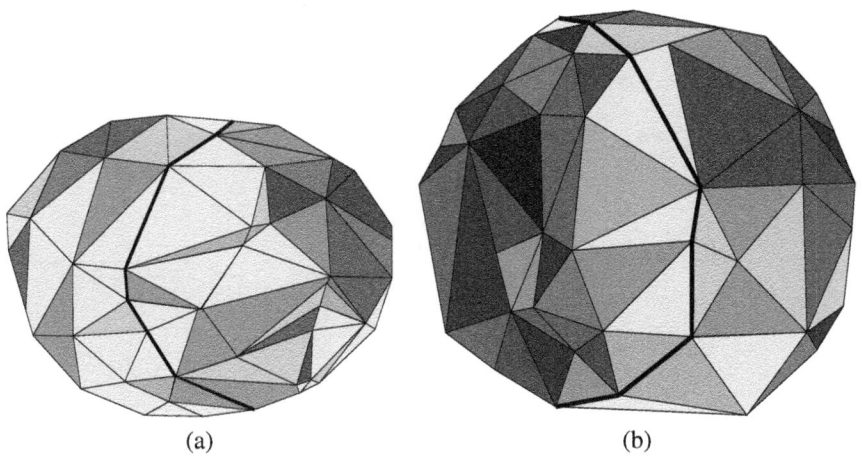

Figure 4.30: (a) Polytope $\mathscr{A}$. (b) Polytope $\mathscr{B}$.

structures. Therefore, in practice, the incremental algorithm is often preferred due to its simplicity and easier implementation.

4.3 Exercises

Exercise 4.1 Given an unsorted array of segments in the plane that form a convex polygon, implement an algorithm with time complexity $\mathscr{O}(n\log n)$ that reconstructs the convex polygon from this array.

Exercise 4.2 Given an unsorted array of segments in the plane that form a convex polygon, implement an algorithm with time complexity $\mathscr{O}(n)$ that reconstructs the convex polygon from this array.

Exercise 4.3 Prove that the incremental algorithm for computing the convex hull always converges to a final solution.

Exercise 4.4 Prove that if $\mathscr{P}$ is a set of n points sampled from a uniform distribution over the unit square, then the expected number of points on the convex hull of $\mathscr{P}$ is of order $\mathscr{O}(\log n)$.

Exercise 4.5 Implement object-oriented versions of the algorithms for computing the convex hull in the plane.

Exercise 4.6 Construct point sets in the plane that represent the best-case (worst-case) scenarios for the following algorithms: *Gift Wrapping*, *Graham Scan*, *Incremental Algorithm*.

Exercise 4.7 Design a linear-time algorithm for computing the convex hull of a simple polygon consisting of n vertices.

Exercise 4.8 Prove that sorting a set of numbers can be reduced to computing a convex hull in $\mathscr{O}(n\log n)$ time.

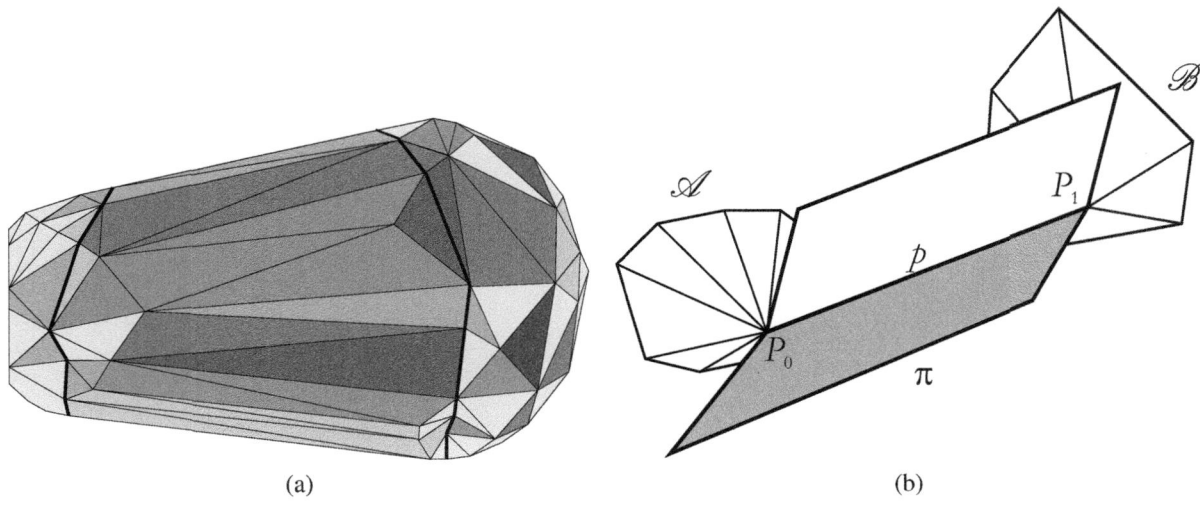

(a)   (b)

Figure 4.31: (a) Merging of the recursively computed polytopes $\mathscr{A}$ and $\mathscr{B}$. (b) The folded plane π around the line p, rotated around the polytopes $\mathscr{A}$ and $\mathscr{B}$.

Exercise 4.9 Let $\mathscr{S}$ denote a set of n points given in the plane. Design an algorithm that finds a convex hull $\mathscr{H}$ consisting of three points from the set $\mathscr{S}$ such that the perimeter of $\mathscr{H}$ is minimized (maximized).

Exercise 4.10 It is known that a line l best fits the points of a set $\mathscr{S}$ if it minimizes the total distance between the elements of $\mathscr{S}$ and the line itself. Find such a line in the plane, given the convex hull of the set $\mathscr{S}$.

Exercise 4.11 It is known that in the MergeHull algorithm, the lowest and highest points of the merging sets always lie on the tangents connecting the two sets. Find a point set for which this is not the case.

Exercise 4.12 Prove that the number of faces of a 3D convex hull obtained using the incremental algorithm is not greater than $6n - 20$.

Exercise 4.13 Let $\mathscr{Q}$ be a tetrahedron and let P be a point outside of it. Determine the minimum (maximum) number of faces that the convex hull $\mathscr{Q} \cup P$ can have. Is this number of faces always odd? Prove or disprove.

Exercise 4.14 Let the sets $\mathscr{C}_1$ and $\mathscr{C}_2$ represent two disjoint cubes in space, such that cube $\mathscr{C}_2$ is a translation of cube $\mathscr{C}_1$. Determine the minimum (maximum) number of faces that the convex hull of their union can have.

Exercise 4.15 Design an algorithm for computing the 3D convex hull as an extension of the 2D Graham Scan algorithm.

5. Polygon Triangulation Methods

Polygon triangulation is one of the oldest problems in geometry, whose study led to the discovery of the Catalan numbers [162, 185]. In general, polygon triangulation is not unique, as there are multiple ways to perform it. This makes the task of decomposing a polygon into triangles particularly challenging, especially for concave polygons. However, when considering only convex polygons—where all diagonals lie entirely within the polygon—the number of possible triangulations becomes limited and depends solely on the number of vertices, not the shape of the polygon. Polygon triangulation has wide applications in various fields, including terrain modeling, point location in space, visibility problems in art galleries, robotics, and mesh generation [57]. For this reason, triangulation is regarded as one of the fundamental subroutines in many geometric algorithms. For example, algorithms that fill the interior of a polygon often begin by triangulating it and then progressively color the resulting individual triangles from this decomposition. In the remainder of this chapter, we consider simple polygons defined by a finite set of line segments forming a simple closed path $\partial \mathscr{P}$. It will be shown that any such polygon $\mathscr{P}$ with n vertices can be triangulated into exactly $n-2$ triangles using $n-3$ diagonals [50].

5.1 Properties of Simple Polygons

In this section, we will formulate and prove statements that are essential for the development of polygon triangulation algorithms. A set of n given points $\{P_0, P_1, \cdots, P_{n-1}\}$ in the plane defines a polygon $\mathscr{P}$ *if and only if* the following conditions are satisfied:

- $s_i \cap s_{i+1} = P_i$, for every $i = \overline{0, n-2}$;
- $s_j \cap s_{i+1} = \emptyset$, for every $j \neq i+1$.

Here, each segment $s_i = \overline{P_i P_{i+1}}$ represents a side of the polygon, with endpoints P_i and P_{i+1}. A polygon $\mathscr{P}$ defined in this way divides the plane into an interior and an exterior region, such that if a walker moves along the sides of the polygon in a counterclockwise direction, the interior lies to the left of the walker, and the exterior lies to the right.

Definition 5.1.1 A vertex of a polygon is said to be *convex* if its interior angle is less than or equal to π.

Definition 5.1.2 A vertex of a polygon is said to be *strictly convex* if it is not collinear with its adjacent vertices.

© The Author(s), under exclusive license to Springer Nature Switzerland AG 2026
A. Alihodžić, *Exploring Computational Geometry*, Texts in Computer Science,
https://doi.org/10.1007/978-3-032-06393-9_5

Definition 5.1.3 A vertex of a polygon is said to be *reflex* if its interior angle is greater than π.

From the above definitions, it directly follows that a vertex is strictly convex if the interior angle it forms with its adjacent vertices is strictly less than π.

Lemma 5.1.1 Every polygon $\mathscr{P}$ has at least one strictly convex vertex.

Proof. To prove the existence of at least one such vertex, it is necessary to orient the polygon sides in the counterclockwise direction. In that case, the vertex with the largest x-coordinate and the smallest y-coordinate represents a strictly convex vertex. Let this vertex be denoted by V. Let l be a line passing through it and parallel to the x-axis. Observing the traversal in the counterclockwise direction, the interior of the polygon $\mathscr{P}$ always lies to the left of the line l, that is, above it. Therefore, an edge that is not contained in line l, and is simultaneously incident to vertex V, must lie above l. This implies that while passing through V, a left turn occurs, which means that vertex V is not collinear with its adjacent vertices. Based on Definition 5.1.2, it follows that vertex V is strictly convex, which was to be proven. ∎

Definition 5.1.4 The segment $\overline{P_i P_j}$ is called a *diagonal* of the polygon $\mathscr{P}$ if it connects two non-adjacent vertices of the polygon and lies entirely within it.

It follows directly from this definition that a diagonal of a convex polygon does not intersect any of its sides except at the endpoints to which it is incident. Moreover, it is easy to show that every pair of non-adjacent vertices of a convex polygon forms a diagonal.

Lemma 5.1.2 Every polygon $\mathscr{P}$ has at least one diagonal.

Proof. Based on Lemma 5.1.1, every polygon has at least one strictly convex vertex. Let this vertex be V, and let V_- and V_+ denote its adjacent vertices. If the segment $\overline{V_- V_+}$ is a diagonal of the polygon, then the proof is complete. Otherwise, the segment $\overline{V_- V_+}$ either intersects the polygonal chain $\partial\mathscr{P}$ of the polygon $\mathscr{P}$ (see Fig. 5.1 (a)), or it does not lie within its interior (see Fig. 5.1 (b)).

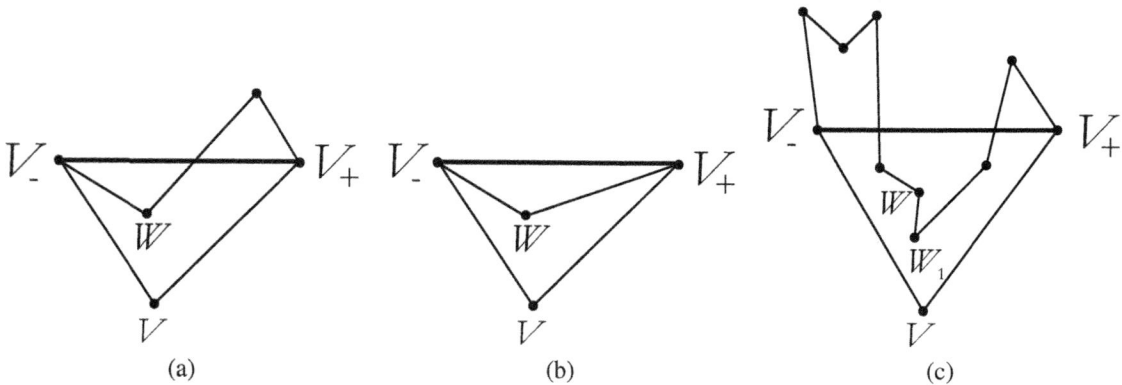

Figure 5.1: (a) The diagonal $\overline{V_- V_+}$ intersects the polygonal chain $\partial\mathscr{P}$ of the polygon $\mathscr{P}$. (b) The diagonal $\overline{V_- V_+}$ does not lie in the interior of the polygon $\mathscr{P}$. (c) Existence of the nearest vertex W_1 with respect to the strictly convex vertex V.

In both of the previously described cases, the triangle $\triangle V_- V V_+$ contains at least one vertex that is not coincident with its corners (In Fig. 5.1, it is the vertex W). Within this triangle, one can identify the vertex that is closest to vertex V in terms of Euclidean distance (In Fig. 5.1 (c), it is the vertex W_1). It is easy to show that the segment $\overline{VW_1}$ represents a diagonal of the polygon. Namely, the choice of vertex W_1

directly implies that the segment $\overline{VW_1}$ lies inside the polygon. Moreover, this segment does not intersect the polygonal chain $\partial\mathscr{P}$ of the polygon $\mathscr{P}$ except at the vertices V and W_1. Otherwise, there would exist a point U where the segment $\overline{VW_1}$ intersects $\partial\mathscr{P}$, which would imply that vertex W_1 is not the closest to vertex V, contradicting its selection. Hence, every polygon contains at least one diagonal, which completes the proof. ∎

Theorem 5.1.1 Any polygon $\mathscr{P}$ composed of n vertices can be triangulated using a single diagonal ($n = 4$) or multiple diagonals ($n \geq 5$).

Proof. The proof of the theorem is carried out by mathematical induction on the number of vertices n of the polygon $\mathscr{P}$. For $n = 4$, there is exactly one diagonal regardless of whether the polygon is convex or concave (see Fig. 5.2 (a), Fig. 5.2 (b)).

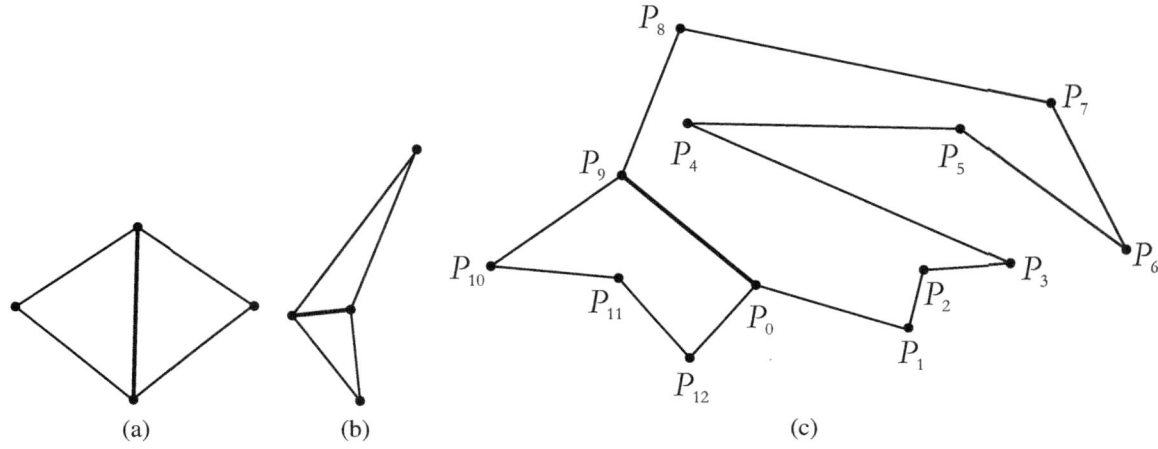

Figure 5.2: (a) Convex polygon. (b) Concave polygon. (c) Division of the polygon $\mathscr{P}$ into two subpolygons $\mathscr{P}_1$ and $\mathscr{P}_2$.

Let the statement be true for a polygon $\mathscr{P}' \subset \mathscr{P}$ with fewer than n vertices. Based on Lemma 5.1.2, there exists at least one diagonal of the polygon $\mathscr{P}$ (In Fig. 5.2 (c), it is the segment $\overline{P_0P_9}$), which divides the polygon $\mathscr{P}$ into two subpolygons $\mathscr{P}_1$ and $\mathscr{P}_2$ ($\mathscr{P}_1, \mathscr{P}_2 \subset \mathscr{P}$). According to the inductive hypothesis, the polygons $\mathscr{P}_1 = \{P_0, P_9, P_{10}, P_{11}, P_{12}\}$ and $\mathscr{P}_2 = \{P_0, P_1, P_2, P_3, P_4, P_5, P_6, P_7, P_8, P_9\}$ can be triangulated. Since the diagonal $\overline{P_0P_9}$ is a common side of these polygons, merging their triangulations yields the triangulation of the original polygon $\mathscr{P}$, thus completing the proof of the theorem. ∎

It is important to emphasize that the number of triangulations is not unique, but is characterized by the n-th Catalan number C_n. In general, in combinatorial mathematics, Catalan numbers are a sequence of natural numbers used to solve various counting problems and are often associated with recursively defined objects. These numbers are named after the French-Belgian mathematician Eugène Charles Catalan (1814–1894). The n-th Catalan number C_n is expressed using binomial coefficients as:

$$C_n = \frac{1}{n+1}\binom{2n}{n} = \frac{(2n)!}{n!(n+1)!}. \tag{5.1}$$

Based on this number, the number of triangulations of an arbitrary polygon $\mathscr{P}$ consisting of $n+2$ vertices is greater than one and less than C_n. In the case of a convex polygon $\mathscr{P}$, the total number of triangulations, denoted as T_n, can be determined using the following relation:

$$T_n = \frac{(2(n-2))!}{(n-2)!(n-1)!}. \tag{5.2}$$

Using mathematical induction on the number n, it can be proven that the total number of triangulations T_n is given by the relation 5.2, which is left to the reader as a useful exercise.

> **Observation 5.1.2** Based on Theorem 5.1.1, after identifying a diagonal—accomplished in Lemma 5.1.2—the polygon is split into two subpolygons, to which the same procedure for finding the remaining diagonals is then recursively applied. This approach leads to a recursive algorithm for polygon triangulation. Since finding a diagonal requires linear time, it follows that, in the worst case, a polygon can be triangulated in quadratic time.

The answer to the question: *"How many triangles, or diagonals, can be obtained when triangulating an arbitrary simple polygon?"* is given by the following lemma.

> **Lemma 5.1.3** Any triangulation of a polygon $\mathscr{P}$ consisting of n vertices $(n \geq 3)$ contains exactly $n-3$ diagonals and $n-2$ triangles.

Proof. The proof of the lemma is carried out by mathematical induction on the number of vertices n of the polygon $\mathscr{P}$. If $n = 3$, then there is exactly one triangle and zero diagonals, so the statement holds in this case. Suppose the statement holds for some polygon $\mathscr{P}' \subset \mathscr{P}$. According to Lemma 5.1.2, the polygon $\mathscr{P}$ can be decomposed into two subpolygons $\mathscr{P}_1$ and $\mathscr{P}_2$, which lie within $\mathscr{P}$ and share only the diagonal along which they are separated. Let n_1 and n_2 denote the number of vertices of these subpolygons, respectively. Then, $n = n_1 + n_2 - 2$, since two vertices incident to the separating diagonal are excluded. Since $\mathscr{P}_1$ is strictly contained in $\mathscr{P}$, we have $n_1 < n$. Analogously, $n_2 < n$. By the inductive hypothesis, it follows that:

    a) the number of diagonals in polygon $\mathscr{P}_1$ is $n_1 - 3$, and the number of triangles is $n_1 - 2$;

    b) the number of diagonals in polygon $\mathscr{P}_2$ is $n_2 - 3$, and the number of triangles is $n_2 - 2$.

Based on a) and b), the total number of triangles in polygon $\mathscr{P}$ is: $n_1 - 2 + n_2 - 2 = n_1 + n_2 - 4 = n + 2 - 4 = n - 2$. Similarly, the total number of diagonals in polygon $\mathscr{P}$ is: $n_1 - 3 + n_2 - 3 + 1 = n_1 + n_2 - 5 = n + 2 - 5 = n - 3$. By the principle of mathematical induction, any polygon $\mathscr{P}$ with n vertices contains exactly $n - 2$ triangles and $n - 3$ diagonals after triangulation, which was to be proven. ∎

> **Observation 5.1.3** The sum of the interior angles of a polygon $\mathscr{P}$ consisting of n vertices is equal to $(n-2)\pi$.

> **Lemma 5.1.4** Let $\triangle ABC$ be a triangle in the plane such that the vertices A, B, and C are oriented in the counterclockwise direction. Then, the area of the triangle is given by
>
> $$\mathscr{A}(\triangle ABC) = \mathscr{A}(\triangle DAB) + \mathscr{A}(\triangle DBC) + \mathscr{A}(\triangle DCA), \tag{5.3}$$
>
> where D is an arbitrary point in the plane.

Proof. Since the point D is chosen arbitrarily, two cases may occur: the point D lies either inside the triangle $\triangle ABC$ or outside of it (see Fig. 5.3). Suppose that the point D lies outside the triangle $\triangle ABC$ (see Fig. 5.3 (a)). Given that the vertices of the triangles $\triangle DBC$ and $\triangle DCA$ are oriented counterclockwise, their areas are positive, and their sum equals the area of the quadrilateral $\square DBCA$. On the other hand, the vertices of the triangle $\triangle DAB$ are oriented clockwise, hence its area is negative. By summing the area of triangle $\triangle DAB$ with the area of the quadrilateral $\square DBCA$, the total area of triangle $\triangle ABC$ is obtained. In the case when the point D lies inside the triangle $\triangle ABC$ (see Fig. 5.3 (b)), all triangles $\triangle DAB$, $\triangle DBC$, and $\triangle DCA$ are positively oriented, i.e., their vertices are oriented counterclockwise, so the area of each of these triangles is positive, and their sum gives the total area of the triangle $\triangle ABC$. This completes the proof of the lemma.

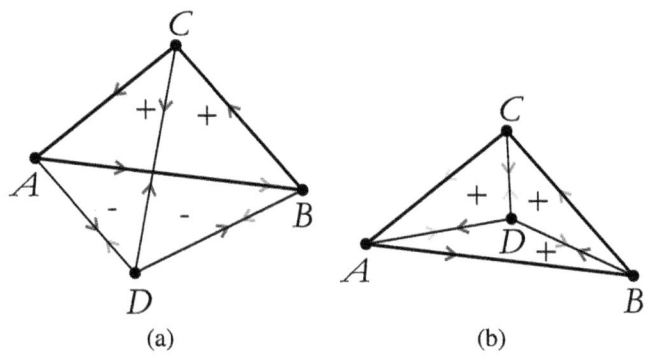

(a)   (b)

Figure 5.3: (a) Point D does not belong to triangle $\triangle ABC$. (b) Point D lies inside triangle $\triangle ABC$.

∎

Theorem 5.1.4 Let $\mathscr{P}$ be a simple polygon consisting of n vertices $P_0(x_0,y_0)$, $P_1(x_1,y_1)$, $P_2(x_2,y_2)$, $\cdots$, $P_{n-1}(x_{n-1},y_{n-1})$ oriented in the counterclockwise direction. Then, the area of the polygon $\mathscr{P}$ is equal to:

$$\mathscr{A}(\mathscr{P}) = \frac{1}{2}\sum_{i=0}^{n-1}(x_i y_{i+1} - x_{i+1}y_i) = \frac{1}{2}\sum_{i=0}^{n-1}(x_{i+1}+x_i)(y_{i+1}-y_i), \tag{5.4}$$

where $P_n(x_n,y_n) = P_0(x_0,y_0)$.

Proof. Relation 5.4 can be derived in two ways. The first method involves the use of Green's theorem, while the second method relies on mathematical induction. The first approach enables the derivation of the formula for computing the area of a polygon, whereas the second approach provides the correctness of that formula.

First method: Green's theorem

In this section, Green's theorem will be exploited to derive a formula for computing the area of a simple polygon $\mathscr{P}$. Green's theorem was introduced by the British scientist **George Green** (1793–1841). This theorem, which is a special case of the more general Stokes' theorem, establishes a connection between the line integral along a simple closed curve $\mathscr{C}$ and the double integral over the region $\mathscr{D}$ bounded by that curve. According to Green's theorem, for a simple, closed, positively oriented curve $\mathscr{C}$ in the plane, and the region $\mathscr{D}$ it encloses, the following holds:

$$\oint_{\mathscr{C}} P(x,y)dx + Q(x,y)dy = \iint_{D}\left(\frac{\partial Q}{\partial x} - \frac{\partial P}{\partial y}\right)dA, \tag{5.5}$$

where the functions $P(x,y)$ and $Q(x,y)$ have continuous partial derivatives on an open region that contains the region $\mathscr{D}$. The curve $\mathscr{C}$ is piecewise smooth. It is clear that the area of the region $\mathscr{D}$ is equal to the double integral $\iint_D dA$. This is achieved when the functions P and Q are taken to be: $P(x,y) = 0$, $Q(x,y) = x$. Now, based on relation 5.5, the area of the region $\mathscr{D}$, denoted by $\mathscr{A}$, is given by

$$\mathscr{A} = \oint_{\mathscr{C}} x\,dy. \tag{5.6}$$

The interior region of the polygon $\mathscr{P}$ can be bounded by a piecewise smooth curve $\mathscr{C} = \mathscr{C}_0 \cup \mathscr{C}_1 \cup \cdots \cup \mathscr{C}_{n-1}$, such that each $\mathscr{C}_k$ starts at point (x_0, y_0) and ends at the next point along the polygon's boundary, assuming the vertices are traversed in a counterclockwise direction (see Fig. 5.4).

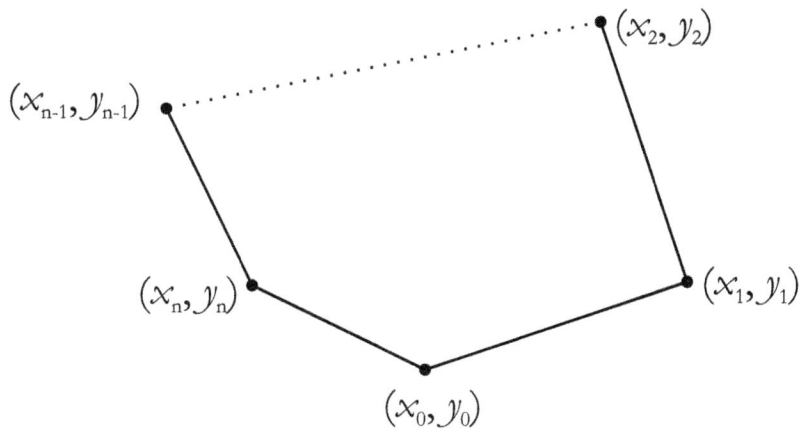

Figure 5.4: Traversal of polygon vertices in counterclockwise direction.

It is known that for piecewise smooth curves, line integrals are additive over their length, so relation 5.6 can be expressed as a sum of line integrals as follows:

$$\mathscr{A} = \oint_{\mathscr{C}} x\,dy = \sum_{i=0}^{n-1} \int_{\mathscr{C}_i} x\,dy. \tag{5.7}$$

To compute any i-th line integral in relation 5.7, it is necessary to express the i-th segment $\overline{P_i P_{i+1}}$ in parametric form. Thus,

$$\mathscr{C}_i : \Big(x_i + t(x_{i+1} - x_i),\ y_i + t(y_{i+1} - y_i) \Big),\, t \in [0, 1]. \tag{5.8}$$

After parametrization, the i-th line integral takes the following form:

$$\int_{\mathscr{C}_i} x\,dy = \begin{vmatrix} \textbf{Substitution:} \\ x : x_i + t(x_{i+1} - x_i) \\ y : y_i + t(y_{i+1} - y_i) \\ t \in [0,1], dy = (y_{i+1} - y_i)dt \end{vmatrix} = \int_0^1 \Big(x_i + t(x_{i+1} - x_i) \Big)(y_{i+1} - y_i)dt = \frac{1}{2}(x_{i+1} + x_i)(y_{i+1} - y_i).$$
$$\tag{5.9}$$

It is easy to observe that the point $P(x, y)$ slides along the segment $\overline{P_i P_{i+1}}$ as the parameter t takes values in the closed interval $[0, 1]$. Based on the last relation and Equation 5.7, after summation, it follows that the total area of the polygon $\mathscr{P}$ is equal to the area given by Equation 5.4, which completes the proof.

Second Approach: Mathematical Induction

The proof of Equation 5.4 is conducted by mathematical induction on the number n. For $n = 3$, based on Lemma 5.1.4, we obtain

$$\mathscr{A}(\mathscr{P}) = \mathscr{A}(\triangle PP_0P_1) + \mathscr{A}(\triangle PP_1P_2) + \mathscr{A}(\triangle PP_2P_0),$$

where the vertex $P(x_3, y_3)$ may lie either inside or outside the triangle $\triangle P_0 P_1 P_2$. These areas can be computed using the vector cross product. Hence, the following holds:

$$\mathscr{A}(\triangle P P_0 P_1) = \frac{1}{2}[x_0(y_1 - y_3) + x_1(y_3 - y_0) + x_3(y_0 - y_1)],$$

$$\mathscr{A}(\triangle P P_1 P_2) = \frac{1}{2}[x_1(y_2 - y_3) + x_2(y_3 - y_1) + x_3(y_1 - y_2)],$$

$$\mathscr{A}(\triangle P P_2 P_0) = \frac{1}{2}[x_0(y_3 - y_2) + x_2(y_0 - y_3) + x_3(y_2 - y_0)].$$

By summing the above areas and assuming that $P(x_3, y_3) = P_0(x_0, y_0)$ due to the closed nature of the polygon $\mathscr{P}$, and after rearranging the factors, the following relation is obtained:

$$\mathscr{A}(\mathscr{P}) = \frac{1}{2}[x_0(y_1 - y_2) + x_1(y_2 - y_0) + x_2(y_0 - y_1)] = \frac{1}{2}\sum_{i=0}^{2}(x_i y_{i+1} - x_{i+1} y_i).$$

Thus, the claim holds for $n = 3$. Assume that the equality in relation 5.4 is valid for all polygons $\mathscr{P}'$ having $n - 1$ vertices. Theorem 5.1.1 states that every polygon can be triangulated and contains $n - 2$ triangles and $n - 3$ diagonals. Without loss of generality, let the vertices $P_{n-2}(x_{n-2}, y_{n-2})$, $P_{n-1}(x_{n-1}, y_{n-1})$, and $P_0(x_0, y_0)$ form the triangle that is removed from the polygon $\mathscr{P}$ during the triangulation. If these vertices do not initially form a triangle, the vertex labeling can always be adjusted so that they do. After removing the triangle $\triangle P_{n-2} P_{n-1} P_0$ from the polygon $\mathscr{P}$, a new polygon $\mathscr{P}_{n-1}$ consisting of $n - 1$ vertices is obtained. Applying the inductive assumption to this polygon yields:

$$\mathscr{A}(\mathscr{P}_{n-1}) = \frac{1}{2}\sum_{i=0}^{n-2}(x_i y_{i+1} - x_{i+1} y_i) = \sum_{i=0}^{n-3}\mathscr{A}(\triangle P P_i P_{i+1}) + \mathscr{A}(\triangle P P_{n-2} P_0). \tag{5.10}$$

Based on the previous relation, the area of the polygon $\mathscr{P}$ is equal to the sum of the areas of the polygon $\mathscr{P}_{n-1}$ and the triangle $\triangle P_{n-2} P_{n-1} P_0$. According to Lemma 5.1.4, the area of the triangle $\triangle P_{n-2} P_{n-1} P_0$ is given by

$$\mathscr{A}(\triangle P_{n-2} P_{n-1} P_0) = \mathscr{A}(\triangle P P_{n-2} P_{n-1}) + \mathscr{A}(\triangle P P_{n-1} P_0) + \mathscr{A}(\triangle P P_0 P_{n-2}).$$

Since $\mathscr{A}(\triangle P P_{n-2} P_0) = -\mathscr{A}(\triangle P P_0 P_{n-2})$, and due to the closedness of the polygon it holds that $P_n = P_0$, the area of the triangle $\mathscr{A}(\triangle P_{n-2} P_{n-1} P_0)$ becomes

$$\mathscr{A}(\triangle P_{n-2} P_{n-1} P_0) = \mathscr{A}(\triangle P P_{n-2} P_{n-1}) + \mathscr{A}(\triangle P P_{n-1} P_n) - \mathscr{A}(\triangle P P_{n-2} P_0).$$

Finally, the area of the polygon $\mathscr{P}$ is given by:

$$\mathscr{A}(\mathscr{P}) = \mathscr{A}(\mathscr{P}_{n-1}) + \mathscr{A}(\triangle P_{n-2} P_{n-1} P_0) = \sum_{i=0}^{n-2}\mathscr{A}(\triangle P P_i P_{i+1}) + \mathscr{A}(\triangle P P_{n-1} P_0) = \sum_{i=0}^{n-1}\mathscr{A}(\triangle P P_i P_{i+1}).$$
$$\tag{5.11}$$

Since the last relation has the same form as relation 5.10, it follows that it represents the area of the polygon $\mathscr{P}$, which was to be proven.   ■

5.2　Algorithms for Triangulating a Simple Polygon

In this section, four algorithms for triangulating a simple polygon without holes will be presented: the naive algorithm, the ear clipping algorithm, the recursive algorithm, and the algorithm based on the sweep line paradigm.

5.2.1　Naive Algorithm

Naive triangulation of a polygon $\mathscr{P}$ with n vertices is based on generating all possible segments between pairs of non-adjacent vertices. There can be at most $\frac{n(n-3)}{2}$ such segments. In the first phase, among them, all segments are eliminated that:

- do not lie entirely within the polygon (i.e., segments not fully contained within $\mathscr{P}$);
- intersect any of the polygon's sides $\partial\mathscr{P}$, except possibly at their endpoints.

This phase requires $\mathscr{O}(n^3)$ time, since for each of the $\mathscr{O}(n^2)$ candidates, up to $\mathscr{O}(n)$ intersection checks may be needed. After this, k segments remain ($k < n^2$). In the second phase, it is necessary to select among them those that do not mutually intersect, except at shared endpoints. This check can be efficiently performed using the sweep line algorithm, with a time complexity of $\mathscr{O}(k\log k)$, which is significantly more efficient than the cubic complexity of the previous phase. As a result, the overall efficiency is improved, although this approach remains inferior compared to optimized triangulation algorithms, such as the ear clipping algorithm or the monotone partitioning algorithm.

5.2.2　Ear Clipping Algorithm

In this section, the basic idea behind the ear clipping algorithm will be presented, followed by its implementation. Let $\mathscr{P}$ be a polygon with n vertices. In order to decompose this polygon into triangles, it is necessary to find all its internal diagonals. If the polygon is convex, then all of its diagonals are internal, allowing triangulation in linear time by connecting any vertex to all non-adjacent vertices. Convexity of a polygon can be checked in linear time by analyzing the orientation of the triangles: $\triangle P_0P_1P_2$, $\triangle P_1P_2P_3$, $\dots$, $\triangle P_{n-2}P_{n-1}P_0$. If all orientations have the same sign, the polygon is convex; otherwise, it is not. In some cases, only two orientation checks are sufficient to conclude that the polygon is not convex. In the following, it is assumed that the polygon is not convex, which implies that some of its diagonals are not internal, and a procedure for identifying them must be described. Let the vertices of the polygon $\mathscr{P}$ be denoted as $P_0, P_1, \dots, P_{n-1}$ and given in clockwise order. Since the vertices are stored in a doubly linked circular list, the predecessor of vertex P_0 is P_{n-1}, and its successor is P_1. The process of searching for diagonals starts from the vertex P_0. In the initial phase, the potential endpoints of a diagonal d are vertices P_{n-1} and P_1, i.e., $d = \overline{P_{n-1}P_1}$. For d to be a valid internal diagonal, it must lie inside polygon $\mathscr{P}$ and must not intersect its boundary $\partial\mathscr{P}$. Validation of whether a segment is an internal diagonal can be performed in constant time using the *Cone method* . This method first checks whether one of the endpoints of the diagonal is convex or reflex (see Fig. 5.5). Without loss of generality, let $A = P_0$, $B = P_2$, $A_- = P_1$, $A_+ = P_{n-1}$. In the cone method, a vertex A is said to be convex if the vertices A, A_+, and A_- of triangle $\triangle AA_+A_-$ are positively oriented (see Fig. 5.5 (a)). If the orientation is negative, then vertex A is considered reflex in the cone method, as shown in Fig. 5.5 (b)).

If vertex A is convex, then the diagonal $\overline{AB}$ lies inside the polygon $\mathscr{P}$, i.e., it passes through the cone A_-AA_+ *if and only if* the vertices A, B, and A_-, as well as the vertices B, A, and A_+, are positively oriented. In Fig. 5.5 (a), the segment $\overline{AB}$ is indeed an interior diagonal of the polygon $\mathscr{P}$. If vertex A is reflex, then the diagonal $\overline{AB}$ lies inside the polygon $\mathscr{P}$ *if and only if* the vertices A, B, and A_+ or the vertices B, A, and A_- are negatively oriented. After this descriptive explanation of the procedure for testing whether a segment belongs to the interior of a polygon, the implementation of the method *is_inside_polygon($\cdot$)* of the **Segment2D** class can be performed as follows:

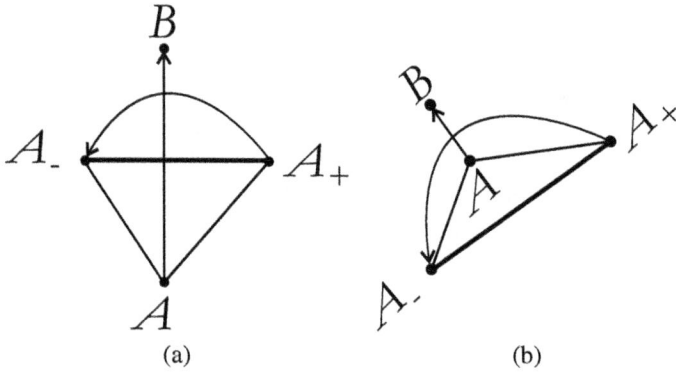

Figure 5.5: (a) Vertex *A* is convex. (b) Vertex *A* is reflex.

```
1 def is_inside_polygon(self, p: 'Polygon') -> bool:
2     s = self; a = s[0]; b = s[1]
3     v = p.neighbor(1)   # Current vertex A
4     aP = v.neighbor(1).vertex_point()   # A+
5     aN = v.neighbor(-1).vertex_point()   # A-
6     if a.classification_m(aP, aN) == TypeP2.LEFT:   # Vertex a is convex
7         if (a.classification_m(b,aN)==TypeP2.LEFT and b.classification_m(a,aP)==
            TypeP2.LEFT): return True
8     else:   # Vertex a is reflex
9         if (a.classification_m(b,aP)==TypeP2.RIGHT or b.classification_m(a,aN)==
            TypeP2.RIGHT): return True
10    return False
```

After describing the procedure for verifying whether a diagonal is interior, the triangulation process of the polygon is based on the gradual removal of diagonals that satisfy this condition. Specifically, if the segment $d = \overline{P_1P_{n-1}}$ is an interior diagonal, it is either stored in the list of identified diagonals or visually displayed, while vertex P_0 is removed from the polygon $\mathscr{P}$. This results in a new polygon $\mathscr{P}'$, on which the search for the remaining diagonals continues. The removal of diagonals is carried out through a procedure known as *Ear Clipping*, where the triangle $\triangle P_{n-1}P_0P_1$, formed by the vertices P_{n-1}, P_0, and P_1, is eliminated from the polygon. This process is repeated iteratively as long as the number of vertices of the remaining polygon is greater than three. The implementation of the algorithm based on the ear clipping method is realized within the function *triangulate_eca()*, whose code is presented below:

```
1 def triangulate_eca(self) -> list[tuple[Point2D, Point2D]]:
2     diagonals = []
3     if self.is_convex():   # polygon is convex
4         a = self.current_vertex(); b = self.neighbor(1)
5         while a.neighbor(-1) != b.neighbor(1):
6             self.move_current(1); b = self.neighbor(1)
7             diagonals.append((a.vertex_point(), b.vertex_point()))
8     else:   # polygon is concave
9         while self.size() > 3:
10            left=self.neighbor(1).vertex_point()
11            right=self.neighbor(-1).vertex_point()
12            s = Segment2D(left, right)
13            if not s.intersects_polygon(self) and s.is_inside_polygon(self):
14                diagonals.append((left, right)); self.remove()
```

```
15        else: self.move_current(-1)
16    return diagonals
```

An analysis of the *triangulate_eca*() method shows that the algorithm has a time complexity of $\mathcal{O}(n)$ if the polygon is convex, while in the case of a concave polygon, the complexity is of the order $\mathcal{O}(n^2)$. Namely, according to Lemma 5.1.3, the total number of diagonals is $n-3$, which means that in the worst case, the algorithm performs $(n-3) \cdot n$ iterations. This results from the fact that the *intersects_polygon*($\cdot$) method of the **Segment2D** class has linear complexity with respect to the number of points n, while the *is_inside_polygon*($\cdot$) method operates in constant time. A graphical interface for computing polygon decomposition can be constructed using the implementation provided in Listing 5.1, as illustrated in Fig. 5.6.

Listing 5.1: Graphical Interface for Visualization of Polygon Decomposition

```python
1  import tkinter as tk
2  import random
3  from geometry import Point2D, Segment2D, Polygon
4  class GeometricVisualizer:
5      def __init__(self, master):
6          self.master = master
7          self.master.title("GUI FOR POLYGON TRIANGULATION-Ear Clipping Algorithm")
8          self.main_frame = tk.Frame(master)
9          self.main_frame.pack(fill=tk.BOTH,expand=True)
10         self.canvas = tk.Canvas(self.main_frame,width=800,height=600,bg="white")
11         self.canvas.pack(side=tk.LEFT,padx=10,pady=10)
12         self.control_frame = tk.Frame(self.main_frame)
13         self.control_frame.pack(side=tk.RIGHT,padx=10,pady=10,fill=tk.Y)
14         self.sim_pol_button = tk.Button(self.control_frame,text="Triangulate",
               command=self.visualise_triangles)
15         self.sim_pol_button.pack(pady=5)
16         self.v_p: List[Point2D] = [] # vertices of polygon
17         self.phase = 'draw_polygon' # phases: draw_polygon -> triangulate polygo
18         self.canvas.bind("<ButtonPress-1>", self.on_left_click)
19         self.canvas.bind("<ButtonPress-3>", self.on_right_click)  # finish polygon
20     def on_left_click(self, e):
21         if self.phase == 'draw_polygon':
22             pt = Point2D(e.x,e.y); self.v_p.append(pt)
23             if len(self.v_p) > 1:
24                 l=self.v_p[-2]; self.canvas.create_line(l[0], l[1], pt[0], pt[1],
                     fill='gray',width=2)
25             self.canvas.create_oval(pt[0]-3,pt[1]-3,pt[0]+3,pt[1]+3,fill='red'
                 )
26     def on_right_click(self, e):
27         if self.phase == 'draw_polygon' and len(self.v_p) >= 3:
28             F= self.v_p[0] #first vertex
29             L= self.v_p[-1] # last vertex
30             self.canvas.create_oval(F[0]-3,F[1]-3,F[0]+3,F[1]+3,fill='red')
31             self.canvas.create_line(L[0],L[1],F[0],F[1],fill='gray',width=2)
32             self.phase = 'triangulate_polygon'
33     def visualise_triangles(self):
34         polygon = Polygon()
35         for i in range(len(self.v_p)): polygon.insert(self.v_p[i])
36         if polygon.area() < 0: polygon.change_orientation()
37         segments=polygon.triangulate_eca()#Call Ear Clipping Algorithm
38         for i in range(len(segments)):
39             seg = segments[i]
```

```
40          x1,y1=seg[0][0],seg[0][1]; x2,y2=seg[1][0],seg[1][1]
41          self.canvas.create_line(x1, y1, x2, y2, fill='black', width=1)
42
43 if __name__ == '__main__':
44 root = tk.Tk()
45 app = GeometricVisualizer(root)
46 root.mainloop()
```

Observation 5.2.1 The triangulation of a polygon using the *triangulate_eca()* method can only be performed if all points are provided in counterclockwise order, which is handled within the *visualise_triangles()* function as shown in Listing 5.1. If some of the points follow one orientation and the remaining points another, it is necessary to renumber them to ensure consistent orientation. In the case of randomly given points, a simple polygon must first be reconstructed from them, then oriented in the counterclockwise direction, and only then can the triangulation process be applied.

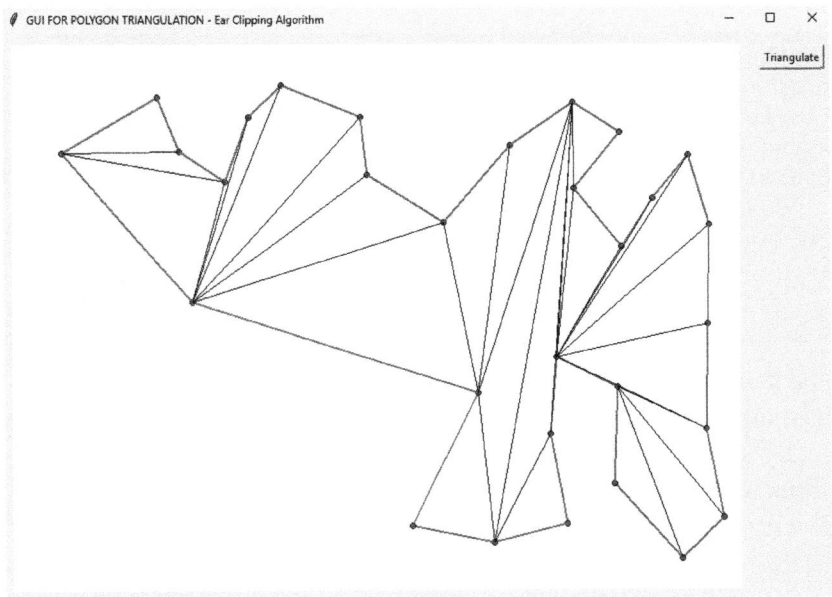

Figure 5.6: Triangulation of a simple polygon consisting of 30 points.

Lemma 5.2.1 Any polygon consisting of n ($n \geq 4$) vertices has at least two ears.

Proof. The proof of this lemma directly follows from Leme 5.1.3 and the fact that each ear corresponds to exactly one triangle. ∎

5.2.3 Recursive Algorithm

According to Lemma 5.1.3, it is possible to construct a recursive algorithm for polygon triangulation. Once an internal diagonal of the initial polygon $\mathscr{P}$ is identified, the algorithm is recursively applied to the subpolygons formed by that diagonal. In the worst-case scenario, the recursion depth reaches $n - 3$, while the time required to find a diagonal is linear with respect to the number of vertices n. Consequently, the total time complexity of the algorithm in the worst case is $\mathcal{O}(n^2)$. For a complete implementation of this algorithm, two additional methods of the **Polygon** class must be implemented. The first method, *get_convex_vertex()*, is used to identify a convex vertex within an arbitrary simple polygon. Let the vertices A, B, and C be given in counterclockwise order. According to the definition of a convex vertex, if vertex B is convex, then point C lies to the left of the segment $\overline{AB}$, indicating a left turn at vertex B. The implementation of this method is provided below:

```
1 def get_convex_vertex(self) -> Vertex:
2     a = self.neighbor(-1); b= self.current; c = self.neighbor(1);
3     while c.classification_m(a.vertex_point(), b.vertex_point()) == TypeP2.RIGHT:
4         a = b; b=self.move_current(1); c = self.neighbor(1)
5     return self.current
```

The second method, *nearest_vertex*($\cdot$), is designed to return the nearest vertex d, if such a vertex exists, relative to a given convex vertex c_v—passed as a formal parameter—according to Lemma 5.1.3. The implementation of this method is presented below:

```
1 def nearest_vertex(self, c_v: Vertex) -> Vertex | None:
2     a = self.neighbor(-1); b = c_v; c = self.neighbor(1); d = None
3     triangle = Polygon(); triangle.insert(a.vertex_point());
4     triangle.insert(b.vertex_point()); triangle.insert(c.vertex_point())
5     smallest_distance = 0.0; v = self.move_current(1)
6     while v != a:
7         if triangle.contains_point(v.vertex_point()):
8             distance=v.distance(Segment2D(c.vertex_point(),a.vertex_point()))
9             if distance >smallest_distance:
10                d = v; smallest_distance = distance
11        v = self.move_current(1)
12    self.update_current(b)
13    return d
```

Based on the implementation above, it is evident that the method *contains_point*($\cdot$) from the **Polygon** class is invoked. Since a triangle is a special case of a polygon, its usage is entirely justified in this context. Naturally, a completely separate function for testing whether a point lies within a triangle could also have been written. Specifically, to determine whether a point P lies inside the triangle $\triangle ABC$, one must connect the point P with the vertices A, B, and C of triangle $\triangle ABC$, and then check the orientation of the triples (P,A,B), (P,B,C), and (P,C,A). If all these orientations have the same sign—i.e., the areas of triangles $\triangle PAB$, $\triangle PBC$, and $\triangle PCA$ share the same sign—then the point P lies inside the triangle $\triangle ABC$. Otherwise, it does not. It is known from earlier that if A is a convex vertex and B is its nearest vertex lying inside the polygon, then the diagonal $\overline{AB}$ splits the polygon $\mathscr{P}$ into two smaller subpolygons, to which the same procedure for finding new diagonals is recursively applied. This process terminates when the number of vertices in each resulting subpolygon is exactly three. Based on the above, the recursive implementation of the *triangulate_recursive*($\cdot$) method of the **Polygon** class can be constructed as follows:

```
1 def triangulate_recursive(self, diagonals: list[tuple[Point2D, Point2D]]):
2     if self.count > 3:
3         d = self.nearest_vertex(self.get_convex_vertex())
4         if d is None:   # No nearest vertex found
5             c = self.neighbor(1)
6             diagonals.append((self.neighbor(-1).vertex_point(), c.vertex_point()))
7             self.move_current(-1); q = self.split(c)
8             self.triangulate_recursive(diagonals)
9             q.triangulate_recursive(diagonals)
10        else:   # Found the nearest vertex
11            diagonals.append((self.point_of_current(), d.vertex_point()))
12            q = self.split(d); self.triangulate_recursive(diagonals)
```

13   q.triangulate_recursive(diagonals)

It is not difficult to observe that the working principle of this algorithm resembles that of the QuickSort algorithm, and that in some cases its complexity may be of order $\mathcal{O}(n\log n)$. Based on experiments conducted by the author of this text, it has been shown that this algorithm is significantly faster compared to the quadratic ear clipping algorithm. A graphical interface for the recursive algorithm for computing the triangulation of a simple polygon, implemented through Listing 5.1, is shown in Fig. 5.7, where the *triangulate_recursive*(·) method is called instead of *triangulate_eca*(). This call is performed by defining a local list of segments (segments= []), which is then passed to the method *triangulate_recursive*(·), i.e., *triangulate_recursive*(segments).

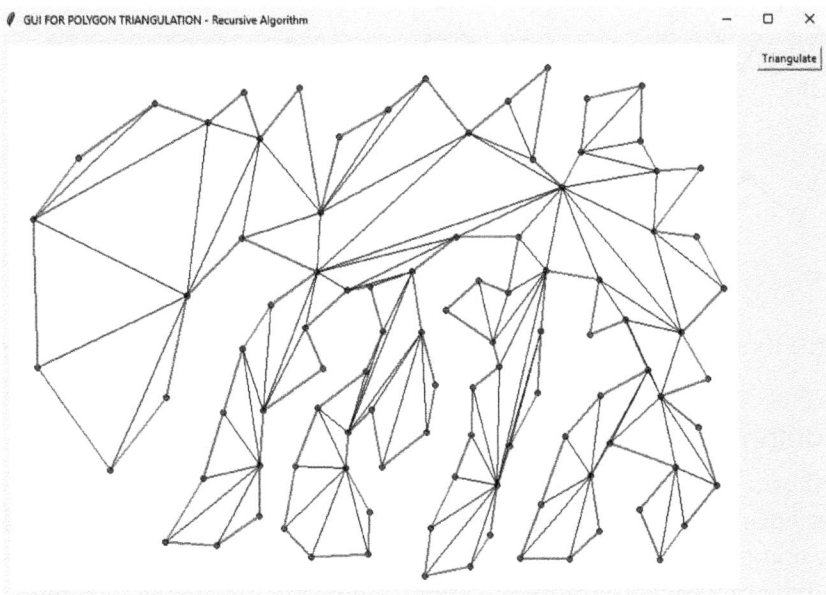

Figure 5.7: Triangulation of a simple polygon for a set of 100 randomly generated points.

5.3 Triangulation of Monotone Polygons

This section presents a linear-time algorithm for the triangulation of monotone polygons. Before providing a detailed description of the algorithm, it is necessary to define the concept of a monotone chain, which forms the foundation of a monotone polygon.

Definition 5.3.1 A chain L consisting of k vertices is said to be *monotone* if an imaginary vertical line intersects it at exactly one point.

If, during its translation from left to right—or when traversing the vertices of the chain in increasing order along the x-axis—a vertical line intersects the chain at more than one point, then, according to Definition 5.3.1, the chain is not monotone (see Fig. 5.8 (b)). An example of a monotone chain is illustrated in Fig. 5.8 (a).

Let the vertices of the polygon be given in a clockwise order. If that is not the case, they can always be reoriented accordingly. The *upper monotone chain* is formed by traversing the vertices from the leftmost to the rightmost vertex, while the *lower monotone chain* is obtained by traversing from the rightmost to the leftmost vertex. The traversal of all vertices is always performed in a clockwise direction. An example of a monotone polygon composed of an upper and lower monotone chain is shown in Fig. 5.9 (a).

Figure 5.8: (a) Monotone vertex chain. (b) Vertex chain is not monotone.

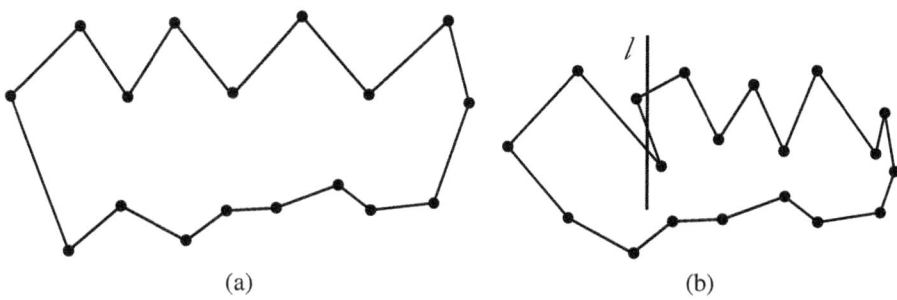

Figure 5.9: (a) Example of a monotone polygon. (b) Example of a non-monotone polygon.

5.3.1 Linear-Time Algorithm for Triangulating a Monotone Polygon

This section describes a linear-time algorithm for triangulating a monotone polygon, along with the data structures that ensure the triangulation process runs in asymptotically $\mathscr{O}(n)$ time. Let $\mathscr{P}$ be a monotone polygon composed of n vertices V_0, V_1, V_2, $\cdots$, V_{n-1}, with a subset of the vertices lying on the upper chain and the remaining ones on the lower chain (see Fig. 5.9 (a)). Within the algorithm, the vertices of the upper and lower chains are processed based on their position along the x-axis. During the algorithm's execution, smaller monotone polygons are generated as intermediate decompositions. For example, a smaller monotone polygon $\mathscr{P}_i$ is obtained by decomposing the current polygon $\mathscr{P}_{i-1}$ into multiple triangles. The algorithm terminates when no further monotone polygons can be decomposed. The final collection of triangles resulting from the decomposition constitutes the triangulation of the original monotone polygon $\mathscr{P}$. For the triangulation of the monotone polygon $\mathscr{P}$, a stack is used as the primary data structure to store and manage the processed polygon vertices. Therefore, the entire vertex processing is tracked via the stack. Let the stack contain t vertices denoted in order as $S_1, S_2, \cdots, S_t$, where S_t is the most recently added vertex and the first to be removed from the stack according to the **LIFO** principle. The rules that must be followed during stack manipulation are as follows:

1. The vertices $S_1, S_2, \cdots, S_t$ are sorted in increasing order with respect to the x-axis and include all vertices of the polygon $\mathscr{P}_{i-1}$ that lie between vertices S_1 and S_t;

2. The vertices $S_1, S_2, \cdots, S_t$ are adjacent vertices or lie entirely on either the upper or lower chain of the polygon $\mathscr{P}_{i-1}$;

3. The vertices $S_1, S_2, \cdots, S_t$ are reflex vertices of the polygon $\mathscr{P}_{i-1}$;

4. In polygon $\mathscr{P}_{i-1}$, vertex V_i can be in exactly one of the following three states (see Fig. 5.10):

    a) V_i is adjacent to S_t but not to S_1;

    b) V_i is adjacent to S_1 but not to S_t;

    c) V_i is adjacent to both S_1 and S_t.

Since items a), b), and c) of Rule 4 are crucial for the implementation of the algorithm, each of them will be explained in detail separately.

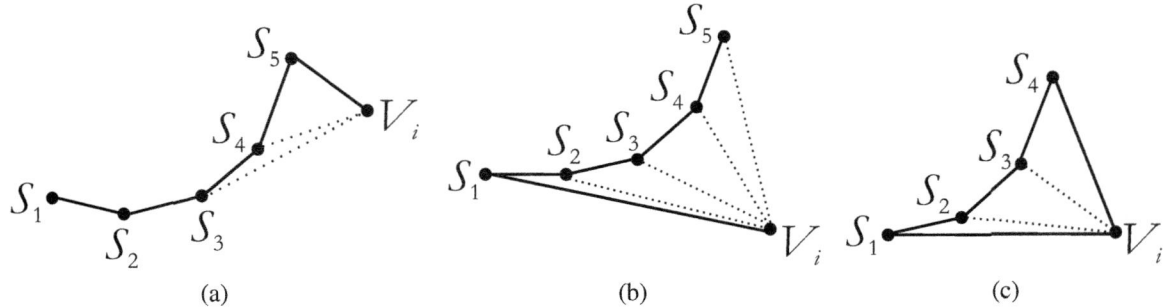

Figure 5.10: Three possible states of Rule 4) in which the vertex V_i may be found.

Case a) If the vertex V_i falls into this state, then while the stack is not empty ($t > 1$) and the angle $\angle V_i S_t S_{t-1} < \pi$, the triangle $\triangle V_i S_t S_{t-1}$ is successively removed from the polygon $\mathscr{P}_{i-1}$, and the stack is updated accordingly, i.e., the processed vertex S_t is popped from the stack. When one of the conditions is no longer satisfied, the triangle removal procedure is terminated, and the vertex V_i is pushed onto the stack. In the implementation of this scenario, instead of checking $\angle V_i S_t S_{t-1} < \pi$, it is more efficient to determine on which side of the vector $\overrightarrow{V_i S_t}$ (i.e., the segment $\overline{V_i S_t}$) the vertex S_{t-1} lies. Namely, if the vertex V_i lies on the upper chain of the polygon $\mathscr{P}_{i-1}$, then $\angle V_i S_t S_{t-1} < \pi$ *iff* the vertex S_{t-1} lies to the left of the segment $\overline{V_i S_t}$. However, if the vertex V_i belongs to the lower chain of the polygon, then $\angle V_i S_t S_{t-1} < \pi$ *iff* the vertex S_{t-1} lies to the right of the segment $\overline{V_i S_t}$.

Case b) In this case, the subpolygon $\mathscr{P}_{i-1}$ defined by the vertices $V_i, S_1, \cdots, S_t$ is separated from the polygon defined by the remaining vertices of polygon $\mathscr{P}$ (see Fig. 5.10 (b)). The extracted part is a convex polygon, so its triangulation is performed by drawing diagonals from the vertex V_i to the other elements of the stack S_i ($i = 1, 2, \cdots, t$). Afterwards, the stack is emptied, and elements S_t and V_i are pushed back onto it. In Fig. 5.10 (b), the vertex S_t corresponds to vertex S_5.

Case c) In this case, the currently processed vertex V_i becomes V_n. This indicates that all vertices have been processed, and the polygon $\mathscr{P}_{i-1}$ composed of vertices $V_i, S_1, \cdots, S_t$ is triangulated as in case b), except that the diagonals are now drawn from vertex V_n. Afterwards, the triangulation process for the monotone polygon is complete (see Fig. 5.10 (c)).

To better understand the above-described linear-time procedure for triangulating a monotone polygon, a step-by-step triangulation of the monotone polygon shown in Fig. 5.11 will be provided in the following example.

■ Example 5.1 Let $\mathscr{P}$ be a given monotone polygon composed of ten vertices ($n = 10$), as shown in Fig. 5.11. Determine its triangulation in linear time with respect to the number of vertices, i.e., in time complexity of order $\mathcal{O}(n)$.   ■

Solution. To compute the triangulation of a monotone polygon, one first identifies the leftmost vertex in time $\mathcal{O}(n)$. In Fig. 5.11, this is vertex V_1, which is then added to the initially empty stack $S = \{\}$, resulting in the stack state $S = \{S_1\}$, where $S_1 \leftarrow V_1$. The algorithm continues by processing vertices of the polygonal chains sorted in increasing order with respect to their x-coordinates. The first such vertex is V_2. Since it belongs to the upper chain and precedes vertex V_5 of the lower chain, it is added to the stack, yielding $S = \{S_1, S_2\}$ with $S_2 \leftarrow V_2$. The next vertex to be processed is V_3. As it is adjacent to

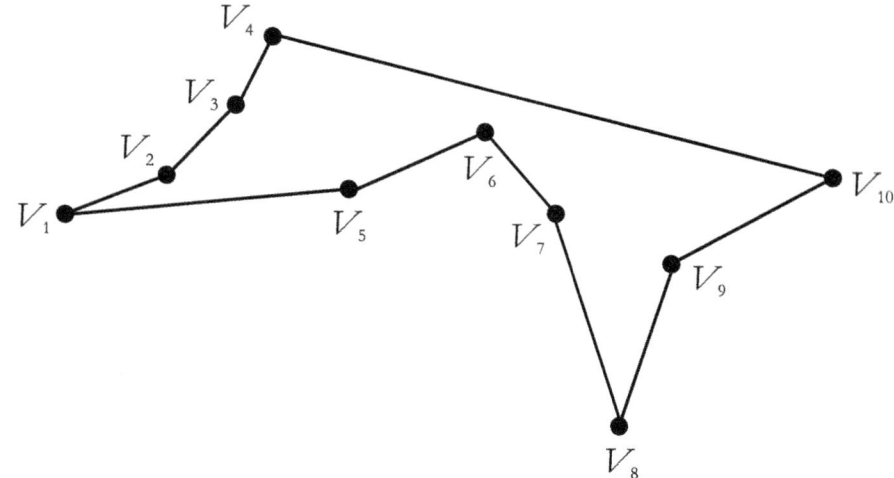

Figure 5.11: A monotone polygon composed of ten vertices.

S_2 ($t = 2$) but not to S_1, scenario 4. a) is triggered. Since S_1 lies to the right of segment $\overline{V_3 S_2}$, vertex V_3 is added to the stack, resulting in $S = \{S_1, S_2, S_3\}$ with $S_3 \leftarrow V_3$. By analogy, it follows that vertex V_4 is also added to the stack, leading to $S = \{S_1, S_2, S_3, S_4\}$ and $S_4 \leftarrow V_4$. Up to this point, no polygon decomposition has occurred, as illustrated in Fig. 5.12 (a). Continuing from V_4, the next vertex is V_5 (adjacent to S_1), and it precedes vertex V_{10} (adjacent to S_4). Now the situation arises where V_5 is incident to S_1 but not to S_4, which triggers scenario 4. b). Accordingly, the convex polygon defined by vertices V_5 and the stack elements S_1, S_2, S_3, and S_4 is triangulated by drawing diagonals from V_5 (see Fig. 5.12 (b)). After this step, the stack is cleared, and elements S_4 and V_5 are pushed back onto it, i.e., $S = \{S_4, S_5\}$ with $S_5 \leftarrow V_5$. From this point on, the triangulated region is not shown graphically, as it has been decomposed (clipped) from the original polygon. The current polygonal state is illustrated in Fig. 5.12 (c). Since S_4 lies to the right of segment $\overline{V_6 S_5}$ and vertex V_6 belongs to the lower chain, scenario 4. a) applies. As a result, triangle $\triangle S_4 V_5 S_6$ is successively extracted from the polygon, and S_5 is removed from the stack. The updated polygon is shown in Fig. 5.12 (d). After this operation, the stack contains only one element ($t = 1$), which terminates the extraction procedure, and vertex V_6 is added to the stack. The new stack state is $S = \{S_4, S_6\}$ with $S_6 \leftarrow V_6$. At this point, five triangles have been decomposed using vertices $\{V_1, V_2, V_3, V_4, V_5, V_6\}$. Continuing analogously, it is shown that no decomposition occurs for the current polygon formed by vertices $\{V_4, V_6, V_7, V_8, V_9, V_{10}\}$. Thus, vertices V_7 and V_8 are added to the stack, updating it to $S = \{S_4, S_6, S_7, S_8\}$. After processing V_9, since S_7 lies to the right of segment $\overline{V_9 S_8}$, triangle $\triangle V_9 S_8 S_7$ is extracted, and S_8 is popped. Similarly, triangle $\triangle V_9 S_7 S_6$ is extracted because S_6 lies to the right of segment $\overline{V_9 S_7}$. The current state of the decomposed polygon is shown in Fig. 5.12 (e). Now S_7 is removed from the stack, giving $S = \{S_4, S_6\}$. Since S_4 does not lie to the right of segment $\overline{V_9 S_6}$, the process halts, and V_9 is added to the stack, yielding $S = \{S_4, S_6, S_9\}$ with $S_9 \leftarrow V_9$. Finally, vertex V_{10} lies on the upper chain and is adjacent to both S_4 and S_9, which corresponds to scenario 4. c). This signals that all vertices have been processed, and the current polygon $\mathscr{P}_{i-1}$ composed of V_{10}, S_4, S_6, and S_9 is triangulated by drawing diagonals from V_{10}. After this, the triangulation process of the monotone polygon is complete. The fully triangulated polygon is shown in Fig. 5.12 (f).

Before implementing the *triangulate_monotone()* method of the **Polygon** class, we first provide the implementation of the *is_monotone()* method. This method is responsible for verifying whether the polygon is monotone. Its implementation is given below:

```
def is_monotone(self) -> bool:
    count=0; c_v=self.current
    for _ in range(self.count):
```

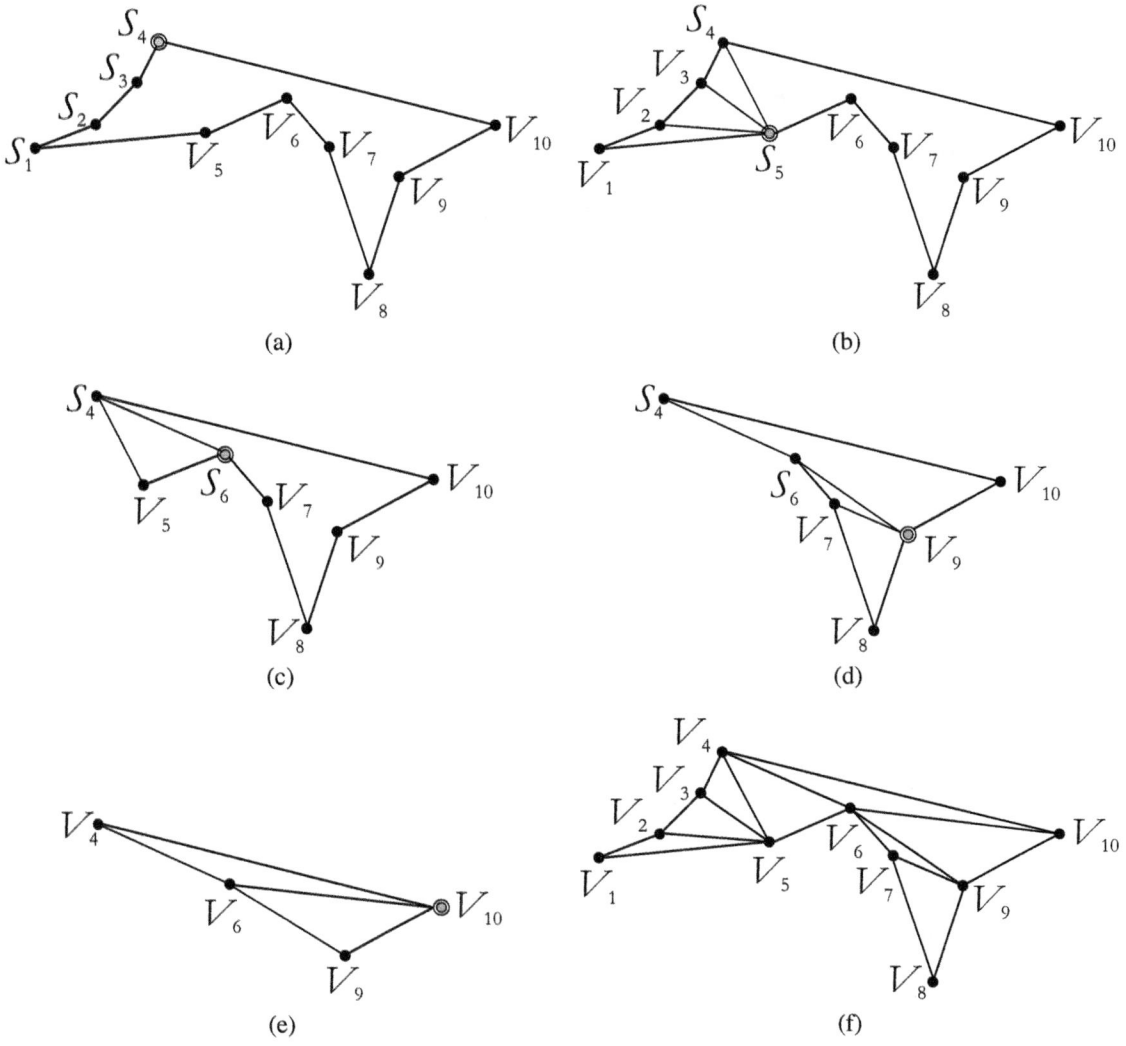

Figure 5.12: Triangulation process of a monotone polygon across steps (a)–(f).

```
4        prev = self.neighbor(1).vertex_point()
5        next = self.neighbor(-1).vertex_point()
6        if self.point_of_current()<prev and self.point_of_current()<next: count+=1
7        if count>1: return False
8        self.move_current(1)
9    self.update_current(c_v)
10   return count == 1
```

If the simple polygon is indeed monotone, then it can be triangulated in $\mathcal{O}(n)$ time, as implemented in the *triangulate_monotone()* method of the **Polygon** class:

```
1 def triangulate_monotone(self) -> List['Polygon']:
2     def are_neighbors(a: Vertex, b: Vertex) -> bool: #help function
3         return b == a.clockwise() or b == a.counter_clockwise()
4
5     def chain_side(u:Vertex,l:Vertex)->tuple[int,Vertex,Vertex,Vertex]:# help fun.
6         if u.clockwise().vertex_point()<l.counter_clockwise().vertex_point():
```

```
7            u=u.clockwise();v=u;return 0, u,l,v #0- is an upper chain
8        else: l=l.counter_clockwise();v=l; return 1, u,l,v #1 is a lower chain
9
10    def triangulate_fan(pol:Polygon, triangle_l: List[Polygon]): #help function
11        v = pol.current_vertex().clockwise().clockwise()
12        for _ in range(2, pol.size()):
13            triangle_l.append(pol.split(v)); v=v.clockwise()
14        triangle_l.append(pol)
15
16    v=self.find_vertex(lambda a, b: -1 if a < b else (1 if a > b else 0));
17    triangles = []; u = l = v; stack = []; stack.append(v)
18    chain, u,l,v =chain_side(u, l); stack.append(v);q=Polygon()
19    while True:
20        chain, u,l,v = chain_side(u,l)
21        if are_neighbors(v,stack[-1]) and not are_neighbors(v,stack[0]):#Case 4.a
22            direction = TypeP2.LEFT if chain == 0 else TypeP2.RIGHT
23            a = stack[-1]; b = stack[-1] if len(stack) == 1 else stack[-2]
24            while stack.size() > 1 and b.vertex_point().classification_m(v.
                     vertex_point(), a.vertex_point()) == direction:
25                if chain == 0: # Upper chain 4. a)
26                    self.update_current(b); triangles.append(self.split(v))
27                else: # Lower chain 4. a)
28                    self.update_current(v); triangles.append(self.split(b))
29                stack.pop();a=b; b=stack[-1] if len(stack)==1 else stack[-2]
30            stack.append(v)
31        elif not are_neighbors(v, stack[-1]): # Case 4. b)
32            st = stack.pop()
33            if chain == 0: #Upper chain 4. b)
34                self.update_current(st); q = self.split(v)
35            else: #Lower chain 4. b)
36                self.update_current(v); q = self.split(st); q.move_current(-1)
37            triangulate_fan(q, triangles)
38            while len(stack)>0: stack.pop()
39            stack.append(st); stack.append(v)
40        else: # Case 4. c)
41            self.update_current(v); triangulate_fan(self, triangles); break
42    return triangles
```

Within the implementation of the *triangulate_monotone*() method of the **Polygon** class, three helper functions are defined: *are_neighbors*(·,·), *chain_side*(·,·), and *triangulate_fan*(·,·). The *are_neighbors*(a, b) function checks whether the vertices a and b are adjacent within the polygonal structure. The *chain_side*(u, l) function determines whether the chain of vertices between two given vertices u and l belongs to the upper or lower chain of a monotone polygon, based on their orientation. Specifically, it compares the vertex reached by u in the clockwise direction with the vertex reached by l in the counterclockwise direction. If the x-coordinate of the point associated with u is smaller, then the chain is considered upper (code 0), and the function returns the tuple $(0, u, l, v)$ with $v = u$. Otherwise, it is considered a lower chain (code 1), and the function returns $(1, u, l, v)$ with $v = l$. The *triangulate_fan*(·, ·) function performs fan triangulation by drawing all interior diagonals from the current vertex to the other vertices in the given list. For example, in Fig. 5.10 (b), diagonals are drawn from vertex V_1 to the vertices S_1, S_2, S_3, S_4, and S_5, effectively decomposing the fan into four triangles.

The graphical interface of the linear-time algorithm for monotone polygon triangulation is shown in Fig. 5.13, and it is implemented based on the code in Listing 5.1. For this purpose, the body of the *visualise_triangles* function should be updated with the following code:

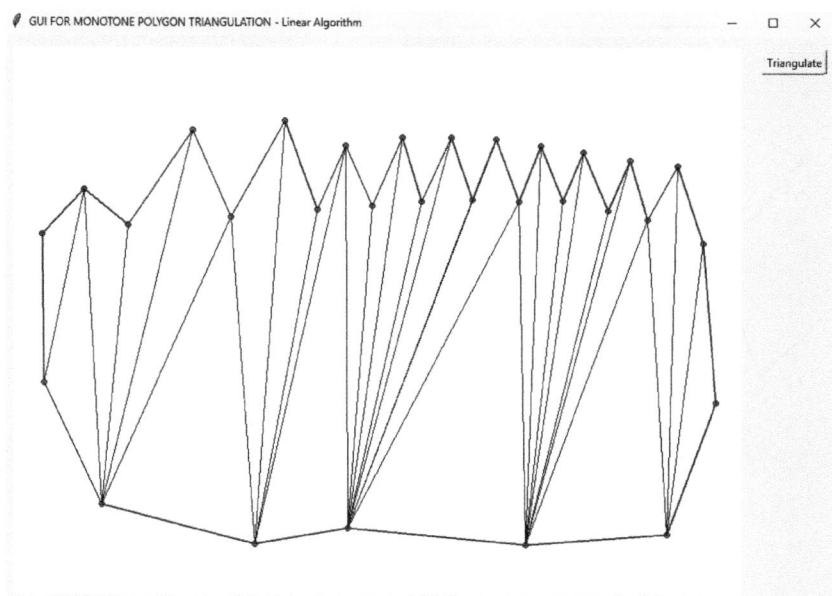

Figure 5.13: Triangulation of a monotone polygon for a set of 30 generated points.

```
1 polygon = Polygon()
2 for v in self.v_p:polygon.insert(v)
3 if polygon.area() < 0: polygon.change_orientation()
4 if not polygon.is_monotone(): messagebox.showwarning("Warning: ", "Polygone is not
      monotone."); return
5 for triangle in polygon.triangulate_monotone():
6     for _ in range(triangle.size()):
7         seg = triangle.current_edge()
8         triangle.move_current(1)
9         x1,y1=seg[0][0],seg[0][1]; x2,y2=seg[1][0],seg[1][1]
10        self.canvas.create_line(x1, y1, x2, y2, fill='black', width=1)
```

5.4 Triangulation of a Polygon Using the Sweep Line Paradigm

This section describes the technique of transforming an arbitrary simple polygon into a sequence of monotone polygons using the sweep line paradigm, with a time complexity of $\Theta(n \log n)$. The algorithm can be implemented in two variants: vertical and horizontal. The vertical variant involves moving the sweep line from top to bottom, during which the polygon is decomposed into one or more y-monotone polygons. The horizontal variant treats the case where the sweep line moves from left to right, partitioning the polygon into several smaller x-monotone polygons. Both variants require processing an event queue, and the horizontal variant can be seen as a $90°$ counterclockwise rotation of the vertical one. For implementation purposes, the decomposition of a simple polygon into several smaller x-monotone polygons will be considered, where the vertices of the polygon are assumed to be ordered in a clockwise direction, as done previously.

Let a simple polygon be given as shown in Figure 5.14, together with the labels of events that will be described in detail below. As the sweep line moves from top to bottom, five different types of events are processed:

E1. **START** — A vertex V is a START vertex if it is convex and both its adjacent vertices lie below it.

E2. **END** — A vertex V is an END vertex if it is convex and both its adjacent vertices lie above it.

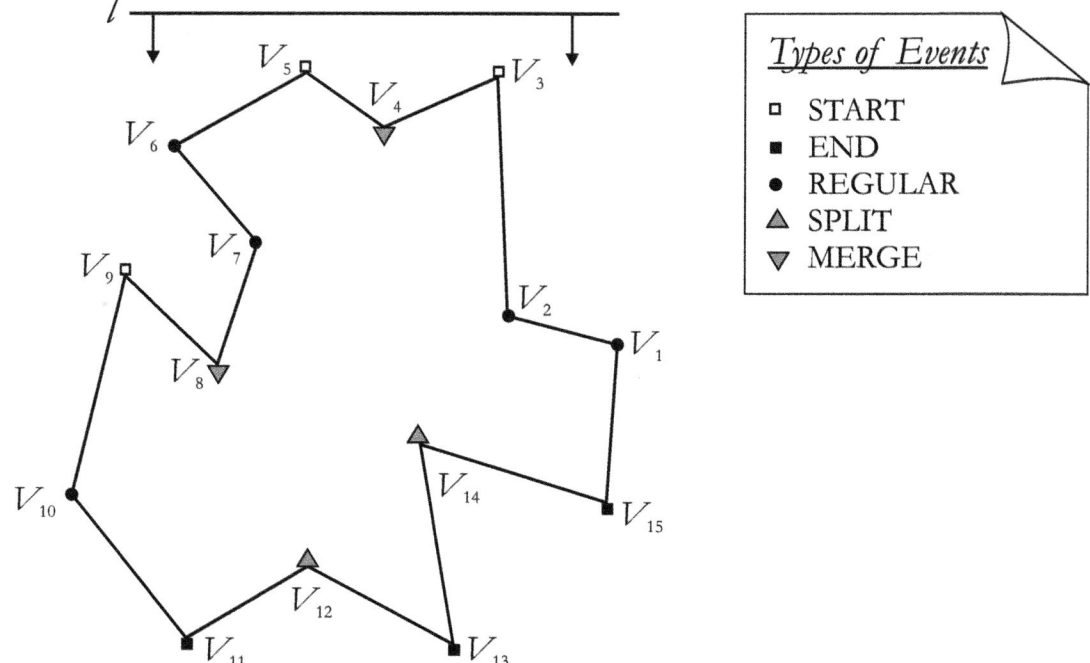

Figure 5.14: Graphical representation of events: *START*, *END*, *REGULAR*, *SPLIT* and *MERGE*.

E3. **SPLIT** — A vertex V is a SPLIT vertex if it is reflex and both its adjacent vertices lie below it.

E4. **MERGE** — A vertex V is a MERGE vertex if it is reflex and both its adjacent vertices lie above it.

E5. **REGULAR** — A vertex V is a REGULAR vertex if none of the above cases apply. That is, V is regular if one adjacent vertex lies above and the other lies below it.

In the event types listed above, the terms *above* and *below* are used, which are defined as follows.

Definition 5.4.1 Let $\mathscr{P}$ be a given polygon, and let V' and V'' be two adjacent vertices of that polygon. Then, vertex V' is said to be *below* of the vertex V'' *if and only if* $V'_y < V''_y$, or $V'_y = V''_y$ and $V'_x > V''_x$.

Definition 5.4.2 Let $\mathscr{P}$ be a given polygon such that the vertices V' and V'' are its neighbors. Then, vertex V' is said to be *above* of the vertex V'' *if and only if* $V'_y > V''_y$, or $V'_y = V''_y$ and $V'_x < V''_x$.

The following lemma states that if the vertices of types MERGE and SPLIT are removed from a simple polygon $\mathscr{P}$, then it becomes a y-monotone polygon.

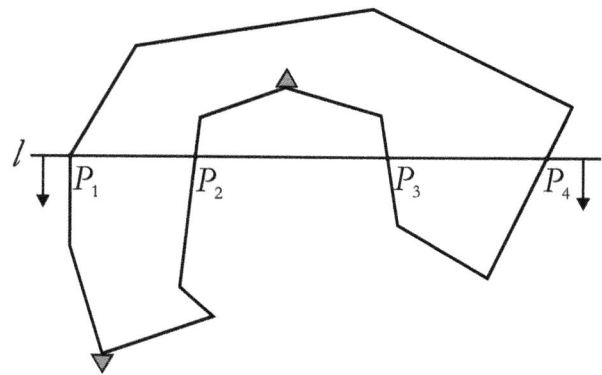

Figure 5.15: Locating MERGE and SPLIT vertices in a non-y-monotone polygon.

Lemma 5.4.1 Let the polygon $\mathscr{P}$ contain no MERGE or SPLIT vertices. Then, $\mathscr{P}$ is a y-monotone polygon.

Proof. In the proof of the lemma, the law of contraposition is used, that is, $A \Rightarrow B \Leftrightarrow \neg B \Rightarrow \neg A$, where the premise A states that the polygon $\mathscr{P}$ has no MERGE or SPLIT vertices, while the conclusion B claims that $\mathscr{P}$ is a y-monotone polygon. Thus, suppose that polygon $\mathscr{P}$ is not y-monotone, i.e., the statement $\neg B$ holds. It remains to prove that $\neg A$ holds as well, meaning that polygon $\mathscr{P}$ contains either a MERGE or a SPLIT vertex. According to the assumption, $\mathscr{P}$ is not a monotone polygon, so there exists a line l parallel to the x-axis that intersects the polygon in more than two points (see Fig. 5.15). Without loss of generality, assume that the intersection points of the line l with the boundary of the polygon $\mathscr{P}$ are denoted by P_1, P_2, P_3, and P_4, as illustrated in Fig. 5.15. It is not difficult to observe that a SPLIT vertex appears if one starts traversing the polygon sides $\mathscr{P}$ from the point P_2 in a clockwise direction, such that the interior of the polygon remains on the left side of the imagined walker. Since $\mathscr{P}$ is not y-monotone, there necessarily exists another intersection point between the polygon and the sweep line l exists reached during this traversal. In the figure, this is the point P_3. It is evident that along the path from P_2 to P_3, a vertex with a y-coordinate greater than those of P_2 and P_3 is encountered. That vertex is a SPLIT vertex (marked in gray), since it is reflex and its neighboring vertices lie below it. Similarly, if one starts from point P_2 and traverses polygon $\mathscr{P}$ downward in the clockwise direction, one eventually reaches the point P_1, another intersection point between the polygon and the sweep line l. Along that path, a MERGE vertex (also shown in gray) is encountered, which is characterized by having a y-coordinate smaller than those of its neighbors, who lie above it, and being reflex as well. This completes the proof of the lemma. ∎

Based on the proven lemma, it follows that the polygon $\mathscr{P}$ becomes y-monotone if all turning vertices are removed. These turning vertices can be eliminated by adding diagonals in such a way that each SPLIT vertex is assigned a diagonal directed upward, and each MERGE vertex a diagonal directed downward, such that these diagonals do not intersect each other. In the following section, the procedure for adding these diagonals will be described.

5.4.1 Removing SPLIT Vertices

Let V_1, V_2, $\cdots$, V_n be the vertices of polygon $\mathscr{P}$, oriented in the counterclockwise direction, and let the edges be denoted as e_1, e_2, $\cdots$, e_n such that $e_i = \overline{V_i V_{i+1}}$ for $i = \overline{1, n-1}$, and $e_n = \overline{V_n V_1}$. Let the sweep line move downward, processing only event points such as SPLIT vertices, which are stored in a priority queue. Among two vertices, the one with a larger y-coordinate has higher priority; if the y-coordinates are equal, the one with the smaller x-coordinate takes precedence. Since the vertices of polygon $\mathscr{P}$ are stored in a list, it is possible to determine which vertices are of type SPLIT in linear time. Therefore, they can be added in advance to the priority queue, sorted according to the criteria mentioned above. This priority queue can be implemented in several ways; however, in this chapter, it will be realized by SortedDict() dictionary. As previously stated, the removal of a SPLIT vertex V is based on finding a diagonal whose one endpoint is the vertex V, while the other endpoint W needs to be determined. As the sweep line moves downward, the diagonal will eventually reach the SPLIT vertex V, as shown in Fig. 5.16.

Let e_j be a side of the polygon $\mathscr{P}$ intersected by the sweep line l such that the vertex V lies to its right, and let e_k be another side intersected by the sweep line such that the vertex V lies to its left. Then, the vertex V can always be connected to the lowest vertex W (if it exists) that lies above the sweep line and between the edges e_j and e_k. Furthermore, the segment $\overline{VW}$ must be an internal diagonal of the polygon $\mathscr{P}$. By finding the diagonal $\overline{VW}$, the SPLIT vertex V is eliminated, dividing the polygon $\mathscr{P}$ into two sub-polygons $\mathscr{P}_1$ and $\mathscr{P}_2$, which are subsequently further divided into smaller polygons until all SPLIT vertices are removed. For each newly created polygon, it must be checked whether it contains any MERGE vertices, and if so, those vertices must also be eliminated in order to ultimately obtain y-monotone polygons, which can be triangulated in linear time relative to the number of their vertices.

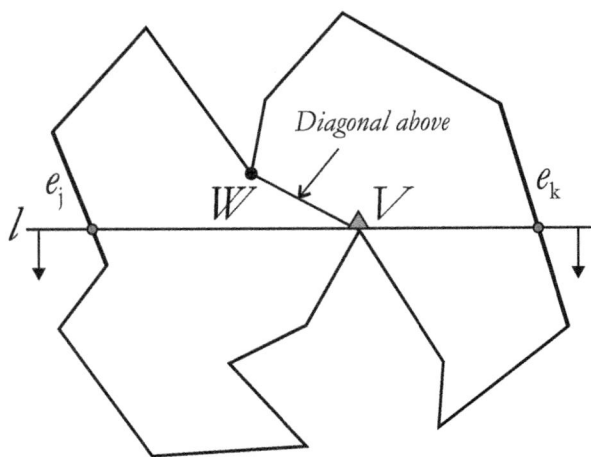

Figure 5.16: Determining the vertex W after the sweep line l reaches the SPLIT vertex V.

5.4.2 Removing MERGE Vertices

In this section, the procedure for removing MERGE vertices is described. As previously mentioned, in order to eliminate a MERGE vertex V, it is necessary to draw a lower diagonal from it and identify a vertex W located below it, which will serve as the second endpoint of the diagonal. In this case, the situation is somewhat more complex than in the case of eliminating SPLIT vertices, because when the sweep line l reaches (hits) vertex V, the part of the polygon lying below the sweep line has not yet been explored. However, thanks to the fact that MERGE vertices are simply the inversion of SPLIT vertices (obtained from one another by a 180-degree rotation), their elimination becomes straightforward. Namely, let the sweep line l hit the MERGE vertex V, as shown in Fig. 5.17. It is necessary to connect the MERGE vertex V with the highest vertex W located just below the sweep line l, such that vertex W lies between the edges e_j and e_k of the polygon $\mathscr{P}$. At the moment the sweep line hits vertex V, the appropriate vertex W with which V should be connected may not yet be known, but as soon as the sweep line reaches the next vertex W, vertex V should then be connected to vertex W and it should be verified whether the segment $\overline{VW}$ is an internal diagonal of the polygon. When vertex W becomes a SPLIT vertex and the segment $\overline{VW}$ is an internal diagonal, then $\overline{VW}$ is added to the list, and pointers to the diagonal are added to the tree so that the SPLIT vertex can later be eliminated. Additionally, it may occur that vertex W lies lower than the endpoints of segment e_k, in which case vertex V is connected to the lower endpoint of segment e_j intersected by the sweep line l.

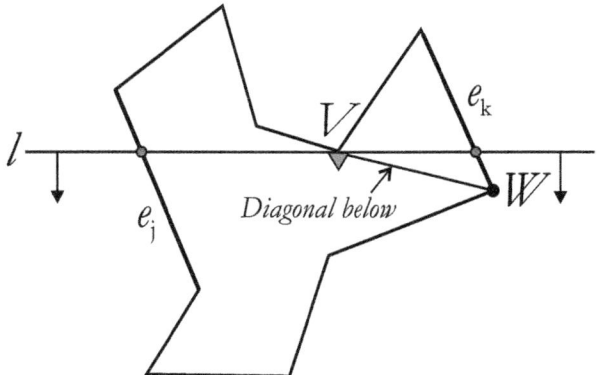

Figure 5.17: Determining vertex W after the sweep line l hits the MERGE vertex V.

5.4.3 Adding Edges to the Binary Tree

To ensure that the time complexity of decomposing a simple polygon is of order $\Theta(n \log n)$, it is necessary to store the polygon edges in a data structure such that, for each SPLIT and MERGE vertex being removed, the lookup of edges e_j and e_k can be performed in $\Theta(\log n)$ time. The edges e_j and e_k are those located immediately to the left and right of the mentioned vertices, with respect to the y-coordinate of the sweep line l. Such a structure is a binary search tree, where the external nodes (leaves) store polygon sides intersected by the sweep line. In that case, the order of edges from left to right in the tree leaves corresponds to the order of edges immediately to the left and right of the sweep line. Only pointers to edges for which the interior of the polygon $\mathscr{P}$ lies to the right of the sweep line are stored in the tree. The diagonals found during the removal of SPLIT and MERGE vertices are stored in a list, which also contains the original polygon edges. Clearly, adding diagonals requires constant time, as it only involves redirecting pointers.

5.4.4 Event Handling in x-Monotone Polygons

In this section, we examine the events that occur when the sweep line, translating from left to right, encounters vertices of a simple polygon that need to be decomposed into x-monotone polygons, as such components are essential for the implementation. By removing vertices such as SPLIT and MERGE, we obtain subpolygons that are x-monotone. In the case of decomposing a simple polygon into x-monotone parts, the xOy-plane is rotated by $90°$ counterclockwise, which transforms the previously used relations "above" and "below" into "left" and "right", respectively.

Definition 5.4.3 Let $\mathscr{P}$ be a given polygon, and let V' and V'' be two adjacent vertices of $\mathscr{P}$. Vertex V' is said to be to the *left* of vertex V'' *if and only if* $V'_x < V''_x$ or $V'_x = V''_x$ and $V'_y > V''_y$.

Definition 5.4.4 Let $\mathscr{P}$ be a given polygon, and let V' and V'' be two adjacent vertices of $\mathscr{P}$. Vertex V' is said to be to the *right* of vertex V'' *if and only if* $V'_x > V''_x$ or $V'_x = V''_x$ and $V'_y < V''_y$.

Definition 5.4.5 Let $\mathscr{P}$ be a given polygon. A reflex vertex V is said to be a *spike* if both of its adjacent vertices lie to its left or to its right.

Based on Definitions 5.4.3, 5.4.4, 5.4.5, as well as previously introduced definitions, it follows that the vertices referred to as **spikes** are representatives of SPLIT and MERGE vertices.

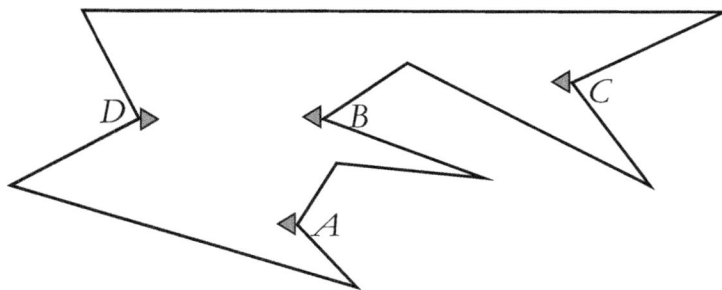

Figure 5.18: Vertices A, B, C, and D are spikes, i.e., representatives of SPLIT and MERGE vertices.

In Fig. 5.18, the marked vertices are representatives of spike vertices. If the polygon $\mathscr{P}$ contains no such vertices, then it is referred to as a monotone polygon. More precisely, vertex D is a MERGE vertex because it lies to the right of its neighboring vertices. The remaining vertices A, B, and C are SPLIT vertices because they lie to the left of their neighboring vertices.

In the following, we describe the events that occur during the translation of the sweep line l from left to right. Prior to that, Fig. 5.19 graphically illustrates the process of removing the SPLIT vertex V and

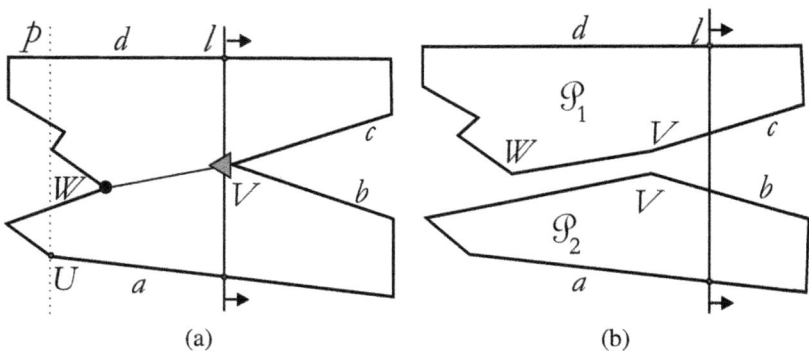

Figure 5.19: (a) Detection and elimination of a SPLIT vertex. (b) Splitting the polygon $\mathcal{P}$ into two parts.

splitting the polygon $\mathcal{P}$ into two subpolygons $\mathcal{P}_1$ and $\mathcal{P}_2$. From Fig. 5.19 (a), it can be seen that vertex W is the leftmost vertex located to the left of the sweep line l, between segments a and d, which are vertical neighbors with respect to the vertical sweep line l. Furthermore, vertex W lies inside the trapezoid bounded by segments a, d, the sweep line l, and the line p that is parallel to l and passes through vertex U. If there is no vertex of the polygon inside the trapezoid, then the diagonal $\overline{VU}$ will split the polygon $\mathcal{P}$ into two parts, i.e., vertex W becomes vertex U. Also, vertex U may represent the left endpoint of segment a or segment d. Thus, if the rightmost vertex W exists within the trapezoid, it will be connected to vertex V. After splitting polygon $\mathcal{P}$ into two parts (see Fig. 5.19 (b)), the old vertex V no longer holds the status of a SPLIT vertex in the resulting polygons $\mathcal{P}_1$ and $\mathcal{P}_2$. Based on this, it is evident that during the sweep line's movement from left to right, none of the vertices located to the left of line l will remain SPLIT vertices. Since the event type depends on the type of vertex, the vertices will now be classified based on the position of their neighbors relative to the sweep line movement. Therefore, three types of vertices will be used in the implementation of the algorithm:

- **BEGIN** – a vertex where both of its neighbors lie behind the sweep line, i.e., to its right;
- **BEND** – a vertex where one of its neighbors lies behind the sweep line and the other in front, or vice versa;
- **TERMINATE** – a vertex where both of its neighbors lie in front of the sweep line, i.e., to its left.

It is not difficult to observe that the aforementioned events correspond to the START, SPLIT, END, MERGE, and REGULAR events, depending on whether the sweep line is translating from left to right or from right to left. Namely, if the sweep line moves from left to right, then the BEGIN event represents a START vertex, since it is a convex vertex and both of its neighbors lie to its right. Analogously, the TERMINATE event corresponds to the END event, as both of its neighbors lie to its left, and the vertex itself is also convex. If the neighbors of a vertex lie on both sides of the sweep line that the given vertex touches, then regardless of the direction in which the sweep line is moving, it is clear that this is a BEND event, i.e., a REGULAR event. An example of these events during the left-to-right movement of the sweep line is shown in Fig. 5.20.

On the other hand, if the direction of the sweep line l is reversed, for example, from right to left, then the BEGIN and TERMINATE events correspond to the SPLIT and MERGE events, respectively (see Fig. 5.21).

In this way, depending on the direction of the sweep line movement, it is necessary to handle only three types of events at any given moment: BEGIN, BEND, and TERMINATE. From an implementation point of view, this can be achieved by writing the function $create\_monotone\_partitions(\cdot, \cdot)$, which processes all vertex types depending on the direction of the sweep line. The implementation of the function is shown in

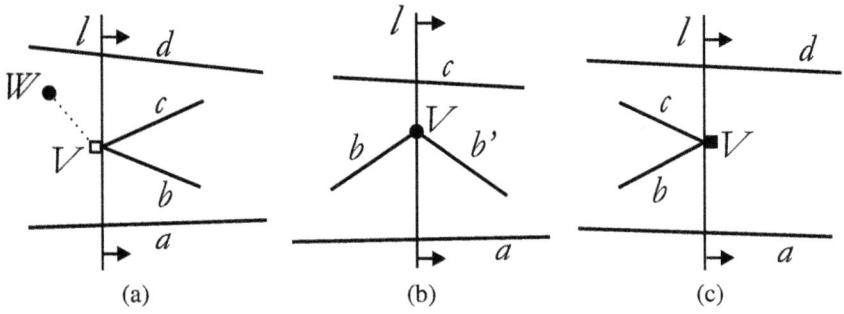

Figure 5.20: (a) BEGIN event. (b) BEND event. (c) TERMINATE event.

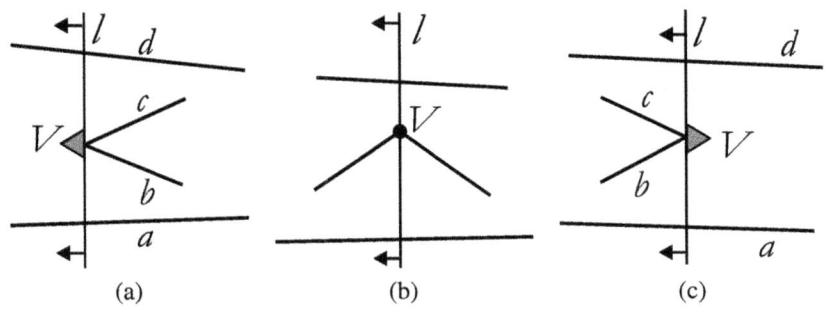

Figure 5.21: (a) SPLIT event. (b) BEND event. (c) MERGE event.

the code snippet below:

```
 1 def create_monotone_partitions(pol: Polygon, direction: int)->list[Polygon]:
 2     if direction == 0:criterion = leftmost_vertex   # Sort from left to right
 3     else:criterion = rightmost_vertex   # Sort from right to left
 4     sorted_vertices = sort_vertices(pol, criterion)
 5     sweep=SortedDict(); pol_list=[]
 6     sweep[EdgeEnd2D(Point2D(0, -1e10),direction,TypeE2.BEGIN)]=Edge2D()
 7     for s_v in sorted_vertices:
 8         event_type=classify_event_type(s_v,criterion)
 9         if event_type==TypeE2.BEGIN:handle_begin(s_v,sweep,direction,event_type)
10         elif event_type==TypeE2.BEND:handle_bend(s_v,sweep,direction,event_type)
11         elif event_type==TypeE2.TERMINATE:handle_terminate(s_v,sweep,pol_list,
               direction,event_type)
12     pol.update_current(None)
13     return pol_list
```

In the function *create_monotone_partitions*($\cdot,\cdot$), the following functions are invoked, which will later be described and implemented: *sort_vertices*($\cdot,\cdot$), *handle_begin*($\cdot,\cdot,\cdot,\cdot$), *handle_bend*($\cdot,\cdot,\cdot,\cdot$), and *handle_terminate*($\cdot,\cdot,\cdot,\cdot,\cdot$). Depending on the values of the variables event_type and direction, all five event types are handled. For example, if the value of the variable direction is set to zero, then the events **START**, **END**, and **REGULAR** will be processed; whereas if the value is one, then the events **SPLIT**, **MERGE**, and **REGULAR** are processed. Moreover, if the variable direction is set to zero or one, then the vertices of the polygon are sorted based on the criteria defined by the functions *leftmost_vertex*($\cdot,\cdot$) and *rightmost_vertex*($\cdot,\cdot$), whose implementations are provided in the second chapter of this textbook.

Sorting of polygon vertices is performed using the function *sort_vertices*($\cdot$,$\cdot$), whose implementation is given below:

```python
def sort_vertices(polygon, criterion):
    vertices = []
    for _ in range(polygon.size()):
        vertices.append(polygon.current_vertex()); polygon.move_current(-1)
    vertices.sort(key=cmp_to_key(criterion))
    return vertices
```

After sorting the vertices, a corresponding action must be taken based on the type of event. To determine the type of event associated with a given vertex V, the function *classify_event_type*($\cdot$,$\cdot$) is used. This function categorizes any vertex according to the position of its neighboring vertices. Its implementation is shown in the code snippet below:

```python
def classify_event_type(v: Vertex, criterion) -> TypeE2:
    a=criterion(v.clockwise(),v); b = criterion(v.counter_clockwise(),v)
    if a<=0 and b<=0: return TypeE2.TERMINATE
    elif a>0 and b>0: return TypeE2.BEGIN
    else: return TypeE2.BEND
```

The return type of the function *classify_event_type*($\cdot$,$\cdot$) is an enumerated type TypeE2:

```python
class TypeE2(Enum):
    BEGIN = 1
    BEND = 2
    TERMINATE = 3
```

5.4.5 Sweep Line Structure

To represent the sweep line structure, a SortedDict() dictionary in Python is used to store the active polygon sides $\mathcal{P}$. Active edges are those that intersect the sweep line l, and they are maintained in ascending order with respect to the y-coordinates of their intersection points with the sweep line l. The dictionary sweep is initialized at the beginning of the *create_monotone_partitions*($\cdot$,$\cdot$) function. Within the dictionary, the active polygon sides $\mathcal{P}$ are stored as instances of the class **Edge2D** (see Listing 5.3), which publicly inherits from the abstract class **Object2D** (see Listing 5.2). Additionally, a point with the smallest y-coordinate is inserted into the sweep dictionary, acting as a *sentinel point*, ensuring that it lies below all polygon edge endpoints that will later be added to the dictionary.

Listing 5.2: Definition of an Abstract Base Class Object2D

```python
from abc import ABC, abstractmethod
class Object2D(ABC):
    def __init__(self, type: int):
        self._type = type  # 0 -> edge, 1 -> point
    def get_type(self) -> int: return self._type
    @abstractmethod
    def get_y(self,x_sl: float) -> float: pass
    def get_edge(self) -> Segment2D: return Segment2D()
    def get_slope(self) -> float: return 0.0
```

Listing 5.3: Definition of Class Edge2D

```
1 class Edge2D(Object2D):
2     def __init__(self, v=None, r=0, w=None):
3         super().__init__(0) #0 indicates that it is an edge
4         self.v = v  # one end of the active edge
5         self.w = w  # the other end the active edge(SPLIT vertex)
6         self.r = r  # a flag for switching from one edge to another
7     def get_edge(self) -> Segment2D:
8         return Segment2D(self.v.vertex_point(), self.v.clockwise().vertex_point())
9     def get_y(self,x_sl: float) -> float: return self.get_edge().y_coord(x_sl)
10    def get_slope(self) -> float: return self.get_edge().slope()
11    def get_r(self) -> int: return self.r
12    def __getitem__(self, i): return self.v if i == 0 else self.w
13    def __setitem__(self, i, value):
14        if i == 0: self.v = value
15        else: self.w = value
16    def get_v(self): return self.v
17    def get_w(self): return self.w
18    def update_w(self, w): self.w = w
```

When the sweep line encounters an event V of type **SPLIT** or **MERGE**, it is necessary to determine the vertex W located between the active polygon edges that the sweep line intersects. Since the active edges are stored in a dictionary sweep, the vertex W must also be stored in the dictionary as an instance of the class **EdgeEnd2D**, whose definition is given in Listing 5.4.

Listing 5.4: Definition of Class EdgeEnd2D

```
1 class EdgeEnd2D(Object2D):
2     def __init__(self, p, s_d, e_t):
3         super().__init__(1)
4         self.p = p
5         self.sweep_direction = s_d
6         self.event_type = e_t
7     def __lt__(self, other): return self.compare_objects(other) < 0
8     def __eq__(self, other): return self.compare_objects(other) == 0
9     def __hash__(self): return id(self)
10    def get_y(self): return self.p[1]
11    def get_point(self): return self.p
12    def compare_objects(self, other):
13        y01 = self.get_y(); y02 = other.get_y(); sign = 1
14        if y01 < y02: return -1
15        elif y01 > y02: return 1
16        if self.get_type() == 1 and other.get_type() == 1: return 0
17        elif self.get_type() == 1: return -1
18        elif self.get_type() == 1: return 1
19        if (self.sweep_direction == 0 and self.event_type==TypeE2.BEGIN) or (self.
               sweep_direction == 1 and self.event_type==TypeE2.TERMINATE): sign = -1
20        n01 = self.get_slope(); n02 = other.get_slope()
21        if n01 < n02: return sign
22        elif n01 > n02: return -sign
23        return 0
```

Since the dictionary sweep maintains its elements in sorted order, it relies on a comparator to determine the relative positioning of entries. This comparison logic is encapsulated within implemented method *compare_objects*$(\cdot,\cdot)$ of the class **EdgeEnd2D**, which defines the ordering criteria between active objects. Its task is to compare two active objects (either points or edges), o_1 and o_2, based on the y-coordinates of their intersection points with the sweep line. If both edges intersect the sweep line at the same point, then either o_1 is considered to lie below o_2, or vice versa. Additionally, active edges are compared using the y-coordinates of their intersections with the sweep line. If these intersections are identical, the ordering is determined based on their slopes with respect to the x-axis. When the sweep line moves from left to right and the event point is a BEGIN (or TERMINATE) vertex, the edge with the smaller slope lies below (or above) the edge with the larger slope. Conversely, if the sweep line moves from right to left and the event point is a BEGIN (or TERMINATE) vertex, then the edge with the smaller slope lies above (or below) the edge with the larger slope. Essentially, the roles of BEGIN and TERMINATE vertices are reversed depending on the direction of the sweep line.

5.4.6 Event Handling

In this section, the procedures for processing vertices such as: **BEGIN, BEND**, and **TERMINATE** are described and implemented. These procedures, among other things, assist the algorithm, which operates in two phases, to decompose the original polygon into x-monotone parts. In the first phase of the algorithm, the initial polygon is split into smaller parts (sub-polygons stored in a list) by translating the sweep line from left to right, whereby some of the resulting polygons will be x-monotone, while others may not. In the second phase of the algorithm, when the sweep line translates from right to left, all polygons from the list obtained in the first phase are tested for x-monotonicity. Those that were not x-monotone are further decomposed into new sub-polygons which eventually become x-monotone. In this way, the resulting polygons stored in the polygon list truly represent x-monotone polygons. The first function to be implemented for this purpose is the function *handle_begin*$(\cdot,\cdot)$. Let the sweep line l translate from left to right and let it first encounter a convex START vertex V (see Fig. 5.20 (a)). At that moment, the active edges a and d between which vertex V lies are located in the dictionary sweep, if they exist. When vertex V becomes incident to edges b and c, these edges are added to the dictionary, and vertex V is designated as the target vertex for the following edge pairs: a-b, b-c, and c-d. On the other hand, if vertex V is not convex, then the current polygon is divided into two parts along the internal diagonal $\overline{VW}$ with respect to V. For the division, the method *split*$(\cdot)$ of the class **Vertex** is used. In this case as well, active edges are added to the dictionary and the target vertex W is updated. The complete implementation of the function *handle_begin*$(\cdot,\cdot)$ is given below:

```python
def handle_begin(v, sweep: SortedDict,direction,event_type):
    key = EdgeEnd2D(v.vertex_point(),direction,event_type)
    keys = list(sweep.keys()); i=0;
    if key in sweep: i=keys.index(key)
    e = sweep[keys[i]]
    w = e.get_w()
    if not v.is_convex():# Processing a SPLIT vertex
        wp = v.split(w)
        sweep[EdgeEnd2D(wp.clockwise().vertex_point(),direction,event_type)] = \
            Edge2D(wp.clockwise(), -1, wp.clockwise())
        sweep[EdgeEnd2D(v.counter_clockwise().vertex_point(),direction,event_type)
            ] = Edge2D(v.counter_clockwise(), 1, v)
        if direction == 0: e.update_w(wp.counter_clockwise())
        else: e.update_w(v)
    else: # Processing a START vertex
        sweep[EdgeEnd2D(v.counter_clockwise().vertex_point(),direction,event_type)
            ] = Edge2D(v.counter_clockwise(), 1, v)
        sweep[EdgeEnd2D(v.vertex_point(),direction,event_type)] = Edge2D(v, -1, v)
        e.update_w(v)
```

The function for processing a BEND vertex will now be defined. Let the sweep line l hit a REGULAR (BEND) vertex V, as shown in Fig. 5.20 (b). To process this bend vertex, the edges a, b, and c are first located in the dictionary, and it is then specified that for the pairs a-b and b-c, the target vertex W is in fact the vertex V. Additionally, depending on the direction of movement of the sweep line, the target vertex of edge b is updated accordingly. Based on this, the function $handle\_bend(\cdot,\cdot)$ can be implemented as follows:

```python
def handle_bend(v, sweep: SortedDict,direction,event_type):
    key = EdgeEnd2D(v.vertex_point(),direction,event_type)
    keys = list(sweep.keys()); i=0;
    if key in sweep: i=keys.index(key)
    a = sweep[keys[i]]; b = sweep[keys[(i+1)%len(keys)]]
    if a is not None and b is not None:
        a[1]=v; b[1]=v; b[0]=(b[0]).neighbor(b.get_r())
```

The last remaining task is to implement the function for processing the TERMINATE vertex. Let the sweep line l reach the END vertex V, as shown in Fig. 5.20 (c). To process this vertex, the active edges a, b, c, and d must first be located in the dictionary. If the END vertex V is convex, then it must be the rightmost vertex in its polygon (up to that point discovered), because otherwise the polygon containing vertex V could have an edge directed to the left of V, which contradicts the direction of the sweep line. Therefore, since V is the rightmost vertex in its polygon, the polygon defined by this vertex is added to the list of polygons. On the other hand, if vertex V is reflex, then it becomes the target vertex for the edge pair $a - d$. Finally, it is necessary to remove the active edges b and c from the dictionary. Based on the above, the implementation of the function $handle\_terminate(\cdot,\cdot)$ becomes quite simple, as can be seen from the code snippet below:

```python
def handle_terminate(v: Vertex, sweep: SortedDict, polygons: list[Polygon],
    direction,event_type):
    key = EdgeEnd2D(v.vertex_point(),direction,event_type)
    keys = list(sweep.keys()); i=0;
    if key in sweep: i=keys.index(key)
    a = sweep[keys[i]]; b = sweep[keys[(i+1)%len(keys)]]
    c = sweep[keys[(i+2)%len(keys)]]
    if a is not None and b is not None and c is not None:
        if v.is_convex():polygons.append(Polygon().from_vertex(v))# Proc. END ver.
        else: a.update_w(v) # MERGE vertex was processed
        del sweep[keys[(i+1)%len(keys)]]; del sweep[keys[(i+2)%len(keys)]]
```

The graphical interface of the sweep-ine algorithm for monotone polygon triangulation is shown in Fig. 5.22, and it is implemented based on the code in Listing 5.1. For this purpose, the body of the *visualise_triangles* function should be updated with the following code:

```python
polygon = Polygon()
for v in self.v_p:polygon.insert(v)
if polygon.area() < 0:polygon.change_orientation()
#First phase of the algorithm
partitions = create_monotone_partitions(polygon, 0) #Split from left to right
list_monotone = [] # List of all monotone polygons
for pol in partitions:
    if pol.is_monotone():list_monotone.append(pol)
    else: #Split from right to left
        list_monotone.extend(create_monotone_partitions(pol, 1)) # Second phase
list_trian_pol = [] # Triangulation of all monotone polygons
```

```
12 for pol in list_monotone:
13     if pol.size() == 3: list_trian_pol.append(pol)
14     else: list_trian_pol.extend(pol.triangulate_monotone())
15 #Drawing all triangles
16 for pol in list_trian_pol:
17     for _ in range(pol.size()):
18         seg = pol.current_edge()
19         x1, y1 = seg[0][0], seg[0][1]; x2, y2 = seg[1][0], seg[1][1]
20         self.canvas.create_line(x1, y1, x2, y2, fill='black', width=1)
21         pol.move_current(1)
```

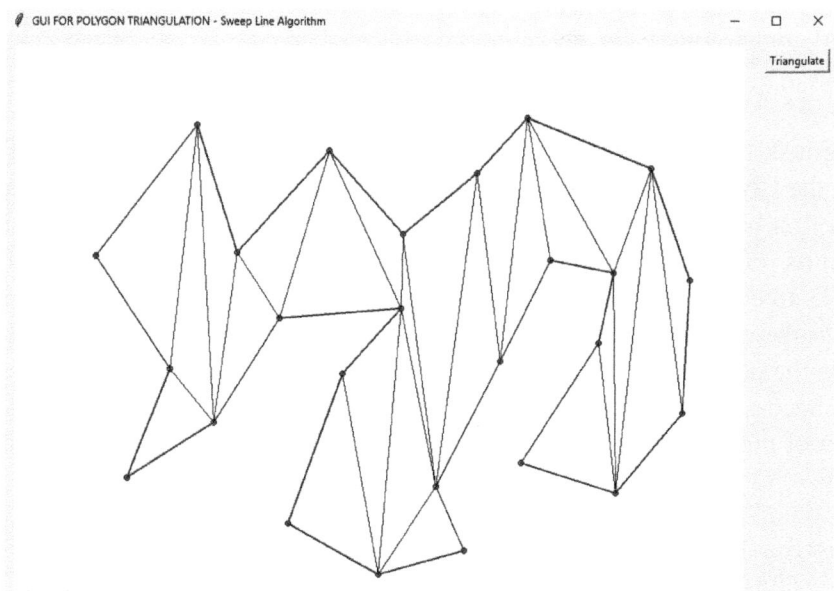

Figure 5.22: Triangulation of a simple polygon after its decomposition into monotone parts.

5.4.7 Algorithm Analysis

To analyze the complexity of the algorithm for decomposing a simple polygon into x-monotone pieces using the sweep-line paradigm, it is sufficient to examine the time complexity of lines 5 through 10 in the *visualise_triangles*() function. Let $\mathcal{P}$ be a simple polygon consisting of n vertices oriented in the clockwise direction. In line 5, the function *create_monotone_partitions*($\cdot$, $\cdot$) is invoked during the left-to-right sweep phase. This function requires $\Theta(n \log n)$ time in the worst case, as it may need to process up to n events by calling the following procedures: *handle_begin*($\cdot,\cdot,\cdot,\cdot$), *handle_bend*($\cdot,\cdot,\cdot,\cdot$), and *handle_terminate*($\cdot,\cdot,\cdot,\cdot,\cdot$). Each of these functions takes at most $\Theta(\log n)$ time, as they involve accessing, inserting, or removing certain elements from a dictionary SortedDict. During this phase, a partial decomposition of the initial polygon into a number of smaller sub-polygons is performed. These are later further processed in the second phase, when the sweep line moves from right to left. In that phase, all sub-polygons obtained previously are subjected to decomposition again via another call to the *create_monotone_partitions*($\cdot$, $\cdot$) function (see Line 10). It is evident that the original polygon $\mathcal{P}$ is split into two sub-polygons $\mathcal{P}_1$ and $\mathcal{P}_2$ during the removal of a SPLIT or MERGE vertex V. In such cases, the vertex V is processed twice in each sweep direction—once for each of the resulting sub-polygons $\mathcal{P}_1$ and $\mathcal{P}_2$. Thus, the vertex V is processed four times in total. Let k be the number of vertices involved in the decomposition of the original polygon $\mathcal{P}$. Then, at most $4k$ processing steps are required for those vertices, which is $\mathcal{O}(n)$ since k is strictly less than n. The remaining $n - k$ vertices are each processed exactly twice, which is also $\mathcal{O}(n)$.

Since each vertex is processed by calling one of the functions *handle_begin*($\cdot,\cdot,\cdot,\cdot$), *handle_bend*($\cdot,\cdot,\cdot,\cdot$), and *handle_terminate*($\cdot,\cdot,\cdot,\cdot,\cdot$), the total time complexity of the algorithm is $\Theta(n \log n)$, because each of the $\mathcal{O}(n)$ transitions requires $\mathcal{O}(\log n)$ time to handle the corresponding vertex.

5.5 Art Gallery Problem

The works of famous painters, in addition to being popular among art enthusiasts, are also attractive to criminals due to their high market value. It is well known that the prices of artworks are extremely high, they are easy to transport, and surprisingly quick to sell. For these reasons, *Art Galleries* take great care in securing the paintings they display. It is known that during the day, gallery visitors can somewhat safeguard the artworks, while at night this task is handled by surveillance cameras mounted on ceilings, rotating around an imaginary vertical axis by 360°. The video feeds from these cameras are monitored by security personnel in a control room. The greater the number of cameras, the more monitors are required, thereby increasing the burden on observers. Thus, it is desirable to reduce the number of cameras where possible. Reducing the number of cameras also lowers the cost of securing the gallery, both in terms of personnel and technology, as it reduces not only the number of monitors but also the number of storage disks needed to store approximately 25 images per second from a single camera. While attempting to minimize the number of cameras, care must be taken not to leave parts of the gallery unmonitored [70]. Therefore, cameras should be placed at strategic positions such that each one covers as large a portion of the gallery as possible [106]. This optimal placement of cameras is known as the *Art Gallery Problem* (**AGP**) [53, 141]. The Art Gallery Problem lies at the intersection of robotics, optimization, and computer graphics, with visibility being a key component in all of these domains [3, 114]. In computational geometry, this problem is known as the *Visibility Problem* (**VP**) [77]. It originates from the task of guarding an art gallery with the minimum number of stationary guards capable of overseeing the entire space. Assuming the gallery can be modeled as a simple polygon, and each guard (camera) is represented as a vertex of the polygon, a natural question arises: *"How many guards (cameras) must be placed within the gallery so that every room is always visible?"* In addition to cameras, the determination of visual sensors in a 2D environment is often modeled as an art gallery problem. The main challenge is to cover the interior of a concave polygon with the optimal number of sensors, which constitutes a complex combinatorial problem [5]. In Fig. 5.23, only three guards (cameras) are needed, even though the gallery is modeled as a polygon with 27 vertices. From this, it is not immediately apparent how many guards are actually necessary.

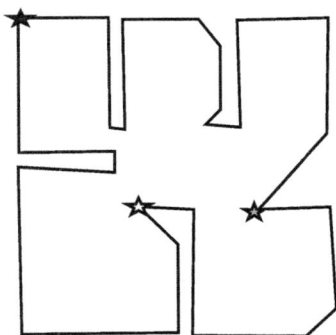

Figure 5.23: Covering a simple polygon using three guards.

Back in 1973, Václav Chvátal proposed a complex mathematical proof for determining the number of guards (cameras), under the assumption that each camera has a field of view ranging from 0 to 360 degrees [45]. However, five years later, Steve Fisk demonstrated that this problem can be solved much more efficiently using graph coloring on a triangulated polygon [62].

Definition 5.5.1 Let $\mathscr{P}$ be a simple polygon consisting of n vertices modeling the rooms of a gallery. A vertex $V \in \mathscr{P}$ *sees the vertex* $W \in \mathscr{P}$ *if and only if* the segment $\overline{VW}$ lies entirely within the interior of the polygon $\mathscr{P}$ such that $\overline{VW} \cap \partial \mathscr{P} \subseteq \{V, W\}$.

Let $\mathscr{P}$ be a simple polygon composed of n vertices. In his proof, Chvátal demonstrated that $\lfloor n/3 \rfloor$ guards are sufficient to cover a gallery represented by the simple polygon $\mathscr{P}$. It is assumed here that the guards are located at the vertices of the polygon, although the same upper bound remains valid even if they are placed at arbitrary points within the polygon. However, this upper bound of $\lfloor n/3 \rfloor$ can be improved for certain types of polygons, such as orthogonal polygons [4]. In the case of orthogonal polygons, whose sides (walls) meet at right angles, exactly $\lfloor n/6 \rfloor$ guards are sufficient (see Fig. 5.24 (c)). Clearly, for convex polygons, only one guard is always needed (see Fig. 5.24 (d)). In Fig. 5.24 (a), we see that in the case of a **comb polygon**, exactly $\lfloor n/3 \rfloor$ guards are required to fully cover the gallery. For galleries with holes, the model is extended to allow simple polygons (holes) inside the gallery, where guards are not allowed to be placed [10, 83]. In Fig. 5.24 (b), only three guards are necessary. It has been proven that the minimum number of guards required for such a model with holes is given by the expression $\lfloor (w + h + z_h)/3 \rfloor$, where h is the number of holes, w is the number of walls of the gallery, and z_h denotes the number of walls of all holes within the gallery.

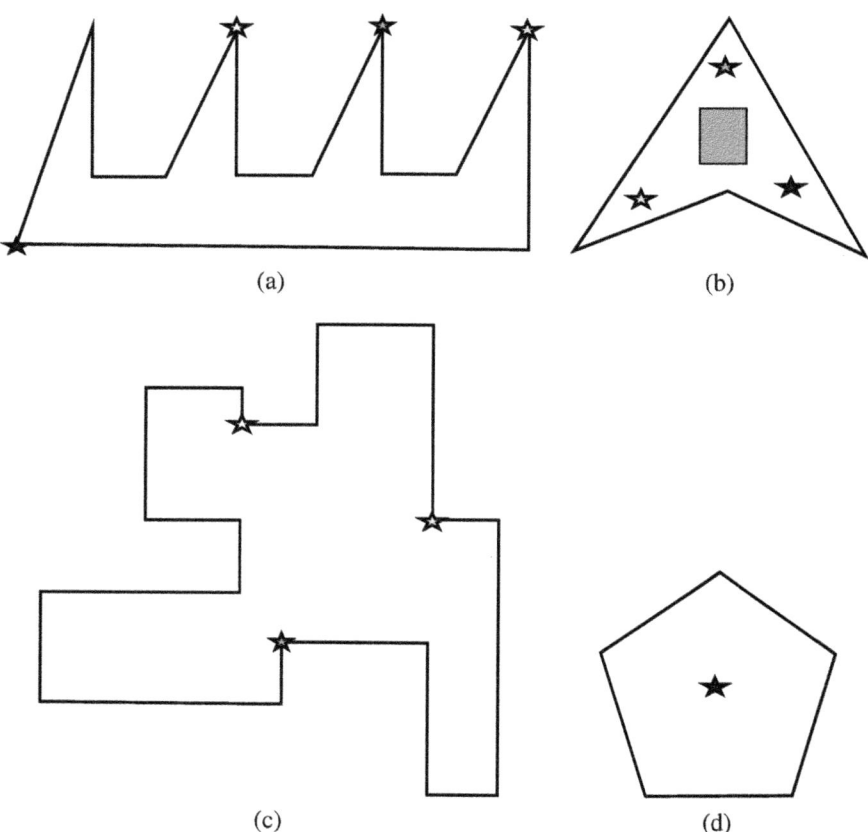

Figure 5.24: (a) Comb polygon. (b) Polygon with a hole. (c) Orthogonal polygon. (d) Convex polygon.

5.6 Steve Fisk's Proof of the Three-Colorability of Planar Triangulations

Let $\mathscr{P}$ be a simple polygon consisting of n vertices. Fisk's proof for determining the minimal number of guards required to cover the polygon $\mathscr{P}$ consists of the following steps (see Fig. 5.25):

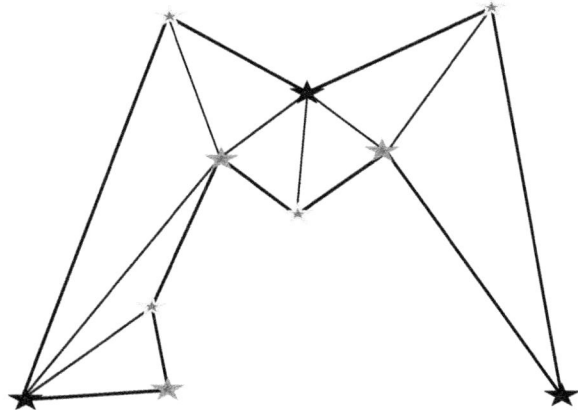

Figure 5.25: Three-coloring of a simple polygon.

A. Perform a triangulation of the simple polygon $\mathscr{P}$, resulting in $n-2$ triangles;

B. Color each triangle in the triangulation using colors a, b, and c, thereby forming vertex sets P_a, P_b, and P_c, whose elements are colored with a, b, and c, respectively;

C. Among the sets P_a, P_b, and P_c, choose the one with the fewest elements. The elements of this set serve as the gallery guards.

It will now be shown, based on steps A), B), and C), that the selected set $\mathscr{P} = \min\{|P_a|, |P_b|, |P_c|\}$ contains at most $\lfloor n/3 \rfloor$ elements. Specifically, if one camera is placed inside each triangle, then $n-2$ cameras are required to cover the entire gallery. A more efficient approach is to place cameras along well-chosen diagonals, in which case each camera can cover two triangles, leading to a total of $\lfloor n/2 \rfloor$ cameras in the best case. However, if cameras are placed at vertices that are incident to three or more triangles, then in the worst case, $\lfloor n/3 \rfloor$ cameras are needed, while the actual number may be smaller in better cases. The worst case occurs when each selected vertex is incident to exactly three triangles. If each of these triangles is colored with three distinct colors a, b, and c, then the set $\mathscr{P}$ contains vertices of a single color, which, in the worst case, are incident to exactly three triangles. Since $|\mathscr{P}| = n$, it follows that $|\mathscr{P}| \leq \lfloor n/3 \rfloor$, meaning the total number of such monochromatic vertices is less than or equal to $\lfloor n/3 \rfloor$, which completes the proof.

5.7 Exercises

Exercise 5.1 Implement the naive algorithm for triangulating a simple polygon with n vertices, whose time complexity is $O(n^3)$.

Exercise 5.2 Prove that the number of distinct triangulations of a convex polygon $\mathscr{P}$ with $n+2$ vertices is equal to the n-th Catalan number C_n.

Exercise 5.3 Show that any polygon can be formed by combining appropriately selected half-planes using intersection and union operations.

Exercise 5.4 Using mathematical induction, show that every polygon composed of four or more vertices has at least two ears.

Exercise 5.5 Find a polygon composed of n vertices ($n > 3$) that has a unique triangulation.

Exercise 5.6 Let polygon $\mathscr{P}$ with h holes have n vertices, including the vertices of the holes. Find a formula for determining the number of triangles in an arbitrary triangulation of polygon $\mathscr{P}$.

Exercise 5.7 Prove that there exists a diagonal between any two non-adjacent vertices of polygon $\mathscr{P}$ *if and only if* polygon $\mathscr{P}$ is convex.

Exercise 5.8 Let polygon $\mathscr{P}$ have $n + 2$ vertices. Prove that the number of triangulations of polygon $\mathscr{P}$ lies between 1 and C_n.

Exercise 5.9 Find a polygon consisting of n vertices ($n > 3$) that has exactly two triangulations.

Exercise 5.10 Prove that there does not exist a polygon $\mathscr{P}$ with $n + 2$ vertices ($n \geq 3$) that has exactly $C_n - 1$ triangulations.

Exercise 5.11 Give an example of an orthogonal polygon $\mathscr{P}$ where only $\lfloor n/4 \rfloor$ cameras are sufficient to cover its interior, where n denotes the number of vertices of the polygon $\mathscr{P}$.

Exercise 5.12 Implement a linear-time algorithm for coloring a triangulated simple polygon using exactly three colors.

Exercise 5.13 Propose an efficient algorithm for determining whether the simple polygon $\mathscr{P}$ is monotone or not.

Exercise 5.14 Let $\mathscr{P}_1$ be a simple polygon of cardinality m_1, along with its triangulation and its pockets, where pockets are regions outside the polygon but inside its convex hull. Let $\mathscr{P}_2$ be a convex polygon of cardinality m_2. Show that the intersection of polygons $\mathscr{P}_1$ and $\mathscr{P}_2$ can be computed in $\mathscr{O}(m_1 + m_2)$ time.

6. Delaunay Triangulation

In the previous chapter, a very useful and practical topic was covered—namely, the decomposition of a simple polygon into triangles. In this chapter, we consider the triangulation of a set of points in the plane, which is used to solve a significant number of problems in science and engineering [39, 54]. Delaunay triangulation is named after the Russian mathematician Boris Nikolaevich Delaunay (1890–1980), who studied optimal methods for dividing space into simple geometric structures. This triangulation plays a key role in computational geometry, computer graphics, geographic information systems, and numerical simulations. Its most important feature is that it maximizes the minimum interior angle among all possible triangulations of a given set of points, thereby avoiding the formation of extremely elongated triangles and achieving better regularity. Such triangulations can also be used to create models of a region on Earth. The generated model should be able to respond or estimate, at any point within a given region, the elevation, temperature, or air pressure. If the terrain is described by some function $f : A \subset \mathbb{R}^3 \to \mathbb{R}$, which assigns to each element a from the domain A a height value $f(a) \in \mathbb{R}$, then due to the uncountability and infiniteness of the set A, it is not possible to measure the height $f(a)$ for every $a \in A$—they can only be estimated (see Fig. 6.1 (a)).

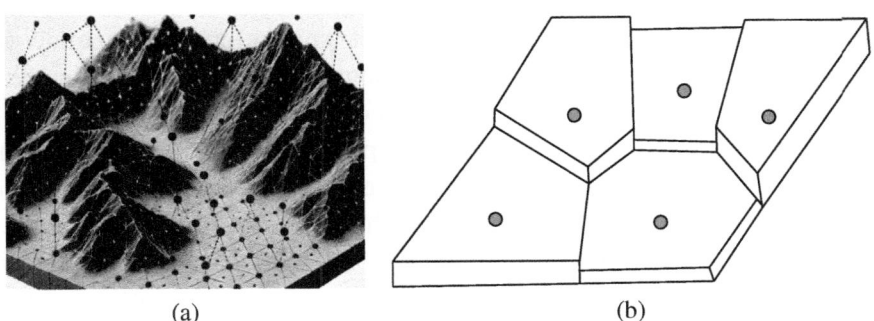

(a) (b)

Figure 6.1: (a) Sampling the terrain with a finite set of measurements. (b) Discrete terrain.

Estimation is possible if the terrain is modeled using triangles in space. In other words, based on a finite set of measured values, other values (e.g., elevations) at remaining points can be approximately estimated (in the plane, estimations are typically done using the least squares method). Thus, based on the elevation values of the sampled points, the goal is to approximate the elevations of the remaining points. The

© The Author(s), under exclusive license to Springer Nature Switzerland AG 2026
A. Alihodžić, *Exploring Computational Geometry*, Texts in Computer Science,
https://doi.org/10.1007/978-3-032-06393-9_6

simplest approach is to assign to each point the elevation of its nearest sampled point, resulting in a discrete terrain, as shown in Fig. 6.1 (b). Terrain approximation using triangles in space is performed by projecting each sampled point onto the appropriate plane, and then triangulating the resulting planar points. As a result of the triangulation, planar triangles are obtained, and by assigning the measured elevations to their vertices, they are transformed into 3D triangles, as illustrated in Fig. 6.2.

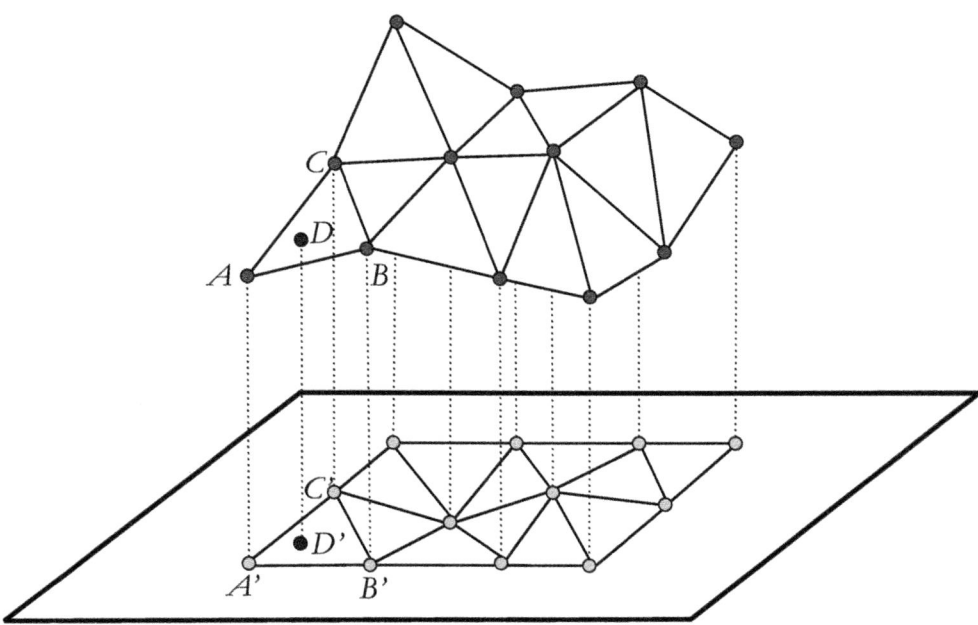

Figure 6.2: Generation of a polyhedral terrain from the planar triangulation of sampled points.

By uniting the triangles in space, a polyhedral terrain is formed, which serves as an approximation of the original surface. For example, if the temperatures at the vertices A, B, and C of triangle $\triangle ABC$ are known (see Fig. 6.2), the question arises: what is the temperature at point D, which lies inside that triangle? If point D lies on one of the sides of the triangle, its temperature can be determined using one-dimensional interpolation (e.g., linear interpolation along the edge). In the case where the point is strictly inside the triangle, the temperature is estimated using two-dimensional interpolation. There are various methods for triangulating points in the plane, and in many applications, triangulations that generate triangles closer to regular shapes are preferred. One of the most suitable triangulations for interpolating terrain elevation is the *Delaunay Triangulation* (**DT**). Figure 6.3 shows two different triangulations of the same terrain. It can be observed that the triangulation in b) creates a steeper depression in the mountain ridge, whereas the triangulation in a) is of higher quality. This is because, in the right triangulation, point Q lies at the midpoint of an edge between two elongated triangles with very sharp angles (see Fig. 6.3 (b)). Flipping that edge by 90 degrees results in the left triangulation, which produces more regular triangles and thus improves interpolation. This edge-flipping technique is the foundation of Delaunay triangulation and other types of high-quality planar triangulations, which will be described in more detail later. It should be noted that, although Delaunay triangulation is of very high quality, it is not the most optimal triangulation for a planar point set. Namely, a more optimal approach for finding the best triangulation is the *Minimum Weight Triangulation* (**MWT**) [7, 8]. While the DT is slightly less efficient than the MWT, it is widely used in practice, primarily because a polynomial-time algorithm exists for computing it. On the other hand, no polynomial-time algorithm is known for computing MWT, as it has been proven to be an NP-hard problem [138]. Due to space constraints, the Minimum Weight Triangulation will not be discussed in this textbook.

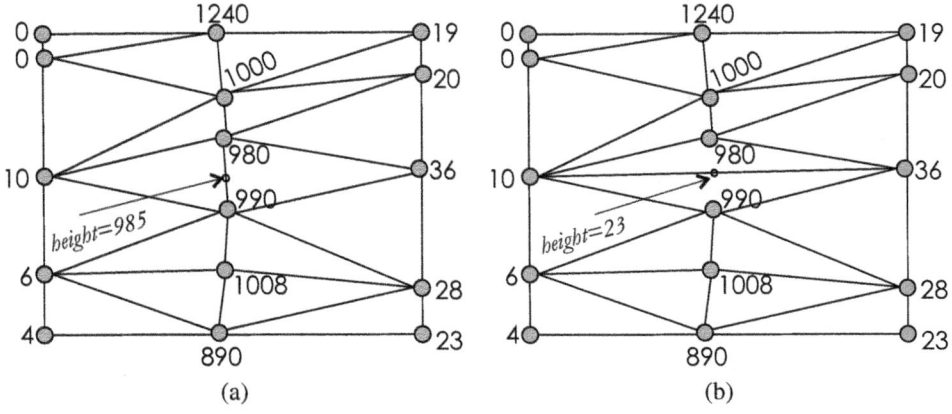

Figure 6.3: a) Higher-quality triangulation. b) Lower-quality triangulation.

6.1 Triangulation of a Planar Point Set

This section describes the triangulation of a planar point set, which is closely related to the triangulation of a simple polygon in the plane.

Definition 6.1.1 A graph $G = (V, E)$ is called a *planar graph* if it can be embedded or drawn in the plane such that its edges intersect only at vertices.

Definition 6.1.2 A triangulation of a planar point set $\mathscr{P}$ generates a set of line segments with endpoints from $\mathscr{P}$ that intersect only at their endpoints.

An example of a planar triangulation, that is, a triangulation of a planar point set, is shown in Fig. 6.4. Based on the definition of planar triangulation, the edges obtained during this process actually represent the edges of a planar graph. In Fig. 6.4, the edges of the planar graph are "attached" to the convex hull $CH(\mathscr{P})$ of polygon $\mathscr{P}$. Moreover, each edge of the triangulation is incident to two faces. Specifically, each interior edge is shared by two triangles, while each edge on the convex hull is incident to one triangle and one unbounded face. There exist several different types of triangulations for a given set of planar points $\mathscr{P}$, although every triangulation yields the same number of triangles and edges. The following lemma addresses this.

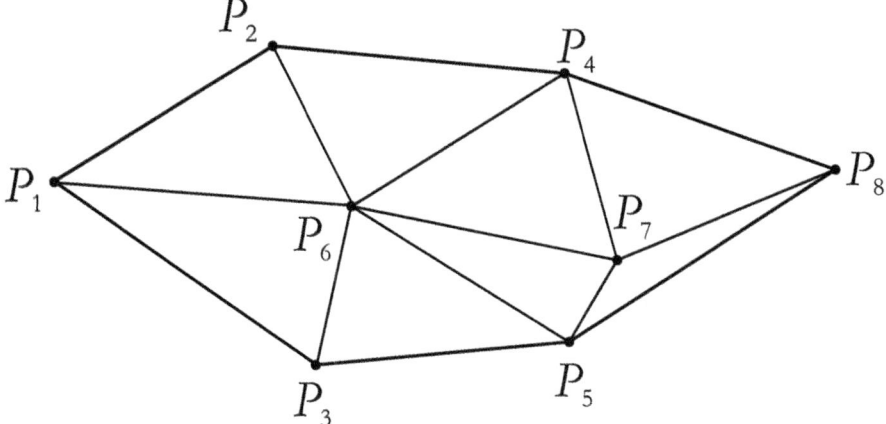

Figure 6.4: Triangulation of a planar point set $\mathscr{P}$ bounded by the convex hull $CH(\mathscr{P})$.

Lemma 6.1.1 Let $\mathscr{P}$ be a set of $n \geq 3$ points in the plane that are not all collinear. Let i denote the number of points inside the convex hull $CH(\mathscr{P})$. Then every triangulation contains exactly $n+i-2$ triangles and $n+2i-3$ interior edges.

Proof. Assuming that i denotes the number of interior points of the convex hull $CH(\mathscr{P})$, and given that the set $\mathscr{P}$ consists of n points, it follows that the convex hull $CH(\mathscr{P})$ contains $n-i$ points on its boundary. Based on Lemma 5.1.3, the triangulation of a simple polygon with n vertices contains $n-2$ triangles and $n-3$ diagonals. Since the convex hull is a simple polygon, it follows that $CH(\mathscr{P})$ consists of $n-i-2$ triangles and $n-i-3$ diagonals. Given that there are i interior points, each must be added to the convex hull $CH(\mathscr{P})$. Let P_{i_1} be the first such point to be added. During this addition, the point will either lie strictly within one of the triangles formed during the triangulation of the convex polygon $CH(\mathscr{P})$ (see Fig. 6.5 (a)) or be coincident with an edge of one of the triangles (see Fig. 6.5 (b)).

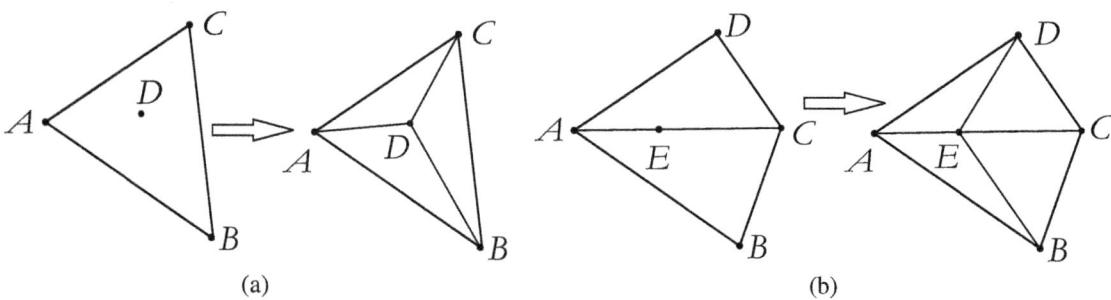

(a)   (b)

Figure 6.5: (a) The point D lies strictly inside the triangle $\triangle ABC$. (b) The point E lies on the diagonal $\overline{AC}$ of the quadrilateral $ABCD$.

Let the point P_{i_1} lie inside a triangle, as shown in Fig. 6.5 (a), where $D = P_{i_1}$. In this case, the number of existing triangles increases by 2, meaning that the total number of triangles after incorporating this point into the existing triangulation becomes $n-i-2+2 = n-i$. If this procedure is repeated for the remaining $(i-1)$ points, the total number of triangles becomes: $n-i+2+2+\cdots+2 = n-i+2(i-1) = n+i-2$. Thus, the statement holds in this first case. Now, suppose the point P_{i_1} lies on the edge of some triangle, as in the case of point E in Fig. 6.5 (b), where $E = P_{i_1}$. Once again, the number of triangles increases by two, meaning the total number of triangles becomes $n-i-2+2 = n-i$ after incorporating this point. Whether the first or second case occurs for the remaining $(i-1)$ points, it follows that each point increases the triangle count by two, yielding a final total of $n+i-2$ triangles after all i points are added. This proves the claim regarding the number of triangles. Similarly, when incorporating the point P_{i_1} into the existing triangulation, the number of interior edges increases by three, regardless of whether the point lies strictly inside a triangle or coincides with an interior edge. Since this process is repeated i times, the total number of interior edges becomes $n-i-3+3i = n+2i-3$. This completes the proof of the lemma in terms of both the number of triangles and edges. ∎

Observation 6.1.1 Based on the proof of Lemma 6.1.1, an efficient algorithm can be constructed for determining the planar triangulation of a point set. Specifically, by applying Graham's algorithm to the given point set $\mathscr{P} = \{P_1, P_2, \ldots, P_n\}$, the convex hull $CH(\mathscr{P})$ can be computed in $\Theta(n\log n)$ time. Then, a triangulation of the convex hull $CH(\mathscr{P})$ can be constructed in $\mathcal{O}(|CH(\mathscr{P})|)$ time, consisting of $|CH(\mathscr{P})|-2$ triangles. Next, at most $|CH(\mathscr{P})|-2$ checks are needed to determine which triangle contains the first interior point. Once located, the number of triangles increases by two, resulting in a total of $|CH(\mathscr{P})|$ triangles. For the second interior point, at most $|CH(\mathscr{P})|$ checks are needed, and the triangle count increases to $|CH(\mathscr{P})|+2$. Continuing this process, the worst-case number of checks needed for the i-th point is $|CH(\mathscr{P})|+2i-4$. Thus, for i interior points, the worst-case total number of checks is $i|CH(\mathscr{P})|+(i-2)(i-1)-2$. Since generally $i<n$, it follows that the proposed algorithm belongs to the class of quasi-quadratic algorithms, with time complexity on the order of $\Theta(n\log n)+i(n-i)+(i-2)(i-1)-2$.

Lemma 6.1.2 Let $\mathscr{P}$ be a set of $n\geq 3$ planar points that are not all collinear. Let k denote the number of points that lie on the convex hull $CH(\mathscr{P})$. Then, any triangulation of the set $\mathscr{P}$ contains exactly $3(n-1)-k$ edges and $2(n-1)-k$ triangles.

Proof. The proof of this lemma will be presented in two ways.

First method: The proof relies on the application of Lemma 6.1.1, according to which the number of interior points is $i=n-k$. From the mentioned lemma, there are $n+i-2=n+(n-k)-2=2n-k-2=2(n-1)-k$ triangles, and $n+2i-3=n+2(n-k)-3=3n-2k-3=3(n-1)-2k$ internal edges. Since k points lie on the convex hull by assumption, there are an additional k edges forming the hull. Therefore, the total number of edges is $3(n-1)-2k+k=3(n-1)-k$, which is what we aimed to prove.

Second method: In this approach, the claim is proven using Euler's formula for connected planar graphs. This formula states that a planar graph divides the plane into $f=m-n+2$ regions, where n is the number of vertices, m is the number of edges, and f is the number of regions. It is easy to observe that the number of regions bounded by the convex hull $CH(\mathscr{P})$ is equal to the number of triangles in the triangulation plus one unbounded exterior region. Thus, the number of regions is $f=\text{number\_of\_triangles}+1$. Since $|CH(\mathscr{P})|=k$, the initial triangulation contains $k-2$ triangles. By incorporating the $n-k$ interior points into the $k-2$ triangles, we obtain $2(n-k)+(k-2)=2n-k-2$ triangles, and the number of regions becomes $f=2n-k-1$. According to Euler's formula, the total number of edges is $m=f+n-2=2n-k-1+n-2=3n-k-3=3(n-1)-k$ edges, which completes the proof. ∎

6.2 Angle-Optimal Triangulation

In many practical applications, it is necessary to construct a triangulation of a point set in such a way that poorly shaped triangles are avoided. For this reason, various criteria have been developed to define what constitutes a high-quality triangulation. One of the most commonly used criteria is based on the requirement that triangles be as regular as possible, meaning their interior angles should be approximately equal. For example, a triangulation composed of *equilateral* or *equiangular triangles* is often considered high quality. Figure 6.6 shows two different triangulations, $\mathbb{T}_1$ and $\mathbb{T}_2$, for the same set of points, where triangulation $\mathbb{T}_2$ is not suitable for approximating the modeled object. The following section describes the conditions that a triangulation must satisfy to be considered optimal. Let $\mathscr{P}$ be a set of n points in the plane. Let $\mathbb{P}$ be a triangulation of the point set $\mathscr{P}$ consisting of $m=2(n-1)-i$ triangles, where $i=|CH(\mathscr{P})|$. Let the angles $\alpha_1,\alpha_2,\cdots,\alpha_m$ denote the smallest angles of the triangles obtained by the triangulation $\mathbb{P}$, respectively. By sorting these angles in increasing order, we obtain a new sequence of angles β_i ($i=\overline{1,m}$) such that $\beta_i\leq\beta_j$ for $i<j$. The *triangulation indicator* $I(\mathbb{T})$ is defined as the vector $\vec{\beta}=(\beta_1,\beta_2,\cdots,\beta_m)$, such that if $\vec{\beta}$ is strictly increasing, its first component β_1 represents the smallest angle, while the last component β_m represents the largest one. On the other hand, since each angle α_i represents the smallest angle of the i-th triangle, it follows that the largest angle β_m among all triangles in the triangulation can be computed as

$$\beta_m=\max_i\alpha_i=\max_i\min_{\alpha,\beta,\gamma\in T_i}(\alpha,\beta,\gamma),$$

which actually represents the *Max-Min* criterion.

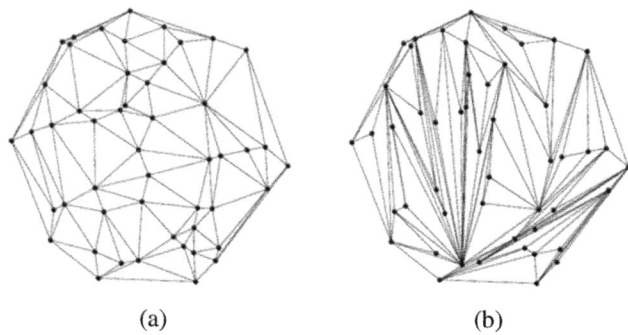

(a)   (b)

Figure 6.6: (a) Relatively good triangulation $\mathbb{T}_1$. (b) Poor triangulation $\mathbb{T}_2$.

Accordingly, any two triangulations $\mathbb{T}$ and $\mathbb{T}'$ can be compared using their triangulation indicators. Specifically, triangulation $\mathbb{T}$ is considered better than triangulation $\mathbb{T}'$ if and only if $I(\mathbb{T}) > I(\mathbb{T}')$. The condition $I(\mathbb{T}) > I(\mathbb{T}')$ implies that there exists an index $k \in \{1, 2, \cdots, m\}$ such that $\beta_j = \beta_j'$ for all $j < k$ and $\beta_j > \beta_j'$ for $j \geq k$. Therefore, triangulation $\mathbb{T}$ is considered angle-optimal relative to triangulation $\mathbb{T}'$ if holds $I(\mathbb{T}) \geq I(\mathbb{T}')$. Angle-optimal triangulations play a crucial role in constructing polyhedral terrains over a sample point set. It is important to note that such triangulations are not necessarily unique. To demonstrate this, it is first necessary to define the cocircular points.

Definition 6.2.1 The points A, B, C, and D are called *cocircular points* if they lie on the boundary of some circle, that is, on a circumference.

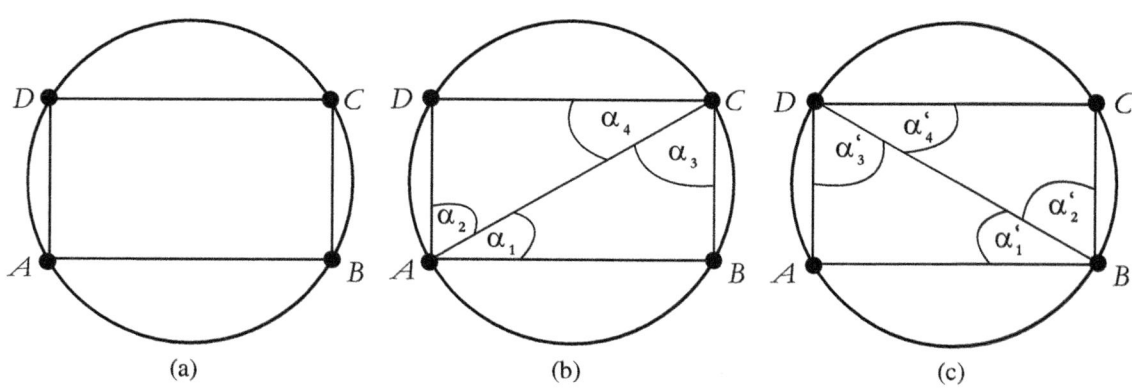

(a)   (b)   (c)

Figure 6.7: a) Cocircular points A, B, C, and D. b) Triangulation $\mathbb{T}_1$. c) Triangulation $\mathbb{T}_2$.

If the points in a triangulation are cocircular, then the angle-optimal triangulation is not unique. Namely, let the points A, B, C, and D represent the vertices of a rectangle, as shown in Fig. 6.7 (a). In that case, two triangulations, $\mathbb{T}_1$ and $\mathbb{T}_2$, can be formed depending on the choice of the internal diagonal. It is not difficult to observe that both triangulations are angle-optimal. From Figs. 6.7 (b) and 6.7 (c), it is evident that both triangulations contain two right angles. Furthermore, the following equalities hold: $\alpha_1 = \alpha_4$, $\alpha_2 = \alpha_3$, $\alpha_1' = \alpha_4'$, $\alpha_2' = \alpha_3'$. Based on Thales' theorem (see Fig. 6.8), it directly follows that $\alpha_1 = \alpha_4'$ (chord $\overline{BC}$), and that $\alpha_3 = \alpha_3'$ (chord $\overline{AB}$). From this, it follows that both triangulations have equal angles, and are therefore both optimal. In order for an optimal triangulation to be unique, it is necessary that the set of planar points does not contain four cocircular points, and that not all points are collinear. A point set that satisfies these conditions is called a set in *general position*. In other words, a point set is said to be in general position if no four points lie on the same circumference. For further characterization of optimal triangulations, certain results from elementary geometry are used, such as Thales' theorem, which is stated here without proof.

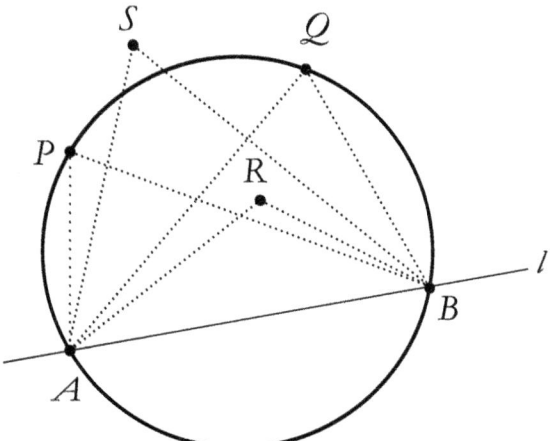

Figure 6.8: Illustration of Thales' Theorem.

Theorem 6.2.1 (*Thales' Theorem*) Let the line l intersect the circle at points A and B. Let the points P, Q, R, and S be located on the same side of line l, where point R lies inside the circle, points P and Q lie on the circle, and point S lies outside the circle. Then the following holds:

$$\angle ARB > \angle APB = \angle AQB > \angle ASB.$$

Lemma 6.2.1 Let $\square P_1P_2P_3P_4$ be a convex quadrilateral. Point P_2 does not lie on the circle C_1 circumscribed about triangle $\triangle P_1P_3P_4$ *if and only if* point P_4 does not lie on the circle C_2 circumscribed about triangle $\triangle P_1P_2P_3$.

Proof. The proof of the statement is carried out using the equivalence $P \Leftrightarrow Q$ *if and only if* $\neg P \Leftrightarrow \neg Q$. Suppose that point P_4 lies on circle C_2. Then the quadrilateral $\square P_1P_2P_3P_4$ is a cyclic quadrilateral (see Fig.6.9 (a)). Based on the property of cyclic quadrilaterals, the triangles $\triangle P_1P_2P_3$ and $\triangle P_1P_3P_4$ share the same circumscribed circle. Since, by assumption, C_1 is the circle circumscribed about triangle $\triangle P_1P_3P_4$, and C_2 is the circle circumscribed about triangle $\triangle P_1P_2P_3$, it follows that circles C_1 and C_2 coincide ($C_1 \cong C_2$), which further implies that point $P_2 \in C_1$, as was to be proven. ∎

Lemma 6.2.2 Let $\square P_1P_2P_3P_4$ be a convex quadrilateral. Point P_4 lies inside the circle C_1 circumscribed about triangle $\triangle P_1P_2P_3$ *if and only if* point P_1 lies outside the circle C_2 circumscribed about triangle $\triangle P_2P_3P_4$.

Proof. Suppose that point P_4 lies inside the circle C_1. Using Thales' theorem, it can be observed that point P_1 lies outside the circle C_2 (see Fig. 6.9 (b)). Namely, if the chord $\overline{P_2P_3}$ is considered, then it follows that $\angle P_2P_4P_3 > \angle P_2P_1P_3$. This means that point P_1 lies outside the circle C_2 circumscribed about triangle $\triangle P_2P_3P_4$. Conversely, suppose that point P_1 lies outside the circle C_2. According to Thales' theorem, if we again consider the chord $\overline{P_2P_3}$, it follows that $\angle P_2P_4P_3 > \angle P_2P_1P_3$. This implies that point P_4 lies inside the circle C_1, which was to be proven. This completes the proof of the lemma. ∎

If the quadrilateral $\square P_1P_2P_3P_4$ is convex, then there exist two triangulations, $\mathbb{T}_1$ and $\mathbb{T}_2$. In order to determine which of them is better, that is, which one satisfies the *Max-Min* criterion, it is necessary to

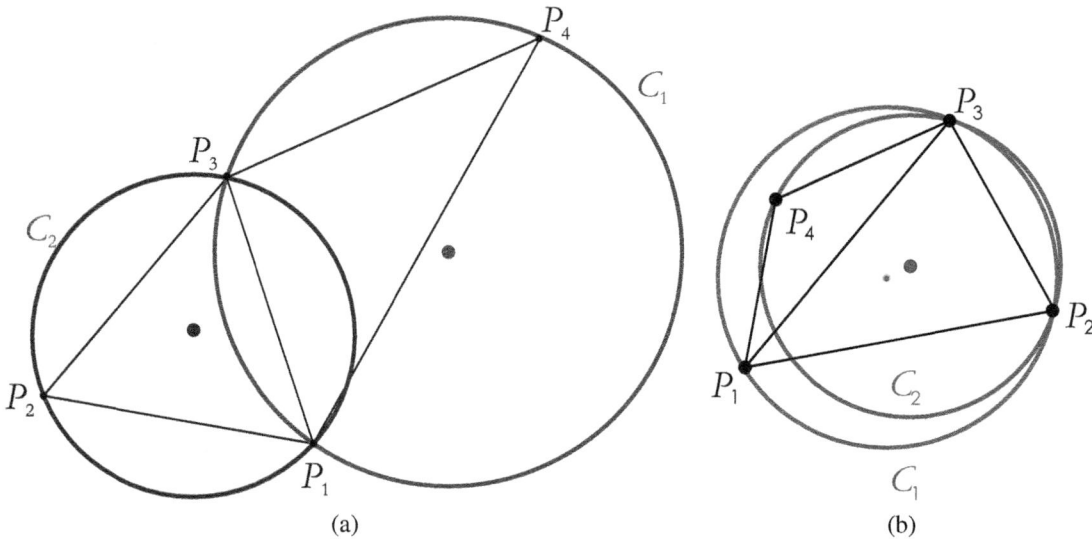

Figure 6.9: (a) Illustration related to the proof of Lemma 6.2.1. (b) Illustration related to the proof of Lemma 6.2.2.

choose an internal diagonal such that the smallest angle of the first triangulation $\mathbb{T}_1$ is greater than the smallest angle of the second triangulation $\mathbb{T}_2$. The following lemma provides a characterization of this.

Lemma 6.2.3 Let $\square P_1P_2P_3P_4$ be a convex quadrilateral. A necessary and sufficient condition for choosing the edge $\overline{P_2P_4}$ according to the Max-Min criterion is that point P_3 lies outside the circle C_1 circumscribed about triangle $\triangle P_1P_2P_4$.

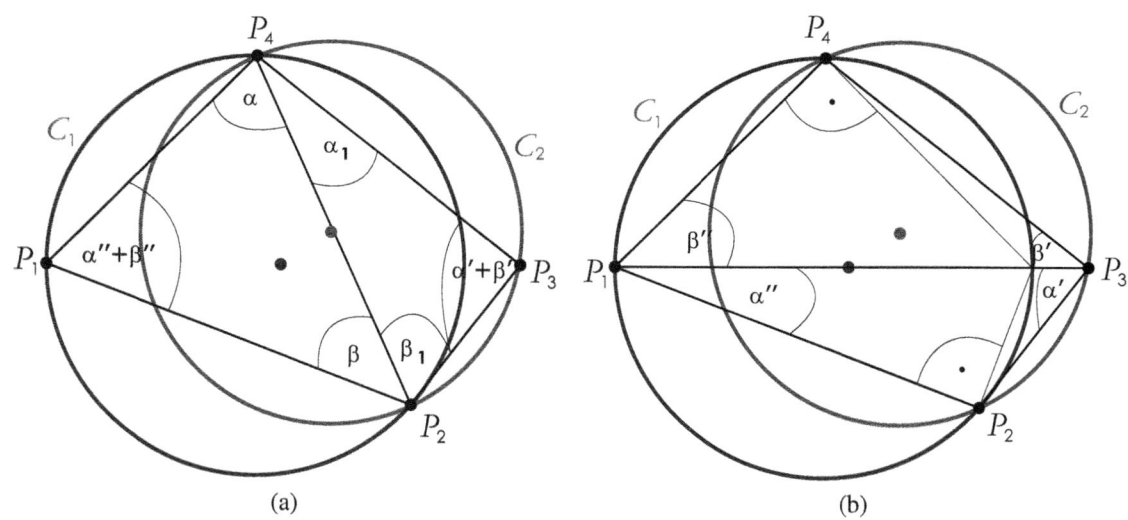

Figure 6.10: (a) Triangulation $\mathbb{T}_1$. (b) Triangulation $\mathbb{T}_2$.

Proof. Let $\mathbb{T}_1$ and $\mathbb{T}_2$ be two triangulations such that triangles $\triangle P_1P_2P_4$ and $\triangle P_2P_3P_4$ are formed by the first triangulation, and triangles $\triangle P_1P_2P_3$ and $\triangle P_1P_3P_4$ by the second triangulation. In order to prove that the Max-Min criterion selects the edge $\overline{P_2P_4}$ as optimal rather than the edge $\overline{P_1P_3}$, it is *necessary and sufficient* to show that the smallest angle among the triangles of the first triangulation is greater than the smallest angle among the triangles of the second triangulation (see Fig. 6.10). According to Thales' theorem, it holds that $\alpha > \alpha'$ (considering chord $\overline{P_1P_2}$) and $\beta > \beta'$ (chord $\overline{P_1P_4}$). Based on the lemma's assumption, the quadrilateral $\square P_1P_2P_3P_4$ is convex, so the sum of opposite angles equals π. Since point P_3 lies outside the circle C_1, it follows that angles $\angle P_1P_4P_3$ and $\angle P_1P_2P_3$ are greater than the angle $\frac{\pi}{2}$. Therefore, the candidates for the smallest angles in triangulation $\mathbb{T}_2$ are: α', α'', β', β''. In the following, it will be shown that the smallest angle of triangle $\triangle P_1P_2P_4$ in triangulation $\mathbb{T}_1$ is greater than the smallest angles of triangles $\triangle P_1P_2P_3$ and $\triangle P_1P_3P_4$ in triangulation $\mathbb{T}_2$. Since $\alpha > \alpha'$, $\beta > \beta'$, $\alpha'' + \beta'' > \alpha''$, and $\alpha'' + \beta'' > \beta''$, it follows that hold: $\min\{\alpha, \beta, \alpha'' + \beta''\} > \min\{\alpha', \beta', \alpha'', \beta''\}$. Thus, the smallest angle of triangle $\triangle P_1P_2P_4$ from the first triangulation is greater than the smallest angles of triangles $\triangle P_1P_2P_3$ and $\triangle P_1P_3P_4$ from the second triangulation. It remains to show that the smallest angle of triangle $\triangle P_2P_3P_4$ from $\mathbb{T}_1$ is greater than the smallest angles of triangles $\triangle P_1P_2P_3$ and $\triangle P_1P_3P_4$ from $\mathbb{T}_2$. To prove this, it is sufficient to show that $\alpha_1 > \alpha''$ and $\beta_1 > \beta''$. According to Lemma 6.2.1, point P_1 lies outside the circle C_2 circumscribed about triangle $\triangle P_2P_3P_4$, given that point P_3 lies outside the circle C_1 as assumed in the lemma. By Thales' theorem, we obtain that $\beta_1 > \beta''$ (using chord $\overline{P_3P_4}$) and $\alpha_1 > \alpha''$ (using chord $\overline{P_2P_3}$). Finally, since $\alpha_1 > \alpha''$, $\beta_1 > \beta''$, $\alpha' + \beta' > \alpha'$, and $\alpha' + \beta' > \beta'$, it implies the following: $\min\{\alpha_1, \beta_1, \alpha' + \beta'\} > \min\{\alpha'', \beta'', \alpha', \beta'\}$. Thus, in this case as well, the smallest angle of triangle $\triangle P_2P_3P_4$ from triangulation $\mathbb{T}_1$ is greater than the smallest angles of triangles $\triangle P_1P_2P_3$ and $\triangle P_1P_3P_4$ from triangulation $\mathbb{T}_2$. Therefore, the Max-Min criterion is satisfied:

$$\max\left\{\min\{\alpha, \beta, \alpha'' + \beta''\}, \min\{\alpha_1, \beta_1, \alpha' + \beta'\}\right\} > \max\left\{\min\{\alpha', \beta', \alpha'', \beta''\}, \min\{\alpha'', \beta'', \alpha', \beta'\}\right\}.$$

Additionally, it is easy to see that the Min-Min criterion is also satisfied. This completes the proof of the lemma. ∎

6.2.1 Edge Flipping

Let $\mathscr{P} = \{P_1, P_2, \cdots, P_n\}$ be a set of n points in the plane, and let $\mathbb{P}$ be a triangulation of these points. Furthermore, let $\overline{P_iP_j}$ be an interior edge of the triangulation $\mathbb{P}$. If this edge is not incident to any boundary edge, then it is incident to two triangles, i.e., it is the shared side of triangles $\triangle P_iP_jP_k$ and $\triangle P_iP_jP_l$ in triangulation $\mathbb{T}$. If the vertices of these triangles form a convex quadrilateral $\square P_iP_kP_jP_l$, then a new triangulation $\mathbb{T}'$ can be obtained by replacing the edge $\overline{P_iP_j}$ with the edge $\overline{P_kP_l}$. This operation of replacing edges is called *edge flipping*, as illustrated in Fig. 6.11. From the figure, it can be observed that as soon as the old edge $\overline{P_iP_j} \in \mathbb{T}$ is flipped or rotated into the new edge $\overline{P_kP_l} \in \mathbb{T}'$, the initial angles α_i ($i = \overline{1,6}$) of triangulation $\mathbb{T}$ are replaced by the angles α_i' ($i = \overline{1,6}$) of triangulation $\mathbb{T}'$.

Definition 6.2.2 The edge $\overline{P_iP_j}$ is said to be *illegal* if $\min\limits_{i=\overline{1,6}} \alpha_i < \min\limits_{i=\overline{1,6}} \alpha_i'$ holds.

An example of an illegal edge is shown in Fig. 6.12 (a). In order to check the legality of an edge within a quadrilateral $\square P_iP_kP_jP_l$, it is not necessary to compute all the angles α_i and α_i' for $i = \overline{1,6}$. Instead, a simpler criterion is used, formulated in the form of the following lemma.

Lemma 6.2.4 Let the edge $s = \overline{P_iP_j}$ be the common side of triangles $\triangle P_iP_jP_k$ and $\triangle P_iP_jP_l$, and let C_1 be the circle circumscribed about triangle $\triangle P_iP_jP_k$. Then the edge s is illegal *if and only if* point P_l lies inside the circle C_1.

Proof. The proof of the lemma follows directly from the proof of the previous lemma. Namely, according to Lemma 6.2.3, the edge s is legal *if and only if* point P_l lies outside the circle C_1. ∎

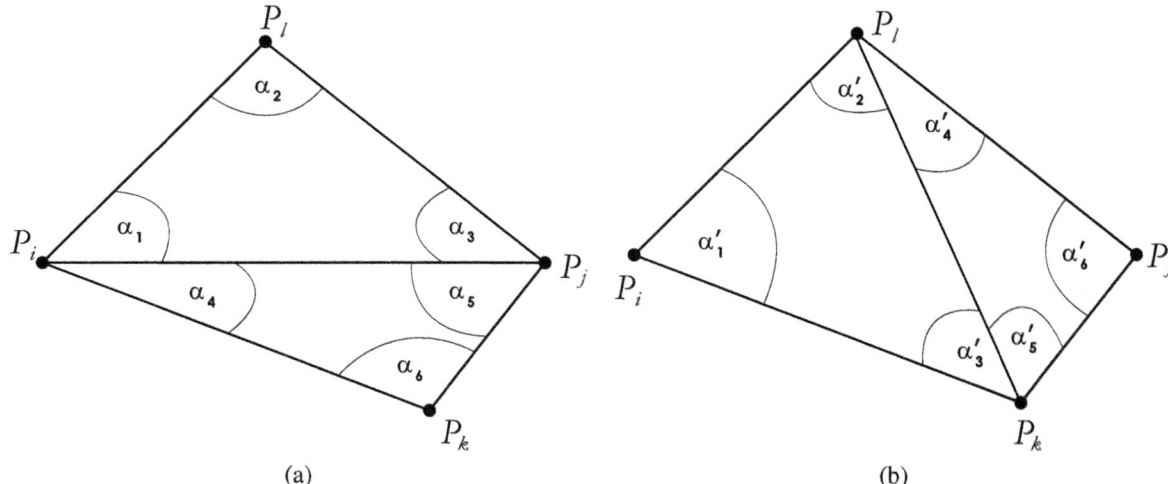

Figure 6.11: (a) Initial triangulation $\mathbb{T}$. (b) Triangulation $\mathbb{T}'$ induced by introducing the edge $\overline{P_kP_l}$.

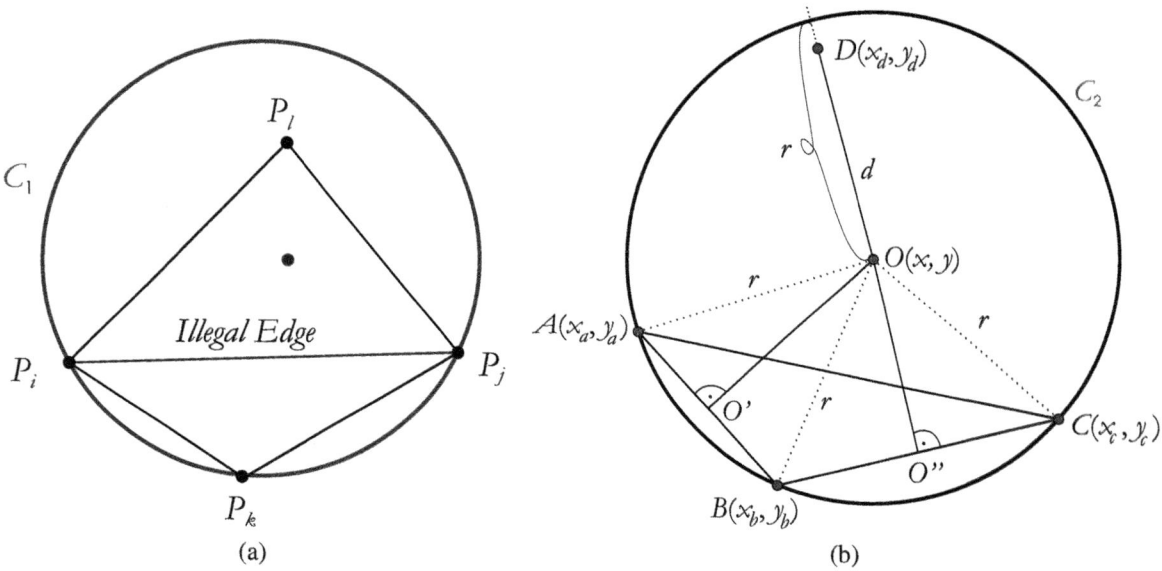

Figure 6.12: (a) Illustration of the illegal edge $\overline{P_iP_j}$. (b) Illustration related to the proof of Lemma 6.2.5.

The following lemma provides an efficient method for checking whether point D lies inside the circle C_2 circumscribed about triangle $\triangle ABC$ (see Fig. 6.12 (b)).

Lemma 6.2.5 Let $\triangle ABC$ be a given triangle with vertices $A(x_a, y_a)$, $B(x_b, y_b)$, and $C(x_c, y_c)$. A necessary and sufficient condition for point $D(x_d, y_d)$ to lie inside the circle C_2 circumscribed about triangle $\triangle ABC$ is that the sign of the determinant E is positive, i.e.,

$$E = \begin{vmatrix} x_a & y_a & x_a^2 + y_a^2 & 1 \\ x_b & y_b & x_b^2 + y_b^2 & 1 \\ x_c & y_c & x_c^2 + y_c^2 & 1 \\ x_d & y_d & x_d^2 + y_d^2 & 1 \end{vmatrix} > 0. \tag{6.1}$$

Proof. The proof of the lemma uses the diagram from Fig. 6.12 (b), where point O is the center of the circle C_2 circumscribed about triangle $\triangle ABC$. This center is obtained as the intersection of the perpendicular bisectors s_1 and s_2 of sides $\overline{AB}$ and $\overline{BC}$, respectively. To show that the line s_1, which passes through points O and O', is indeed the perpendicular bisector of segment $\overline{AB}$, it is sufficient to prove that triangles $\triangle AOO'$ and $\triangle BOO'$ are congruent. Let point O' be the midpoint of segment $\overline{AB}$. Then the coordinates of O' are $O'\left(\frac{x_a+x_b}{2}, \frac{y_a+y_b}{2}\right)$. Since the lengths of segments $\overline{AO}$ and $\overline{BO}$ are both equal to r, and the length of segment $\overline{AO'}$ is equal to the length of segment $\overline{BO'}$, it follows that the triangles are congruent and therefore have equal angles. This implies that $\angle AO'O = \angle BO'O$. Now, since the sum of these two angles is equal to π, it follows that each of them is $\frac{\pi}{2}$, meaning that the line s_1, which contains segment $\overline{OO'}$, is indeed the perpendicular bisector of side $\overline{AB}$. Similarly, it can be shown that the line s_2, defined by segment $\overline{OO''}$, is the perpendicular bisector of segment $\overline{BC}$. The bisectors s_1 and s_2 intersect at point $O(x,y)$, whose coordinates x and y need to be determined in order to compute the distance from point D to the center O of the circle C_2, and thus determine whether point D lies inside the circle C_2. First, the equation of the bisector s_1 must be found, i.e., the line passing through point O' and perpendicular to segment $\overline{AB}$. In analytic geometry, the equation of a line l passing through points A and B is given by:

$$l : \frac{x - x_a}{x_b - x_a} = \frac{y - y_a}{y_b - y_a} \tag{6.2}$$

The general form of the equation of a line l is $ax + by + c = 0$. Since the line l passes through points $A(x_a, y_a)$ and $B(x_b, y_b)$, it follows that $a = y_b - y_a$ and $b = x_a - x_b$. Moreover, $\vec{a} = (a, b)$ is the normal vector of line l, which is also the direction vector of the bisector s_1, since s_1 is perpendicular to l. The normal vector of the bisector s_1 then has the form $\vec{a}_1 = (b, -a)$, because $\vec{a} \cdot \vec{a}_1 = 0$. Therefore, the equation of the bisector s_1 is $bx - ay + c_1 = 0$. The coefficient c_1 can be determined from the condition that the line s_1 passes through the point $O'\left(\frac{x_a+x_b}{2}, \frac{y_a+y_b}{2}\right)$, that is, $c_1 = -b\left(\frac{x_a+x_b}{2}\right) + a\left(\frac{y_a+y_b}{2}\right) = \frac{1}{2}(-x_a^2 + x_b^2 - y_a^2 + y_b^2)$. Thus, the equation of the bisector s_1 has the form $a_1 x + b_1 y + c_1$, where $a_1 = b$ and $b_1 = -a$. Similarly, the equation of the bisector s_2 can be written as $a_2 x + b_2 y + c_2$, where $a_2 = x_b - x_c$, $b_2 = y_b - y_c$, and $c_2 = \frac{1}{2}(-x_b^2 + x_c^2 - y_b^2 + y_c^2)$. Finally, the coordinates x and y can be found by solving the system of two equations with two unknowns. The mentioned system can be solved in various ways (Gaussian elimination, Cramer's rule, the Kronecker–Capelli theorem, etc.). Additionally, the above system can be represented in matrix form as $A\mathbf{z} = \mathbf{c}$, where $A = \begin{bmatrix} a_1 & b_1 \\ a_2 & b_2 \end{bmatrix}$ is a 2×2 matrix. The components of the column vector $\mathbf{z} = [x\ y]^T$ are obtained by multiplying the inverse matrix A^{-1} with the column vector $\mathbf{c} = [-c_1\ -c_2]^T$. Solving the above system yields the coordinates x and y:

$$x = \frac{x_c^2(y_a - y_b) + x_b^2(-y_a + y_c) + (y_b - y_c)[x_a^2 + (y_a - y_b)(y_a - y_c)]}{2[x_c(y_a - y_b) + x_a(y_b - y_c) + x_b(y_c - y_a)]},$$

$$y = \frac{(x_b - x_c)(-x_a^2 + x_b^2 - y_a^2 + y_b^2) + (x_a - x_b)(x_b^2 - x_c^2 + y_b^2 - y_c^2)}{2[x_c(y_a - y_b) + x_a(y_b - y_c) + x_a(y_c - y_b)]}.$$

After the formulas for the coordinates x and y of point $O(x,y)$ have been determined, the radius r of the circumscribed circle C_2, as well as the distance d between points $D(x_d, y_d)$ and $O(x,y)$, are computed as follows:

$$r = \sqrt{(x - x_c)^2 + (y - y_c)^2}, \quad d = \sqrt{(x - x_d)^2 + (y - y_d)^2}. \tag{6.3}$$

For computational efficiency, instead of calculating the square root, it is sufficient to compute only the values of R^2 and d^2. Namely, to determine whether point D lies on the circle C_2, inside it, or outside it, it is enough to analyze the following three cases:

- point D lies on the circle C_2 *if and only if $r = d$*;
- point D lies inside the circle C_2 *if and only if $d < r$*;
- point D lies outside the circle C_2 *if and only if $d > r$*.

Therefore, all three cases reduce to examining the sign of the difference $r - d$. Since $r^2 - d^2 = (r - d)(r + d)$ and $r + d > 0$, to determine the sign of $r - d$, it is sufficient to consider the sign of the squared difference $r^2 - d^2$. After a few elementary operations, this difference simplifies to the expression $E/2P$, where E denotes the determinant defined by equation 6.1, and P is the area of triangle $\triangle ABC$, defined as

$$P = \frac{1}{2}[x_a(y_b - y_c) + x_b(y_c - y_a) + x_c(y_a - y_b)]. \tag{6.4}$$

Finally, $E = 2P(r + d)(r - d)$, so the sign of the difference $r - d$ depends solely on the sign of the determinant E. Therefore, if $E > 0$, it follows that $r > d$, and point $D(x_d, y_d)$ lies inside the circle C_2; if $E = 0$, point D lies on the circle C_2; and if $E < 0$, point D lies outside the circle C_2. This completes the proof of the lemma.   ∎

It is not difficult to observe that if the convex quadrilateral $\square P_i P_k P_j P_l$ is not cyclic (see Fig. 6.12 (a)), then exactly one of its diagonals is an illegal edge. An illegal edge in a convex quadrilateral can always be replaced by a legal one, thereby increasing the smallest angle, which results in a locally improved triangulation. In other words, replacing an illegal edge with a legal one yields a triangulation that consists of less acute triangles compared to the one based on the illegal edge.

Definition 6.2.3 A triangulation is said to be *legal* if it contains no illegal edges.

Based on what has been stated so far, a pseudocode algorithm can be proposed for finding a legal triangulation of a planar point set. Algorithm 7 starts from an initial triangulation (e.g., a triangulation obtained using Observation 6.1.1), and then performs edge flipping of illegal edges until all edges in the triangulation become legal.

Algorithm 7: Pseudocode of the algorithm for finding a legal triangulation.

Input : Initial triangulation $\mathbb{P}$ of the planar point set $\mathscr{P} = \{P_1, P_2, \cdots, P_n\}$.

Step 1: While $\mathbb{T}$ contains an illegal edge $\overline{P_i P_j}$ **do**:

Replace the illegal edge $\overline{P_i P_j}$ with the legal edge $\overline{P_k P_l}$.

Output : Legal triangulation

It is not difficult to conclude that Algorithm 7 will terminate after a finite number of iterations. Namely, due to the finite number of possible triangulations obtained by replacing illegal edges with legal ones, the algorithm must terminate, thereby producing a legal triangulation $\mathbb{T}'$ of the initial point set $\mathscr{P}$. For this triangulation, it holds that $I(\mathbb{T}') > I(\mathbb{T})$, which is guaranteed by the following lemma.

Lemma 6.2.6 Let $\mathbb{T}$ be the initial triangulation of the point set $\mathscr{P} = \{P_1, P_2, \cdots, P_n\}$, and let $\mathbb{T}'$ be the triangulation obtained from $\mathbb{T}$ by flipping illegal edges into legal ones. Then it holds that $I(\mathbb{T}') > I(\mathbb{T})$.

Proof. Let β_i and β_j be two components of the vector $I(\mathbb{T})$, representing the smallest angles of the triangles whose common side is the illegal edge s. Let $i < j$; then $\beta_i \leq \beta_j$, since these angles are sorted in ascending order. Since the illegal edge s is replaced with the legal edge s' according to the Max-Min criterion, it follows that the smallest angle β_i' of the triangles sharing edge s' is strictly greater than the angle $\beta_i = \min\{\beta_i, \beta_j\}$. Therefore, we obtain that $I(\mathbb{T}') > I(\mathbb{T})$, which completes the proof.   ∎

6.3 Properties of Delaunay Triangulation

Definition 6.3.1 The circle C_1 circumscribed about triangle $\triangle P_i P_j P_k$ is called the *largest empty circle* if its interior contains no point.

Definition 6.3.2 A triangulation of a finite point set $\mathscr{P} = \{P_1, P_2, \cdots, P_n\}$ is called a *Delaunay triangulation* if for each of its triangles there exists a largest empty circle, i.e., a circle whose interior contains no point from the set $\mathscr{P}$.

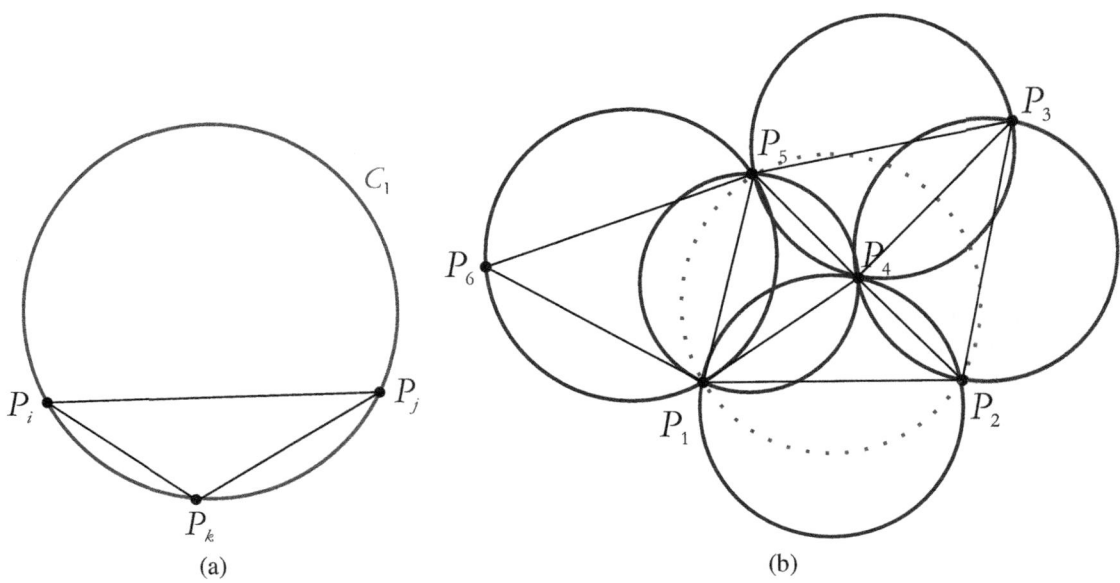

Figure 6.13: (a) Illustration of the largest empty circle C_1. (b) Delaunay triangulation.

An example of the largest empty circle and Delaunay triangulation for a set of six points is shown in Fig. 6.13. As can be seen in Fig. 6.13 (b), for each triangle in the triangulation, a circle can be drawn that contains no point in its interior. Additionally, the same figure shows a dashed circle that does not satisfy the condition of being the largest empty circle, since point P_4 lies inside it. However, this circle does not violate the Delaunay triangulation, as it is not circumscribed about any triangle in the triangulation. It is important to note that the Delaunay triangulation is not necessarily unique. Namely, in the case of a convex quadrilateral whose vertices are cocircular, there may exist two different Delaunay triangulations, as illustrated in Fig. 6.14 (a). Moreover, the choice of the internal diagonal of a convex quadrilateral may result in a triangulation that is not a Delaunay triangulation, as shown in Fig. 6.14 (b). On the other hand, Fig. 6.14 (c) shows a Delaunay triangulation, where an appropriate choice of diagonal ensures that the largest empty circle can be drawn around each triangle, which was not the case in Fig. 6.14 (b). The following lemma addresses the uniqueness of the Delaunay triangulation.

Lemma 6.3.1 Let $\square P_1 P_2 P_3 P_4$ be a given convex quadrilateral such that its vertices are not cocircular. Then there exists a unique Delaunay triangulation of this quadrilateral.

Proof. Let $\square P_1 P_2 P_3 P_4$ be a convex quadrilateral such that its vertices are not cocircular. Then there exist two triangulations, $\mathbb{T}_1$ and $\mathbb{T}_2$, of the given quadrilateral. Let the first triangulation contain the diagonal $\overline{P_2 P_4}$ and the second the diagonal $\overline{P_1 P_3}$, as shown in Fig. 6.15. In what follows, it will be shown that selecting the diagonal $\overline{P_2 P_4}$ in triangulation $\mathbb{T}_1$ results in a Delaunay triangulation of the quadrilateral $\square P_1 P_2 P_3 P_4$. Let C_1 and C_2 be the circles circumscribed about triangles $\triangle P_1 P_2 P_4$ and $\triangle P_2 P_3 P_4$ (see

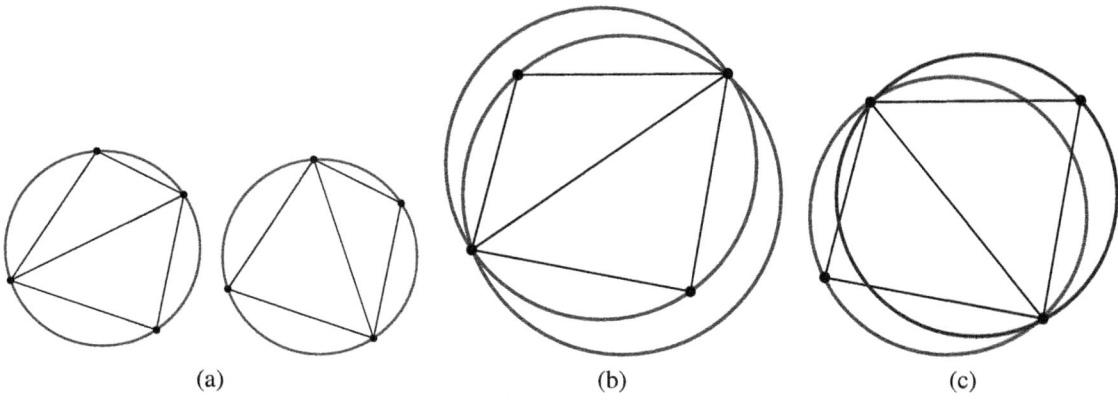

Figure 6.14: (a) Two Delaunay triangulations. (b) Not a Delaunay triangulation. (c) Delaunay triangulation.

Fig. 6.15 (a)), respectively. Also, let $\mathscr{C}_1$ denote the family of circles passing through points P_2 and P_4. Since circles C_1 and C_2 both pass through P_2 and P_4, it follows that they belong to the family $\mathscr{C}_1$. According to Lemma 6.2.3, the edge $\overline{P_2P_4}$ is legal (optimal) *if and only if* point P_3 lies outside circle C_1. Given the assumption that the points are not cocircular, the quadrilateral $\square P_1P_2P_3P_4$ is not cyclic, and the circles C_1 and C_2 are not identical, so the point $P_3 \in C_2$ does not lie on C_1, which implies, by Lemma 6.2.3, that the edge $\overline{P_2P_4}$ is legal. Therefore, $\mathbb{T}_1$ is a Delaunay triangulation. In other words, by traversing the family of circles $\mathscr{C}_1$ from circle C_1 to circle C_2, one obtains the largest empty circles. According to Definition 6.3.2, $\mathbb{T}_1$ is a Delaunay triangulation. It remains to be shown that choosing the diagonal $\overline{P_1P_3}$ in triangulation $\mathbb{T}_2$ does not yield a Delaunay triangulation. Since the vertices of the quadrilateral $\square P_1P_2P_3P_4$ are not cocircular, the quadrilateral is not cyclic, and thus there exists only one legal edge that generates the angle-optimal triangulation. What follows is a demonstration that triangulation $\mathbb{T}_2$ is not such a triangulation, and hence $\mathbb{T}_1$ is the unique Delaunay triangulation. Let $\mathscr{C}_2$ denote the family of circles passing through points P_1 and P_4 (see Fig. 6.15 (b)). Also, let circles C_1 and C_2 in triangulation $\mathbb{T}_2$ be the circles circumscribed about triangles $\triangle P_1P_2P_4$ and $\triangle P_1P_3P_4$, respectively. According to Lemma 6.2.2, point P_2 lies inside circle C_2 *if and only if* point P_3 lies outside circle C_1. By assumption, point P_3 lies outside circle C_1 (since $\square P_1P_2P_3P_4$ is not cyclic), which implies that P_2 lies inside circle C_2. This can also be seen by traversing the family of circles $\mathscr{C}_2$ from circle C_1 to circle C_2. Thus, since point P_2 lies in the interior of circle C_2, it follows that C_2 is not the largest empty circle, and therefore $\mathbb{T}_2$ is not a Delaunay triangulation, which completes the proof. ∎

Based on the previous considerations, it can be concluded that angle-optimal triangulations are, in fact, Delaunay triangulations. Their characterization will be presented through the following two theorems, which are stated without proof, as they can be relatively easily derived from the material previously discussed.

Theorem 6.3.1 Let $\mathbb{T}$ be a triangulation of the planar point set $\mathscr{P} = \{P_1, P_2, \cdots, P_n\}$. Then $\mathbb{T}$ is a Delaunay triangulation *if and only if* the circles circumscribed about the triangles in $\mathbb{T}$ contain no point from $\mathscr{P}$ in their interior.

Theorem 6.3.2 A triangulation $\mathbb{T}$ of the planar point set $\mathscr{P} = \{P_1, P_2, \cdots, P_n\}$ is a Delaunay triangulation *if and only if* it is a legal triangulation.

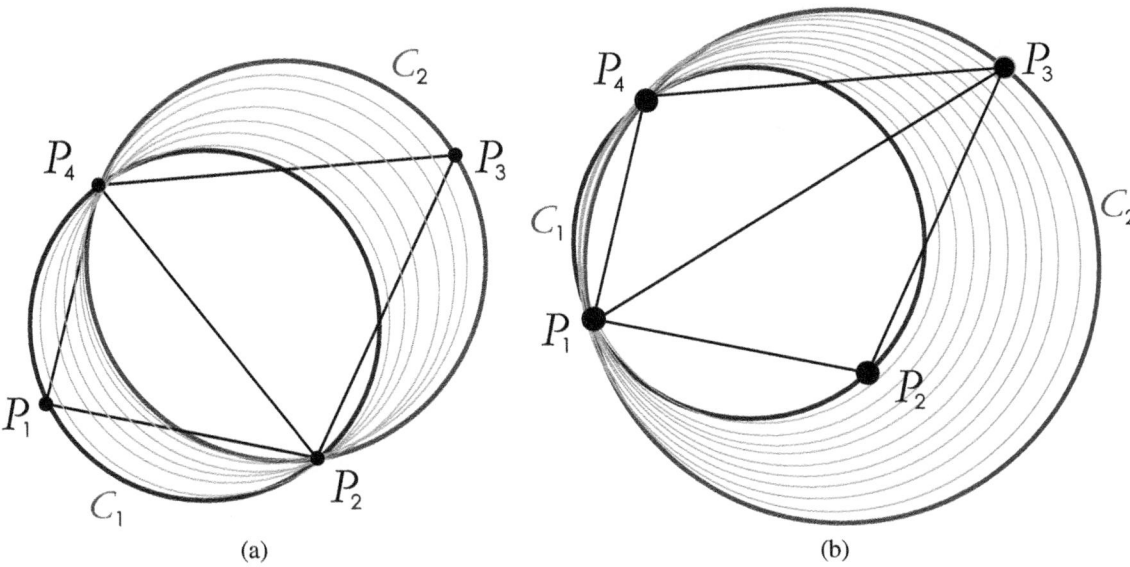

Figure 6.15: (a) Translation of circles from C_1 to C_2 through the family $\mathscr{C}_1$. (b) Translation of circles from C_1 to C_2 through the family $\mathscr{C}_2$.

6.4 Computing the Delaunay Triangulation

In this section, two algorithms for computing the Delaunay triangulation will be presented: the **Flip-Edge Algorithm** and the **Incremental Algorithm** [21, 82, 115].

6.4.1 Flip-Edge Algorithm

The Flip-Edge Algorithm begins by identifying an extreme edge e for a given set of points in the plane. Then, for the identified extreme edge, the algorithm searches for the *mate of the edge*, i.e., a point such that the circumscribed circle passing through that point and the endpoints of edge e is the largest empty circle. In each iteration of the algorithm, a triangle is determined to serve as the face associated with edge e. Initially, the edge e represents the *frontier* of the current triangulation. The definition of the frontier is based on the following scheme, according to which each edge in the Delaunay triangulation is classified as:

- *Dormant Edge* – an edge that has not yet been discovered by the algorithm;
- *Live Edge* – an edge that has been discovered by the algorithm, but for which only one of its incident faces (a triangle or the exterior region) is known;
- *Dead Edge* – an edge that has been fully processed by the algorithm and for which both incident faces are known.

The Flip-Edge Algorithm consists of four steps. In the first step, the algorithm searches for an extreme edge e from the set $\mathscr{P} = \{P_1, P_2, \ldots, P_n\}$ of cardinality n, where this search is performed in $\mathscr{O}(n)$ time. The extreme edge is determined by first selecting an anchor point. This anchor can be defined as the point with the smallest x-coordinate; if several points share the same x-value, the one with the smallest y-coordinate is chosen. Alternatively, the anchor may be taken as the point with the largest x-coordinate; in this case, ties are resolved by selecting the point with the largest y-coordinate. This anchor point is found in $\mathscr{O}(n)$ time. Once the anchor point P_{i_1} is found, it is swapped with the first point in the set $\mathscr{P}$, i.e., with point P_1. The anchor point becomes the starting point of the extreme edge e. The other endpoint P_{i_2} of the extreme edge is determined by selecting, at each step, only those points in the set $\mathscr{P}$ that lie to the left of the segment $\overline{P_{i_1}P_{i_2}}$, or between the points P_{i_1} and P_{i_2}, since points to the right of that segment are not candidates for the endpoint of the extreme edge. Initially, the point P_{i_2} is set to the second point in the set $\mathscr{P}$, i.e., $P_{i_2} \leftarrow P_2$, while P_1 is the anchor point. After all elements of the set $\mathscr{P}$ have been processed—that is, after at most n iterations—the index m is found such that $P_{i_2} \leftarrow P_m$, which defines the endpoint of the extreme edge e, i.e., $e \leftarrow \overline{P_1P_m}$. The following code snippet demonstrates how to find the extreme edge e in linear time:

```python
def extreme_edge(points: list[Point2D]) -> Segment2D:
    m = 0; n = len(points)
    for i in range(1, n):
        if points[i] < points[m]:m = i
    points[0], points[m] = points[m], points[0] #swap elements
    m = 1
    for i in range(2, n):
        t_c = points[i].classification_m(points[0], points[m])
        if t_c==TypeP2.BETWEEN or t_c==TypeP2.RIGHT: m = i
    return Segment2D(points[0], points[m])
```

In the second step of the algorithm, edge storage is optimized using a `SortedDict`, which maintains edges classified into one of the following states: dormant, live, or dead. Each edge inserted into the dictionary is assigned a priority determined by the function *compare_edges*($\cdot, \cdot$), whose implementation is provided below:

```python
def compare_edges(a: Segment2D, b: Segment2D) -> bool:
    a_ordered = (min(a.s, a.e), max(a.s, a.e))
    b_ordered = (min(b.s, b.e), max(b.s, b.e))
    return a_ordered < b_ordered
```

Since *compare_edges*($\cdot, \cdot$) is used as the comparison criterion when inserting edges (segments) into the `SortedDict`, it is necessary to invoke this comparison function within the `__lt__` method of the **Segment2D** class. Once the extreme edge e is identified from the list `points`, it is inserted into the boundary dictionary. In addition, a list named `delaunay_triangles` is initialized to store the computed triangles of the Delaunay triangulation. The following code snippet illustrates this process:

```python
boundary = SortedDict();   delaunay_triangles = []
e = extreme_edge(points); boundary[e] = True
```

Once the edge e is inserted into the dictionary boundary, it is assigned the status of a live edge. In the following, the process of finding the mate of edge e is described. The candidates for the mate can only be the points located to the right of edge e, since the edge was selected such that no points exist on its left side. The principle of finding a mate becomes clearer when demonstrated through an example (see Fig. 6.16). In Fig. 6.16, eight points P_i $(i = \overline{1,8})$ are given, with edge $e = \overline{AB}$ representing the extreme edge. Let p denote the line defined by edge e, described by the parametric equation $p(s) = A + s(B-A)$, where $s \in \mathbb{R}$. The midpoint of edge e is obtained by setting $s = 0.5$. The perpendicular bisector of edge e is determined by first computing the segment $\overline{CD}$, obtained by rotating edge e around its midpoint. A parametric equation $q(r)$ is then assigned to this segment $\overline{CD}$, where points P_1 and P_2 correspond to points A and B (i.e., $P_1 \leftarrow A$, $P_2 \leftarrow B$). To find the mate P_k $(k > 2)$, the algorithm iterates over the remaining points and seeks the smallest value of parameter r. This value is obtained as the intersection of the lines $q(r)$ and $r(t)$, where $q(r)$ is the bisector of segment $\overline{AB}$, and $r(t)$ is the bisector of segment $\overline{P_2P_k}$. In Fig. 6.16, point $P_3 \leftarrow E$ represents the mate of edge e since it yields the smallest parameter value $r = r_1 < r_2 < 1$, while all other values are greater than 1. This choice ensures the formation of triangle $\triangle ABE \cong \triangle P_1P_2P_3$, around which the largest empty circle is circumscribed, as formalized in the following lemma.

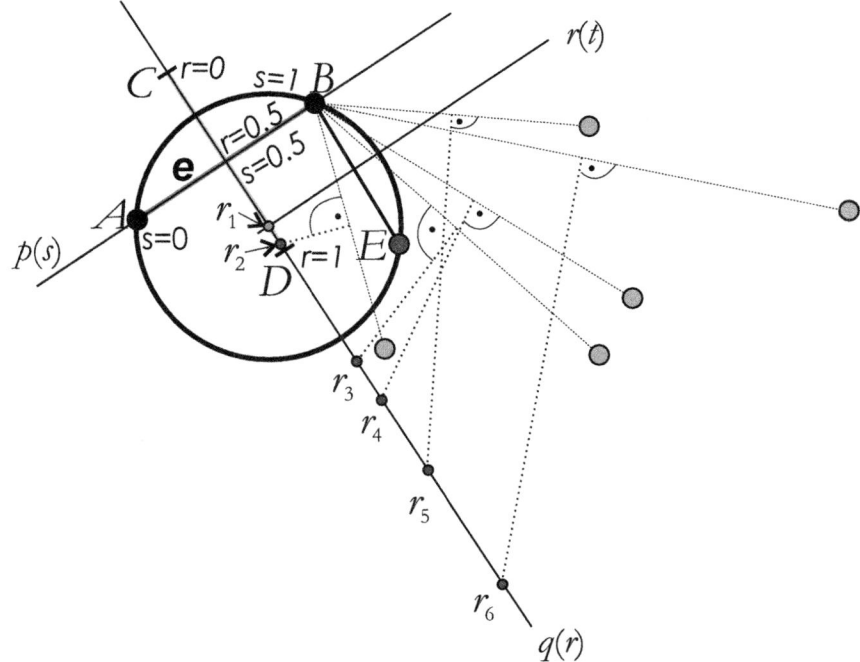

Figure 6.16: Graphical illustration of finding the mate, i.e., point E.

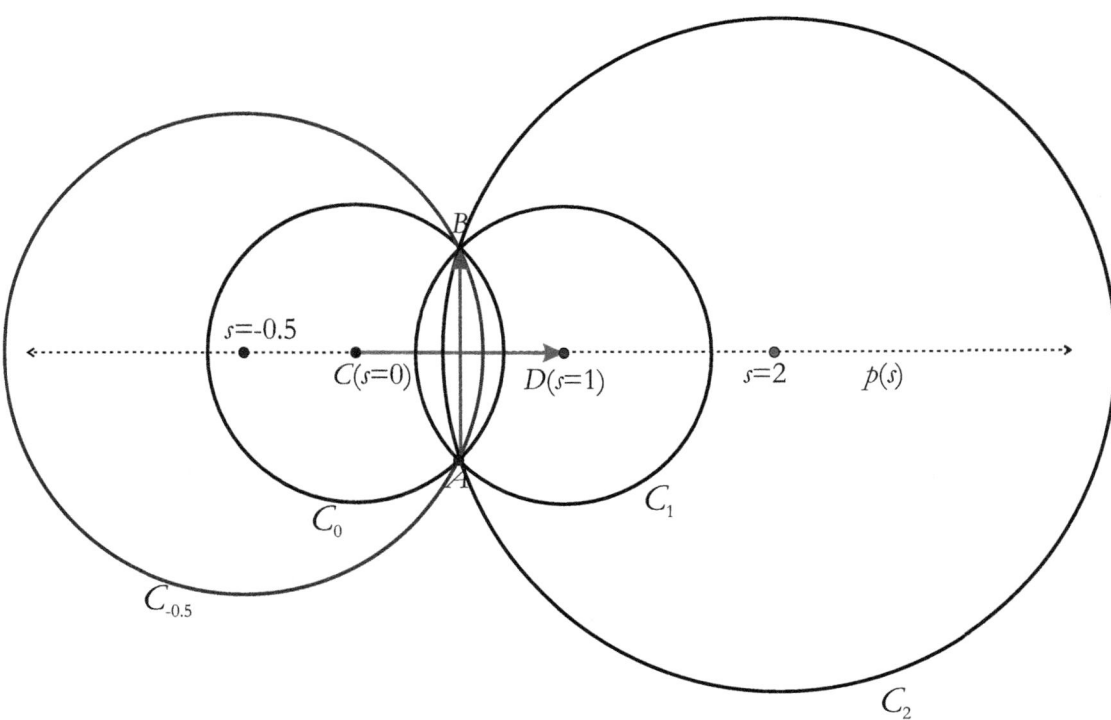

Figure 6.17: Four circles from the family $\mathscr{C}(A, B)$ defined by edge $\overline{AB}$ and the parametric values s of the line $p(s)$.

Lemma 6.4.1 Let $e = \overline{AB}$ be the extreme edge, and let the candidates for its mate be the points located to its right. The mate of edge e is the point P_k for which the intersection of the bisectors of edges $\overline{AB}$ and $\overline{BP_k}$ corresponds to the smallest value of the parameter r ($r < 1$), and the triangle $\triangle ABP_k$ defines the largest empty circle.

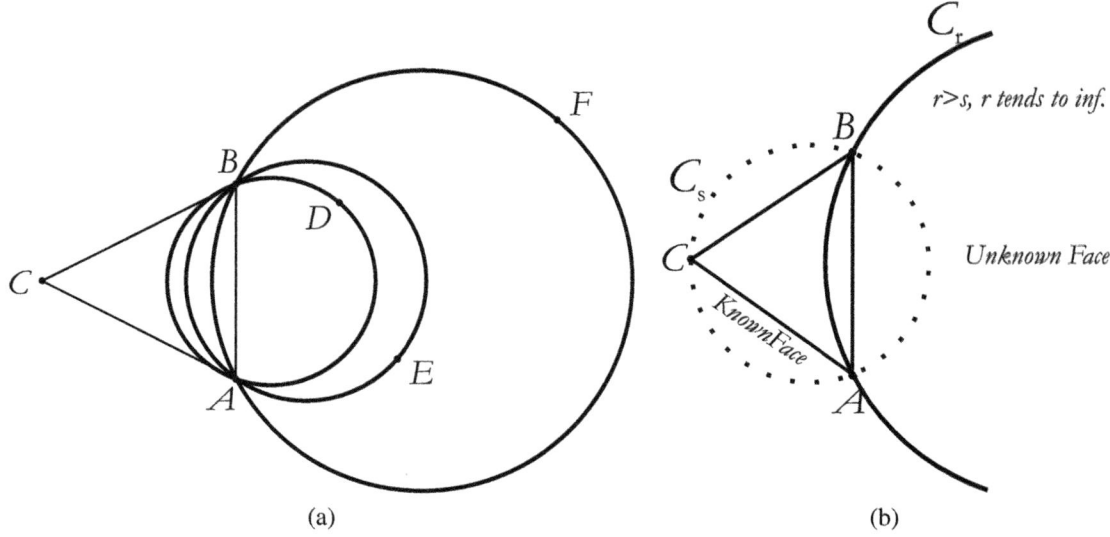

Figure 6.18: (a) Finding the mate D of edge $\overline{AB}$. (b) Case when edge $\overline{AB}$ has no mate.

Proof. Let $\mathscr{C}(A,B)$ denote the family of circles passing through points A and B, as illustrated in Fig. 6.17. These circles are defined based on the segment $\overline{AB}$ and the parametric values of the line $p(s)$, which represents the perpendicular bisector of segment $\overline{AB}$. As $s \to -\infty$ or $s \to +\infty$, the circle $C_s \in \mathscr{C}(A,B)$ degenerates into a corresponding half-plane containing the segment $\overline{AB}$: the left half-plane for $s \to -\infty$, and the right half-plane for $s \to +\infty$. As s varies over the set of real numbers, an infinite number of circles passing through points A and B is generated, with centers determined by the parameter s. This implies that $\mathscr{C}(A,B)$ forms an infinite family of circles. Let C_s be the circle circumscribed about the known face (In Fig. 6.18 (b), it is triangle $\triangle ABC$), defined via the edge $\overline{AB}$. If the face is unbounded and $s \to -\infty$, the circle C_s becomes the half-plane lying to the left of segment $\overline{AB}$. When determining the mate P_k, the algorithm searches for the smallest value of the parameter $r > s$ such that there exists a point in the set of n points (excluding the endpoints of $\overline{AB}$) that lies on the circle C_r. In Fig. 6.18 (a), this point is labeled as $D = P_k$. This process can be interpreted as a gradual expansion of a circle through the edge $\overline{AB}$. Intuitively, one can imagine inflating a balloon along the edge $\overline{AB}$. The first point from the input set that the balloon touches is called the mate—in this case, point D. On the other hand, if no such minimal value $r > s$ exists that produces such a point, then edge $\overline{AB}$ has no mate. Visually, this means the balloon expands to fill the entire half-plane to the right of $\overline{AB}$ without ever touching a point from the input set. Formally, it must be proven that C_r is indeed the largest empty circle. Let the known face with edge $\overline{AB}$ be bounded by the largest empty circle C_s, and let the unknown face be bounded by the circle C_r. Clearly, if $r \to \infty$ and $r > s$, then edge $\overline{AB}$ has no mate (see Fig. 6.18 (b)). Therefore, edge $\overline{AB}$ has a mate in two cases. The first case occurs when $s \to -\infty$ and $r > s$ is the smallest possible value. The second case occurs when $s \to +\infty$ and $r < s$. Since the second case can be reduced to the first, only the first case is considered, where $s \to -\infty$ and $r > s$ is minimal. It must now be shown that no point from the input set lies in the interior of circle C_r. Indeed, on the left side of segment $\overline{AB}$, the circular sector bounded by segment $\overline{AB}$ and the arc of C_r is fully contained within the largest empty circle C_s, implying that no point lies within C_r on that side. It is also clear that no point lies within C_r on the right side of segment $\overline{AB}$. If such a point existed, there would be a circle $C_u \in \mathscr{C}(A,B)$ containing that point, implying $s < u < r$, which contradicts the minimality of r. Therefore, circle C_r is indeed empty. Moreover, this circle is the largest, because if there existed a larger empty circle, its center would lie farther along the bisector than the center of C_r, implying that the mate of edge e would not be point P_k, contradicting the construction. Hence, C_r is the largest empty circle, and triangle $\triangle ABP_k$ is a Delaunay triangle, as was to be proven. ∎

Based on the proof presented in Lemma 6.4.1, it is clear that the time required to find the mate is linear with respect to the number of points, which is also evident from the implementation of the function *has_edge_mate*(·, ·):

```python
def has_edge_mate(edge: Segment2D, points: list[Point2D])-> Point2D:
    nearest_point = None; min_distance = 1e10
    f=Segment2D(edge[0],edge[1]); f.rotate()
    for i in range(len(points)):
        if points[i] == edge[0] or points[i] == edge[1]:continue
        if points[i].classification_m(edge[0], edge[1]) == TypeP2.LEFT:
            g = Segment2D(edge[1], points[i]); g.rotate()
            p = [0]; f.intersection_lines(g, p)
            if p[0]< min_distance: nearest_point = points[i]; min_distance=p[0]
    return nearest_point
```

From the implementation of the function *has_edge_mate*(·, ·), it can be observed that the function returns the mate if one is found, and otherwise returns **None**. Once the mate is found, a triangle is formed, causing the live edge $\overline{P_1P_2}$ to transition to the dead state, while the dormant edges $\overline{P_1P_3}$ and $\overline{P_2P_3}$ become live. These changes affect the state of the dictionary: the live edge $e \leftarrow \overline{P_1P_2}$ changes its status to a dead edge, and the new edges $\overline{P_1P_3}$ and $\overline{P_2P_3}$ are added to the dictionary as live edges, since they were not previously present. In other words, when edge e is removed from the dictionary using the method *popitem*(-1), and it is determined that it has a mate, the newly created triangle is appended to the list delaunay_triangles. Additionally, the edges connecting the mate to the endpoints of edge e are updated in the tree structure, as illustrated in the following code snippet:

```python
e1, _ = boundary.popitem(-1)
mate = has_edge_mate(e1, points)
if mate is not None:
    update_boundary(boundary, mate, e1[0])
    update_boundary(boundary, e1[1], mate)
    p = Polygon(); p.insert(e1[0]); p.insert(e1[1]); p.insert(mate)
    delaunay_triangles.append(p)
```

In the code snippet above, the function *update_boundary*(·, ·, ·) is invoked. Its purpose is to assign the unbounded region (the unknown face) of an edge—being added to the dictionary for the first time—to its right side, while the bounded region, i.e., the triangle, lies on its left side. This follows from the fact that the mate of an edge is always searched for on its right side. Therefore, before an edge is added to the dictionary, it is necessary to perform edge flipping, which is implemented within the function *update_boundary*(·, ·, ·):

```python
def update_boundary(boundary: SortedDict, a: Point2D, b: Point2D):
    s = Segment2D(a, b);
    if s in boundary: boundary.pop(s);
    else: s.flip(); boundary[s]=s
```

After the implementation of the auxiliary functions, the main function *delaunay_triangulation_fe*(·) for generating the Delaunay triangulation is presented below:

```python
def delaunay_triangulation_fe(points: list[Point2D]) -> list[Polygon]:
    boundary = SortedDict(); delaunay_triangles = []
    e = extreme_edge(points); boundary[e] = True
```

```
4      while boundary:
5          e1, _ = boundary.popitem(-1)
6          mate = has_edge_mate(e1, points)
7          if mate is not None:
8              update_boundary(boundary, mate, e1[0])
9              update_boundary(boundary, e1[1], mate)
10             p = Polygon(); p.insert(e1[0]); p.insert(e1[1]); p.insert(mate)
11             delaunay_triangles.append(p)
12     return delaunay_triangles
```

From the previous implementation, the counting while loop continues executing as long as there are edges in the dictionary boundary. This implies that the algorithm performs at most $\mathcal{O}(n)$ iterations, since, according to Lemma 6.1.1, the total number of edges for n given points on the canvas is on the order of $\mathcal{O}(n)$. Given that the function *has_edge_mate*$(\cdot, \cdot)$ has a time complexity of $\mathcal{O}(n)$, while the remaining invoked functions run in $\mathcal{O}(\log k)$ or $\mathcal{O}(1)$ time, it follows that the worst-case time complexity of the Flip-Edge algorithm is quadratic. More precisely, within each iteration of the while loop, the total time is $\mathcal{O}(n) + \mathcal{O}(\log k)$, where k ($k \ll n$) is the number of elements in the dictionary. The $\mathcal{O}(\log k)$ component arises from operations performed on the dictionary boundary. Specifically, all fundamental operations on the **SortedDict**—such as insertion, lookup, deletion, and membership testing—have time complexity $\mathcal{O}(\log k)$, owing to its internal structure based on a balanced binary search tree, typically implemented as a Red-Black Tree or an AVL Tree variant. Since $\log k < \log n < n$, the expression $\mathcal{O}(n) + \mathcal{O}(\log k)$ simplifies to $\mathcal{O}(n)$, confirming that the overall time complexity of the Flip-Edge algorithm is $\mathcal{O}(n^2)$.

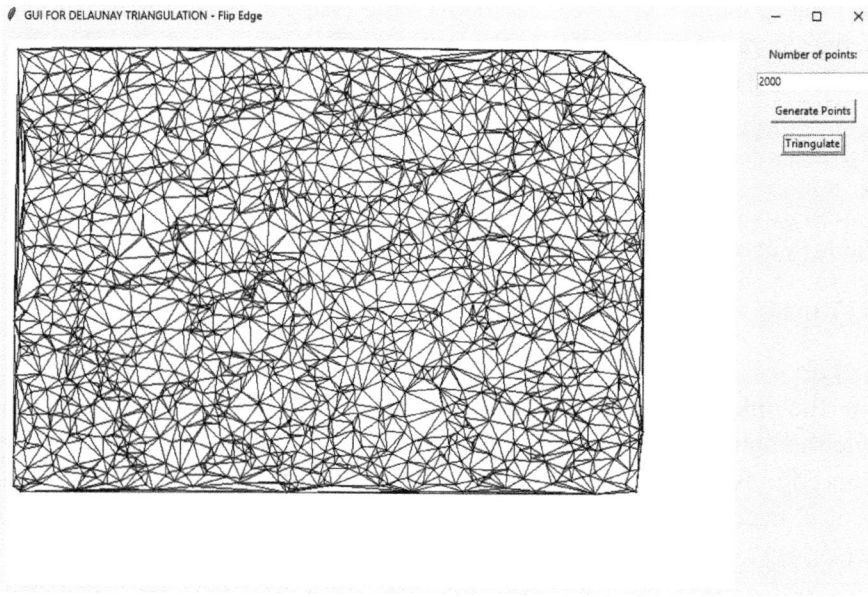

Figure 6.19: Delaunay triangulation for 2000 randomly generated points.

For graphical visualization of the algorithm—implemented in the Python programming language—that computes the Delaunay triangulation using the Flip-Edge method, an equivalent code listing is employed, analogous to the one used for constructing a simple polygon (see Listing 4.2 in Chapter 4). The only difference is the replacement of the function *visualise_simple_polygon*() with a new function called *visualise_delaunay_triangles*(), whose implementation is given below:

```
1  def visualise_delaunay_triangles(self):
2      dt_triangles = delaunay_triangulation_fe(self.points)
3      for pol in dt_triangles: #Drawing all triangles
```

```
4    for _ in range(pol.size()):
5        seg = pol.current_edge()
6        x1, y1 = seg[0][0], seg[0][1]; x2, y2 = seg[1][0], seg[1][1]
7        self.canvas.create_line(x1, y1, x2, y2, fill='black', width=1)
8        pol.move_current(1)
```

Figure 6.19 demonstrates the computation of the Delaunay triangulation for a set of 2000 randomly generated points computed using the Flip-Edge algorithm.

6.4.2 Incremental Algorithm

This section describes the *Incremental Algorithm* (**IA**), which incrementally constructs the Delaunay triangulation in two steps with a time complexity of $\mathcal{O}(n \log n)$. In the first step, the algorithm generates a sufficiently large triangle $\triangle ABC$ that encloses all planar points from the input set $\mathscr{P} = \{P_1, P_2, \cdots, P_n\}$. The vertices of triangle $\triangle ABC$ are selected such that they cannot lie within any circle defined by any three points from the set $\mathscr{P}$. This selection can be performed in $\mathcal{O}(n)$ time. Specifically, the algorithm finds the point in $\mathscr{P}$ with the maximum absolute coordinate value. Let this value be denoted as $M = \max\{|x_1|, |y_1|, |x_2|, |y_2|, \cdots, |x_n|, |y_n|\}$. All points from the set $\mathscr{P}$ then lie within the rectangle $\square A_1 B_1 C_1 D_1$, whose vertices are defined as follows: $A_1(-M, M)$, $B_1(M, M)$, $C_1(M, -M)$, and $D_1(-M, -M)$ (see Fig. 6.20).

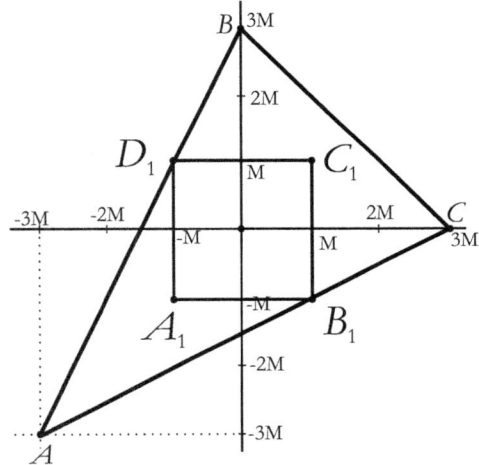

Figure 6.20: Selection of coordinates for triangle $\triangle ABC$.

To ensure that the rectangle $\square A_1 B_1 C_1 D_1$ lies entirely within triangle $\triangle ABC$, the triangle's vertices are selected as follows: $A = (-3M, -3M)$, $B = (0, 3M)$, and $C = (3M, 0)$. It can be easily shown that the points A_1 and C_1 lie strictly inside triangle $\triangle ABC$, as they are located to the left of segments $\overline{AC}$, $\overline{CB}$, and $\overline{BA}$ (see Fig. 6.20). Furthermore, points B_1 and D_1 lie on the sides $\overline{AC}$ and $\overline{AB}$ of triangle $\triangle ABC$, respectively, since they are collinear with points A and C, and points A and B. In the second step of the algorithm, the points from the input set $\mathscr{P}$ are incrementally added to triangle $\triangle ABC$ in a random order. In other words, a random permutation $\{i_1, i_2, \cdots, i_n\}$ of the index set $\{1, 2, \cdots, n\}$ is generated, according to which the points are inserted into triangle $\triangle ABC$. Suppose the first point added is P_{i_1}. By connecting this point to the vertices of triangle $\triangle ABC$, an initial triangulation $\mathbb{T}$ is formed, consisting of three triangles. The algorithm proceeds incrementally by taking the next point P_{i_2} and inserting it into triangulation $\mathbb{T}$. If point P_{i_2} lies strictly inside one of the existing triangles, it is connected to the triangle's vertices, forming a new triangulation $\mathbb{T}'$, i.e., the original triangulation $\mathbb{T}$ is updated to include the new point P_{i_2}. However, if point P_{i_2} lies on a shared edge between two adjacent triangles in $\mathbb{T}$, it is connected to the vertices of those triangles that are not incident to the shared edge (see Fig. 6.5 (b)). The resulting triangulation $\mathbb{T}'$ is not

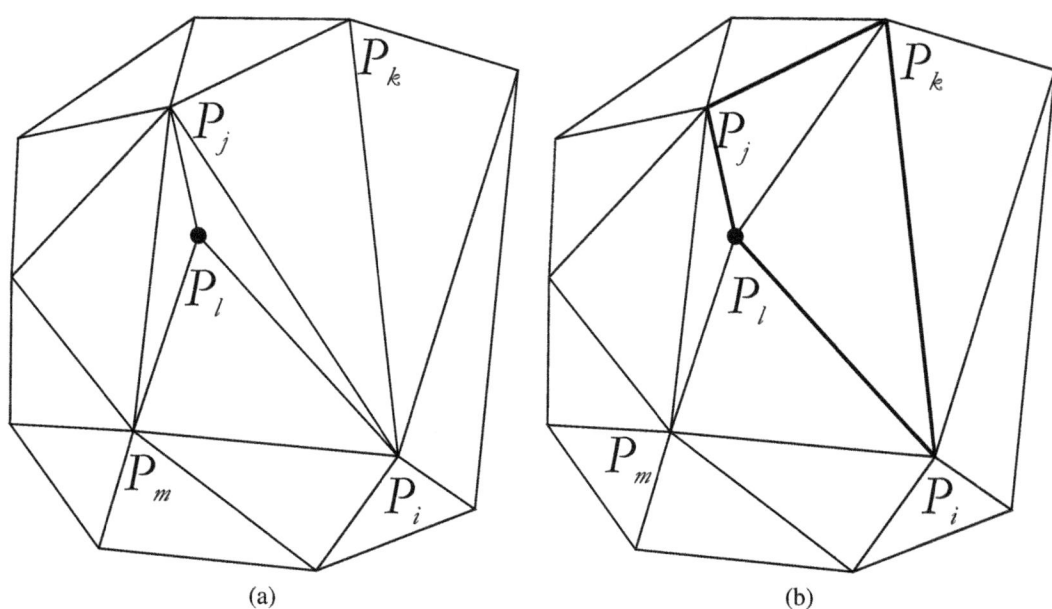

(a)   (b)

Figure 6.21: (a) By inserting point P_l into $\triangle P_m P_i P_j$, the illegal edge $\overline{P_i P_j}$ becomes legal in the new triangulation. (b) The illegal edge $\overline{P_i P_j}$ is substituted by the legal one $\overline{P_l P_k}$ in the new triangulation.

necessarily a Delaunay triangulation. In fact, inserting a new point may cause previously legal edges to become illegal (see Fig. 6.21). Therefore, it is necessary to check the legality of a subset of edges, as not all of them are affected—this will be formally proven later. Additionally, not all triangles in the triangulation are modified when a new point is inserted, but only those that no longer satisfy the empty-circle criterion. If a new point is inserted into the interior of a triangle, the edges created by connecting it to the triangle's vertices remain unchanged, as they are not diagonals of a convex quadrilateral. Consequently, the only candidates for edge flipping are the sides of the newly formed triangles that are not incident to the inserted point. In Fig. 6.21 (a), the candidates for flipping are segments $\overline{P_m P_i}$, $\overline{P_i P_j}$, and $\overline{P_j P_m}$. The same principle applies when point P_l lies on an existing edge. It is important to note that flipping an edge can cause other edges to become illegal. In other words, after flipping one edge, four new candidates emerge, of which only two can become illegal. Specifically, in Fig. 6.21 (a), after the illegal edge $\overline{P_i P_j}$ is replaced by the legal edge $\overline{P_l P_k}$, four new candidates are created: $\overline{P_l P_i}$, $\overline{P_i P_k}$, $\overline{P_k P_j}$, and $\overline{P_j P_l}$ (see Fig. 6.21 (b)). Among them, only the segments $\overline{P_i P_k}$ and $\overline{P_k P_j}$ can become illegal edges, since they are opposite point P_l in the quadrilateral $\square P_l P_i P_k P_j$. The following lemma formally confirms this claim.

Lemma 6.4.2 Each replacement of an illegal edge with a legal one generates at most two new illegal edges that need to be flipped.

Proof. The legal edge $\overline{P_i P_j}$ of the quadrilateral $\square P_i P_k P_j P_m$ becomes an illegal edge after inserting point P_l into triangle $\triangle P_i P_j P_m$ (see Fig.6.21 (a)). This edge is then replaced by the legal edge $\overline{P_l P_k}$ within the quadrilateral $\square P_l P_i P_k P_j$, generating four new edge-flip candidates: $\overline{P_l P_i}$, $\overline{P_i P_k}$, $\overline{P_k P_j}$, and $\overline{P_j P_l}$, out of which at most two may result in new illegal edges (In Fig. 6.21 (b), the candidates are highlighted in bold). The circle C circumscribed about triangle $\triangle P_i P_k P_n$ contains point P_l in its interior, making edge $\overline{P_i P_k}$ illegal. It is therefore replaced by the legal edge $\overline{P_l P_n}$, since the circle C', circumscribed about triangle $\triangle P_k P_l P_n$, contains no other point in its interior, and thus satisfies the empty-circle property (see Fig. 6.22). Furthermore, edge $\overline{P_k P_j}$ is legal, as the circle C'' circumscribed about triangle $\triangle P_k P_j P_l$ is also an empty circle, and thus no replacement is needed. It remains to be shown that edges $\overline{P_j P_l}$ and $\overline{P_l P_i}$, which lie within quadrilaterals $\square P_k P_j P_m P_l$ and $\square P_k P_l P_m P_i$, respectively, cannot be illegal. Suppose, for the sake of contradiction, that edge $\overline{P_j P_l}$ is illegal and the quadrilateral $\square P_k P_j P_m P_l$ is convex. According to Lemma 6.2.4, point P_m must lie inside circle C''. However, since C'' is the largest empty circle, it cannot contain any point in its interior—a contradiction. Thus, edge $\overline{P_j P_l}$ is legal. An analogous argument shows that edge $\overline{P_l P_i}$ is also legal; otherwise, point P_k would lie inside the largest empty circle C', again leading to a contradiction. Therefore, at most two of the four candidate edges can be replaced (In Fig. 6.22, these are segments $\overline{P_i P_k}$ and $\overline{P_k P_j}$, although in this case edge $\overline{P_k P_j}$ was already legal), which completes the proof. ∎

Algorithm 8: LegalizeEdge(P_l, $\overline{P_i P_j}$, $\mathbb{T}$)

Step 1: If edge $\overline{P_i P_j}$ is illegal, **do**:
    a) replace the illegal edge $\overline{P_i P_j}$ with the legal edge $\overline{P_k P_l}$.
    b) recursively call LegalizeEdge(P_l, $\overline{P_i P_k}$, $\mathbb{T}$).
    c) recursively call LegalizeEdge(P_l, $\overline{P_k P_j}$, $\mathbb{T}$).

Algorithm 9: DelaunayTriangulation($\mathscr{P}$)

Input : Planar point set $\mathscr{P} = \{P_1, P_2, \cdots, P_n\}$.

Step 1: Determine the coordinates of points A, B, and C such that all points from the set $\mathscr{P}$ lie strictly inside triangle $\triangle ABC$.

Step 2: Set the initial triangulation $\mathbb{T}$ to be triangle $\triangle ABC$, and then generate a permutation $\{i_1, i_2, \cdots, i_n\}$ of the index set $\{1, 2, \cdots, n\}$, where $i_j \in \{1, 2, \cdots, n\}$ for all $j = \overline{1, n}$. Insert the point $P_{i_1} \in \mathscr{P}$ into triangulation $\mathbb{T}$ and connect it with edges to the vertices of triangle $\triangle ABC$, resulting in a new triangulation $\mathbb{T}'$. Replace $\mathbb{T}$ with $\mathbb{T}'$, i.e., set $\mathbb{T} \leftarrow \mathbb{T}'$.

Step 3: For $l \leftarrow 2$ to n **do**:

    a) Insert $P_{i_l} \in \mathscr{P}$ into the current triangulation $\mathbb{T}$, then recursively identify the triangle from $\mathbb{T}$ that contains point P_{i_l}. Denote this triangle as $\triangle P_i P_j P_k$.

    b) **If** point P_{i_l} lies strictly inside triangle $\triangle P_i P_j P_k$ **then**

        • draw edges from vertices P_i, P_j, and P_k to point P_{i_l};
        • call the procedure LegalizeEdge(P_{i_l}, $\overline{P_i P_j}$, $\mathbb{T}$);
        • call the procedure LegalizeEdge(P_{i_l}, $\overline{P_i P_k}$, $\mathbb{T}$);
        • call the procedure LegalizeEdge(P_{i_l}, $\overline{P_j P_k}$, $\mathbb{T}$).

    c) **Else**

        • draw edges from point P_{i_l} to the opposite vertices P_k and P_m of the triangles that share edge e, where $e \leftarrow \overline{P_i P_j}$ and $P_{i_l} \in e$;
        • call the procedure LegalizeEdge(P_{i_l}, $\overline{P_i P_m}$, $\mathbb{T}$);
        • call the procedure LegalizeEdge(P_{i_l}, $\overline{P_m P_j}$, $\mathbb{T}$);
        • call the procedure LegalizeEdge(P_{i_l}, $\overline{P_j P_k}$, $\mathbb{T}$);
        • call the procedure LegalizeEdge(P_{i_l}, $\overline{P_k P_i}$, $\mathbb{T}$).

    d) Assign the triangulation $\mathbb{T}'$ obtained in steps b) or c) to the current triangulation $\mathbb{T}$, i.e., $\mathbb{T} \leftarrow \mathbb{T}'$.

Step 4: Remove the vertices A, B, and C, along with all edges incident to them, from $\mathbb{T}$.

Output : Edges and triangles of the Delaunay triangulation.

Based on the discussion so far, the procedure for checking the legality of an edge $\overline{P_i P_j}$ is given in the form of pseudocode in Algorithm 8. As previously explained, the status of an edge may change after the insertion of a point P_l, when triangles $\triangle P_i P_j P_k$ and $\triangle P_i P_j P_l$ become incident to the edge $\overline{P_i P_j}$. According to Lemma 6.4.2, only the edges $\overline{P_i P_k}$ and $\overline{P_k P_j}$ need to be checked for legality, since only these edges may

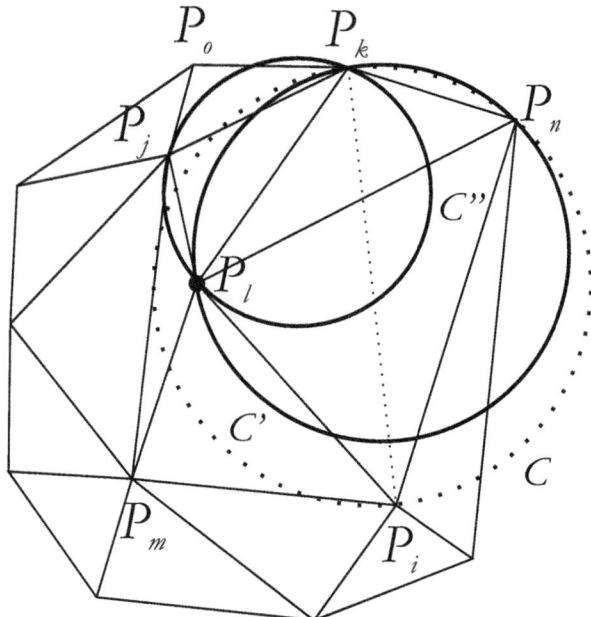

Figure 6.22: Graphical illustration used in the proof of Lemma 6.4.2.

potentially be flipped in a triangulation $\mathbb{T}$. Finally, the incremental algorithm for computing the Delaunay triangulation of a given planar point set $\mathscr{P}$ is presented in the form of pseudocode in Algorithm 9. The correctness of Algorithm 9 will now be verified. To prove its correctness, it must be shown that after executing the procedure *LegalizeEdge*($\cdot$, $\cdot$, $\cdot$), no illegal edges remain. Every edge created by inserting point P_{i_l} must be incident to that point. It has also been stated earlier that an edge can become illegal only if one of the neighboring triangles, relative to the triangle into which the point was inserted, is modified. Since Algorithm 9 checks all edges that could become illegal (substeps b) and c) in Step 3)), it follows that the algorithm is correct, as all possible cases are covered. Moreover, the algorithm must terminate in a finite number of iterations, since each edge replacement lexicographically increases the triangulation indicator of $\mathbb{T}$.

6.4.2.1   Implementation of the Incremental Algorithm for Computing the Delaunay Triangulation

To implement the incremental algorithm, a *tree structure* is introduced, denoted by $\mathscr{D}$. The main purpose of this structure is to enable efficient storage and retrieval of triangles formed during the incremental insertion of points from the input set of cardinality n. This design allows the incremental algorithm to achieve a best-case time complexity of $\mathscr{O}(n\log n)$. Without the tree structure, the algorithm would require traversing $\mathscr{O}(n)$ iterations, and for each newly inserted point, it would have to identify the triangle that contains it. This would entail a time complexity of $\mathscr{O}(2(n-1)-k)$, since, according to Lemma 6.1.2, there are $\mathscr{O}(2(n-1)-k)$ triangles, where k ($k \ll n$) represents the number of extreme vertices of the convex hull. Therefore, without using a tree, the overall execution time of the algorithm would be quadratic. The tree structure $\mathscr{D}$ is modeled as a directed acyclic graph (DAG), where the leaf nodes correspond to the newly created triangles of the current triangulation $\mathbb{T}$, while the internal nodes store previously created triangles that will be removed upon insertion of a new point P_{i_l} or upon edge replacement. Initially, the root of the tree $\mathscr{D}$ stores the triangle $\triangle ABC$. When point P_{i_l} is inserted and lies inside triangle $\triangle ABC$, that triangle is split into three new triangles (see Fig. 6.23 (a)). If the point lies on one of the triangle's sides, two new triangles are formed. In that case, new nodes corresponding to the newly formed triangles are added to the tree $\mathscr{D}$, and pointers are established from triangle $\triangle ABC$ to its children (see Fig. 6.23 (b)). Thus, triangle $\triangle ABC$ is replaced by triangles $\triangle ACD$, $\triangle ABD$, and $\triangle BCD$, making it an internal node of the tree

$\mathscr{D}$, while the newly formed triangles become its leaves, as illustrated in Fig. 6.23 (b).

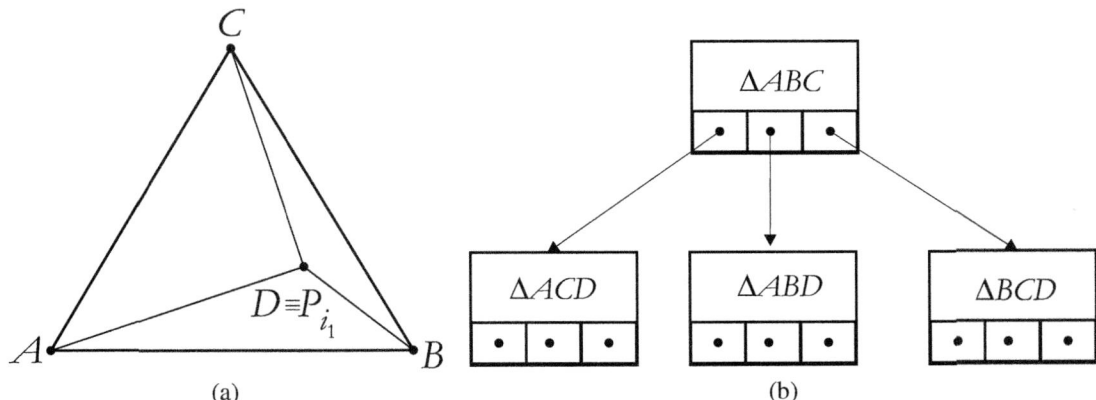

(a)   (b)

Figure 6.23: (a) Decomposition of triangle $\triangle ABC$ into three parts. (b) Tree structure $\mathscr{D}$ after the decomposition of triangle $\triangle ABC$.

Since the nodes of the tree $\mathscr{D}$ store triangles, they will be represented in the implementation as instances of the **Triangle2D** class, whose definition is given in Listing 6.1. For simplicity, the Triangle2D class is equipped with two constructors and four methods. The simplest among them is the *vertex*($\cdot$) method. This method returns a vertex of the triangle from the list T based on the index provided as a formal parameter, using the moduo 3 operation.

Listing 6.1: Definition of the class **Triangle2D**

```
1  class Triangle2D:
2      def __init__(self, a=None, b=None, c=None):
3          if a is None or b is None or c is None:
4              self.T=[Point2D(0,0), Point2D(0,0), Point2D(0,0)]
5          else:
6              if a.orientation(b,c)<0: self.T=[a, c, b]
7              else: self.T=[a, b, c]
8      def vertex(self, i: int) -> Point2D: return self.T[(i+3)%3]
9      def position(self, p: Point2D) -> int:
10         p01=p.orientation(self.T[0], self.T[1])
11         p12=p.orientation(self.T[1], self.T[2])
12         p20=p.orientation(self.T[2], self.T[0])
13         if p12==0 and p20==p01: return 0   #Opposite to the vertex A
14         elif p20==0 and p01==p12: return 1 #Opposite to the vertex B
15         elif p01==0 and p12==p20: return 2 #Opposite to the vertex C
16         elif p01!=0 and p01==p12 and p01==p20: return 3 # Inside the triangle
17         else: return -1 # Out of traingle
18     def is_in_circumcircle(self, p: Point2D) -> bool:
19         a=self.T[0][0]-p[0]; b=self.T[0][1] - p[1]
20         c=self.T[0][0]**2-p[0]**2+self.T[0][1]**2-p[1]**2
21         d=self.T[1][0]-p[0]; e=self.T[1][1]-p[1]
22         f=self.T[1][0]**2-p[0]**2+self.T[1][1]**2-p[1]**2
23         g=self.T[2][0]-p[0]; h=self.T[2][1]-p[1]
24         i=self.T[2][0]**2-p[0]**2+self.T[2][1]**2-p[1]**2
25         det=a*(e*i-f*h)-b*(d*i-f*g)+c*(d*h-e*g)
26         return det>0
27     def draw(self, canvas, color='blue', w=1):
```

```
28        for i in range(3):
29            if not self.T[i].get_id() and not self.T[(i+1)%3].get_id():
30                x1,y1=self.T[i][0],self.T[i][1]
31                x2,y2=self.T[(i+1)%3][0],self.T[(i+1)%3][1]
32                canvas.create_line(x1,y1,x2,y2, fill=color, width=w)
```

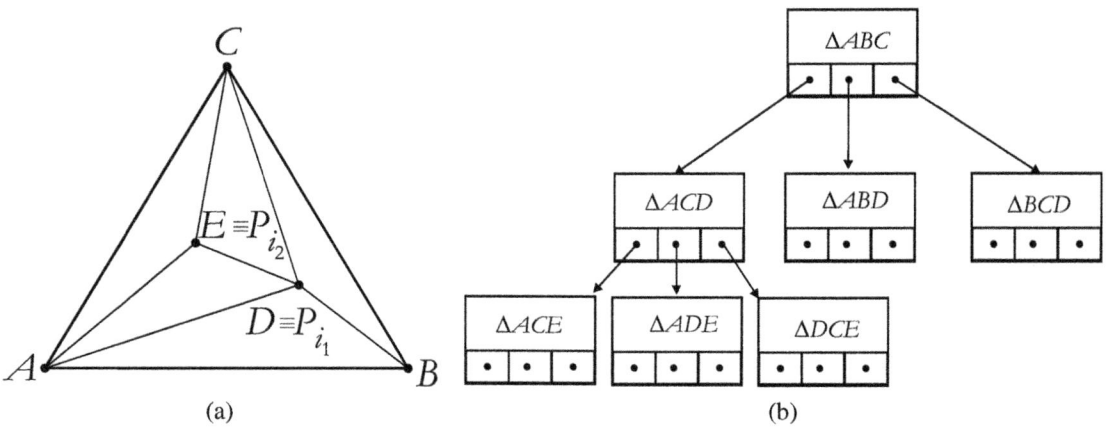

(a)   (b)

Figure 6.24: (a) Decomposition of triangle $\triangle ACD$ into three parts. (b) The state of the tree $\mathscr{D}$ after the decomposition of triangle $\triangle ACD$.

The method *position*($\cdot$) determines the relative location of the given point with respect to the triangle. It returns a value of -1 if the point lies outside the triangle, while the value 3 indicates that the point is strictly inside the triangle. If the point lies on one of the triangle's sides, the method returns 0, 1, or 2, depending on whether the point is located on the side opposite to the vertex with the corresponding index. The implementation of the method *is_in_circumcircle*($\cdot$) is fairly straightforward, as it reduces to checking the sign of a determinant (see Lemma 6.2.5). The final method, *draw*($\cdot$, $\cdot$, $\cdot$), defined in the **Triangle2D** class, is also simple in its implementation: it draws the edges connecting the triangle's vertices. This is achieved using the *create_line*(x1, y1, x2, y2, ..., options) method from the tkinter.Canvas class, which is invoked on the formal parameter canvas, an instance of the same class.

In the second iteration of the incremental algorithm, the point P_{i_2} is inserted into triangle $\triangle ABC$. Without loss of generality, assume that it lies inside the triangle $\triangle ACP_{i_1}$, as shown in Fig. 6.24 (a). Since the point P_{i_2} lies strictly inside triangle $\triangle ACD$, edges are drawn from P_{i_2} to the vertices A, C, and D. Consequently, the procedure *LegalizeEdge*($\cdot$,$\cdot$,$\cdot$) is called three times to verify the legality of the edges $\overline{AC}$, $\overline{AD}$, and $\overline{CD}$ with respect to the current triangulation shown in Fig. 6.23 (a). Since these edges are legal, the triangulation itself remains unchanged; however, the corresponding tree structure is updated (see Fig. 6.24 (b)) by adding three new child nodes, i.e., the triangles $\triangle ACE$, $\triangle ADE$, and $\triangle DCE$. The following section presents the implementation of the incremental algorithm. For the first time, in the context of planar triangulation—specifically Delaunay triangulation—a class named **DelaunayTriangulation** is designed, which will include, among other things, the method *incremental_algorithm*($\cdot$). Naturally, this class may also incorporate a method named *flip_edge_algorithm*($\cdot$), allowing the construction of Delaunay triangulations using the Flip-Edge algorithm. In general, this design paradigm can be applied to a wide range of geometric problems, including *simple polygon triangulation*, *convex hull computation*, *Voronoi diagram construction*, and many others. The definition of the **DelaunayTriangulation** class is given in Listing 6.2.

```
 1 class DelaunayTriangulation:
 2     class CGNode:
 3         def __init__(self, tr:Triangle2D):
 4             self.triangle = tr; self.visited = False
 5             self.neighbors = [None] * 3; self.children = [None] * 3
 6         def set_neighbors(self, n0,n1,n2): self.neighbors=[n0,n1,n2]
 7         def set_children(self,ch0,ch1,ch2=None): self.children=[ch0,ch1,ch2]
 8         def opposite_vertex(self, neighbor):
 9             for i in range(3):
10                 if all(neighbor.triangle.vertex(i) != self.triangle.vertex(j) for
                        j in range(3)): return i
11             return 0
12         def is_legal(self, neighbor, i=0):pass
13         def legalize(self, i=0): pass
14         def add_point(self, p): pass
15     # The methods of the class DelaunayTriangulation
16     def __init__(self, triangle=None):
17         self.root = None if triangle is None else self.CGNode(triangle)
18     def insert_point(self, p):
19         if self.root and self.root.triangle.position(p)>=0:self.root.add_point(p)
20     def mark_node(self, node):
21         if node is None or not node.visited: return
22         for child in node.children: self.mark_node(child)
23         node.visited = False
24     def erase_node(self, node:CGNode): pass
25     def draw_node(self, node:CGNode, canvas): pass
26     def draw(self, canvas):
27         self.draw_node(self.root,canvas); self.mark_node(self.root)
28     def incremental_algorithm(self, points):
29         for p in points:self.insert_point(p)
```

From Listing 6.2, it can be seen that the class **DelaunayTriangulation** contains an inner class named **CGNode**, which is designed to implement the tree structure described earlier in detail. The **CGNode** class has four attributes related to triangle operations: *triangle storage*, *triangle visitation status*, *triangle neighbors*, and *children triangles* resulting from decomposition. The **CGNode** class includes a constructor and six methods closely tied to tree-based operations and Delaunay triangle generation procedures. The first three methods are implemented immediately, while the remaining three — namely *is_legal*($\cdot,\cdot$), *legalize*($\cdot$), and *add_point*($\cdot$) — will be implemented later. The constructor, as well as the methods *set_neighbors*($\cdot,\cdot,\cdot$) and *set_children*($\cdot,\cdot,\cdot$), are intuitive and require no further explanation. The method *opposite_vertex*($\cdot$) returns the index of the vertex opposite to a shared edge between the current triangle and one of its neighboring triangles. For example, if two neighboring triangles $\triangle ABC$ and $\triangle BCD$ share the edge $\overline{BC}$, then passing the node containing triangle $\triangle BCD$ as an argument to the method *opposite_vertex*($\cdot$) will return index 2. This is because vertex D is the vertex opposite to triangle $\triangle ABC$ with respect to the shared edge $\overline{BC}$, as it lies outside of triangle $\triangle ABC$ along that edge. In this context, vertices A and D are considered opposite with respect to triangle $\triangle BCD$, since they are located on opposite sides of the line containing edge $\overline{BC}$.

Within the inner class **CGNode**, the method *is_legal*($\cdot,\cdot$) evaluates the legality of an edge formed by inserting a new point. Since the procedure for this check has already been described in detail earlier, the implementation must now account for several edge cases (e.g., whether the edge endpoints belong to the big-triangle, whether the quadrilateral is convex, etc.) that help determine the edge's legality. It is clear that the time complexity of this method is constant. Its implementation is provided below:

```
1 def is_legal(self, neighbor, i=0):
2     if neighbor is None: return 0, True # Edge on convex hull is legal
3     prev=self.triangle.vertex(i-1); curr=self.triangle.vertex(i)
4     nxt=self.triangle.vertex(i+1); j=self.opposite_vertex(neighbor)
5     neighbor_triangle=neighbor.triangle
6     curr_n=neighbor_triangle.vertex(j); curr_p=curr_n
7     if not curr_n.get_id():
8         if not neighbor_triangle.vertex(j-1).get_id() and not neighbor_triangle.
            vertex(j+1).get_id():
9             return j, not neighbor_triangle.is_in_circumcircle(self.triangle.
                vertex(i))
10    else:
11        left_id=neighbor_triangle.vertex(j-1).get_id()
12        right_id=neighbor_triangle.vertex(j+1).get_id()
13        if not left_id and not right_id: return j, True
14        if left_id: y_id=left_id
15        elif right_id: y_id=right_id
16        if curr_n.get_id() > y_id: return j, True
17        curr_p=curr
18    return j, not (
19        nxt.orientation(prev, curr) != nxt.orientation(prev, curr_p) and
20        curr.orientation(curr_n, prev) != curr.orientation(curr_n, nxt)
21    )
```

The method *legalize*($\cdot$) performs the legalization of an edge with respect to the vertex at index *i* in the given node, where the index is passed as a formal parameter. It is important to emphasize that its implementation follows the procedure described in Algorithm 8. During the replacement of an illegal edge with a legal one, all necessary updates must be synchronized with the **CGNode** class and its associated operations, as explained in detail below. Since the method recursively processes elements of the tree, its time complexity is logarithmic. The implementation of the method is given below:

```
1 def legalize(self, i=0):
2     if any(self.children): return # No legalization for an internal node
3     n=self.neighbors[i]; j, leg_edge=self.is_legal(n, i);
4     if leg_edge: return # If edge is legal, do nothing
5     n1=DelaunayTriangulation.CGNode(Triangle2D(self.triangle.vertex(i),self.
        triangle.vertex(i+1),n.triangle.vertex(j)))
6     n2=DelaunayTriangulation.CGNode(Triangle2D(self.triangle.vertex(i),n.triangle.
        vertex(j),n.triangle.vertex(j+1)))
7     prev=self.neighbors[(i+2)%3]; nxt=self.neighbors[(i+1)%3]
8     n_prev=n.neighbors[(j+2)%3]; n_nxt=n.neighbors[(j+1)%3]
9     n1.set_neighbors(n_nxt,n2,prev)
10    if n_nxt: k=n1.opposite_vertex(n_nxt); n_nxt.neighbors[k]=n1
11    if prev: k=n1.opposite_vertex(prev); prev.neighbors[k]=n1
12    n2.set_neighbors(n_prev,nxt,n1)
13    if n_prev: k=n2.opposite_vertex(n_prev); n_prev.neighbors[k]=n2
14    if nxt: k=n2.opposite_vertex(nxt); nxt.neighbors[k]=n2
15    self.set_children(n1,n2); n.set_children(n2,n1)
16    n1.legalize(); n2.legalize()
```

The final method of the internal class **CGNode** is *add_point*($\cdot$). This method represents a crucial component of the incremental algorithm, as it enables the recursive insertion of points into appropriate triangles in logarithmic time. Additionally, the tree structure must be updated to include the newly created triangles, and the legality of edges formed by the addition of new points must be verified. All illegal edges must be replaced with legal ones to ensure that the triangles stored in the tree satisfy the Delaunay condition. A verbal description of the point insertion procedure is provided in the following code snippet:

```python
def add_point(self, p):
    for child in self.children: # Check whether point p belongs to the triangle
        if child and child.triangle.position(p)>-1: child.add_point(p); return
    pos=self.triangle.position(p)
    if pos==3:# the point p lies strictly inside the triangle
        np01=DelaunayTriangulation.CGNode(Triangle2D(p,self.triangle.vertex(0),
            self.triangle.vertex(1)))
        np12=DelaunayTriangulation.CGNode(Triangle2D(p,self.triangle.vertex(1),
            self.triangle.vertex(2)))
        np20=DelaunayTriangulation.CGNode(Triangle2D(p,self.triangle.vertex(2),
            self.triangle.vertex(0)))
        np01.set_neighbors(self.neighbors[2],np12,np20)
        if self.neighbors[2]:i=np01.opposite_vertex(self.neighbors[2]); self.
            neighbors[2].neighbors[i]=np01
        np12.set_neighbors(self.neighbors[0],np20,np01)
        if self.neighbors[0]:i=np12.opposite_vertex(self.neighbors[0]); self.
            neighbors[0].neighbors[i]=np12
        np20.set_neighbors(self.neighbors[1],np01,np12)
        if self.neighbors[1]:i=np20.opposite_vertex(self.neighbors[1]); self.
            neighbors[1].neighbors[i]=np20
        self.set_children(np01,np12,np20)
        np01.legalize(); np12.legalize(); np20.legalize()
    else: #the point p lies on the side of the triangle
        n=self.neighbors[pos]; i=self.opposite_vertex(n)
        n1=DelaunayTriangulation.CGNode(Triangle2D(p,self.triangle.vertex(pos),
            self.triangle.vertex(pos+1)))
        n2=DelaunayTriangulation.CGNode(Triangle2D(p,self.triangle.vertex(pos-1),
            self.triangle.vertex(pos)))
        n3=DelaunayTriangulation.CGNode(Triangle2D(p,n.triangle.vertex(i-1),n.
            triangle.vertex(i)))
        n4=DelaunayTriangulation.CGNode(Triangle2D(p,n.triangle.vertex(i),n.
            triangle.vertex(i+1)))
        prev=self.neighbors[(pos+2)%3]; nxt=self.neighbors[(pos+1)%3]
        n_prev=n.neighbors[(i+2)%3]; n_nxt=n.neighbors[(i+1)%3]
        n1.set_neighbors(prev,n3,n2)
        if prev: j=n1.opposite_vertex(prev); prev.neighbors[j]=n1
        n3.set_neighbors(n_nxt,n4,n1)
        if n_nxt: j=n3.opposite_vertex(n_nxt); n_nxt.neighbors[j]=n3
        n4.set_neighbors(n_prev,n2,n3)
        if n_prev: j=n4.opposite_vertex(n_prev); n_prev.neighbors[j]=n4
        n2.set_neighbors(nxt,n1,n4)
        if nxt: j=n2.opposite_vertex(nxt); nxt.neighbors[j]=n2
        self.set_children(n2,n1); n.set_children(n3,n4)
        n1.legalize(); n3.legalize(); n4.legalize(); n2.legalize()
```

After implementing the methods of the **CGNode** class, the following section provides the implementations of two methods from the **DelaunayTriangulation** class. The remaining methods—*incremental_algorithm*(·), *insert_point*(·), *mark_node*(·), and *draw*(·, ·)—are implemented directly in place due to their simplicity and brevity. The first such method is *erase_node*(·), which recursively deletes all nodes as soon as they become leaves. Its implementation is as follows:

```python
def erase_node(self, node:CGNode):
    if node is None or node.visited: return
```

```
3    is_leaf = True
4    for child in node.children:
5        if child: is_leaf = False; self.erase_node(child)
6    node.visited = True
7    if is_leaf: del node #no more children, so the node is deleted
```

The second method is *draw_node*($\cdot$,$\cdot$). It recursively draws nodes as soon as they become leaves by invoking the *draw*($\cdot$,$\cdot$,$\cdot$) method of the **Triangle2D** class, which is responsible for rendering the triangles stored in the leaf nodes of the **CGNode** class. Its implementation is carried out as follows:

```
1 def draw_node(self, node:CGNode, canvas):
2     if node is None or node.visited:return
3     is_leaf=True
4     for child in node.children:
5         if child: is_leaf=False; self.draw_node(child, canvas)
6     node.visited = True
7     if is_leaf: node.triangle.draw(canvas, 'red')
```

Finally, the process of generating a planar Delaunay triangulation using the incremental algorithm becomes remarkably straightforward, as demonstrated in the implementation of the function *visualise_delaunay_triangles*():

```
1 def visualise_delayunay_triangles(self):
2     dim=max(int(self.canvas['width']), int(self.canvas['height']))
3     big_triangle=Triangle2D(Point2D(-1,-1,1),Point2D(2*dim,1,2),Point2D(-1,2*dim,3)
        )
4     DT=DelaunayTriangulation(big_triangle)
5     DT.incremental_algorithm(self.points)
6     DT.draw(self.canvas)
```

The graphical user interface of the incremental algorithm for computing the Delaunay triangulation, implemented in the Python programming language, is shown in Fig. 6.25.

6.4.3 Comparative Performance Analysis of Delaunay Triangulation Algorithms

To evaluate the computational performance of the implemented algorithms, we measured their execution times on randomly generated point sets of increasing size: $n = 100, 500, 900, 1300, 1700, 2100$, and 2500. The comparison includes the *Flip-Edge Algorithm* and the *Incremental Algorithm*, both implemented in Python using consistent data structures. The results, presented in Table 6.1, provide insights into the scalability and runtime behavior of both methods as the input size grows steadily.

Table 6.1: Execution times (in seconds) for Flip-Edge and Incremental algorithms on various point set sizes.

Number of Points (n)	Flip-Edge Algorithm	Incremental Algorithm
100	0.119457	0.019742
500	2.930945	0.119754
900	9.439547	0.237878
1300	19.563329	0.343245
1700	33.186537	0.461848
2100	50.747612	0.588321
2500	71.471452	0.713107

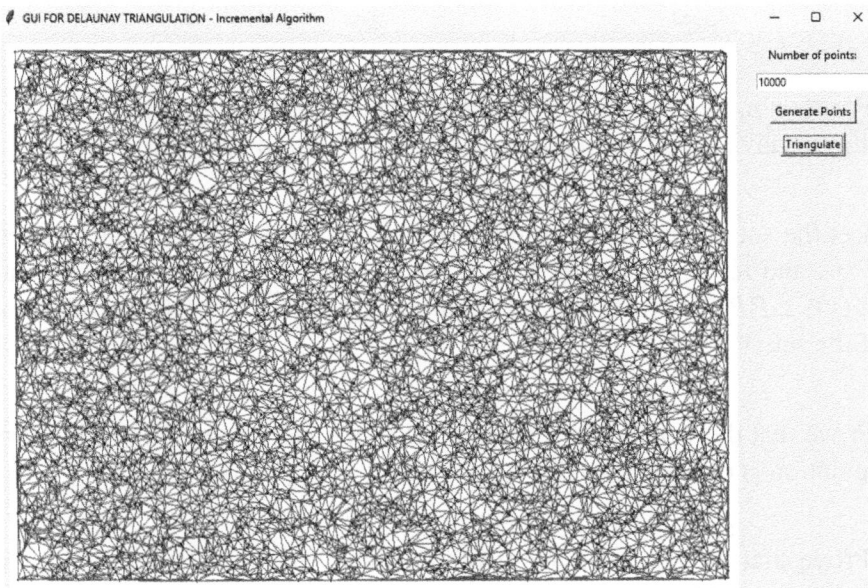

Figure 6.25: Delaunay triangulation for 10,000 randomly generated points computed using the Incremental Algorithm.

The results presented in Table 6.1 reveal a substantial difference in the scalability and computational efficiency of the two algorithms. While both approaches perform satisfactorily for small input sizes (e.g., $n = 100$), the *Flip-Edge Algorithm* exhibits a steep rise in execution time as the number of points increases. For instance, its runtime exceeds 70 seconds for $n = 2500$, indicating a super-linear, and likely cubic, growth in complexity. In contrast, the *Incremental Algorithm* demonstrates significantly better scalability, with execution times increasing gradually and remaining below one second even for the largest tested instance. Notably, this algorithm completes triangulation for $n = 10,000$ points in just 3.326933 seconds. These findings indicate that the Incremental Algorithm is considerably more suitable for large-scale triangulation tasks, offering clear advantages in both computational efficiency and practical applicability.

6.5 Exercises

Exercise 6.1 Prove that any set consisting of n planar points can be triangulated in at most $2^{\binom{n}{2}}$ ways.

Exercise 6.2 Prove that there exist sets of n planar points that can be triangulated in at least $2^{n-2\sqrt{n}}$ different ways.

Exercise 6.3 Provide an example of a set of n points in the plane such that, regardless of how the set is triangulated, there always exists a point that is incident to $n - 1$ edges.

Exercise 6.4 Prove that any two triangulations of a planar point set can always be transformed into each other via edge flipping.

Exercise 6.5 Prove that the smallest angle is same in all triangulations of a convex polygon whose vertices lie on a circle, from which it directly follows that the Delaunay triangulation maximizes this smallest angle.

Exercise 6.6 Propose an iterative version of the algorithm for the procedure *LegalizeEdge*. State the advantages and/or disadvantages of this method in comparison to the recursive approach.

Exercise 6.7 Let the set $\mathscr{P}$ contain n points in general position. Let a point $Q \notin \mathscr{P}$ lie within the convex hull of $\mathscr{P}$, and let P_i, P_j, and P_k be the vertices of a triangle in the Delaunay triangulation of $\mathscr{P}$ such that $Q \in \triangle P_i P_j P_k$. Prove that the segments $\overline{QP_i}$, $\overline{QP_j}$, and $\overline{QP_k}$ are edges of the Delaunay triangulation of the set $\mathscr{P} \cup \{Q\}$.

Exercise 6.8 Prove that the worst-case running time of the incremental algorithm for computing the Delaunay triangulation is of order $\Omega(n^2)$.

Exercise 6.9 Prove that the set of edges of the Delaunay triangulation contains the edges of the minimum spanning tree. The *minimum spanning tree* of a weighted graph is a subgraph that connects all its vertices with the minimum total edge length.

Exercise 6.10 The Gabriel graph of a planar point set $\mathscr{P}$ is defined as follows: two points (vertices) $P, Q \in \mathscr{P}$ are connected by an edge (arc) of the Gabriel graph if and only if the circle with diameter $r = \text{dist}(P, Q)$ contains no other point from the set $\mathscr{P}$ except for P and Q. Prove that the Delaunay triangulation of the set $\mathscr{P}$ contains the Gabriel graph of that set, and that such graph can be computed in linear time if the Delaunay triangulation is known.

Exercise 6.11 A partition of the set $\mathscr{P}$ of cardinality n into k non-empty subsets (clusters) $\mathscr{P}_1$, $\mathscr{P}_2$, $\cdots$, $\mathscr{P}_k$ is called a k-clustering of the set $\mathscr{P}$. The minimum distance between clusters $\mathscr{P}_i$ and $\mathscr{P}_j$, denoted by $\text{dist}(\mathscr{P}_i, \mathscr{P}_j)$, is defined as

$$\text{dist}(\mathscr{P}_i, \mathscr{P}_j) := \min_{P \in \mathscr{P}_i, U \in \mathscr{P}_j} \text{dist}(P, U).$$

Assume that the minimum distance between the clusters $\mathscr{P}_i$ and $\mathscr{P}_j$ is attained at points $P \in \mathscr{P}_i$ and $U \in \mathscr{P}_j$. Prove that the segment $\overline{PU}$ is an edge of the Delaunay triangulation of the set $\mathscr{P}$.

Exercise 6.12 Prove that the Delaunay triangulation is not the minimum-weight triangulation. A *minimum-weight triangulation* is a triangulation in which the total sum of the weights assigned to the edges is minimal.

7. Voronoi Diagrams

In the previous chapter of this book, a beneficial and practical topic related to the triangulation of a set of points into Delaunay triangles was discussed for a planar set of points. In this chapter, for the planar set of points $\mathscr{P} = \{P_1, P_2, \cdots, P_n\}$, very efficient algorithms are considered, which, among other things, will answer the question of which point in the planar set $\mathscr{P}$ is closest to an arbitrarily chosen point P outside that set. For example, suppose the points in the set $\mathscr{P}$ represent specific centers (e.g., schools, clinics, etc.), and point P represents a location (GPS coordinate) of a pedestrian. In that case, the algorithms discussed in this chapter, related to searching Voronoi diagrams, will quickly answer questions like, "Which clinic or school is closest to the pedestrian P?" This concept pertains to the proximity problem, precisely the nearest neighbor problem, which involves the wealthy geometry of the Voronoi diagram. It is important to note that many natural and social phenomena can be described using Voronoi diagrams, such as forestry, crystallography, ecology, art, geophysics, meteorology, geodesy, economics, biophysics, and more. In 1644, Descartes utilized Voronoi diagrams, while 1850 Dirichlet used them to study quadratic forms. In 1854, British physician John Snow used a Voronoi diagram to demonstrate that most people who died in a cholera epidemic lived closer to the infected Broad Street pump than any other water pump. The Voronoi diagram was also studied by Russian mathematician Georgy Fedosseevich Voronoi, who 1908 defined and examined generalized n-dimensional spaces. More information about the applications of Voronoi diagrams can be found at the link: https://www.voronoi.com.au. Moreover, there is a profound connection between the Voronoi diagram and Delaunay triangulation and their relationship with the 3D convex hull, which will be discussed later in this chapter.

7.1 Definitions and Basic Properties of Voronoi Diagrams

This section introduces the basic definitions of the Voronoi diagram and describes several of its basic properties.

Definition 7.1.1 A Voronoi model assigns to each point P in the plane the region of all points that are closer to P than to any other point. The partitioning of the plane into such regions is called a *Voronoi diagram*.

Definition 7.1.2 A graph $G = (V, E)$ is *planar* if placed in a plane, so its edges intersect only at vertices.

■ **Example 7.1** Figure 7.1 shows the planar graph K_4 and the non-planar graph $K_{3,3}$. ■

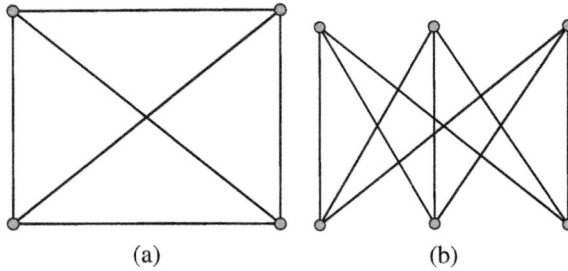

Figure 7.1: (a) Planar K_4 graph. (b) Nonplanar $K_{3,3}$ graph.

In a graph $G = (V, E)$, a region or area denoted as f is a part of the surface bounded by a contour (see Fig. 7.2). The set of these regions is denoted by $F(G)$, where V is the set of all vertices and E is the set of all edges.

■ **Example 7.2** Figure 7.2 illustrates the set of faces $F(G) = \{f_1, f_2, f_3, f_4, f_5\}$, for a graph with the vertex set $V = \{v_1, v_2, v_3, v_4, v_5\}$. ■

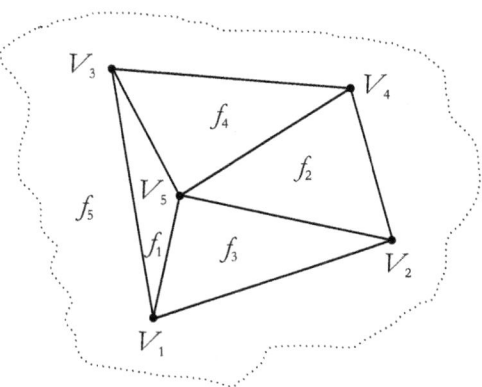

Figure 7.2: Planar graph regions.

Definition 7.1.3 The *degree of a vertex* v in a graph $G = (V, E)$, denoted as $d(v)$, is the number of edges incident to v.

In Fig. 7.2 it can be seen that: $d(v_i) = 3$, for $i = 1, 2, 3, 4$, while $d(v_5) = 4$.

Corollary 7.1.1 For each graph $G = (V, E)$ the following equality holds

$$\sum_{v \in V(G)} d(v) = 2|E(G)|. \tag{7.1}$$

Proof. Let M be the incidence matrix of the graph $G = (V, E)$, so that the graph G has n vertices and m branches, i.e. $n = |V(G)|$ and $m = |E(G)|$, and the matrix $M = (a_{ij})_{n \times m}$ is given like this

$$M = \begin{pmatrix} a_{11} & a_{12} & \ldots a_{1m} \\ \vdots & \ddots & \\ a_{n1} & a_{n2} & \ldots a_{nm} \end{pmatrix}.$$

Without loss of generality, it can be assumed that the degree of an arbitrary vertex v_i is equal to $d(v_i) = \sum_{j=1}^{m} a_{ij}$, where $a_{ij} \in \{0, 1\}$ and that it is also worth:

$$a_{ij} = \begin{cases} 1, & \text{if the } i\text{-th vertex of } v_i \text{ is incident to the } j \text{ branch of } e_j, \\ 0, & \text{otherwise} \end{cases}$$

It is clear that the edges e_j ($\forall j = 1, 2, \cdots, m$) represent the columns of the matrix M, while the vertices v_i ($\forall i = 1, 2, \cdots, n$) indicate its rows. From $d(v_i) = \sum_{j=1}^{m} a_{ij}$ it is obtained that $\sum_{i=1}^{n} d(v_i) = \sum_{i=1}^{n} \sum_{j=1}^{m} a_{ij}$. However, since each edge e_j is incident to exactly two vertices v_i and v_j, it turns out that $\sum_{i=1}^{n} a_{ij} = 2$ holds ($\forall j$). It further implies

$$\sum_{i=1}^{n} d(v_i) = \sum_{i=1}^{n} \sum_{j=1}^{m} a_{ij} = \sum_{j=1}^{m} \sum_{i=1}^{n} a_{ij} = \sum_{j=1}^{m} 2 = 2m = 2|E(G)|. \tag{7.2}$$

In the relation 7.2, sums (rows with finitely many terms) can replace sites since they are finite (and therefore concurrent). It completes the proof of the corollary. ∎

Definition 7.1.4 Let the set $\mathscr{F} = \{P_1, P_2, \cdots, P_n\}$ represent a series of planar given points (sites). The *Voronoi diagram* of the set $\mathscr{F}$ in the notation $Vor(\mathscr{P})$ represents the division of the plane into n Voronoi cells (regions) so that each cell corresponds to one and only one site of the set $\mathscr{F}$ with the property that the point Q lies in the cell determined by the site P_k *if and only if* $d(Q, P_k) < d(Q, P_j)$, $\forall P_j \in \mathscr{F}$ ($k \neq j$).

In Definition 7.1.4, a Voronoi cell can either be a half-plane or a convex polygon. Figure 7.3 provides a graphical illustration of the *Voronoi diagram if and only if.*

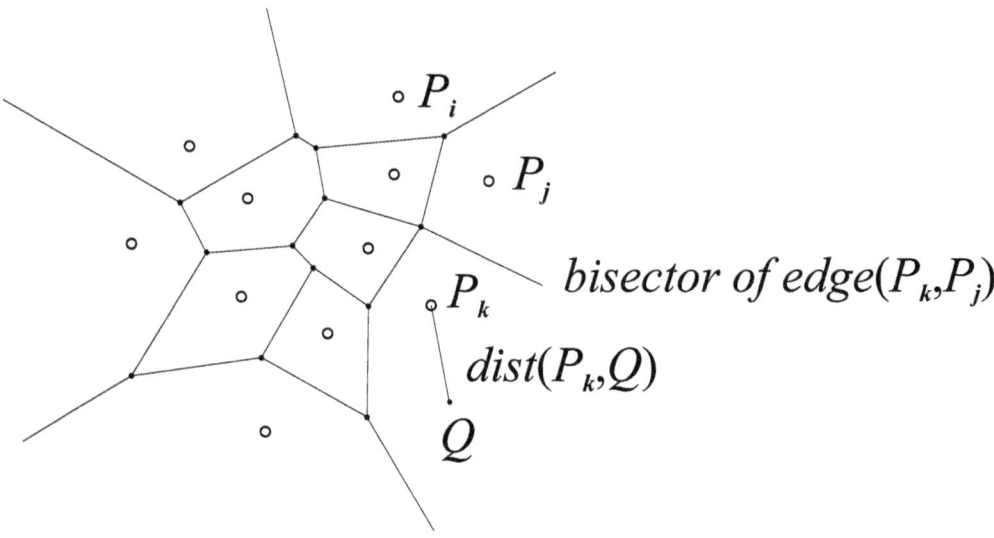

Figure 7.3: Voronoi diagram composed of 11 sites.

In Fig. 7.3, the sites, represented as circles, could correspond to post offices or other facilities in a city where citizens visit the closest one. In this example, the nearest post office for the citizen represented by point Q is site P_k, as Q lies within the region, or Voronoi cell, uniquely determined by site P_k. Further details on how this and the other cells are constructed will be provided.

Definition 7.1.5 The *Voronoi cell* of the site $P_k \in \mathscr{F}$ in the label $V(P_k)$ is defined as

$$V(P_k) = \{Q \in \mathbb{R}^2 : \|Q - P_k\| \le \|Q - P_j\|, \; \forall P_j \in \mathscr{F}\},$$

where the norm $\|\cdot\|$ denotes the Euclidean distance between sites.

Observation 7.1.1 According to Definition 7.1.6, points located on the boundaries between Voronoi cells do not have a unique nearest site. As will be explained later, these boundaries are the bisectors of the lines connecting the sites of the Voronoi diagram.

Definition 7.1.6 The line denoted as $B(P_j, P_k)$, between points P_j and P_k, is the *bisector* of the line segment $\overline{P_j P_k}$.

A bisector divides a plane into two half-planes. An open half-plane denoted as $H(P_j, P_k)$, which contains the point P_j and does not contain the point P_k, is defined as follows:

$$H(P_j, P_k) = \{Q \in \mathbb{R}^2 : \|Q - P_j\| \le \|Q - P_k\|\}.$$

A graphical illustration of the Voronoi diagram obtained as a section of half-planes is shown in Fig. 7.4. It can be observed that three points P_1, P_2, and P_3 are given, and each Voronoi cell is obtained as an intersection of two half-planes.

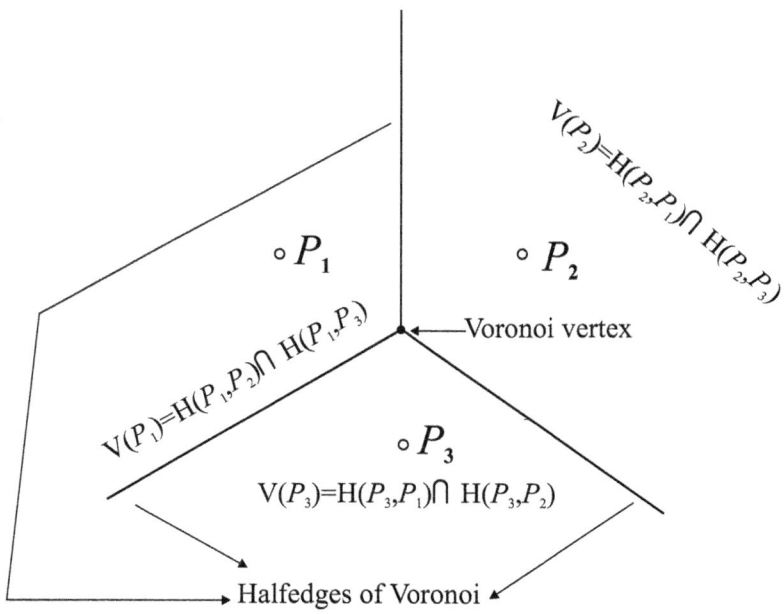

Figure 7.4: Voronoi diagram expressed as a union of Vornoi cells $V(P_1)$, $V(P_2)$ and $V(P_3)$.

Observation 7.1.2 The Voronoi cell $V(P_i)$ of the site P_i is obtained as an intersection of the other half-planes $H(P_i, P_j)$, i.e. for every $i \ne j$ holds

$$V(P_i) = \bigcap_{1 \le j \le n, i \ne j} H(P_i, P_j).$$

In other words, the i-th Voronoi cell $V(P_i)$ is obtained as the intersection of $n - 1$ half-planes in the case where n sites in the plane are given. Figure 7.4 shows the creation of Voronoi cells when $n = 3$, i.e., when exactly three sites are given.

Definition 7.1.7 The region F is *convex* if for $\forall x_1, x_2 \in F$ and for $\forall \lambda \in [0,1]$, the vector $\mathbf{x} = \lambda x_1 + (1-\lambda)x_2 \in F$.

The following Corollary represents a fundamental result of discrete geometry.

Corollary 7.1.2 The intersection of convex sets (not necessarily finite) is again a convex set.

Proof. Without loss of generality, it can be assumed that two convex sets A and B are given and that the set C is their intersection. It is proved analogously in the case of countably many given convex sets. In order to prove that the set C is convex, first it is taken arbitrarily that $x_1, x_2 \in C$, $\lambda \in [0,1]$, then it is shown that $\lambda x_1 + (1-\lambda)x_2 \in C$. Since A and B are convex and $x_1, x_2 \in A \cap B$, it follows that $\lambda x_1 + (1-\lambda)x_2 \in A$ and $\lambda x_1 + (1-\lambda)x_2 \in B$. Hence, $\lambda x_1 + (1-\lambda)x_2 \in A \cap B$ implies that the set C is convex, thus completing proof of the corrolary. ∎

Since all half-planes $H(P_i, P_j)$ are convex, it follows that the Voronoi cell $V(P_i)$ is a convex polygonal region, bounded by at most $n-1$ vertices. As illustrated in Figure 7.4, bisectors' intersections represent the Voronoi diagram's vertices. However, not all bisector's intersections define the vertices of $\text{Vor}(\mathscr{P})$ (Fig. 7.5). One of the upcoming theorems characterizes when these intersections truly determine the Voronoi vertices.

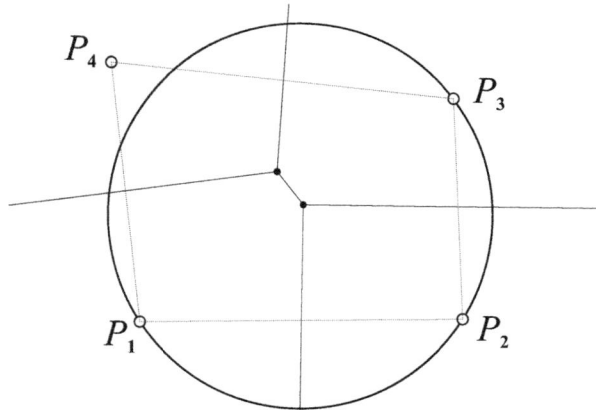

Figure 7.5: Not all bisector intersections define vertices of the Voronoi diagram.

Definition 7.1.8 The circle denoted by $C_F(Q)$ is the *largest empty circle* centered at point Q that contains no site $P_i \in \mathscr{F}$ in its interior.

Theorem 7.1.3 Let $\mathscr{F}$ be a set of n points in the plane, identified as sites in $\text{Vor}(\mathscr{P})$. A point Q is a Voronoi vertex *if and only if* the largest empty circle $C_F(Q)$ contains three or more sites on its boundary.

Proof. Let Q be a vertex of $\text{Vor}(\mathscr{P})$. Then it is incident with at least three edges of $\text{Vor}(\mathscr{P})$, corresponding to at least three Voronoi cells, such as $V(P_i)$, $V(P_j)$, and $V(P_k)$. This further implies that the vertex Q is equidistant from the sites P_i, P_j, and P_k. It implies that these sites uniquely determine a circumcircle enclosing a circle centered at Q. It is necessary to show that this resulting circle is the largest empty circle, meaning no site exists in its interior. To demonstrate this, we can apply the law of contraposition. Specifically, if a site P_l were present within the circle, it would be closer to the point Q, implying that the

Voronoi cells $V(P_i)$, $V(P_j)$, and $V(P_k)$ would not meet at Q, which is a contradiction. Therefore, the sites P_i, P_j, and P_k uniquely determine the largest empty circle $C_F(Q)$.

Conversely, let $C_F(Q)$ contain at least three sites P_i, P_j, and P_k on its boundary. Then these sites are the vertices of the triangle $\triangle P_i P_j P_k$, around which the circumcircle enclosing the circle $C_F(Q)$ is described. Thus, the point Q is the intersection point of the perpendicular bisectors of the sides of this triangle. Since $\|Q - P_i\| = \|Q - P_j\| = \|Q - P_k\| = r$ (r is the radius of the circle $C_F(Q)$), it follows that the point Q lies on the boundary of the Voronoi cells $V(P_i)$, $V(P_j)$, and $V(P_k)$, making it a vertex of $\mathrm{Vor}(\mathscr{P})$.

∎

■ Example 7.3 Construct a set of n points, or sites, in the plane such that the Voronoi diagram for this set has no Voronoi vertices.   ■

■ Example 7.4 For the following set of points $\mathscr{F} = \{(1,3),(1,9),(1,11),(3,6),(4,9),(6,6)\}$, draw the Voronoi diagram.   ■

It is easy to observe in Fig. 7.5 that some Voronoi edges are segments while others are half-lines. Additionally, some Voronoi edges are parts of bisectors. However, not all bisectors determine Voronoi edges, meaning there are Voronoi edges that are not segments of bisectors (in Fig. 7.5, this refers to the shortest Voronoi edge connecting two Voronoi vertices). Specifically for $n = 3$ (Fig. 7.4), all Voronoi edges are half-lines incident with a common vertex. The following theorem provides a geometric property that characterizes the situation when the bisector of sites becomes a Voronoi edge.

> **Theorem 7.1.4** Let $\mathscr{F}$ be a set of n points in the plane, identified as sites in $\mathrm{Vor}(\mathscr{P})$. The bisector $B(P_i, P_j)$ of the sites P_i and P_j, or any of its parts (subsets), is a Voronoi edge if and only if for every point Q on the bisector or its part, the circle $C_F(Q)$ contains exactly two sites P_i and P_j on its boundary.

Proof. Let Q be an arbitrary point on the bisector $B(P_i, P_j)$ or its part, such that the largest empty circle $C_F(Q)$ with center at point Q contains exactly two sites P_i and P_j on its boundary. This implies that $\|Q - P_i\| = \|Q - P_j\| \leq \|Q - P_k\|$ for any other site P_k outside the circle ($k \neq i, k \neq j$). Consequently, point Q is either a vertex of $\mathrm{Vor}(\mathscr{P})$ or lies on its edge. Based on Theorem 7.1.3, point Q cannot be a vertex. Hence, it follows that point Q lies on the edge of $\mathrm{Vor}(\mathscr{P})$.

Conversely, let the bisector $B(P_i, P_j)$ or its part be a Voronoi edge. It must be shown that the circle $C_F(Q)$ contains exactly two sites P_i and P_j on its boundary for every point Q on the bisector or its part. If the circle $C_F(Q)$ contains more than two sites on its boundary, for example, if circle $C_F(Q)$ contains sites P_i and P_j as well as a third site P_k on its boundary, then point Q becomes a vertex of $\mathrm{Vor}(\mathscr{P})$ based on Theorem 7.1.3. However, since every vertex is incident with at least three Voronoi edges, point Q is incident with at least three edges. This last statement is a contradiction with the choice of point Q, so it follows that the circle $C_F(Q)$ contains only two sites on its boundary, thus proving the theorem.

∎

In the previous illustrations, it is evident that some edges of $\mathrm{Vor}(\mathscr{P})$ are segments, while others are half-lines. Specifically, for $n = 3$, all edges of $\mathrm{Vor}(\mathscr{P})$ are half-lines incident to a single common vertex. The following theorem addresses the question of under what circumstances Voronoi edges are lines.

> **Theorem 7.1.5** Let the set $\mathscr{F}$ represent n sites of the Voronoi diagram. Then $\mathrm{Vor}(\mathscr{P})$ contains $n - 1$ parallel lines and n cells if all sites of the set $\mathscr{F}$ are collinear points.

Proof. The proof of the theorem is conducted using the equivalence $P \iff Q \iff \neg P \iff \neg Q$. Assume that $\mathrm{Vor}(\mathscr{P})$ does not contain $n - 1$ parallel lines or does not contain n cells. First, assume that $\mathrm{Vor}(\mathscr{P})$ does not contain $n - 1$ parallel lines, which can be denoted as $e_1, e_2, \ldots, e_{n-1}$. This further implies that there exists some line e_j that intersects the other lines e_i ($i \neq j$). Without loss of generality, let this line be $e_i = e_{n-1}$. Since the lines e_i are Voronoi lines, it follows that e_i is the bisector of the segment

$\overline{P_i P_{i+1}}$, and specifically, e_{n-1} is the bisector of the segment $\overline{P_{n-1} P_n}$. Since the line e_{n-2} is the bisector of the segment $\overline{P_{n-2} P_{n-1}}$, it follows that the intersection point of the lines e_{n-2} and e_{n-1} is the center of the circumcircle of triangle $\triangle P_{n-2} P_{n-1} P_n$. This further implies that the points P_{n-2}, P_{n-1}, and P_n are not collinear, which is a contradiction. Thus, starting from the statement $\neg P$, we arrive at the statement $\neg Q$. Similarly, the other part of the claim is proven by assuming that Vor($\mathscr{P}$) does not contain n cells. Specifically, let the number of cells in Vor($\mathscr{P}$) be less than n. They are then, based on Dirichlet's principle (when $n+1$ arbitrary objects are distributed into n boxes, at least one box contains at least two objects), at least two sites belong to the same cell, which contradicts the definition of a Voronoi cell. Furthermore, if the number of cells is greater than n, then at least one will undoubtedly remain empty, which contradicts the principle of creating Voronoi cells. Thus, the proof of the theorem is complete.

■

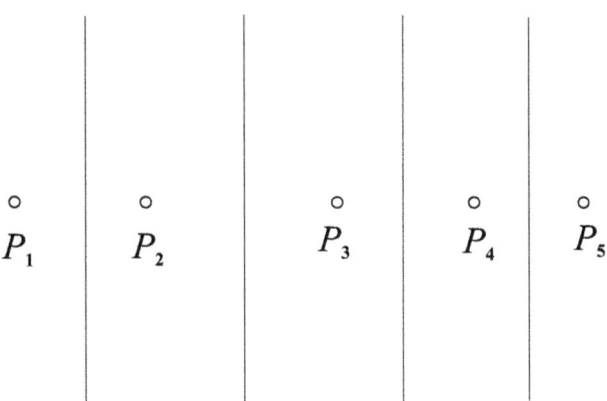

Figure 7.6: Creating Voronoi diagram in the case of collinear sites.

An example of seeking a Voronoi diagram for a set of five sites represented by collinear points is depicted in Fig. 7.6. The figure clearly illustrates that the Voronoi diagram is not a connected graph, as the following corollary states.

Corollary 7.1.3 Let the set $\mathscr{F}$ contains n sites of Vor($\mathscr{P}$). Then Vor($\mathscr{P}$) is not connected *if and only if* all elements of the set $\mathscr{F}$ are collinear points.

Proof. Let Vor($\mathscr{P}$) is not connected. Then, a Voronoi cell $V(P_i)$, defined by the site P_i, separates the plane into two disjoint regions. Since the Voronoi cell $V(P_i)$ is a convex set, its hull must consist of two parallel lines. It further implies, based on Theorem 7.1.5, that the sites of Vor($\mathscr{P}$) must be collinear because otherwise, the hull of cell $V(P_i)$ would not be parallel lines, which was to be proven.

■

Behind constructing the Voronoi diagram for n sites given in the plane, the question arises: How many vertices and edges can the diagram have maximally? The answer to this question is provided by the following theorem, which states that this number is proportional to $O(n)$.

Theorem 7.1.6 Let the set $\mathscr{F}$ represent n sites of Vor($\mathscr{P}$). Then, the number of vertices in the Voronoi diagram is at most $2n-5$, and the number of edges is $3n-6$.

Proof. If the sites of Vor($\mathscr{P}$) are collinear, then the number of vertices is zero, and the number of edges is $n-1$ since they can be considered as lines of Vor($\mathscr{P}$), making the proof of the theorem trivial in this case. Let us assume the sites are not collinear. Let n_v denote the number of vertices of Vor($\mathscr{P}$), n_e the number of edges, while n is the number of sites in Vor($\mathscr{P}$). We need to show that $n_v \leq 2n-5$ and

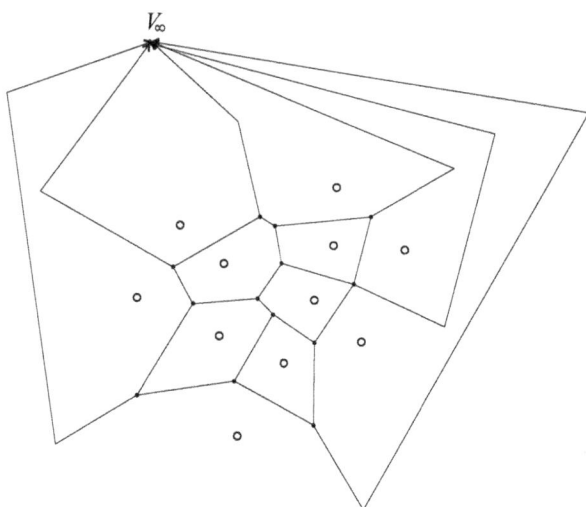

Figure 7.7: Adding the vertex V_∞ to Vor($\mathscr{P}$) and connecting it with infinite half-lines.

$n_e \leq 3n - 6$. It can be demonstrated using Euler's formula for planar graphs. If the graph is not connected, then the following inequality holds $m_v - m_e + m_f \geq 2$, where m_v denotes the number of vertices in the graph, m_e the number of edges in the graph, and m_f the number of faces in the plane such that only the outer face is unbounded. Equality holds in the case of a connected graph. Unfortunately, Euler's formula cannot be directly applied to Vor($\mathscr{P}$) because Vor($\mathscr{P}$) has infinite rays, and thus some Voronoi cells are unbounded. Specifically, the cells associated with the sites that represent the vertices of the convex hull of the set $\mathscr{F}$ are the unbounded ones. Therefore, to apply Euler's formula to Vor($\mathscr{P}$), it is necessary to add some vertex v_∞ at infinity (Fig. 7.7) and connect it to all infinite rays of Vor($\mathscr{P}$). It ensures the application of Euler's formula because, in this case, we obtain a connected planar graph where all faces, except the outer one, are bounded. This graph $G = (V, E)$ consists of $m_v = n_v + 1$ vertices ($|V| = n_v + 1$) and $m_e = n_e$ edges. Each site P_i, $i = \overline{1, n}$ is associated with exactly one region in the graph, so $m_f = n$. Since each vertex of Vor($\mathscr{P}$) has a degree of at least 3, based on Corollary 7.1.1, it follows that $\sum_{v \in V} d(v) = 2|E| \geq 3|V| = 3(n_v + 1)$. Finally, based on Euler's formula, we have $(n_v + 1) - m_e + n = 2$, which further implies $2m_e = 2(n_v + 1 + n - 2) = 2(n_v - 1 + n) = 2n_v + 2n - 2 \geq 3n_v + 3$. From the last inequality, we obtain $n_v \leq 2n - 5$. Finally, from $m_e = n_v + n - 1$ and $n_v \leq 2n - 5$, it follows that $n_e \leq 3n - 6$, which is what we aimed to prove. ∎

Based on the proven theorem, it is evident that the number of vertices and edges of the Voronoi diagram is linear concerning n, or the number of sites of Vor($\mathscr{P}$). Without this theorem, if one naively considers it, one might conclude that there are $\binom{n}{2}$ bisectors for the sites of Vor($\mathscr{P}$), suggesting that the relationship would be quadratic, which is incorrect. Therefore, due to the linear dependence, algorithms based on the Voronoi diagram can execute very quickly.

■ **Example 7.5** Draw the Voronoi diagram when its sites represent the vertices of a regular polygon. ■

■ **Example 7.6** Let $\mathscr{F}$ be a set of n sites. Prove that the Voronoi cell $V(P_i)$ of the site P_i is unbounded if and only if the site P_i is a vertex of the convex hull $CH(\mathscr{F})$. ■

■ **Example 7.7** Let $\mathscr{F}$ be a set of n sites. Prove that a Voronoi cell's average number of vertices is less than six. ■

7.2 **Algorithms for Constructing Voronoi Diagrams**

Due to the importance of Voronoi diagrams and their practical applications, this section will propose several algorithms, among which will be the most efficient algorithm for determining Voronoi diagrams based on the sweep paradigm, which has a time complexity of $\Theta(n \log n)$.

7.2.1 **Naive Approach**

This section will describe an exhaustive method for finding the Voronoi diagram for a given set of points $\mathscr{F} = \{P_1, P_2, \ldots, P_n\}$. To find the Voronoi diagram, that is, to determine the Voronoi cells for each point P_i $(i = \overline{1, n})$, a rectangle R encompassing all points is first created. The rectangle R is uniquely defined by two points (x_{min}, y_{max}) and (x_{max}, y_{min}), where the coordinates $x_{min}, x_{max}, y_{min}$, and y_{max} represent the minimum and maximum x and y-coordinates of the points P_i $(i = \overline{1, n})$ of the Voronoi diagram, respectively. After constructing the rectangle R, the Voronoi cell $V(P_i)$ for each point P_i is determined as the intersection of the half-planes $H(P_i, P_j)$ for every $j \neq i$. This approach is easy to implement, as seen in the pseudocode of algorithm 10. The drawbacks of this approach are that there is much unnecessary work, as the intersections of bisectors far from the point P_i have no impact on the cell $V(P_i)$.

Algorithm 10: Pseudocode of the algorithm for finding the Voronoi diagram.

Input: Sites P_i $(i = \overline{1, n})$ of the Voronoi diagram.
Step 1: Create a rectangle R that encompasses the sites of the Voronoi diagram.
Step 2: Initialize an empty list $\mathscr{L}$ $(\mathscr{L} \leftarrow \{\})$ that will contain all Voronoi cells $V(P_i)$, $i = \overline{1, n}$.
Step 3: For **each** site P_i, do the following:

    i) Initialize the polygon $\mathscr{A}$ as empty, i.e., $\mathscr{A} \leftarrow \{\}$. Create the polygon $\mathscr{R}$ based on the rectangle R so that $\mathscr{R} \leftarrow R$.

    ii) For **each** point P_j $(j \neq i)$, **do**:
    a) Find the perpendicular bisector of the line segment $\overline{P_iP_j}$. Let this line be l.
    b) Find the polygon resulting from dividing polygon $\mathscr{R}$ by the line l such that the new polygon contains the point P_i. Assign this polygon to $\mathscr{A}$.
    d) Assign the polygon $\mathscr{A}$ to $\mathscr{R}$, i.e., $\mathscr{R} \leftarrow \mathscr{A}$.

    iii) Add the polygon $\mathscr{R}$ to the list $\mathscr{L}$.

Output: Voronoi diagram composed of n Voronoi cells.

■ **Example 7.8** Apply Algorithm 10 to find the Voronoi diagram for the sites $P_1(1,1)$, $P_2(4,1)$, and $P_3(3,4)$.

Solution: Let the rectangle R encompass the sites P_1, P_2, and P_3, as shown in Fig. 7.8 (a). For sites P_1, P_2, and sites P_1, P_3, the bisectors s_1 and s_2 are found (Fig. 7.8 (b)). The bisector s_1 intersects the rectangle $\mathscr{R}$ at points C_1 and C_2, forming the polygon $\mathscr{A}_1$. According to the algorithm, $\mathscr{A}_1$ contains the point P_1, with vertices C_1, D, A, and C_2, i.e., $\mathscr{A}_1 \leftarrow \{C_1, D, A, C_2\}$. Next, polygon $\mathscr{A}$ is assigned $\mathscr{A}_1$, which is then assigned to polygon $\mathscr{R}$, i.e., $\mathscr{R} \leftarrow \mathscr{A}$. The bisector s_2 intersects polygon $\mathscr{R}$ at points B_1 and B_2, creating polygon $\mathscr{A}_2$ (Fig. 7.8 (c)). Then, polygon $\mathscr{A}_2$ is added to $\mathscr{R}$. Since all points have been processed, this results in the Voronoi cell $V(P_1)$ for point P_1 (Fig. 7.8 (d)). It remains to find the Voronoi cells $V(P_2)$ and $V(P_3)$ for points P_2 and P_3, respectively. Before doing so, the rectangle R is re-assigned to polygon $\mathscr{R}$ when searching for Voronoi cells $V(P_2)$ and $V(P_3)$. These cells are found analogously to cell $V(P_1)$, where for cell $V(P_2)$, the bisectors s_1' and s_2' of segments $\overline{P_2T_1}$ and $\overline{P_2T_3}$ are found (Fig. 7.8 (e)), and for cell $V(P_3)$, the bisectors s_1'' and s_2'' of segments $\overline{P_3T_1}$ and $\overline{P_3T_2}$, respectively (Fig. 7.8 (f)). By uniting the Voronoi cells $V(P_1)$, $V(P_2)$, and $V(P_3)$, the Voronoi diagram for points P_1, P_2, and P_3 is obtained.   ■

Building upon the geometric primitives and algorithms developed in the preceding chapters, the imple-

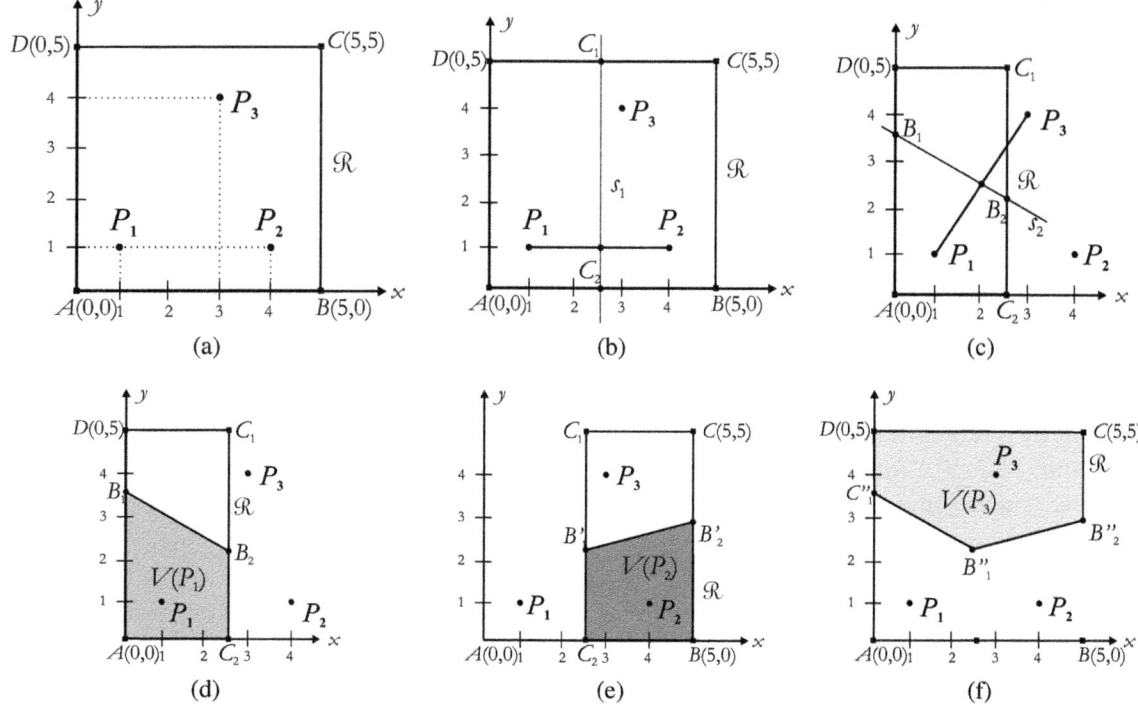

Figure 7.8: Iterative determination of the Voronoi diagram through steps (a) to (f).

mentation of the naive algorithm 10 becomes conceptually straightforward. This is illustrated through the functions *convex_polygon_intersection*($\cdot,\cdot$), *half_plane_intersection*($\cdot,\cdot,\cdot$), *voronoi_cell*($\cdot,\cdot,\cdot,\cdot$), and *naive_voronoi_method*($\cdot,\cdot,\cdot$). While Chapter 3 provides optimized implementations of the functions *convex_polygon_intersection* and *half_plane_intersection*, this section presents intentionally simplified versions. The aim is to facilitate a more pedagogical exposition, thereby enhancing the reader's comprehension of the geometric principles underlying convex polygon and half-plane intersections. The function *convex_polygon_intersection*($\cdot,\cdot$) computes the intersection of two polygons in quadratic time, following an approach similar to the Sutherland–Hodgman algorithm (see Chapter 3), which is traditionally used for clipping rectangles and polygons. Specifically, this function takes polygon P and systematically clips it along the polygon sides Q, thereby generating their intersection.

```
1 def convex_polygon_intersection(pol1: Polygon, pol2: Polygon) -> Polygon:
2     res=pol1.to_list(); pol2_list=pol2.to_list()
3     for i in range(len(pol2_list)):
4         input_list=res; res=[]
5         A=pol2_list[i]; B=pol2_list[(i+1)%len(pol2_list)]
6         for j in range(len(input_list)):
7             P=input_list[j]; Q=input_list[(j+1)%len(input_list)]
8             s1=Segment2D(P,Q); s2=Segment2D(A,B); p=[0]
9             if Q.is_on_segment(s2):
10                 if not P.is_on_segment(s2):
11                     if s1.intersection_lines(s2,p)==TypeS2.INTERSECT:
12                         res.append(s1.point_at(p[0]))
13                 res.append(Q)
14             elif P.is_on_segment(s2):
15                 if s1.intersection_lines(s2,p)==TypeS2.INTERSECT:
16                     res.append(s1.point_at(p[0]))
```

```
17        return Polygon.from_points(res)
```

As previously mentioned, the function *half_plane_intersection*(·,·,·) can be implemented with a time complexity of $\mathscr{O}(n^2 \log n)$ (see Chapter 3). However, in this context, it will be implemented with cubic time complexity, which arises from the quadratic cost required to compute the intersection of convex polygons at each step. The implementation is presented below:

```
 1 def half_plane_intersection(S: List[Segment2D], n: int, b_box: Polygon)->Polygon:
 2     pol1=Polygon(); pol2=Polygon()
 3     pol1=clip_polygon_with_segment(b_box.copy(), S[0])
 4     pol2=clip_polygon_with_segment(b_box.copy(), S[1])
 5     pol1.ensure_clockwise_orientation();
 6     pol2.ensure_clockwise_orientation()
 7     pol2=convex_polygon_intersection(pol1, pol2)
 8     for i in range(2,n):
 9         pol1=clip_polygon_with_segment(b_box.copy(), S[i])
10         pol1.ensure_clockwise_orientation();
11         pol2.ensure_clockwise_orientation()
12         pol2=convex_polygon_intersection(pol1, pol2)
13     return pol2
```

The implementation of the function *voronoi_cell*(·,·,·,·) directly follows step 3(ii) of Algorithm 10. Its overall time complexity is governed by the underlying complexity of the *half_plane_intersection*(·,·,·) function, leading to a total time complexity of $\mathscr{O}(n^2 \log n)$, or in the worst case, $\mathscr{O}(n^3)$, as is the case with the implementation provided below.

```
 1 def voronoi_cell(p:Point2D, points:List[Point2D], n:int, R:Polygon)->Polygon:
 2     bisectors =[Segment2D(p, points[i]) for i in range (n)]
 3     for i in range (n):
 4         bisectors[i].rotate() #Create bisectors
 5         # Check if the point p is to the left of bisector
 6         if p.classification_m(bisectors[i][0],bisectors[i][1])==TypeP2.LEFT:
 7             bisectors[i].flip()
 8     # Find polygon P as intersection of polygon R and bisectors
 9     P=half_plane_intersection(bisectors,n,R)
10     return P
```

Finally, the function *naive_voronoi_method*(·,·,·) calls the *voronoi_cell*(·,·,·,·) function *n* times to process all cells in the Voronoi diagram, resulting in a time complexity of $O(n^3 \log n)$ or, at worst, $O(n^4)$. Further analysis is unnecessary since its implementation directly follows Algorithm 10.

```
 1 def naive_voronoi_method(points:List[Point2D], n:int, R:Polygon):
 2     all_voronoi_cells=[]#All Voronoi cells
 3     for i in range (n): # For each point P_i
 4         p=points[i]; points[i]=points[n-1]# Replace A[i] with the last point
 5         v_c=voronoi_cell(p,points,n-1,R)#For each point P_j(j!=i)
 6         if v_c: all_voronoi_cells.append(v_c)
 7         points[i]=p # Restore original value
 8     return all_voronoi_cells
```

The graphical user interface for computing the Voronoi diagram builds upon the Listing previously used for constructing the Delaunay triangulation. The key difference lies in the substitution of the function *visualise_delaunay_triangles*() with a newly defined function *visualise_voronoi_cells*(), whose implementation is provided below. The referenced listing imports the module **ch7_helper_functions**, which contains the previously implemented functions, including: *convex_polygon_intersection*($\cdot,\cdot$), *half_plane_intersection*($\cdot,\cdot,\cdot$), *voronoi_cell*($\cdot,\cdot,\cdot,\cdot$), *naive_voronoi_method*($\cdot,\cdot,\cdot$).

```python
def visualise_voronoi_cells(self):
    R=Polygon(); w_c=int(self.canvas['width'])
    R.insert(Point2D(-10,-10)); R.insert(Point2D(w_c+10,-10))
    h_c=int(self.canvas['height']); R.insert(Point2D(w_c+10,h_c+10))
    R.insert(Point2D(-10,h_c+10))
    list_V_C=naive_voronoi_method(self.points, len(self.points),R)
    for pol in list_V_C: #Drawing all cells
        for _ in range(pol.size()):
            seg = pol.current_edge()
            x1, y1 = seg[0][0], seg[0][1]; x2, y2 = seg[1][0], seg[1][1]
            self.canvas.create_line(x1, y1, x2, y2, fill='black', width=1)
            pol.move_current(1)
```

Figure 7.9 displays the graphical interface of the Naive Voronoi Approach for generating Voronoi diagrams implemented in Python.

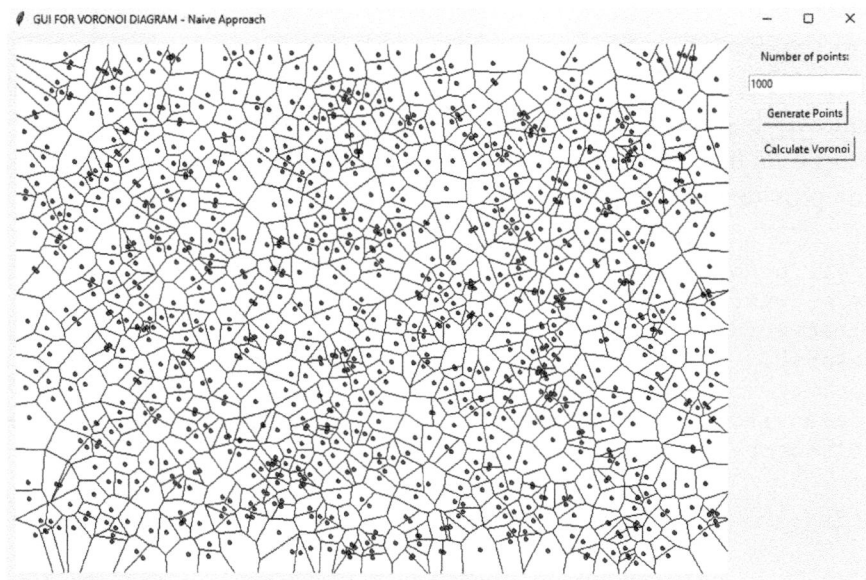

Figure 7.9: The Voronoi diagram was generated from 1000 random points using Algorithm 10.

■ **Example 7.9** Using the analysis from Algorithm 10, provide a detailed assessment of the time complexity for the "naive_voronoi_method" function.

■

■ **Example 7.10** Evaluate the time complexity of the Voronoi edge detection algorithm after constructing the Voronoi diagram using the Naive Approach.

■

7.2.2 Recursive Algorithm

The direct method for finding the Voronoi diagram is based on Observation 7.1.2. According to that observation, each Voronoi cell can be obtained as the intersection of the remaining $n-1$ half-planes. Thus, for each point P_i ($i = \overline{1,n}$), the intersection of the half-planes $H(P_i,P_j)$, where $i \neq j$, is calculated using the algorithm 11.

Algorithm 11: HalfPlane_Intersection($\mathscr{H}$).

Input : $\mathscr{H} = \{H(P_i, P_j) : \forall i, j, \ i \neq j\}$

Step 1: If $|\mathscr{H}| = 1$ **then** $\mathscr{C} \leftarrow \mathscr{H}$. **Otherwise**, the set $\mathscr{H}$ is recursively divided into two smaller subsets $\mathscr{H}_1$ and $\mathscr{H}_2$ that are approximately the same size.

Step 2: $\mathscr{C}_1 \leftarrow$ HalfPlane_Intersection($\mathscr{H}_1$).

Step 3: $\mathscr{C}_2 \leftarrow$ HalfPlane_Intersection($\mathscr{H}_2$).

Step 4: $\mathscr{C} \leftarrow$ Intersection_Convex_Polygons($\mathscr{C}_1, \mathscr{C}_2$)

Output : Voronoi cell $\mathscr{C}$.

The procedure "Intersection_Convex_Polygons" determines the intersection of two convex polygonal regions in linear time concerning the total number of vertices of those polygons, as demonstrated in the third chapter of this book. Consequently, the time complexity of the procedure **HalfPlane_Intersection** is of order $O(n \log n)$. Thus, to determine any Voronoi cell, $O(n \log n)$ time is required. Therefore, a total of $O(n^2 \log n)$ time is necessary to find the Voronoi diagram.

7.2.3 Incremental Algorithm

In this section, the incremental algorithm of quadratic complexity from 1977, authored by Peter Green and Robin Sibson, will be described. The fundamental idea of this algorithm is very similar to the concept used in the incremental algorithm for constructing the convex hull. This algorithm incrementally builds the Voronoi diagram by starting from an initial Voronoi diagram (created based on a few points) and incrementally processing points that did not participate in the construction of the initial diagram, thereby creating new Voronoi cells and updating the previously formed cells. In other words, let a Voronoi diagram be created for n given points in the plane for k points ($k > 1$), specifically $P_1, P_2, \cdots, P_k$. During the implementation of this algorithm, it is assumed that $k = 2$, meaning that the algorithm begins with the assumption that two Voronoi cells $V(P_1)$ and $V(P_2)$ have already been created. These cells are found by drawing the perpendicular bisector of the segment $\overline{P_1 P_2}$, which divides (intersects) a rectangle R containing all the sites of the Voronoi diagram into two parts (cells). The following procedure is performed to create the Voronoi cell for a new site P that is not in the existing Voronoi diagram. First, the Voronoi cell containing site P is identified. Let this cell be $V(P_l)$ ($1 \leq l \leq k$). This cell is detected in linear time relative to the number of created cells, as it is sufficient to find the cell's site closest to site P. Next, a segment $\overline{X_1 X_2}$ is drawn to be orthogonal to the perpendicular bisector of the segment $\overline{P_l P}$. Continuing from point X_2, the previously described process is conducted for the neighboring cells of the Voronoi cell $V(P_l)$ in the opposite direction of the clockwise movement until returning to point X_1. Once point X_1 is reached again, this indicates that the Voronoi cell for point P has been created, and the neighboring cells intersecting with $V(P)$ need to be updated based on the new intersection between them and cell $V(P)$. Based on this description, it immediately follows that the time complexity of this algorithm is quadratic.

■ **Example 7.11** Using the Incremental algorithm, determine the Voronoi cell $V(P)$ for the site P based on the previously constructed Voronoi diagram shown in Fig. 7.10 (a).

Solution: Let the rectangle R encompass all points $P_1, P_2, \cdots, P_{12}$, as shown in Fig. 7.10 under (a). Based on the description of the incremental algorithm, the Voronoi cell $V(P_l)$, which contains the site P, is first identified. In Fig. 7.10 (a), this cell is $V(P_{10})$, so we have $P_l = P_{10}$, or $l = 10 \leq k = 12$. Next, the bisector of the segment $\overline{PP_{10}}$ is found, which intersects cell $V(P_{10})$ at points X_1 and X_2 (Fig. 7.10 (b)). The endpoints X_1 and X_2 are chosen so that the points P, X_1, and X_2 are oriented in the opposite direction of clockwise movement. It is easy to see that the intersection of the cell and the bisector reduces to clipping a convex polygon and a segment (algorithm implemented in Chapter 3). The algorithm continues from the point X_2, which lies on the Voronoi edge between cell $V(P_{10})$ and its neighboring region $V(P_6)$. Following the previously described procedure, the bisector of the segment $\overline{PP_6}$ is found, which intersects cell $V(P_{10})$ at point X_2 and cell $V(P_6)$ at point X_3. Since Voronoi cells are convex regions, the bisector will intersect

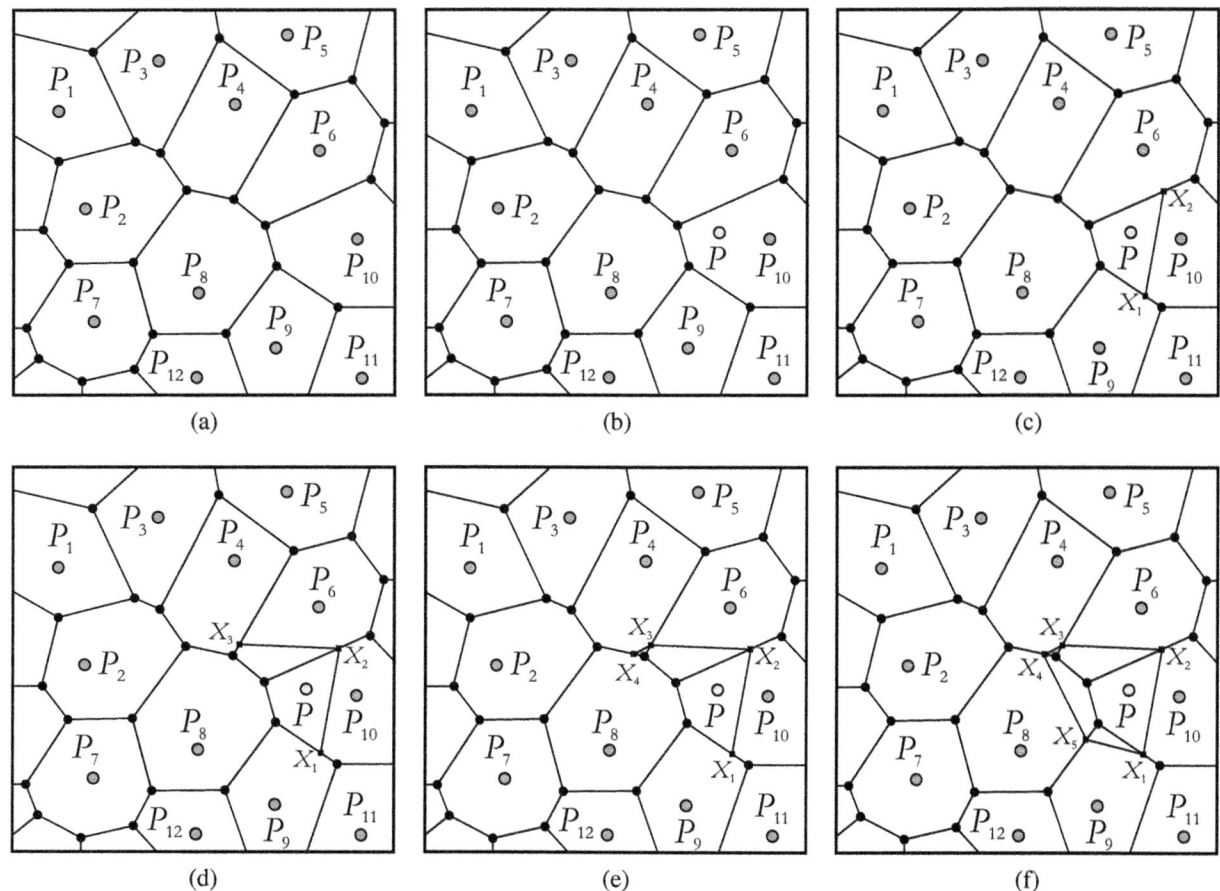

Figure 7.10: Detection of region $V(P)$ for the site P through steps (b) to (f).

them at exactly two points. At this point, it is important to mention that the membership of point X_2 is checked only for a few immediate neighboring regions of cell $V(P_{10})$ (Fig. 7.10 (b), this is the region $V(P_6)$). Therefore, in implementing the incremental algorithm, each region should keep track of which regions are its neighbors. Since point X_3 lies on the edge of region $V(P_6)$, and its immediate neighbor containing that point is region $V(P_4)$, the bisector of segment $\overline{PP_4}$ is sought, which passes through point X_3 and intersects the Voronoi cell $V(P_4)$ at point X_4 (Fig. 7.10 (d)). Since point X_4 lies on the edge of cell $V(P_8)$, the bisector of segment $\overline{PP_9}$ is sought, which intersects the edge of cell $V(P_8)$ at point X_5 (Fig. 7.10 (e)). Finally, since point X_5 lies in cell $V(P_9)$, and point X_1 lies on the edge of that same cell, the algorithm concludes by connecting point X_5 with a segment to point X_1, thereby finally creating the Voronoi cell $V(P)$ for site P (Fig. 7.10 (f)). In Fig. 7.10 (f), it is also necessary to update the cells for points P_4, P_6, P_8, P_9, and P_{10}. In general, neighboring Voronoi cells are updated by deleting those vertices that strictly lie within the Voronoi cell of the point being added and adding the vertices of the newly formed Voronoi cell that lie on their edges. For example, the Voronoi cell $V(P_4)$ is updated by deleting the vertex that strictly lies within cell $V(P)$ and adding vertices X_3 and X_4 of cell $V(P)$. Another method for updating cells is based on finding the intersection (some polygon) between the updated cell and the newly formed cells, which is then removed from the updating cell. Effectively, this is a difference operation between convex polygons, which can be reduced to their intersection (algorithm implemented in Chapter 3).

■

7.2.4 Plane Sweep Algorithm

The plane sweep algorithm, Fortune's Algorithm, is a very efficient method for finding Voronoi diagrams. This algorithm, based on the sweep line paradigm, was invented by Steve Fortune in 1987. The time complexity of this algorithm is $O(n \log n)$, and since sorting numbers can be performed at this time, it follows that this algorithm is asymptotically optimal. The strategy of Fortune's algorithm involves drawing an imaginary vertical (horizontal) line from left to right (top to bottom) while concurrently constructing the Voronoi diagram. Thus, sweeping from left to right (top to bottom) means moving from the point with the smallest to the point with the largest x-coordinate (or from the point with the largest to the point with the smallest y-coordinate). During this sweep, information about the intersection of the sweep line and the calculated Voronoi diagram is updated. The information must not be updated continuously as the sweep line moves, but it should be updated at particular Event points.

Definition 7.2.1 An *event point* is a point in the plane when the sweep line hits a new site.

Maintaining information between the sweep line l and the Voronoi diagram is not straightforward because the part of the diagram to the right of the line l depends on both the sites that lie to the left of l and those that lie to the right of l. In other words, when the sweep line reaches the vertex with the highest x coordinate in some Voronoi cell $V(P_i)$, the corresponding site P_i has yet to be computed. Therefore, instead of maintaining the intersection of the Voronoi diagram with the sweep line, information is maintained about the sites to the left of the line l (which belong to some part of Vor(P)) that the sites cannot change to the right of l. The close half-plane containing the sites to the left of the line l is denoted by l^-. The question arises whether there exists a part of Vor(P) in which the points from the half-plane l^- have indeed found their nearest site, which will remain the same by further translation of the sweep line to the right. The following Corollary answers this question.

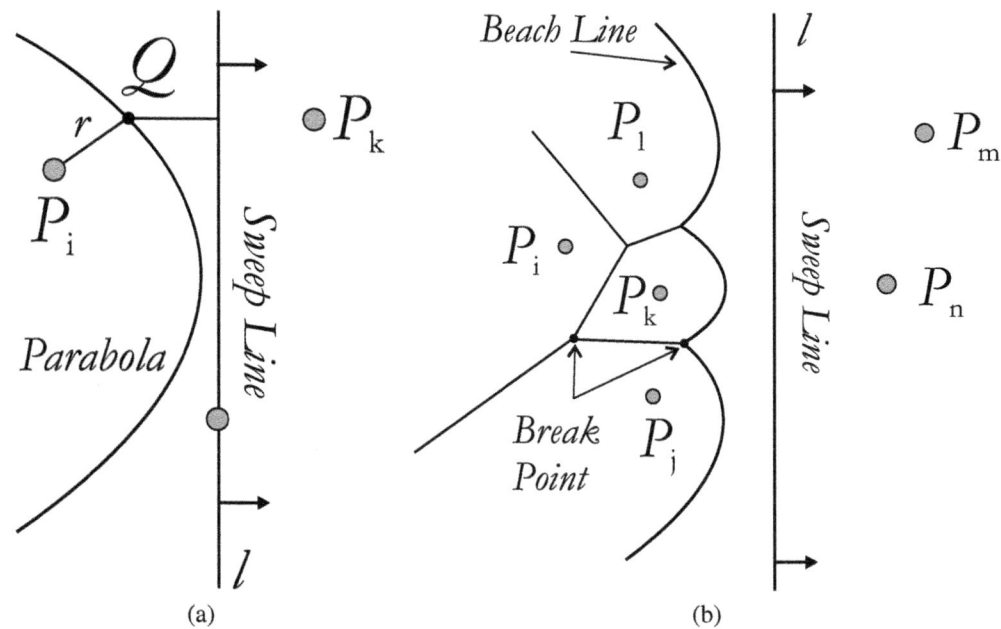

(a) (b)

Figure 7.11: (a) An illustration of a parabola and sweep line. (b) Illustration of beachline, break point and sweep line.

Corollary 7.2.1 For any point $Q \in l^-$, there exists a part of Vor(P) such that the nearest site to the point Q will not be changed by translating the sweep line to the right.

Proof. It is clear that $dist(Q, P_k) > dist(Q, P_i)$, where $Q \in l^-$ is any point, P_i is any site to the left of l, and P_k is any site to the right of the sweep line l. In other words, the nearest site to the point $Q \in l^-$ cannot lie to the right of the line l if point Q is at least as close to that site from l^- as it is to the line l. Thus, this implies that all points $Q \in l^-$ that are closer to the site $P_i \in l^-$ than to the sweep line l are grouped in their cell and bounded by a parabolic arc (Fig. 7.11 (a)), so the nearest site cannot be changed by translating the sweep line to the right. Therefore, the Corollary is proven. ∎

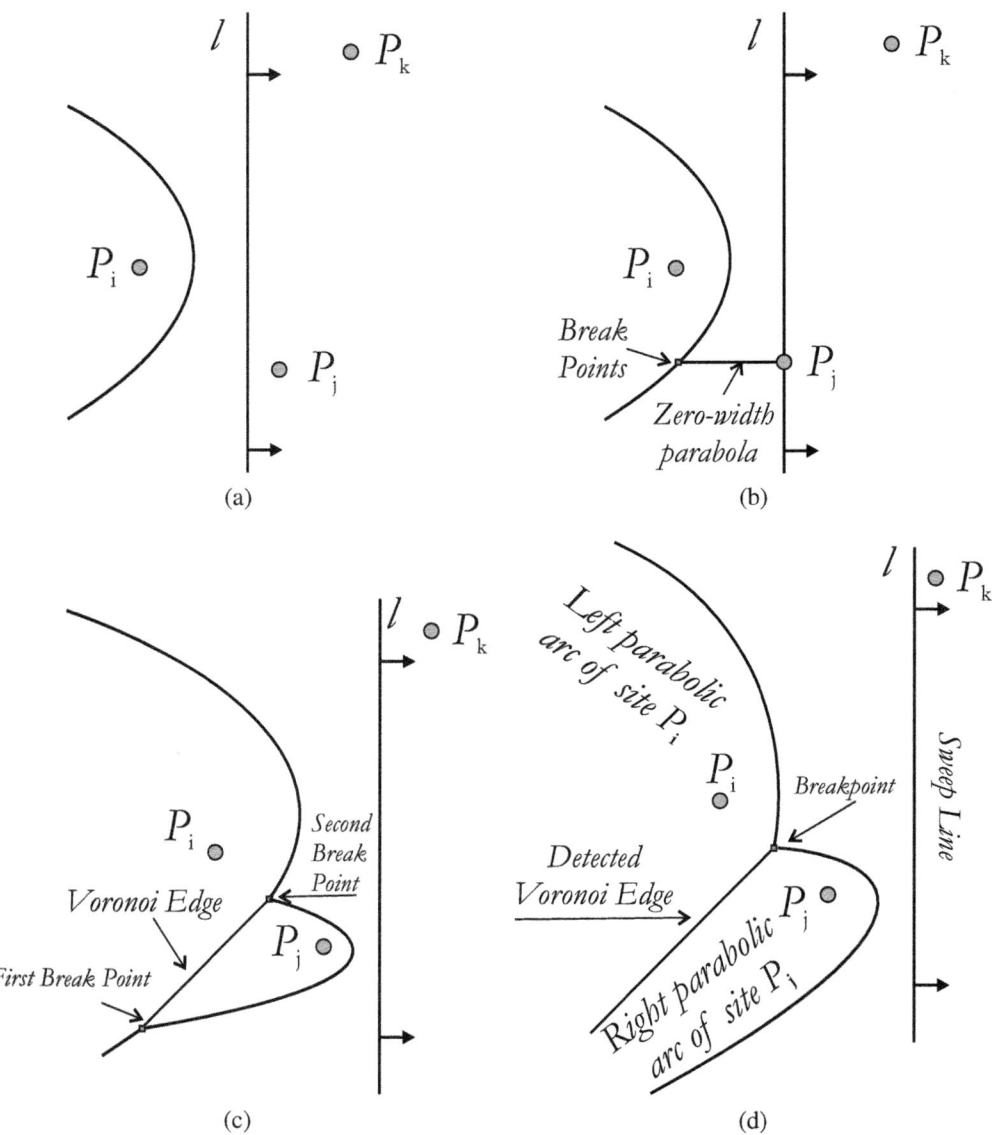

Figure 7.12: The appearance of a new arc on the parabolic front during the translation of sweep line from left to right.

Definition 7.2.2 A *beach line* is a curve formed by parabolic arcs closest to the sweep line l concerning its x-coordinate.

Definition 7.2.3 A *breakpoint* is a point on the beach line which separates two parabolic arcs.

The breakpoints cross parts of the bisectors drawn between sites of the Voronoi diagram, while the sweep line translates from left to right. With the introduction of the beach line or parabolic front, information about the intersection of Vor(P) with the sweep line changes to maintaining the beach line while translating the sweep line is maintained. The following steps describe the emergence of arcs on the beach line. The emergence of an arc on the parabolic front occurs when the sweep line intersects a Vor(P) site. The parabola defined by this site is initially degenerated to a width of zero, i.e., a line segment connecting the struck site to the beach line. The line segment transforms into a parabolic arc as the sweep line continuously translates to the right. This process of emerging a new parabolic arc is illustrated in Fig. 7.12 through steps (a) to (d).

Definition 7.2.4 The event indicating that a new site has been calculated is a *site event*.

Two break points are identified as a single point in a site event. Then, by translating the sweep line to the right, the breakpoints separate in opposite directions, thereby tracing a part of the bisector of Vor($\mathscr{P}$), revealing the edges of the Voronoi diagram. The question arises as to how many ways a new arc can appear on the beach line. The following theorem answers this question.

Theorem 7.2.1 A new arc can appear on the beach line only through a site event.

Proof. The proof of the theorem is derived using the law of contraposition. Let us assume that a site event is not the only way a new arc can appear on the beach line. Furthermore, let the existing parabola β_j defined by the site P_j intersect the beach line (see Fig. 7.13 (a)). It can occur in two ways:

   A) The parabola β_j penetrates through the midpoint of the arc β_i on the beach line, specifically at the point M;
   B) The parabola β_j appears between two arcs (two sequences of parabolas) on the beach line.

In case A), the arc β_j penetrates through the midpoint of the arc β_i on the beach line, and they touch at the point $M(x,y)$, where the x-coordinate of the sweep line l at that moment is equal to l_x. Furthermore, let $r = dist(P_j, M)$, $\rho = dist(M, L)$, where $L \in l$. Then it holds that $\rho = L_x - M_x$ and $r = \sqrt{(M_x - P_{j,x})^2 + (M_y - P_{j,y})^2}$. Since β_j is a parabola, it follows that r is equal to ρ, i.e., $r = \rho$. Based on this, the parabola β_j for the site P_j is determined as follows:

$$\beta_{j,x} := \frac{1}{2(P_{j,x} - l_x)}(y^2 - 2P_{j,y}y + P_{j,y}^2 + P_{j,x}^2 - l_x^2), \tag{7.3}$$

where $y = P_{j,y}$. The parabola β_i for the site P_i is determined similarly. Given that $P_{i,x} < l_x$ and $P_{j,x} < l_x$, it follows that the parabolas β_i and β_j have more than one common point, which is a contradiction. Therefore, the parabola β_j never penetrates through the midpoint of another β_i and thus cannot appear on the beach line outside a site event. In case B), let the parabola β_j appear between two arcs (two sequences of parabolas) β_i and β_k on the beach line (see Fig. 7.13 (b)). Let Q be the intersection point of the arcs β_i and β_k at which the arc β_j must appear. Then there exists a circle C passing through the sites P_i, P_j, and P_k defined by the parabolas β_i, β_j, and β_k, respectively (see Fig. 7.13 (c)). Let the circle C be tangent to the sweep line l at the point P_l, and let it be oriented in the direction of clockwise movement so that the following arrangement of points holds: $P_i - P_j - P_k$. Suppose a small arbitrary movement of the sweep line l to the right is made while ensuring it remains tangent to the circle C. In that case, it follows that the interior of the circle C' (where C' is derived from circle C) is not empty, i.e., either $P_i \in C'$ or $P_k \in C'$ (see Fig. 7.13 (d)). Thus, in a sufficiently small neighborhood around the point Q, the parabola β_j cannot

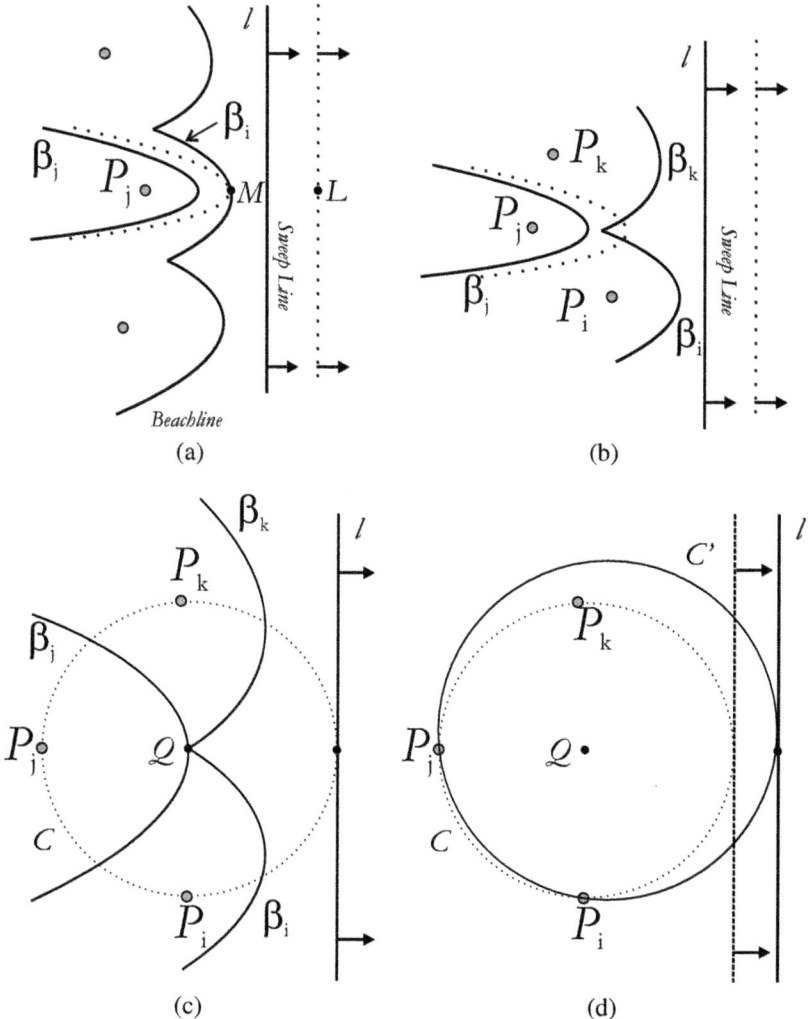

Figure 7.13: (a) The penetration of arc β_j through the midpoint of arc β_i. (b) Representation of arc β_j between arcs β_i and β_k. (c) The largest empty circle C defined by points P_i, P_j, and P_k. (d) Representation of the circle C' that results from a tiny movement of the sweep line l.

appear on the beach line when the sweep line is shifted to the right because, in that case, the points P_i or P_k would be closer to the sweep line l than the site P_j, which is a contradiction. Therefore, the theorem does not hold in this case either. Last rejects the assumption that the appearance of a new arc can occur outside of a site event, thus completely proving the theorem. ■

Observation 7.2.2 The beach line contains at most $2n-1$ parabolic arcs (each processed site generates one new arc and splits at most one of the existing ones into two) and $2n-2$ points, which define the beginning and the end of the parabolic arcs.

Definition 7.2.5 The event when the sweeping line touches a point (the point belongs to the edge of the circle defined by three sites that define consecutive arcs on the beach line) with the largest x-coordinate is called a *circle event*.

Theorem 7.2.3 An existing arc can disappear from the beach line only through a circle event.

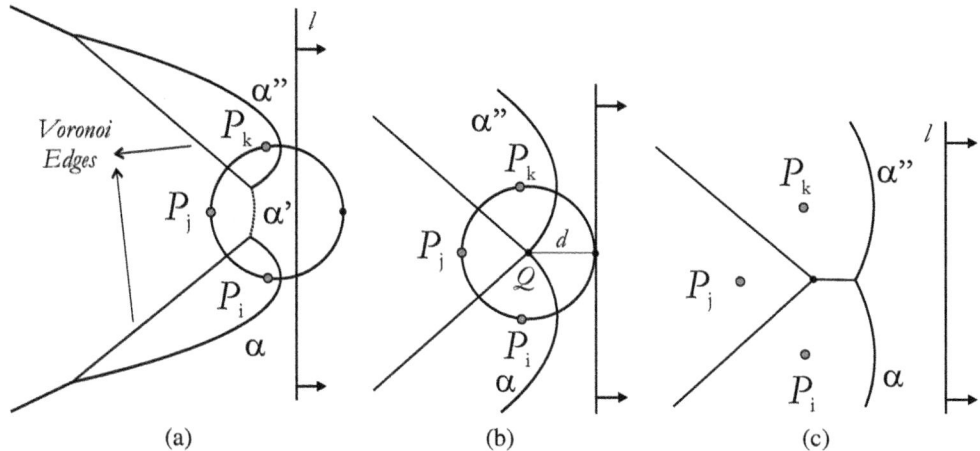

Figure 7.14: Illustration of the disappearance of arc α' from the parabolic front through steps (a), (b), and (c).

Proof. Let α' be the arc that disappears from the beach line, and α and α'' be its two neighboring arcs. Arcs α, α', and α'' are defined by the sites P_i, P_j, and P_k, respectively (see Fig. 7.14 (a)). At the moment of the disappearance of the arc α', the mentioned parabolas pass through the common point Q (see Fig. 7.14 (b)). Since it holds that $dist(Q,P_i) = dist(Q,P_j) = dist(Q,P_k) = d$, it follows that there exists a circle C centered at point Q, which passes through the sites P_i, P_j, and P_k (see Fig. 7.14(a)), and at the moment of the disappearance of the arc α' (see Fig. 7.14(b)), the sweep line is tangent to the circle C at the point with the largest x-coordinate. It is easy to notice that this defined circle is the largest empty circle centered at Q. Based on Theorem 7.1.3, it follows that the point Q is a vertex of the Voronoi diagram (see Fig. 7.14 (c)). This obtained result is not accidental, as the beach line breakpoints intersect certain Voronoi edge segments. Thus, when an arc disappears from the beach line and two breakpoints meet, the two Voronoi edges also meet, forming a vertex of the Voronoi diagram. Based on this, it is clear that an arc can disappear only through a circle event. ∎

7.2.5 Data Structures for Computing Voronoi Diagrams

In the first chapter of this textbook, binary search trees are introduced, which have been used several times so far (intersection of segments, triangulation of a simple polygon, union of rectangles, etc.), and will also be used to construct Voronoi diagrams, as would preserve the time complexity at $O(n \log n)$. The connection between the descendants of the tree and the beach line can be established as follows (see Fig. 7.15 (a)). Namely, the largest left descendant of the tree is joined by the largest left arc, then the next descendant, the second largest arc, etc. Each descendant of the tree commits a site that defines an arc on the beach line. The internal nodes in the tree record the division points on the parabolic front using the ordered pair of sites (P_k, P_j), where the sites P_k and P_j are used to create parabolas to the right and left of the division point M, respectively (see Fig. 7.15 (b)). Using a binary search tree to represent the beach line, an arc on the beach line that lies above the new location can be found in time proportional to $O(\log n)$. The tree also stores pointers to two other data structures, such as **priority event queue** and **singly linked list** . Each child in the tree, which shows some arc α, also commits a pointer to a node in the priority queue, which represents the circle event in which the arc α disappears. In addition, each internal node has a pointer to the **half-line** of the Voronoi diagram, which is deleted using the breakpoint. A singly linked list (discussed in the first chapter of the textbook) is used during its construction to store the sites of the Voronoi diagram, since the number of sites is never known in advance. Since a priority order is used when constructing a Voronoi diagram, the priority of events such as a site event or a circle event is defined via the x-coordinate of those events. So the priority queue will store known events. In site events, each site is dealt with separately, while in circle events, the largest site in the circle is saved. Also, in site events, a pointer to a descendant in the tree is committed. That descendant represents the arc that will disappear through the circle event. It is important to note that all site events are known in advance, while circle events are unfortunately not. This situation is known as *circle event detection*. A circle event is inserted into the priority queue, if the circle defined by the points of Vor($\mathscr{P}$) intersects the sweep line. However, if the circle lies entirely to the left of the sweep line or contains a site in its interior, then it is not added to the priority queue.

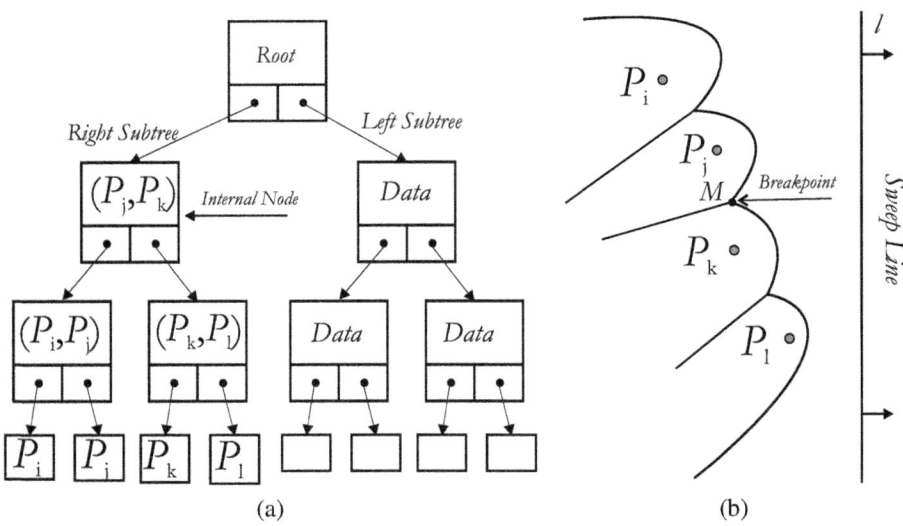

Figure 7.15: A link between the descendants of the tree and the arcs on the beach line, where the descendants keep the sites that define the arcs.

Theorem 7.2.4 Each Voronoi vertex is detected through a circle event.

Proof. Let Q be a vertex of the Voronoi diagram. Then based on the theorem 7.1.3, the circle $C_F(Q)$ contains at least three sites P_i, P_j and P_k on its edge and does not contain any other site in its interior. For simplicity, we will prove the case when no other site lies inside the circle $C_F(Q)$ and the largest point on the circle is not the sites P_i, P_j and P_k. Without diminishing the generality, if one goes around the circle $C_F(Q)$ in the clockwise direction from the point on it with the highest x-coordinate, then the sites P_i, P_j and P_k are detected (see Fig. 7.16 (a)). It is necessary to show that on the beach line there are three adjacent arcs α, α' and α'' defined by points P_i, P_j and P_k, before the sweep line hits the point of the circle with the largest x-coordinate, since then the circle event will certainly occur. A slight movement of the sweep line to the left (after it touched the point of the circle with the highest x-coordinate), induces a circle $C'_F(Q')$, which is created from the circle $C_F(Q)$, and which contains on its edge only sites P_i and P_j, and tangerine with sweep line l (see Fig. 7.16 (a)). Based on this, it follows that on the beach line there are adjacent arcs α and α' defined by points P_i and P_j. Analogously, there are adjacent arcs α' and α'' defined by points P_j and P_k. However, this means that on the beach line there are three adjacent ports α, α' and α'' defined by sites P_i, P_j and P_k. Therefore, the corresponding circle event is in the priority queue before the tangent of the sweep line to the point of the circle that has the largest x-coordinate. This implies that indeed the Voronoi vertex Q was detected through the circle event, which should have been proved. ∎

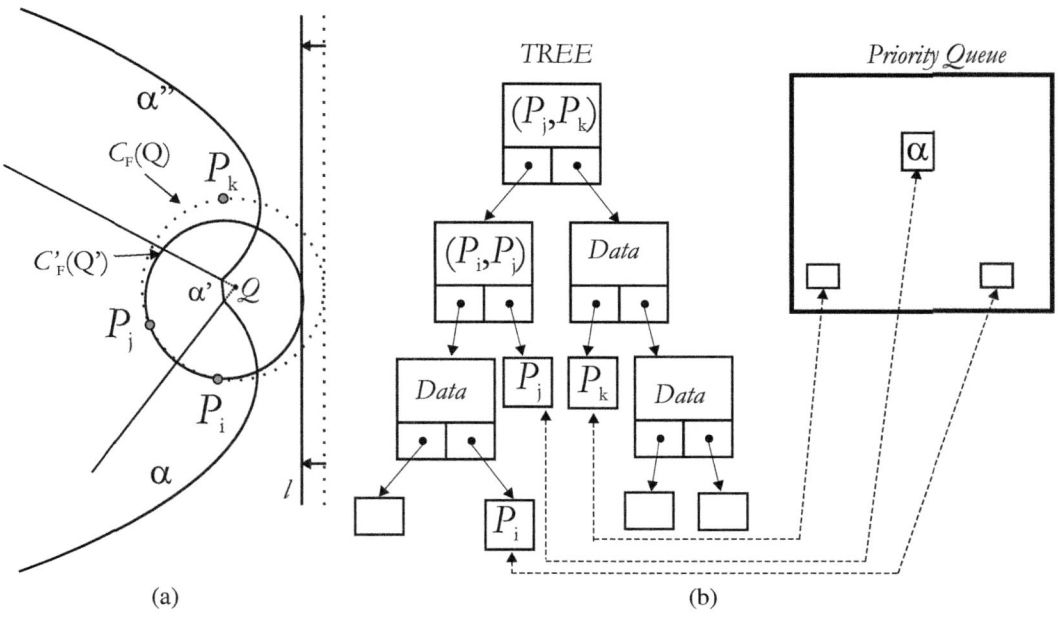

Figure 7.16: (a) Inducing the circle $C'_F(Q')$ at infinitesimal displacement of the sweep line. (b) Correlation between tree and priority queue.

Observation 7.2.5 During the movement of the sweep line, the beach line changes its topological structure in each event. This means that three new arcs in a row can appear in all events. In a site event, a new arc appears on the beach line and it joins an existing triple consecutive pair of arcs. In a circle event, the existing arc disappears from the beach line and adjacent arcs define a new triple arc. It is important to note that when an arc disappears in a circle event, then all other triple arcs associated with that destroyed arc no longer represent consecutive triple arcs on the beach line. When a new arc appears through a site event, the existing arc is split, so the triple arc that is bound to the split arc can be deleted. A circle event occurs in priority queue only if triple consecutive arcs are alive, until the sweep line reaches the smallest point of the circle. Thus, the row contains the circle event **if** there are three consecutive arcs on the beach line, so that the circle passing through the sites defined by those arcs intersects the sweep line and has not yet been deleted from the row. In order to insert the circle event into the queue it is necessary to check the following: *Whether the newly found triple of consecutive arcs is defined by three different sites.* If not, then that triple is discarded and it is not a candidate to define the circle event. However, if it is, then it is checked whether the condition is satisfied: *The circle event is wrong, and the circle intersects the sweep line.* If the given condition is true, then the circle event is inserted into the queue, otherwise it is not inserted. Additionally, there is the question of what happens in the queue when a trio of consecutive arcs are destroyed. Namely, when a trio of consecutive arcs is destroyed, then the corresponding event of the circle is deleted from the row, assuming that it happened in it.

Algorithm 12: Pseudocode of Fortune's algorithm for searching Voronoi diagrams.

Input: Sites P_i ($i = \overline{1,n}$) of the Voronoi diagram.

Step 1: Sort the sites P_i ($i = \overline{1,n}$) of the Voronoi diagram. Initialize the sequence of events with input events, i.e. sites P_1, P_2, $\cdots$, P_n, and set the randomized search tree and the singly linked list of edges to empty.

Step 2: Until the priority queue is empty **Do**:

    i) Select the event Q from the row with the smallest x or the largest y-coordinate, depending on whether the sweep line moves from left to right or from top to bottom.

    ii) If event Q occurring at location P_i is a *site event*, then it is processed using algorithm 13. **Otherwise**, using the algorithm 14, process the circle event Q for the arc α, where α is treated as a leaf of the tree.

    iii) Delete event Q from priority queue.

Step 3: Internal nodes are still present in the tree and they correspond to half-lines in Vor($\mathscr{P}$). Therefore, a rectangle is determined, containing in its interior all the vertices of the diagram to which half-lines are added by means of an adequate update of the singly linked list of edges.

Step 4: Iterate over all the half-lines in the singly linked list to preserve the Voronoi cells, as well as pointers from them to something else and pointers from something else to them.

Output: Voronoi diagram composed of n Voronoi cells.

Figure 7.16 (b) shows the correlation between the tree and the priority queue during the disappearance of the arc α from the beach line. In order to delete the event of the arc circle disappearing from the beach line, it is necessary to search in the tree for the descendant that does the site that determines the arc α. In that child, the stored pointer to the circle event is dequeued. Two other circle events involving the same arc α can be found through the previous and next descendants in the tree. These children have a pointer to the node in priority queue, which must be deleted. Finally, the descendant from the tree is also deleted. After all the events that happen during the construction of the Voronoi diagram and after the priority queue becomes empty, the beach line is still not destroyed. The breakpoints that are still present correspond to the half-lines in the diagram. However, since a singly connected edge list cannot display half-lines, a *bounding box* must be introduced in which infinite half-lines are attached. Based on what has been said so far, the global structure of Fortune's algorithm is rounded off in the form of pseudocode of the algorithm 12.

Algorithm 13: Site event processing algorithm pseudocode.

Input: Site P_i Voronoi diagram.

Step 1: If the tree is empty, **then** site P_i is added to it.

Step 2: An arc α vertically above the location P_i is searched for in the tree. If the tree leaf representing the arc α has a pointer to a circle event in the priority queue, then that event is deleted from the queue.

Step 3: Replace the leaf in the tree representing the arc α with a subtree that has three leaves. The middle leaf of that subtree stores the location P_i, while the other two leaves store the location P_j, which was originally assigned to the arc α. Store the pairs (P_j, P_i) and (P_i, P_j), which represent new points of division into two new internal nodes. Rebalance the tree if necessary.

Step 4: Store the half-line in a singly linked list of edges that separates the Voronoi cells $V(P_i)$ and $V(P_j)$, and will be detected (redrawn) by two new break points.

Step 5: For a triple of consecutive arcs, where the new arc of site P_i is the left arc, test whether the division points approach, i.e. converge to a single point. If yes, then the circle event is added to the priority queue, as well as the pointers between the nodes in the tree and the queue. The same is done for three consecutive arcs when the new arc of the site is the right arc.

Output: Updated data storage structures such as tree, queue and singly linked list.

In step 1 of the algorithm 12, if the sweep line moves from left to right, then the sites P_i $(i = \overline{1,n})$ are sorted in ascending order by the x-coordinate , and if two sites have the same x-coordinate, then they are sorted by the smaller y-coordinate. Since Fortune's algorithm can be implemented to translate the sweep line from top to bottom, then the sorting of the sites in step 1 is done in descending order by the y-coordinate, and if two sites have the same y-coordinate, then the sorting is done by the smaller x-coordinates.

Algorithm 14: Pseudocode of the circle event processing algorithm.

Input: The largest point X_j on the circle defined by the points of the Voronoi diagram.

Step 1: Delete the leaf of the tree representing the arc α that disappears from the beach line. Next, update the pairs representing the break points in the internal nodes. Rebalance the tree if necessary.

Step 2: Delete all circle events from the queue of events representing the arc α. These events in the tree are found in constant time via pointers to the predecessors and successors of the leaf representing the arc α.

Step 3: Add the center of the circle that causes the circle event as a vertex in a singly linked list of edges. Then, memorize the two half-lines that end in the center of the circle, and correspond to the new division point on the Voronoi diagram. Place suitable pointers between them.

Step 4: Test for a new triple of consecutive arcs in which the middle arc was the previous left neighbor of the arc α, whether the two break points of the triple converge. If this is the case, then the corresponding circle event is inserted into the priority queue, and the pointers between the tree leaf and the new circle event from the queue are updated. The procedure is analogous for the triplet in which the previous right neighbor of the arc α is exactly the middle arc.

Output: Updated data storage structures such as tree, priority queue and singly linked list.

Theorem 7.2.6 The plane sweep algorithm takes $O(n\log n)$ time and uses $O(n)$ storage in the plane.

Proof. Primitive operations in a binary tree and in a queue, such as inserting or deleting an element take $O(\log n)$ time. Primitive operations related to a singly linked list take constant time. In order to process an event, usually a constant number of primitive operations are performed, thus spending $O(\log n)$ time for its processing. Based on the Theorem 7.2.4, each vertex of the Voronoi diagram is detected through the circle event, and since the number of vertices $\text{Vor}(\mathscr{P})$ cannot be greater than $2n - 5$ (Theorem 7.1.6), it follows that the total number of circle events is of order $O(n)$. The number of site events is known in advance and is equal to the number n. Based on these facts, it follows that the computation of the Voronoi diagram has a time complexity of the order of $O(n\log n)$. To save n sites on the canvas, as well as to store among the results (meaning the objects of the structures used in the implementation of Fortune's algorithm), in the worst case it is necessary to spend $O(n)$ memory. ∎

7.2.6 Simulation of Fortune's Algorithm

In this section, the interface of the classes used to implement Fortune's algorithm will be presented, as well as the simulation for finding the Voronoi diagram, which is implemented in Python programming language in accordance with the pseudocode of the algorithm 12. A graphical user interface (GUI) is employed to visualize the simulation, in a manner analogous to that used for the naive method (see Fig. 7.17). Due to the volume of the implementation itself, it is not given here, but through the simulation of Fortune's algorithm, in a very clear way, the process of constructing the Voronoi diagram, along with the drawing of Voronoi edges, circles, arcs, and the beach line itself, is shown step by step. Fortune's algorithm can be implemented procedurally or object-oriented (OO). The simulation of his work itself is performed in an object-oriented way based on the use of ten classes (see Fig. 7.18). Since the implementation of Fortune's algorithm is written in an object-oriented spirit, it follows that four postulates of OO programming are represented in it: hiding, encapsulation, inheritance and polymorphism.

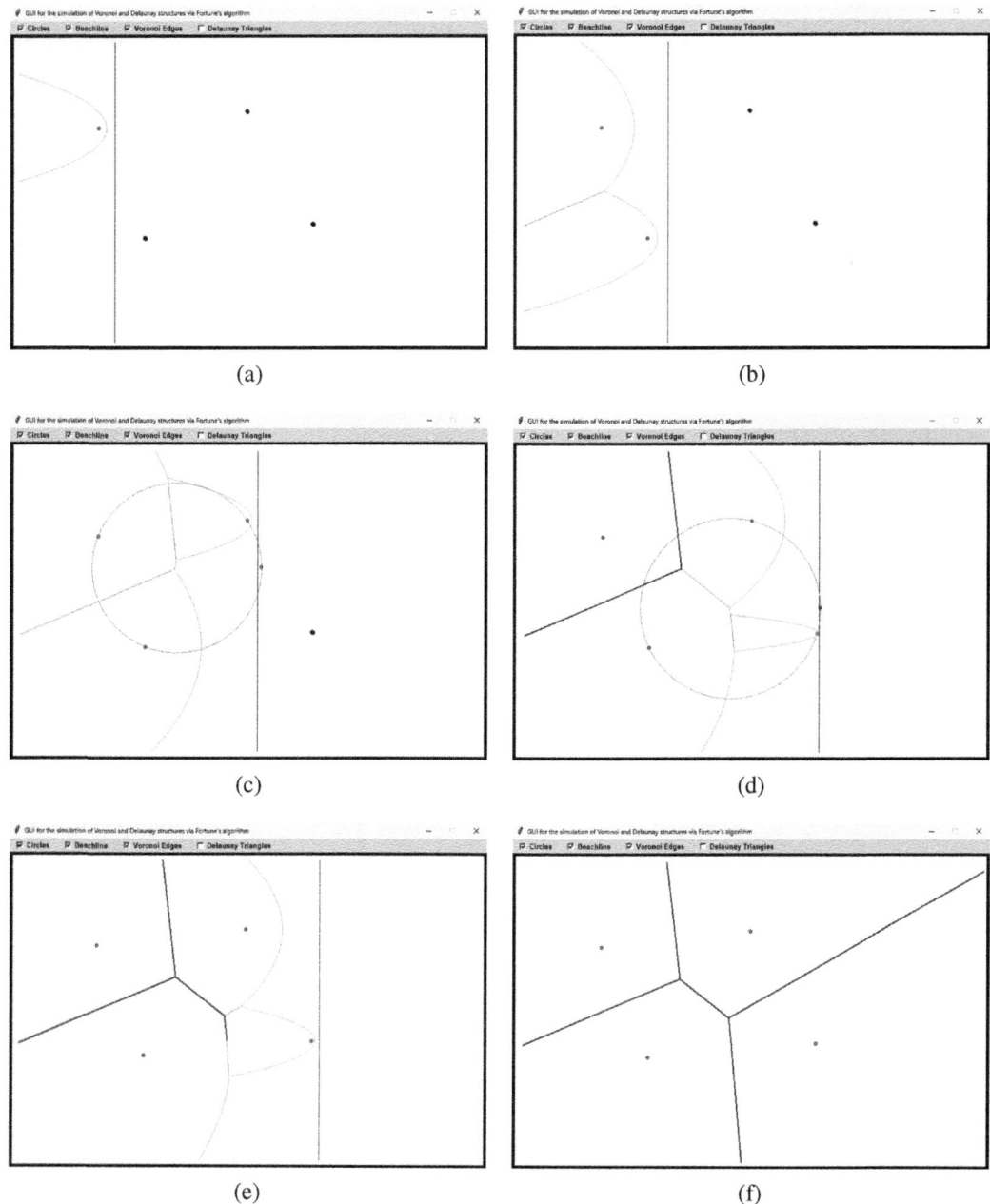

Figure 7.17: Simulation of Fortune's algorithm operation through steps (a) to (f).

For the purposes of demonstration of the simulation of Fortune's algorithm, four sites are set on the canvas of the graphical user interface (see Fig. 7.17). After the sweep line l hits the first site (the site event happened), and after that it moves very slightly to the right, then a parabolic arc is drawn for that site, as in Fig. 7.17 (a). After the sweep line reaches the second site, then a parabola is drawn for that site, which intersects with the parabola of the first site, thus revealing the bisector of the length of the first two sites through the break points (see Fig. 7.17 (b)). It is important to point out that the found parabolas, after being connected to each other, create a beach line. When the sweep line reaches the third site, a new parabola appears for that site, as well as the circle defined by the first three sites. The parabola of the third site splits or updates the existing line of the beach, so it now consists of four arcs (see Fig. 7.17 (c)). Also,

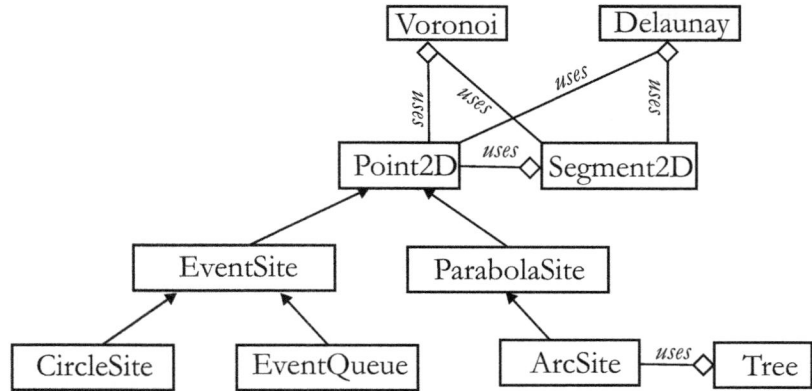

Figure 7.18: Illustrative presentation of class hierarchies that participate in the implementation of Fortune's algorithm.

the appearance of a new arc induces new division points that reveal the bisector of the length between the first and third sites. Thus, the second Vornoi edge is revealed. At the moment of tangent of the sweep line with and the point of the circle with the largest x-coordinate, the third arc from top to bottom disappears from the beach line, so the third edge of the Voronoi diagram is revealed through the break points, i.e. a longer bisector between second and third site is in sight. Finally, after the tangent of the sweep line with the fourth site of Vor($\mathscr{P}$), analogously as before, the arc of that site is created, as well as the circle defined by sites two, three and four (see Fig. 7.17 (d)). By creating an arc, break points appear that reveal the fourth edge of Vor($\mathscr{P}$), i.e. bisector longer sites two and four. After the sweep line reaches the point of the last circle with the largest x-coordinate, the existing arc disappears from the beach line, which is an indicator to detect the last Voronoi edge (see Fig. 7.17 (e)). By translating the sweep line to the right, we finally get the four-site division of the plane induced by the Voronoi diagram, which is shown in Fig. 7.17 (f).

7.2.7 Experimental Evaluation of Voronoi Diagram Construction Algorithms

In computational geometry, the efficiency of an algorithm is typically evaluated based on its theoretical time complexity. However, real-world performance often depends on additional factors such as implementation details, memory access patterns, and the characteristics of the input data. Therefore, empirical analysis plays a crucial role in understanding the practical behavior of geometric algorithms. In this section, we present a comparative study of two algorithms for computing Voronoi diagrams: the naive approach with a time complexity of $O(n^4)$, and the sweep line algorithm, which achieves significantly better asymptotic performance. Both algorithms are evaluated using the same set of randomly generated sites, sampled from a uniform distribution over the plane. This controlled setup ensures a fair benchmarking environment, allowing execution times to be compared directly on identical input data. The results, presented in Table 7.1, provide insights into the scalability and runtime behavior of both methods as the input size grows steadily.

The results presented in Table 7.1 highlight a substantial performance gap between the Naive approach and the Plane Sweep algorithm for computing Voronoi diagrams. As the number of input points increases, the execution time of the Naive method grows rapidly, consistent with its theoretical time complexity of $O(n^4)$. For instance, when $n = 1700$, the Naive method requires over 427 seconds to complete, making it impractical for larger datasets. In contrast, the Plane Sweep algorithm exhibits significantly better scalability, with execution times remaining well below one second across all tested instances. These empirical findings confirm the theoretical advantage of the sweep line technique and reinforce its suitability for efficient Voronoi diagram construction in practical applications involving large point sets.

Table 7.1: Comparative execution times (in seconds) of the Naive and Sweep Line algorithms for constructing Voronoi diagrams over varying input sizes.

Number of Points (n)	Naive Approach	Plane Sweep Algorithm
100	1.347647	0.021742
500	33.948914	0.229154
900	111.472758	0.327878
1300	232.453144	0.413245
1700	427.641849	0.561148

7.3 Duality Between the Voronoi Diagram and the Delaunay Triangulation

In this section, we demonstrate an elegant and fundamental connection between Voronoi diagrams and Delaunay triangulations. Specifically, the problems of constructing the Voronoi diagram and the Delaunay triangulation for the same set of points are dual to one another. This duality implies that if a Voronoi diagram is constructed for a given point set, and if one connects the generating points of those Voronoi cells that share a common edge, the resulting set of segments forms the Delaunay triangulation for the given set of points (see Fig. 7.19). The mentioned connection between the Voronoi diagram and the Delaunay triangulation is valid only in the case when all Voronoi vertices have a degree equal to the number three (see Fig. 7.19). Otherwise, if there are Voronoi vertices of degree greater than three, the described joining procedure does not produce Delaunay triangles everywhere. More precisely, every degenerate Voronoi vertex of degree k will have a corresponding k-corner.

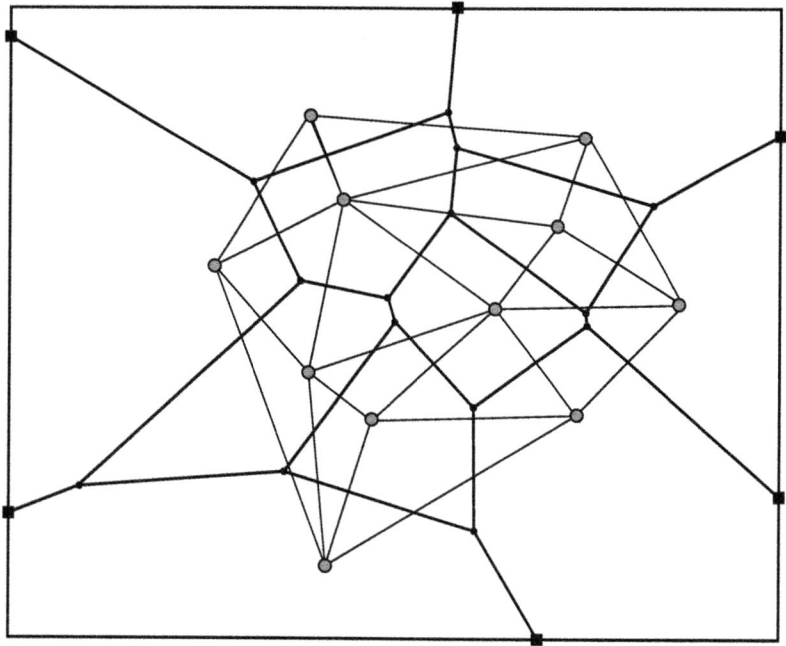

Figure 7.19: Connection between Voronoi diagram and Delaunay triangulation.

This results in something that is not strictly a Delaunay triangulation, but a so-called Delaunay graph. However, if any triangulation of those polygons that are not triangles is performed in the Delaunay graph, Delaunay triangulation is obtained as a result. This is actually the case when the Delaunay triangulation is not unique. The described connection between the Voronoi diagram and the Delaunay triangulation is not difficult to prove, comparing their basic properties. Thus, it is proved that the point Q is the vertex of the Voronoi diagram if the largest empty circle centered at the point Q passes through three or more sites. Also, it was shown that the bisector of a length connecting some two sites P_i and P_j determines the edge of the Voronoi diagram if on that bisector there is a point Q such that the largest empty circle with the center at that point that does not contain threads one site in its interior passes through the sites P_i and P_j, but does not pass through any other place. Apart from this, it is known that Delaunay is a planar triangulation of a set of points in which there are no illegal edges, as well as that the edge connecting the sites P_i and P_j, and belonging to the triangle, whose third vertex is some point P_k, is a legal edge if the largest empty circle passes through places P_i, P_j and P_k. By carefully relating these properties, the proof of the statement about the connection between the Voronoi diagram and the Delaunay triangulation follows. Based on this connection, it follows that it is possible to modify in linear time any algorithm that finds a Voronoi diagram into an algorithm that determines Delaunay triangulation and vice versa. Therefore, Fortune's algorithm can be easily modified for the purpose of finding the Delaunay triangulation, whereby the modified algorithm is even slightly simpler than the original algorithm for finding Voronoi diagrams, since there is no need to update the Voronoi edges and the coordinates of their ends, thus obtaining an algorithm that guaranteed to find the Delaunay triangulation in $(n \log n)$ time. Namely, if the only goal is to find the edges of the Delaunay triangulation, i.e. of the sides of the triangles that make up that triangulation, it is sufficient, every time a dividing point is detected, to write that there is an edge of the Delaunay triangulation connecting the sites P_i and P_j (given that the Voronoi cells corresponding to the sites really share a common Voronoi edge). On the other hand, if it is necessary to keep a list of triangles that form a Delaunay triangulation, then whenever a Voronoi vertex is detected (i.e. when processing a circle event), it is the center of the circumcircle defined by three sites that form a triangle in the triangulation. Therefore, it is possible to create a Delaunay triangle and record it in the list of triangles. Conversely, it is possible to modify an arbitrary algorithm for creating Delaunay triangulation into an algorithm for finding Voronoi diagrams. Indeed, Voronoi vertices are the centers of circumscribed circles around the triangles that make up the Delaunay triangulation, while Voronoi edges are the lengths joining two Voronoi vertices corresponding to pairs of adjacent triangles. Admittedly, this is not true for Voronoi edges that are semi-real (or even real in the degenerate case), but such edges are not hard to find either. Namely, they are the bisectors of the outer edges in the Delaunay triangulation, that is, those sides that belong to only one triangle (that is, which are not common to some two triangles) (see Fig. 7.19). At the same time, if they are half lines, their starting points coincide with the centers of the circumcircles of such triangles. Voronoi cells are a bit more difficult to determine, but it's not too difficult either, following the information about which triangles are adjacent to each other.

7.4 The Relationship Between Voronoi Diagrams and 3D Convex Hulls

In this section, the correlation between the Voronoi diagram and the convex hull in space will be described. More precisely, a connection will be established between the Delaunay triangulation and the 3D convex hull, which is a direct connection with the Voronoi diagram, since it is obtained as a dual of the Delaunay triangulation. This connection was discovered back in 1979 by Kevin Brown, and researchers Herbert Edelsbrunner and Raimund Seidel developed it in the early 80s of the last century. The key idea behind the connection between the Delaunay triangulation (Voronoi diagram) and the 3D convex hull relies on the introduction of a unit paraboloid defined by $z = x^2 + y^2$. To explain this connection, let $\mathscr{P}$ be the set of n points located in the xy-plane such that no four points are cocircular. An arbitrary point $P_i(x_i, y_i) \in \mathbb{R}^2$ $(i = \overline{1,n})$ of the set $\mathscr{P}$ is joined by z_i-coordinates so that $z_i = x_i^2 + y_i^2$. This means that the point $P_i \in \mathbb{R}^2$ maps to the point $P_i'(x_i, y_i, z_i) \in \mathbb{R}^3$, which lies on the unit paraboloid. By applying any of the algorithms for computing the 3D convex hull (see Chapter 4 of the textbook) to the set of points $P_i'(x_i, y_i, z_i)$, a convex hull in space is found. Based on what was said in the fourth chapter, the 3D convex hull consists of upper and lower faces, which are usually represented by 3D triangles. The Delaunay triangulation is obtained by projecting the lower faces of the 3D convex hull onto the xy-plane, which is explained by the following corollary.

Corollary 7.4.1 Let $\mathscr{P} = \{P_1, P_2, \cdots, P_n\}$ be a set of n points in the xy-plane. The Delaunay triangulation of the set $\mathscr{P}$ is obtained as the projection of the points of the lower convex hull onto the xy-plane.

Proof. The points of the lower convex hull in space are of the form $P_i'(x_i, y_i, z_i)$, where $z_i = x_i^2 + y_i^2$ ($\forall i \in \{1, 2, \cdots, n\}$). In order to prove that the projections of the points of the lower 3D convex hull, i.e. the projections of its triangles are actually Delaunay triangles, it is necessary to show that the projections of the ellipse on the xy-plane are actually the largest empty circles whose edges represent the circles described around the Delaunay triangles. Ellipses in space are obtained by the intersection of the unit paraboloid and the tangential plane defined by the triangles of the convex hull, where the vertices of those triangles lie on the paraboloid. From calculus we know that the tangent plane π at the point $P_a(x_a, y_a)$ is defined as follows

$$z = 2(x_a x + y_a y) - (x_a^2 + y_a^2). \tag{7.4}$$

By translating the plane π upwards along the z axis by a distance r^2, a new plane π' is obtained, which is given as follows

$$z = 2(x_a x + y_a y) - (x_a^2 + y_a^2 - r^2). \tag{7.5}$$

Let the plane π' be defined over the lower face of the convex hull. When it descends along the z axis for some distance r^2, then it starts with the unit paraboloid $z = x^2 + y^2$ at the point $(x_a, x_b, x_a^2 + y_b^2)$. Before its descent, it intersects the paraboloid in space along the ellipse containing the vertices of the faces (3D triangle $\mathbb{T}$). The equation for the projection of this ellipse on the xy-plane is obtained by eliminating the z axis, i.e. by including the equation of the paraboloid in the relation 7.5. Therefore, the projection of the ellipse on the xy-plane ($z = 0$) actually represents the equation of the circle in the xy-plane with the center at the point $P_a(x_a, y_a)$ and the radius r. As the plane π' is defined by the lower face of the convex hull, it follows that the vertices of the other triangles lie above it (based on the definition of the convex hull), so it will be projected outside the triangle $\mathbb{T}$ whose edge is described by the circle C of radius r. This means that the circle C defined by the projected vertices of the lower face must be empty (in its interior there are no projected vertices of the other faces of the lower convex hull), because if this were not the case, then the two faces would intersect, which is impossible based on the definition of 3D convex hull. Thus, the circle C is empty, which implies that the projected face located in the π'-plane is really a Delaunay triangle in the xy-plane. Since what has been said so far is valid for all other faces of the lower convex hull, we get two all projected triangles on the xy-plane are indeed Delaunay triangles, which should have been proved. ∎

Based on the proven lemma, it follows that the Voronoi diagram and the Delaunay triangulation can be computed very efficiently based on the computation of the convex hull in space. Moreover, the calculation of the convex hull in n dimensional space implies the determination of the Delaunay triangulation in the space of dimension minus one.

7.5 Recovering Sites from a Voronoi Diagram

In this section, a linear complexity algorithm for the construction of a Voronoi space based on a predetermined division of the plane into a certain number of convex polygons will be described. Let the division of the plane into n convex polygons, which should be checked if they form Voronoi cells (In Fig. 7.20 (a), there are eleven convex regions). Without loss of generality, some division of the plane is created using the algorithm for finding Voronoi cells (see Fig. 7.20 (b)). It will be shown later that it is necessary to slightly modify the desired algorithm in order to work in the general case, i.e. when it is not known in advance whether the division was made through algorithms for creating Voronoi diagrams or not. One example of dividing a plane, and finding a site for it, is illustrated in Fig. 7.20. It is important to notice that if one site

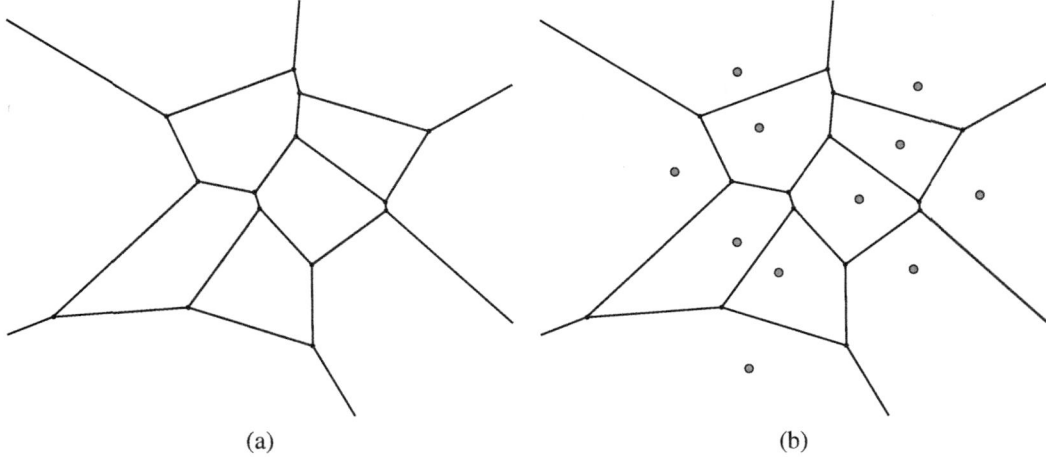

(a)   (b)

Figure 7.20: Determining the location of Voronoi cells through steps (a) and (b).

of Vor($\mathscr{P}$) is found, then the other sites can be found in linear time, which is what the following lemma says.

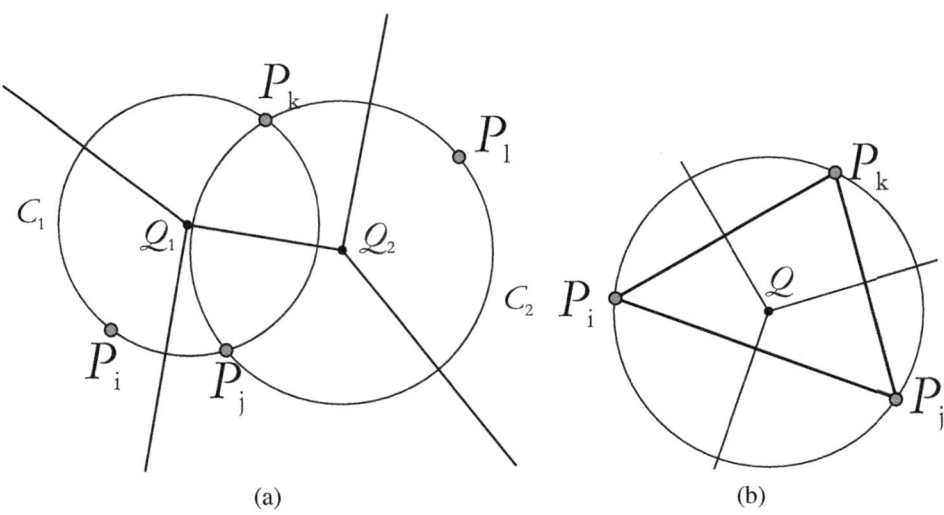

(a)   (b)

Figure 7.21: (a) Illustration of the circles C_1 and C_2 defined by sites of Vor($\mathscr{P}$). (b) Vertex Q at the same distance from Vor($\mathscr{P}$)'s site.

Lemma 7.5.1 Consider the subdivision of the plane induced by the Voronoi diagram and an arbitrary site. Then, in linear time, other sites can be constructed in relation to the total number of sites.

Proof. Let there be such a data structure, i.e. a Voronoi diagram representation that stores information about:

- Voronoi cells from which the Voronoi diagram is built;
- to neighbors of Voronoi cells so that for each Voronoi cell one knows who is its neighbor;
- Voronoi edges that divide two adjacent Vorono cells;
- Voronoi vertices.

Every two adjacent sites P_i and P_j of the Voronoi diagram are divided by some Voronoi edge that represents the bisector of edge $\overline{P_iP_j}$. In this way, for an arbitrary location P_k of the Voronoi cell $V(P_k)$ (assuming that it is indeed a true Voronoi diagram), its neighboring locations can be found by checking against each edge l_i^k of the cell $V(P_k)$ construct the points N_i^k, so that the edges l_i^k are bisectors longer than $\overline{P_kN_i^k}$, where m_k is the number of edges of the cell $V(P_k)$ ($i = \overline{1, m_k}$). The newly constructed points N_i^k correspond to the locations of the cells bordering the cell $V(P_k)$ with respect to the edges l_i^k. The construction of the point N_i^k is done in constant time, because for a given site $P_k(x_k, y_k)$ and the edge l_i^k (represented by a linear equation of the form $y = ax + b$), the coordinates of the site $N_i^k(x_i^k, y_i^k)$ are found like this

$$x_i^k = \frac{2(x_k + a_i^k(y_k - b_i^k))}{a_i^{2k} + 1} - x_k, \ y_i^k = 2\left[\frac{a_i^k(x_k + a_i^k(y_k - b_i^k))}{a_i^{2k} + 1} + b_i^k\right] - y_k. \tag{7.6}$$

After constructing the site N_i^k ($i = \overline{1, m_k}$) with respect to the given site P_k of the Voronoi cell $V(P_k)$, the other sites for the remaining Voronoi cells are constructed analogously for the reason that based on the assumption, it is known for each cell who is its neighbor. After determining the cell $V(P_k)$, the *Breadth-First Search* (BFS) algorithm is initiated from this cell to systematically explore adjacent unvisited cells, thereby enabling the reconstruction of the associated sites. Since it is necessary to spend a constant time to construct the location of one cell, and since there are n cells in total, it follows that all locations can be constructed in time of the order of $O(n)$. This completes the proof of the lemma. ∎

Lemma 7.5.1 says that to determine all sites of Vor($\mathscr{P}$) it is enough to have located any site of the Voronoi diagram. Finding a site of Vor($\mathscr{P}$) can be done in constant time (see Lemma 7.5.3). Earlier it was proved that Voronoi vertices are centers of circles that pass through three adjacent sites (see Fig. 7.21 (a)). Also, the vertex of the Voronoi diagram is equally distant from at least three neighboring sites (see Fig. 7.21 (b)). Therefore, each Voronoi vertex is located in the center of the circle described around the triangle formed by its three adjacent points. Moreover, every Voronoi edge separating two sites P_i and P_j is also the bisector of the edge $\overline{P_iP_j}$. In other words, three adjacent Voronoi points form a triangle, so that the bisectors of the sides of that triangle correspond to the Voronoi edges, which bound the Voronoi cells of the corresponding sites, and the intersection of those bisectors corresponds exactly to the Voronoi vertex, which is equidistant from the three adjacent Voronoi points (see Fig. 7.21 (b)).

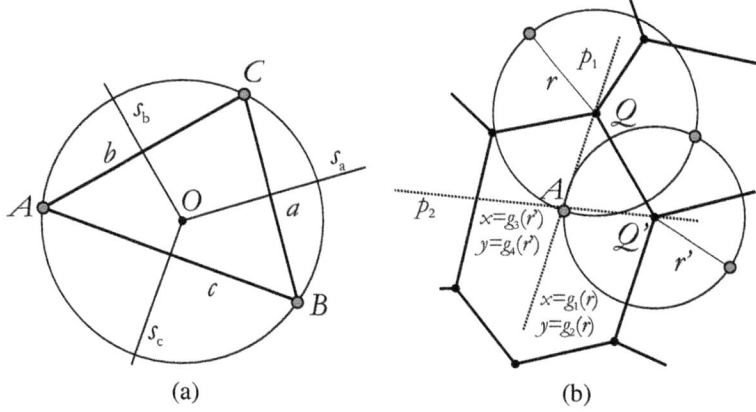

(a)   (b)

Figure 7.22: (a) Locating the vertex of the triangle $\triangle ABC$ via the radius r and the bisectors s_a, s_b and s_c. (b) Intersection of lines p_1 and p_2 defined by equations $x = g_1(r), y = g_2(4)$ and $x = g_3(r'), y = g_4(r')$, respectively.

Corollary 7.5.2 The radius r of the circumcircle of the triangle $\triangle ABC$, and its side bisectors s_a, s_b and s_c uniquely determine the coordinates of the vertex of the triangle.

Proof. The center of the described circle $O(x_o, y_o)$ is located as the intersection of the bisectors of the sides s_a, s_b and s_c of the triangle $\triangle ABC$ (see Fig. 7.22 (a)), which are defined by the following equations

$$
\begin{aligned}
s_a &: y = k_1 x + n_1, \\
s_b &: y = k_2 x + n_2, \\
s_c &: y = k_3 x + n_3,
\end{aligned}
\tag{7.7}
$$

where the coefficients k_i, n_i ($i \in \{1,2,3\}$) belong to the set of real numbers. The equations of the lines p_a, p_b and p_c on which the sides a, b and c of the triangle $\triangle ABC$ lie are given as follows

$$
\begin{aligned}
p_a &: y = k_a x + n_a, \\
p_b &: y = k_b x + n_b, \\
p_c &: y = k_c x + n_c,
\end{aligned}
\tag{7.8}
$$

where k_a, k_b, k_c, n_a, n_b, n_c are from $\mathbb{R}$, and the coefficients k_a, k_b and k_c hold $k_a = -1/k_1$, $k_b = -1/k_2$, $k_c = -1/k_3$. The described circle around the triangle $\triangle ABC$ is given as follows

$$
(x - x_o)^2 + (y - y_o)^2 = r^2,
\tag{7.9}
$$

where $(x_o, y_o) \in \mathbb{R}^2$ denotes the center of the circle. Based on the equations 7.7, 7.8 and 7.9, and the fact that the points $A(x_A, y_A)$, $B(x_B, y_B)$ and $C(x_C, y_C)$ lie both on the directions of the sides of the triangle and on the described circle, a system of nine equations in nine variables x_A, y_A, x_B, y_B, x_C, y_C is obtained , n_a, n_b and n_c. By solving this system, the values of the point coordinates are obtained depending on the parameters k_a, k_b, k_c, x_o, y_o and r. In other words, there are functions f_1 and f_2 such that $x_A = f_1(k_a, k_b, k_c, x_o, y_o, r)$ and $y_A = f_2(k_a, k_b, k_c, x_o, y_o, r)$. Thus, the completeness corollary follows. ∎

Corollary 7.5.3 In a Voronoi diagram, the corresponding site can be located in constant time.

Proof. From the constructed Voronoi diagram, any of its vertices can be accessed in constant time. Namely, from the representation of the Voronoi diagram, one simply takes the first vertex Q from the list, and next to that vertex, information can be obtained about the Voronoi edges coming out of it (among other things, the equations of the directions on which they lie), as well as about the Voronoi cells that contain it. they touch. In other words, the coefficients of the directions k_a, k_b and k_c on which the edges connecting the sites closest to the vertex Q lie can be calculated in a constant time. Therefore, the coefficients $k_a = -1/k_1$, $k_b = -1/k_2$, $k_c = -1/k_3$ are calculated in constant time, where k_1, k_2 and k_3 are the coefficients Voronoi edges emanating from vertex Q. Without loss of generality, let the degree of vertex Q be equal to three, i.e. there are sites $A(x_A, y_A)$, $B(x_B, y_B)$ and $C(x_C, y_C)$ that are closest to it. Let x_Q and y_Q be the coordinates of the vertex Q. If the radius r of the circle centered at Q and passing through the sites A, B, and C can be computed in constant time, then, by the previous lemma, the coordinates x_A, y_A, x_B, y_B, and x_C, y_C can also be computed in constant time. In the expressions $x_A = f_1(k_a, k_b, k_c, x_Q, y_Q, r)$ and $y_A = f_2(k_a, k_b, k_c, x_Q, y_Q, r)$ only r is unknown, so they can be written as $x_A = g_1(r)$, $y_A = g_2(r)$, where g_1 and g_2 are unknowns to be determined (see Fig. 7.22 (b)). But this is precisely the parametric record of the curve according to the parameter r, where the site A is certainly located. More precisely, it is easy to show that it is not a curve but a direction. Therefore, one can find the direction according to the parameter r where the site A is located. However, this is not the only direction where A lies. Therefore, another direction can be found from the Voronoi vertex Q' adjacent to the vertex Q such that it passes through the site A (see Fig. 7.22 (b)). For that direction, it is also true that there are functions g_3 and g_4 (analogously counted as g_1 and g_2) such that $x_A = g_3(r'), y_A = g_4(r')$. By solving the system

$$
\begin{aligned}
g_1(r) &= g_3(r'), \\
g_2(r) &= g_4(r'),
\end{aligned}
\tag{7.10}
$$

there are the radii r and r', and therefore the coordinates of the site A. Coordinates for sites B and C are found in a completely analogous way. This completes the proof of the lemma. ■

It remains to extend the given solution so that it checks whether the given Voronoi diagram is valid. It is said that only a small modification of the original algorithm is sufficient. Namely, it is enough to construct an opposite site for each neighboring Voronoi cell with the BFS algorithm when visiting each Voronoi cell. For those neighboring cells that were previously visited, that is, for which a site has already been constructed, it is checked whether the constructed site matches the existing one. If it does not match, then the given Voronoi diagram is not valid.

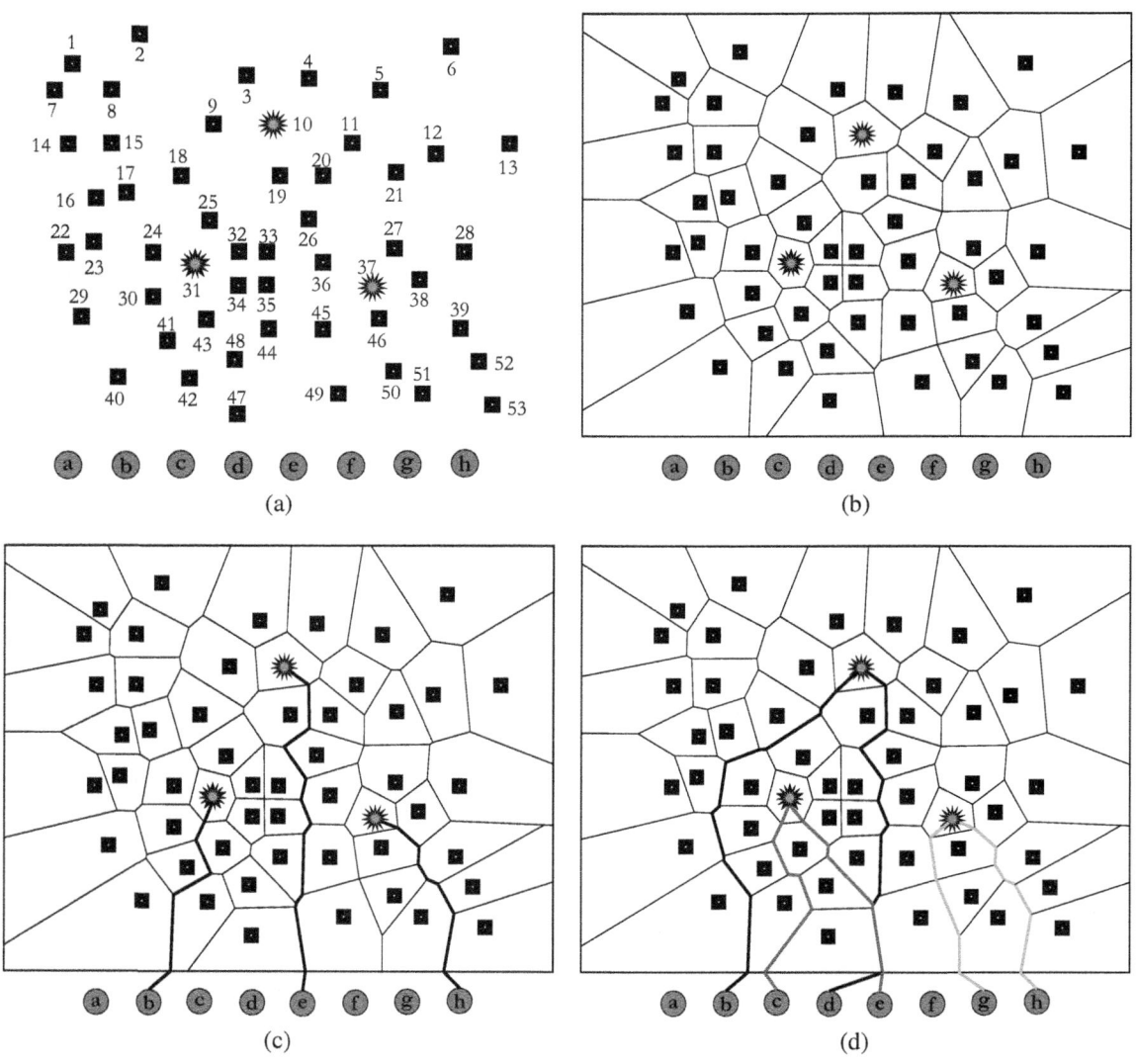

Figure 7.23: (a) Illustration of a battlefield. (b) Planning routes for drone movement using Voronoi diagrams. (c) Path optimization using one drone. (d). Path optimization using multiple drones.

7.6 Voronoi Diagram-Based Path Planning for Unmanned Aerial Vehicles

Unmanned aircraft are aircraft without a pilot and a crew whose weight and size varies depending on their purpose. They are controlled from remote locations from control rooms via joysticks or using a programmed flight plan. In the modern world, unmanned aerial vehicles or drones are used in various fields, such as medicine, logistics, military, etc. For military purposes, drones are more than 10 meters long and weigh between 500 kilograms and one ton. The *Battlefield* on which the aircraft fly is usually 100km × 100km in size. During the flight, it is necessary to ensure that the unmanned aerial vehicle does not collide with physical obstacles (trees, buildings, etc.), as well as with various radars in order to avoid being located. In practice, *unmanned aerial vehicles for electronic jamming* **JUAV** are also sent on the battlefield, which interfere with the operation of radars and help combat aircraft in achieving the intended goal. Optimal route planning is of crucial importance for all aircraft, which must be the shortest possible, and at the same time safe, so that they can fly safely from the starting location A to the desired destination B, of course with the satisfaction of all preset restrictions. In the following, it will be described how to calculate the optimal route of an unmanned aerial vehicle when it is exploited for military purposes. Let there be n_o dangers or enemy radars on the battlefield, n_m targets that the drones should hit, and n_b bases from where the drones take off. In Fig. 7.23 (a), dangers are marked as squares, targets as bombs, and drone bases as circles. The goal is to find safe and shortest paths for drones to hit targets as quickly as possible. If dangers and targets are treated as sites of the Voronoi diagram (see Fig. 7.23 (a) there are a total of 53 of them), it is clear that the creation of the Voronoi diagram will allow them to be located in its cells at a safe distance from its edges, which implies that its edges can be used for the safe movement of unmanned aerial vehicles (see Fig. 7.23 (b)). Voronoi diagram edges are most commonly assigned weights based on their distance from surrounding obstacles. By applying *Dijkstra's algorithm* (Edsger W. Dijkstra, 1930–2002) or an alternative graph-based algorithm, one can compute a path that minimizes the total accumulated weight along the route. The best-known graph algorithm for such occasions is the algorithm for creating graph visibility, which will be discussed in more detail in Chapter 11. There are two ways targets can be destroyed. The first way is to optimally select the base stations from which drones are sent (one per target) in order to destroy the targets (see Fig. 7.23 (c)). In Fig. 7.23 (c), the base stations b, e and h from which the drones were sent were chosen, because the optimal paths to the desired targets were found from them. Since in reality the environment of the battlefield is quite complex, the targets are difficult to see, and the radars and anti-aircraft defense are very strengthened, it often happens that it is not enough to send one drone per target, since in a large number of cases the mission is not successful. Therefore, as another way to attack targets is the strategy of sending more than one drone per target (see Fig. 7.23 (d)). This was done in Fig. 7.23 (d), where a total of six drones were sent, two drones per target, from base stations (b,d), (c,e) and (g,h). Of course, the choice from which base stations the drones are sent must be coordinated so that the total length of the path is the shortest, in order to complete the entire mission as quickly as possible without major damage or destruction of the drones.

7.7 Exercises

Exercise 7.1 Let $\mathscr{P}$ denote the set of n points in the plane. Describe an algorithm of time complexity $O(n \log n)$ that finds the two closest points of the set $\mathscr{P}$.

Exercise 7.2 Prove that for $n > 3$ there exists a set of n sites in the plane such that one of the cells of $\mathrm{Vor}(\mathscr{P})$ contains $n - 1$ vertices.

Exercise 7.3 Prove that the mean number of vertices of $\mathrm{Vor}(\mathscr{P})$ is less than six.

Exercise 7.4 Let $\mathscr{P}$ denote the set of n points in the plane. Describe an algorithm of time complexity $O(n\log n)$ that for each point $P \in \mathscr{P}$ finds another point $U \in \mathscr{P}$ that is closest to it.

Exercise 7.5 Let $\mathscr{P}$ denote the set of n points in the plane. Prove that the Voronoi diagram of P is an unbounded cell if the point P lies on the convex hull of the set $\mathscr{P}$.

Exercise 7.6 Describe in the incremental algorithm how to handle the case when the point being incrementally added does not fall directly into the Voronoi cell, but on its edge or vertex.

Exercise 7.7 Describe a divide-and-conquer algorithm for the construction of Voronoi diagrams for a set of n planarly assigned locations.

Exercise 7.8 Describe in detail the geometric properties of one-dimensional Voronoi diagrams for n locations given on the real axis. Design an algorithm for computing the Voronoi diagram in this case, and analyze its time complexity.

Exercise 7.9 Let $n-1$ points on the real axis be given. Devise a method to verify that the arrangement of these points matches their 1D Voronoi diagram.

Exercise 7.10 Let the Delaunay triangulation for the set $\mathscr{P}$ composed of n points be given. Describe the algorithm that computes the Delaunay triangulation when some points are deleted from the set $\mathscr{P}$. Explain how such an algorithm will change if the deleted point lies on the convex hull of the set $\mathscr{P}$ or in its interior.

Exercise 7.11 Let $\mathscr{P}$ be a planar set of points. Prove that the vertices P and Q are adjacent in the Gabriel graph if the Delaunay edge $\overline{PQ}$ intersects its dual Voronoi edge.

Exercise 7.12 The faces of the lower 3D convex hull are known to project onto Delaunay triangles. Explain to which 2D objects the faces of the upper convex hull will be projected.

8. Visualization Techniques

In this chapter, various algorithms for visualizing objects in space will be presented and implemented. Some of these algorithms require significant memory resources, while others are computationally intensive. The choice of an appropriate algorithm depends on the nature of the problem, the available hardware, and the characteristics of the scene being visualized. When rendering objects from a particular viewpoint, typically only a portion of the object is visible. Therefore, hidden surfaces are removed prior to rendering using a technique known as *Hidden Surface Removal* [52]. Additionally, parts of an object may be occluded by other objects, a problem partially addressed by the *Painter's Algorithm* [22], also referred to as the *Depth-Sort Algorithm* [21]. However, this algorithm does not provide optimal results in all scenarios, as will be demonstrated later in the chapter. Consequently, the *Z-buffer Algorithm* [176] or its improved variant, based on a modification of the depth-sort algorithm, is frequently employed in practice. Nevertheless, the modified algorithm has a time complexity of order $\Theta(n^3)$ due to the underlying data structures, while the Z-buffer algorithm consumes a large amount of RAM memory. To accelerate the modified Painter's Algorithm, advanced concepts such as *Binary Space Partition Trees (BSP Trees)* [87, 157] are introduced. BSP trees find broad application in various fields, including *shadow generation* [149], *set operations on polyhedra* [177], *visibility preprocessing for interactive walkthroughs* [26], *range searching* [23], and *cell decomposition in motion planning* [50]. BSP trees are widely used in graphic design, video games (e.g., Doom, Quake, RPGs), virtual simulations (VRML), animation, video [149], and Geographic Information Systems (GIS) [144]. Furthermore, structures such as *kd-trees* [150] and *quadtrees* [117] represent special cases of BSP trees, where the *splitting planes* are orthogonal to the z-axis.

8.1 Basics of Rendering and Visibility in Three-Dimensional Scenes

Three-dimensional computer graphics involves modeling a scene in space, where the process of creating a 3D image is referred to as *Rendering of a 3D Scene*. To render a scene correctly, the *Viewing Position* must first be defined, determining the perspective from which the scene will be displayed. A key challenge in rendering lies in the fact that not the entire scene is displayed, but only its visible parts. Surfaces that are not within the *Field of View (FOV)* are occluded by other objects and are thus discarded, significantly accelerating the rendering process. Furthermore, parts of the scene located outside the *Visible Field of View (VFOV)* are also omitted from display, further optimizing the rendering process. The viewing field, commonly referred to as the frustum, is typically modeled as a cone-shaped region that encompasses

A. Alihodžić, *Exploring Computational Geometry*, Texts in Computer Science,
https://doi.org/10.1007/978-3-032-06393-9_8

the points visible to the camera (see Fig. 8.1 (c)). Figure 8.1 (a) illustrates a conference room modeled using several thousand spatial triangles. It is evident that navigation through the scene is significantly accelerated when non-visible parts are excluded, as this reduces the total number of triangles that must be rendered. The problem of hidden surface removal can be formulated as the elimination of invisible objects, which are most often occluded by other opaque objects (see Fig. 8.1 (c)). Without loss of generality, let us assume the scene consists of a finite number of 3D triangles. If the scene is represented by quadrilaterals in space, they can be triangulated, thus reducing the problem to rendering a triangulated scene. For example, consider a scene composed of a quadrilateral $\square P_1 P_2 P_3 P_4$ in space. Its triangulation begins by projecting the vertices $P_1(x_1, y_1, z_1)$, $P_2(x_2, y_2, z_2)$, $P_3(x_3, y_3, z_3)$, and $P_4(x_4, y_4, z_4)$ onto a plane. This process involves determining the viewing positions of the vertices in 3D and then projecting them onto the screen, resulting in 2D points $P_1'(u_1, v_1)$, $P_2'(u_2, v_2)$, $P_3'(u_3, v_3)$, and $P_4'(u_4, v_4)$. Each vertex of the quadrilateral $\square P_1 P_2 P_3 P_4$ is assigned a label (1, 2, 3, and 4), which is preserved after projection, so the vertices P_1', P_2', P_3', and P_4' define a polygon in the plane. This polygon is then triangulated using algorithms for triangulating simple polygons. Once the triangulation of the quadrilateral $\square P_1' P_2' P_3' P_4'$ in the plane is obtained, the triangulation of the quadrilateral $\square P_1 P_2 P_3 P_4$ in space can be easily reconstructed using the vertex labels.

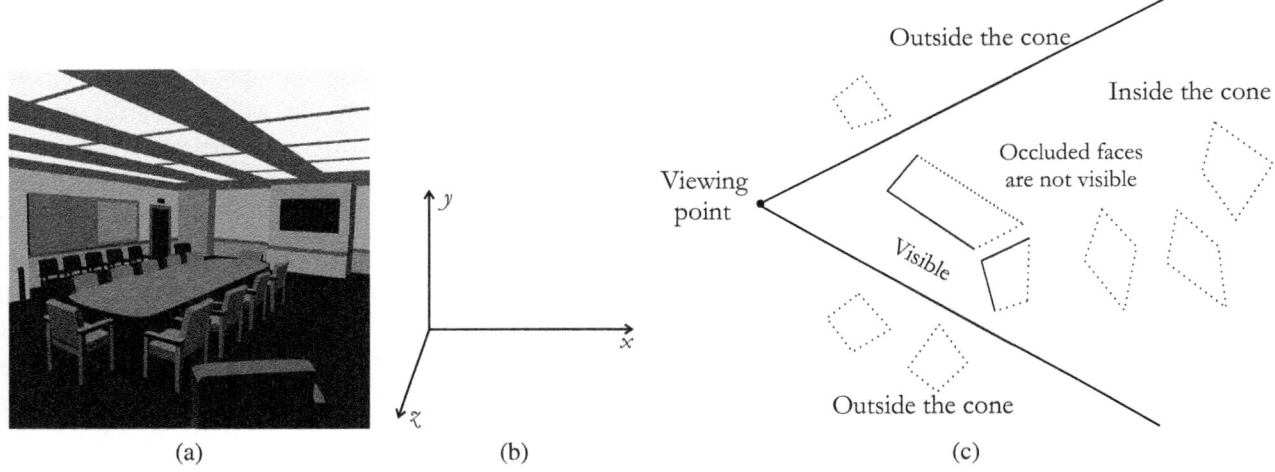

(a)   (b)   (c)

Figure 8.1: (a) The scene was created in Blender 3D as part of the visualization process. (b) Right-handed coordinate system. (c) Illustration of camera visibility.

Rendering of the scene is performed in a right-handed coordinate system (see Fig. 8.1 (b)), assuming the viewing point $P_v(x_p, y_p, z_p)$ is located behind the xy-plane, that is, within the half-space containing the negative z-axis, while the scene is situated in the opposite half-space containing the positive z-axis. Intuitively, this implies that objects appear farther away when moving toward the viewing point, whereas they appear closer when moving from the viewing point toward the positive z-axis. The triangles used to model the scene are typically assigned outward-pointing normals, defined by normal vectors $\vec{n}_i$ ($i = 1, \ldots, k$), where k denotes the total number of triangles. The angle $\alpha_i = \angle(\vec{n}_i, \vec{p}_i)$ between the normal vector $\vec{n}_i$ and the viewing direction vector $\vec{p}_i$ (defined by the viewing point P_v and the intersection point P_i) is used to detect the visible sides of the triangles (see Fig. 8.2 (a)). Specifically, let $\vec{n} = (a, b, c)$ be the outward-pointing normal vector of a triangle's face, and let $\vec{p}$ be the viewing direction vector pointing from the viewing point toward the face. If the dot product $\vec{n} \cdot \vec{p}$ is positive, the corresponding face lies in the background, as the angle $\alpha = \angle(\vec{n}, \vec{p})$ belongs to the intervals $[0, \pi/2)$ or $(3\pi/2, 2\pi]$. In this case, the face is discarded, as its visualization is unnecessary—it is hidden from the viewing point. Conversely, if the dot product is negative (i.e., $\alpha \in (\pi/2, 3\pi/2)$), the face is visible from the viewing point, and it is rendered. If the dot product equals zero, only the edges of the face are visualized. This special case can be used for visualizing hidden or occluded faces, for example, by rendering their edges as dashed lines. This is accomplished by maintaining a separate list of hidden faces, which are subsequently rendered as dashed edges after the visible faces have been drawn. In Fig. 8.2 (a), the faces $\square P_1P_2P_3P_4$ and $\square P_3P_6P_7P_4$ are visible, while the face $\square P_2P_5P_6P_3$ is not. In this manner, hidden faces (or triangles) are eliminated at an early stage, a process known as *Back-Face Culling*.

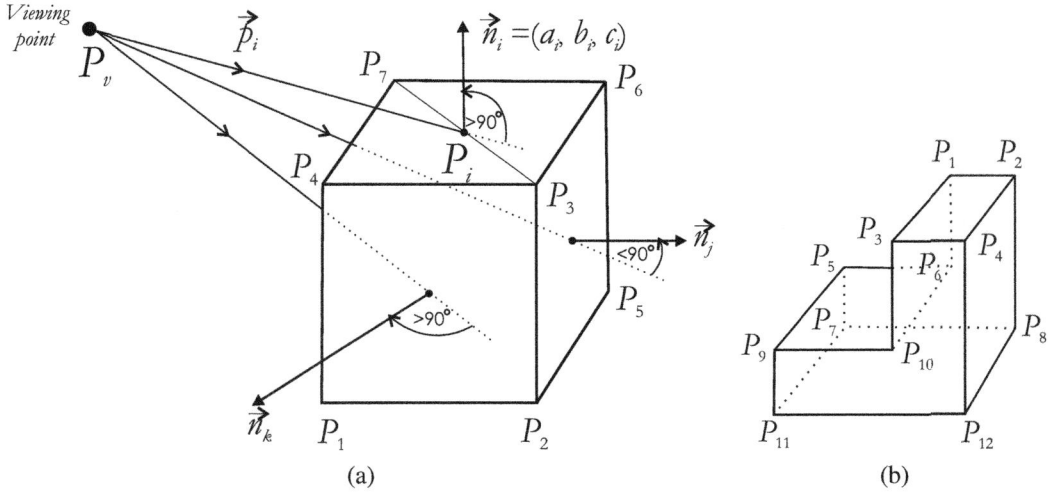

Figure 8.2: (a) A testing of visibility. (b) An examole of concave polyhedron.

Back-Face Culling technique assumes that the viewing point is located outside the object. If the viewing point were placed inside the object, only the interior faces would be visible, resulting in the elimination of all faces and preventing correct visualization. This technique is particularly effective for removing hidden opaque faces of convex polyhedra, where each face is either entirely visible or entirely hidden. In such cases, all faces that are not culled are fully visible. Unfortunately, back-face culling is not applicable to concave polyhedra (see Fig. 8.2 (b)). Its use is appropriate only when dealing with well-defined polyhedra that do not contain redundant or missing polygons, such as a cube open on one side. Based on these observations, a basic version of the back-face culling algorithm can be expressed in the form of pseudocode, as shown in Algorithm 15.

Algorithm 15: Pseudocode of the Back-Face Culling Algorithm.

Input : A set of n triangles $\mathbb{T}_i = \triangle A_iB_iC_i$ ($i = 1,\ldots,n$), which are tested for visibility from the viewing point $P_v = (x_p, y_p, z_p)$.

Step 1. For each face, i.e., triangle $\mathbb{T}_i$, the outward normal vector $\vec{n}_i = (a_i, b_i, c_i)$ is computed.

Step 2. If the visualization is performed in a left-handed coordinate system and $c_i > 0$ holds, then the face is not visualized. Otherwise, the face is added to the list of visible faces.

Step 3. If the visualization is performed in a right-handed coordinate system and $c_i < 0$ holds, then the face is not visualized. Otherwise, the face is added to the list of visible faces.

Step 4. In the case where $c_i = 0$, only the edges of the face are visualized.

Output : A list of visible faces and those edges that are subject to visualization.

In certain situations, it is desirable to render the edges of hidden or occluded faces of a polyhedron to improve visual comprehension. To facilitate this, such edges are first collected into a separate container or list. After all visible faces have been rendered, the edges of hidden faces are drawn using dashed lines (see Fig. 8.1). This approach, however, encounters challenges when applied to concave polyhedra, which often contain partially visible faces. As shown in Fig. 8.2 (b), the technique successfully discards fully occluded faces such as $\square P_5P_7P_{11}P_9$, $\square P_1P_6P_{10}P_3$, and $\square P_1P_2P_8P_7P_5P_6$. Nevertheless, the partially visible face $\square P_5P_9P_{10}P_6$ remains undetected and is not culled, even though it is partially hidden behind the face $\square P_3P_{10}P_9P_{11}P_{12}P_4$. The Back-Face Culling technique can be implemented efficiently by utilizing the geometric primitives introduced in Chapter 2. Furthermore, Chapter 4, which is devoted to the implementation of the naive algorithm for computing the 3D convex hull, provides a simple description of the procedures for rotating points in three-dimensional space, projecting them onto a plane, and converting coordinates from the Cartesian system to the screen coordinate system. Building on that exposition and the associated formulas, the implementations of the following functions are provided: *rotate_around_axes*($\cdot,\cdot,\cdot,\cdot$), *project_to_2d*($\cdot,\cdot$), and *map_to_screen*($\cdot,\cdot,\cdot,\cdot,\cdot,\cdot,\cdot$). These functions perform, respectively, the rotation of a 3D point about the coordinate axes, its projection onto a plane, and its mapping from planar coordinates to screen space:

```python
def rotate_around_axes(p, alpha, beta, gamma)->Point3D:
    SA=math.sin(alpha); CA=math.cos(alpha)
    SB=math.sin(beta); CB=math.cos(beta)
    SG=math.sin(gamma); CG=math.cos(gamma)
    # Rotation around the x-axis
    p1=Point3D(p[0],p[1]*CA-p[2]*SA,p[1]*SA+p[2]*CA)
    # Rotation around the y-axis
    p2=Point3D(CB*p1[0]+SB*p1[2],p1[1],-SB*p1[0]+CB*p1[2])
    # Rotation around the z-axis
    p3=Point3D(CG*p2[0]-SG*p2[1],SG*p2[0]+CG*p2[1],p2[2])
    return p3
```

```python
def project_to_2d(p: Point3D, d: float) -> Point2D:
    return Point2D(d*p[0]/(d-p[2]),d*p[1]/(d-p[2]))
```

```python
def map_to_screen(p,x1,x2,y1,y2,wc,hc)->Point2D:
    ax=wc/(x2-x1); bx=-ax*x1; ay=hc/(y1-y2); by=-ay*y2
    return Point2D(ax*p[0]+bx,ay*p[1]+by)
```

Based on the pseudocode provided in Algorithm 15, the function *create_2d_triangles*($\cdot,\cdot,\cdot,\cdot,\cdot,\cdot,\cdot$) is implemented. This function internally calls the previously defined routines to support the screen visualization of a tetrahedron defined by the vertices $A(0,0,5)$, $B(2,0,0)$, $C(0,3,0)$, and $D(-2,-1,0)$. As its output, the function returns two lists: one containing the visible triangles and the other containing the invisible ones, as determined from the viewing point $P_v(0,0,-d)$, where d represents the distance between the projection plane and the center of projection (i.e., the viewpoint).

```python
def create_2d_triangles(pts:List[Point3D],d:float,wc:int,hc:int,alpha,beta,gamma):
    vp=Point3D(0,0,-d); rvp=rotate_around_axes(vp,alpha,beta,gamma)
    vs=[(0,1,2),(0,1,3),(0,2,3),(1,2,3)] #vs-vertices of tetrahedron sides
    visible_faces=[]; invisible_faces=[]
    for i in range(4):
        face=vs[i]; rotations=[]
        for j in range(3):
            rotations.append(rotate_around_axes(pts[face[j]],alpha,beta,gamma))
        tr=Triangle3D(rotations[0],rotations[1],rotations[2])
        normal=tr.get_normal()
        if normal*(tr[0]-rvp)>0:#Check the orientation of the normal
            tr=Triangle3D(rotations[0],rotations[2],rotations[1])
```

```
13        normal=tr.get_normal() #Now, the normal points outward
14     pol=Polygon(); visible_face=False
15     if (tr[0]-rvp)*normal<0:visible_face=True
16     for j in range(3):
17         p=project_to_2d(rotations[j],d)
18         pol.insert(map_to_screen(p,-5.0, 5.0, -5.0, 5.0,wc,hc))
19     if visible_face: visible_faces.append(pol)
20     else: invisible_faces.append(pol)
21  return visible_faces, invisible_faces
```

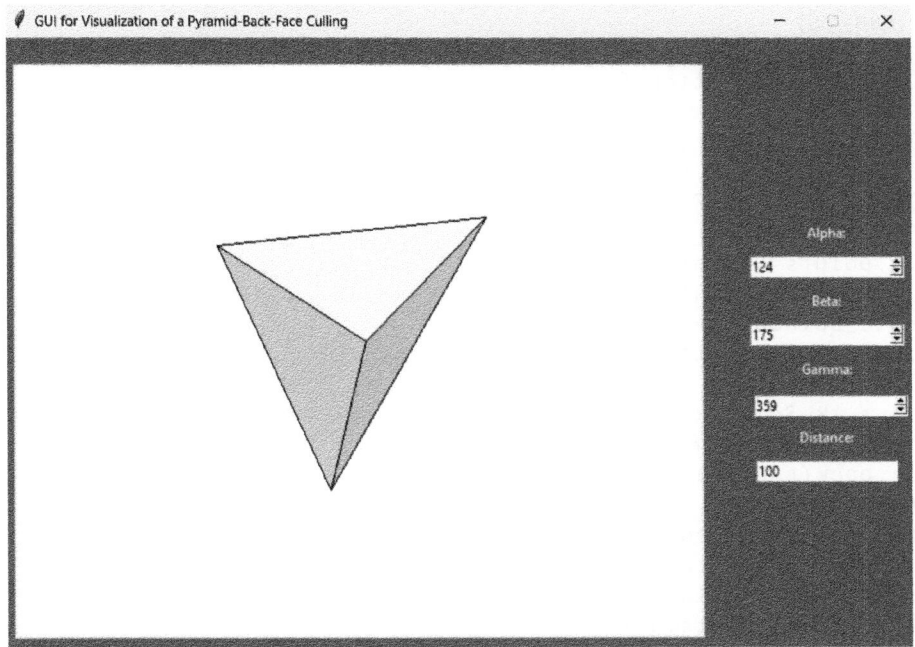

Figure 8.3: Illustration of Visible Faces of the Pyramid Using the Back-Face Culling Technique.

Figure 8.3 presents the visualization of a pyramid, where only its visible faces are rendered during rotation by applying the Back-Face Culling technique. This method significantly enhances the efficiency of the rendering process, particularly in scenes composed of several thousand triangles. The figure was generated based on the implementation shown in Listing 8.1, which, with minor modifications, will serve as a foundation for the 3D visualization of the remaining algorithms discussed in this chapter.

Listing 8.1: Simple GUI for 3D Visualization: Back-Face Culling Algorithm

```
1 import tkinter as tk
2 from tkinter import Canvas
3 import random
4 import math
5 from geometry import Point2D,Point3D
6 from ch8_helper_functions import create_2d_triangles
7 class GeometricVisualizer:
8    def __init__(self, root):
9        self.root = root
10       self.root.title("GUI for Visualization of a Pyramid-Back-Face Culling")
11       ww=800; wh=550 # ww-window width, wh-window height
12       sw=root.winfo_screenwidth() #sw-screen window
13       sh=root.winfo_screenheight()#sh-screen height
```

```
14    x=(sw//2)-(ww//2); y=(sh//2)-(wh//2) #Determine x i y to center the window
15    root.geometry(f"{ww}x{wh}+{x}+{y}")#Set geometry
16    root.resizable(False, False)#Disable resizing of window
17    self.main_frame = tk.Frame(self.root, bg="gray")
18    self.main_frame.pack(fill=tk.BOTH, expand=True)
19    # Canvas for object rendering
20    self.canvas = Canvas(self.main_frame, bg="white", width=600, height=500)
21    self.canvas.pack(side=tk.LEFT, padx=10, pady=10)
22    # Side panel for controls
23    self.button_frame = tk.Frame(self.main_frame, bg="gray")
24    self.button_frame.pack(side=tk.RIGHT, padx=10, pady=10)
25    tk.Label(self.button_frame,text="Distance:",fg="white",bg="gray").pack(
          pady=5)
26    self.entry_var = tk.StringVar(value="100")
27    tk.Entry(self.button_frame,textvariable=self.entry_var).pack(pady=5)
28    # Spinboxes for alpha, beta, gamma
29    self.alpha = self.create_spinbox("Alpha:")
30    self.beta = self.create_spinbox("Beta:")
31    self.gamma = self.create_spinbox("Gamma:")
32    # Example 3D points of a Tetrahedron
33    self.points=[Point3D(0.0,0.0,5.0),Point3D(2.0,0.0,0.0),
34                 Point3D(0.0,3.0,0.0),Point3D(-2.0,-1.0,0.0)]
35 def create_spinbox(self, label_text):
36    tk.Label(self.button_frame, text=label_text, fg="white", bg="gray").pack(
          pady=5)
37    spin = tk.Spinbox(self.button_frame, from_=0, to=359, command=self.
          visualise_tetrahedron)
38    spin.pack(pady=5)
39    return spin
40 def visualise_tetrahedron(self):
41    self.canvas.delete("all")# clear canvas
42    alpha=int(self.alpha.get())*math.pi/180
43    beta=int(self.beta.get())*math.pi/180
44    gamma=int(self.gamma.get())*math.pi/180
45    d=float(self.entry_var.get()) # d denotes distance
46    visible,_=create_2d_triangles(self.points,d,682,514,alpha,beta,gamma)
47    colors = ['lightblue', 'lightgreen', 'lightpink', 'lightyellow']; i=0
48    for i, face in enumerate(visible):
49        points = []
50        for _ in range(face.size()):
51            pt = face.current_vertex(); points.extend([pt[0],pt[1]])
52            face.move_current(1)
53        self.canvas.create_polygon(points, fill=colors[i], outline='black',
              width=1)
54 if __name__ == '__main__':
55    root = tk.Tk(); app = GeometricVisualizer(root); root.mainloop()
```

Additionally, in concave polyhedra, a face that is not culled may be entirely hidden behind another face, further complicating visibility determination. Although back-face culling does not resolve visibility issues in non-convex polyhedra, it is often used as a preprocessing step. This significantly accelerates visibility algorithms in complex and computationally demanding operations. For instance, by applying this technique during preprocessing, faces that are certainly not visible are immediately discarded, reducing the number of faces that need to be processed by more advanced algorithms. In practice, this technique typically eliminates about 50% of faces in the initial phase, which substantially speeds up further processing, particularly when using advanced methods such as the *Modified Painter's Algorithm*.

8.2 The 3D Rendering Pipeline: From Transformation to Illumination

The visualization of objects in space refers to the display of three-dimensional objects on two-dimensional devices such as computer screens, tablets, or mobile phones. In addition to projection, it enables interactive manipulations such as rotation, translation, scaling, and other transformations. To achieve this, it is essential to employ appropriate mathematical tools, including transformation matrices, projection methods for representing 3D objects on a 2D surface, and shading techniques, all of which will be discussed in detail in the following sections.

8.2.1 Transformation Matrices

Transformation Matrices represent a fundamental mathematical tool in graphics applications, enabling efficient and concise representation of transformations applied to graphical objects, which often consist of a large number of points. They are particularly important for understanding perspective projection, which will be discussed in the following section. Transformations include operations such as *translation, rotation, scaling, reflection*, and *shearing*, which can be combined to create more complex transformations.

8.2.1.1 Rotation Matrix

Let the point $M(x,y)$ lie on the unit circle centered at the origin $O(0,0)$, and let it be rotated counterclockwise by an angle γ with respect to the origin $O(0,0)$ (see Fig. 8.4 (c)). The coordinates of the rotated point $M_0(x_0,y_0)$, expressed using sine and cosine functions, take the form $x_0 = \cos(\gamma_0 + \gamma)$, $y_0 = \sin(\gamma_0 + \gamma)$, where γ_0 denotes the angle between point $M(x,y)$ and the positive x-axis in the xy-plane $(z = 0)$. By applying the *Addition Formulas*, the coordinates x_0 and y_0 can be rewritten as

$$x_0 = x\cos\gamma - y\sin\gamma, \quad y_0 = x\sin\gamma + y\cos\gamma.$$

These expressions can be compactly represented in matrix form as $M_0 = R_{z,\gamma} \cdot M$, that is,

$$\begin{pmatrix} x_0 \\ y_0 \end{pmatrix} = \begin{pmatrix} \cos\gamma & -\sin\gamma \\ \sin\gamma & \cos\gamma \end{pmatrix} \cdot \begin{pmatrix} x \\ y \end{pmatrix}, \tag{8.1}$$

where the points M and M_0 are represented as column vectors, while $R_{z,\gamma}$ denotes the rotation matrix about the z-axis by an angle γ. It is important to emphasize that the rotation is performed counterclockwise. If, instead, the rotation were performed clockwise, the angle γ in the matrix $R_{z,\gamma}$ would be replaced with $-\gamma$, as can be easily verified. The rotation of a point in space within a right-handed coordinate system about the x-, y-, or z-axis (see Fig. 8.5 (a)) can be carried out in a manner analogous to rotation in the plane. Specifically, consider rotating a point $M(x,y,z)$ about the z-axis by an angle γ. It is evident that the z-coordinate remains unchanged during this transformation. The corresponding 3D rotation matrix is obtained by augmenting the 2D rotation matrix with an additional row and column, where the first, second, and third columns correspond to the unit vectors $\vec{i} = (1,0,0)$, $\vec{j} = (0,1,0)$, and $\vec{k} = (0,0,1)$, respectively. Thus, the rotation of the point $M(x,y,z)$ by an angle γ about the z-axis (see Fig. 8.4 (c)) is given by $M_0 = R_{z,\gamma} \cdot M$, where the z-coordinate of the rotated point $M_0(x_0,y_0,z_0)$ remains unchanged, i.e., $z_0 = z$. A similar conclusion holds for rotation about the y-axis by an angle β (see Fig. 8.4 (b)) and about the x-axis by an angle α (see Fig. 8.4 (a)). In these cases, the coordinates x_0 and y_0 remain unchanged when rotating about the x-axis and y-axis, respectively. Based on these observations, the rotation matrices about the x-, y-, and z-axes for angles α, β, and γ, respectively, are given below:

$$R_{x,\alpha} = \begin{bmatrix} 1 & 0 & 0 \\ 0 & \cos\alpha & -\sin\alpha \\ 0 & \sin\alpha & \cos\alpha \end{bmatrix}, R_{y,\beta} = \begin{bmatrix} \cos\beta & 0 & \sin\beta \\ 0 & 1 & 0 \\ -\sin\beta & 0 & \cos\beta \end{bmatrix}, R_{z,\gamma} = \begin{bmatrix} \cos\gamma & -\sin\gamma & 0 \\ \sin\gamma & \cos\gamma & 0 \\ 0 & 0 & 1 \end{bmatrix}. \tag{8.2}$$

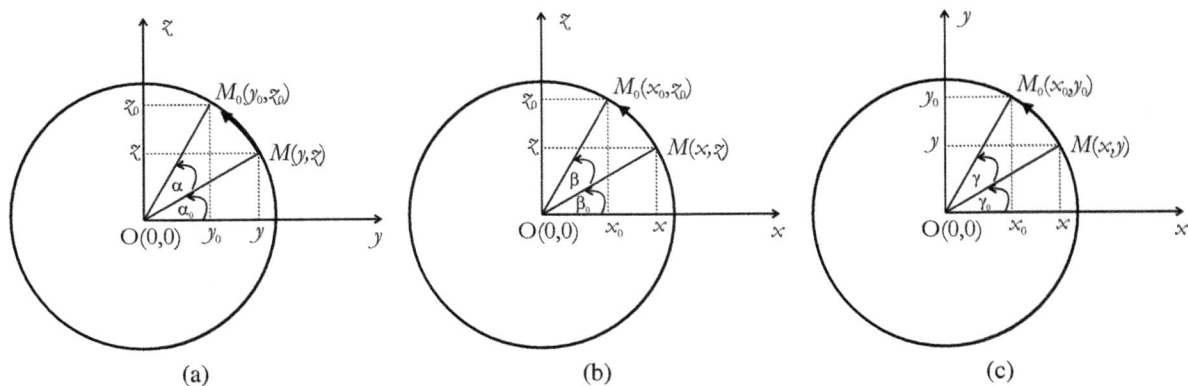

Figure 8.4: (a) Rotation about the x-axis by angle α. (b) Rotation about the y-axis by angle β. c) Rotation about the z-axis by angle γ.

8.2.1.2 Translation, Scaling, Reflection, and Shearing Matrices

A point $M(x,y)$ is translated along the vector (d_x, d_y) to a new point $M_0(x_0, y_0)$ by adding d_x to the x-coordinate and d_y to the y-coordinate, that is, $x_0 = x + d_x$, $y_0 = y + d_y$. More compactly, this can be expressed using homogeneous coordinates as $[x_0 \ y_0 \ 1]^T = T \cdot [x \ y \ 1]^T$, where T is the translation matrix. A point $M(x,y)$ is scaled to a new point $M_0(x_0, y_0)$ by multiplying its x- and y-coordinates by scaling factors s_x and s_y, respectively, so that $x_0 = s_x \cdot x$, $y_0 = s_y \cdot y$. In matrix form, this is written as $[x_0 \ y_0 \ 1]^T = S \cdot [x \ y \ 1]^T$, where S is the scaling matrix. Reflection of a point $M(x,y)$ can be performed with respect to the x-axis or y-axis. If the reflection is taken with respect to the x-axis, the point M is mapped to $M_0(x_0, y_0)$ where $x_0 = x$ and $y_0 = -y$. Similarly, reflection with respect to the y-axis gives $x_0 = -x$ and $y_0 = y$. These reflections can be expressed compactly as $[x_0 \ y_0 \ 1]^T = R_x \cdot [x \ y \ 1]^T$, $\quad [x_0 \ y_0 \ 1]^T = R_y \cdot [x \ y \ 1]^T$, where R_x and R_y are the reflection matrices with respect to the x- and y-axes, respectively. Shearing of a point $M(x,y)$ to a new point $M_0(x_0, y_0)$ is performed by assigning $y_0 = y$ and $x_0 = x + y \tan \beta$, where β is the shear angle. In matrix notation, this can be written as $[x_0 \ y_0 \ 1]^T = S_m \cdot [x \ y \ 1]^T$, where S_m is the shear matrix. Based on the above, the translation, scaling, reflection, and shear matrices are given below:

$$T = \begin{bmatrix} 1 & 0 & d_x \\ 0 & 1 & d_y \\ 0 & 0 & 1 \end{bmatrix}, S = \begin{bmatrix} s_x & 0 & 0 \\ 0 & s_y & 0 \\ 0 & 0 & 1 \end{bmatrix}, R_x = \begin{bmatrix} 1 & 0 & 0 \\ 0 & -1 & 0 \\ 0 & 0 & 1 \end{bmatrix}, R_y = \begin{bmatrix} -1 & 0 & 0 \\ 0 & 1 & 0 \\ 0 & 0 & 1 \end{bmatrix}, S_m = \begin{bmatrix} 1 & \tan \beta & 0 \\ 0 & 1 & 0 \\ 0 & 0 & 1 \end{bmatrix}.$$

It is evident that, for translating a point $M(x,y,z)$ along a vector (d_x, d_y, d_z), the translation matrix T is extended by adding a new row and column such that the last column contains the vector $[d_x \ d_y \ d_z \ 1]^T$. A similar procedure is followed to construct the corresponding matrices for scaling, reflection, and shearing transformations in three-dimensional space. To perform translation using matrix operations, homogeneous coordinates are introduced. These coordinates are particularly useful for matrix multiplication and for ensuring dimensional consistency. A point expressed in standard (non-homogeneous) coordinates is transformed into a point with homogeneous coordinates by introducing an additional coordinate w, which represents an extra dimension. Specifically, a point $P(x,y)$ in the plane or $P(x,y,z)$ in space is transformed into its homogeneous counterpart by multiplying each of its coordinates by w (typically set to 1), and then appending the coordinate w. In other words, homogenization replaces the point $P(x,y,z)$ with its homogeneous form $P(x,y,z,1)$. Conversion back from homogeneous to standard coordinates is performed by dividing all components of the homogeneous point by the value of w and discarding the last coordinate.

8.2.1.3 Composite Matrix Transformations

In many situations, it is necessary to perform composite matrix transformations. One common example is the composition of a translation and a rotation. Although such a composite transformation can be executed by applying the individual transformations sequentially (e.g., first performing the translation followed by the rotation, or vice versa), this approach is not recommended—especially when the composition involves a larger number of transformations and needs to be applied to a large set of points. For instance, consider a composite transformation consisting of a rotation followed by a translation, applied to a set of 1000 points. If this is implemented as a single matrix operation, the computation requires 9027 multiplications and 6018 additions. In contrast, if the translation and rotation are applied separately to each point, a total of 18,000 multiplications and 12,000 additions are required—more than double the number of operations. This difference becomes even more pronounced as the number of transformations in the composition increases, which is frequently the case in practice. A typical example is when an object must first be translated by the vector $(-d_x, -d_y)$, then scaled by the factors (s_x, s_y), rotated by an angle α about the z-axis, and finally translated back by the vector (d_x, d_y). This sequence of transformations can be efficiently expressed as a single composite transformation defined by $T \circ R \circ S \circ T^{-1}$. In some cases, it is necessary to rotate a 3D object not only around the coordinate axes x, y, and z, but also around an arbitrary line in space, or its direction vector. Without loss of generality, let us consider a counterclockwise rotation of a point $M(x, y, z)$ about a vector $\vec{v}$, with one endpoint at the origin O and the other at a point $A(x_1, y_1, z_1)$, as illustrated in Fig. 8.5 (b). The figure shows that the vector $\vec{v}$ can be defined in two ways. The first approach updates the Cartesian coordinates x_1, y_1, and z_1 of point A. The second approach expresses the direction of vector $\vec{v}$ using spherical angles θ and φ, where θ is the angle between the positive x-axis and the projection of $\vec{v}$ onto the xy-plane, and φ is the angle between vector $\vec{v}$ and the positive z-axis. If the coordinates of point A are given, then the angles θ and φ can be computed as $\theta = \arctan \frac{y_1}{x_1}$, $\varphi = \arctan \frac{\sqrt{x_1^2 + y_1^2}}{z_1}$.

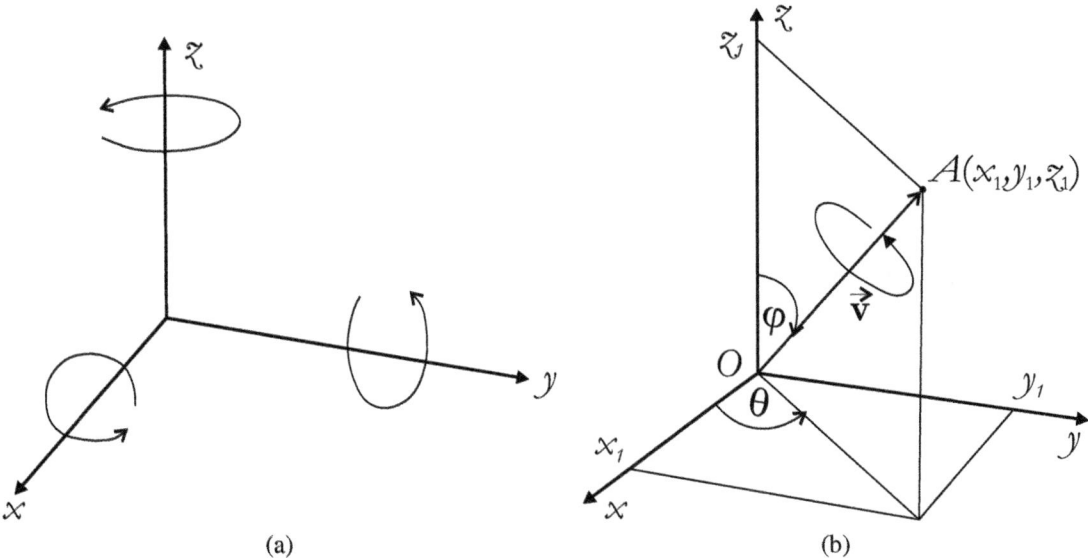

(a)   (b)

Figure 8.5: (a) Rotation about axes in a right-handed coordinate system. (b) Rotation of a point $M(x, y, z)$ about a vector $\vec{v}$.

The matrix R_α, which enables the rotation of a point $M(x, y, z)$ about a vector $\vec{v}$ by an angle α, is in fact a composite matrix transformation represented as the composition $R_\alpha = R_z^{-1} R_y^{-1} R_v R_y R_z$, where the matrices R_z, R_y, and R_v are defined below

$$R_z = \begin{bmatrix} \cos\theta & -\sin\theta & 0 \\ \sin\theta & \cos\theta & 0 \\ 0 & 0 & 1 \end{bmatrix}, R_y = \begin{bmatrix} \cos\varphi & 0 & \sin\varphi \\ 0 & 1 & 0 \\ -\sin\varphi & 0 & \cos\varphi \end{bmatrix}, R_v = \begin{bmatrix} \cos\alpha & -\sin\alpha & 0 \\ \sin\alpha & \cos\alpha & 0 \\ 0 & 0 & 1 \end{bmatrix},$$

while the inverse matrices R_z^{-1} and R_y^{-1} are obtained by substituting the angles θ and φ with $-\theta$ and $-\varphi$, respectively. The matrix R_α performs the rotation of the point $M(x,y,z)$ around the vector $\vec{v}$ by first aligning $\vec{v}$ with the z-axis using the composition R_yR_z, then applying the rotation R_v about the z-axis (which now corresponds to $\vec{v}$), and finally restoring the original orientation via the inverse transformation $R_z^{-1}R_y^{-1}$. Thus, the overall composition R_α effectively rotates the point $M(x,y,z)$ about the arbitrary vector $\vec{v}$. To optimize performance, especially when rotating an entire 3D object, it is more efficient to compute the matrix product representing the full composition once, rather than applying individual transformations to each point. The resulting matrix R_α can be expressed as

$$R_\alpha = \begin{bmatrix} a_1a_2a_3 - b_2b_3 & -a_1a_3b_2 - a_2b_3 & a_3b_1 \\ a_1a_2b_3 + a_3b_2 & -a_1b_2b_3 + a_2a_3 & b_1b_3 \\ -a_2b_1 & b_1b_2 & a_1 \end{bmatrix},$$

where $a_1 = \cos\varphi$, $a_2 = \cos\theta$, $a_3 = \cos(\alpha - 2\theta)$, $b_1 = \sin\varphi$, $b_2 = \sin\theta$, $b_3 = \sin(\alpha - 2\theta)$. This matrix formulation is particularly suitable for implementation, as it allows for a reduction in the number of arithmetic operations—for example, the product a_1a_2 appears multiple times and can be computed once and stored. The matrix R_α is used when the vector of rotation $\vec{v}$ has one endpoint at the coordinate origin. If this is not the case, the vector must first be translated so that its base lies at the origin. After performing the rotation using R_α, the inverse translation is applied to restore the vector to its original position. This sequence is expressed as the composition $T^{-1}R_\alpha T$, where T is a 4×4 translation matrix that translates points by (d_x, d_y, d_z), and T^{-1} is its inverse, performing translation by $(-d_x, -d_y, -d_z)$. In order to allow matrix multiplication within the composition, the matrix R_α must be extended with one row and one column—i.e., converted to homogeneous coordinates. Let R_k denote the product of the matrices in the composition, that is, $R_k = (T^{-1})^T R_\alpha^T T^T$. Then, after applying the rotation of a point $M(x,y,z)$ about the vector $\vec{v}$, the transformed point $M_0(x_0, y_0, z_0)$ is obtained as $[x_0\ y_0\ z_0\ 1] = [x\ y\ z\ 1]R_k$.

8.2.2 Perspective Projection and View Transformation

Perspective projection is widely used in painting to depict realistic three-dimensional objects, relying on a natural visual perception similar to that produced by photography. Since a photograph represents a projection from three-dimensional to two-dimensional space, perspective projection also plays a central role in the human visual system. A key phenomenon associated with this type of projection is known as *Perspective Foreshortening*, which refers to the fact that, in perspective projection, the apparent size of an object varies inversely with its distance from the eye or camera. There exists a strong analogy between the human eye and the photographic camera. Although the camera merely imitates the function of the eye, it will be used in the subsequent discussion as a reference viewing point from which object visualization is performed. Accordingly, it is important to note that the visual appearance of objects depends on the position of the viewing point.

Let the coordinate axes x, y, and z of the *world*, *camera*, and *screen* coordinate systems be denoted by x^w, x^c, x^s, y^w, y^c, y^s, z^w, and z^c, respectively. It is important to note that the world coordinates x^w, y^w, and z^w correspond to the axes of a standard Cartesian coordinate system and will therefore be denoted simply as x, y, and z in the remainder of the text. To project a 3D object defined in world coordinates (x, y, z) onto the screen, it is first necessary to transform these coordinates into camera coordinates (x^c, y^c, z^c) via the *view transformation*, and subsequently apply a perspective projection to obtain screen coordinates (x^s, y^s). The view transformation defines how a 3D object, centered at the origin $O(0,0,0)$, is visualized from the viewing point O_c of the camera coordinate system (see Fig. 8.6 (a)). If the object is not initially centered

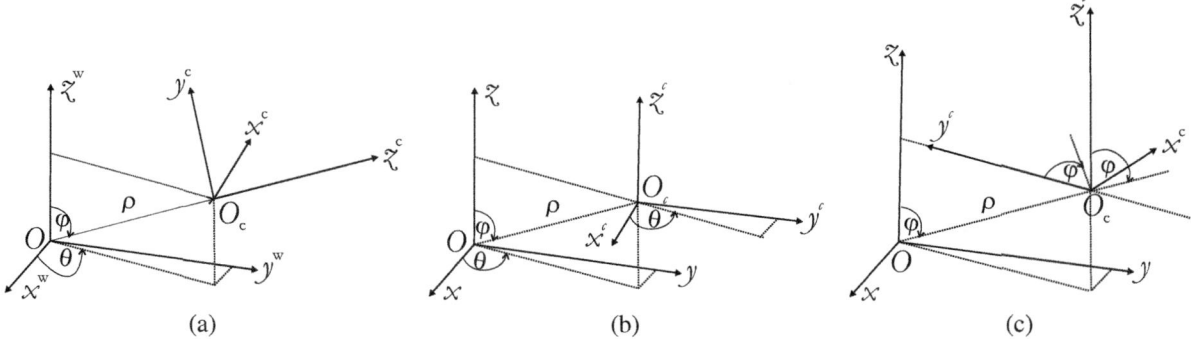

Figure 8.6: (a) Camera coordinate system. (b) Rotation about the z-axis. (c) Rotation about the x-axis.

at the origin, it can be easily repositioned as part of the implementation process. Let the viewing point (camera position) O_c be specified in spherical coordinates (ρ, φ, θ), such that

$$x_1^c = \rho \sin \varphi \cos \theta, \quad y_1^c = \rho \sin \varphi \sin \theta, \quad z_1^c = \rho \cos \varphi,$$

where ρ is the norm of the vector $\overrightarrow{OO_c}$, and the angles φ and θ carry the same meaning as previously defined. The point O_c corresponds to the point $A(x_1, y_1, z_1)$ in Cartesian coordinates (see Fig. 8.5 (b)). The camera coordinate system $O_c(x^c, y^c, z^c)$ is constructed by placing its origin at the viewing point O_c such that its z^c-axis aligns with the line $q(O, O_c)$ passing through the origin and O_c, while its x^c- and y^c-axes are orthogonal to this line (see Fig. 8.6 (a)). Given a point (x, y, z) in world coordinates, its corresponding camera coordinates (x^c, y^c, z^c) are obtained via the transformation:

$$\begin{bmatrix} x^c & y^c & z^c & 1 \end{bmatrix} = \begin{bmatrix} x & y & z & 1 \end{bmatrix} \cdot M_p,$$

where the view matrix M_p is a 4×4 matrix defined as the product

$$M_p = (T^{-1})^T R_z^T R_x^T,$$

with $(T^{-1})^T$ denoting the inverse translation matrix, and R_z^T and R_x^T representing the transposed rotation matrices about the z-axis and x-axis, respectively. These matrices are of size 4×4 and are presented below:

$$(T^{-1})^T = \begin{bmatrix} 1 & 0 & 0 & 0 \\ 0 & 1 & 0 & 0 \\ 0 & 0 & 1 & 0 \\ -x_1^c & -y_1^c & -z_1^c & 0 \end{bmatrix}, R_z^T = \begin{bmatrix} -\sin \theta & -\cos \theta & 0 & 0 \\ \cos \theta & -\sin \theta & 0 & 0 \\ 0 & 0 & 1 & 0 \\ 0 & 0 & 0 & 1 \end{bmatrix}, R_x^T = \begin{bmatrix} 1 & 0 & 0 & 0 \\ 0 & \cos \varphi & -\sin \varphi & 0 \\ 0 & \sin \varphi & \cos \varphi & 0 \\ 0 & 0 & 0 & 1 \end{bmatrix}.$$

In the composite matrix M_p, the inverse translation matrix T^{-1} translates the camera origin O_c to the origin of the world coordinate system O. The matrix R_z performs a rotation of the world coordinate system $Oxyz$ about the z-axis by an angle of $-(\theta + \pi/2)$ (see Fig. 8.6 (b)), while the matrix R_x rotates it about the x-axis by an angle of $-(\varphi + \pi/2)$ (see Fig. 8.6 (c)). Accordingly, the resulting matrix M_p, after matrix multiplication, takes the following form:

$$M_p = \begin{bmatrix} -\sin \theta & -\cos \varphi \cos \theta & \sin \varphi \cos \theta & 0 \\ \cos \theta & -\cos \varphi \sin \theta & \sin \varphi \sin \theta & 0 \\ 0 & \sin \varphi & \cos \varphi & 0 \\ 0 & 0 & -\rho & 1 \end{bmatrix}.$$

If the coordinate z_c is discarded, the remaining camera coordinates x_c and y_c are said to represent an orthographic projection. Since orthographic projection does not produce realistic images, the following section will describe how perspective images (i.e., 2D representations) can be mathematically generated from 3D objects.

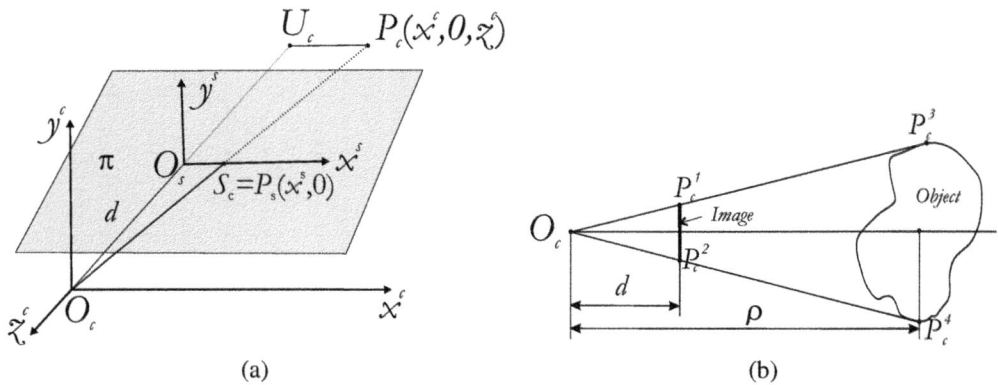

Figure 8.7: (a) Determination of screen coordinates. (b) Determination of the distance d.

Without loss of generality, let $P_c(x^c, y^c, z^c)$ be an arbitrarily chosen but fixed point in the camera coordinate system that is to be projected onto the screen point $P_s(x^s, y^s)$. Let there be a projection plane π located between the point P_c and the viewing point (eye of camera) O_c, such that the line p defined by the points P_c and O_c intersects the plane π at the point S_c (see Fig. 8.7 (a)). In this figure, the projection plane π is in fact the plane $z^c = -d$, which contains the point $O_s(0, 0, -d)$ and is orthogonal to the z^c-axis. The value d represents the distance between the points O_c and O_s. The point O_s is defined as the origin of the screen coordinate system, where its axes x^s and y^s are parallel to the corresponding axes of the camera coordinate system, i.e., $x^c \parallel x^s$ and $y^c \parallel y^s$. Furthermore, the point S_c in the camera coordinate system has coordinates $(x^s, 0)$, that is, $S_c = P_s(x^s, 0)$. For simplicity, assume that the y^c-coordinate of the point P_c is zero, and let U_c denote the projection of the point P_c onto the z^c-axis. From the similarity of triangles $\triangle O_c P_c U_c$ and $\triangle O_c S_c O_s$, it follows that hold $\frac{P_c U_c}{S_c O_s} = \frac{O_c U_c}{O_c O_s}$. This implies the relationship $\frac{x^c}{x^s} = \frac{-z^c}{d}$, so that $x^s = -d \cdot \frac{x^c}{z^c}$. Similarly, it holds $y^s = -d \cdot \frac{y^c}{z^c}$. These formulas for the screen coordinates x^s and y^s are valid under the assumption that the point O_s lies at the center of the screen or drawing surface. If, instead, the center of the screen is located at the bottom-left corner, the screen coordinates must be shifted by adding $WC/2$ and $HC/2$, respectively, where WC and HC represent the width and height of the canvas. It remains to determine the distance d between the viewing point O_c and the projection plane π, or equivalently, the screen. This distance can be computed based on the similarity of triangles $\triangle O_c P_c^1 P_c^2$ and $\triangle O_c P_c^3 P_c^4$ (see Fig. 8.7 (b)). From their similarity, one obtains the expression $d = \rho \cdot \frac{DC}{DO}$, where ρ is the distance from the viewing point O_c to the center of the object, while DC and DO denote the dimensions of the canvas (e.g., width or height) and the object, respectively. In practice, the object size is typically approximated by taking the maximum among its height, width, and depth. The same approach is used for estimating the canvas size.

8.2.3 Shading of Objects

In computer graphics, object shading refers to the process of determining the surface color of a 3D object in order to achieve a photorealistic appearance and convey a sense of volume. This effect depends on the surface orientation relative to the light source, as well as its distance from it. In essence, shading involves coloring the object's surface based on illumination conditions. From a physics perspective, when light strikes a surface, it may be absorbed, reflected, or refracted. Absorbed light is converted into heat, while reflected and refracted light enables the object to become visible to the human eye. To simulate these phenomena, mathematical shading models are employed, which approximate complex physical processes. The models presented in this section are *local illumination models*, meaning they do not account for secondary reflections—that is, light that has been reflected by multiple surfaces before reaching the viewer. According to the principles of optical physics, shading is governed by three key components. The first is *reflection*, where a portion of the light is reflected off the object's surface. The second is *refraction*, where light passes through transparent materials and exits on the opposite side. The third is *absorption*, in which part of the light is absorbed by the surface and transformed into heat. Since only reflection and refraction contribute to the visual perception of an object, they determine the apparent color and brightness of its surface. The color of an object depends on the intensity of the reflected and refracted light, which in turn is influenced by the wavelength of the incident light and the material's absorption properties. Accurate computation of reflection and refraction requires knowledge of the light's spectral distribution, surface reflectivity and transmissivity, as well as factors such as geometry, texture, optical properties of the material, and the position of the light source. Due to the complexity of these parameters, practical shading models rely on approximations tailored to specific applications. Basic shading models assume point light sources and opaque objects with smooth surfaces, neglecting refraction and ambient diffuse light. Moreover, since light absorption does not contribute to the visual effect, it is typically excluded from these models, which focus solely on reflection.

8.2.3.1 Types of Light and Illumination

This section outlines the types of illumination used to model the interaction of light with specific points on the surface of a 3D object in order to determine its shading. The shade at a given surface point depends on multiple factors, including ambient and diffuse light, specular reflection (governed by the material's reflectivity), light refraction, inter-object reflection, shadows, and material properties such as transparency, texture, and surface relief. An illumination model also considers:

- *light source attributes* – shape, intensity, color, position, and direction of light;
- *object surface attributes* – color, reflectivity, and transparency;
- *light-object interaction* – the object's orientation in space;
- *object-observer interaction* – viewing direction.

Illumination types are categorized into local (direct light) and global (indirect light) models. Local illumination models account only for fundamental factors: the light source, observer position, and object material properties. In contrast, global illumination models incorporate more complex interactions, where light reflected from other objects in the scene contributes to the final appearance of the illuminated object.

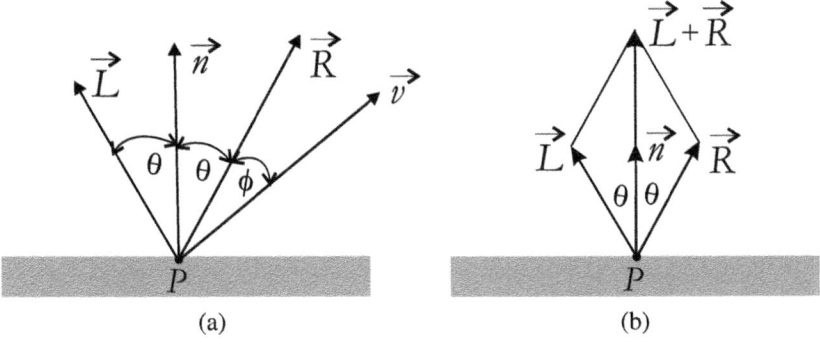

Figure 8.8: (a) Specular reflection. (b) Light, normal, and reflection vectors.

Ambient Lighting arises from background light that diffuses throughout the environment and serves as a simplified approximation of global illumination. It is generated by the reflection of light from other objects in the scene, where ambient reflection plays a key role in producing diffuse lighting that softens harsh shadows and enhances spatial perception. The intensity of ambient reflected light I_A can be approximated using the formula $I_A = L_A M_A$, where L_A denotes the intensity of ambient illumination in the scene, and M_A represents the ambient reflection coefficient of the object, which depends on the material properties. This coefficient ranges between 0 and 1 for each of the RGB color components. Unlike other lighting models, ambient light does not depend on the position of the light source, the orientation of the object in the scene, or the viewing angle. Moreover, the surface normal and the direction of the incoming light are not considered. Different materials reflect varying amounts of ambient light, thereby influencing their perceived appearance in a virtual scene.

Diffuse Lighting refers to a type of illumination in which light, upon striking a surface, is reflected uniformly in all directions. Consequently, the intensity of the reflected light does not depend on the observer's position, but solely on the direction of the incoming light. The key factor in computing diffuse lighting is the amount of light a surface receives from the light source. This form of illumination is based on Lambert's cosine law, which models the behavior of an ideal diffusely reflecting surface. Such a surface reflects light equally in every direction, resulting in a constant perceived color and light intensity regardless of the viewer's position, provided that the illumination is uniform. According to Lambert's law, the intensity of diffuse reflection I_D at point P is proportional to the cosine of the angle $\theta = \angle(\vec{L}, \vec{n})$ between the direction of incoming light $\vec{L}$ and the surface normal vector $\vec{n}$ (see Fig. 8.9 (b)). Thus, the diffuse reflection intensity is given by the formula $I_D = I_d K_d \cos\theta = I_d K_d (\vec{L} \cdot \vec{n})$, where I_d is the intensity of the light striking the surface, and $K_d \in (0,1)$ is the diffuse reflection coefficient. This formula implies that I_D is influenced solely by the angle of incoming light and is independent of the viewing angle or reflection direction. It is evident that I_D reaches its maximum (minimum) when θ is zero (ninety) degrees. If $\theta < 0$, the light source is positioned behind the surface, and the light does not reach point P. In the RGB color model, the diffuse reflection coefficient K_d consists of three components—K_{dr}, K_{dg}, and K_{db}—corresponding to red, green, and blue reflection coefficients, respectively. These components together define the surface color. Similarly, the light intensity I_d may be divided into three components—I_r, I_g, and I_b—allowing the surface to be shaded by assigning these respective values.

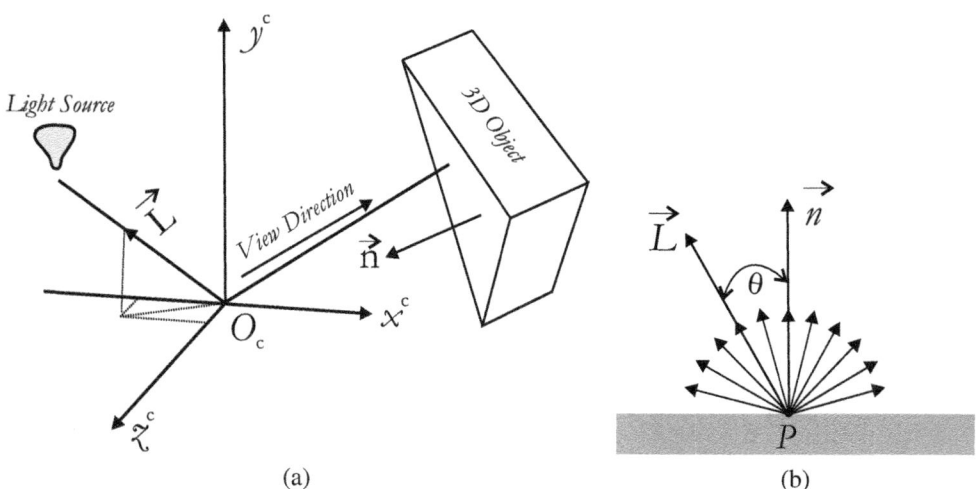

(a)   (b)

Figure 8.9: (a) Light source vector $\vec{L}$, unit normal vector of the face $\vec{n}$. (b) Diffuse reflection at point P.

Specular Lighting is based on the Phong illumination model and describes the way light reflects off smooth, glossy surfaces such as metal or polished glass. While diffuse lighting yields realistic results for rough surfaces (e.g., walls or paper), it does not account for mirror-like reflections that occur on smooth surfaces exposed to a light source. When a light ray strikes a smooth surface, a specular reflection is produced. Let $\vec{n}$ be the surface normal at point P, and let $\phi \in [0, \pi/2]$ denote the angle between the normal vector $\vec{n}$ and the viewing direction vector $\vec{v}$ (see Fig. 8.8 (a)). The incident light ray is then reflected symmetrically with respect to the normal, producing a reflection vector $\vec{R}$ forming the same angle θ on the opposite side. The vector $\vec{R}$ is computed using a unit parallelogram, as illustrated in Fig. 8.8 (b)). Since both $\vec{R}$ and $\vec{L}$ are unit vectors, the projection of $\vec{L}$ onto $\vec{n}$ equals $\vec{L} \cdot \vec{n} = \cos \theta$, and the length of the vector $\vec{L} + \vec{R}$ is $2 \cos \theta$. Thus, the reflection vector is given by $\vec{R} = (2 \cos \theta, \vec{n} - \vec{L})$. Specular reflection, as defined by the Phong model, is computed using the formula $I_S = I_d K_s (\cos \varphi)^n = I_d K_s (\vec{v} \cdot \vec{R})^n$, where K_s is the specular reflection coefficient, and n is the Phong exponent. This formula indicates that specular reflection depends on the viewing direction and the intensity of the incoming light. Specifically, for fixed values of I_d and K_s, the reflection is strongest when $\phi = 0$. Moreover, the intensity gradually diminishes as the viewing direction $\vec{v}$ diverges from the reflection vector $\vec{R}$. Taking into account all three types of illumination described—ambient, diffuse, and specular—the resulting realistic lighting according to the Phong model is given by the sum $I = I_A + I_D + I_S$.

8.2.3.2 Shading Models

This section presents three algorithms corresponding to three distinct shading models: *Flat Shading*, *Gouraud Shading*, and *Phong Shading*. In flat shading, lighting is computed at a single point per polygon. Specifically, only one vertex, its associated normal, and material properties are considered for a given planar polygon, and the entire polygon is rendered using the same shade. The primary advantage of flat shading lies in its computational efficiency, as only one lighting calculation is required per polygon. However, compared to other shading models such as Phong, Gouraud, Blinn-Phong, or Lambertian, flat shading produces visibly sharp polygon edges, significantly reducing the realism of the rendered objects. Despite its limitations, flat shading can be effectively used when polygons are sufficiently small, the light source is relatively distant, or the observer is far from the object. The following explanation outlines how a polygon can be shaded depending on its orientation relative to the light source. Let the polygon lie in a plane π described by the equation $ax + by + cz = h$, where $\vec{n} = (a, b, c)$ is the unit normal vector to the plane, satisfying $a^2 + b^2 + c^2 = 1$. Furthermore, let $\vec{L} = \frac{1}{\sqrt{3}}(-1, 1, 1)$ denote the unit vector representing the light direction, oriented from the object toward the light source in the camera coordinate system (see Fig. 8.9 (a)). The intensity of reflected light (which determines the color code) can be computed as the dot product $\vec{n} \cdot \vec{L}$ and is typically modeled using RGB components. It is important to note that in the camera coordinate system, the x-axis points from the object toward the observer. Therefore, the negative sign in the x-component of $\vec{L}$ indicates that the light source is positioned in front of the object. Clearly, a larger dot product $\vec{n} \cdot \vec{L}$ results in a brighter color for the rendered 3D triangle.

Following the theoretical and mathematical analysis of visualization and shading methods for 3D objects, the subsequent section presents the implementation. To realize the visualization, a class named **Object3D** has been developed, whose definition is provided in Listing 8.2.

Listing 8.2: Definition of the class **Object3D**

```
1 import math
2 from typing import List
3 from geometry import Point2D, Point3D, Triangle3D
4 class Object3D:
5     def __init__(self):
6         #Attributes related to the camera and screen
7         self.d=self.rho=self.min_rho=self.max_rho=0.0
8         self.phi=1.3; self.theta=0.3
```

```
9       #Dimensions of 3D object
10      self.min_x=self.min_y=self.min_z=float('inf')
11      self.max_x=self.max_y=self.max_z=float('-inf')
12      #Attributes for shading object
13      self.range_scal_prod=0.0; self.screen_center=Point2D(0.0, 0.0)
14      self.min_scal_prod= float('inf'); self.max_scal_prod=float('-inf')
15      self.world_points:List[Point3D]=[]; self.camera_points:List[Point3D]=[]
16      self.screen_points:List[Point2D]=[]
17      self.triangle_list:List[Triangle3D]=[]
18      self.render_triangles:List[Triangle2D]=[]; sqrt3=math.sqrt(3.0)
19      self.light=Point3D(-1.0/sqrt3,1.0/sqrt3,1.0/sqrt3)
20  def get_color_code(self, pt: Point3D) -> int:
21      dot = pt*self.light
22      return round(((dot-self.min_scal_prod)/self.range_scal_prod)*255)
23  def get_render_triangles(self) -> List[Triangle2D]:return self.
        render_triangles
24  def get_camera_points(self)-> List[Point3D]: self.camera_points
25  def get_screen_center(self) -> Point2D: return self.screen_center
26  def get_light(self) -> Point3D:return self.light
27  def add_triangles(self, triangles: List[Triangle3D]): pass
28  def center_object(self): pass
29  def determine_rho(self): pass
30  def update_angles(self, dt:float, dp:float, dr:float)->bool: pass
31  def calculate_camera_and_screen_coordinates(self,width:int,height:int): pass
32  def set_plane_coefficients(self): pass
33  def shade_triangles(self): pass
```

The **Object3D** class encapsulates the essential methods and attributes required for the visualization and shading of three-dimensional objects, thereby enabling a realistic rendering of geometric scenes. Building upon the previously established mathematical foundations, this section presents the implementation of the class methods in the Python programming language. The class constructor is defined within the class declaration itself, where it performs the initialization of all relevant attributes. Notably, the unit light vector is set using the attribute self.light, which determines the direction and intensity of lighting used in the shading process. To facilitate the input of a 3D object represented as a collection of triangles, the method *add_triangles*(·) is implemented. This method is responsible for accepting and storing the triangle data necessary for rendering. Its implementation is given below:

```
1 def add_triangles(self, triangles: List[Triangle3D]):
2   for tr in triangles:
3       self.triangle_list.append(tr)
4       for i in range(3):
5           pt = tr[i]
6           self.max_x=max(self.max_x,pt[0]);self.min_x=min(self.min_x, pt[0])
7           self.max_y=max(self.max_y,pt[1]);self.min_y=min(self.min_y, pt[1])
8           self.max_z=max(self.max_z,pt[2]);self.min_z=min(self.min_z,pt[2])
9           self.world_points.append(Point3D(pt[0], pt[1], pt[2]))
10  self.center_object(); self.determine_rho()
```

The method *add_triangles*(·) inserts the vertices of the triangles into the list self.world_points, accepting them over a formal parameter in the form of a list. Simultaneously, it computes the minimum and maximum coordinate values, which are subsequently used for approximate estimation of the object's dimensions. In addition, this method invokes two member functions: *center_object*() and *determine_rho*(). The method *center_object*() translates the center of the 3D object toward the origin point $O(0,0,0)$ by shifting all points of the object along the vector $(-\frac{min\_x+max\_x}{2}, -\frac{min\_y+max\_y}{2}, -\frac{min\_z+max\_z}{2})$. Although the object could be precisely centered at the origin by computing its centroid, the presented method of translation is sufficient for practical rendering purposes. Owing to its clear logic, the implementation of the method is straightforward and intuitive, as illustrated in the following code excerpt:

```python
def center_object(self):
    cx=(self.min_x+self.max_x)/2.0; cy=(self.min_y+self.max_y)/2.0
    cz=(self.min_z+self.max_z)/2.0
    for p in self.world_points: p[0]-=cx; p[1]-=cy; p[2]-=cz
```

The method *determine_rho*() approximates the distance between the object's center and the viewpoint O_c.

```python
def determine_rho(self):
    dx=self.max_x-self.min_x; dy=self.max_y-self.min_y; dz=self.max_z-self.min_z
    self.min_rho=0.6*math.sqrt(dx**2+dy**2+dz**2)
    self.rho=3*self.min_rho; self.max_rho=1000*self.min_rho
```

Since the rotation of the 3D object is performed using the angles φ and θ, it is necessary to implement the method *update_angles*($\cdot,\cdot,\cdot$), which updates the values of the attributes φ, θ, and ρ via formal parameters. It is evident that if the object needs to be rotated left/right or forward/backward, a value of 1.0 should be passed as the third parameter of this method. After updating the value of the attribute ρ, it is essential to verify whether the new value falls within the interval (min_rho, max_rho). If it does not, the previous value of the attribute ρ is retained, as demonstrated in the implementation below:

```python
def update_angles(self, dt:float, dp:float, dr:float)->bool:
    self.theta+=dt; self.phi+=dp; new_rho=dr*self.rho
    if new_rho>self.min_rho and new_rho<self.max_rho:
        self.rho = new_rho; return True
    return False
```

The next highly important method of the class **Object3D** is *calculate_camera_and_screen_coordinates*($\cdot,\cdot$).

```python
def calculate_camera_and_screen_coordinates(self, width:int, height:int)->float:
    self.screen_points.clear(); self.camera_points.clear()
    sinf=math.sin(self.phi); cosf=math.cos(self.phi)
    sint=math.sin(self.theta); cost=math.cos(self.theta)
    a12=-cosf*cost; a13=sinf*cost; a22=-cosf*sint; a23=sinf*sint
    min_sx=min_sy=float('inf'); max_sx=max_sy=float('-inf')
    for pt in self.world_points:
        xc=-sint*pt[0]+cost*pt[1]
        yc=pt[0]*a12+pt[1]*a22+pt[2]*sinf
        zc=pt[0]*a13+pt[1]*a23+pt[2]*cosf-self.rho
        self.camera_points.append(Point3D(xc,yc,zc))
        xs=-xc/zc; ys=-yc/zc;
        self.screen_points.append(Point2D(xs,ys))
        min_sx=min(min_sx,xs); max_sx=max(max_sx,xs)
        min_sy=min(min_sy,ys); max_sy=max(max_sy,ys)
    delta_x=max_sx-min_sx; delta_y=max_sy-min_sy
    self.d=0.95*min(width/delta_x,height/delta_y)
    self.screen_center=Point2D(self.d*(max_sx+min_sx)/2,self.d*(max_sy+min_sy)/2)
    for pt in self.screen_points: pt[0]*=self.d; pt[1]*=self.d
    return self.d*max(delta_x,delta_y)
```

It remains to implement the member functions *set_plane_coefficients*() and *shade_triangles*(). The method *set_plane_coefficients*() will be implemented first, in accordance with the theoretical background previously presented.

```python
def set_plane_coefficients(self):
    for i in range(0, len(self.triangle_list), 2):
        tr=Triangle3D(self.camera_points[3*i],self.camera_points[3*i+1],self.
            camera_points[3*i+2],0)
        normal=tr.get_normal(); d=normal*tr[0]; dot=normal*self.light
        self.triangle_list[i].update_plane(normal,d)
        self.triangle_list[i+1].update_plane(normal,d)
        self.min_scal_prod=min(self.min_scal_prod,dot)
        self.max_scal_prod=max(self.max_scal_prod,dot)
    self.range_scal_prod=self.max_scal_prod-self.min_scal_prod
```

The method *shade_triangles*() appends 2D triangles to the list `render_triangles`. These planar triangles are constructed based on the screen coordinates of the corresponding 3D triangles. To enable shading, their color is determined by invoking the method *get_color_code*(·), whose implementation is grounded in the theoretical framework previously discussed.

```python
def shade_triangles(self):
    self.render_triangles.clear()
    for i in range(len(self.triangle_list)):
        tr=Triangle2D(
            A=self.screen_points[3*i],
            B=self.screen_points[3*i+1],
            C=self.screen_points[3*i+2],
            code=self.get_color_code(self.triangle_list[i].get_plane_coeff())
            d=(self.camera_points[3*i][2]+self.camera_points[3*i+1][2]+self.
                camera_points[3*i+2][2])/3
        )
        self.render_triangles.append(tr)
```

For the purposes of the **Object3D** class, a triangle in the plane is constructed as follows:

```python
from dataclasses import dataclass
@dataclass
class Triangle2D:
    A: Point2D
    B: Point2D
    C: Point2D
    code: int = 0
    d:    float=0.0 # depth
```

Upon completing the design of the **Object3D** class, it is subsequently employed for the visualization of two cuboids, as depicted in Fig. 8.10. This is achieved using the implementation provided in Listing 8.3.

Listing 8.3: Simple GUI for Visualization of 3D Objects with Shading

```python
import tkinter as tk
from tkinter import Canvas
import math
from geometry import Point2D,Point3D,Triangle3D
from Object3D import Object3D
```

```python
6  class Visualizer3DApp:
7      def __init__(self, root):
8          self.root=root; ww=800; wh=550 #define window width and height
9          self.root.title("Visualization of 3D Objects with Shading")
10         sw=root.winfo_screenwidth(); sh=root.winfo_screenheight()
11         x=(sw//2)-(ww//2); y=(sh//2)-(wh//2)#Centering of window
12         root.geometry(f"{ww}x{wh}+{x}+{y}")#Setting the window geometry
13         root.resizable(False, False) #Disable size of window
14         self.main_frame = tk.Frame(self.root, bg="gray")# Main Frame
15         self.main_frame.pack(fill=tk.BOTH, expand=True)
16         # Canvas for object rendering
17         self.canvas=Canvas(self.main_frame,bg="white",width=600,height=500)
18         self.canvas.pack(side=tk.LEFT, padx=10, pady=10)
19         self.button_frame = tk.Frame(self.main_frame, bg="gray")
20         self.button_frame.pack(side=tk.RIGHT, padx=10, pady=10)
21         self.create_buttons() # Create four buttons
22         self.triangles=[]; self.create_cuboids() # Create objects
23         self.create_3d_objects(); self.draw_3d_objects("red")
24     def iX(self, y:float, w:int, p:Point2D)-> int: return round(w//2-y+float(p[1])
           )
25     def iY(self, y:float, h:int,p:Point2D)-> int: return round(h//2-y+float(p[1]))
26     def create_cuboids(self):
27         coords=[
28             (0, 0.624, 4.79), (0, 0.624, 0), (0, 0, 0), (0, 0, 4.79),
29             (1, 0.624, 4.79), (1, 0.624, 0), (1, 0, 0), (1, 0, 4.79),
30             (4.79, -0.624, 0), (-3, -0.624, 0), (-3, 0, 0), (4.79, 0, 0),
31             (4.79, -0.624, 1), (-3, -0.624, 1), (-3, 0, 1), (4.79, 0, 1)
32         ]
33         pts=[Point3D(x, y, z) for x, y, z in coords]
34         i1=[(0,1,2),(0,2,3),(6,5,4),(6,4,7),(0,4,5),(0,5,1),
35             (1,5,6),(1,6,2),(2,6,7),(2,7,3),(3,7,4),(3,4,0)]
36         i2=[(8,9,10),(8,10,11),(14,13,12),(14,12,15),(8,12,13),(8,13,9),
37             (9,13,14), (9,14,10),(10,14,15),(10,15,11),(11,15,12),(11,12,8)]
38         t1=[Triangle3D(pts[i],pts[j],pts[k],l) for l,(i,j,k) in enumerate(i1)]
39         t2=[Triangle3D(pts[i],pts[j],pts[k],l+12) for l,(i,j,k) in enumerate(i2)]
40         self.triangles.extend(t1[:12] + t2[:12])
41     def create_3d_objects(self):
42         self.object_3d=Object3D()
43         self.object_3d.add_triangles(self.triangles)
44     def draw_3d_objects(self, color):
45         #Set parameters before drawing
46         width=int(self.canvas.cget("width"))
47         height=int(self.canvas.cget("height"))
48         self.object_3d.calculate_camera_and_screen_coordinates(width,height)
49         c_i=self.object_3d.get_screen_center() #center of image
50         self.object_3d.set_plane_coefficients()
51         self.object_3d.shade_triangles()
52         # The rendering of the objects onto the canvas
53         rendering_tr=self.object_3d.get_render_triangles(); alpha=255
54         for tr in rendering_tr:
55             a, b, c, code = tr.A, tr.B, tr.C, tr.code
56             R, G, B = [x//256 for x in self.canvas.winfo_rgb(color)]
57             r_c=int(code*R/alpha); g_c=int(code*G/alpha); b_c=int(code*B/alpha)
58             f_color = f"#{r_c:02x}{g_c:02x}{b_c:02x}"
59             x1,y1=self.iX(a[0],width-1,c_i),self.iY(a[1],height-1,c_i)
60             x2,y2=self.iX(b[0],width-1,c_i),self.iY(b[1],height-1,c_i)
61             x3,y3=self.iX(c[0],width-1,c_i),self.iY(c[1],height-1,c_i)
62             self.canvas.create_polygon(x1,y1,x2,y2,x3,y3,fill=f_color,outline="")
```

```python
63    def create_buttons(self):
64        buttons=[
65            ("U","red","white",self.move_up,0,1,5,0),
66            ("D","green","white",self.move_down,2,1,5,0),
67            ("L","blue","white",self.move_left,1,0,0,5),
68            ("R","yellow","black",self.move_right,1,2,0,5)
69        ]
70        for t,b,f,cd,r,c,y,x in buttons:
71            tk.Button(self.button_frame,text=t,bg=b,fg=f,font=("Arial",16),
72            command=cd).grid(row=r,column=c,pady=y,padx=x)
73    def move_left(self):
74        self.canvas.delete("all")
75        if self.object_3d.update_angles(0.1,0.0,1.0): self.draw_3d_objects("red")
76    def move_right(self):
77        self.canvas.delete("all")
78        if self.object_3d.update_angles(-0.1,0.0,1.0): self.draw_3d_objects("red")
79    def move_up(self):
80        self.canvas.delete("all")
81        if self.object_3d.update_angles(0.0,0.1,1.0): self.draw_3d_objects("red")
82    def move_down(self):
83        self.canvas.delete("all")
84        if self.object_3d.update_angles(0.0,-0.1,1.0): self.draw_3d_objects("red")
85
86 if __name__ == "__main__":
87 root = tk.Tk()
88 app = Visualizer3DApp(root)
89 root.mainloop()
```

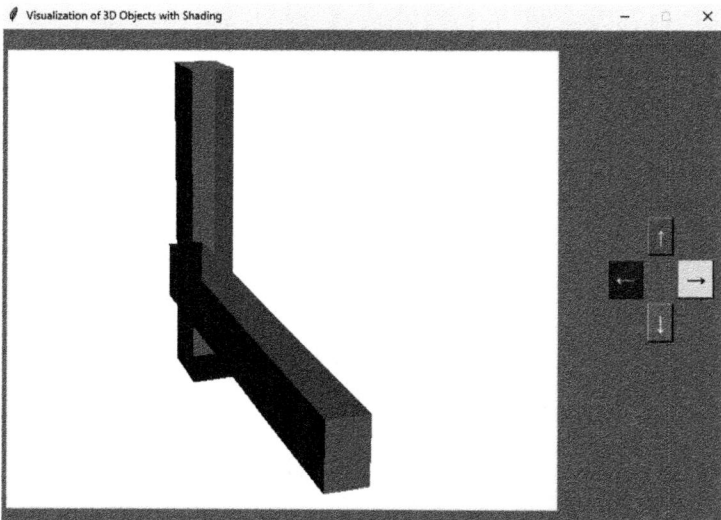

Figure 8.10: Visualization of Two Cuboids in 3D Space with Shading.

Within Listing 8.3, the function *create_cuboids*() defines the cuboids through a list of their vertices, based on which the list of triangles self.triangles is constructed. Subsequently, the method *create_3d_objects*() instantiates the object self.object_3d of the **Object3D** class, upon which the method *add_triangles*(·) is invoked, with the previously created list self.triangles passed as an actual parameter. Finally, the function *draw_3d_objects*(·) is called to render the cuboids on the canvas. This function internally invokes the methods *iX*(·,·,·) and *iY*(·,·,·), which perform coordinate translation in the context of 2D visualization.

8.3 Painter's Algorithm

The painter's algorithm, also known as the depth-sorting algorithm, is inspired by the traditional technique employed by painters, particularly when working with oil paints. Artists typically begin by painting the background and then progressively add elements, starting with those furthest from the viewer and advancing toward the foreground. In doing so, closer objects partially or fully occlude those behind them, effectively removing the hidden parts from view. This concept can be extended to the visualization of 3D objects, where object faces are rendered in order, starting from the most distant relative to the viewpoint and subsequently overlaying nearer faces. Naturally, this approach is only feasible when the rendering medium supports pixel-level color overwriting, such as on a computer screen. On physical media such as printed paper, this method is not directly applicable. Therefore, instead of rendering directly to the output medium, the process is carried out in an off-screen buffer—a pixel matrix that acts as a virtual canvas. Rather than immediately drawing each pixel to the screen, the corresponding element in the matrix is updated. Once all objects have been processed, the final image is transferred to the target medium using the values stored in the pixel matrix. The faces or sides of the visualized objects are represented as spatial polygons, which are typically triangulated to simplify processing and then displayed on the screen. Suppose one needs to visualize a collection of objects composed of three triangles, as illustrated in Fig. 8.11 (a). The visualization process begins by rendering the most distant triangle (Fig. 8.11 (b)), followed by the incremental addition of closer triangles that overlap previously drawn elements. This process continues until the triangle nearest to the observation point is rendered, as shown in Figs. 8.11 (b)–(d).

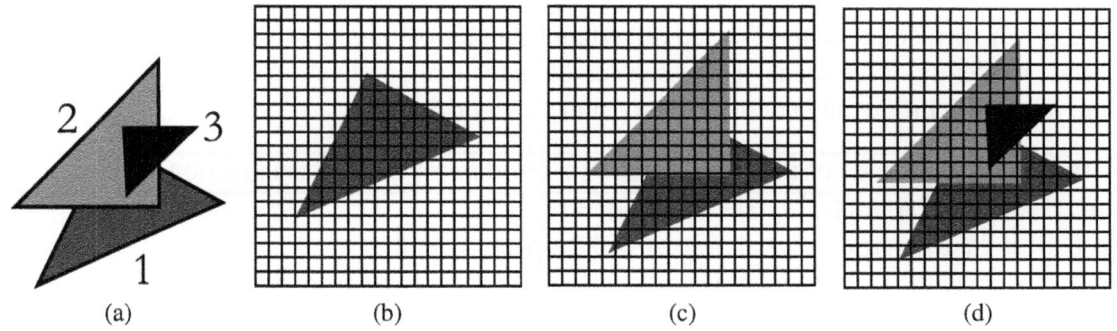

Figure 8.11: Gradual rendering of faces 1, 2, and 3 from (a), shown step by step in (b)–(d).

To ensure the correct rendering order, triangles are initially sorted in descending order according to their distance from the viewpoint, i.e., by their depth, which constitutes the core principle of the depth-sorting algorithm. A fundamental challenge in this process is determining which triangle is closer or farther from the viewpoint, especially given that different vertices of a single triangle may exhibit varying distances. It is customary to estimate the triangle's distance based on a representative point, such as the centroid of the triangle. In practice, sorting by the z-coordinate of the centroid—rather than by its actual Euclidean distance from the viewpoint—yields nearly identical results. This approximation proves particularly effective when the distance between the viewpoint and the size of the triangle is relatively large. Consequently, this method is commonly adopted in the implementation of the painter's algorithm. Based on these considerations, the visualization of objects using the painter's algorithm is presented in the pseudocode of Algorithm 16. It is important to emphasize that back-face culling should preferably be performed prior to applying the painter's algorithm. This avoids rendering surfaces that will ultimately be completely occluded by other parts of the object. For example, when visualizing a cube, if back-face culling is not applied, three hidden faces would be rendered first, only to be overwritten later by the one

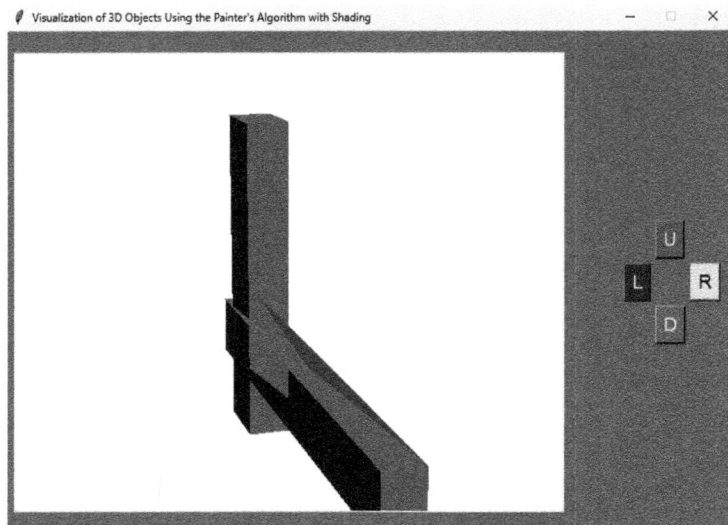

Figure 8.12: Visualization of 3D objects using the Painter's algorithm.

visible face—resulting in unnecessary and inefficient processing. To implement the painter's algorithm described in Algorithm 16, it is sufficient to slightly modify the *draw_3d_objects*($\cdot$) function in Listing 8.3. Specifically, the line `rendering_tr.sort(key=lambda t: t.d)` should be inserted immediately after line 53 to enable depth-based sorting of triangles stored in the `rendering_tr` list. Figure 8.12 illustrates the visualization of two cuboids in 3D space using the painter's algorithm. However, it is evident that the visualization is incorrect due to the overlap of certain triangles belonging to the cuboids, which results in an inaccurate rendering of the scene. This issue serves as the main motivation for introducing the Z-buffer algorithm, as well as improved versions of the painter's algorithm.

Algorithm 16: Pseudocode of the basic painter's algorithm for object visualization.

Input   : A set of n triangles $\mathbb{T}_i$ $(i = 1, \cdots, n)$.
Step 1. Sort the triangles $\mathbb{T}_i$ $(i = 1, \cdots, n)$ with respect to depth.
Step 2. Visualize the sorted triangles on the canvas or append them to the list.
Output : Visualization of visible faces.

8.4 Z-Buffer Algorithm

The limitations of the painter's algorithm are overcome by employing the Z-buffer algorithm, which is natively supported by most modern graphics cards. This algorithm relies on two interdependent buffers for rendering images on the screen: the color buffer and the depth buffer. During the visualization of visible parts of 3D objects, the color buffer stores the color values of each pixel in the image, while the depth buffer maintains the corresponding z-coordinates. The Z-buffer algorithm implements these buffers using two 2D matrices of size $m \times n$, where m denotes the height and n the width of the rendering screen. To accurately display 3D objects on the screen, a projection from three-dimensional space to a two-dimensional plane must first be performed. This is followed by transforming the objects' logical coordinates into physical (screen) coordinates and rendering them according to the selected coordinate system. In other words, each point in space, represented by logical coordinates, must be mapped to a planar point with physical coordinates to ensure correct visualization. The matrix representing the color buffer initially holds the background color value—typically 255, corresponding to white color. Conversely, the depth buffer matrix is initialized to very large values, such as 10^{10}, to enable the proper update of depth information during execution. This matrix retains only the z-coordinates of the points closest to the viewpoint, with closer points having smaller z-values than those farther away, in accordance with the assumption that the viewpoint lies within the negative half-space of a right-handed coordinate system. Based on this rationale, the pseudocode for the Z-buffer algorithm for visualizing 3D objects is presented in Algorithm 17.

Algorithm 17: Pseudocode of the Z-buffer algorithm.

Input : A set of n faces F_i ($i = \overline{1,n}$), which are tested for visibility from the viewpoint $P_v = (x_v, y_v, z_v)$. The width $j_{\max}$ and height $i_{\max}$ represent the dimensions of the canvas used for visualization.

Step 1. (*Initialization*): The elements of the 2D matrices depth_buffer and color_buffer, of dimensions $m \times n$, where $m = i_{max}$ and $n = j_{max}$, are initialized to the large values.

Step 2. (*Color and depth updates for overlapping faces*):

For each face F_k and each projected point $P_k(x, y)$ of that face represented by the pixel $p_k = (i, j)$, compute the depth z of the pixel p_k.

if $z < depth\_buffer[i, j]$ **then**

$depth\_buffer[i, j] = z$;
$color\_buffer[i, j] = intensity(p_k)$;

Output : Visualization of visible faces on the screen.

The following describes how to determine the depth z of a given pixel. Let $A(x_a, y_a, z_a)$, $B(x_b, y_b, z_b)$, and $C(x_c, y_c, z_c)$ be the vertices of a 3D triangle, and let $A'(x'_a, y'_a)$, $B'(x'_b, y'_b)$, and $C'(x'_c, y'_c)$ denote their central projections, i.e., their screen coordinates. Assume the point $P'(x'_p, y'_p)$ lies on the segment $\overline{A'B'}$ (see Fig. 8.13). Then, it holds that $x'_p = x'_a + \lambda(x'_b - x'_a)$, $y'_p = y'_a + \lambda(y'_b - y'_a)$, where $\lambda \in [0, 1]$. The question arises: *How can one determine the corresponding point $P(x_p, y_p, z_p)$ in 3D space such that P' is its central projection?* It is evident that once the depth coordinate z_p is known, the spatial coordinates x_p and y_p can be computed as $x_p = -x'_p z_p / d$ and $y_p = -y'_p z_p / d$, respectively. Therefore, the key task is to determine the depth value z_p. Since point P lies on the spatial segment $\overline{AB}$, its z-coordinate can be linearly interpolated as $z_p = z_a + \lambda(z_b - z_a)$. However, for the purpose of implementing the Z-buffer algorithm, the inverse depth value is used instead: $1/z_p = 1/z_a + \lambda(1/z_b - 1/z_a)$, denoted as z_{pi}, i.e., $z_{pi} = 1/z_p$.

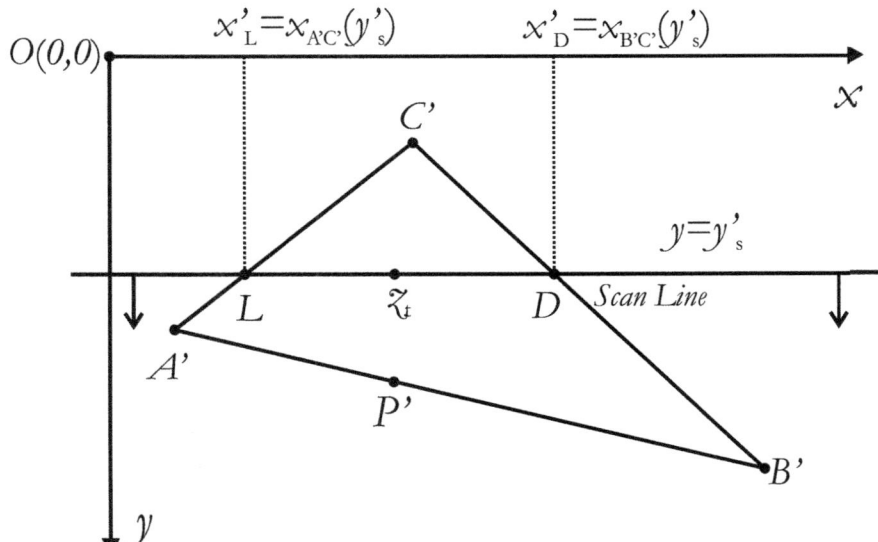

Figure 8.13: Illustration of pixel depth determination in the physical coordinate system.

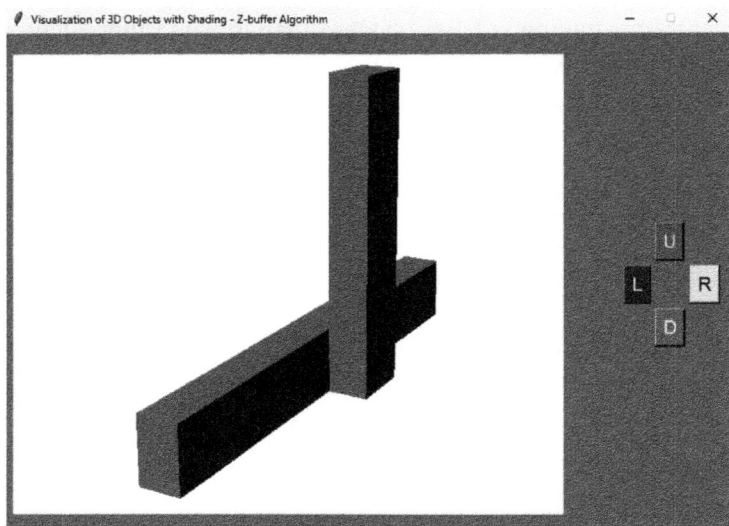

Figure 8.14: Correct visualization of a cuboid in 3d space using the Z-buffer algorithm.

For simplicity, the notation z_i is used instead of z_{pi}, as it is understood to refer to the point P. Let $D'(x'_d, y'_d)$ denote the centroid of triangle $\triangle A'B'C'$, computed as $x'_d = (x'_a + x'_b + x'_c)/3$ and $y'_d = (y'_a + y'_b + y'_c)/3$. Similarly, let $z_{di} = (z_{ai} + z_{bi} + z_{ci})/3$. In Fig. 8.13, for a specific scanline at $y = y'_s$ (obtained by moving the scanline from the vertex of triangle $\triangle A'B'C'$ with the smallest y-coordinate y'_C to the vertex with the largest y-coordinate y'_B), the intersection points x'_L and x'_D are computed. Within the closed interval $[x'_L, x'_D]$, the depth values z_i are then determined using linear interpolation. It is clear that the values x'_L and x'_D are obtained by substituting $y = y'_s$ into the equations of the lines corresponding to the triangle edges. Specifically, the determination of x'_L and x'_D depends on which edges are intersected by the scanline. Hence, the parameters are defined as follows:

$$x'_L = \min\left(x_{B'C'}(y'_s), \min(x_{A'C'}(y'_s), x_{A'B'}(y'_s))\right), \quad x'_D = \max\left(x_{B'C'}(y'_s), \max(x_{A'C'}(y'_s), x_{A'B'}(y'_s))\right).$$

The key task is to estimate, via interpolation, how the depth value z_i changes when point P is shifted one pixel to the right or downward, i.e., when screen coordinates x' and y' increase by one unit. This change can be modeled using partial derivatives $\partial z_i/\partial x'$ (rightward shift) and $\partial z_i/\partial y'$ (downward shift). In the implementation of the Z-buffer algorithm, these partial derivatives are denoted simply as dzdx and dzdy, respectively. Let the points (x', y', z_i) lie on a plane $\pi : ax + by + cz = k$. Then, the depth satisfies the plane equation $ax' + by' + cz_i = k$. Taking partial derivatives yields:

$$\frac{\partial z_i}{\partial x'} = -\frac{a}{c}, \quad \frac{\partial z_i}{\partial y'} = -\frac{b}{c}.$$

Assume the plane π is defined by the triangle $\triangle A''B''C''$ whose vertices are given by $A''(x'_a, y'_a, z_{ai})$, $B''(x'_b, y'_b, z_{bi})$, and $C''(x'_c, y'_c, z_{ci})$. Since the ordered triple (a, b, c) represents the normal vector of the triangle $\triangle A''B''C''$, it can be computed as the cross product of vectors $\overrightarrow{A''B''}$ and $\overrightarrow{A''C''}$. That is, the components of the normal vector $\vec{n} = (a, b, c)$ are computed as:

$$a = (y'_b - y'_a)(z_{ci} - z_{ai}) - (z_{bi} - z_{ai})(y'_c - y'_a),$$
$$b = (z_{bi} - z_{ai})(x'_c - x'_a) - (x'_b - x'_a)(z_{ci} - z_{ai}),$$
$$c = (x'_b - x'_a)(y'_c - y'_a) - (y'_b - y'_a)(x'_c - x'_a).$$

As previously noted, triangle $\triangle A'B'C'$ is vertically scanned from y'_C to y'_B, where:

$$y'_C = \min(y'_a, y'_b, y'_c), \quad y'_B = \max(y'_a, y'_b, y'_c).$$

Finally, the depth value z_{li} at pixel position (x'_L, y'_s) is computed using the formula:

$$z_{li} = z_{di} + (y' - y'_d)\frac{\partial z}{\partial y'} + (x'_L - x'_d)\frac{\partial z}{\partial x'}.$$

For implementation purposes, this is approximated by:

$$z_i = 1.01 z_{di} + (y' - y'_d) \cdot \text{dzdy} + (x'_L - x'_d) \cdot \text{dzdx}.$$

Based on the pseudocode of Algorithm 17 and the pixel depth computation procedure, the implementation of the function *draw_3d_objects_za*($\cdot$) is presented below. The visualization of a cuboid in space using the Z-buffer algorithm, as illustrated in Fig. 8.14, is achieved by replacing the existing function *draw_3d_objects*($\cdot$) in Listing 8.3 with the function *draw_3d_objects_za*($\cdot$). In contrast to the painter's algorithm, the Z-buffer algorithm provides a correct rendering.

```
def draw_3d_objects_za(self, color):
    width=int(self.canvas.cget("width"))
    height=int(self.canvas.cget("height"))
    self.object_3d.calculate_camera_and_screen_coordinates(width,height)
    c_i=self.object_3d.get_screen_center() # Center of the image
    self.object_3d.set_plane_coefficients()
    self.object_3d.shade_triangles()
    # Rendering of Objects Using the Z-Buffer Algorithm
    depth_buffer=np.full((width-1,height-1), float('inf'), dtype=np.float32)
    rendering_tr=self.object_3d.get_render_triangles(); i=0
    cam_pts=self.object_3d.get_camera_points(); alpha=255
    for tr in rendering_tr:
        A, B, C, code = tr.A, tr.B, tr.C, tr.code
        r, g, b = [x//256 for x in self.canvas.winfo_rgb(color)]
        r_c=int(code*r/alpha); g_c=int(code*g/alpha); b_c=int(code*b/alpha)
        fill_color = f"#{r_c:02x}{g_c:02x}{b_c:02x}"
        zAi,zBi,zCi=1/cam_pts[3*i][2],1/cam_pts[3*i+1][2],1/cam_pts[3*i+2][2]
        D,E,F=Point3D(A[0],A[1],zAi),Point3D(B[0],B[1],zBi),Point3D(C[0],C[1],zCi)
        i+=1; cross_prod=(E-D)%(F-D) # Cross product
        if cross_prod[2]<=0: continue
        dzdx, dzdy = -cross_prod[0]/cross_prod[2], -cross_prod[1]/cross_prod[2]
        x_d, y_d, z_di=(A[0]+B[0]+C[0])/3, (A[1]+B[1]+C[1])/3, (zAi+zBi+zCi)/3
        y_top, y_bottom = min(A[1], B[1], C[1]), max(A[1], B[1], C[1])
        for y in range(math.ceil(y_top), math.floor(y_bottom)+1):#Scanning of rows
            xa=xb=xc=float('inf'); xa1=xb1=xc1=float('-inf')
            if (y-B[1])*(y-C[1])<=0 and B[1]!=C[1]:
                xa=xa1=C[0]+(y-C[1])/(B[1]-C[1])*(B[0]-C[0]) # Line BC
            if (y-C[1])*(y-A[1])<=0 and C[1]!=A[1]:
                xb=xb1=A[0]+(y-A[1])/(C[1]-A[1])*(C[0]-A[0]) # Line AC
            if (y-A[1])*(y-B[1])<=0 and A[1]!=B[1]:
                xc=xc1=B[0]+(y-B[1])/(A[1]-B[1])*(A[0]-B[0]) # Line AB
            x_left,x_righty=min(xa,xb,xc),max(xa1,xb1,xc1)
            iy=self.iY(y,height-1,c_i);i_xl=self.iX(float(x_left+0.5),width-1,c_i)
            i_xr=self.iX(float(x_right-0.5),width-1,c_i)
            if iy<=0 or iy>=height-1: continue
            zi=1.01*z_di+(y-y_d)*dzdy+(x_left-x_d)*dzdx
            start_x, x_start = False, 0
            if i_xl<0: i_xl=0
            if i_xr>=width-1: i_xr=width-2
            for ix in range(i_xl, i_xr+1): # Scanning of columns
                if zi<depth_buffer[ix][iy]:
                    depth_buffer[ix][iy]=zi
```

```
43              if not start_x: x_start,start_x=ix,True
44              elif start_x:
45                  start_x=False
46                  self.canvas.create_line(x_start,iy,ix,iy,fill=fill_color)
47              zi+=dzdx
48          if start_x:
49              self.canvas.create_line(x_start,iy,i_xr+1,iy, fill=fill_color)
```

8.5 Modified Painter's Algorithm

As previously discussed, the Painter's Algorithm is not always reliable, particularly in cases where triangles overlap, as illustrated in Fig. 8.15. There are scenarios—such as the one in Fig. 8.15 (b)—in which no drawing order of triangles can guarantee a correct visualization. Although the Painter's Algorithm may yield correct rendering for certain viewpoints (e.g., in Fig. 8.15 (a), a suitable triangle ordering exists), there are frequent situations in which no sequence of drawing operations produces accurate results, as exemplified in Fig. 8.15 (b). For instance, when rendering triangles $\triangle P_1 P_2 P_3$ and $\triangle P_4 P_5 P_6$ in Fig. 8.15 (a), if $\triangle P_4 P_5 P_6$ is drawn first, followed by $\triangle P_1 P_2 P_3$, the visualization will be incorrect. This occurs because, depending on the viewpoint, a portion of $\triangle P_1 P_2 P_3$—which intersects with the plane containing $\triangle P_4 P_5 P_6$—cannot be rendered correctly. A similar issue arises when the triangles are drawn in reverse order. Although in certain cases—depending on the viewpoint—a correct visualization may be achieved (e.g., the order $\triangle P_4 P_5 P_6$ followed by $\triangle P_1 P_2 P_3$), it is generally not possible to obtain an accurate rendering without splitting some of the triangles, as will be discussed in detail below. The question of whether the Painter's Algorithm can be modified to ensure correct rendering has a positive answer. The key step in this process is establishing a correct depth order. This is accomplished by intersecting a given triangle with a plane π, thereby dividing it into two parts. If the plane π does not contain any of the triangle's vertices, the intersection yields a triangle and a quadrilateral; otherwise, the result consists of two new triangles.

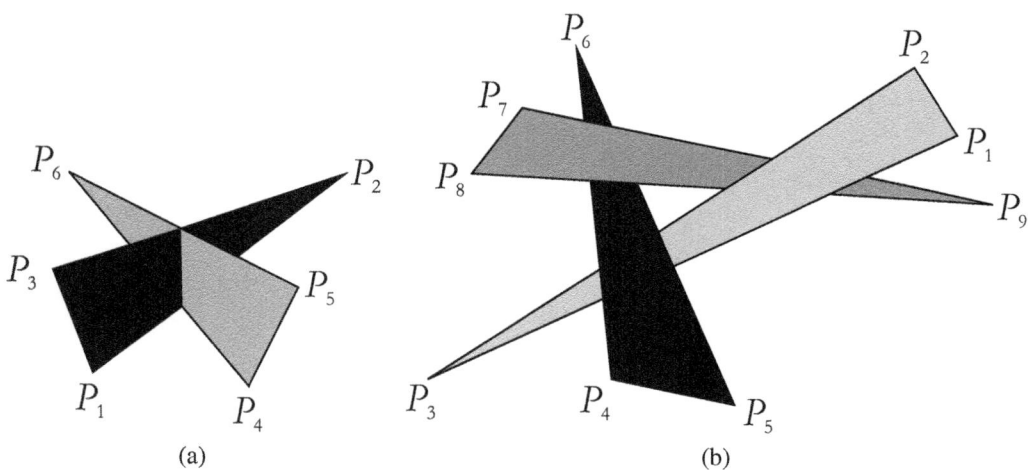

(a)   (b)

Figure 8.15: (a) Eventual visualization. (b) Impossible object visualization using the Painter's algorithm.

In Figure 8.16 (a), the triangle $\mathbb{T}_1 \cong \triangle P_1 P_2 P_3$ is intersected by a plane π defined by the triangle $\mathbb{T}_2 \cong \triangle P_4 P_5 P_6$, resulting in the division of $\mathbb{T}_1$ along a cutting line that remains entirely visible—i.e., it is not occluded by any other triangle. This cutting line divides $\mathbb{T}_1$ into two parts: the first is a triangle $\mathbb{T}_1' \cong \triangle P_1' P_2 P_3'$, and the second is a quadrilateral $\square P_1 P_1' P_3' P_3$, which is subsequently triangulated into two new triangles: $\mathbb{T}_1'' \cong \triangle P_1 P_1' P_3'$ and $\mathbb{T}_1''' \cong \triangle P_1 P_3' P_3$. Hence, the original triangle $\mathbb{T}_1$ is transformed into three new triangles: $\mathbb{T}'_1$, $\mathbb{T}''_1$, and $\mathbb{T}'''_1$ (see Fig. 8.16 (a)). This decomposition allows for the establishment of a valid depth ordering: first, draw triangle $\mathbb{T}'_1$, followed by $\mathbb{T}_2$, then $\mathbb{T}'''_1$, and finally $\mathbb{T}''_1$. This ordering is denoted as $\mathbb{T}'_1$–$\mathbb{T}_2$–$\mathbb{T}'''_1$–$\mathbb{T}''_1$.

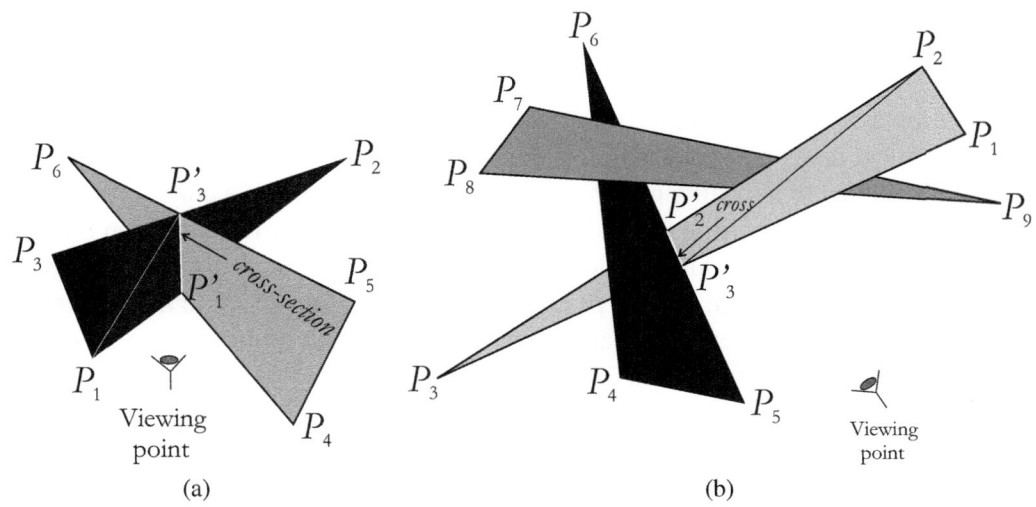

Figure 8.16: (a) Correct order $\mathbb{T}'_1$ - $\mathbb{T}_2$ - $\mathbb{T}'''_1$ - $\mathbb{T}''_1$. (b) Correct order $\mathbb{T}'_1 - \mathbb{T}_2 - \mathbb{T}_3 - \mathbb{T}''_1 - \mathbb{T}'''_1$.

Algorithm 18: Pseudocode of the Modified Painter's Algorithm.

Input : A set of n triangles $\mathbb{T}_i$ $(i = 1, \ldots, n)$ in space, tested for visibility from the viewpoint P_v.

Output : Visualization of the visible faces on screen.

Step 1 (*Sorting triangles*): Sort the triangles $\mathbb{T}_i$ $(i = 1, \ldots, n)$ in descending order according to the distance between the viewpoint P_v and the maximal z-coordinate of their bounding box projected onto the z-axis. Add sorted triangles into the list L_s.

Step 2 (*Reordering triangles after sorting*): Let $\mathbb{T}'_j$ be the first element of the sorted list L_s obtained in Step 1. For each triangle $\mathbb{T}'_k \in L_s$, test whether triangle $\mathbb{T}'_j \in L_s$ $(j \neq k)$ occludes it.

    a) **If** $\mathbb{T}'_j$ does not occlude any triangle $\mathbb{T}'_k$ $(k = 1, \ldots, n, k \neq j)$, **then** visualize $\mathbb{T}'_j$ and remove it from list L_s.

    b) **If** $\mathbb{T}'_j$ occludes a triangle $\mathbb{T}'_k$ from list L_s, **then** check whether $\mathbb{T}'_k$ occludes $\mathbb{T}'_j$ or whether $\mathbb{T}'_k$ is marked.

    c) **If** either of the two conditions from (b) holds, **then** split triangle $\mathbb{T}'_k$ with plane π $(\pi \supset \mathbb{T}'_j)$ and update the list L_s by replacing $\mathbb{T}'_k$ with the two new triangles resulting from the split.

    d) **If** neither of the two conditions from (b) is met (i.e., $\mathbb{T}'_k$ does not occlude $\mathbb{T}'_j$ and is not marked), **then** swap the positions of triangles $\mathbb{T}'_k$ and $\mathbb{T}'_j$ in the list L_s.

From the viewpoint, such an order guarantees that all triangles are correctly rendered on the screen—none will be incorrectly occluded during drawing. A similar scenario arises when more than two triangles are involved, as shown in Figure 8.16 (b). Specifically, if one attempts to render triangles $\mathbb{T}_1 \cong \triangle P_1 P_2 P_3$, $\mathbb{T}_2 \cong \triangle P_4 P_5 P_6$, and $\mathbb{T}_3 \cong \triangle P_7 P_8 P_9$ in any arbitrary order, it can be verified that the rendering will fail—at least one triangle will always be occluded by another. For instance, if triangle $\mathbb{T}_2$ is drawn first, followed by $\mathbb{T}_3$, it becomes impossible to draw $\mathbb{T}_1$, as it will be obscured by $\mathbb{T}_2$. A similar conclusion is reached with other triangle orderings, such as $\mathbb{T}_1$–$\mathbb{T}_2$–$\mathbb{T}_3$, where drawing $\mathbb{T}_1$ first, then $\mathbb{T}_2$, and finally $\mathbb{T}_3$, also fails. To resolve this, triangle $\mathbb{T}_1$ can be split by a plane π containing triangle $\mathbb{T}_2$, resulting in three new triangles: $\mathbb{T}'_1 \cong \triangle P_3 P'_3 P'_2$, $\mathbb{T}''_1 \cong \triangle P'_3 P_2 P'_2$, and $\mathbb{T}'''_1 \cong \triangle P'_3 P_1 P_2$. The following depth order: $\mathbb{T}'_1 - \mathbb{T}_2 - \mathbb{T}_3 - \mathbb{T}''_1 - \mathbb{T}'''_1$ ensures that triangles $\mathbb{T}_1$, $\mathbb{T}_2$, and $\mathbb{T}_3$ are correctly visualized on the screen. This process of reorganizing triangles to resolve visibility issues is known as refinement. A fundamental question that arises in this context is: "How can one correctly choose the plane that will split a given triangle and enable a proper depth-based ordering?" The answer to this question is provided by the algorithm presented below. Broadly speaking, the process begins with an approximate ordering of the triangles by sorting the initial set in descending order based on the distance between the viewpoint and the maximum z-coordinate of the bounding box that contains each triangle. This method enables an initial sorting from the farthest to the nearest triangles, similar to the Painter's algorithm. Subsequently, the approximate order is refined by inserting newly generated triangles to ensure a correct rendering sequence. This procedure is carried out according to the pseudocode of Algorithm 18. Based on this pseudocode, the algorithm can be implemented using previously introduced geometric data structures. Hence, let the function *reorder_triangles*($\cdot$) implement the pseudocode of Algorithm 18. The implementation of this function reveals that it relies on several auxiliary procedures involving sorting, swapping, refinement, and comparison criteria for ordering triangles in 3D space.

```python
def reorder_triangles(triangles: List[Triangle3D]) -> List[Triangle3D]:
    sorted_tr= sorted(triangles, key=cmp_to_key(compare_triangles))
    reorder_triangles= []
    while len(sorted_tr) > 0:
        tj=sorted_tr[0]; changed = False; i = 1
        while i<len(sorted_tr) and tj.overlaps(sorted_tr[i],2):
            tk=sorted_tr[i]
            if tj.occludes(tk):
                if tk.get_mark() or tk.occludes(tj):
                    reorder_list(sorted_tr, tj, i)
                else:
                    change_elements(sorted_tr,tj,i)
                    changed=True; break
            i+=1
        if not changed:
            reorder_triangles.append(tj); sorted_tr.pop(0)
    return reorder_triangles
```

The function *reorder_triangles*($\cdot$) returns a list of non-overlapping triangles in space, which can therefore be directly visualized. What remains is to implement the comparison function *compare_triangles*($\cdot,\cdot$), along with two auxiliary functions: *change_elements*($\cdot,\cdot,\cdot$) and *reorder_list*($\cdot,\cdot,\cdot$). The comparison function is employed to establish an approximate ordering of the initially defined triangles. Its implementation is based on comparing any two triangles according to their maximum depth, as shown in the code snippet below:

```python
def compare_triangles(t1: Triangle3D, t2: Triangle3D) -> int:
    z1 = t1.get_box()[1][2]; z2 = t2.get_box()[1][2]
    if z1 > z2: return 1
    elif z1 < z2: return -1
    return 0
```

The logic of the *change_elements*($\cdot,\cdot,\cdot$) function is straightforward, and its implementation is as follows:

```python
def change_elements(tr_list: List[Triangle3D],tj:Triangle3D,idx: int):
    if idx+1>=len(tr_list): return # no change
    tk=tr_list[idx]; tk.set_mark(True) # mark triangle T_k
```

```
4    tr_list[idx]=tj # T_k is updated with T_j
5    tr_list[idx+1]=tk # T_j is updated with T_k
```

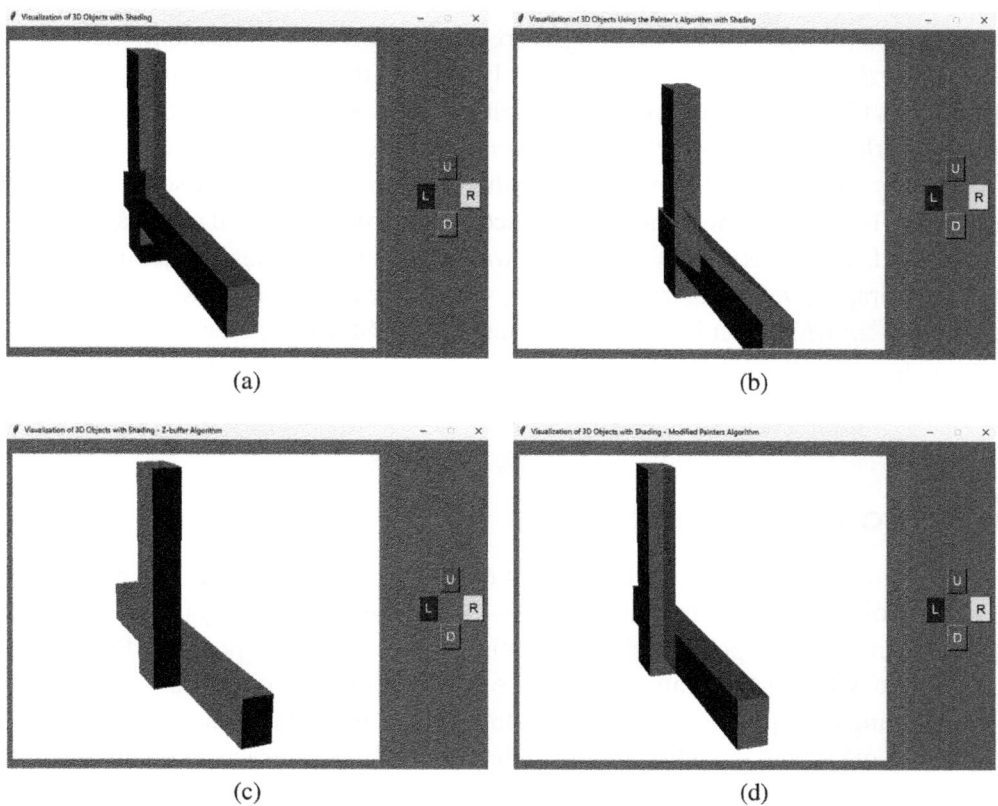

(a)   (b)

(c)   (d)

Figure 8.17: (a) Naive Rendering. (b) Painter's Algorithm. (c) Z-Buffer Algorithm. (d) Modified Painter's Algorithm.

The remaining task is to implement the function *reorder_list*$(\cdot,\cdot,\cdot)$. This function takes three formal parameters. The first parameter is a list of triangles from which the triangle $\mathbb{T}_k$ is extracted as the current element using the index idx, passed as the third formal parameter. The current triangle is then partitioned into two or more parts by the plane defined by triangle $\mathbb{T}_j$, which is passed as the second parameter. After the partitioning, triangle $\mathbb{T}_k$ is replaced by two or three new triangles resulting from the splitting process. Two triangles are generated in the case where the splitting plane contains a vertex of $\mathbb{T}_k$. The implementation of this function is provided below:

```
1 def reorder_list(tr_list: list[Triangle3D], tj: Triangle3D, idx: int):
2    tk=tr_list[idx]
3    num_parts,tk1,tk2,tk3=tk.intersection(tj)
4    if num_parts>1:
5        tr_list.pop(idx) #The tk is removed from the list since it is split
6        # Insert the new parts in place of the original triangle
7        tr_list.insert(idx, tk2); tr_list.insert(idx, tk1)
8        if num_parts==3: tr_list.insert(idx,tk3)
```

Based on the preceding discussion, it is evident that the visualization of cuboids using the modified Painter's algorithm can be implemented via Listing 8.3 by inserting the command self.triangles =

reorder_triangles(self.triangles) immediately after line 42 within the *create_3d_objects*() function. Additionally, at the beginning of the listing, it is necessary to import the *reorder_triangles* function from the file ch8_helper_functions.py, which also contains definitions of the following functions: *reorder_list*, *change_elements*, *compare_triangles*, and *reorder_triangles*. Figure 8.17 presents a comparative visualization of two cuboids in 3D space using the previously described methods. From the visual results, it is clear that only images (c) and (d) provide fully correct visualizations of the mentioned 3D objects. The definition of the *reorder_triangles*($\cdot$) function clearly implies that the time complexity of the modified Painter's algorithm is $\Theta(n^2)$. This runtime is not a critical issue when the viewpoint changes infrequently. However, in real-world scenarios—such as flight simulations or computer games—the viewpoint often changes dynamically, significantly slowing down the rendering of complex scenes containing a large number of triangles. To alleviate this problem, advanced data structures based on binary space partitioning have been introduced, known as *Binary Space Partition* (BSP) trees. These structures were first studied from a theoretical perspective by Paterson and Yao, who proved that for any set of $(d-1)$-dimensional objects embedded in $\mathbb{R}^d$ $(d \geq 3)$, it is possible to construct a BSP tree of size $\mathcal{O}(n^{d-1})$. In particular, for planar objects such as orthogonal rectangles, they demonstrated that a BSP tree of size $\mathcal{O}(n^{\frac{3}{2}})$ can be constructed.

8.6 BSP Trees in Two-Dimensional Space

To develop an intuitive understanding of the concept of BSP trees in the plane, it is best to begin with the analysis the content of Fig. 8.18, as the saying goes—"a picture is worth a thousand words." In Fig. 8.18 (a), five planar objects (simple polygons) are depicted, while the corresponding BSP tree is shown in Fig. 8.18 (b). Figure 8.18 (a) illustrates a recursive binary partitioning of the plane, starting with the selection of a separating line l_1, which is chosen randomly. This line divides the plane into two half-planes: one above (to the left of) l_1, and the other below (to the right of) it. The process continues recursively—the half-plane above l_1 is further divided using line l_2, and the half-plane below l_1 is partitioned by line l_3, resulting in additional subdivisions. The lines that divide the plane are referred to as *splitting lines*. These lines not only partition the plane but may also intersect the objects, fragmenting them into smaller pieces. The subdivision continues until each region contains exactly one fragment. The BSP tree depicted in Fig. 8.18 (b) is constructed by inserting line l_1 into the root (parent node). The left and right subtrees are then generated as follows: the left children store lines that divide the half-plane on the right (below) the line stored in the parent node. These lines are stored in the internal nodes of the left subtrees. Similarly, the right children are constructed by storing lines that divide the left (above) half-plane in the internal nodes of the right subtrees. The leaves, which have no descendants, contain the object fragments located either to the left or to the right of the splitting lines stored in their parent nodes. For instance, the object o_4, which lies to the right of both l_3 and l_1, is stored in a leaf node of the left subtree descending from the internal node where line l_3 is stored.

Definition 8.6.1 The half-plane h^+ is called the *positive half-plane* if it lies to the right of the line l, while the half-plane h^- is *negative* if it lies to the left of that line.

Definition 8.6.1 naturally extends to higher dimensions. Specifically, let h be a hyperplane in a d-dimensional space. This hyperplane can be expressed as $a_1x_1 + a_2x_2 + \cdots + a_dx_d + a_{d+1} = 0$, where the positive (negative) half-space h^+ (h^-) consists of all points $(x_1, x_2, \cdots, x_d) \in \mathbb{R}^d$ satisfying $h > 0$ ($h < 0$). A BSP tree for a set of objects $\mathcal{O}$ in the plane is a binary tree $\mathscr{B}$ with the following properties:

- If the cardinality of the set $\mathcal{O}$ is less than or equal to one, then $\mathscr{B}$ is a leaf node, and the object from $\mathcal{O}$ ($|\mathcal{O}| \neq 0$) is explicitly stored in that leaf. If this leaf is denoted by v, then the set $\mathcal{O}(v)$ represents the objects stored in node v.

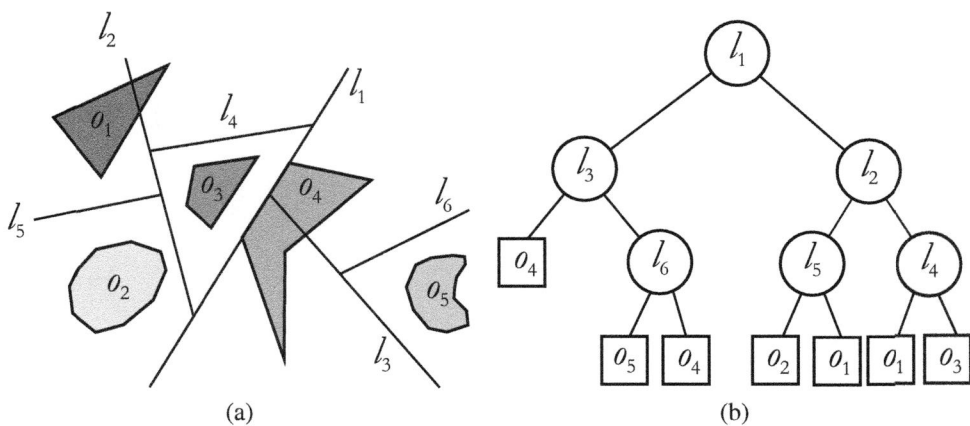

Figure 8.18: (a) Binary partitioning of the plane. (b) Structure of the BSP tree after partitioning.

- If $|\mathcal{O}| > 1$, then the root node v of the tree $\mathcal{B}$ stores a hyperplane h_v, along with the set of objects $\mathcal{O}(v)$ lying on h_v. The left subtree corresponds to the BSP tree $\mathcal{B}^-$ for the set $\mathcal{O}^- = \{h_v^- \cap o : o \in \mathcal{O}\}$, while the right subtree corresponds to the BSP tree $\mathcal{B}^+$ for the set $\mathcal{O}^+ = \{h_v^+ \cap o : o \in \mathcal{O}\}$.

As illustrated in Fig. 8.18 (a), when the hyperplane h_v is associated with the line l_1 (i.e., $h_v \leftarrow l_1$), it follows that $\mathcal{O}^- = \{o_1, o_2, o_3\}$ and $\mathcal{O}^+ = \{o_4, o_5\}$. The size of the BSP tree is defined as the total number of elements in the sets $\mathcal{O}(v)$, taken over all nodes v in the binary tree. In other words, the size of the tree corresponds to the total number of fragments (which may be entire objects from $\mathcal{O}$ or parts resulting from splitting) generated during the BSP tree construction. For instance, in Fig. 8.18 (b), the tree size is 7, as it stores seven fragments. The splitting lines used in BSP construction can be arbitrarily selected. For practical implementation, however, the set of candidate splitting lines is typically restricted. Specifically, for segments defined in the plane, candidate splitting lines are those associated with the segments themselves. Such candidates induce what is known as an *auto-partition* in the BSP tree. In three-dimensional space, auto-partitions are induced by planes associated with triangles that approximate a polyhedron. As will be shown later, the size of the BSP tree depends directly on the choice of auto-partition, i.e., on the selection of splitting lines (or planes) in the plane (or space).

8.6.1 Constructing BSP Trees in the Plane

This section provides a detailed description of the construction process of a BSP tree for a predefined set of segments in the plane, assuming that the segments are opaque and non-intersecting. Let $\mathcal{S}$ be a given set consisting of n opaque segments positioned in the plane such that they do not intersect one another (see Fig. 8.19 (a)).

Assume that a BSP tree partition is constructed as illustrated in Fig.8.19(b), where, without loss of generality, the splitting line is selected randomly. In Fig. 8.19 (b), the splitting line is chosen to contain segment a. A key question arises: *How should the segments from the set $\mathcal{S}$ be organized, or more precisely, into which data structure should they be stored to enable correct visualization on the canvas from an arbitrary viewpoint P_v?* Since the segments are opaque, rendering segment e first from viewpoint P_v (see Fig.8.19 (a)) would obscure segment f, preventing its correct visualization. Although the correct visibility order of segments from point P_v can be manually determined from Fig. 8.19 (a) (e.g., $f - e - b - c - d - a$), it is crucial to ensure an algorithmic approach to compute this order. Therefore, it is necessary to design a data structure that supports automatic localization and sorting of segments within the BSP tree, enabling the efficient generation of a sequence that guarantees correct rendering at any moment. It has been demonstrated that triangles in three-dimensional space can be correctly ordered for rendering—even in the

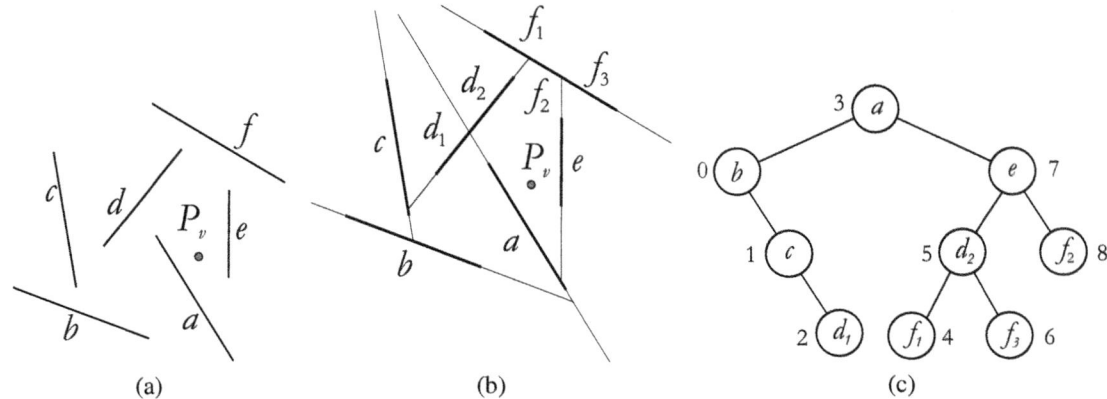

Figure 8.19: (a) A set of six opaque segments. (b) BSP auto-partition. (c) BSP tree construction.

presence of intersections—by employing a modified painter's algorithm or the Z-buffer algorithm. An analogous situation arises in the planar case with segments; however, the Z-buffer algorithm is memory-intensive, while the modified painter's algorithm may yield suboptimal performance when handling a large number of objects. Consequently, constructing a BSP tree becomes a preferred approach for visualization. The construction of a BSP tree proceeds as follows: let l denote a separating line associated with an arbitrary segment $s \in \mathcal{S}$, such that l contains s ($l \ni s$).

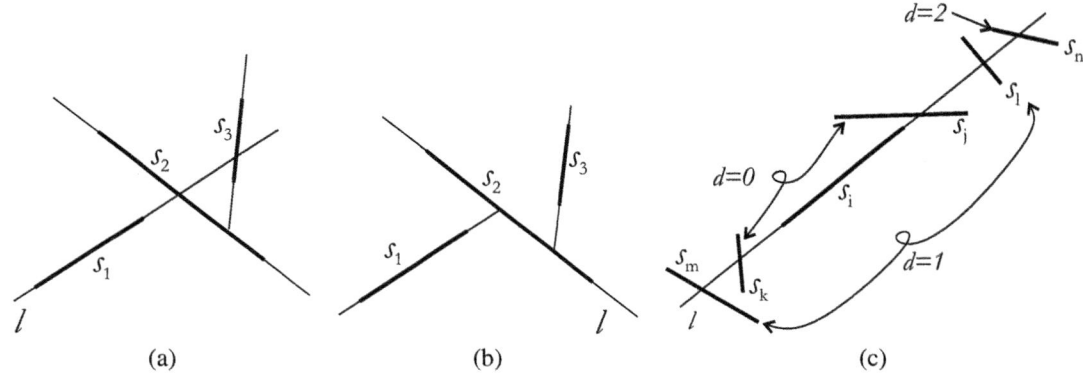

Figure 8.20: (a) The size of the BSP tree is not optimal. (b) The line l defined by segment s_2 yields an optimal BSP tree size. (c) The distance of segment s_j relative to segment s_i.

Without loss of generality, let segment s in Fig. 8.19 (a) be segment a. The construction begins by creating the root of the tree and assigning it the line l defined by segment a. This line partitions the remaining segments into two groups, $\mathcal{S}_a^+$ and $\mathcal{S}_a^-$, as illustrated in Fig. 8.19 (b). The set $\mathcal{S}_a^+$ contains segments or segment fragments located on the right side of the line l, specifically d_2, e, and f, so that $\mathcal{S}_a^+ = \{d_2, e, f\}$, where d_2 is the portion of segment d lying to the right of l. Similarly, $\mathcal{S}_a^-$ consists of segments on the left side of l, namely $\mathcal{S}_a^- = \{b, c, d_1\}$. The construction proceeds recursively: the left subtree is built over the set $\mathcal{S}_a^-$ and the right subtree over $\mathcal{S}_a^+$, relative to node a of the original segment set $\mathcal{S}$. After several recursive steps, the resulting BSP tree is shown in Fig. 8.19 (c). The left subtree from node a is built by arbitrarily selecting a segment from $\mathcal{S}_a^- = \{b, c, d_1\}$, say b, and defining a line l_1 such that $l_1 \ni b$. This line partitions $\mathcal{S}_a^-$ into two subsets: $\mathcal{S}_b^- = \{\emptyset\}$ and $\mathcal{S}_b^+ = \{c, d_1\}$. Analogously, the right subtree from node a is built by selecting a segment from $\mathcal{S}_a^+ = \{d_2, e, f\}$, for example e, and defining the line l_2 such that $l_2 \ni e$. This partitions the set into $\mathcal{S}_e^- = \{d_2, f'\}$ and $\mathcal{S}_e^+ = \{f_3\}$, where $f' = f_1 \cup f_2$, given that l_2 splits segment f into two subsegments f' and f_3 (see Fig. 8.19 (c)). Based on this procedure, the process of constructing a BSP tree in the plane for n non-intersecting segments is formalized in the pseudocode of Algorithm 19.

Algorithm 19: Pseudocode of the algorithm for constructing a BSP tree in the plane.

Input : A set $\mathcal{S}$ consisting of n planar segments.

Step 1. If $|\mathcal{S}| \leq 1$, then the tree $\mathcal{B}$ is created consisting of exactly one leaf node that stores the elements of the set $\mathcal{S}$—specifically, it holds a single segment from $\mathcal{S}$ or no segments at all if $\mathcal{S}$ is empty.

Step 2. If $|\mathcal{S}| > 1$, then using the separating line $l(s_1)$ ($l \ni s_1$, $s_1 \in \mathcal{S}$), the set $\mathcal{S}^+ := \{s \cap l(s_1)^+ : s \in \mathcal{S}\}$ is first constructed. The right subtree $\mathcal{B}^+$ is then recursively created with respect to this set by passing $\mathcal{S}^+$ to the algorithm. Similarly, the set $\mathcal{S}^- := \{s \cap l(s_1)^- : s \in \mathcal{S}\}$ is constructed, and the left subtree $\mathcal{B}^-$ is recursively generated with respect to it. Finally, the algorithm returns the tree $\mathcal{B}$ with root node v, where $\mathcal{B}^-$ and $\mathcal{B}^+$ are its left and right subtrees, respectively, and $\mathcal{S}(v) = \{s \in \mathcal{S} : s \subset l(s_1)\}$.

Output: A BSP tree for storing segments in the plane, i.e., the elements of the set $\mathcal{S}$.

It is important to emphasize that the size of the BSP tree constructed by Algorithm 19 is not minimal and can be significantly optimized depending on the choice of the initial separating line. For instance, in Fig. 8.20 (a), the initial separating line l is chosen as $l(s_1)$, as in Algorithm 19, which results in a BSP tree with five leaves. This is because the separating line splits segments s_2 and s_3 into subsegments s_2', s_2'', s_3', and s_3'', respectively. Thus, the BSP tree stores the segments s_1, s_2', s_2'', s_3', and s_3''. However, if one chooses the separating line $l(s_2)$ instead of $l(s_1)$, then segments s_1 and s_3 remain unsplit, and the tree stores only three segments: s_1, s_2, and s_3 (see Fig. 8.20 (b)). Experimental results have shown that the most optimal size of the BSP tree is typically achieved when the initial separating line is selected randomly. In other words, a permutation of the segment indices of the set $\mathcal{S}$ is generated, and the first element of the permutation is used to define the separating line. In Fig. 8.20 (b), instead of the permutation $\{1, 2, 3\}$, the permutation $\{2, 1, 3\}$ is used. More generally, for a set of segments $\mathcal{S} = \{s_1, s_2, \ldots, s_n\}$, one constructs a permuted set $\mathcal{S}' = \{s_{i_1}, s_{i_2}, \ldots, s_{i_n}\}$, where $(i_1, i_2, \ldots, i_n)$ is a permutation of $\{1, 2, \ldots, n\}$ generated uniformly at random. The permuted set $\mathcal{S}'$ is then passed as input to Algorithm 19. Since the size of the BSP tree may vary depending on the chosen permutation, the following lemma provides a characterization of the tree size, i.e., the number of elements stored in the tree, when considering all $n!$ permutations of the set $\{1, 2, \ldots, n\}$.

Lemma 8.6.1 Let n be the number of non-intersecting segments given in the plane. If the initial separating line is chosen completely at random, then the number of fragments generated by Algorithm 19 is proportional to $\mathcal{O}(n \log n)$.

Proof. Let $s_i \in \mathcal{S}$ be an arbitrarily selected and fixed segment used to define the separating line l. It will be shown that, on average, the total number of fragments (resulting from the intersection of the line $l(s_i)$ with other segments in $\mathcal{S}$) does not exceed $2 \ln n$. The distance between two segments s_i and s_j is defined as:

$$d(s_i, s_j) := \begin{cases} b, & \text{if the line } l(s_i) \text{ intersects segment } s_j \\ \infty, & \text{otherwise} \end{cases}, \tag{8.3}$$

where b denotes the number of segments between s_i and s_j that intersect the line $l(s_i)$. In Fig. 8.20 (c), there are no segments between s_i and s_j ($d(s_i, s_j) = 0$), nor between s_i and s_k ($d(s_i, s_k) = 0$), that intersect the line $l(s_i)$. On the other hand, there is exactly one segment, s_j or s_k, between s_i and s_l, or between

s_i and s_m, intersecting $l(s_i)$, which implies $d(s_i, s_l) = 1$ and $d(s_i, s_m) = 1$. Furthermore, there are two segments s_j and s_l between s_i and s_n, yielding $d(s_i, s_n) = 2$. It is easy to observe that if the distance is finite, then there are at most two such segments at that distance—one on each side of s_i. Suppose $k = d(s_i, s_j)$. Then there exist k segments $s_{j_1}, s_{j_2}, \ldots, s_{j_k}$ between s_i and s_j. The key question is: *What is the probability that the line $l(s_i)$ intersects segment s_j when chosen as the separating line?* For this to happen, s_i must appear before s_j in the random ordering, and also before every intermediate segment s_k between s_i and s_j. In Fig. 8.20 (c), the line $l(s_i)$ intersects segment s_n, which lies beyond s_i, while s_i appears before s_j and s_l, the segments located between s_i and s_n. Thus, this configuration implies that the index ordering is $i - j - l - n$. More generally, with respect to the index set $\{i, j, j_1, j_2, \ldots, j_k\}$, the index i must be the smallest, i.e., it must appear first. Since the segments are randomly ordered, each segment in the set $\mathscr{S}_a = \{s_i, s_j, s_{j_1}, s_{j_2}, \ldots, s_{j_k}\}$ has an equal probability of appearing first, which is $1/(k+2)$, as $|\mathscr{S}_a| = k + 2$. Thus, the following inequality holds:

$$0 \leq P(\text{line } l(s_i) \text{ intersects segment } s_j) \leq \frac{1}{k+2}, \tag{8.4}$$

where $P(\text{line } l(s_i) \text{ intersects segment } s_j)$ denotes the probability that the line $l(s_i)$ intersects s_j when chosen as the separating line in Algorithm 19. The next step is to estimate the expected maximum number of fragments induced by introducing the separating line $l(s_i)$. According to the theory of probability, the expectation in the discrete case can be approximated by the mean. From inequality 8.4, we derive the bound:

$$E\left[P(\text{line } l(s_i) \text{ intersects segment } s_j)\right] \leq \sum_{i \neq j} \frac{1}{d(s_i, s_j) + 2} \leq 2 \sum_{k=0}^{n-2} \frac{1}{k+2} \leq 2 \ln n. \tag{8.5}$$

Since for any fixed segment s_i, the expected number of fragments is at most $2 \ln n$, it follows that by processing the remaining $n - 1$ non-intersecting segments, the expected total number of fragments is at most $2(n-1) \ln n$. Including the n initially given segments, the total number of fragments generated by Algorithm 19 is bounded above by $n + 2(n-1) \ln n$, implying that the total number of fragments is proportional to $\mathcal{O}(n \log n)$, which concludes the proof. ∎

The following theorem addresses the amount of time required to construct a Random BSP tree of size $\mathcal{O}(n \log n)$.

> **Theorem 8.6.1** Given n non-intersecting segments in the plane, a Random BSP tree of size $\mathcal{O}(n \log n)$ can be constructed in expected time $\mathcal{O}(n^2 \log n)$.

Proof. Based on Lemma 8.6.1, the number of elements in the BSP tree is proportional to $\mathcal{O}(n \log n)$. Since each recursive call of Algorithm 19 processes a subset of the input segments or their fragments, it follows that the total number of recursive calls is also proportional to the total number of fragments, i.e., $\mathcal{O}(n \log n)$. At this point, the duration of the recursive calls themselves is disregarded. Furthermore, generating a random permutation can be performed in linear time $\mathcal{O}(n)$. In addition, each recursive call consists of checking for intersections and splitting fragments, which in the worst case requires time proportional to the number of input fragments processed in that call. Although the number of fragments decreases with tree depth, the total cost of such operations across all calls may accumulate to $\mathcal{O}(n)$ for each of the $\mathcal{O}(n \log n)$ fragments. Therefore, the overall expected time complexity for constructing the random BSP tree is $\mathcal{O}(n^2 \log n)$. This completes the proof of the theorem. ∎

Based on the previously presented theory, and in particular the pseudocode of Algorithm 19, the implementation of a BSP tree in the plane can be realized using the classes **BSPTree2D** and **BSPNode2D**, whose definitions are provided in Listing 8.4. The class **BSPTree2D** is equipped with a constructor and two methods: *build_tree*(·) and *inorder_traversal*(·,·). On the other hand, the class **BSPNode2D** contains a constructor and the method *inorder_traversal*(·,·), whose purpose is to generate the correct ordering of visible segments from a given viewpoint. Since the constructors of both classes are relatively straightforward, they are implemented within the class definitions for the sake of clarity. The same applies to the *inorder_traversal*(·,·) method of the **BSPTree2D** class, which simply delegates the traversal to the corresponding method in the **BSPNode2D** class.

Listing 8.4: Definition of the BSPTree2D and BSPNode2D Classes

```
from typing import List
from geometry import Point2D, Segment2D, TypeP2
class BSPNode2D:
    def __init__(self,segment):
        self.segment=segment # Segment defining the splitting line
        self.left=None # A negative half-plane
        self.right=None # A positive half-plane
    def inorder_traversal(self, pt:Point2D, output_list:List[Segment2D]): pass

class BSPTree2D:
    def __init__(self, segments):
        self.root = self.build_tree(segments)
    def build_tree(self, seg_list:List[Segment2D]): pass
    def inorder_traversal(self, view_point:Point2D, res_list:List[Segment2D]):
        if self.root: self.root.inorder_traversal(view_point, res_list)
```

The method *build_tree*(·) recursively constructs the BSP tree by assigning segments to appropriate half-planes with respect to the selected separating line. Segments located to the left of the separating line are placed in the negative half-plane, while those to the right are placed in the positive half-plane. These half-planes are represented through the corresponding subtrees. In the case where the separating line intersects a segment, the segment is split into two parts—one part is assigned to the negative, and the other to the positive half-plane. If a segment lies exactly on the separating line, it may be assigned to either half-plane. This approach accounts for all possible scenarios, thereby enabling the implementation of the method, as demonstrated in the code snippet below:

```
def build_tree(self, seg_list:List[Segment2D]):
    if not seg_list: return None
    if len(seg_list) == 1: return BSPNode2D(seg_list[0])
    pos_list = []; neg_list = []; s=seg_list[0] #s is splitting line
    for e in seg_list[1:]: # TypeP2.RIGHT -> 2
        cl=[e[0].classification(s[0],s[1]),e[1].classification(s[0],s[1])]
        if (cl[0]==TypeP2.LEFT and cl[1]==TypeP2.LEFT) or \
            (cl[0]==TypeP2.LEFT and cl[1].value>2) or \
            (cl[0].value>2 and cl[1]==TypeP2.LEFT): pos_list.append(e)
        elif (cl[0]==TypeP2.RIGHT and cl[1]==TypeP2.RIGHT) or \
            (cl[0]==TypeP2.RIGHT and cl[1].value>2) or \
            (cl[0].value>2 and cl[1]==TypeP2.RIGHT): neg_list.append(e)
        elif cl[0].value>2 and cl[1].value>2: pos_list.append(e)
        else: # segment e intersects splitting line l(s)
            p=[0]; s.intersection_segments(e,p); pt=s.point_at(p[0])
            if s[0].orientation(s[1],e[0])==-1:
                neg_list.append(Segment2D(e[0],pt))
                pos_list.append(Segment2D(pt,e[1]))
            else:
                pos_list.append(Segment2D(e[0],pt))
```

```
21                 neg_list.append(Segment2D(pt,e[1]))
22      node=BSPNode2D(s)
23      node.left=self.build_tree(neg_list); node.right=self.build_tree(pos_list)
24      return node
```

What remains is the implementation of the *inorder_traversal*(·,·) method of the **BSPNode2D** class, whose purpose is to enable the correct retrieval of segments or their fragments from the BSP tree, ensuring accurate scene visualization from a given viewpoint. This is achieved through a modified inorder traversal of the binary tree. In standard inorder traversal, the left subtree (L) is visited first, followed by the current node (N), and finally the right subtree (R), which is denoted as L-N-R. However, in the modified inorder traversal, the viewpoint P_v is also taken into account. The procedure begins with the segment s stored in the root node, after which the position of the viewpoint relative to this segment is evaluated. If the viewpoint P_v lies to the right of the separating line $l(s)$, then the segments stored on the left side of this line neither occlude s nor any segments on the right side of the line. Therefore, those segments should be drawn first via recursive traversal. Since the segment s itself does not occlude the segments on the right side of $l(s)$, it is drawn next. Finally, the segments on the right side of $l(s)$ are recursively processed. Conversely, if the viewpoint P_v lies to the left of the separating line $l(s)$, the process is applied analogously but in reverse order: first, the right subtree is traversed recursively, followed by the current segment s, and finally the left subtree is traversed. This approach ensures a correct visualization order of the segments, yielding an accurate reconstruction of the scene from any given viewpoint. Specifically, for the BSP tree illustrated in Fig. 8.19 (c), the modified inorder traversal produces the correct segment sequence: $b - c - d_1 - a - f_1 - d_2 - f_3 - e - f_2$. A verbal description of this algorithm can be further formalized using the pseudocode in Algorithm 20.

Algorithm 20: Pseudocode of the modified inorder traversal.

Input : The viewpoint P_v and the segment s that defines the separating line $l(s)$.
Step 1. If the viewpoint P_v lies to the right of segment s, **then**

    a) Recursively traverse the left subtree relative to the root storing segment s;
    b) Visualize or add segment s to the list;
    c) Recursively traverse the right subtree relative to the root storing segment s.

Step 2. If the viewpoint P_v is not located to the right of segment s, **then**

    a) Recursively traverse the right subtree relative to the root storing segment s;
    b) Visualize or add segment s to the list;
    c) Recursively traverse the left subtree relative to the root storing segment s.

Output : Correct reading order of segments from the viewpoint.

Following the pseudocode presented in Algorithm 20, the recursive implementation of the *inorder_traversal*(·) method in the **BSPNode2D** class is given as follows:

```
1 def inorder_traversal(self, pt:Point2D, output_list:List[Segment2D]):
2     if pt.orientation(self.segment[0],self.segment[1])==1: # pt lies right of line
3         if self.left: self.left.inorder_traversal(pt,output_list)
4         output_list.append(self.segment)
5         if self.right: self.right.inorder_traversal(pt,output_list)
6     else: # pt is left of or on the line
7         if self.right: self.right.inorder_traversal(pt,output_list)
8         output_list.append(self.segment)
9         if self.left: self.left.inorder_traversal(pt,output_list)
```

To illustrate the correct visualization of BSP tree elements relative to a dynamically specified viewpoint, a GUI application has been developed based on the code presented in Listing 8.5. The application is shown in Fig. 8.21.

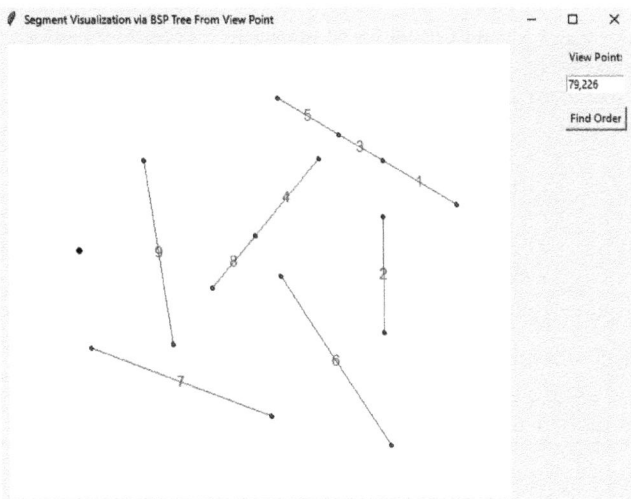

Figure 8.21: Visualization of segment visibility from the viewpoint $P_v = (79, 226)$.

Figure 8.21 presents the correct visualization of six segments, labeled a, b, c, d, e, and f, relative to the viewpoint $P_v(79, 226)$, with the proper rendering order indicated by numbers from 1 to 9. Since the separating line is defined by segment s_1, i.e., segment a (see Fig. 8.19 (b)), the visualization sequence in Fig. 8.21 begins with segment $1(f_3)$, followed by $2(e)$, then $3(f_2)$, and finally segment $9(c)$.

Listing 8.5: GUI for Visualization of Segments by Using BSP Trees in Plane

```
from tkinter import Canvas, Entry, Button
from typing import List
from geometry import Point2D, Segment2D, TypeP2
from BSP import BSPTree2D
class SegmentVisualizer:
    def __init__(self, root):
        self.root=root; self.root.geometry("700x520")
        self.root.title("Segment Visualization via BSP Tree From View Point")
        self.canvas = Canvas(root, width=550, height=500, bg="white")
        self.canvas.pack(side=tk.LEFT, padx=10, pady=10)
        right_panel = tk.Frame(root, width=200)
        right_panel.pack(side=tk.RIGHT, fill=tk.Y, padx=10, pady=10)
        tk.Label(right_panel, text="View Point:").pack(pady=5)
        self.text_input= Entry(right_panel, width=10)
        self.text_input.pack(pady=5); self.text_input.insert(0,"79,226")
        self.button=Button(right_panel,text="Find Order",command=self.find_order)
        self.button.pack(pady=10); self.segments=[]; self.create_segments()
    def create_segments(self):
        self.segments=[
            Segment2D(Point2D(420,440), Point2D(300,254)),#s1
            Segment2D(Point2D(289,408), Point2D(92,333)), #s2
            Segment2D(Point2D(182,329), Point2D(150,128)),#s3
            Segment2D(Point2D(225,267), Point2D(342,126)),#s4
            Segment2D(Point2D(413,316), Point2D(412,189)),#s5
            Segment2D(Point2D(493,176), Point2D(297,60))  #s6
        ]
```

```
27      for s in self.segments:
28          self.canvas.create_line(s[0][0],s[0][1],s[1][0],s[1][1],fill='red')
29      def find_order(self): #Correct rendering of segments from view point
30          x, y=self.text_input.get().split(',')
31          p_v=Point2D(int(x),int(y)); self.canvas.delete("all")
32          self.canvas.create_oval(p_v[0]-3,p_v[1]-3,p_v[0]+3,p_v[1]+3,fill='black')
33          tree=BSPTree2D(self.segments); res_list=[]; i=0
34          tree.inorder_traversal(p_v, res_list)
35          for s in res_list:
36              x1,y1,x2,y2=s[0][0],s[0][1],s[1][0],s[1][1]
37              self.canvas.create_line(x1,y1,x2,y2,fill='red')
38              self.canvas.create_oval(x1-2,y1-2,x1+2,y1+2,fill='red')
39              self.canvas.create_oval(x2-2, y2-2,x2+2,y2+2,fill='red')
40              a, b =(x1+x2)//2, (y1+y2)//2; i+=1
41              self.canvas.create_text(a,b,text=str(i),fill='red',font=('Arial',12))
42
43 if __name__ == "__main__":
44 root = tk.Tk(); app = SegmentVisualizer(root); root.mainloop()
```

> **Observation 8.6.2** Although the construction time of a Random BSP tree in the plane is on the order of $\mathcal{O}(n^2 \log n)$, in some applications the tree is generated only once, making the construction time less critical. This time complexity can be reduced to $\mathcal{O}(n \log n)$ by employing a deterministic algorithm. However, in such cases, automatic partitioning is not used, and the resulting BSP tree is slightly larger than $\mathcal{O}(n \log n)$. Researchers Paterson and Yao demonstrated that for a set of n non-intersecting planar segments—specifically, those that are all vertical or all horizontal—a BSP tree of size $\mathcal{O}(n)$ can be constructed. Furthermore, Tóth showed that it is possible to construct segments in the plane (not necessarily all vertical or horizontal) such that the size of the BSP tree grows proportionally to $\Omega\left(\frac{n \log n}{\log \log n}\right)$. This result may be considered a lower bound, while the upper bound for arbitrary segments remains $\mathcal{O}(n \log n)$.

8.7   BSP Trees in Three-Dimensional Space

This section generalizes the BSP tree construction algorithm from the plane to higher dimensions. Instead of disjoint segments in the plane, the focus is on non-intersecting triangles in three-dimensional space. Moreover, instead of separating lines, partition planes are introduced—defined by triangles that serve to approximate polyhedral surfaces in space. The pseudocode of the 3D BSP tree construction algorithm is derived from Algorithm 19 by replacing planar segments with 3D triangles and separating lines with partition planes. Analogous to the two-dimensional case, the size of the tree depends on the spatial arrangement of triangles—that is, on the order in which partition planes are selected. If the triangles are initially shuffled in a completely random manner, the resulting BSP tree in space will have a size on the order of $\mathcal{O}(n^2)$, as established by the following lemma.

> **Lemma 8.7.1** Let there be n non-intersecting triangles in three-dimensional space. If the triangles are randomly shuffled at the beginning, then the maximum number of fragments in the resulting BSP tree is upper bounded by $\mathcal{O}(n^2)$.

Proof. Let the set $\mathscr{T}$ contain n triangles in three-dimensional space, and let $\mathbb{T}_k \in \mathscr{T}$ be an arbitrarily selected but fixed triangle. It will be shown that the average number of fragments (triangles or quadrilaterals) generated when the next partitioning plane is chosen as the plane $\pi(\mathbb{T}_k)$ does not exceed n^2. The plane $\pi(\mathbb{T}_k)$ is defined by the triangle $\mathbb{T}_k$. Triangles $\mathbb{T}_i \in \mathscr{T}$ $(i < k)$ for which the planes $\pi(\mathbb{T}_i)$ intersect the partitioning plane $\pi(\mathbb{T}_k)$ can generate at most $k-1$ lines l_i in space. Hence, if all $k-1$-planes intersect the partitioning plane $\pi(\mathbb{T}_k)$, then the lines $l_i = \pi(\mathbb{T}_i) \cap \pi(\mathbb{T}_k)$ ($i = 1, \ldots, k-1$) lie within the plane $\pi(\mathbb{T}_k)$. Clearly, there exist planes $\pi(\mathbb{T}_j)$ that do not intersect the triangle $\mathbb{T}_k$ (see Fig. 8.22 (a)). Figure 8.22 (a) illustrates the intersections between the partitioning plane $\pi(\mathbb{T}_k)$ and other planes defined by the triangles $\mathbb{T}_1$, $\mathbb{T}_2$, $\mathbb{T}_3$, and $\mathbb{T}_4$. As seen in the figure, the resulting intersections are obtained via perspective projection from space onto the plane, where the projected version of line l_2 does not intersect the projected triangle $\mathbb{T}_k$. Let segment s_i denote the intersection between line l_i and triangle $\mathbb{T}_k$ in space, and let the set $\mathscr{S}$ contain all such intersections s_i. Then the cardinality of $\mathscr{S}$ cannot exceed $k-1$, and the number of resulting fragments (obtained by splitting the triangles) is not equal to the number of faces induced by the set $\mathscr{S}$. Specifically, let segment s_{k-1} denote the intersection between line l_{k-1} and triangle $\mathbb{T}_k$ (see Fig. 8.22 (b)). In this case, triangle $\mathbb{T}_k$ is divided into a triangle and a quadrilateral in space. Moreover, segment s_{k-1} intersects several elements from the set $\mathscr{S} \setminus s_k$. It is easy to observe that the partitioning plane $\pi(\mathbb{T}_{k-1})$ intersects only the exterior faces incident to the edges of triangle $\mathbb{T}_k$. Furthermore, it can be shown that the expected number of fragments generated by splitting triangle $\mathbb{T}_k$ and induced by the partitioning plane $\pi(\mathbb{T}_k)$ is proportional to $\mathscr{O}(k)$. In fact, the expected number of fragments of triangle $\mathbb{T}_k$ remains constant when the remaining partitioning planes $\pi(\mathbb{T}_1), \pi(\mathbb{T}2), \ldots, \pi(\mathbb{T}_{k-1})$ are considered. This property becomes especially evident in the case of a cube modeled using twelve triangles in space. Since splitting any of the n triangles produces $\mathscr{O}(k)$ fragments, it follows that the total number of fragments is upper bounded by $\mathscr{O}(n^2)$, which completes the proof.

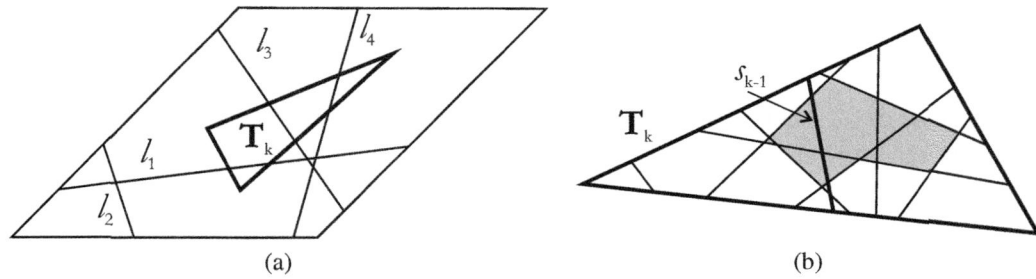

(a)　(b)

Figure 8.22: (a) Intersection of the projected plane $\pi(\mathbb{T}_k)$ with the projected planes $\pi(\mathbb{T}_1)$, $\pi(\mathbb{T}_2)$, $\pi(\mathbb{T}_3)$, and $\pi(\mathbb{T}_4)$. (b) Projected intersections between the line l_{k-1} and the triangle $\mathbb{T}_k$, including the elements of the set $\mathscr{S} \setminus s_k$.

∎

Observation 8.7.1 The size of a BSP tree in space does not depend on automatic partitioning; that is, any selection of partition planes will not result in a tree size smaller than n^2. On the other hand, in practice, the size of a BSP tree rarely reaches the order of $\mathscr{O}(n^2)$, especially in scenarios where the scene is modeled using nearly equilateral triangles (e.g., those generated by Delaunay triangulation). Thus, when Delaunay triangles are constructed from a cloud of n given points in space, it is possible to design a BSP tree whose size is proportional to the number of triangles.

The implementation of a BSP tree in three-dimensional space follows a similar approach as in the plane, with the primary distinction being the use of the classes **Point3D** and **Triangle3D** instead of **Point2D** and **Segment2D**. Most methods from the classes **BSPTree2D** and **BSPNode2D** can be directly adapted, except for the *build_tree*(·) method, whose implementation requires specific modifications to operate in three-dimensional space. As a useful exercise, the reader is encouraged to implement this version independently.

8.8 Exercises

Exercise 8.1 Explain how BSP trees are utilized in graphical algorithms for real-time rendering, particularly in the context of video game development.

Exercise 8.2 In the implementation of BSP trees, each partitioning plane is typically defined by one of the triangles in the scene. Implement a version of BSP trees in which the partitioning planes are determined according to a different criterion. Discuss the advantages of using planes defined by triangles during the partitioning process.

Exercise 8.3 Consider a modification of BSP trees in which the partitioning planes are not selected based on the existing triangles. What alternative criteria could potentially yield better performance, and why? Provide a reasoned explanation.

Exercise 8.4 Compare the computational and memory requirements of the Z-buffer algorithm and BSP trees. In which situations is it preferable to use one approach over the other? Provide a reasoned explanation.

Exercise 8.5 How is the accuracy issue in depth storage addressed in the Z-buffer? Explain how floating-point precision is utilized in modern GPU architectures.

Exercise 8.6 Given six triangles in 3D space, how can they be correctly sorted for rendering using the Painter's algorithm, assuming that no two triangles are strictly parallel?

Exercise 8.7 Prove the correctness of the Painter's algorithm by showing that if any part of object A is rasterized before any part of object B, then object A cannot lie in front of object B.

Exercise 8.8 Let $\mathscr{S}$ be a set of n non-intersecting segments in the plane for which there exists a BSP tree of size n. Prove that any automatic partitioning of the set $\mathscr{S}$ contains at least $\lfloor 4n/3 \rfloor$ elements.

Exercise 8.9 Let $\mathscr{S}$ be a set of n disjoint 2D segments. Prove that any automatic partitioning of the set $\mathscr{S}$ has depth $\Omega(n)$.

Exercise 8.10 Given a set of n segments in the plane, devise a deterministic algorithm based on the *divide-and-conquer* paradigm that constructs a BSP tree of size $\mathscr{O}(n\log n)$.

Exercise 8.11 Let $\mathscr{P}$ be a set consisting of m polygons in the plane with a total of n vertices, for which there exists a BSP tree of size k. Prove that the total complexity of the fragments generated by the BSP is of order $\mathscr{O}(n+k)$.

Exercise 8.12 Let $\mathcal{D}$ be a set of n disjoint unit disks. Prove that there exists a BSP tree for this set of size $\mathcal{O}(n)$.

Exercise 8.13 Provide an example of a set of n triangles with constant density such that any automatic partitioning, or BSP tree that exclusively uses separating planes defined by the input triangles, has size $\Omega(n^2)$.

9. Algorithms for Space Exploration

In this chapter, we present several methods used for efficient space exploration in a geometric context, particularly within the framework of computational geometry. These methods are commonly applied for optimizing query performance in relational database systems such as MySQL or PostgreSQL [109]. The connection between geometric space searching and tuple retrieval from database tables becomes evident when each tuple composed of n attributes is interpreted as a point in n-dimensional Euclidean space. For instance, querying a table with three attributes corresponds geometrically to searching within the three-dimensional space $\mathbb{R}^3$ for points satisfying a given constraint. This geometric analogy can be illustrated through a personnel management database containing a table named **EMPLOYEE**, which includes attributes such as *Name*, *Address*, *Age*, *Savings*, and so forth. A common query might be: *List all employees born between 1950 and 1955 whose savings range from €50,000 to €100,000.*

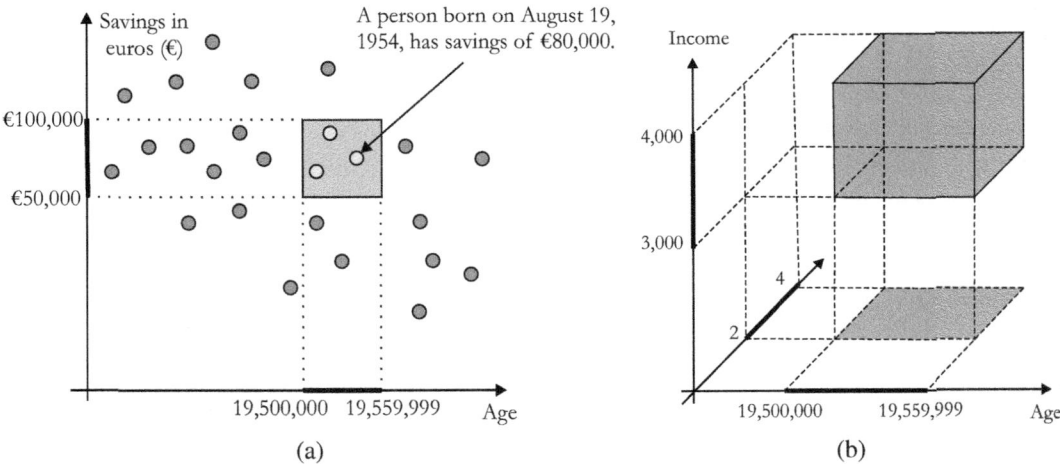

Figure 9.1: (a) Geometric interpretation of the query in 2D. (b) Geometric interpretation of the query in 3D.

From a geometric perspective, this query can be interpreted as follows:

- Each employee record is modeled as a point in $\mathbb{R}^n$ (in this case, $n = 4$).

- Since only the attributes *Age* and *Savings* are used in the query, the problem reduces to a 2D range search.
- Let E denote the set of points representing employees. The query corresponds to retrieving all points $E \in \mathbb{R}^2$ that satisfy:

$$19500000 \le E.x \le 19559999 \quad \text{and} \quad 50000 \le E.y \le 100000,$$

where the x-coordinate encodes the date of birth using the transformation:

$$E.x = 10000 \times \text{year} + 100 \times \text{month} + \text{day},$$

and $E.y$ represents the savings in euros.

This geometric viewpoint provides a foundation for applying spatial data structures to efficiently answer such queries, leveraging methods such as range trees, k-d trees, and quadtrees. Figure 9.1 (a) illustrates a geometric range search in the two-dimensional plane. From a geometric standpoint, it is straightforward to extend the interpretation of queries involving three attributes to a spatial search within a cuboid or, more generally, a polyhedron. Consider a database query aiming to retrieve all employees:

- whose birth year lies between 1950 and 1955,
- whose salary ranges from €3000,00 to €4000,00,
- and who have between two and four children.

In the geometric model, each record in the **EMPLOYEE** table is represented as a point in three-dimensional space, where:

- the x-coordinate encodes the date of birth (e.g., using the transformation $10000 \times \text{year} + 100 \times \text{month} + \text{day}$),
- the y-coordinate corresponds to the salary,
- and the z-coordinate denotes the number of children.

Thus, the query translates into a geometric range search over the Cartesian product:

$$[19500000, 19559999] \times [3000, 4000] \times [2, 4],$$

as visually demonstrated in Figure 9.1 (b). More generally, for a database table composed of d attributes, each record can be mapped to a point in $\mathbb{R}^d$ space. Efficient query processing in such cases can be achieved by employing established multidimensional searching techniques tailored for high-dimensional spaces, such as range trees, k-d trees, or R-trees [34].

9.1 One-Dimensional Geometric Range Searching

This section introduces fundamental techniques for searching numerical values within a given interval on the real line. To ensure efficiency in geometric search tasks, a key strategy involves decomposing the space into smaller, manageable subregions or partitions. For instance, calculating the area of a polygon becomes significantly more tractable once the shape is partitioned into simpler components—such as triangles—allowing the total area to be computed as the sum of individual triangle areas. Spatial decomposition strategies vary in structure and complexity; however, they are most commonly realized through recursive subdivision, though efficient iterative methods (e.g., polygon triangulation via the ear-clipping algorithm) are also widely used in practice. In one-dimensional (1D) space, a prototypical example of recursive decomposition arises in interval searching over a sorted array of real numbers. Let us consider an array of n real values. To determine the presence or location of a specific element within this array, a binary search algorithm may be employed, yielding a logarithmic time complexity of $O(\log n)$—provided the array is pre-sorted. If the array is unsorted, an initial sorting step requires $O(n \log n)$ time, after which binary search can be efficiently applied. The trade-off between naive and binary search depends on the number of queries k:

- If only a few interval queries are expected (e.g., $k \ll n$), a naive linear search, with overall complexity $O(kn)$, may be preferable to the combined cost of sorting and binary search, which is $O(n \log n + k \log n)$.
- Conversely, if frequent querying is required (e.g., thousands of times), the initial investment in sorting is justified, as each subsequent query benefits from the efficiency of binary search.

An illustrative implementation of binary search is provided in the following code snippet.

```python
def binary_search_recursive(el, A, s, e):
    if s>e: return -1   # The element el not found
    mid=(s+e)//2
    if el == A[mid]: return mid
    elif el < A[mid]: return binary_search_recursive(el, A, s, mid - 1)
    else: return binary_search_recursive(el, A, mid + 1, e)
```

The function call $binary\_search\_recursive(x, A, 0, n-1)$ is used to determine whether a given element el is present in a sorted array A of size n. If the element el is found, the function returns its index. Otherwise, it returns -1, indicating that the element is not present in the array. This function can be extended to support the retrieval of all elements in A that lie within a specified interval $[a, b]$, where $a < b$. In such cases, binary search can be employed to locate the interval boundaries efficiently. If there are k such elements, their identification requires a total time complexity of $\mathcal{O}(k \log n)$, assuming an efficient extended search algorithm is used on the sorted sequence.

The iterative version for identifying all elements within an array A that belong to a specified interval $[a, b]$ (where $a < b$) can be efficiently implemented by locating two key indices:

- the smallest index l such that $A[i] \geq a$ for all $i \geq l$,
- the largest index r such that $A[i] \leq b$ for all $i \leq r$.

Once the indices l and r are determined, all elements satisfying the interval constraint lie between positions l and r in the array. These indices can be computed either iteratively or recursively, depending on the implementation. The following code snippet illustrates the iterative approach for computing both bounds:

```python
def find_indices_iterative(a: float, b: float, A: List[float]) -> Tuple[int, int]:
    n=len(A); l=1; end=n+1
    while l<end:
        mid=(l+end)//2
        if A[mid-1]>= a: end=mid
        else: l=mid+1
    l-=1; r=1; end=n
    while r<end:
        mid=1+(r+end)//2
        if A[mid-1]>b: end=mid-1
        else: r=mid
    r-=1
    return l, r
```

An analysis of the function $find\_indices\_iterative$ reveals that locating the boundary indices l and r requires $O(\log n)$ time. Specifically, both indices are determined using the standard principle of dichotomic search (i.e., halving the search space), which guarantees logarithmic time complexity in the worst-case scenario. Thus, the total complexity of the algorithm is:

$$O(\log n) + O(\log n) = O(\log n).$$

This method is particularly efficient in cases where the number of target elements k falling within the interval $[a, b]$ is relatively small. In such scenarios, binary search combined with index-based access provides a substantial performance advantage over naive linear search. However, when the number of elements within the interval is large (e.g., $k \approx n$), the naive method may become more favorable, as it avoids the overhead of sorting and indexing. It is important to note that in practical applications, the number of elements within a given interval is often limited—especially when the data is uniformly distributed, and the interval width $b - a + 1$ is significantly smaller than the range $A_{\max} - A_{\min}$, where $A_{\max}$ and $A_{\min}$ denote the maximum and minimum values in the array, respectively. For example, consider the sorted array:

$$A = [1, 3, 6, 9, 12],$$

and suppose we wish to retrieve all elements within the interval $[3, 9]$. A call to the function:

```
l, r=find_indices_iterative(3, 9, A)
```

returns the values $l = 1$ and $r = 3$, indicating that elements $A[1]$, $A[2]$, and $A[3]$ satisfy the search criteria. A total of three elements are found within the closed interval, including its boundaries. These elements can be printed using a simple Python loop:

```
for i in range(l,r+1): print(A[i])
```

This example demonstrates how the combination of binary search and index identification enables efficient processing of range queries in one-dimensional numerical arrays. The boundary indices l and r can also be determined using a recursive approach. This is implemented through the functions *find_left_index_recursive*($\cdot,\cdot,\cdot,\cdot$) and *find_right_index_recursive*($\cdot,\cdot,\cdot,\cdot$), whose Python implementations are given below:

```python
def find_left_index_recursive(a, A, l, k):
    # Recursive implementation for determining the left index l
    if l>=k: return l
    mid=(l+k)//2
    if A[mid]>=a:
        return find_left_index_recursive(a,A,l,mid)
    else:
        return find_left_index_recursive(a,A,mid+1,k)

# Recursive implementation for determining the right index r
def find_right_index_recursive(b,A,r,k):
    if r>=k:return r
    mid=(r+k)//2
    if A[mid]>b:
        return find_right_index_recursive(b,A,r,mid)
    else:
        return find_right_index_recursive(b,A,mid+1,k)
```

To extract all elements from a sorted array that fall within a given closed interval $[a, b]$, the above recursive functions can be invoked as follows:

```
1 A = [1, 3, 6, 9, 12]; n = len(A); a, b = 3, 9
2 l = find_left_index_recursive(a, A, 0, n)
3 r = find_right_index_recursive(b, A, 0, n)
4 for j in range(l, r): print(A[j])
```

For example, given the sorted array $A = [1, 3, 6, 9, 12]$ and the interval $[3, 9]$, the recursive functions correctly identify $l = 1$ and $d = 3$, corresponding to the subarray $[3, 6, 9]$. This demonstrates the correctness and efficiency of the recursive approach in handling range-based searches, especially when the array is pre-sorted and the number of required queries is small to moderate.

Listing 9.1: GUI for Performing One-Dimensional Search Using Three Methods

```
1 import tkinter as tk
2 import numpy as np
3 import time
4 from ch9_helper_functions import find_indices_iterative, find_left_index_recursive
5 from ch9_helper_functions import find_right_index_recursive
6
7 class OneSearchGUI:
8     def __init__(self, master):
9         self.master = master
10         self.master.title("GUI FOR ONE DIMENSIONAL SEARCH - Three Methods")
11         self.master.configure(bg='gray')
12         tk.Label(master, text="Number of elements:", bg="gray", fg="white").place(
            x=20, y=20)
13         self.field_num = tk.Entry(master, width=10)
14         self.field_num.place(x=140, y=20); self.field_num.insert(0, "10000")
15         tk.Label(master, text="Interval (a,b):", bg="gray", fg="white").place(x
            =250, y=20)
16         self.field_a = tk.Entry(master, width=10)
17         self.field_a.place(x=360, y=20); self.field_a.insert(0, "-100")
18         self.field_b = tk.Entry(master, width=10)
19         self.field_b.place(x=450, y=20); self.field_b.insert(0, "100")
20         self.button_generate = tk.Button(master, text="Generate Randomly", command
            =self.generate_random_array)
21         self.button_generate.place(x=560, y=17)
22         tk.Label(master, text="Array elements:", bg="gray", fg="white").place(x
            =20, y=70)
23         self.listbox = tk.Listbox(master, height=5, width=10)
24         self.listbox.place(x=120, y=70)
25         tk.Label(master,text="Search for k elements:",bg="gray",fg="white").place(
            x=20,y=170)
26         tk.Label(master,text="from interval (c,d):",bg="gray",fg="white").place(x
            =20,y=190)
27         tk.Label(master,text="k:",bg="gray",fg="white").place(x=180, y=180)
28         self.field_k=tk.Entry(master,width=10)
29         self.field_k.place(x=200,y=180); self.field_k.insert(0, "100")
30         tk.Label(master, text="c:", bg="gray", fg="white").place(x=60, y=240)
31         self.field_c = tk.Entry(master, width=10)
32         self.field_c.place(x=90, y=240); self.field_c.insert(0, "-50")
33         tk.Label(master, text="d:", bg="gray", fg="white").place(x=180, y=240)
34         self.field_d = tk.Entry(master, width=10)
35         self.field_d.place(x=210, y=240); self.field_d.insert(0, "50")
36         self.button_recursive = tk.Button(master, text="Recursive Search", command
            =self.run_recursive_search)
37         self.button_recursive.place(x=350, y=160)
```

```
38    self.recursive_time = tk.Label(master, text="Execution time (s):", bg="
          gray", fg="white")
39    self.recursive_time.place(x=460, y=160)
40    self.button_iterative = tk.Button(master, text="Iterative Search", command
          =self.run_iterative_search)
41    self.button_iterative.place(x=350, y=200)
42    self.iterative_time = tk.Label(master, text="Execution time (s):", bg="
          gray", fg="white")
43    self.iterative_time.place(x=460, y=200)
44    self.button_naive = tk.Button(master, text="Naive Search", command=self.
          run_naive_search)
45    self.button_naive.place(x=350, y=240)
46    self.naive_time = tk.Label(master, text="Execution time (s):", bg="gray",
          fg="white")
47    self.naive_time.place(x=440, y=240)
48    self.global_array = []
49
50    def generate_random_array(self):
51        try:
52            size = int(self.field_num.get())
53            a=int(self.field_a.get()); b=int(self.field_b.get())
54            seed=int(time.time()*1000); rng=np.random.default_rng(seed)
55            arr=rng.integers(a,b+1,size=size).tolist()
56            self.global_array=arr; self.listbox.delete(0,tk.END)
57            for num in arr[:100]:self.listbox.insert(tk.END, num)
58        except ValueError:
59            print("Enter valid numbers!")
60
61    def run_recursive_search(self):
62        start=time.time();arr=sorted(self.global_array)
63        c=int(self.field_c.get());d=int(self.field_d.get())
64        l = find_left_index_recursive(c, arr, 0, len(arr))
65        r = find_right_index_recursive(d, arr, 0, len(arr))
66        end = time.time()
67        self.recursive_time.config(text=f"Execution time (s): {end - start:.6f},
            Elements found: {r-l-1}")
68
69    def run_iterative_search(self):
70        start=time.time(); arr=sorted(self.global_array)
71        c=int(self.field_c.get()); d=int(self.field_d.get())
72        l,r = find_indices_iterative(c, d, arr)
73        end = time.time()
74        self.iterative_time.config(text=f"Execution time (s): {end - start:.6f},
            Elements found: {r-l}")
75
76    def run_naive_search(self):
77        start=time.time(); total=0
78        c=int(self.field_c.get()); d=int(self.field_d.get())
79        for x in self.global_array:
80            if c <= x and x<=d: total+=1
81        end = time.time()
82        self.naive_time.config(text=f"Execution time (s): {end - start:.6f},
            Elements found: {total-1}")
83
84 if __name__ == '__main__':
85 root = tk.Tk()
86 root.geometry("800x320")
87 app = OneSearchGUI(root)
```

```
88 root.mainloop()
```

Figure 9.2, generated from Listing 9.1, presents a comparative analysis of the naive, iterative, and recursive methods with respect to their execution times when searching for $k = 100$ elements within the interval $(-50, 50)$. Specifically, the time in seconds is measured to determine how long each algorithm takes to repeatedly locate k elements from the interval $(-50, 50)$ within an array A consisting of 10^4 elements uniformly distributed over $(-100, 100)$. The results indicate that the iterative and recursive versions require the least execution time. In scenarios involving more frequent searches, the performance gap becomes even more pronounced—highlighting the significant advantage of the iterative approach over the naive method.

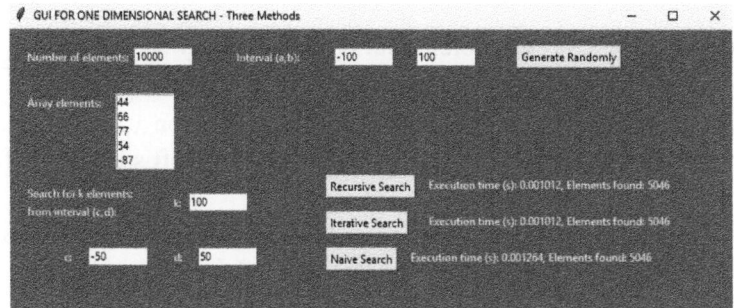

Figure 9.2: Comparison of algorithms in the case of one-dimensional search.

Although frequent range searches are not common in the one-dimensional (1D) case, such situations often occur in two-dimensional (2D) contexts. A representative example of 2D searching where it makes sense to initially sort the points arises in algorithms that repeatedly need to determine whether a given point lies inside a polygon. In the worst-case scenario, a naïve approach requires $O(n)$ time to check if a point belongs to a polygon. However, if the array of points is sorted in advance and binary search is then applied, the time required to determine point inclusion is reduced to $O(\log n)$. This type of 2D search is widely used in solving the art gallery problem. A slightly more efficient approach than binary search involves storing numbers or points within a balanced binary search tree. The primary advantage of this structure is that it enables efficient future modifications such as insertion, deletion, or updating. In contrast, if elements are stored in an array, each insertion or deletion in the worst case requires $O(n)$ time, which is significantly higher than the $O(\log n)$ time needed for similar operations in a tree, where elements are maintained in sorted order. Consider a balanced binary search tree constructed to store the elements [3, 10, 19, 23, 30, 37, 49, 59, 62, 70, 80, 89, 100, 105], as shown in Fig. 9.3.

In Fig. 9.3, the leaf nodes of the tree store the elements of the array, while the internal nodes contain the so-called splitting values—elements that induce the partitioning of the tree and thereby guide the search process. Let x_v denote the value stored in node v; this value divides the tree into two subtrees. For instance, the value 49 stored at the root node partitions the tree into a left and a right subtree. By convention, the left subtree of a node v contains nodes whose values are less than or equal to x_v, whereas the right subtree holds nodes with values strictly greater than x_v. The extraction of elements within a closed interval $(a, b]$ (where $a < b$) is performed using the pseudocode provided in Algorithm 21.

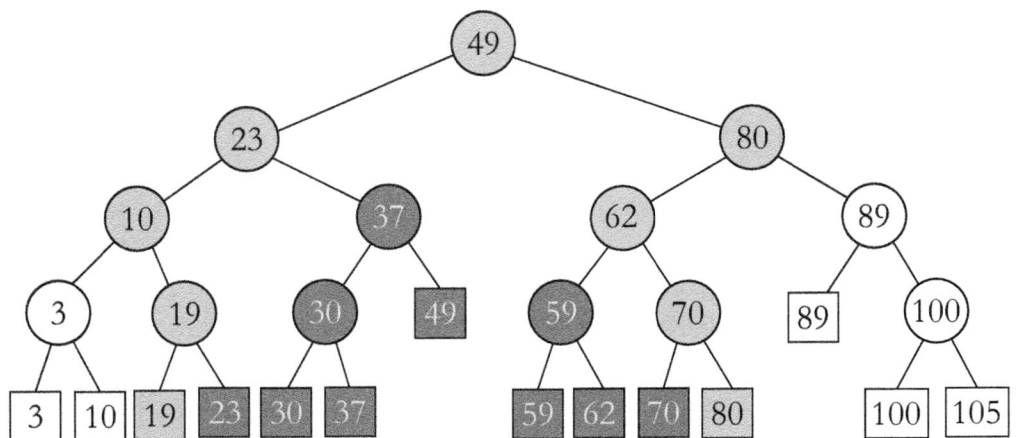

Figure 9.3: Representation of a number sequence within a balanced binary search tree.

Algorithm 21: Pseudocode for searching elements within a binary search tree.

Input: A binary search tree containing n elements, and a closed interval $(a,b]$.

Step 1: Starting from the root node x, check whether the condition $x_v \leq a$ is satisfied. If true, recursively search the right subtree, if it exists, and ignore the left subtree. If false, proceed to search the left subtree.

Step 2: If the condition $x_v > b$ holds, recursively search the left subtree while skipping the right subtree. Otherwise, search the right subtree whenever $x_v \leq b$.

Step 3: If neither of the conditions from Step 1 nor Step 2 holds, i.e., $a < x_v \leq b$, then print the value x_v and recursively continue the search in both the left and right subtrees, if they exist.

Output: Print all elements that lie within the interval $[a,b)$.

Figure 9.3 illustrates the process of extracting values from a balanced binary search tree that lie within the closed interval $(19,70]$. As shown, the leaf nodes containing the qualifying values are shaded dark gray, while the branches leading to the recursively explored subtrees are depicted in bold. All nodes that were visited during the search are colored light gray or dark gray, whereas those that were not involved in the search remain white. It is important to note that the extracted nodes need not be directly connected—for example, nodes 23 and 30 are not contiguous within the tree structure. According to the pseudocode in Algorithm 21, the time complexity of retrieving k elements from the interval $(a,b]$ is $\mathscr{O}(k\log n)$, which matches the complexity of a method based on searching a sorted array. However, a key advantage of using a tree over a sorted array lies in its generality: the tree-based approach can be naturally extended to higher dimensions. That is, it enables efficient search among multidimensional geometric objects, unlike array-based techniques that are limited to one-dimensional data, such as sequences of real numbers.

9.2 Two-Dimensional Spatial Search

This section discusses algorithms for two-dimensional spatial searching, specifically for identifying points in the plane that lie within a given range. When the points are enclosed by regular geometric shapes—such as a rectangle, circle, square, or ellipse—the search process becomes relatively straightforward. For instance, one may retrieve all points located within a rectangle defined by the corner points $A(x_1, y_1)$ and $B(x_2, y_2)$, as illustrated in Fig. 9.4 (b). However, the problem becomes considerably more complex when the search region is defined by an irregular structure (see Fig. 9.4 (a)). One viable strategy to address this challenge is to approximate the boundary of the irregular region using a large number of linear segments, thereby forming a closed polygonal chain—a simple polygon. Subsequently, this polygon can be triangulated, and the problem of determining which points lie within the irregular region is reduced

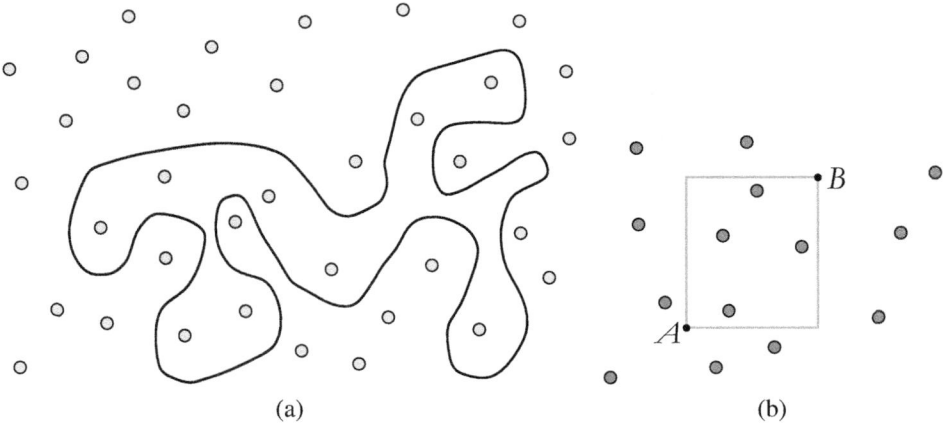

Figure 9.4: (a) Search using an irregular structure. (b) Search using a regular structure.

to testing whether they belong to any of the constituent triangles whose union covers the region. Given n points to be tested, this method allows the determination of those lying within the irregular region in $O(n \log n)$ time. Specifically, assume that the irregular region is defined by an implicit curve $F(x,y) = 0$, or more conveniently, by a parametric representation. By sampling N points along this curve, a simple polygon $\mathscr{P}$ consisting of N vertices can be constructed. In the worst-case scenario, verifying whether n points lie inside $\mathscr{P}$ requires $O(nN)$ time. Although a rectangle is a special case of a polygon, it is sometimes more practical to implement a dedicated class for representing rectangles in computer memory. Such an implementation is provided in Chapter 3. The *contains_point*($\cdot$) method of the Rectangle class enables a straightforward implementation of range queries through naive sequential scanning. Specifically, one can determine in $O(n)$ time whether a given set of n points lies within a query rectangle R. Despite its simplicity, this naive approach is frequently exploited in large-scale database systems. In practice, queries are often pre-collected and grouped into batches, enabling their joint evaluation during a single iteration over all points (i.e., records) stored in a virtual table (or view). In large databases—where data is typically stored in external files—the time required to access a single record can be significant. Consequently, the total time needed to read all records from disk often dominates the overall query processing time. To mitigate this, queries can be loaded into internal memory and executed simultaneously in a single pass over the dataset. This strategy significantly reduces I/O overhead and enhances performance, particularly when the database can be held entirely in memory or when multiple queries target the same dataset. From a geometric perspective, this approach can be interpreted as follows: all points (records) are stored in a list (internal memory), and for each query rectangle, the list is iterated over to extract those points that lie within the specified range. If, for instance, ten query rectangles are evaluated, iterating through the list ten times is substantially faster than performing equivalent operations directly on disk-based records—even with modern SSD storage—due to the considerable difference in access latency between internal and external memory. Thus, while naive, this method remains effective and justified in scenarios where query batching is feasible or where the data volume permits in-memory processing.

9.2.1 Projection Method

A natural question arises in the context of spatial search: Given a set of n points in the plane, is it possible to retrieve k points (e.g., those lying within a rectangle) in time proportional to $O(k \log n)$, analogous to the one-dimensional case? To address this question, one must consider several algorithmic strategies related to the two-dimensional range searching problem. The first such approach is the well-known projection method, which offers a semi-sequential mechanism for spatial querying. This method partially relies on the principles of binary search as applied in the one-dimensional case. The process begins by sorting the points in ascending order with respect to their x-coordinates. Once sorted, the method projects the points onto the x-axis, resulting in a sorted sequence of real values. A binary search is then performed on this sequence to identify all projections that fall within the interval $[A.x, B.x]$, where points A and B represent the bottom-left and top-right corners of a rectangular query region R. The use of binary search on one coordinate dimension allows for the identification of points bounded by vertical lines $x_1 = A.x$ and $x_2 = B.x$ in $O(\log n)$ time. This principle is illustrated in Fig. 9.5, where the initial reduction of the search space along one axis significantly improves efficiency before any further filtering by the y-coordinate is applied.

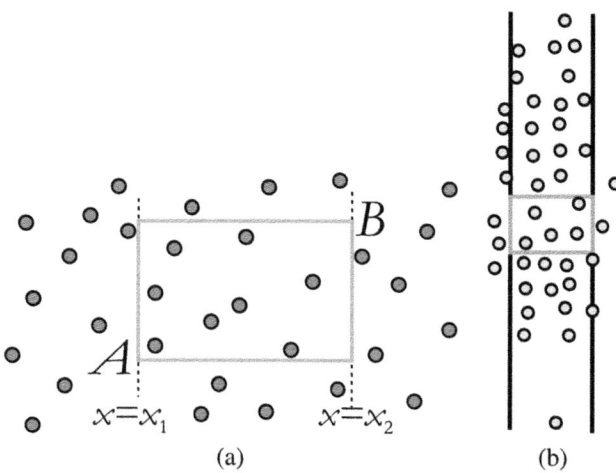

(a)   (b)

Figure 9.5: (a) Sequential search of points within a vertical strip. (b) It is more efficient to project along the y-axis first, and then along the x-axis, rather than the reverse.

In order to apply binary search, it is sufficient to sort the set of n points once at the beginning, which requires $O(n \log n)$ time. When evaluating whether each of the k randomly generated rectangles contains specific points, the total time complexity of the process is approximately $O(k \log n + n \log n + kl)$, where l denotes the maximum number of points lying within the vertical strip defined by any given rectangle. This conceptual explanation is reflected in the implementation of the function *projection_Method*($\cdot$, $\cdot$), whose structure is presented below:

```
1 def projection_method(points:List['Point2D'],rectangles:List['Rectangle'])->int:
2     count = 0; points.sort(key=lambda p: p)# Sort points based on x-coordinate
3     x_coords = [p[0] for p in points]# Extract x-coordinates from points
4     for rect in rectangles:
5         l1,d1=find_indices_iterative(rect[0][0],rect[1][0],x_coords)
6         for j in range(l1, d1 + 1):
7             if rect.contains_point(points[j]): count += 1
8     return count
```

It is evident that binary search efficiently eliminates a significant number of points located outside the vertical strip bounded by the lines $x = x_1$ and $x = x_2$. However, some of the remaining points within this vertical strip may still fall outside the horizontal boundaries defined by the lines $y = y_1$ and $y = y_2$. To filter only the relevant points—those truly contained within the query rectangle—it is necessary to perform a sequential scan over the subset of points found in the vertical strip. This sequential pass requires $O(kl)$ time in the worst case, where k is the number of rectangles, and l denotes the maximum number of points contained within any single vertical strip among the rectangles. During this scan, all points whose *y*-coordinates do not lie within the interval [*A.y*, *B.y*] are discarded. The remaining points represent those contained within the desired query rectangle. The function *enhanced_projection_method*(·, ·) implements the aforementioned logic, as presented below.

```python
def enhanced_projection_method(points: List['Point2D'], rectangles: List['
    Rectangle']) -> int:
    count = 0; points_x = copy.deepcopy(points); points_y = copy.deepcopy(points)
    points_x.sort(key=lambda p: p[0])# sort by x
    points_y.sort(key=lambda p: p[1])# sort by y
    x_coords = [p[0] for p in points_x]; y_coords = [p[1] for p in points_y]
    for rect in rectangles:
        l1, d1 = find_indices_iterative(rect[0][0], rect[1][0], x_coords)
        l2, d2 = find_indices_iterative(rect[0][1], rect[1][1], y_coords)
        if (d1 - l1) < (d2 - l2):
            for j in range(l1, d1 + 1):
                if rect.contains_point(points_x[j]):count += 1
        else:
            for j in range(l2, d2 + 1):
                if rect.contains_point(points_y[j]):count += 1
    return count
```

Although approach presented in the *enhanced_projection_method*(·, ·) might initially appear more costly than the naive method, it offers a substantial advantage: once the initial preprocessing step—sorting the points—is completed, each subsequent query can be resolved in only $O(\log n + m)$ time, where m is the number of points within the vertical strip. This is significantly more efficient than the $O(n)$ time required by the naive approach, especially when $m \ll n$. The efficiency of the projection method becomes particularly pronounced in scenarios where the number of relevant points within a rectangle is small. Such cases frequently arise in vector graphics applications—for example, in CorelDRAW—where numerous objects (points, rectangles, lines, circles, etc.) are stored in vector form. During editing sessions, users often perform operations such as selection, translation, or rotation of graphical elements. These manipulations rely heavily on range-searching techniques, and the projection method enables such interactions to be executed far more efficiently than the naive approach. Conceptually, each selection operation corresponds to a rectangular query that returns all objects contained within the specified region.

Listing 9.2: GUI for Performing Two-Dimensional Search Using Three Methods

```python
import tkinter as tk
from tkinter import ttk
import random
import time
from geometry import Point2D, Rectangle
from ch9_helper_functions import projection_method, enhanced_projection_method

class RangeSearchApp:
    def __init__(self, root):
        root.title("GUI FOR TWO-DIMENSIONAL SEARCH - Three Methods")
        self.root = root
        self.canvas = tk.Canvas(root, width=600, height=500, bg='white')
        self.canvas.grid(row=0, column=0, rowspan=10, padx=10, pady=10)
        tk.Label(root, text="Number of points:").grid(row=0, column=1, sticky='w')
        self.num_points_entry = tk.Entry(root)
        self.num_points_entry.insert(0, "10000")
        self.num_points_entry.grid(row=0, column=2)
```

```
18    tk.Button(root, text="Generate Points", command=self.generate_points).grid
          (row=0, column=3, padx=5)
19    tk.Label(root, text="Number of rectangles:").grid(row=1, column=1, sticky=
          'w')
20    self.num_rectangles_entry = tk.Entry(root)
21    self.num_rectangles_entry.insert(0, "1000")
22    self.num_rectangles_entry.grid(row=1, column=2)
23    tk.Button(root, text="Random Generate", command=self.generate_rectangles).
          grid(row=1, column=3, padx=5)
24    tk.Button(root, text="Naive Method", command=self.run_naive).grid(row=2,
          column=1)
25    self.naive_time = tk.Label(root, text="Execution time (s):")
26    self.naive_time.grid(row=2, column=2, columnspan=1, sticky='w')
27    tk.Button(root, text="Projection Method", command=self.run_projection).
          grid(row=3, column=1)
28    self.projection_time = tk.Label(root, text="Execution time (s):")
29    self.projection_time.grid(row=3, column=2, columnspan=1, sticky='w')
30    tk.Button(root, text="Enhanced Projection Method", command=self.
          run_improved_prijection).grid(row=4, column=1)
31    self.improved_time = tk.Label(root, text="Execution time (s):")
32    self.improved_time.grid(row=4, column=2, columnspan=1, sticky='w')
33    self.points = []; self.rectangles = []
34
35    def generate_points(self):
36        n=int(self.num_points_entry.get())
37        self.points=[Point2D(random.randint(0, 600), random.randint(0, 500)) for _
              in range(n)]
38        for point in self.points:
39            x=point[0]; y=point[1]
40            self.canvas.create_oval(x, y, x+1, y+1, fill='black')
41
42    def generate_rectangles(self):
43        self.rectangles=[]; n=int(self.num_rectangles_entry.get())
44        for _ in range(n):
45            x1,y1=random.randint(0,500),random.randint(0,400)
46            x2,y2=x1+random.randint(20,100),y1+random.randint(20,100)
47            self.rectangles.append(Rectangle(Point2D(x1, y1), Point2D(x2, y2)))
48            self.canvas.create_rectangle(x1,y1,x2,y2,outline=random.choice(["red",
                  "green","blue","purple"]))
49
50    def run_naive(self):
51        start = time.time(); count=0
52        for rect in self.rectangles:
53            A=rect[0]; B=rect[1]
54            for point in self.points:
55                px=point[0]; py=point[1]
56                if A[0]<=px<=B[0] and A[1]<=py<=B[1]: count+=1
57        duration=time.time()-start
58        self.naive_time.config(text=f"Execution time (s): {duration:.6f}, Points
              found: {count}")
59
60    def run_projection(self):
61        start=time.time()
62        count=projection_method(self.points, self.rectangles)
63        duration=time.time()-start
64        self.projection_time.config(text=f"Execution time (s): {duration:.6f},
              Points found: {count}")
65
```

```
66    def run_improved_prijection(self):
67        start=time.time()
68        count=enhanced_projection_method(self.points, self.rectangles)
69        duration=time.time()-start
70        self.improved_time.config(text=f"Execution time (s): {duration:.6f},
              Points found: {count}")
71
72 if __name__ == "__main__":
73 root = tk.Tk()
74 app = RangeSearchApp(root)
75 root.mainloop()
```

The projection method yields highly effective results when the points are well distributed with respect to both coordinate axes. More precisely, if the points are approximately uniformly distributed within a large rectangular region $\mathscr{R}$, such that their x-coordinates are nearly uniformly spread over the interval $[x_{min}, x_{max}]$ and their y-coordinates over $[y_{min}, y_{max}]$, then the expected ratio of the number of points located within a query rectangle $\mathscr{Q}$ (defined by points A and B) to the total number of points n is equal to the ratio of the area of the rectangle $\mathscr{Q}$ to the area of the entire region $\mathscr{R}$, that is:

$$\frac{\mathscr{A}_{\mathscr{Q}}}{\mathscr{A}_{\mathscr{R}}} = \frac{(B.x - A.x)(B.y - A.y)}{(x_{max} - x_{min})(y_{max} - y_{min})}. \tag{9.1}$$

Equation 9.1 can be employed to estimate, in percentage terms, the proportion of points that will be discarded during projection onto the coordinate axes. Consider a rectangular region $\mathscr{R}$ of size 16×16, meaning that $x_{max} - x_{min} = y_{max} - y_{min} = 16$. Let the query rectangle $\mathscr{Q}$ have dimensions 4×6, i.e., $B.x - A.x = 4$ and $B.y - A.y = 6$. When projecting the points onto the x-axis, the proportion of points retained is $4/16 = 1/4$, or 25%, implying that 75% of the points are eliminated. Similarly, projection onto the y-axis retains $6/16 = 37.5\%$ of the points, thus discarding 62.5%. This analysis reveals that projection along the x-axis is more selective and therefore more efficient in reducing the candidate set of points within rectangle $\mathscr{Q}$ compared to projection along the y-axis. Such observations motivate further refinement and optimization of the projection method by selecting the projection axis that yields the highest reduction in the number of points considered in subsequent filtering steps.

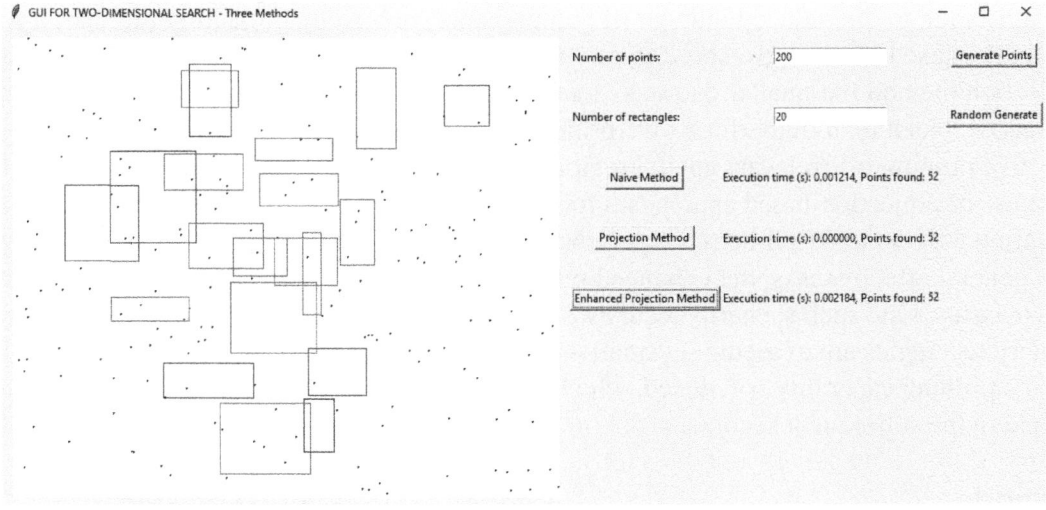

Figure 9.6: Comparison of algorithms in two-dimensional searching.

The projection method can be further optimized by performing two types of sorting during the preprocessing phase: sorting the set of points by their x-coordinates and separately by their y-coordinates. Once sorted, binary search is applied to identify two subsets of points with cardinalities k_1 and k_2, corresponding to the intervals $[A.x, B.x]$ and $[A.y, B.y]$, respectively. In this process, index pairs (l_1, d_1) and (l_2, d_2) are computed such that $k_1 = d_1 - l_1$ and $k_2 = d_2 - l_2$. Following index generation, a comparison is made between k_1 and k_2. If $k_1 < k_2$, a sequential search is conducted within the vertical strip defined by the interval $[A.x, B.x]$, requiring $O(k_1)$ time. Otherwise, the search is conducted within the horizontal strip $[A.y, B.y]$, with time complexity $O(k_2)$. For example, in Fig. 9.5 (b), it is significantly more efficient to project onto the y-axis first, yielding only eight candidate points to verify against the rectangle $\mathscr{Q}$, compared to 33 points when projecting along the x-axis. This results in a 4.125-fold improvement in performance. The asymptotic complexity of this improved method, excluding the one-time preprocessing step of sorting (which requires $O(n \log n)$ time), is $O(\min(k_1, k_2) + \log n)$. A graphical illustration of point querying within a given number of rectangles is provided in Fig. 9.6, which was generated based on the implementation shown in Listing 9.2. The benefits of this optimization become particularly evident when applied to large-scale datasets—for instance, with $n = 10{,}000$ points and $k = 10{,}000$ query rectangles—as demonstrated in Table 9.1, which presents a comprehensive analysis across varying numbers of points (n) and rectangles (k).

Table 9.1: Comparative execution times (in seconds) of three point-in-rectangle query algorithms for different values of n (points) and k (rectangles).

Algorithm	$n = 10^2, k = 10^2$	$n = 10^3, k = 10^2$	$n = 10^3, k = 10^3$	$n = 10^4, k = 10^4$	$n = 10^5, k = 10^4$
Naive Method	0.002025	0.020628	0.203673	20.182557	201.138447
Projection Method	0.000557	0.005771	0.043360	4.175595	42.296952
Enhanced Projection Method	0.002016	0.014675	0.048425	3.824495	41.587194

The execution times reported in Table 9.1 reveal clear distinctions in both the efficiency and scalability of the three evaluated point-in-rectangle query algorithms. As anticipated, the *Naive method* yields the least favorable performance, with execution time increasing approximately linearly with respect to both the number of points (n) and the number of query rectangles (k). For the largest tested instance ($n = 10^5$, $k = 10^4$), its runtime exceeds 200 seconds, making it unsuitable for large-scale applications. In contrast, the *Projection method* achieves a substantial reduction in execution time across all tested input sizes, demonstrating an order-of-magnitude improvement over the naive baseline. This efficiency gain is primarily attributed to the reduced number of comparisons enabled by projecting the search space onto the coordinate axes. Interestingly, the *Enhanced projection method*, while marginally slower than the basic projection method for smaller datasets, demonstrates comparable or even superior performance on larger instances. Notably, it outperforms the projection method when $n = 10^4$ and $n = 10^5$, likely due to more effective pruning of irrelevant spatial regions during the query phase. Overall, the results strongly support the use of projection-based approaches for efficient point-in-rectangle querying, with the enhanced variant offering the best trade-off between preprocessing overhead and query efficiency at scale. However, despite its general effectiveness, the enhanced method may exhibit performance degradation in specific pathological cases. One such scenario occurs when the distribution of points forms an L-shaped pattern and the query rectangles are exceedingly small—often containing only a single point. In these instances, the method's pruning capability is reduced, which motivates the exploration of alternative techniques, to be addressed in the subsequent sections.

9.2.2 Grid Method

This section presents the grid method for range searching, in which the query time is proportional to $\mathscr{O}(k)$—assuming a uniform distribution of points and excluding the initial preprocessing phase, which requires $\mathscr{O}(n)$ time. Here, k denotes the number of points located within a given query rectangle $\mathscr{R}$. The fundamental idea behind this method lies in preserving spatial proximity between points. Specifically, the search space is partitioned into a grid of small square cells, and during the preprocessing phase, each point is assigned to its corresponding cell. This classification step incurs a time complexity of $\mathcal{O}(n)$. Within the grid method framework, the structure of the grid is represented as follows:

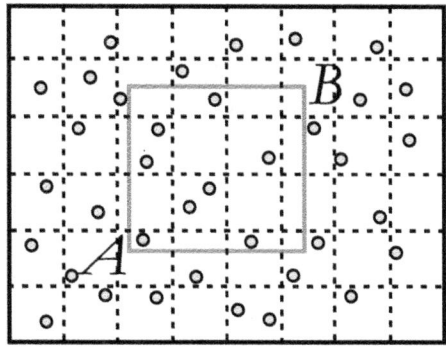

Figure 9.7: A grid of dimensions 8×6 cells overlaid on 37 planar points.

- as a dynamic matrix of cells, where each cell is associated with a list that stores zero, one, or more points contained within that cell;
- as a vector of vectors of vectors, where each cell holds a vector of points;
- as a vector of vectors of lists, where each cell contains a list of points.

Once the grid is constructed, searching for points within a given rectangle $\mathcal{R}$ requires examining only those cells that are either fully contained in or intersected by $\mathcal{R}$. Consider a scenario where 37 points are distributed in the plane, over which a grid of very small square cells has been superimposed, as illustrated in Fig. 9.7. In this figure, a rectangle $\mathcal{R}$ is also shown, encompassing 16 such cells. Consequently, to retrieve points lying within $\mathcal{R}$, it is sufficient to examine only those 16 intersected cells. Among them, only 6 cells actually contain points—resulting in a total of 8 points within $\mathcal{R}$. In the grid method, points that lie on the boundaries or between adjacent cells are assigned to one and only one of the neighboring cells. A widely adopted convention in spatial partitioning associates points lying on the left or bottom boundary of a cell with that cell, while points situated on the right or top boundary are assigned to the neighboring cell to the right or above, respectively. The implementation of the grid-based range search method is realized through the **Grid** class, whose full definition is provided in Listing 9.3.

Listing 9.3: Definition of the **Grid** class

```python
import math
from typing import List
from geometry import Point2D, Rectangle

class Grid:
    def __init__(self,x_d,y_d=None,points=None,m1=None,m2=None,eps=1.0):
        if y_d is None and m1 is None and m2 is None:# Square grid constructor
            self.m_x=math.ceil(math.sqrt(len(points)/eps)); self.m_y=self.m_x
            self.create_grid(x_d,x_d,points)
        elif points is not None and m1 is not None and m2 is not None:
            #Rectangular grid constructor
            self.m_x=m1; self.m_y=m2; self.create_grid(x_d,y_d,points)
        else:
            raise ValueError("Invalid constructor arguments for Grid")

    def create_grid(self, dim_x: float, dim_y: float, points: List[Point2D]): pass
    def range_query(self, rect: Rectangle) -> int: pass
```

Based on the definition of the **Grid** class, it is evident that the grid is internally represented as a matrix of dimensions $m_x \times m_y$, where each element is a list that stores one or more instances of **Point2D** class. These lists enable efficient grouping of points that fall within the same grid cell. Before implementing the class methods, it is crucial to appropriately determine the grid structure by selecting its dimensions. If the grid is too coarse—i.e., the cells are too large—then each cell will contain a large number of points, and even those cells that are only slightly intersected by the query rectangle $\mathscr{R}$ will require exhaustive checking. Conversely, if the grid is too fine-grained—with very small cells—then a large number of cells must be checked even for small rectangles, many of which will likely be empty. A commonly used heuristic for determining the grid resolution is to establish a correlation between the total number of cells (*TNC*) and the total number of points (*TNP*). This can be expressed as:

$$TNC = \frac{TNP}{\varepsilon},$$

where ε is a small constant close to one. Proper tuning of ε is essential: if it is significantly less than one, the total number of cells increases drastically, which in turn reduces the performance of the grid-based range query. To control the number of cells along the x and y axes, the parameter $m_x = m_y$ is set according to:

$$m_x = \left\lfloor \sqrt{\frac{n}{\varepsilon}} \right\rfloor,$$

where n is the total number of input points. This is the approach taken in the default (square grid) constructor. An alternative constructor is provided for rectangular grids, where the number of cells along the x-axis (m_x) and y-axis (m_y) is explicitly specified by the user. In both constructors, the attributes m_x and m_y are initialized with user-provided values, after which the *create_grid*(x_d, y_d, *points*) method is invoked. This method allocates memory for the grid and distributes the given list of points into their corresponding cells based on their spatial positions. The x_d and y_d parameters correspond to the spatial extent of the grid in the x and y directions, respectively. In practice, these are usually set to $x_{max} + 1$ and $y_{max} + 1$, where x_{max} and y_{max} denote the maximum x and y-coordinates among all input points. The implementation of the method *create_grid*($\cdot$, $\cdot$, $\cdot$) is provided below.

```
1 def create_grid(self, x_d: float, y_d: float, points: List[Point2D]):
2     self.cell_width=x_d/self.m_x; self.cell_height=y_d/self.m_y
3     self.grid = [[[] for _ in range(self.m_y)] for _ in range(self.m_x)]
4     for point in points:
5         i=int(point[0]/self.cell_width)#i is the column index of the cell
6         j=int(point[1]/self.cell_height)#j is the row index of the cell
7         if 0<=i<self.m_x and 0<=j<self.m_y: self.grid[i][j].append(point)
```

The next method to be implemented is *range_query*($\cdot$). Its is responsible for determining the number of points contained within a specified query rectangle. Given a rectangle rect, defined by its bottom-left and top-right corners, the algorithm computes the range of grid cells that either intersect or are fully enclosed by the rectangle. This is achieved by converting the x and y-coordinates of the rectangle's corners into corresponding grid cell indices. More precisely, the indices of the starting and ending columns are calculated by dividing the x-coordinates of the rectangle by the cell width, while the starting and ending rows are obtained by dividing the y-coordinates by the cell height. These index boundaries define a submatrix of cells that must be examined. The algorithm then iterates over each cell within the computed index range and inspects all points stored in those cells. For each point, it checks whether the point lies within the given rectangle by invoking the *contains_point*($\cdot$) method ot the class **Rectangle**. If the point satisfies this condition, a counter is incremented. This approach ensures that only the relevant subset of the grid is searched, thereby reducing the number of unnecessary point-in-rectangle checks. The final count of points found within the query rectangle is returned as the result of the method. Based on this, the implementation of the aforementioned range query method is as follows:

```python
def range_query(self, rect: Rectangle) -> int:
    start_col=int(rect[0][0]/self.cell_width)#considered from the start column
    end_col=int(rect[1][0]/self.cell_width)#cons. up to the end of the last column
    start_row=int(rect[0][1]/self.cell_height)#considered from the start row
    end_row=int(rect[1][1]/self.cell_height)#cons. up to the end of the last row
    count=0
    for i in range(start_col, end_col+1):
        for j in range(start_row, end_row+1):
            if 0 <= i < self.m_x and 0 <= j < self.m_y:
                for point in self.grid[i][j]:
                    if rect.contains_point(point):count += 1
    return count
```

Figure 9.8 was generated based on the source code provided in Listing 9.4, which constitutes an extension of the previously presented Listing 9.2.

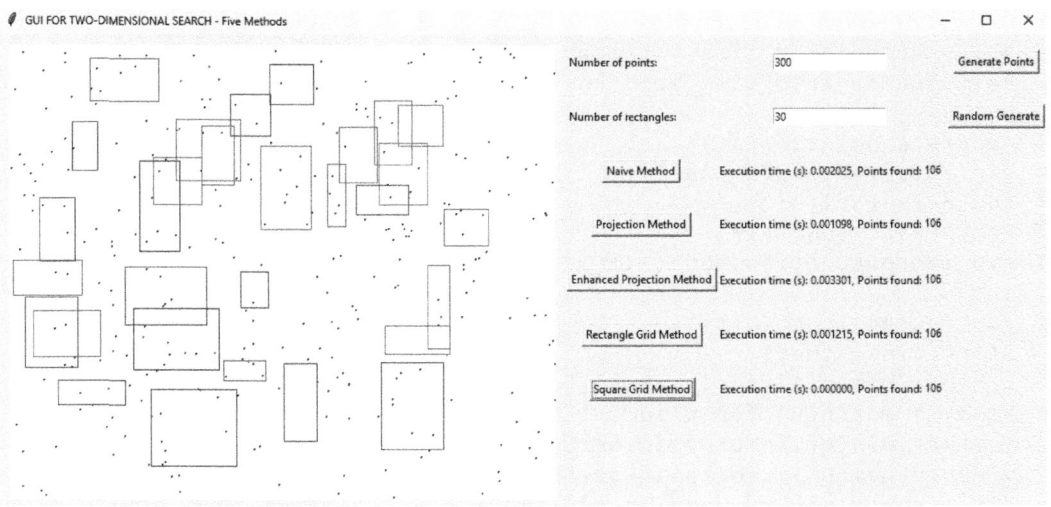

Figure 9.8: Comparison of five techniques for two-dimensional range searching.

Figure 9.8 presents a graphical user interface that extends the one shown in Fig. 9.6 by incorporating two additional range searching techniques: a square grid method and a rectangular grid method.

Table 9.2: Runtime comparison of two point-in-rectangle query algorithms over varying point and rectangle counts.

Algorithm	$n = 10^2$, $k = 10^2$	$n = 10^3$, $k = 10^2$	$n = 10^3$, $k = 10^3$	$n = 10^4$, $k = 10^4$	$n = 10^5$, $k = 10^4$
Rectangle Grid method	0.001012	0.003042	0.013893	0.714571	6.963153
Sqaure Grid method	0.001002	0.002015	0.011841	0.755594	7.446959

Based on the experimental results presented in Table 9.2, obtained under the same conditions as in Table 9.1, it is evident that the use of grid-based techniques leads to substantially faster execution times for range queries when compared to the previously evaluated methods. For instance, in the scenario involving 10,000 points and 10,000 rectangles, the fastest previously tested method, *enhanced_projection_method*$(\cdot, \cdot)$, required 3.824495 seconds to identify 1,246,353 points lying within the specified rectangles. In contrast, both grid-based approaches—particularly the rectangular grid method—achieved the same result in less than one second, with the rectangular grid method completing the query in just 0.714571 seconds, yielding an approximate speedup factor of 5.35. These findings underscore the efficiency and practical value of grid-based spatial partitioning for large-scale range search tasks.

Listing 9.4: Extended GUI for Performing Two-Dimensional Search Using Five Methods

```python
#Same as earlier
from Grid import Grid # New Added
class RangeSearchApp:
    def __init__(self, root):
        # Same as earlier
        # New added
        tk.Button(root, text="Rectangle Grid Method", command=self.
            run_rectangle_grid).grid(row=5, column=1)
        self.rectangle_grid_time = tk.Label(root, text="Execution time (s):")
        self.rectangle_grid_time.grid(row=5, column=2, columnspan=1, sticky='w')

        tk.Button(root, text="Square Grid Method", command=self.run_square_grid).
            grid(row=6, column=1)
        self.square_grid_time = tk.Label(root, text="Execution time (s):")
        self.square_grid_time.grid(row=6, column=2, columnspan=1, sticky='w')

    def generate_points(self): # Same as earlier
    def generate_rectangles(self): # Same as earlier
    def run_naive(self): # Same as earlier
    def run_projection(self): # Same as earlier
    def run_improved_prijection(self): # Same as earlier

    def run_rectangle_grid(self): # New added
        start=time.time()
        x_min = min(p[0] for p in self.points)
        x_max = max(p[0] for p in self.points)
        y_min = min(p[1] for p in self.points)
        y_max = max(p[1] for p in self.points)
        dim = max(x_max, y_max); grid=Grid(x_max+1,y_max+1,self.points,45,50)
        count=sum(grid.range_query(rect) for rect in self.rectangles)
        duration=time.time()-start
        self.rectangle_grid_time.config(text=f"Execution time (s): {duration:.6f},
            Points found: {count}")
    def run_square_grid(self): # New added
        start=time.time()
        x_min = min(p[0] for p in self.points)
        x_max = max(p[0] for p in self.points)
        y_min = min(p[1] for p in self.points)
        y_max = max(p[1] for p in self.points)
        dim=max(x_max,y_max); grid=Grid(dim+5,None,self.points)
        count=sum(grid.range_query(rect) for rect in self.rectangles)
        duration=time.time()-start
        self.square_grid_time.config(text=f"Execution time (s): {duration:.6f},
            Points found: {count}")

if __name__ == "__main__":
    root=tk.Tk(); app=RangeSearchApp(root);root.mainloop()
```

The following section analyzes the time complexity of the proposed method. Since the constructors generate either a rectangular or square matrix and distribute n points into its cells, the execution time of the *create_grid*$(\cdot,\cdot,\cdot)$ method is quadratic and pertains to the preprocessing phase. On the other hand, when points are uniformly distributed in the plane, the *range_query*$(\cdot)$ method operates, on average, in $\mathcal{O}(r)$ time, where r denotes the number of points located within the query rectangle $\mathcal{R}$. Specifically, if r is the number of points returned by the *range_query*$(\cdot)$ method that fall inside rectangle $\mathcal{R}$, then r is typically proportional to the number of grid cells intersected by $\mathcal{R}$. As each cell generally contains a very small number of points, retrieving the contents of these cells requires nearly constant time, i.e., $\mathcal{O}(1)$ on average. Consequently, the overall time complexity of the method is $\mathcal{O}(r)$ in the *average-case* scenario, where the number of examined cells scales with the number of points r. The worst-case time complexity of this method is $\mathcal{O}(n)$, where the rectangle $\mathcal{R}$ covers all grid cells and every point must be examined. Here, n denotes the total number of points stored in the grid. It is worth noting that this type of grid-based method is frequently employed in archaeological applications. However, it is not without limitations. Certain degenerate cases can significantly degrade performance. These drawbacks are effectively mitigated through the use of more advanced techniques, which will be introduced in the next chapter. These methods are based on 2D binary search structures that partition the search space in a non-uniform manner, thereby adapting to the actual spatial distribution of points.

9.2.3 Method Based on Binary Trees

In this section, we begin by describing two-dimensional binary search trees, a specific instance of Kd-trees. These trees constitute a dynamic and adaptive data structure, closely related to classical binary search trees, with the key distinction that they partition the plane (in 2D) or space (in 3D) to support various range-searching operations and other geometric problems. Two-dimensional binary search trees recursively subdivide the plane using vertical and horizontal lines, where the splitting lines alternate by tree depth: vertical lines are used at even levels (including the root), while horizontal lines are employed at odd levels (see Fig. 9.9).

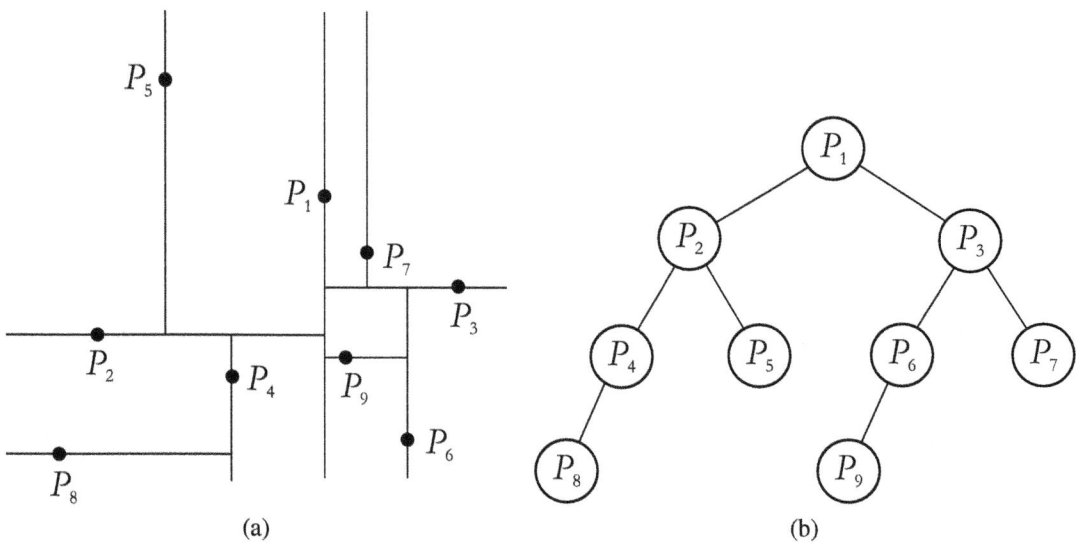

(a)   (b)

Figure 9.9: (a) Recursive subdivision of the plane using alternating vertical and horizontal lines. (b) Corresponding 2D binary search tree structure.

For implementation purposes, we adopt the convention that each node in the tree corresponds to exactly one point in the plane, and that a splitting line always passes through that point. This recursive subdivision results in a hierarchical spatial partitioning, which facilitates efficient geometric queries. The principle is illustrated in Fig. 9.9, where part (a) shows the recursive subdivision of the plane using alternating vertical and horizontal lines, and part (b) presents the corresponding binary search tree. Together, these visualizations elucidate the structural relationship between the spatial decomposition and its associated tree representation. To better understand the construction process of a 2D search tree, consider the point set $\mathscr{S} = \{P_1, P_2, P_3, \cdots, P_9\}$ in the plane, as illustrated on Fig. 9.9 (a). We now describe the procedure for recursively partitioning the plane using alternating vertical and horizontal lines. The construction begins by determining the median point of the set, which is obtained by sorting the points according to a given coordinate. First, the set $\mathscr{S}$ is sorted by the x-coordinates of its points, yielding the ordered set $\mathscr{X} = \{P_8, P_2, P_5, P_4, P_1, P_9, P_7, P_6, P_3\}$. Then, the same set is sorted by y-coordinates to obtain the set $\mathscr{Y} = \{P_8, P_6, P_4, P_9, P_2, P_3, P_7, P_1, P_5\}$. These two auxiliary sets, $\mathscr{X}$ and $\mathscr{Y}$, alternate throughout the recursive construction of the binary tree. The first median is selected from set $\mathscr{X}$, giving point P_1. This point becomes the root of the tree, and a vertical line is drawn through it, dividing the point set into two subsets: $\mathscr{S}_L = \{P_8, P_4, P_2, P_5\}$, consisting of points to the left of the splitting line, and $\mathscr{S}_R = \{P_6, P_9, P_3, P_7\}$, with points on the right. The left subtree of the root node P_1 is constructed recursively. Since the next tree level is odd, a horizontal line is used as the splitting line, and the sets are updated as $\mathscr{X} \leftarrow \mathscr{S}_L, \mathscr{Y} \leftarrow \mathscr{X}$. When a horizontal line is used, points "to the left" of the line are those below it, while those "to the right" are above it. The median of $\mathscr{X}$ is now P_2, which becomes the left child of P_1, and a horizontal line is drawn through it, partitioning the set into $\mathscr{S}_L = \{P_8, P_4\}$ and $\mathscr{S}_R = \{P_5\}$. Continuing recursively, the next level uses a vertical splitting line. The sets are $\mathscr{X} \leftarrow \{P_8, P_4\}$ and $\mathscr{Y} \leftarrow \{P_8, P_4, P_2, P_5\}$. The median is P_4, and the resulting subsets are $\mathscr{S}_L = \{P_8\}$ and $\mathscr{S}_R = \emptyset$. Thus, P_4 becomes the left child of P_2. At the next level (level 3), a horizontal line is used again. The only remaining point in $\mathscr{X}$ is P_8, which becomes the left leaf of P_4. Since there is no right child at this level, the recursion returns to process the right child of P_2, which is P_5. The right subtree of P_1, consisting of $\mathscr{S}_R = \{P_6, P_9, P_3, P_7\}$, is processed analogously. The entire tree construction procedure is illustrated in Fig. 9.9 (b). After introducing the recursive procedure for constructing a 2D search tree, we now present two Python classes that enable its implementation. The first class, **Node2DTree**, represents a node in the 2D binary search tree and is defined as follows:

Listing 9.5: Definition of the class **Node2DTree**

```
1 class Node2DTree:
2     def __init__(self, point: Point2D):
3         self.point=point
4         self.left:Optional['Node2DTree']=None #Left vert. line or lower half-plane
5         self.right:Optional['Node2DTree']=None #Right vertical line or upper h.p.
6     def query_range(self, rect: Rectangle, split_axis: int = 0): pass
```

Within the **Node2DTree** class, the left subtree stores points that lie either to the left of a vertical splitting line or below a horizontal splitting line, depending on the tree level—vertical for even levels and horizontal for odd ones. Conversely, the right subtree contains points located to the right of the vertical line or above the horizontal line. For instance, as illustrated in Fig. 9.9 (b), point P_3 may lie to the right of the vertical line defined by point P_1, while point P_7 may be positioned above the horizontal line defined by P_3. Prior to defining the recursive tree construction method, we introduce two custom comparison functions that preserve the required sorting order during the tree-building process.

```
1 def cmp(a,b): return (a>b)-(a<b)
2 def left_before_right(p1: Point2D, p2: Point2D) -> int:
3     return cmp((p1[0], p1[1]), (p2[0], p2[1]))
4 def bottom_before_top(p1: Point2D, p2: Point2D) -> int:
5     return cmp((p1[1], p1[0]), (p2[1], p2[0]))
```

Following the previous definition of the structure of binary tree nodes, we proceed by introducing the primary class **Binary2DTree**, which encapsulates the logic for both tree construction and range query execution.

Listing 9.6: Definition of the class **Binary2DTree**

```
1 from functools import cmp_to_key
2 class Binary2DTree:
3     def __init__(self, points: List[Point2D]):
4         points_x=sorted(points,key=cmp_to_key(left_before_right))
5         points_y=sorted(points,key=cmp_to_key(bottom_before_top))
6         self.root=self.build_tree(points_x,points_y,0)
7
8     def range_search(self, rect: Rectangle)->List[Point2D]:
9         if not self.root: return []
10        return self.root.query_range(rect,0)
11    def build_tree(self, X: List[Point2D], Y: List[Point2D], depth: int): pass
```

The range query procedure performs alternating comparisons along the *x* and *y* axes, recursively descending into the appropriate subtrees based on the position of the bounding rectangle's corners. In the provided implementation of the *range_search*($\cdot$) method, the query is simply delegated to the root node. Prior to this, within the constructor, the input point set is independently sorted with respect to both *x* and *y*-coordinates. The tree's root is then initialized by invoking the recursive method *build_tree*($\cdot,\cdot,\cdot$), which realizes a divide-and-conquer strategy structured as follows:

```
1 def build_tree(self,X:List[Point2D],Y:List[Point2D],depth:int)->Optional[
      Node2DTree]:
2     n=len(X)
3     if n == 0: return None
4     if n == 1: return Node2DTree(X[0])
5     m=n//2; split_axis=depth%2; left_Y = []; right_Y = []; root=Node2DTree(X[m])
6     cmp=left_before_right if split_axis==0 else bottom_before_top
7     for p in Y:
8         if p==X[m]:continue
9         elif cmp(p,X[m])<0:left_Y.append(p)
10        else:right_Y.append(p)
11    root.left=self.build_tree(left_Y, X[0:m],1+depth)
12    root.right=self.build_tree(right_Y,X[m+1:n],1+depth)
13    return root
```

The recursive method *build_tree*($\cdot,\cdot,\cdot$) selects the median point $X[m]$ along the current splitting axis—alternating between *x* and *y*-coordinates—and recursively partitions the point set to construct the left and right subtrees. What remains is the implementation of the method *query_range*($\cdot,\cdot$) within the **Node2DTree** class, which traverses the tree structure and retrieves all points located within the specified rectangular region.

```
1 def query_range(self, rect: Rectangle, split_axis: int = 0) -> List[Point2D]:
2     results=[]
3     if rect.contains_point(self.point): results.append(self.point)
4     cmp=left_before_right if split_axis == 0 else bottom_before_top
5     if self.left and cmp(rect[0], self.point) <= 0:
6         results.extend(self.left.query_range(rect, 1-split_axis))
7     if self.right and cmp(rect[1], self.point) >= 0:
8         results.extend(self.right.query_range(rect, 1-split_axis))
9     return results
```

Figure 9.10, generated using the code in Listing 9.7, which extends the implementation from Listing 9.4, illustrates the efficiency of the binary search tree–based range search method. In the case of 1000 points and 100 query rectangles, this method demonstrates significantly faster execution times compared to most other approaches, with the exception of the grid-based methods and projection method.

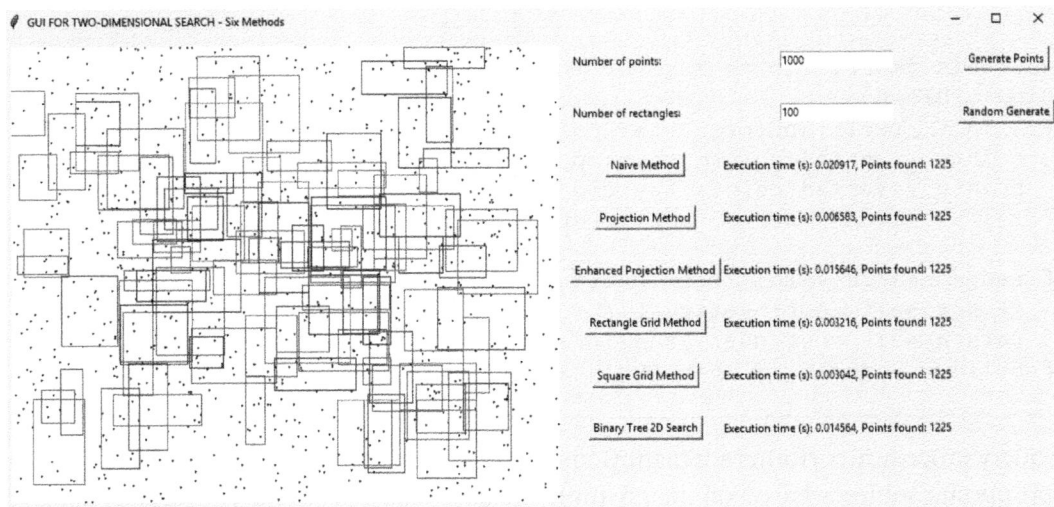

Figure 9.10: Comparative analysis of six techniques for two-dimensional range searching.

Figure 9.10 presents a graphical user interface that extends the one shown in Fig. 9.8 by incorporating binary tree 2d search method.

Listing 9.7: Extended GUI for Performing Two-Dimensional Search Using Six Methods

```python
from Binary2DTree import Binary2DTree
class RangeSearchApp:
    def __init__(self, root):
        # Same as earlier
        # New added
        tk.Button(root, text="Binary Tree 2D Search", command=self.
            run_binary_tree_search).grid(row=7, column=1)
        self.binary_tree_time = tk.Label(root, text="Execution time (s):")
        self.binary_tree_time.grid(row=7, column=2, columnspan=1, sticky='w')

    def run_binary_tree_search(self):  # New added
        start=time.time(); count=0; tree=Binary2DTree(self.points)
        for rect in self.rectangles:
            result = tree.range_search(rect); count+=len(result)
        duration = time.time()-start
        self.binary_tree_time.config(text=f"Execution time (s): {duration:.6f},
            Points found: {count}")

if __name__ == "__main__":
    root=tk.Tk(); app=RangeSearchApp(root);root.mainloop()
```

Finally, it is worth noting that the time required to construct a 2D binary search tree storing n points is proportional to $\mathcal{O}(n \log n)$, as the execution time $T(n)$ satisfies the following recurrence relation:

$$T(n) = \begin{cases} \mathcal{O}(1), & \text{if } n = 1 \\ \mathcal{O}(n) + 2T(\lceil n/2 \rceil), & \text{if } n > 1 \end{cases}$$

Regardless of whether the input points are randomly or uniformly distributed, it can be shown that the range query operation has a time complexity of $\mathcal{O}(k + \sqrt{n})$, where k denotes the number of points contained within the query rectangle $\mathscr{R}$ whose sides are aligned with the coordinate axes. In practice, 2D binary search trees exhibit performance comparable to that of grid-based methods and frequently outperform them, especially in cases where the uniform distribution assumption is violated. This approach is notably more robust in the presence of point clusters and less sensitive to the spatial distribution of data within the bounding region.

9.3 Multidimensional Search

Thus far, we have described several methods for performing two-dimensional range searching. It is not difficult to envision how these approaches could be generalized to support queries in higher-dimensional spaces. However, the inherent complexity of high-dimensional spaces requires special attention, particularly with respect to execution time. In principle, the performance of such generalizations is difficult to predict, and in many cases, they may not offer improvements over a naive linear search. The utility of these methods strongly depends on the specific application context, and empirical evaluation is often necessary to assess their practical benefit.

9.3.1 Grid Method Generalization

To extend the grid-based method to k dimensions, the search space must be divided into k-dimensional *hyperrectangles*, which represent the natural generalization of 2D rectangles and 3D cuboids. This involves constructing a k-dimensional matrix whose cells store lists of points (typically requiring a $(k+1)$-dimensional data structure). A major challenge lies in determining a suitable cell granularity. With increasing dimensionality, the total number of cells grows rapidly, even when each dimension is partitioned modestly. For example, if $k = 10$ and each axis is divided into five intervals, the total number of cells is 5^{10}, most of which will remain empty. This leads to excessive memory consumption and renders the method impractical for large values of k.

9.3.2 Generalization of 2D Trees

A more structured and widely adopted multidimensional generalization of 2D binary trees is the *kd-tree* (short for k-dimensional tree). This structure cyclically alternates the splitting dimension at each tree level: at level 0, points are compared by their first coordinate; at level 1, by their second; and so forth, returning to the first coordinate after k levels. Under the assumption that the input point set is randomly shuffled, the resulting tree retains structural properties similar to those of balanced binary search trees. Moreover, the kd-tree construction mirrors a simple geometric partitioning of space. In 3D, each node divides its associated region by a plane; in general k-dimensional space, the partition is induced by a $(k-1)$-dimensional hyperplane. This elegant correspondence between spatial decomposition and tree structure facilitates efficient range querying in low-dimensional settings.

9.3.3 Challenges in High-Dimensional Spaces

Despite these appealing characteristics, kd-trees suffer from serious limitations as dimensionality increases. In high-dimensional spaces, the resulting trees tend to become poorly balanced, and the effectiveness of range searching deteriorates significantly. In the worst case, performance degrades to that of linear search, while introducing additional structural overhead. This phenomenon arises from the *curse of dimensionality*: in high dimensions, a vastly larger number of points is needed to achieve uniform distribution, and in practice, datasets often exhibit high redundancy. For example, in a personnel database, many "points" (employees) may share common attributes such as city of residence, year of birth, or salary. Such correlations lead to large clusters of identical coordinate values, causing heavily skewed trees with many nodes branching in only one direction.

9.3.4 Heuristic Improvement: Adaptive Splitting

To mitigate the imbalance, a common strategy involves choosing the splitting coordinate adaptively at each node, selecting the dimension that best partitions the data—ideally resulting in balanced subtrees. While this approach requires storing the chosen dimension at each node, the gain in balance and performance, especially in high-dimensional scenarios, often justifies the additional storage cost. Notably, this heuristic can be employed not only in kd-trees but also in their 2D counterparts to improve query efficiency.

9.4 Exercises

Exercise 9.1 Refactor the existing grid-based range searching implementation by replacing the fixed-size two-dimensional array with a dictionary-based data structure. Ensure that the initialization of an $m \times m$ grid over a set of n points is performed in $\mathcal{O}(m+n)$ time, where m denotes the number of occupied cells.

Exercise 9.2 Design and implement a three-dimensional binary search tree (3D tree) as a direct generalization of the 2D tree structure. The primary goal is to support efficient orthogonal range searching in three-dimensional space. Your implementation should:

- Construct the tree by recursively partitioning the 3D point set using axis-aligned planes, alternating the splitting dimension cyclically among x, y, and z;
- Enable queries that retrieve all points within a specified axis-aligned rectangular box (cuboid);
- Analyze and discuss the time complexity of both tree construction and range query operations;
- Evaluate the performance of your implementation on synthetic datasets of varying size and distribution.

Exercise 9.3 Explain why the constructor of the class Binary2DTree fails when provided with a list of points that includes duplicates. Specifically, discuss how the presence of identical points affects the recursive partitioning strategy and leads to infinite recursion. Modify the constructor to robustly handle duplicate points, ensuring correct and finite construction of the 2D binary range tree. The updated implementation should preserve the expected asymptotic time complexity of $\mathcal{O}(n \log n)$ and maintain the structural properties of the tree.

Exercise 9.4 Extend the implementation of the range query in 2D binary search trees by incorporating a mechanism to detect whether a given node is fully contained within the query range. If such a node is identified as a "surrounding node"—meaning that the entire subtree rooted at that node lies entirely within the query rectangle—optimize the traversal by directly collecting all descendant points without further inclusion checks.

Exercise 9.5 Formulate an efficient solution to the disk range searching problem, which requires organizing a given set $\mathscr{S}$ of points in the Euclidean plane to support circular (disk) queries of the form: given a query point P and radius $r > 0$, list all points in $\mathscr{S}$ whose Euclidean distance from P is less than or equal to r. Implement and compare two approaches to this problem: one based on spatial grid partitioning and the other using 2D binary search trees.

Exercise 9.6 Consider a set $\mathcal{T}$ of n triangles embedded in the Euclidean plane. An inverse range counting query is defined as follows: For a given query point Q, determine the number of triangles from $\mathcal{T}$ that contain Q as an interior or boundary point.

i) Devise a data structure that supports efficient inverse range counting queries, aiming for near-linear space complexity. Formally analyze both the storage requirements and the query time of your proposed solution.

ii) Investigate whether the complexity bounds can be improved under the additional assumption that all triangles in $\mathcal{T}$ are pairwise disjoint. Justify your reasoning and propose an optimized solution, if possible.

Exercise 9.7 Design a data structure that supports triangular range searching with a query time of $\mathcal{O}(\log^3 n)$. Clearly describe the structure of your data representation, detailing the preprocessing steps and the organization of geometric information. Formulate the associated query algorithm precisely, including how a given triangle is used to report all points lying inside it. Provide a formal analysis of both the space complexity and the query time, justifying how the desired query bound is achieved.

Exercise 9.8 Given a set $\mathcal{S}$ of n weighted points in the plane, design two data structures to support half-plane maximum-weight queries:

- One with linear storage complexity;
- One with logarithmic query time.

For each, describe the structure, preprocessing, and query algorithm, and analyze both space and time complexity, emphasizing trade-offs between storage and efficiency.

Exercise 9.9 In geometric range searching, the input objects are often more complex than points.

i) Given a set $\mathcal{S}$ of n axis-aligned rectangles in the plane, design a data structure using $\mathcal{O}(n\log^3 n)$ space that returns all rectangles fully contained in a query rectangle in $\mathcal{O}(\log^4 n + k)$ time.

ii) Extend the approach to a set $\mathcal{P}$ of n arbitrary polygons and design a structure with the same asymptotic bounds.

Exercise 9.10 Let $\mathcal{P}$ be a set of n points in $\mathbb{R}^d$.

i) Formally describe a query algorithm that answers d-dimensional orthogonal range queries on $\mathcal{P}$. Prove that the query time is bounded by $\mathcal{O}(n^{1-1/d} + k)$, where k is the number of reported points.

ii) Show that the storage complexity is $\mathcal{O}(dn)$ when d is treated as a variable parameter (i.e., not constant). Additionally, analyze the construction time and query time with respect to d, clearly identifying their dependence on the dimensionality.

10. Quadtrees

In this chapter, we introduce a specialized hierarchical spatial data structure known as the *quadtree* [202–204, 208]. As a recursive partitioning method, the quadtree plays a central role in efficiently organizing two-dimensional spatial information. In contrast to binary trees, where each internal node has at most two children, a quadtree divides the space into four disjoint subregions—referred to as quadrants—at every internal node. These subdivisions are generally square or rectangular in shape, depending on the application context, and they enable a structured, hierarchical decomposition of the spatial domain. The recursive nature of quadtrees facilitates adaptive resolution: subregions are further subdivided only when necessary, typically guided by the spatial distribution of the data. An example of such an adaptive decomposition is depicted in Fig. 10.1 (a), where the spatial region is recursively partitioned according to point density. This adaptive behavior is particularly advantageous in situations where the data is non-uniformly distributed—dense in some areas while sparse in others—as it allows for selective refinement. Consequently, quadtrees significantly reduce memory usage and computational overhead in comparison to uniform grid-based methods, which lack such flexibility. The primary motivation for employing quadtrees stems from their ability to localize computational effort, enabling efficient spatial indexing, range searching, and collision detection. Their hierarchical organization supports logarithmic-depth traversal and localized updates, making them well-suited for real-time applications and dynamic environments. As a result, quadtrees are widely used across various domains, including:

- *Orthogonal Range Searching*: Efficient identification of points lying within a query rectangle, particularly when point distribution is uneven [30].

- *Image Processing and Compression*: Widely used in fractal image compression, where recursive spatial decomposition exploits self-similarity [123].

- *Collision Detection in Computer Graphics and Games*: Applied in real-time rendering engines to detect collisions among moving objects by limiting pairwise checks to nearby quadrants [160].

- *Particle Collision Detection*: In particle simulations (e.g., molecular dynamics, fluid dynamics), quadtrees enable fast detection of interactions between nearby particles, significantly reducing the computational burden from $\mathscr{O}(n^2)$ to near-linear time [93].

- *Geographic Information Systems* (GIS): Support fast spatial indexing, map overlay operations, and efficient data retrieval [161].

A. Alihodžić, *Exploring Computational Geometry*, Texts in Computer Science,
https://doi.org/10.1007/978-3-032-06393-9_10

10.1 Geometric Modeling and Thermal Simulation of PCBs

Modern electronic devices—ranging from electric shavers and phones to televisions and computers—almost invariably incorporate electronic components organized into combinational circuits essential for proper functioning. These components are mounted on printed circuit boards (PCBs), and among the most commonly used elements are VLSI circuits (*Very Large-Scale Integration*), transistors, resistors, capacitors, and various other electronic components. The term VLSI refers to the design of high-density integrated circuits (ICs), enabling millions of MOS transistors to be embedded onto a single chip. VLSI-based devices include microprocessors, memory units, and similar components. The design process of a PCB (see Fig. 10.1 (b)) consists of two fundamental stages:

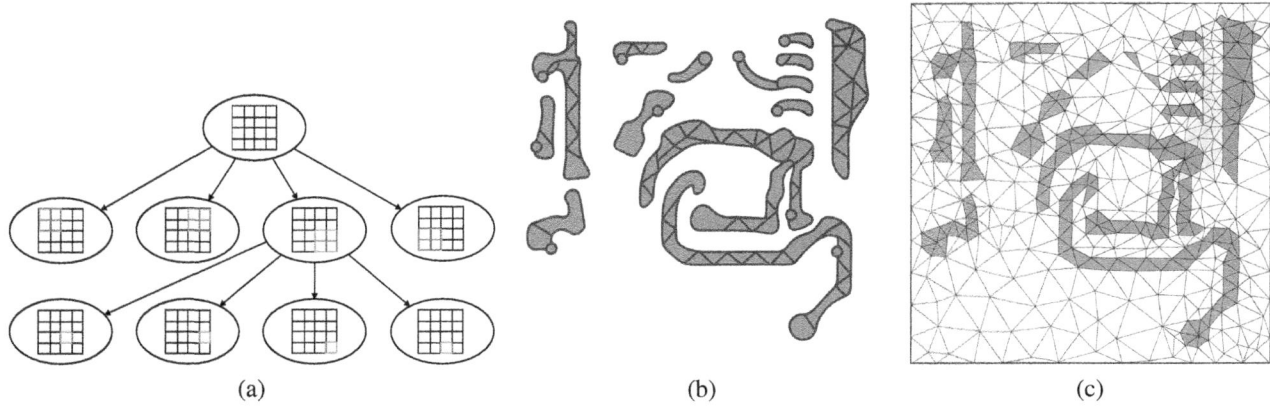

(a)   (b)   (c)

Figure 10.1: (a) An illustration of a quadtree structure. (b) Smoothed conductive tracks of a PCB layout without triangulation. (c) Delaunay triangulation of PCB routing paths approximated by a set of simple polygons.

- determining the physical placement of each component,
- and defining the optimal layout of interconnections among components.

This naturally leads to a computationally complex optimization problem, which—when viewed from a geometric perspective—can be formulated as a mesh generation problem over the component layout. One of the central challenges in PCB design is thermal dissipation. As components operate, they emit heat, whose intensity and spatial distribution depend on the relative arrangement of components and the topology of their interconnections. For the system to function reliably, the heat levels must remain below critical thresholds. Historically, thermal performance was assessed by physically manufacturing PCB prototypes and empirically measuring heat distribution. This process was time-consuming and costly, often requiring multiple redesigns. Today, however, thermal behavior is efficiently simulated using numerical methods, which allow for:

- early detection of suboptimal thermal configurations,
- significant acceleration of the development cycle,
- and optimized thermal profiles without the need for physical prototyping.

The use of simulations in PCB thermal analysis greatly enhances the efficiency and reliability of the design process, ensuring long-term performance and stability of electronic systems. Moreover, such simulation-based approaches find applications in various domains, including collision detection in particle systems, fractal image compression, and layout optimization in CAD systems for electronic circuit design. Heat transfer between different materials on a printed circuit board (PCB) is an inherently complex physical process, and its accurate modeling is essential for optimizing the performance of electronic components. For this purpose, the *finite element method* (FEM) is commonly employed, as it provides a numerical approximation for solving partial differential equations over geometrically complex domains. The FEM approach begins by discretizing the domain of interest—partitioning the PCB into a finite number of elements. Typically, these elements are triangular or quadrilateral in shape (see Fig. 10.1 (c)). Each element is assigned a known temperature value, and the thermal interactions between neighboring elements are modeled based on their conductive properties. Using the known boundary conditions and inter-element interactions, a large system of linear equations is constructed. This system is then solved numerically to obtain the temperature distribution across the entire board. The accuracy of FEM solutions is directly dependent on the mesh resolution. A finer mesh—comprised of smaller and more numerous elements—yields more accurate results but significantly increases computational complexity. Since the number of elements has an exponential effect on execution time, an adaptive strategy is typically employed: finer meshes are used only in regions where high temperature gradients are expected. In addition to granularity, it is crucial that each mesh element belongs exclusively to a single functional region, avoiding any overlap between regions. Moreover, the geometric shape of the elements plays an important role in the stability and convergence of the numerical solution. Poorly shaped elements, such as "thin triangles" with high aspect ratios, often lead to ill-conditioned systems and slow convergence rates.

10.2 Uniform and Non-Uniform Meshes

To explore how (non) uniformity affects mesh-based problem solving, we begin by analyzing a square printed circuit board domain composed of four disjoint polygonal components (i.e., simple polygons), as illustrated in Fig. 10.2 (b). The square domain is defined by vertices $(0,0)$, $(U,0)$, (U,U), and $(0,U)$, where U typically assumes values of the form $U = 2^j$, for some $j \in \mathbb{N}$. The coordinates of the components are constrained to the interval $[0,U]$. In most cases, the edges of the components are restricted to four orientations, forming angles of $0°$, $45°$, $90°$, and $135°$ with respect to the positive x-axis. To enable triangulation of the square mesh (i.e., decomposition into triangles), the mesh must satisfy the following four criteria (see Fig. 10.2 (b)):

(A) *Conformity:* A triangle must not contain a vertex of another triangle in the interior of its sides.
(B) *Input Preservation:* All component edges must be present in the union of mesh triangle edges.
(C) *Shape Quality:* The internal angles of each triangle must lie within the interval $[45°, 90°]$, thus avoiding poorly shaped (sliver) triangles.
(D) *Nonuniformity:* The mesh should be fine (dense) near the edges of the components and coarser further away from them.

A naive triangulation of the square domain that disregards these properties would likely fail to meet multiple criteria. At first glance, Delaunay triangulation appears to be a viable solution, as it can handle point sets comprising mesh vertices and component vertices. However, this approach introduces two significant problems:

- Delaunay triangulation does not inherently preserve input edges (violating property **B**), as the resulting edges may not include all component edges.
- Even if the component vertices are arranged to satisfy property **B**, the resulting triangulation may include extremely small triangles, which violates property **C**.

To illustrate these challenges, consider a 16×16 square mesh with a 1×1 embedded square component as ilustrated in Fig. 10.3 (a). The application of Delaunay triangulation to this setup yields 10 triangles, some of which have angles below $5°$, clearly violating the shape quality criterion. Importantly, it is not required that triangle vertices be limited to mesh or component vertices. Additional points—known as *Steiner points*—can be introduced within the domain to improve triangle quality. When properly chosen, these points enable the construction of a *Steiner triangulation*, which can satisfy all mesh criteria. For

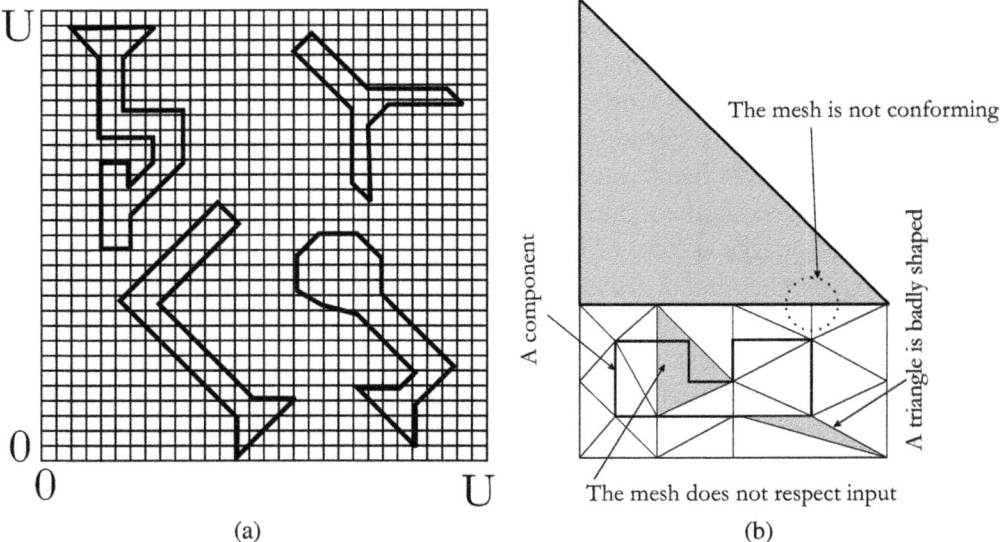

Figure 10.2: (a) A square printed circuit board domain composed of four disjoint polygonal components. (b) A square mesh with partial triangulation illustrating common issues such as non-conforming elements, input mismatch, and poorly shaped triangles.

instance, a dense grid of Steiner points placed at intersections of uniformly spaced horizontal and vertical lines (spacing 1 unit apart) results in a uniform mesh composed of 200 isosceles right triangles (with two $45°$ and one $90°$ angle each) as ilustrated in Fig.s 10.3 (b). While such a uniform mesh satisfies criteria **A–C**, it fails to satisfy **D**, as it populates the entire domain with small triangles, leading to inefficiency. A manual attempt to coarsen the mesh in regions far from component edges—by replacing many small triangles with fewer large ones—would often result in a non-conforming mesh, thus violating property **A**. An effective alternative is to gradually increase triangle size with increasing distance from key features (e.g., from the top-left corner), thereby creating a nonuniform mesh that preserves all four criteria. As shown in Fig. 10.3 (c), such a mesh consists of only 52 triangles—nearly ten times fewer than in the uniform case—while maintaining high-quality triangle shapes and full conformity. This approach leads naturally to the use of *quadtree structures*, which will be described in the next section.

10.3 Quadtree Structure Construction

In this section, we describe a method for generating a nonuniform mesh based on the quadtree structure. As previously introduced, a quadtree is a hierarchical data structure in which every internal node has exactly four children. There exists a one-to-one and bidirectional correspondence between internal nodes of the tree and square regions of the domain. Formally, if a node v in the quadtree has children, the square associated with v is subdivided into four smaller squares, each assigned to one of its child nodes as ilustrated in Fig. 10.4 (b). These subdivided squares become the leaf nodes of the tree if they do not have further subdivisions. Conversely, if a square associated with a child node undergoes additional subdivision, that node becomes an internal node. This recursive subdivision process defines a spatial decomposition known as a *quadtree subdivision*, in which the domain is adaptively partitioned based on local geometric or data-driven criteria. An illustration of such a quadtree-induced subdivision is provided in Fig. 10.4 (a). The root of the quadtree presented in Fig. 10.4 (a) corresponds to the initial bold-outlined square in Fig. 10.4 (b), which is subdivided into four smaller squares, reflecting the four branches emanating from the root node. Since the top-right (North-East, NE) and bottom-right (South-East, SE) quadrants are not further

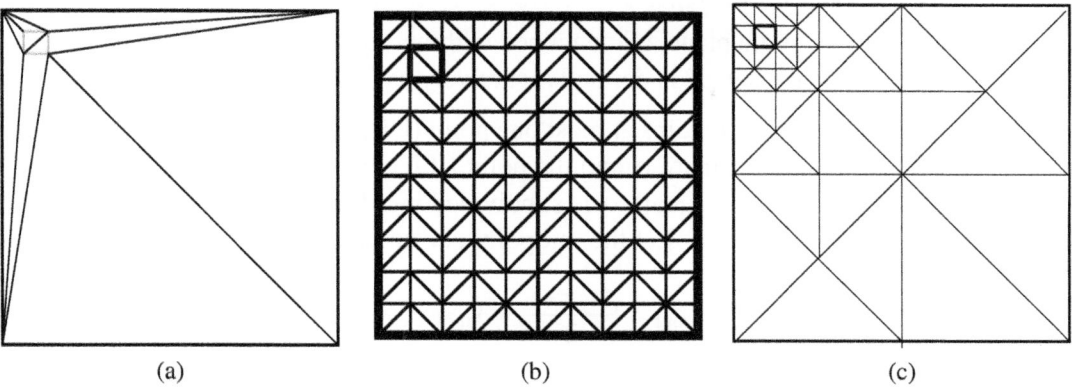

Figure 10.3: (a) Illustration of a 16×16 square mesh with an embedded 1×1 component highlighting triangulation challenges. (b) A uniform mesh of 200 isosceles right triangles generated by a dense grid of Steiner points. (c) A nonuniform mesh of 52 triangles preserving mesh quality and conformity.

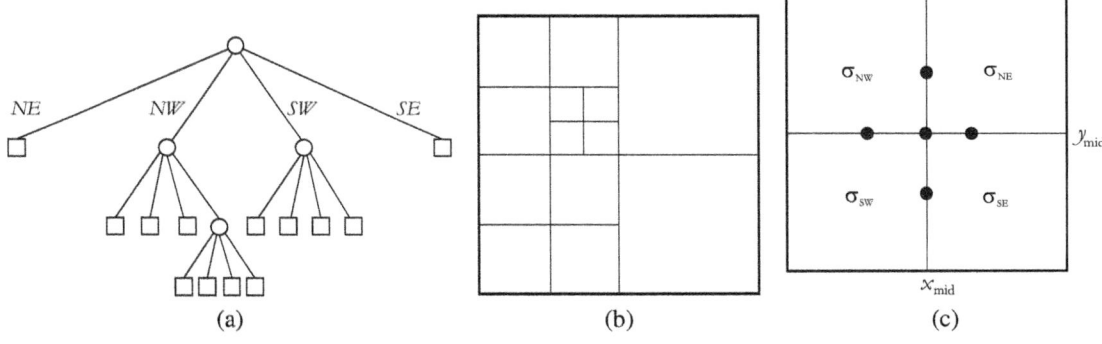

Figure 10.4: (a) Quadtree-induced subdivision of a square domain. (b) One-to-one correspondence between internal nodes and square subregions in a quadtree. (c) Subdivision of a square into four equal quadrants σ_{NE}, σ_{NW}, σ_{SW}, and σ_{SE} in the context of quadtree construction.

subdivided, they are represented in the quadtree as leaf nodes—graphically depicted as small squares. In contrast, the bottom-left quadrant (South-West, SW) undergoes subdivision into four smaller squares, and is thus represented in the tree as an internal node—denoted graphically as a circle—from which four branches emerge, each corresponding to a leaf node for the new sub-squares. The top-left quadrant (North-West, NW) is similarly divided into four smaller squares at level 1 of the tree. Among these, the South-East sub-square is further subdivided into four additional squares. Consequently, it becomes an internal node in the tree, connected to four leaf nodes representing the final level of subdivision. Before proceeding further, we adopt the convention of referring to all faces induced by the quadtree subdivision as "squares," even when their shape deviates from the geometric square and their number of vertices exceeds four. For example, simple polygons with five or more vertices will still be referred to as "squares" within the context of this subdivision. This flexibility highlights the expressive power of the quadtree structure: it can accommodate various types of spatial data. For instance, it may be used to store a set of planar points by recursively subdividing the domain until each square contains at most one or two points.

10.3.1 Recursive Construction of a Quadtree Structure for a Point Set

Let $\mathscr{P}$ be a finite set of points in the plane, all contained within a square region $\sigma = [x_1, x_2] \times [y_1, y_2]$. The construction of a quadtree for the set $\mathscr{P}$ is defined recursively as follows:

(a) *Base case:* If the point set $\mathscr{P}$ contains at most one point ($|\mathscr{P}| \leq 1$), the quadtree consists of a single leaf node that stores both the square σ and the point (if it exists).

(b) *Recursive case:* If $|\mathscr{P}| > 1$, the square σ is subdivided into four equal quadrants: σ_{NE}, σ_{NW}, σ_{SW}, σ_{SE}, as illustrated in Fig. 10.4 (c). Let the midpoint coordinates be defined as:

$$x_{\mathrm{mid}} = \frac{x_1 + x_2}{2}, \quad y_{\mathrm{mid}} = \frac{y_1 + y_2}{2}.$$

Based on this, partition the point set $\mathscr{P}$ into four subsets:

$$\mathscr{P}_{NE} = \{p \in \mathscr{P} : p.x > x_{\mathrm{mid}} \text{ and } p.y > y_{\mathrm{mid}}\},$$
$$\mathscr{P}_{NW} = \{p \in \mathscr{P} : p.x \leq x_{\mathrm{mid}} \text{ and } p.y > y_{\mathrm{mid}}\},$$
$$\mathscr{P}_{SW} = \{p \in \mathscr{P} : p.x \leq x_{\mathrm{mid}} \text{ and } p.y \leq y_{\mathrm{mid}}\},$$
$$\mathscr{P}_{SE} = \{p \in \mathscr{P} : p.x > x_{\mathrm{mid}} \text{ and } p.y \leq y_{\mathrm{mid}}\}.$$

(c) *Node expansion:* The root node v of the current quadtree stores the square σ, denoted as $\sigma(v)$. This node has exactly four children:

- The NE child is the root of the quadtree for the point set $\mathscr{P}_{NE}$,
- The NW child is the root of the quadtree for the point set $\mathscr{P}_{NW}$,
- The SW child is the root of the quadtree for the point set $\mathscr{P}_{SW}$,
- The SE child is the root of the quadtree for the point set $\mathscr{P}_{SE}$.

The resulting recursive algorithm can be summarized as follows: *"Subdivide the current square and partition the point set accordingly; then recursively construct the quadtree for each quadrant and its corresponding subset of points. The recursion terminates when the point set assigned to a region contains at most one point"*.

Bounding the Initial Square. A natural question arises: how to determine the initial square (or more generally, a bounding rectangle) that encloses all points in $\mathscr{P}$? This can be done efficiently by identifying the extreme points in both the x and y directions, which requires only linear time in the number of points.

Properties of the Resulting Tree. At each step of the construction, the square region is subdivided into four smaller squares. However, this does not imply that the associated point set is evenly divided; in fact, all points may reside in a single quadrant. As a result, the quadtree may become highly unbalanced. Consequently, the tree's depth and size cannot be expressed solely as a function of the number of points it stores. The following lemma, which will be presented later, formalizes the relationship between the tree's depth and the minimum distance between stored points, and between the tree's size and the dimensions of the initial bounding square.

> **Lemma 10.3.1** Let $\mathscr{P}$ be a set of points in the plane. Then the depth of the quadtree structure satisfies
>
> $$\mathrm{depth} \leq \log\left(\frac{s}{c}\right) + \frac{3}{2},$$
>
> where c is the shortest distance between any two points in $\mathscr{P}$, while s is the side length of the initial square that encloses all points of $\mathscr{P}$.

Proof. When traversing a quadtree from an internal node (associated with a square) to its children, the side length of the corresponding square is halved. More generally, the side length of a square stored at an

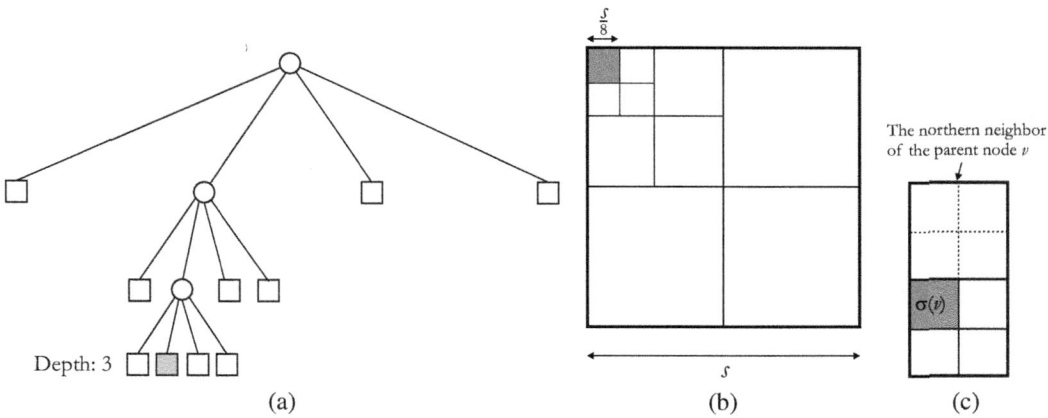

Figure 10.5: (a) A quadtree structure of depth 3 illustrating hierarchical subdivision. (b) Quadtree subdivision illustrating that the side length of a square at depth i is $\frac{s}{2^i}$. (c) Illustration of the northern neighbor query in a quadtree, where the goal is to find a node v' such that $\sigma(v')$ is adjacent to $\sigma(v)$ from the north.

internal node at depth i is given by $\frac{s}{2^i}$, where s denotes the side length of the root square. This is illustrated in Fig. 10.5 (b). The maximum possible distance between any two points within a square corresponds to the length of its diagonal. For the initial square (at level 0), this maximum distance is $s\sqrt{2}$. Consequently, the diagonal of a square at depth i is $\frac{s\sqrt{2}}{2^i}$. By definition, each internal node in the quadtree must store at least two points (see Fig. 10.5 (a)). Therefore, the distance c between any two such points must satisfy $c \le \frac{s\sqrt{2}}{2^i}$. Rearranging this inequality yields an upper bound on the depth i:

$$i \le \log_2\left(\frac{s\sqrt{2}}{c}\right) = \log_2\left(\frac{s}{c}\right) + \log_2\sqrt{2} = \log_2\left(\frac{s}{c}\right) + \frac{1}{2}.$$

Since the depth of the quadtree is exactly one greater than the maximum depth of any internal node, it follows that the total depth of the tree is bounded by $\log_2\left(\frac{s}{c}\right) + \frac{3}{2}$. Rounding this bound up gives the final result:

$$\text{depth} \le \log_2\left(\frac{s}{c}\right) + \frac{3}{2}.$$

■

In the subsequent theorem, we will show that the size of the quadtree (i.e., the total number of nodes) depends on both the tree depth and the number of stored points.

Theorem 10.3.1 A quadtree structure of depth d storing n points contains $\mathcal{O}((d+1)n)$ nodes and can be constructed in $\mathcal{O}((d+1)n)$ time.

Proof. We aim to show that the total number of nodes in a quadtree of depth d that stores n points is bounded above by $\mathcal{O}((d+1)n)$. Since each internal node in a quadtree has exactly four children, the number of leaves grows exponentially with the depth. Specifically:

- At depth $d = 1$, the tree has at most 4 leaves.
- At depth $d = 2$, the tree has at most 16 leaves.
- At depth $d = 3$, the tree has at most 64 leaves.

From this, it can be observed that the total number of leaves n_l in the tree satisfies the recurrence:

$$n_l = 1 + 3 \cdot n_i,$$

where n_i denotes the number of internal nodes. This relationship can be proven by induction on the depth d:

- For $d = 1$: $n_i = 1$ implies $n_l = 1 + 3 \cdot 1 = 4$.
- For $d = 2$: $n_i \leq 5$ implies $n_l \leq 1 + 3 \cdot 5 = 16$.
- For $d = 3$: $n_i \leq 21$ implies $n_l \leq 1 + 3 \cdot 21 = 64$.

Therefore, we obtain:

$$n_l = 1 + 3n_i \quad \Rightarrow \quad n_i = \frac{n_l - 1}{3}.$$

Since each internal node must store at least two points from the set $\mathscr{P}$, the total number of internal nodes n_i is at most n. Consequently, the total number of nodes in the tree, which is bounded by $n_l + n_i$, satisfies:

$$n_l + n_i \leq (1 + 3n) + n = 1 + 4n.$$

This quantity is strictly less than $(d+1)n$ for all $n > \frac{1}{d-3}$, which certainly holds for any non-negative depth d. Hence, the number of nodes in the tree is bounded by:

$$\mathscr{O}((d+1)n).$$

Next, we show that the time required to construct the tree is also $\mathscr{O}((d+1)n)$. Observe that each internal node processes one or more points lying within the square it represents. For a given internal node, the time required to process its associated square is linear in the number of points it contains. Moreover, for each level of the tree, the union of all squares at that level covers all points in $\mathscr{P}$, and no point appears in more than one square at any given level. Therefore, the total number of points processed at each level is at most n. Since the tree has at most $d + 1$ levels, and each level requires $\mathscr{O}(n)$ time to process, the total construction time is:

$$\mathscr{O}((d+1)n).$$

Since, both the size and the construction time of a quadtree of depth d storing n points are bounded above by $\mathscr{O}((d+1)n)$, which completes the proof. ∎

One of the fundamental operations in quadtree structures is the *neighbor finding* procedure. This operation is defined as follows: given a node v and a specified direction (north, east, south, or west), the goal is to identify a node v' such that the square $\sigma(v')$ is adjacent to $\sigma(v)$ in the given direction as ilustrated in Fig. 10.5 (c). A common generalization of this operation assumes that the node v may also be an internal node, and that both v and v' must lie at the same depth. If such a node v' cannot be found, the algorithm attempts to identify the deepest node v' such that $\sigma(v')$ is adjacent to $\sigma(v)$ in the given direction. In cases where no neighboring square exists in the specified direction (e.g., when $\sigma(v)$ shares a boundary with the initial root square), the algorithm returns a sentinel value, typically `nil` (or None in implementation), indicating that no valid neighbor was found. To illustrate the algorithm, consider the task of locating the northern neighbor of a node v. Several cases may arise:

(a) If v is a South-East (SE) or South-West (SW) child of its parent, then its northern neighbor lies within the North-East (NE) or North-West (NW) sibling of the same parent, respectively.

(b) If v is a North-East (NE) or North-West (NW) child, then the algorithm proceeds recursively by attempting to find the northern neighbor μ of v's parent node. Two possibilities then arise:
  - If μ is an internal node, the northern neighbor of v is a corresponding child of μ.
  - If μ is a leaf, then μ itself serves as the northern neighbor of v.

A general algorithm for neighbor finding in a quadtree, derived from the case analysis above, is presented in the form of pseudocode in Algorithm 22.

Algorithm 22: Pseudocode of the algorithm for computing the northern neighbor of node v in the quadtree $\mathcal{T}$.

Input : Given a node v and a quadtree $\mathcal{T}$.

Step 1: If node v is the root node, then it has no northern neighbor (no neighbor exists in the north direction), and in that case, the algorithm returns nil or none in Python implementation.

Step 2: **If** node v is the South-West (SW) child of its parent, **then** return the North-West (NW) child of its parent. Similarly, **if** v is the South-East (SE) child, **then** return the North-East (NE) child of its parent.

Step 3: Recursively find the northern neighbor μ of the parent of node v. **If** μ is nil or a leaf node, **return** μ. Otherwise, check whether v is the North-West (NW) child of its parent. If so, return the South-West (SW) child of node μ; otherwise (i.e., v is the North-East (NE) child), return the South-East (SE) child of node μ.

Output : Return the deepest node v' (if it exists) such that $\sigma(v')$ is the northern neighbor of the square $\sigma(v)$. If no such node exists, return nil.

Based on the proposed algorithm, the time required to find the northern neighbor of a node v in a quadtree $\mathcal{T}$ of depth d is proportional to $\mathcal{O}(d+1)$. Specifically, each recursive call performs a constant number of elementary operations, requiring $\mathcal{O}(1)$ time. Since the depth of the node v is reduced by one with each recursive call, the maximum number of steps in the worst-case scenario is bounded by $d+1$. As previously mentioned, one of the main drawbacks of quadtree structures is their susceptibility to imbalance during recursive subdivision. This occurs when large squares (i.e., nodes at shallow depth) become adjacent to several significantly smaller squares (i.e., nodes at greater depth). An example of this is illustrated in Fig. 10.6 (a), where the top-right quadrant is adjacent to eight smaller quadrants. Such configurations are undesirable in many applications due to inefficiencies in traversal, memory, and spatial locality. To mitigate the imbalance problem, we first define what it means for a quadtree subdivision to be *balanced* [206].

Definition 10.3.1 A subdivision induced by a quadtree is said to be balanced if the side lengths of any two neighboring squares differ by at most a factor of 2. Also, a quadtree structure is considered balanced if its corresponding spatial subdivision satisfies this balance condition.

According to the above definition, a balanced quadtree ensures that any two neighboring leaves correspond to squares whose depths differ by at most one [51]. This property is visually illustrated in Fig. 10.6 (c), while the corresponding balanced quadtree structure is shown in Fig. 10.6 (e). In contrast, the subdivision depicted in Fig. 10.6 (b) is unbalanced, as it contains neighboring squares whose sizes differ by more than a factor of 2. For example, the South-West quadrant at depth 1 is adjacent to a significantly smaller square located in the North-West quadrant, whose corresponding leaf resides at depth 4. Moreover, the internal node representing the square that contains this smallest region is positioned at depth 3, further illustrating the imbalance of the tree structure, as shown in Fig. 10.6 (d).

As previously noted, Figs. 10.6 (c) and (e) illustrate a well-balanced subdivision induced by a quadtree structure. In this configuration, any two adjacent squares differ in depth by at most one, thereby ensuring that the corresponding tree remains balanced. Such balanced trees are highly desirable, as they guarantee a controlled level of uniformity and improved efficiency in spatial operations. The insights discussed above lead to a refinement of Algorithm 22, which is formalized through the pseudocode given in Algorithm 23.

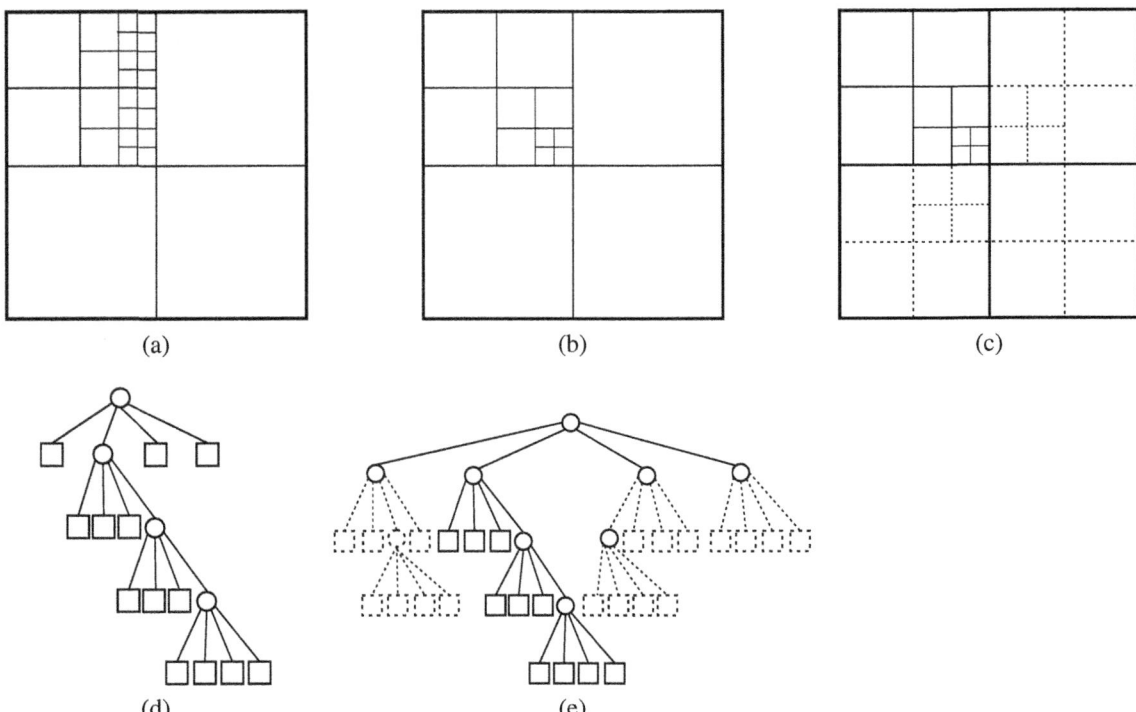

Figure 10.6: (a) An unbalanced quadtree subdivision in which a large square is adjacent to multiple smaller squares, illustrating depth disparity. (b) Illustration of quadtree imbalance: adjacent squares differing in size by a factor greater than two. (c) A balanced quadtree subdivision. (d) An imbalanced tree structure resulting from unbalanced quadtree subdivision. (e) A balanced tree structure induced by a well-balanced quadtree subdivision.

Algorithm 23: Pseudocode for the construction of a balanced quadtree $\mathcal{T}$.

Input : Given a quadtree $\mathcal{T}$.
Step 1: Add all leaf nodes of tree $\mathcal{T}$ to the list $\mathcal{L}$.
Step 2: While the list $\mathcal{L}$ is not empty **do**:

    a) Remove the leaf (i.e., element) μ from the list $\mathcal{L}$.
    b) Check whether the square $\sigma(\mu)$ corresponding to the leaf μ needs to be further subdivided. If so, μ becomes an internal node with four children, represented by four new leaves corresponding to the four quadrants of $\sigma(\mu)$. If node μ stores a point, that point should be reassigned to one of its children, i.e., to one of the new leaves. After the subdivision, insert the four newly created leaves into the list $\mathcal{L}$. Finally, check whether the square $\sigma(\mu)$ had any neighbors that also require further subdivision. If so, insert those neighboring leaves into the list $\mathcal{L}$ as well.

Output : Return the balanced variant of the tree $\mathcal{T}$.

Algorithm 23 outlines the overall procedure for balancing a quadtree. In this section, we provide further clarification on two essential components of the algorithm: (1) determining whether a square should be further subdivided, and (2) verifying whether neighboring squares require refinement.

(1) Subdivision Criterion

To determine whether a square $\sigma(\mu)$ associated with a leaf node μ requires further subdivision, it is sufficient to check whether there exists an adjacent square σ' whose side length is strictly less than half the side length of $\sigma(\mu)$. This test for adjacency and size comparison can be performed using Algorithm 22, which locates a neighboring square σ' and inspects its internal structure. More specifically, such a square σ' exists if and only if Algorithm 22 returns a node whose South-West (SW) or South-East (SE) child is an internal node (i.e., not a leaf). In such cases, the significant size discrepancy implies that μ must be subdivided further to restore balance.

(2) Neighbor Refinement

Once $\sigma(\mu)$ has been processed, it is also necessary to examine whether any of its neighboring squares require additional subdivision. This step is conceptually similar to the previous one and also utilizes Algorithm 22. For instance, if $\sigma(\mu)$ has a northern neighbor whose square is significantly larger, then this neighbor must be subdivided to ensure that the balance condition is maintained. This occurs when Algorithm 22 returns a node whose square is larger than $\sigma(\mu)$.

Theoretical Bound on Balanced Quadtree Construction

It can be rigorously established that a quadtree $\mathcal{T}$ of depth d, consisting of m nodes, retains linear size after the balancing process. Specifically, the balanced version of $\mathcal{T}$ contains at most $\mathcal{O}(m)$ nodes. Moreover, the total computational time required to construct the balanced quadtree is bounded by $\mathcal{O}(m(d+1))$. This result provides a worst-case guarantee on both the space and time complexity of the balancing procedure. The corresponding theorem is stated below without proof.

> **Theorem 10.3.2** Let $\mathcal{T}$ be a quadtree of depth d consisting of m nodes. Then its balanced version contains $\mathcal{O}(m)$ nodes and can be constructed in time proportional to $\mathcal{O}(m(d+1))$.

10.4 Algorithm Implementation for Quadtree Structure Construction

In this section, we briefly revisit the essential concepts related to subdivisions induced by quadtree structures, focusing on the aspects relevant for implementation. As is well known, a quadtree-induced subdivision is defined recursively by partitioning an initial square domain $\mathcal{D}$ into smaller quadrants. The subdivision is performed by drawing one vertical and one horizontal line intersecting at the center of the current square, thereby dividing it into four equal sub-squares. Following the initial partition of the root square, the recursive subdivision proceeds in a fixed order: North-East (top-right quadrant), South-East (bottom-right), South-West (bottom-left), and North-West (top-left). This ordering corresponds to a counter-clockwise traversal starting from the top-right quadrant. The subdivision process gives rise to a tree structure in which each internal node has exactly four children. These children correspond to the four sub-quadrants, and the ordering of the branches matches the order of subdivision: - the leftmost branch corresponds to the North-East quadrant, - followed by the South-East, South-West, - and finally the North-West quadrant associated with the rightmost branch. An example of a quadtree-induced subdivision and its corresponding tree structure is illustrated in Fig. 10.7. As illustrated in Fig. 10.7 (b), the branches corresponding to the North-East (NE), South-East (SE), South-West (SW), and North-West (NW) quadrants are assigned labels 0, 1, 2, and 3, respectively. If the root node of the quadtree is labeled as 0, then the labels of its child nodes can be formed by concatenating the label of the parent with the digit corresponding to the chosen branch. This leads to a hierarchical encoding of quadrants, as shown in Fig. 10.7 (a). Specifically, after the first subdivision induced by the quadtree, the tree consists of four branches labeled 0 through 3, and the initial square is divided into four equally sized sub-quadrants labeled 00, 01, 02, and 03. Continuing the recursive subdivision, the top-right quadrant (labeled 00) is further divided into four quadrants with labels 000, 001, 002, and 003. An important practical question concerns the stopping condition for recursive subdivision: how deep should the subdivision process go?

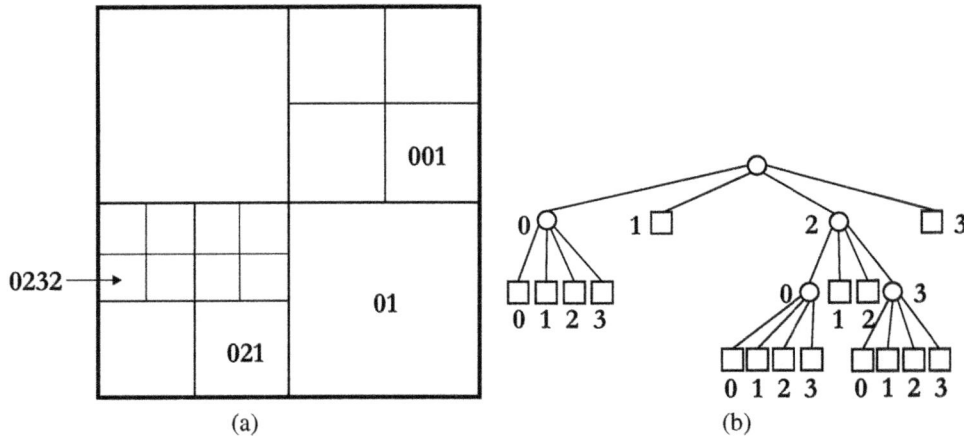

Figure 10.7: (a) Quadtree subdivision. (b) Tree induced by a quadtree subdivision.

In general, subdivision continues until a predefined stopping criterion is satisfied. For example, in the context of range searching, a quadrant is subdivided only if it contains more than m points from a given point set $\mathcal{P}$ in the plane. In other applications, the maximum depth of the tree may be specified in advance as a fixed parameter. It is evident that if the tree grows too deep, operations such as range queries may become computationally expensive. The depth limit that restricts further subdivision of a quadtree is commonly referred to as the *cutoff depth* or *threshold* (denoted as *th*). Based on this constraint, the following conditions characterize any external node (i.e., a leaf) v in the quadtree:

- Node v must not reside at a depth greater than *th*.
- If the depth of v is strictly less than *th*, then the quadrant represented by v continues to subdivide provided it contains more than m points from the point set $\mathcal{P}$.
- If v is not the root node, and its parent quadrant contains more than m points, then further subdivision of the parent may also occur.

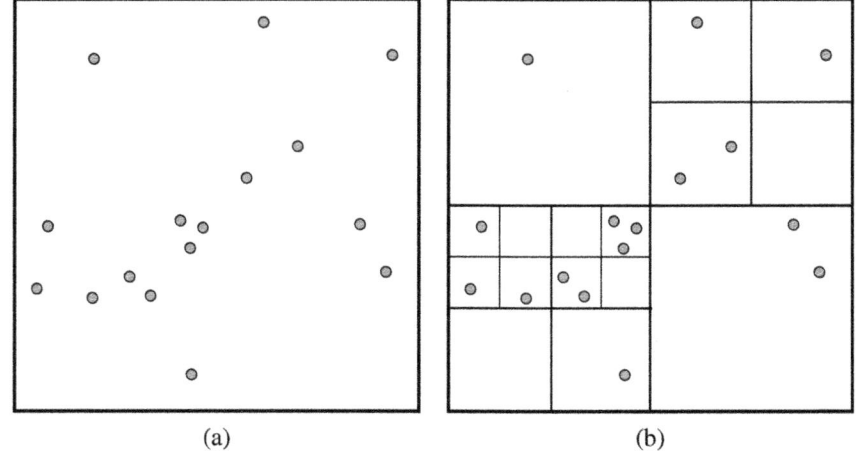

Figure 10.8: (a) The set $\mathcal{P}$ consisting of 16 points. (b) A quadtree subdivision generated for $m = 2$ and $th = 3$.

From the above conditions, it follows that the recursive subdivision process continues as long as a quadrant contains more than *m* points or the current depth does not exceed the specified cutoff depth *th*. An example illustrating this process is shown in Fig. 10.8 , where a set $\mathscr{P}$ consisting of 16 points is partitioned using a quadtree with $m = 2$ and cutoff depth $th = 3$. After the theoretical exposition, we now transition to the practical implementation of the quadtree data structure for performing range queries over a planar point set with respect to a rectangular query region $\mathscr{R}$. The Python implementation provided in Listing 10.1 follows the recursive paradigm inherent to the quadtree and is consistent with the principles previously discussed. Each node in the structure is represented as an instance of the Quadtree class and is defined by its corresponding rectangular region, a threshold on the maximum number of points it may contain, the current depth level within the tree, and a Boolean flag indicating whether the node has been subdivided. Subdivision into four child quadrants is triggered only when the number of points exceeds the specified capacity and the node has not yet reached the maximum allowed depth. The implementation begins with the class constructor, as shown in Listing 10.1.

Listing 10.1: Defintion of Quadtree class

```
1 class Quadtree:
2     def __init__(self,boundary:Rectangle,capacity=4,level=0,max_level=10):
3         self.boundary=boundary; self.capacity=capacity
4         self.level=level; self.max_level=max_level
5         self.divided=False; self.points:List[Point2D]=[]
6     def subdivide(self): pass
7     def insert(self, point: Point2D): pass
8     def query(self, range_rect: Rectangle, found: List[Point2D]): pass
9     def draw(self, canvas): pass
```

The class constructor is designed to initialize all necessary attributes that govern the behavior and structure of a quadtree node. The formal parameter boundary specifies the rectangular domain associated with the current node, thereby defining its spatial extent. The parameter capacity determines the maximum number of points that a node may hold before it becomes eligible for subdivision, while max_level imposes a constraint on the maximum allowed depth of the tree, serving as a termination criterion for recursive subdivision. The attribute self.points maintains a list of all points currently contained within the node, and the Boolean flag self.divided is used to indicate whether the node has already undergone subdivision. The spatial decomposition is handled by the *subdivide()* method, which geometrically partitions the current rectangular region into four equally sized subregions—namely, the North-East (NE), South-East (SE), South-West (SW), and North-West (NW) quadrants—each represented as a new instance of the **Quadtree** class.

```
1 def subdivide(self):
2     sw=self.boundary.sw; ne=self.boundary.ne; c=0.5*(sw+ne)
3     self.ne= Quadtree(Rectangle(c,ne),self.capacity,self.level+1,self.max_level)
4     self.se=Quadtree(Rectangle(Point2D(c[0],sw[1]),Point2D(ne[0],c[1])),self.
          capacity,self.level+1,self.max_level)
5     self.sw= Quadtree(Rectangle(sw,c),self.capacity,self.level+1,self.max_level)
6     self.nw=Quadtree(Rectangle(Point2D(sw[0],c[1]),Point2D(c[0],ne[1])),self.
          capacity,self.level+1,self.max_level)
7     self.divided = True
```

As demonstrated in the implementation of the *subdivide()* method, the subdivision process is initiated by computing the center point *c* of the current rectangular region. This central point serves as the reference for generating four equally sized subrectangles corresponding to the NW, NE, SE, and SW quadrants. Each of these subregions is then instantiated as a separate Quadtree object, thereby preserving the recursive nature of the data structure. Once the node has been subdivided, newly inserted points are distributed among the appropriate subregions according to their spatial coordinates. This logic is encapsulated within the recursive *insert(·)* method, which governs the placement of points within the hierarchical structure of the quadtree.

```
def insert(self, pt: Point2D):
    if not self.boundary.contains_point(pt): return False
    if len(self.points) < self.capacity or self.level >= self.max_level:
        self.points.append(pt); return True
    else:
        if not self.divided: self.subdivide()
        return (self.ne.insert(pt) or self.se.insert(pt) or self.sw.insert(pt) or
            self.nw.insert(pt))
```

The *insert(·)* method begins by verifying whether the input point lies within the boundaries of the current rectangular region. If this condition is satisfied and the number of stored points has not yet reached the predefined capacity, the point is directly appended to the node's local list. Conversely, if the capacity is exceeded and level is less than max_level, the method ensures that the node is subdivided—invoking *subdivide()* if it has not already been executed—and subsequently delegates the insertion task to the appropriate child node based on the point's spatial location. For the purpose of spatial range queries, the *query(·,·)* method is provided. This method traverses the quadtree recursively, collecting all points that lie within a specified rectangular search region. It performs intersection checks to avoid unnecessary traversal of subregions that do not overlap with the query range, thereby improving efficiency.

```
def query(self, range_rect: Rectangle, found: List[Point2D]):
    if not self.boundary.intersects(range_rect): return
    for p in self.points:
        if range_rect.contains_point(p): found.append(p)
    if self.divided:
        self.nw.query(range_rect, found); self.ne.query(range_rect, found)
        self.sw.query(range_rect, found); self.se.query(range_rect, found)
```

The *query(·,·)* method exploits the hierarchical spatial decomposition inherent to the quadtree structure. It begins by evaluating whether the rectangular region associated with the current node intersects the specified query region. In the event of a positive intersection, all points stored at the current node are examined to determine whether they fall within the query bounds. If the node has been subdivided, the method proceeds to recursively query each of the child quadrants. The hierarchical and spatially localized traversal mechanism inherent to the quadtree structure considerably improves the efficiency of range searching, primarily by eliminating subregions that cannot influence the final result set. To assess the performance of the quadtree-based search algorithm, we compare it with three alternative approaches: the Naive method, the Projection-based search method, and the Enhanced projection method introduced in the previous chapter. Figure 10.9 was generated using the implementation provided in Listing 10.2, which builds upon the GUI framework presented in Listing 9.2 of Chapter 9. This figure illustrates the comparative performance of the quadtree-based range search algorithm relative to the aforementioned methods.

Listing 10.2: Extended GUI for Performing Two-Dimensional Search Using Four Methods

```
import tkinter as tk
import random, time
```

```
3 from geometry import Point2D, Rectangle
4 from ch9_helper_functions import projection_method,enhanced_projection_method
5 from Quadtree import Quadtree
6 class RangeSearchApp:
7     def __init__(self, root):
8         # Same as earlier
9         #---------------------------------------------------------------
10         # New added
11         tk.Button(root, text="Quadtree Method", command=self.run_quadtree).grid(
              row=5, column=1)
12         self.quadtree_time = tk.Label(root, text="Execution time (s):")
13         self.quadtree_time.grid(row=5, column=2, columnspan=1, sticky='w')
14
15     # New added
16     def run_quadtree(self):
17         start = time.time(); count = 0
18         x_min,x_max=min(p[0] for p in self.points),max(p[0] for p in self.points)
19         y_min,y_max=min(p[1] for p in self.points),max(p[1] for p in self.points)
20         boundary = Rectangle(Point2D(x_min, y_min), Point2D(x_max, y_max))
21         qt = Quadtree(boundary, capacity=10, level=0, max_level=10)
22         for point in self.points: qt.insert(point)
23         for rect in self.rectangles:
24             found = []; qt.query(rect, found); count += len(found)
25         duration = time.time() - start
26         self.quadtree_time.config(text=f"Execution time (s): {duration:.6f},
              Points found: {count}")
```

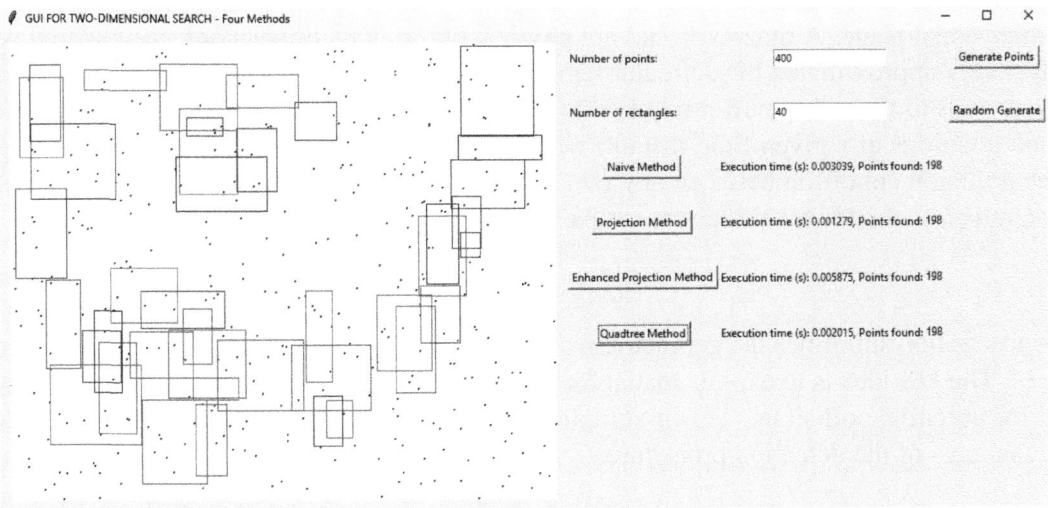

Figure 10.9: Comparison of four techniques for two-dimensional range searching.

The comparative performance results of the quadtree method and the three baseline approaches are presented in Table 10.1. These results clearly demonstrate that the quadtree-based approach consistently outperforms the alternative methods as the size of the dataset increases, particularly in configurations involving a large number of rectangles. The observed efficiency is primarily attributed to the quadtree's inherent ability to hierarchically partition the spatial domain, thereby restricting query operations to relevant subregions and significantly reducing computational overhead. Moreover, the modular and recursive design of the **Quadtree** class offers a robust and extensible foundation for supporting advanced geometric operations such as collision detection, dynamic point insertion, and interactive visualization, making it a suitable solution for a wide range of computational geometry applications.

Table 10.1: Runtime comparison (in seconds) of four point-in-rectangle query algorithms on randomly generated datasets with varying numbers of points (n) and rectangles (k).

Algorithm	$n = 10^2$, $k = 10^2$	$n = 10^2$, $k = 10^3$	$n = 10^3$, $k = 10^3$	$n = 10^3$, $k = 10^4$	$n = 10^4$, $k = 10^4$
Naive Method	0.002026	0.021020	0.202240	2.026417	20.312115
Projection Method	0.000614	0.005814	0.043045	0.426279	4.128851
Enhanced Projection Method	0.001682	0.007532	0.048424	0.382955	3.586139
Quadtree Method	0.002024	0.012891	0.042627	0.375122	1.551381

10.5   Real-Time Collision Detection in Drone Swarms Using Quadtree Structures

In recent years, drone swarms have emerged as a prominent research area in robotics, surveillance, environmental monitoring, and coordinated autonomous systems. A critical aspect in the management of such swarms is the ability to detect and prevent collisions in real time, especially when operating in densely populated or dynamically changing environments. Traditional all-pairs collision detection becomes computationally prohibitive as the number of drones increases, since it requires $\mathcal{O}(n^2)$ comparisons for n agents. To address this limitation, we adopt a spatial partitioning approach based on the quadtree data structure. This section presents a complete solution for drone collision detection using quadtrees, including the theoretical model, algorithmic steps, and implementation in Python.

10.5.1   Modeling Drones as Point Entities

In the context of real-time collision detection, each drone within a swarm is abstracted as a point entity in the two-dimensional plane. Although drones are physical bodies with dimensions, their spatial occupancy can be effectively approximated by a circular region centered at their current position. The radius of this circle corresponds to the safety buffer required to avoid collisions. Let $\mathscr{D} = \{D_1, D_2, \ldots, D_n\}$ denote the set of drone positions at a given time instant, where each $D_i = (x_i, y_i)$ represents the center of the i-th drone. The collision condition between any two drones D_i and D_j is satisfied if the Euclidean distance between them is less than twice the safety radius r, i.e.,

$$\|D_i - D_j\|_2 < 2r.$$

Using this abstraction simplifies the geometric reasoning and aligns with point-based data structures such as quadtrees. The key idea is to exploit spatial locality: only drones located in close proximity need to be compared for potential collisions. This assumption allows for efficient spatial filtering and reduces the computational cost of the detection procedure.

10.5.2   Quadtree-Based Collision Detection Algorithm

The core idea of quadtree-based collision detection lies in exploiting the hierarchical spatial decomposition to efficiently identify potential collision pairs. Given a set of drone positions $\mathscr{D}$ in the plane, we construct a quadtree $\mathscr{Q}$ over the domain containing all points, using a predefined capacity threshold m and maximum tree depth th. Each leaf node of the quadtree stores at most m drones and corresponds to a square region in the plane. The collision detection algorithm operates by recursively traversing the quadtree and performing pairwise distance checks only within local regions, significantly reducing the number of unnecessary comparisons. The algorithm proceeds as follows:

1. Initialize the quadtree $\mathscr{Q}$ to cover the entire flight domain.
2. Insert each drone into $\mathscr{Q}$; split nodes recursively as needed.

3. For each drone d, define a query rectangle of radius $2r$ centered at its position.
4. Retrieve all drones within the query region and check for actual collision using Euclidean distance.

This localized and hierarchical approach drastically reduces computational complexity from $O(n^2)$ in the naive case to approximately $O(n \log n + r)$, where r is the number of detected collision pairs. The quadtree structure effectively filters out spatially distant pairs that cannot possibly collide, ensuring scalability for real-time applications. The execution time is dominated by two factors: quadtree construction and localized pairwise checks. The former operates in $O(n \log n)$ time under balanced subdivision, while the latter is confined to regions containing few drones, making collision checks highly localized and parallelizable. Empirical benchmarks confirm the method's scalability. For instance, in simulations involving $n = 10,000$ drones, the quadtree method consistently achieved collision detection within milliseconds—well within real-time constraints for autonomous navigation systems. Moreover, the structure allows for incremental updates, making it suitable for dynamic environments where drones frequently move and reposition. The real-time performance, combined with the algorithm's adaptability to varying densities and spatial configurations, underscores its utility in practical applications such as coordinated flight control, obstacle avoidance, and safety enforcement in drone airspaces.

10.5.3 Python Implementation

In large-scale drone swarm environments, ensuring real-time responsiveness is of paramount importance. This requirement is effectively addressed by the quadtree-based collision detection algorithm, which leverages spatial decomposition and hierarchical structuring to significantly reduce computational overhead. In contrast to the naïve approach with $\mathcal{O}(n^2)$ complexity—where all pairwise comparisons are performed—the quadtree-based method reduces the complexity to approximately $\mathcal{O}(n \log n)$, rendering it scalable even for high-density scenarios. For implementation purposes, each drone is modeled as an instance of the **Drone** class, whose definition is provided in Listing 10.3. This class encapsulates the essential attributes and behaviors of a drone, including position, motion dynamics, collision detection logic, and visualization capabilities. The modular design of this class supports efficient integration with the quadtree structure and real-time simulation frameworks.

Listing 10.3: Definition of Drone class

```python
import math
import random
from typing import List
from geometry import Point2D, Rectangle

class Drone:
    def __init__(self, x, y, r,c):
        self.center=Point2D(x,y); self.radius=r
        self.direction=Point2D(random.uniform(-1,1),random.uniform(-1,1))
        self.color=c; self.collided=False
    def __getitem__(self,idx):
        return self.center[0] if idx==0 else self.center[1]
    def move(self, delta, w, h): # w-width, h-height
        if not (0<self.center[0]+delta*self.direction[0]<w):self.direction[0]*=-1
        if not (0<self.center[1]+delta*self.direction[1]<h):self.direction[1]*=-1
        self.center[0]+=delta*self.direction[0]
        self.center[1]+=delta*self.direction[1]
    def intersects(self, other):
        dx=self.center[0]-other.center[0]; dy=self.center[1]-other.center[1]
        distance=math.sqrt(dx**2+dy**2)
        return distance<=self.radius+other.radius
    def draw(self, canvas):
        x=self.center[0]; y=self.center[1]; r=self.radius;
```

```
24        canvas.create_oval(x-r,y-r,x+r,y+r,fill=self.color)
```

As shown in Listing 10.3, each drone is modeled as a circular entity whose initial movement direction is randomly assigned. The class **Drone** includes, in addition to the constructor, several essential methods: the move($\cdot,\cdot,\cdot$) method updates the drone's position within the simulation area while reflecting its direction upon encountering the canvas boundaries; the intersects($\cdot$) method determines whether a collision has occurred with another drone based on their Euclidean distance; and the draw($\cdot$) method is responsible for rendering the drone as a filled circle on the canvas. These methods collectively enable autonomous motion, collision checking, and visual representation within the simulation framework. For the purpose of visualizing the planar subdivision induced by the quadtree structure, the Quadtree class is extended with a recursive method draw($\cdot$). This method traverses the hierarchy and renders the boundaries of each quadtree region, thereby illustrating the spatial partitioning. The implementation of this method is provided below.

```
1  def draw(self, canvas):
2      b=self.boundary;
3      canvas.create_rectangle(b[0][0],b[0][1],b[1][0],b[1][1],outline='gray')
4      if self.divided:
5          self.ne.draw(canvas);self.se.draw(canvas)
6          self.sw.draw(canvas);self.nw.draw(canvas)
```

Figure 10.10 illustrates a snapshot of the real-time simulation, generated using the implementation outlined in Listing 10.4.

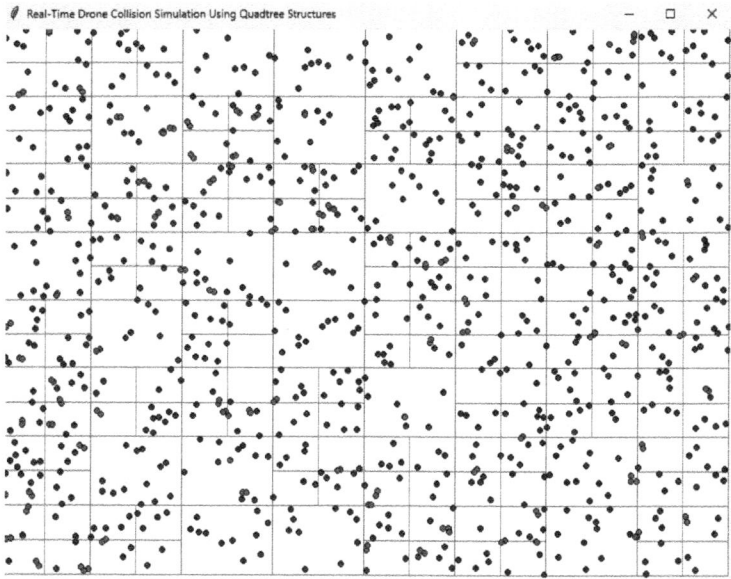

Figure 10.10: Real-time drone simulation with quadtree-based collision detection.

In the simulation environment shown in Fig. 10.10, each drone is graphically represented as a circular object, with its color dynamically reflecting its current collision status. Drones that operate without interference from neighboring agents are rendered in blue, denoting safe and unobstructed movement. Conversely, upon detection of a collision—according to the intersection criterion previously defined—the affected drones are immediately recolored in red. This real-time color transition offers clear and immediate visual feedback, facilitating the identification of collision events and enhancing the interpretability of the underlying quadtree-based detection mechanism.

Listing 10.4: GUI For Real-Time Drone Collision Simulation Using Quadtree Structures

```python
import tkinter as tk
import random
from typing import List
from geometry import Point2D, Rectangle
from Quadtree import Quadtree
from Drone import Drone

class DroneSimulationCollision:
    def __init__(self,root,w=800,h=600,num=1000,cap=10, m_l=10,r=3):
        self.canvas_width=w; self.canvas_height=h;self.num_drones=num
        self.capacity=cap; self.max_level=m_l; self.drone_radius=r
        self.root=root; self.drones = self.generate_drones()
        self.canvas=tk.Canvas(root,width=w,height=h,bg="white")
        self.canvas.pack(); self.run_simulation()

    def generate_drones(self) -> List[Drone]:
        r=self.drone_radius;w=self.canvas_width;h=self.canvas_height;
        return [
            Drone(random.uniform(r,w-r),random.uniform(r,h-r),3,"blue")
            for _ in range(self.num_drones)
        ]

    def quadtree_collision(self):
        rect=Rectangle(Point2D(0,0),Point2D(self.canvas_width,self.canvas_height))
        qt=Quadtree(rect,self.capacity,0,self.max_level)
        for d in self.drones: qt.insert(d)
        for d in self.drones:
            region=Rectangle(
                Point2D(d.center[0]-2*d.radius,d.center[1]-2*d.radius),
                Point2D(d.center[0]+2*d.radius,d.center[1]+2*d.radius)
            )
            found = []; qt.query(region,found)
            for other in found:
                if other!=d and d.intersects(other):
                    d.color="red"; other.color="red"
        return qt

    def update(self):
        self.canvas.delete("all")
        for d in self.drones:
            d.move(1, self.canvas_width, self.canvas_height); d.color="blue"
        qt=self.quadtree_collision(); qt.draw(self.canvas)
        for d in self.drones: d.draw(self.canvas)

    def run_simulation(self):
        self.update(); self.root.after(10, self.run_simulation)

if __name__ == "__main__":
    root = tk.Tk()
    root.title("Real-Time Drone Collision Simulation Using Quadtree Structures")
    app=DroneSimulationCollision(root); root.mainloop()
```

The quadtree structure not only supports efficient spatial indexing but also enables effective visualization of the drone distribution. Each node of the quadtree is depicted as a rectangular region, dynamically updated as drones move, thereby providing intuitive visual cues for detecting clusters, tracking motion, and identifying potential collision zones.

10.5.4 Conclusion

This section has demonstrated that quadtree-based spatial partitioning offers an efficient and scalable solution for real-time collision detection in drone swarms. By abstracting drones as moving particles with safety radii, the algorithm significantly reduces computational complexity while maintaining accurate and responsive collision monitoring. The modular and visually intuitive nature of the implementation makes it suitable for integration into interactive monitoring systems and lays the groundwork for future extensions into three-dimensional environments and predictive swarm coordination.

10.6 Exercises

Exercise 10.1 Implement the octree data structure—an extension of the quadtree to three-dimensional space—for the purpose of solving the range searching problem in three dimensions.

Exercise 10.2 Design and implement a quadtree-based data structure for planar range searching, where each node—whether internal or external—maintains a list of all points from the set $\mathcal{S}$ that fall within its spatial extent. Analyze and compare the memory requirements of this structure relative to the standard quadtree implementation presented in this chapter.

Exercise 10.3 Complete the formal proof that, under the assumption that points are stored in both internal and external nodes, the number of nodes visited during a range query in a quadtree of depth d is bounded above by $\mathcal{O}(2^d)$.

Exercise 10.4 Consider the problem of constructing a triangular mesh within a rectangle of dimensions $1 \times k$, where $k > 1$. The mesh must satisfy the following constraints: no Steiner points are permitted on the boundary, but their placement is allowed in the interior; additionally, all triangle angles must lie strictly within the interval $[30°, 90°]$.

   a) Is it always possible to construct such a mesh under these conditions?

   b) If a mesh satisfying the angle constraints exists for a given rectangle, determine the minimal number of interior Steiner points required to achieve such a triangulation.

Exercise 10.5 A quadtree constructed for a set of n points with real-valued coordinates, confined within a square and having depth d, typically exhibits a worst-case size of $\mathcal{O}((d+1)n)$. However, this size can be reduced to $\mathcal{O}(n)$ by applying a pruning strategy that eliminates any internal node v which possesses only a single child subtree containing points. Specifically, such a node v is removed by redirecting the pointer from its parent directly to its only relevant descendant.

   i) Prove that the size of the pruned quadtree is bounded by $\mathcal{O}(n)$.

   ii) Is it possible to improve the quadtree construction time from $\mathcal{O}((d+1)n)$ under this pruning approach? Provide justification or counterexamples.

Exercise 10.6 In this chapter, a quadtree is defined as balanced if any two adjacent squares in the subdivision differ in size by at most a factor of two. To reduce the constant overhead associated with the additional nodes required to enforce this balance, one could consider a relaxed criterion in which adjacent squares may differ by up to a factor of four.

i) Under this weaker balance condition, is it still possible to complete the quadtree subdivision into a conforming triangulated mesh such that all interior angles lie within the interval $[45°, 90°]$?

ii) Moreover, can this be achieved using only $\mathcal{O}(1)$ triangles per square in the subdivision? Justify your answer.

Exercise 10.7 Consider a stricter balancing condition for quadtrees in which adjacent squares are required to be of exactly the same size, as opposed to allowing a size difference of up to a factor of two as in standard balanced quadtrees.

i) Does the number of nodes in this more strictly balanced quadtree remain asymptotically linear with respect to the number of nodes in the original (unbalanced) quadtree?

ii) If not, provide an analysis or estimate of the asymptotic size of the resulting structure under this constraint.

Exercise 10.8 Design an algorithm for constructing a balanced quadtree directly, without the need for a separate postprocessing phase. Instead of first generating an unbalanced quadtree and subsequently applying a balancing procedure, maintain the quadtree subdivision incrementally using a doubly-connected edge list. During the construction process, whenever a square is subdivided, inspect all of its adjacent squares and recursively apply subdivisions as necessary to enforce the balancing condition.

a) Provide a detailed description of this direct construction algorithm, including the mechanisms for neighbor identification and conditional subdivision.

b) Perform a rigorous analysis of the algorithm's time complexity, and compare it with the two-phase approach.

Exercise 10.9 Quadtrees are frequently employed as a hierarchical data structure for representing digital images. Consider a square image of dimension $2^k \times 2^k$, where k is a non-negative integer. The entire image corresponds to the root node of the quadtree. A recursive subdivision is applied such that a square region is further divided into four equal subsquares if and only if it contains pixels with non-uniform intensity. Formally define the quadtree subdivision process under this model and derive an upper bound on its structural complexity — specifically, the total number of nodes in the resulting quadtree in the worst-case scenario. Justify the bound rigorously.

Exercise 10.10 Let I_1 and I_2 be two binary images of dimension $2^k \times 2^k$, where $k \in \mathbb{N}$. Each pixel in these images takes on one of two possible intensity values: 0 or 1. Assume that both images are represented using quadtree structures as described in the previous exercise, where each node corresponds to a square region, and subdivision occurs only if the region contains pixels of differing intensity. Design efficient algorithms to compute the quadtree representations of the Boolean operations:
pagebreak

a) $I_1 \vee I_2$ (logical disjunction), where a pixel has intensity 1 if it is 1 in at least one of the two images.

b) $I_1 \wedge I_2$ (logical conjunction), where a pixel has intensity 1 if and only if it is 1 in both images.

Your algorithms should take as input the quadtrees for I_1 and I_2, and produce a new quadtree representing the result of the corresponding Boolean operation. Clearly describe the recursive strategy employed, and discuss the conditions under which nodes are subdivided or merged during computation.

11. Robot Motion Planning

This chapter presents foundational techniques for efficient and optimal motion planning in mobile robotics [210]. In recent years, one of the central challenges in robotics has been the design of autonomous systems, i.e., enabling robots to generate their own motion plans in order to accomplish specific tasks. A motion plan, in essence, defines a sequence of admissible movements that transition the robot through its environment to achieve a goal. By definition, a robot is said to be autonomous if it can be instructed *what to do*, without specifying *how to do it*. This implies the robot must be capable of independently planning its own motion. Naturally, to plan its movement, the robot must possess some level of knowledge about its environment [216]. For example, a mobile robot operating within a factory setting must be aware of obstacle locations. Some of this information can be derived from a preloaded map, while additional details must be acquired using onboard sensors. The robot should be capable of detecting unforeseen obstacles not captured in the map, such as humans or mobile machinery. Utilizing this environmental data, the robot can then compute a safe trajectory to reach a target location without collisions. Formally, robot motion planning is a highly non-trivial problem, especially because it must be solved for arbitrary types of robots navigating physical spaces. To make the problem more tractable, we adopt several simplifying assumptions that do not compromise the generality of the discussion. In the context of two-dimensional motion planning, the environment is modeled as a planar workspace populated with polygonal obstacles. The robot is either abstracted as a point (termed a *point robot*) or as a polygonal shape (termed a *polygonal robot*), as illustrated in Fig. 11.1 (a). As depicted, the objective is to plan a valid path for the robot from an initial position A to a target position B, ensuring all obstacles are avoided. In other words, the task is to compute a *collision-free path* that allows the robot to safely reach its destination. A similar planning paradigm applies to aerial drones, with the key distinction that the motion planning is conducted in a three-dimensional space, requiring the incorporation of the vertical (z) coordinate to account for altitude variations [218]. For the purposes of this chapter, we assume that all obstacles are static, even though in realistic scenarios obstacles may be dynamic. If obstacles are capable of motion, the environment becomes time-dependent, and the problem complexity increases significantly. For instance, when dealing with dynamic obstacles, a shortest-path algorithm must adapt to the constantly changing environment, potentially increasing the time required to compute an optimal trajectory. Moreover, not only may obstacles be dynamic, but the start and goal positions may also vary over time, further complicating the planning task. Therefore, in this chapter, we restrict our attention to static environments with fixed start and goal configurations, which enables us to focus on core algorithmic principles without the added complexity of time-varying components. The types of movements a robot can perform depend heavily on its mechanical structure.

A. Alihodžić, *Exploring Computational Geometry*, Texts in Computer Science,
https://doi.org/10.1007/978-3-032-06393-9_11

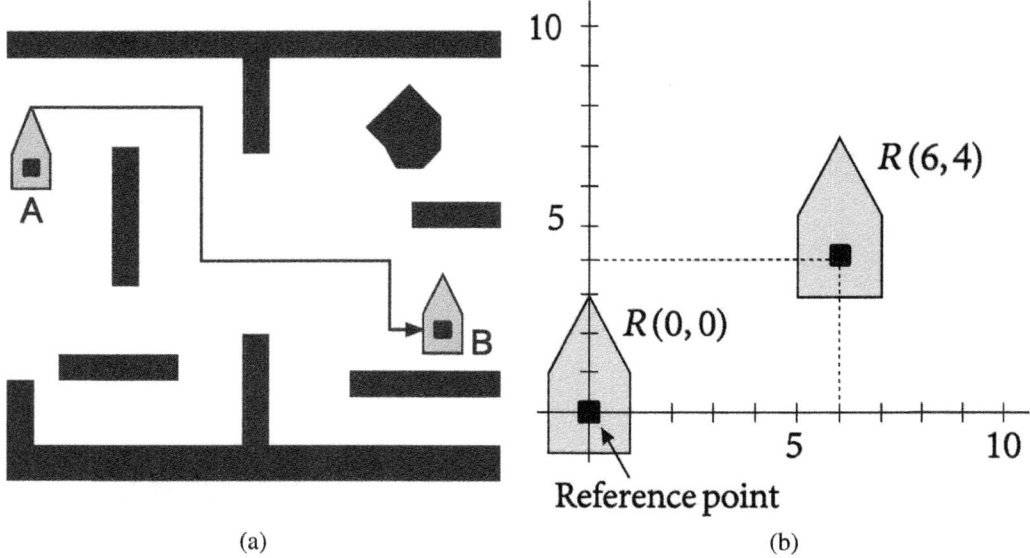

(a)   (b)

Figure 11.1: (a) Example of a robot navigating from point A to point B in a planar environment with polygonal obstacles. (b) Translation of a polygonal robot $\mathcal{R}$ from the initial position $\mathcal{R}(0,0)$ to a new configuration $\mathcal{R}(6,4)$ using a reference point located at the origin.

Some robots are capable of omnidirectional motion, while others face constraints during specific maneuvers. In this chapter, we consider mobile robots that can translate freely in any direction. That is, the robot's motion is restricted to translation only; rotational movements are excluded from the planning process. In addition to external constraints imposed by the environment, internal constraints must also be considered during motion planning. These internal constraints often arise from the robot's mechanical design and include limitations such as:

- **Nonholonomic Constraint** – This type of constraint restricts the robot's ability to move sideways. A typical example is the lateral parking of a car, where the robot (vehicle) cannot instantaneously translate in directions perpendicular to its primary axis of motion.

- **Sensor Constraint** – These constraints occur when physical obstacles (classified as external constraints) obstruct the robot's field of view, such as blocking the camera or other sensors.

It is essential to emphasize that the method by which paths are generated to avoid obstacles must be carefully selected. In this context, two distinct paradigms are commonly employed in path planning:

- **Local Path Planning Paradigm** – This approach relies on limited information about the environment. It enables reactive behavior to unforeseen changes and requires minimal computational resources. However, it typically does not yield optimal paths.

- **Global Path Planning Paradigm** – This method requires comprehensive knowledge of the environment, often in the form of a precise and static world model. While it can produce optimal or near-optimal paths, it demands considerable computational time and lacks flexibility in the presence of dynamic or unexpected changes in the environment.

In what follows, we begin by introducing two fundamental types of configuration spaces used in robot motion planning.

11.1 Configuration Spaces for Robot Motion

In this section, we describe two fundamental spaces used in planning the motion of a mobile robot. Let $\mathscr{R}$ denote a robot operating in a two-dimensional environment populated with t polygonal obstacles, represented as the set $\mathscr{S} = \{P_1, P_2, \ldots, P_t\}$. This environment is referred to as the *work space*, which we assume to be a simple polygon. Conceptually, the workspace represents the physical environment in which the robot operates, as illustrated in Fig. 11.2 (b). In this example, the robot—modeled as a polygon—navigates from its initial configuration using a designated reference point, following a collision-free path that avoids all polygonal obstacles. The configuration of the robot $\mathscr{R}$ can be described using a translation vector. For example, if the robot is translated by the vector $\vec{d} = (d_x, d_y)$ from its current position, then it moves by d_x units along the x-axis and d_y units along the y-axis. The new position of the robot is denoted by $\mathscr{R}(d_x, d_y)$. Consider a polygonal robot $\mathscr{R}$ initially defined by the vertices $(1, -1)$, $(1, 1)$, $(0, 3)$, $(-1, 1)$, and $(-1, -1)$, as illustrated in Fig. 11.1 (b). When translated by the vector $(6, 4)$, the robot assumes a new configuration $\mathscr{R}(6, 4)$, with its vertices relocated to $(7, 3)$, $(7, 5)$, $(6, 7)$, $(5, 5)$, and $(5, 3)$, respectively. Robot translation may also be defined with respect to a reference point. This approach is particularly intuitive when the coordinate origin $(0, 0)$ lies within the interior of the robot at configuration $\mathscr{R}(0, 0)$; in this case, the origin serves as the *reference point*. The new position of the robot is then uniquely determined by specifying the coordinates of its reference point. That is, $\mathscr{R}(d_x, d_y)$ indicates that the robot has been placed such that its reference point lies at point (d_x, d_y). In general, the reference point need not be located inside the robot; it may be defined externally, for example, as if attached to the robot by an invisible rod. Unless otherwise specified, we will assume throughout this chapter that the reference point coincides with the coordinate origin for the configuration $\mathscr{R}(0, 0)$.

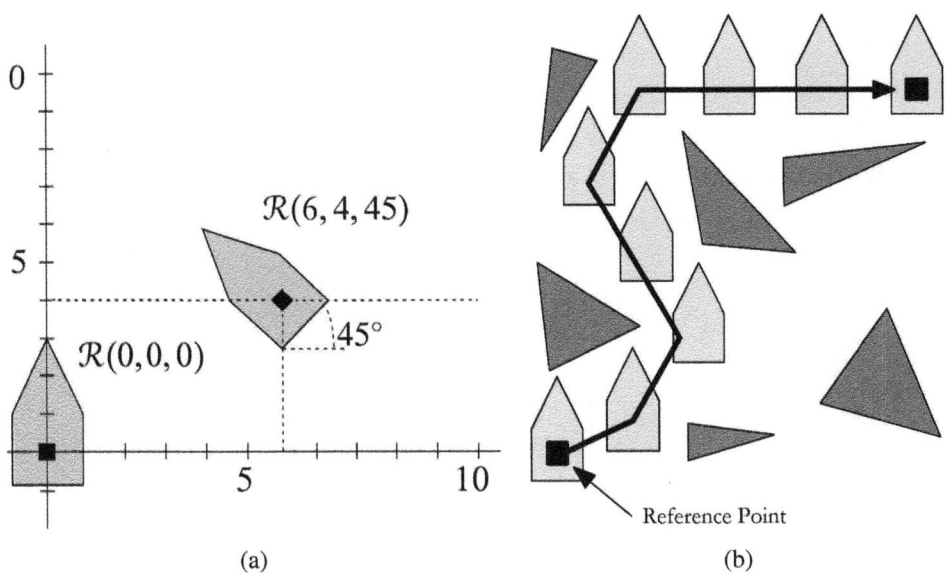

(a)   (b)

Figure 11.2: (a) Translation and rotation of a polygonal robot $\mathscr{R}$ from $\mathscr{R}(0, 0, 0)$ to $\mathscr{R}(6, 4, 45°)$ about a reference point at the origin. (b) Example of a robot navigating through the workspace.

If we assume that the robot is capable of changing its orientation—e.g., by rotating about its reference point—then an additional parameter must be introduced to capture this rotational component. Let this parameter be the angle $\varphi \in [-\pi, \pi)$ (or alternatively, $\varphi \in [0, 2\pi)$), which specifies the robot's orientation relative to a global frame. Thus, the notation $\mathscr{R}(d_x, d_y, \varphi)$ represents a robot positioned at (d_x, d_y) and rotated counterclockwise by angle φ about its reference point. The configuration $\mathscr{R}(0, 0, 0)$ corresponds to the robot's initial position and orientation. An example of such a rotation by 45 degrees can be seen in Fig. 11.2 (a). In general, the positioning of a robot is characterized by a set of parameters equal to its number of *degrees of freedom* (DOF). For example, in 2D motion planning where the robot only translates, two parameters suffice. However, if rotation is also allowed, then three degrees of freedom are required. The number of degrees of freedom increases significantly in higher-dimensional spaces. In 3D, translation alone requires three parameters—corresponding to movement along the x, y, and z axes. If rotation is permitted, three additional parameters must be introduced to define orientation about the coordinate axes, typically denoted by angles α, β, and γ. Hence, a full 3D pose of a rigid body robot in space requires six degrees of freedom: three for translation and three for rotation. We define the space of all possible configurations of the robot $\mathscr{R}$ as its *configuration space*, denoted by $\mathscr{C}(\mathscr{R})$. This space represents the set of all positions and orientations that the robot may assume. There is a natural correspondence between configuration space and work space: a point P in configuration space determines a unique placement of the robot $\mathscr{R}(P)$ in the work space. For instance, planning the motion of a robot that both translates and rotates in a 2D plane results in a 3-dimensional configuration space—one that encodes (x, y, φ). Specifically, a configuration point $P = (x_0, y_0, \varphi)$ corresponds to placing the robot at position (x_0, y_0) and rotating it by angle φ. Note that this configuration space is not strictly $\mathbb{R}^3$, but rather $\mathbb{R}^2 \times [0, 2\pi)$, due to the periodic nature of orientation. If the robot is restricted to translation in the plane, the configuration space coincides with the Euclidean plane $\mathbb{R}^2$, and it becomes equivalent to the work space. Choosing a point in configuration space effectively determines a specific placement of the robot in the physical world. It is important to observe, however, that not every point in configuration space corresponds to a valid or feasible placement. Some configurations result in the robot intersecting one or more obstacles from the set $\mathscr{S}$. Such configurations are termed *forbidden points*, and the set of all forbidden configurations is referred to as the *forbidden configuration space*, denoted by $\mathscr{C}_o(\mathscr{R}, \mathscr{S})$. The complement of this set, comprising all valid configurations in which the robot avoids collisions, is known as the *free configuration space*, denoted by $\mathscr{C}_f(\mathscr{R}, \mathscr{S})$.

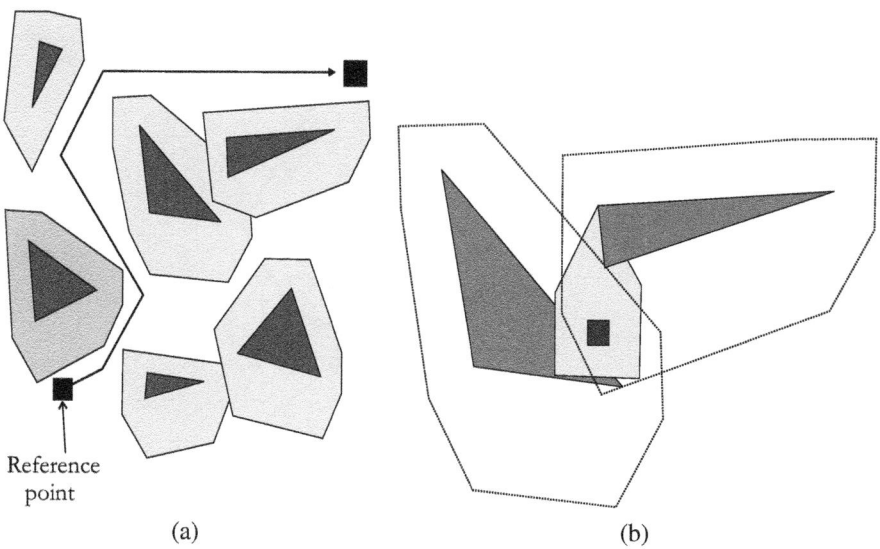

(a)   (b)

Figure 11.3: (a) Representation of a collision-free path in the configuration space. (b) Overlapping configuration-space obstacles resulting from disjoint physical obstacles in the workspace, as induced by the Minkowski sum with a polygonal robot.

An illustrative example is shown in Fig. 11.3 (a), where the robot—abstracted as a point defined by its reference point—traverses the free configuration space while avoiding obstacles generated through

Minkowski sums [29]. A polygonal robot in the work space (see Fig. 11.2 (b)) corresponds to a single point in configuration space (see Fig. 11.3 (a)), and each point in configuration space uniquely determines a placement of the robot in the work space. Although obstacles are also depicted in configuration space, they serve a different purpose: they indicate where configurations result in collisions. The path taken by the robot in the work space maps to a curve in configuration space, and vice versa. More importantly, a collision-free path in the work space corresponds to a continuous path within the free configuration space. By carefully selecting points from the free configuration space, one can construct a *collision-free path* that guarantees safe traversal from a start to a goal configuration. An important question is whether obstacles in the work space can be represented in configuration space. The answer is affirmative. A physical obstacle $\mathscr{O}$ from the work space can be transformed into a set of configurations $\mathscr{C}_O$ in which the robot $\mathscr{R}$ would intersect $\mathscr{O}$. This set is known as a *configuration-space obstacle*. As illustrated in Fig. 11.3 (b), configuration-space obstacles may overlap even when physical obstacles in the work space are disjoint. Such situations arise when certain robot configurations result in simultaneous intersection with multiple obstacles, implying that the robot cannot navigate between them. In the remainder of this text, we adopt the assumption that obstacles are modeled as open sets—permitting the robot to make contact with their boundaries without being classified as in collision. However, this assumption is generally impractical, as operating too close to obstacle boundaries increases the risk of unpredictable behavior or unintended collisions. A widely used remedy is to *inflate* each obstacle by the shape of the robot through the Minkowski sum prior to path planning. Consequently, for analytical consistency and safety, we consider all obstacles as closed sets throughout this chapter.

11.2 Point Robot

Before analyzing the motion of a polygonal robot in the plane, this section first explores how a point robot can be exploited to navigate from one location to another. As previously discussed, for a point robot, the workspace and the configuration space are identical. Let us now assume that a point robot $\mathscr{R}$ is given, along with a set of t disjoint obstacles $\mathscr{O}_1, \mathscr{O}_2, \ldots, \mathscr{O}_t$, each represented as a simple polygon. Let n denote the total number of vertices among all obstacles. The robot's motion from the start to the goal location requires determining a path along which the robot will move. Before computing such a path, it is useful to construct a data structure that stores the free space. This structure can then be reused to compute paths between any arbitrary pair of start and goal positions. This paradigm is particularly efficient when the robot's workspace remains static and path queries are frequent. For simplicity, we restrict the robot's motion to a large bounding box $\mathscr{B}$ that contains all polygonal obstacles. In other words, we add an additional large outer obstacle, visually represented in Fig. 11.4 (a) as the area outside the mentioned box. Accordingly, the free configuration space can be expressed as

$$\mathscr{C}_f = \mathscr{B} \setminus \bigcup_{i=1}^{t} \mathscr{O}_i.$$

As seen in Fig. 11.4 (a), the free space is generally a disconnected region with holes. In what follows, we describe how to find a path that connects the robot's initial position to its goal. Before doing so, we consider a suitable decomposition of the workspace. Several techniques can be used for decomposing the workspace, including:

- Trapezoidal decomposition;
- Decomposition based on the Voronoi diagram;
- Segment-based decomposition;
- Potential field method;
- Attractive-repulsive force method.

In this chapter, we focus solely on trapezoidal decomposition. Given that the workspace consists of disjoint polygonal obstacles, and each obstacle is composed of non-intersecting segments, trapezoidal decomposition of the plane is achieved by extending two vertical rays—one upward and one downward—from each endpoint of every segment, stopping at the next intersected edge, as illustrated in Fig. 11.4 (b).

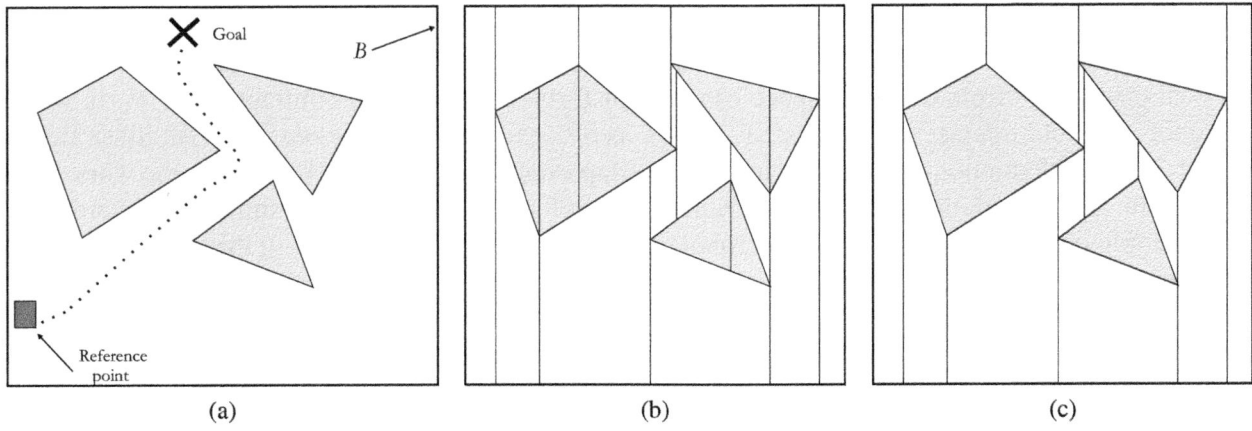

| (a) | (b) | (c) |

Figure 11.4: (a) Illustration of the bounding box (rectangle) $\mathscr{B}$ that encloses all polygonal obstacles, with the free configuration space defined as the region inside $\mathscr{B}$ but outside the obstacles. (b) Trapezoidal decomposition of the workspace using vertical extensions from segment endpoints. (c) Computed free space as the union of trapezoids which do not intersect with obstacles.

As illustrated in Fig. 11.4 (b), by extending vertical segments, we obtain trapezoids as flat surfaces resulting from such a decomposition. A triangle can be considered a special case of a trapezoid where one of the bases has zero length. Each trapezoid is defined by two segment endpoints (referred to as the left and right vertices of the trapezoid) and two subsegments (the upper and lower edges of the trapezoid). An efficient trapezoidal decomposition is performed using a randomized algorithm with a time complexity of $\mathscr{O}(n \log n)$ [127]. Once the workspace has been decomposed into trapezoids, Algorithm 24 is applied to determine the free space.

Algorithm 24: Pseudocode of the algorithm for computing free workspace.

Input : A set $\mathscr{S}$ consisting of t disjoint polygons.

Step 1: Determine the set of edges $\mathscr{E}$ from the set $\mathscr{S}$.

Step 2: Compute the trapezoidal decomposition of the set $\mathscr{E}$.

Step 3: Remove the trapezoids that lie within the interior of polygons (obstacles) and return the resulting decomposition.

Output : Trapezoidal decomposition of the workspace for the point robot $\mathscr{R}$.

According to Algorithm 24, the free space is defined as the union of trapezoids that do not intersect with any obstacles. The removal of an arbitrary trapezoid that lies entirely within the interior of an obstacle can be performed in constant time, $\mathscr{O}(1)$. Specifically, to discard such a trapezoid, it is sufficient to check whether one of its bounding edges lies along the upper or lower boundary of an obstacle (see Fig. 11.4 (c)). In what follows, we state a lemma—without proof—that characterizes the total time required to represent the plane with obstacles as a union of non-overlapping trapezoids.

Lemma 11.2.1 The trapezoidal decomposition of the free configuration space for a point robot navigating among disjoint polygonal obstacles—comprising a total of n edges—can be efficiently computed using a randomized algorithm with time complexity $\mathcal{O}(n\log n)$.

When the number of obstacles is relatively small, a naive algorithm with time complexity $\mathcal{O}(n^2)$ can be employed to compute the free workspace. Consider, for example, three polygonal obstacles represented by simple polygons: $\mathcal{O}_1 = \{P_1, P_2, P_3, P_4\}$, $\mathcal{O}_2 = \{P_5, P_6, P_7\}$, and $\mathcal{O}_3 = \{P_8, P_9, P_{10}\}$, as shown in Fig. 11.5 (a).

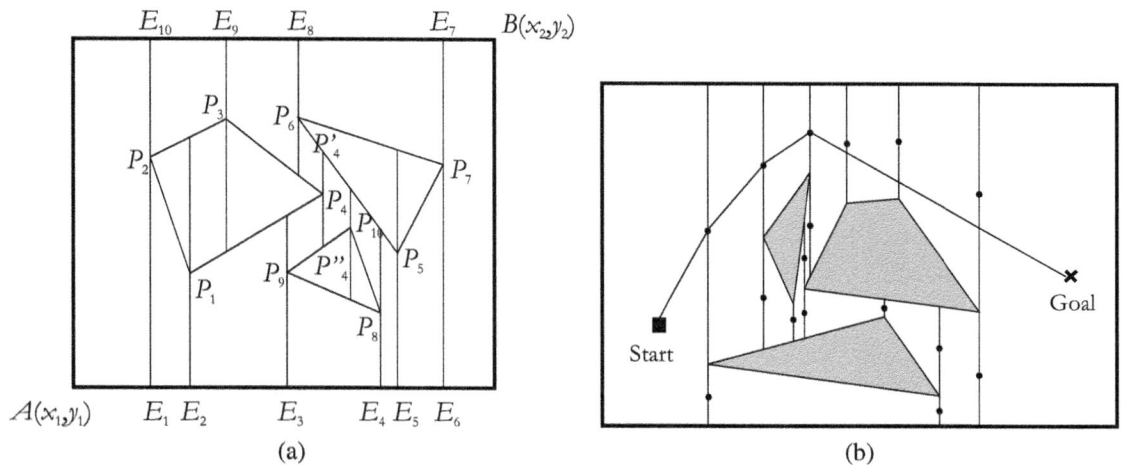

Figure 11.5: (a) Quadratic algorithm for computing the free workspace. (b) Path planning via centers of vertical extensions.

Assume that these obstacles are enclosed within a bounding rectangle defined by two opposite corners $A(x_1, y_1)$ and $B(x_2, y_2)$. As an initial step, we sort the vertices of all obstacles $\mathcal{O}_1$, $\mathcal{O}_2$, and $\mathcal{O}_3$ in ascending order according to their x-coordinates. The sorted sequence is stored in a list L. Based on the arrangement shown in the figure, the sorted order is: P_2–P_1–P_3–P_9–P_6–P_4–P_{10}–P_8–P_5–P_7. Without loss of generality, we assume that there are no vertical polygon edges and no duplicate x-coordinates among the vertices. If such cases arise, they can be resolved by rotating the entire workspace by a small angle. Next, for each point P_i in the list L, we compute two vertical extensions—one upward and one downward. We describe the process for constructing the upward extension; the downward case is entirely analogous. From point P_i, we draw a ray l orthogonal to the segment $\overline{DB}$, where $D = (x_1, y_2)$. Among all polygon edges, we identify the segment $s_j = \overline{P_m P_n}$ that intersects ray l such that the distance from P_i to the intersection point S is minimized. The segment $\overline{P_i S}$ is then defined as the vertical extension of point P_i. As illustrated in Fig. 11.5 (a), the vertical extension of point P_2 is the segment $\overline{P_2 E_{10}}$, where E_{10} is the intersection point of the upward ray from P_2 with the rectangle's top boundary. Since there are n polygon edges inside the bounding rectangle, identifying the appropriate extension for any point requires $\mathcal{O}(n)$ time in the worst case. As each of the n vertices generates two extensions, the total runtime of the algorithm is quadratic. Once all vertical extensions have been computed, those which lie entirely within obstacle interiors are discarded. The remaining extensions, together with polygon vertices, form trapezoids whose union constitutes the free space. As shown in Fig. 11.5 (a), the decomposition yields 13 trapezoids: $\square AE_1E_{10}D$, $\square E_1E_2P_1P_2$, $\square P_2P_3E_9E_{10}$, $\square E_2E_3P_9'P_1$, $\square E_3E_4P_8P_9$, $\square E_4E_5P_5P_8'$, $\square P_8P_8'P_{10}'P_{10}$, $\square P_{10}P_{10}'P_4'P_4''$, $\square P_9P_4''P_4P_9'$, $\square P_4P_4'P_6P_6''$, $\square P_3P_6''E_8E_9$, $\square E_5E_6P_7P_6$, $\square E_6CBE_7$, where $C = (x_2, y_1)$. Once the decomposition is completed, any path from a start location to a goal location is computed within the union of these trapezoids. If the start and goal positions lie within the same trapezoid, the path between them is simply the segment $\overline{AB}$. Otherwise, path planning becomes more complex. Several methods exist for addressing this problem; one intuitive approach is to compute the centers of all vertical extensions and connect them to form a graph that guides the robot from the start to the goal location, as illustrated in Fig. 11.5 (b). Let us describe how the path shown above is constructed. Once the free space is computed, the next step is to generate a roadmap, i.e., a graph that captures all feasible paths from the start to the goal location. Naturally, this graph is embedded within the free space. If we exclude the initial and terminal segments—those that connect the start point A to the graph and the graph to the goal point B—the resulting path is entirely composed of edges belonging to the graph. It is not difficult to observe that any two adjacent trapezoids share a vertical edge, which corresponds to a vertical extension drawn from a polygon vertex. The key question is how to define the graph's vertices. To this end, one vertex is placed at the center of each trapezoid, and an additional vertex is placed at the midpoint of each vertical extension (see Fig. 11.6 (a)). Hence, the graph's nodes consist of the centers of trapezoids and the centers of their vertical extensions.

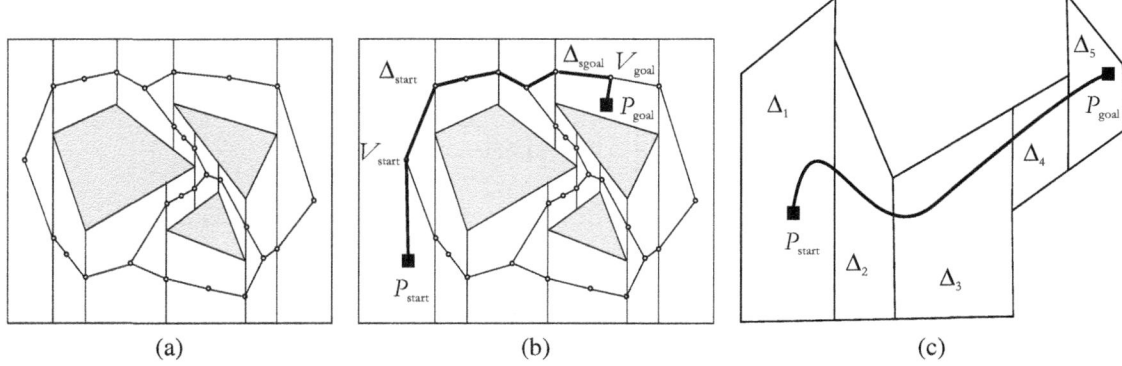

(a)   (b)   (c)

Figure 11.6: (a) An example of vertex and edge construction in the graph. (b) Illustration of a three-part path constructed via trapezoidal decomposition: from Start and Goal positions to trapezoid centers and through the graph core. (c) Illustration used to demonstrate the correctness of Algorithm 25.

The next question concerns the construction of edges. An arc between two nodes is considered a valid edge of the graph if one node lies at the center of a trapezoid and the other lies on its boundary (or vice versa). Conversely, if both endpoints of the arc lie at trapezoid centers or both lie on boundaries, the arc is not considered a valid graph edge. An example of such vertex and edge construction is illustrated in Fig. 11.6 (a). It can be concluded that the graph described above can be constructed in linear time $\mathcal{O}(n)$, by traversing a suitable structure (e.g., a doubly-connected edge list) that stores the edges and vertical extensions. Once the graph is determined, it serves—together with the trapezoidal decomposition—as the basis for defining a path from the start position P_{start} to the goal position P_{goal}. First, the trapezoids Δ_{start} and Δ_{goal} containing the start and goal positions are located. This can be done in linear time, or in $\mathcal{O}(\log n)$ time if more advanced data structures are used. If both P_{start} and P_{goal} lie within the same trapezoid, the path is immediately returned as the direct segment $\overline{P_{start}P_{goal}}$. Otherwise, we identify the centers V_{start} and V_{goal} of the corresponding trapezoids Δ_{start} and Δ_{goal}, respectively, as illustrated in Fig. 11.6 (b). The path constructed between the points P_{start} and P_{goal} consists of three main segments. The first and last segments correspond to the straight-line connections from the start and goal points to the centers of their respective trapezoids, denoted as V_{start} and V_{goal}. The central segment is of primary interest—it represents the core of the path and is computed by finding a sequence of graph edges that connects the vertices V_{start} and V_{goal}. This intermediate path is determined using Algorithm 25. Before analyzing the time complexity of Algorithm 25, let us first examine its correctness. It is straightforward to observe that the path generated by mentioned algorithm does not intersect any obstacles, as it consists of segments entirely contained within trapezoids that belong to the free workspace. We now aim to demonstrate that any feasible path connecting the points P_{start} and P_{goal}, if it exists, must lie entirely within the free space. Consider an arbitrary continuous path connecting points P_{start} and P_{goal}. Based on the construction of the trapezoidal decomposition, these points lie within the interior of trapezoids that belong to the obstacle-free region. Thus, it follows that the path must traverse a sequence of k adjacent trapezoids, denoted by $\Delta_1, \Delta_2, \ldots, \Delta_k$, where $\Delta_1 = \Delta_{\text{start}}$ and $\Delta_k = \Delta_{\text{goal}}$.

Algorithm 25: Pseudocode of the algorithm for computing path.

Input : Trapezoidal decomposition of the free workspace, the graph G, start point P_{start}, and goal point P_{goal}.

Step 1: The trapezoids Δ_{start} and Δ_{goal}, which respectively contain the points P_{start} and P_{goal}, are identified.

Step 2: If the trapezoids Δ_{start} and Δ_{goal} do not exist, **then** the points P_{start} or P_{goal} lie in the forbidden space. In this case, an error is reported and the algorithm terminates.

Step 3: Otherwise, the following steps of the algorithm are executed:

  a) The centers V_{start} and V_{goal} of the trapezoids Δ_{start} and Δ_{goal}, respectively, are identified.
  b) Using the BFS algorithm, the path between the nodes V_{start} and V_{goal} is computed. If such a path exists, the complete trajectory is returned, consisting of the segment connecting P_{start} and V_{start}, followed by the path from V_{start} to V_{goal}, and finally the segment connecting V_{goal} and P_{goal}. If no such path exists, a message indicating that no path is available is returned.

Output : Computed path between points P_{start} and P_{goal}, or a notification of its absence.

As shown in Fig. 11.6 (c), a representative case might involve $k = 5$ trapezoids. Each trapezoid Δ_i is associated with a node V_i in the graph. If the path passes from Δ_i to Δ_{i+1}, these two trapezoids must be adjacent, which implies that they share a common vertical extension. Given the structure of the graph, this adjacency guarantees the existence of an edge connecting the corresponding nodes V_i and V_{i+1}. Consequently, there exists a path in the graph that connects the nodes V_1 and V_k. By applying the Breadth-First Search (BFS) algorithm on this graph, one obtains a valid path from V_{start} to V_{goal}.

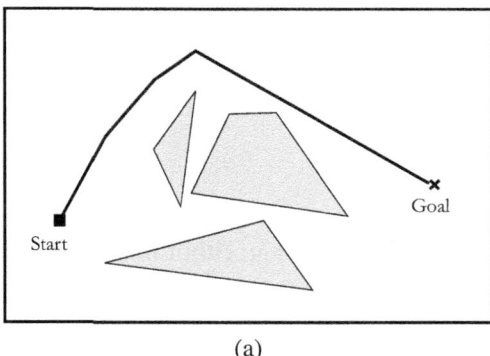
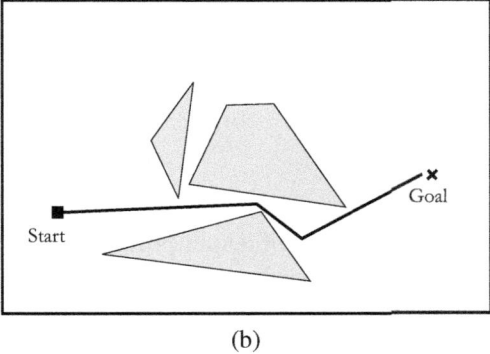

(a)   (b)

Figure 11.7: (a) Path obtained using the Depth-First Search (DFS) algorithm. (b) Path generated by the A* algorithm.

Let us now consider the time complexity of this approach. It is well known that BFS on a graph with n nodes runs in time $\mathcal{O}(n)$. Since each trapezoid and each vertical extension contributes exactly one node to the graph, and the total number of such geometric primitives is proportional to the number of obstacle vertices, the number of graph nodes is $\mathcal{O}(n)$. Moreover, since the graph is planar and constructed with bounded degree, the number of edges is also $\mathcal{O}(n)$. Therefore, BFS determines the path in linear time $\mathcal{O}(n)$ in the worst case. It should be noted, however, that the path obtained by Algorithm 25 is not necessarily optimal in terms of its Euclidean length. In subsequent sections, we will present techniques for refining the path to obtain shorter trajectories within reasonable computational bounds. Finally, although BFS is a natural choice due to its simplicity, other graph search methods such as Depth-First Search (DFS) or A* search can also be employed to compute paths [151, 183], as illustrated in Fig. 11.7. While the A* algorithm typically yields shorter paths compared to those obtained via Depth-First Search (DFS), it is evident that more sophisticated techniques exist for generating significantly shorter and more efficient trajectories, some of which will be introduced in the following section.

11.3   Shortest Path Search

In this section, we introduce several algorithms for computing the shortest path. In the preceding section, we discussed a method for determining a path from a start point to a goal point; however, this path is not guaranteed to be optimal. The previously presented algorithm may generate unnecessarily long detours or involve excessive turning, which can be impractical in real-world scenarios where high-quality paths are essential. The definition of a "high-quality" path is often application-dependent. In general, longer paths result in increased traversal time for the robot. For instance, in an industrial setting, a mobile robot tasked with transporting goods along a longer route will be less productive, reducing overall system efficiency. Hence, finding the shortest feasible path is typically desirable.

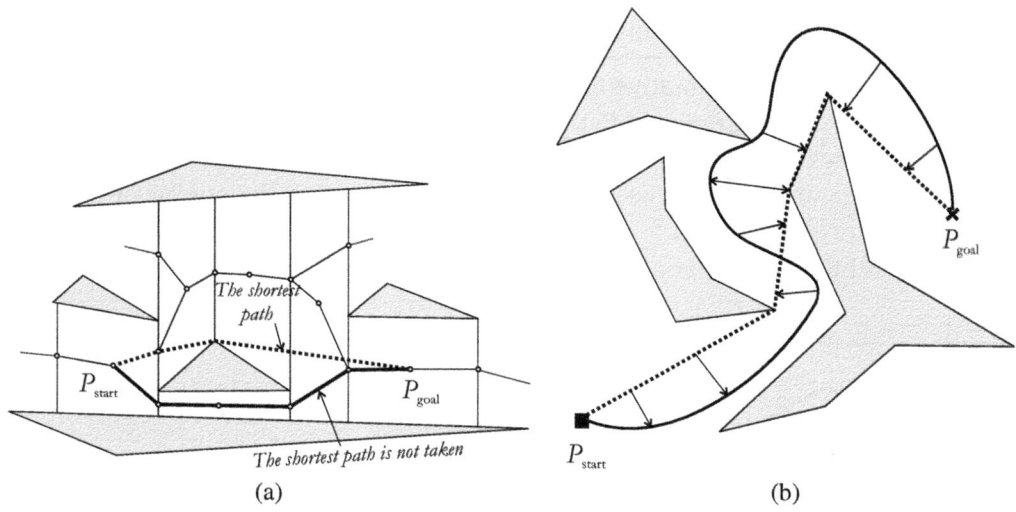

Figure 11.8: (a) Illustration of a suboptimal path returned by Dijkstra's algorithm in a weighted visibility-based graph. (b) Rubber-band metaphor illustrating how obstacles shape the shortest path by constraining its geometry.

Other practical considerations may also arise. For example, some robots can only move in straight lines, requiring them to decelerate, stop, and reorient before proceeding in a new direction. Consequently, each change in direction introduces delays, and for such robots, both the total path length and the number of turns become critical factors. Although such constraints are important in practice, our focus in this chapter will be limited to computing the shortest path for a planar translational robot. We begin by examining how to compute the shortest path from a given start point P_{start} to a goal point P_{goal}, ensuring that the point robot $\mathscr{R}$ avoids collisions with a set of polygonal obstacles $\mathcal{O}$. One major limitation of the previous method—based on trapezoidal decomposition of the free space, graph construction, and breadth-first search (BFS)—is that the resulting path may traverse arcs that are not necessarily the shortest segments. This approach can be refined by assigning edge weights to the graph that correspond to the Euclidean distance between connected vertices, thereby converting it into a weighted graph. A classical graph-search algorithm, such as Dijkstra's algorithm [193], can then be applied to identify a shortest path in this weighted structure. While this refinement appears promising, it does not always yield the true shortest path, as will be illustrated in Fig. 11.8 (a). To compute the shortest path between the points P_{start} and P_{goal} in the presence of obstacles from the set $\mathcal{O}$, we must adopt a refined approach. Instead of relying on the graph induced by trapezoidal decomposition, we consider an alternative graph construction that more effectively captures the geometric constraints of the environment. Intuitively, one may envision the shortest path as an elastic rubber band stretched between the start and goal positions. This metaphor suggests that the obstacles in $\mathcal{O}$ act as constraints that shape the band, forcing it to conform to the permissible region of the configuration space. As illustrated in Fig. 11.8 (b), the resulting path will naturally contour around the obstacles, potentially making contact with their vertices and even sliding along their edges. This behavior aligns with the requirement that obstacles be modeled as open sets—ensuring that the path is allowed to touch obstacle boundaries without intersecting their interior. From this visualization, we observe that the shortest path in a polygonal environment is composed of straight-line segments that connect visible vertices of the obstacles. Importantly, such a path will often pass through critical points such as obstacle corners. This observation forms the foundation of a more formal characterization of shortest paths in polygonal domains. Before introducing a lemma that formalizes this idea, it is essential to note two important aspects: (1) the shortest path between two points in a polygonal environment may not be unique, and (2) we define an *interior vertex* of a path as any vertex that is neither the start nor the goal point. The forthcoming lemma encapsulates the structure of such shortest paths and guides the construction of visibility graphs—an essential tool for determining optimal paths in static environments with polygonal obstacles.

> **Lemma 11.3.1** Any shortest path connecting the start point P_{start} and the goal point P_{goal}, while avoiding a set $\mathcal{S}$ of polygonal obstacles, must consist of a sequence of straight-line segments whose interior vertices coincide with the vertices of the obstacles in $\mathcal{S}$.

Proof. Let τ be an arbitrary shortest path connecting the points P_{start} and P_{goal} while avoiding a set $\mathcal{S}$ of polygonal obstacles. We aim to prove two fundamental properties of τ: (1) the path τ is polygonal, and (2) all of its interior vertices lie at the vertices of obstacles in $\mathcal{S}$. To establish the first claim, we proceed by contraposition. Assume, for contradiction, that τ is not a polygonal path. Since the obstacles in $\mathcal{S}$ are polygonal by definition, the non-polygonal nature of τ implies the existence of a point $P \in \tau$ which lies in the interior of the free space, such that no linear segment containing P is part of the path τ, as illustrated in Fig. 11.9 (a).

Since the point P lies in the interior of the free space, there exists a circle C centered at the point P with a nonzero radius such that it intersects the path τ at two distinct points Q and R. The subpath of τ between Q and R can thus be replaced with the straight-line segment $\overline{QR}$, which lies entirely within the free space. This modification yields a path strictly shorter than τ, contradicting the assumption that τ is a shortest path. Hence, τ must be polygonal. We now turn to the second part of the lemma concerning the nature of the interior vertices of τ. Let v be an arbitrary interior vertex of τ. We aim to prove that v must coincide with a vertex of some polygonal obstacle in $\mathcal{S}$. Suppose, to the contrary, that v is not a vertex of any obstacle. Then two cases may arise:

- **Case 1:** The vertex v lies in the interior of the free space. It is inadmissible since, similar to the argument above, an open disk centered at v would intersect the path τ in two points Q and R, allowing for the replacement of the subpath between them with a shorter segment $\overline{QR}$, violating the optimality of τ.

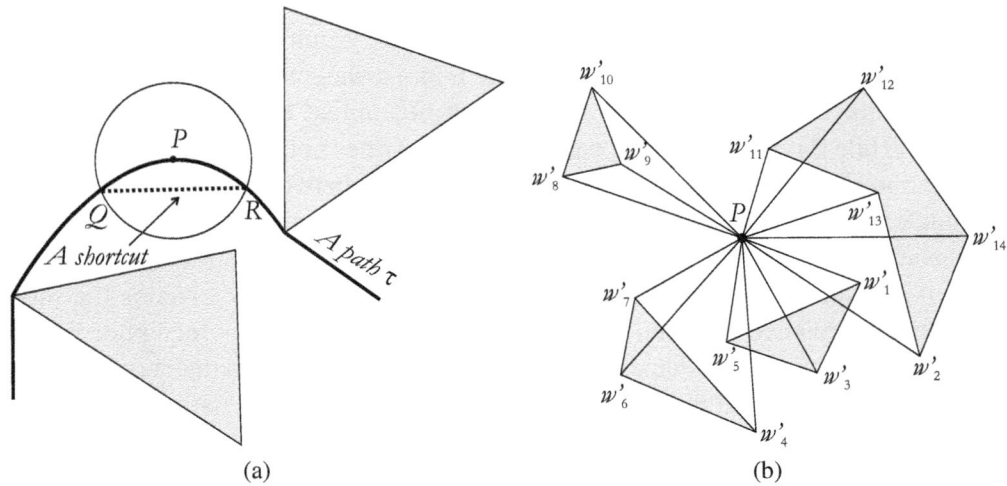

(a)   (b)

Figure 11.9: (a) Illustration used in the proof of Lemma 11.3.1. (b) Clockwise polar angle sorting of obstacle vertices around the query point P.

- **Case 2:** The vertex v lies in the relative interior of an edge e of some polygonal obstacle in $\mathcal{S}$. In this scenario, v does not correspond to a true vertex of any obstacle. As before, it would be possible to locally shortcut the path near v using a straight-line segment that bypasses the current configuration, once again producing a shorter path and contradicting the optimality of τ.

Since both alternative scenarios lead to contradictions, the only viable conclusion is that each interior vertex v of the shortest path τ must be a vertex of some polygonal obstacle in the set $\mathcal{S}$.

∎

Building upon Lemma 11.3.1, we observe a substantial reduction in the search space, as the lemma implies that the optimal path must lie within a specific, well-defined subset of the configuration space shaped by the geometry of the obstacles. This insight paves the way for constructing a more efficient representation of the problem domain—namely, an enhanced roadmap that enables the computation of shortest paths with greater precision. This refined structure is known as the *visibility graph* of the obstacle set $\mathcal{S}$, denoted by $G_{\text{vis}}(\mathcal{S})$. The visibility graph is formally defined as follows: its *nodes* correspond to the vertices of the polygonal obstacles comprising $\mathcal{S}$, while its *edges* are line segments (or arcs) that connect pairs of vertices which are *mutually visible*. That is, there exists an edge between two vertices v and w if and only if the straight-line segment $\overline{vw}$ lies entirely within the free space and does not intersect the interior of any obstacle in $\mathcal{S}$. Such segments are referred to as *visibility edges*. According to Lemma 11.3.1, the shortest path must consist entirely of visibility edges, with the possible exception of the initial and terminal segments connecting the start and goal points to the nearest obstacle vertices. To ensure that these segments are also part of the visibility graph, it is standard practice to augment the set $\mathcal{S}$ by incorporating the start point P_{start} and the goal point P_{goal} as additional vertices. This yields the *extended obstacle set*, defined as $\mathcal{S}^* = \mathcal{S} \cup \{P_{\text{start}}, P_{\text{goal}}\}$. By constructing the visibility graph over the extended set $\mathcal{S}^*$, the shortest path problem can be reformulated as a discrete graph-search problem, where the solution corresponds to the shortest path in $G_{\text{vis}}(\mathcal{S}^*)$. This fundamental observation is formalized in the following Lemma.

Lemma 11.3.2 The shortest path connecting the points P_{start} and P_{goal} while avoiding a set $\mathcal{S}$ of disjoint polygonal obstacles is composed entirely of arcs (edges) of the visibility graph $G_{\text{vis}}(\mathcal{S}^*)$.

Having established this structural insight, we are now in a position to formulate an algorithm for computing the shortest path between the points P_{start} and P_{goal}. The algorithm will operate on the visibility graph $G_{vis}(\mathscr{S}^*)$ and will rely on classical graph-search techniques to identify the optimal trajectory through the free space.

Algorithm 26: Pseudocode of the algorithm for seeking shortest path.

Input : The set $\mathscr{S}$ of disjoint polygonal obstacles, along with the points P_{start} and P_{goal} specified within the free space.

Step 1: Construct the visibility graph of $G_{vis}(\mathscr{S}^*)$ with respect to the set $\mathscr{S}^*$.

Step 2: Assign a weight to each arc (edge) (v,w) in the visibility graph G_{vis}, which represents the Euclidean distance between the vertices v and w.

Step 3: Apply Dijkstra's algorithm to find the shortest path between the vertices P_{start} and P_{goal} in the graph G_{vis}.

Output : The shortest collision-free path connecting the points P_{start} and P_{goal}.

The time complexity of the Algorithm 26 is proportional to $\mathscr{O}(n^2 \log n)$, which corresponds to the computational cost of constructing the visibility graph—a result that will be formally demonstrated later. As before, n denotes the total number of edges defining the polygonal obstacles. From graph theory, it is known that the time complexity of Dijkstra's algorithm is bounded by $\mathscr{O}((n+m)\log n)$, where n denotes the number of vertices and m the number of edges. In the context of Algorithm 26, the number of arcs is bounded by $\mathscr{O}(n^2)$, that is, $k = \mathscr{O}(n^2)$. Consequently, applying Dijkstra's algorithm to the visibility graph G_{vis} requires time proportional to $\mathscr{O}(n^2 \log n)$. Therefore, the total time complexity of Algorithm 26 is $\mathscr{O}(n^2 \log n)$. We now return to the problem of constructing the visibility graph. Without loss of generality, we focus on computing the graph for the set $\mathscr{S}$, rather than for its augmented version $\mathscr{S}^*$. To construct the graph, one must identify all pairs of vertices that are mutually visible. This involves verifying, for each candidate pair (v,w), whether the segment $\overline{vw}$ intersects the interior of any polygonal obstacle in the set $\mathscr{S}$. A naïve approach to this problem would incur a time complexity of $\mathscr{O}(n^3)$, since for each of the $\mathscr{O}(n^2)$ vertex pairs, an intersection test must be performed against all n obstacle edges. This results in a cubic-time procedure.

Algorithm 27: Pseudocode of the algorithm for computing the visibility graph.

Input : The set $\mathscr{S}$ of disjoint polygonal obstacles.

Step 1: Initialization of the graph $G_{vis} = \{V, E\}$, where V is the set of vertices of the polygonal obstacles in the set $\mathscr{S}$, and E is the empty set of edges.

Step 2: For each vertex v in the set V **do**:

    a) Determine the visible vertices $w \in V$ with respect to the vertex v and assign them to the set W;

    b) For each vertex $w \in W$, add the edge (arc) (v,w) to the set E.

Step 3: Return the graph G_{vis}.

Output : Visibility graph G_{vis} of the set $\mathscr{S}$.

A significantly more efficient strategy avoids iterating over all unordered vertex pairs. Instead, it focuses on one vertex at a time and identifies all other vertices that are visible from it. This idea underpins Algorithm 27, which organizes visibility computation in a more structured manner. As will be shown later, the asymptotic time complexity of Algorithm 27 is $\mathscr{O}(n^2 \log n)$, representing a substantial improvement over the naïve cubic-time method. In the following, we first describe a procedure that requires $\mathscr{O}(n \log n)$ time for identifying all vertices which are visible from a fixed vertex v. The goal is to determine, for an arbitrarily selected vertex v in the free space, the set of all obstacle vertices that are mutually visible with v. A straightforward brute-force approach would yield quadratic time complexity. Specifically, to determine whether v can see another vertex w, one must check whether the segment $\overline{vw}$ intersects any of the n obstacle edges from the set $\mathscr{S}$. Repeating this process for each possible vertex w leads to a total of $\mathscr{O}(n^2)$ intersection tests, which becomes computationally prohibitive for large n. A more sophisticated solution leverages the sweep-line paradigm—commonly used in segment intersection algorithms—but with a crucial modification: instead of translating the line horizontally or vertically, the sweep line is rotated clockwise around the fixed vertex v. This angular sweep enables efficient determination of all visible vertices from v by systematically examining their angular ordering and dynamically updating visibility constraints. The details of this angular sweep-based visibility algorithm will be outlined in the subsequent discussion.

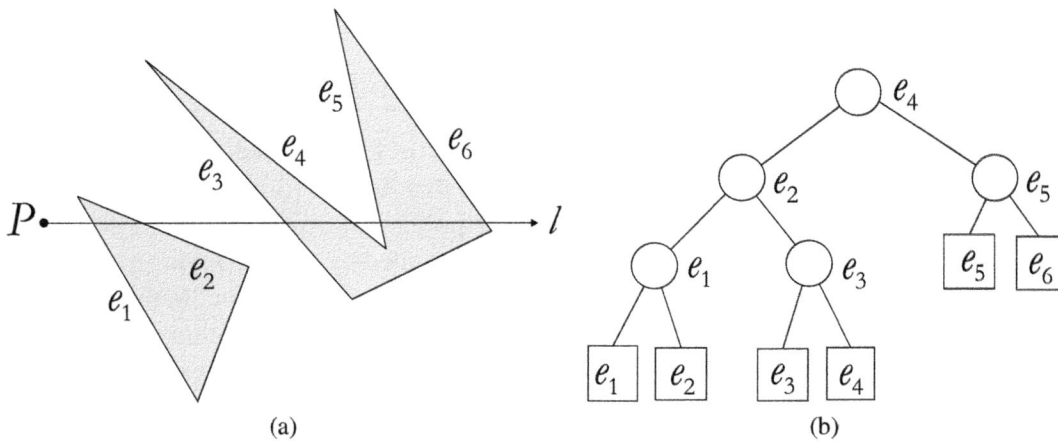

(a)   (b)

Figure 11.10: (a) Intersection of obstacle edges with the rotating sweep line ℓ originating from point P. (b) Search tree $\mathscr{T}$ used in the circular sweep-line algorithm.

The core idea behind the angular sweep algorithm lies in avoiding redundant visibility checks for every pair of points. Instead, previously acquired visibility information is reused to determine the visibility of subsequent vertices. This leads to a significant efficiency gain compared to naïve methods. Before initiating the sweep-line process, all obstacle vertices from the set $\mathscr{S}$ are sorted in a clockwise circular order based on decreasing polar angles with respect to the fixed query point P. The polar angle is defined as the angle between the positive x-axis and the vector $\overrightarrow{Pw_i}$, resulting in an ordered sequence of vertices w_i' sorted around P, as illustrated in Fig. 11.9 (b). As with standard sweep-line algorithms, this method employs two fundamental data structures: a balanced binary search tree $\mathscr{T}$ and an event queue. The tree $\mathscr{T}$ stores obstacle edges from $\mathscr{S}$, while the event queue holds the circularly ordered vertices, which correspond to the endpoints of obstacle edges (see Fig. 11.10 (b)). As the sweep progresses, each vertex from the event queue is processed sequentially. During this process, the tree $\mathscr{T}$ dynamically maintains the set of obstacle edges that intersect the rotating half-line ℓ—originating from the fixed point P and passing through the current event point (see Fig. 11.10 (a)). This half-line serves as the rotating sweep line, sweeping clockwise around the query point P. The leaves of the tree $\mathscr{T}$ store obstacle edges in the order they are intersected by ℓ: the leftmost leaf corresponds to the first intersected edge, the next leaf to the second, and so on. Internal nodes in the tree also store edges, specifically using the following invariant: an internal node v stores a reference edge e_v such that all edges in its left subtree are less than or equal to e_v, and all edges in its right subtree are strictly greater than e_v, with respect to their order of intersection with the rotating sweep line ℓ. An illustrative example of such a search tree construction is provided in Fig. 11.10. Hence, the balanced search tree maintains the obstacle edges—and consequently their endpoints (events)—in a sorted order with respect to the angle each edge forms with the initial position of the rotating ray. This organization ensures that the sweeping ray visits the event points in a clockwise direction. The process of determining all visible vertices of the set $\mathscr{S}$ from the vertex v is formally described in Algorithm 28.

Algorithm 28: Pseudocode of the algorithm for identifying the visible vertices from the point P.

Input : The set $\mathscr{S}$ of disjoint polygonal obstacles and a point P which does not lie in their interior.

Step 1: Sort the obstacle points, i.e., the vertices w_i ($i = 1, \cdots, m$) in decreasing order with respect to the angles α_i, where α_i is defined as the angle between the positive x-axis and the vector $\overrightarrow{Pw_i}$, and m denotes the total number of obstacle points in the set $\mathscr{S}$. In the case of equal angles, sorting is performed based on the distance from point P. After sorting, a sequence of points $w_{i_1}, w_{i_2}, \cdots, w_{i_m}$ is obtained, where $i_k \in \{1, 2, \cdots, m\}$. These points serve as the elements of the event queue in the sweep line algorithm and are traversed by the rotating ray in a clockwise direction. Initialize the list $\mathscr{L}$ as empty.

Step 2: Identify the obstacle edges e from the set $\mathscr{S}$ that are intersected by the ray ℓ (originating at point P and initially aligned with the positive x-axis), and insert them into a balanced search tree $\mathscr{T}$ in the order in which they are intersected by the ray ℓ (i.e., the imaginary sweep line).

Step 3: For each $i = 1$ to n **do**:

    a) If the point P can see the vertex w_i, then add the vertex w_i to the list $\mathscr{L}$.

    b) Update the tree $\mathscr{T}$ as follows:

        i) Insert into the tree the edge from $\mathscr{S}$ that is not yet contained in the tree, which is incident to w_i and its other endpoint w_i' lies to the right of the vector $\overrightarrow{Pw_i}$. Consequently, the points P, w_i, and w_i' are arranged in a clockwise orientation.

        ii) Delete from the tree the edge from $\mathscr{S}$ that is currently in the tree, which is incident to w_i and whose other endpoint w_i' lies to the left of the vector $\overrightarrow{Pw_i}$.

Step 4: Return the list $\mathscr{L}$.

Output : The set of visible vertices from the point P.

To determine whether a given point P can see the vertex w_i in $\mathscr{O}(\log n)$ time, it is necessary to perform a search within a balanced search tree. This search aims to identify whether the edge e, stored in the leftmost leaf of the tree and closest to point P (where closeness is defined as the distance from P to the intersection point between the ray ℓ—originating at P and passing through w_i—and the edge e), actually intersects the segment $\overline{Pw_i}$. Thus, the visibility check can be performed in logarithmic time by testing whether the segment $\overline{Pw_i}$ intersects the edge e, provided such an edge exists in the tree. However, the situation becomes more complex because the edge e may contain additional vertices along its interior. This introduces further ambiguity into the visibility determination. The possible configurations and special cases are illustrated in Fig. 11.11, where the vertices are sorted according to the angles previously discussed.

Let us note that all obstacle vertices are stored in a doubly linked circular list, such that the predecessor of vertex w_i is w_{i-1} and the successor is w_{i+1}. Initially, no visibility information is known, so all vertices are assumed to be invisible from the query point P. If $i = 1$, that is, when testing whether P can see w_1, there are no intermediate vertices along the segment $\overline{Pw_1}$. In this case, it suffices to check for an intersection between this segment and the edge e from the search tree that is closest to P. This constitutes the *first scenario*. For $i > 1$, if the previous vertex w_{i-1} is known to be invisible from P and lies along the segment $\overline{Pw_i}$, it follows that w_i must also be invisible. However, if w_{i-1} is visible from P, as illustrated in Fig. 11.11 (a), the algorithm searches for an edge e in the tree that intersects the segment $\overline{w_{i-1}w_i}$. If such an edge exists, w_i is deemed invisible; otherwise, it is visible (see Fig. 11.11 (b)). This case represents the *second scenario*. The *third* and *fourth scenarios* also assume that w_{i-1} is visible from P. The third scenario occurs when the entire segment $\overline{w_{i-1}w_i}$ lies inside a single obstacle polygon P_j, meaning that both endpoints are

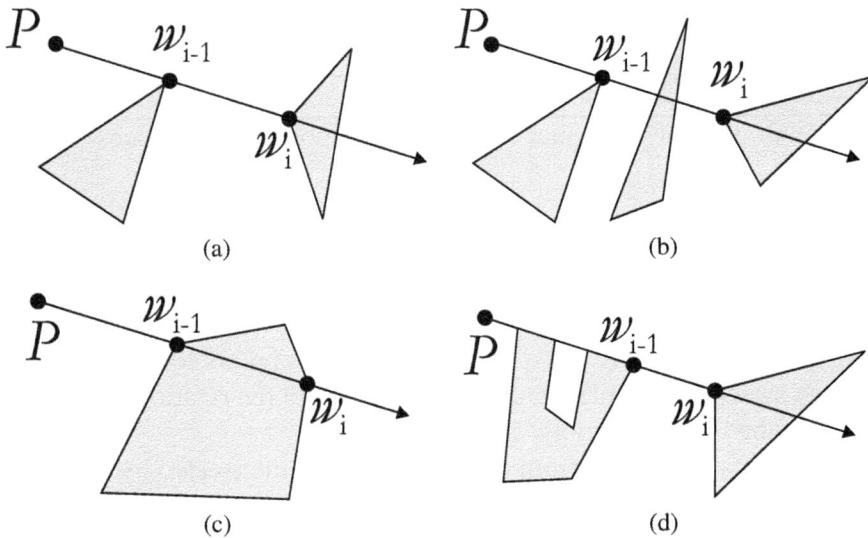

Figure 11.11: Scenarios that may arise when checking whether the point P can see the vertex w_i.

vertices of P_j (see Fig. 11.11 (c)). This condition can be verified in $\mathcal{O}(1)$ time by maintaining a record of which polygon each vertex belongs to. Specifically, if both w_{i-1} and w_i are vertices of the same polygon P_j, and if w_i is not the direct successor of w_{i-1} in the polygonal chain, the segment lies entirely within P_j and is therefore not visible. It is important to emphasize that the indices $i-1$ and i do not necessarily refer to consecutive elements in the circular list, as the vertices have been sorted by polar angle. Finally, the *fourth scenario* applies when w_{i-1} and w_i belong to different obstacles (Fig. 11.11 (d)). In this case, the search tree is queried to determine whether any edge intersects the segment $\overline{w_{i-1}w_i}$.

Based on the preceding discussion, the procedure for determining whether the point P can see the vertex w_i is formally presented in Algorithm 29.

Algorithm 29: Pseudocode of the algorithm for identifying the visible vertices from the point P.

Input : The point P and the vertex w_i being tested for visibility.

Step 1: If the segment $\overline{Pw_i}$ intersects the interior of an obstacle in the vicinity of point w_i, then return **false**.

Step 2: If $i = 1$ or the vertex w_{i-1} does not lie on the segment $\overline{Pw_i}$, then check whether the segment $\overline{Pw_i}$ intersects the edge e from the tree that is closest to point P. If such an edge e exists, it is stored in the leftmost leaf of the tree. If the segment $\overline{Pw_i}$ and the edge e intersect, return **false**. Otherwise, return **true**.

Step 3: If the vertex w_{i-1} is not visible, then return **false**. Otherwise, find the edge e in the tree that intersects the segment $\overline{w_{i-1}w_i}$. If such an edge exists, return **false**; otherwise, return **true**.

Output : Information about whether the vertex w_i is visible from point P.

Based on the pseudocodes of Algorithms 27, 28, and 29, it can be concluded that the time complexity of the visibility graph construction algorithm is proportional to $\mathcal{O}(n^2 \log n)$. This complexity arises due to the following components:

- **Angular Sorting of Vertices**: Sorting obstacle vertices in circular (angular) order relative to a fixed point requires $\mathcal{O}(n \log n)$ time;

- **Balanced Search Tree Operations**: Searching, inserting, and deleting elements (edges) in the balanced search tree during the sweep process each take $\mathcal{O}(\log n)$ time per operation;

- **Geometric Visibility Tests**: The constant-time geometric tests (e.g., orientation, intersection checks) performed during the sweep do not dominate the overall complexity.

In what follows, we present a naive implementation of the visibility graph construction algorithm with cubic time complexity. This method serves as a practical alternative to more sophisticated approaches, especially in scenarios where the number of obstacle vertices is relatively small, and the performance gap becomes negligible.

11.4 Naive Implementation For Seeking Shortest Path with Cubic Time Complexity

While asymptotically optimal algorithms for visibility graph construction achieve a time complexity of $\mathcal{O}(n^2 \log n)$, their practical implementation typically requires advanced data structures such as balanced search trees and meticulous management of geometric edge cases. However, in real-world scenarios, the number of obstacle vertices is often moderate, rendering the performance advantage of such sophisticated algorithms less pronounced. Motivated by this observation, the current section introduces a naive algorithm for constructing the visibility graph with a cubic time complexity of $\mathcal{O}(n^3)$. The implementation is carried out in the Python programming language, prioritizing clarity and pedagogical value. The core idea of the algorithm is to iterate over all pairs of vertices and, for each pair, verify mutual visibility by testing whether the line segment connecting them intersects any obstacle edge. Despite its theoretical inefficiency, this method is straightforward to implement, effective for inputs of moderate size, and serves as a practical baseline for validating the correctness of more advanced approaches. Additionally, it provides valuable insight into the core visibility testing procedure before introducing sweep-line techniques or rotational plane sweep optimizations. Building upon the geometric primitives and algorithms introduced in earlier chapters of this textbook, the implementation of the naive visibility graph algorithm is conceptually straightforward. This is demonstrated in the function *create_visibility_graph*($\cdot$, $\cdot$), which constructs the graph by connecting mutually visible points with weighted edges. The implementation relies on two auxiliary functions, $f(\cdot,\cdot)$ and $g(\cdot,\cdot)$, where f is responsible for detecting whether a given segment s intersects any of the obstacle polygons, and g checks whether a point p lies inside any polygonal obstacle. The algorithm proceeds in two phases. First, it assigns edge weights to the polygon boundaries, ensuring that adjacent vertices of each polygon are connected according to their Euclidean distance. In the second phase, all remaining pairs of vertices (including those outside the polygons) are examined. An edge is added between any two vertices if the corresponding segment does not intersect any obstacle and its midpoint does not lie inside a polygon. This conservative check ensures that the resulting graph respects obstacle boundaries and is suitable for shortest-path queries.

```python
#Check whether segment s intersects any polygon
def f(s, all_polygons):
    for poly in all_polygons:
        if s.intersects_polygon(poly):return True
    return False
#Check whether point p is contained in any polygon
def g(p, polygons):
    for poly in polygons:
        if poly.contains_point(p):return True
    return False
def create_visibility_graph(all_points, all_polygons):
    n = len(all_points); visibility_graph = [[] for _ in range(n)]
    polygon_vertices = all_points[:(n-2)]; total=0
    #Assign weights to the edges of the obstacles (polygons)
    for poly in all_polygons:
        m = poly.size(); p_list=poly.to_list()
        for i in range(m):
```

```
18          u = p_list[i]; v = p_list[(i + 1) % m]
19          idx_u =total+i; idx_v =total+(i + 1) % m
20          d =(v-u).norm()
21          visibility_graph[idx_u].append((idx_v, d))
22          visibility_graph[idx_v].append((idx_u, d))
23      total+=m
24   #Assign weights to the remaining edges in the graph
25   for i in range(n):
26      for j in range(i + 1, n):
27          s=Segment2D(all_points[i],all_points[j])
28          if f(s,all_polygons) or g(s.point_at(0.5),all_polygons): continue
29          d=(s[1]-s[0]).norm()
30          visibility_graph[i].append((j, d)); visibility_graph[j].append((i, d))
31   return visibility_graph
```

Once the visibility graph has been constructed via the function *create_visibility_graph*($\cdot,\cdot$), the next step involves applying an appropriate shortest-path algorithm to determine the optimal route between two points in the scene. As previously discussed, Dijkstra's algorithm was selected for this purpose due to its efficiency and suitability for graphs with non-negative edge weights. The implementation of Dijkstra's algorithm used in this context is presented below.

```
1  def dijkstra(graph, start:Point2D, goal:Point2D):
2     n = len(graph); dist = [float('inf')] * n
3     prev = [None] * n; visited = [False] * n;
4     dist[start] = 0; heap = [(0, start)]
5     while heap:
6         curr_dist, u = heapq.heappop(heap)
7         if visited[u]:continue
8         visited[u] = True
9         if u == goal:break
10        for v, weight in graph[u]:
11            if not visited[v]:
12                alt = dist[u] + weight
13                if alt < dist[v]:
14                    dist[v] = alt; prev[v] = u
15                    heapq.heappush(heap, (alt, v))
16    #Reconstruct the path
17    if dist[goal] == float('inf'): return float('inf'), []
18    path = []; at = goal
19    while at is not None:
20        path.append(at); at = prev[at]
21    path.reverse()
22    return dist[goal], path
```

The graphical user interface (GUI) designed for computing the shortest path is developed based on the code provided in Listing 11.1, whose visual layout is illustrated in Fig. 11.12. The referenced listing imports the module ch11_helper_functions, which contains the previously implemented functions, including: *create_visibility_graph*($\cdot, \cdot$), *f*($\cdot,\cdot$), *g*($\cdot,\cdot$), *dijkstra*($\cdot,\cdot,\cdot$).

Listing 11.1: GUI for Computing the Shortest Path Using a Naive Approach

```
1 import tkinter as tk
2 from tkinter import messagebox
3 from geometry import Point2D, Polygon
4 from ch11_helper_functions import create_visibility_graph,dijkstra
```

```
 5
 6 class PolygonDrawingApp:
 7     def __init__(self, master):
 8         self.master = master
 9         self.master.title("GUI for Computing the Shortest Path Using a Naive
                Approach")
10         self.canvas_width = 800; self.canvas_height = 600
11         self.canvas = tk.Canvas(master, width=self.canvas_width, height=self.
                canvas_height, bg='white')
12         self.canvas.pack()
13         control_frame = tk.Frame(master); control_frame.pack()
14         tk.Label(control_frame, text="Number of Polygons:").pack(side=tk.LEFT)
15         self.poly_count_var = tk.StringVar(value="3")
16         self.poly_count_entry = tk.Entry(control_frame, textvariable=self.
                poly_count_var, width=5)
17         self.poly_count_entry.pack(side=tk.LEFT)
18         self.poly_count_entry.bind("<FocusOut>", self.on_entry_focus_out)
19         self.compute_button = tk.Button(control_frame, text="Find Shortest Path",
                command=self.compute_path)
20         self.compute_button.pack(side=tk.LEFT)
21         self.reset()
22         self.canvas.bind("<Button-1>", self.on_left_click)
23         self.canvas.bind("<Button-3>", self.on_right_click)
24
25     def reset(self):
26         self.num_polygons = int(self.poly_count_var.get())
27         self.pt_A=self.pt_B=None; self.current_polygon_index = 0
28         self.polygons = []; self.current_points = []
29         self.after_polygons = False; self.canvas.delete("all")
30
31     def on_entry_focus_out(self, event):
32         try:
33             self.reset()
34             except ValueError:
35                 messagebox.showerror("Error", "Please enter a valid integer.")
36
37     def on_left_click(self, e):
38         pt = Point2D(e.x, e.y)
39         if not self.after_polygons:
40             if self.current_polygon_index >= self.num_polygons: return
41             self.current_points.append(pt)
42             if len(self.current_points) > 1:
43                 prev = self.current_points[-2]
44                 self.canvas.create_line(prev[0], prev[1],pt[0],pt[1],fill='black')
45             else:
46                 if self.pt_A is None:
47                     self.pt_A=pt; self.canvas.create_oval(pt[0]-4,pt[1]-4,pt[0]+4,pt
                        [1]+4,fill='red')
48                 elif self.pt_B is None:
49                     self.pt_B=pt; self.canvas.create_oval(pt[0]-4,pt[1]-4,pt[0]+4,pt
                        [1]+4,fill='green')
50
51     def on_right_click(self, event):
52         if len(self.current_points)<3: return #Pol. must have at least 3 vertices.
53         first, last = self.current_points[0], self.current_points[-1]
54         self.canvas.create_line(last[0],last[1],first[0],first[1],fill='black')
55         self.polygons.append(Polygon.from_points(self.current_points))
56         self.current_polygon_index += 1; self.current_points = []
```

```
57      if self.current_polygon_index == self.num_polygons:
58          self.after_polygons=True; messagebox.showinfo("Polygons Done", "All
                polygons done. Now draw start point A and goal point B.")
59
60  def compute_path(self):
61      if not self.after_polygons or self.pt_A is None or self.pt_B is None:
62          messagebox.showwarning("Warning", "Please draw all polygons and select
                points A and B first.")
63          return
64      all_points=[]
65      for poly in self.polygons:
66          for _ in range(poly.count):
67              all_points.append(poly.point_of_current()); poly.move_current(1)
68      all_points.append(self.pt_A);all_points.append(self.pt_B)
69      vis_graph=create_visibility_graph(all_points, self.polygons)
70      distance, path = dijkstra(vis_graph, len(all_points)-2, len(all_points)-1)
71      for i in range(1, len(path)):
72          p1 = all_points[path[i - 1]]; p2 = all_points[path[i]]
73          self.canvas.create_line(p1[0],p1[1],p2[0],p2[1],fill='red',width=2)
74  # Run App
75  if __name__ == "__main__":
76      root = tk.Tk()
77      app = PolygonDrawingApp(root)
78      root.mainloop()
```

Figure 11.12, generated based on the implementation provided in Listing 11.1, illustrates the use of a point robot in the visualization of the shortest-path computation from point A to point B. While such an approach is sufficient for point-based models, motion planning involving polygonal robots requires a more advanced geometric treatment. In particular, it becomes necessary to introduce the concept of the Minkowski sum—a fundamental tool that enables the geometric expansion of obstacles, commonly referred to as obstacle inflation. This concept plays a central role in transforming the configuration space to account for the shape and size of the robot during path planning.

11.5 Minkowski Sum

In geometry, the Minkowski sum of two sets of position vectors A and B in Euclidean space is, informally, obtained by adding each vector in A to every vector in B. More formally, the Minkowski sum of two subsets $A \subset \mathbb{R}^2$ and $B \subset \mathbb{R}^2$ is defined as

$$A \oplus B = \{\mathbf{p} + \mathbf{q} : \mathbf{p} \in A, \mathbf{q} \in B\}, \tag{11.1}$$

where $\mathbf{p} + \mathbf{q}$ denotes the vector (componentwise) sum of vectors $\mathbf{p}$ and $\mathbf{q}$. For instance, if $\mathbf{p} = (p_x, p_y)$ and $\mathbf{q} = (q_x, q_y)$, then their sum is given by $\mathbf{p} + \mathbf{q} = (p_x + q_x, p_y + q_y)$. To gain better intuition about the Minkowski sum $A \oplus B$, consider the simpler case where a single vector (or point) $\mathbf{p}$ is summed with a set B. This special case is defined as:

$$\mathbf{p} \oplus B = \{\mathbf{p} + \mathbf{q} : \mathbf{q} \in B\}. \tag{11.2}$$

This operation can be interpreted as a translation of the entire set B by the vector $\mathbf{p}$, resulting in a shifted copy of B whose elements are obtained by adding $\mathbf{p}$ to each $\mathbf{q} \in B$. Extending this idea, the general Minkowski sum $A \oplus B$ represents the union of all such translated copies of B, one for each vector $\mathbf{p}$ in the set A. Equivalently, it can be viewed as the set of all pairwise vector sums $\mathbf{p} + \mathbf{q}$, where $\mathbf{p} \in A$ and $\mathbf{q} \in B$. A geometric illustration of this construction is provided in Fig. 11.13 (a).

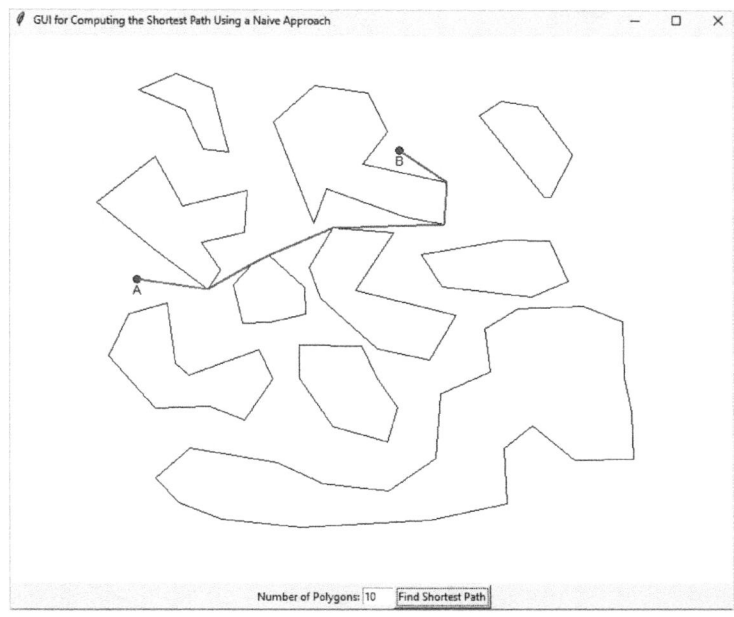

Figure 11.12: Shortest path computation between points A and B with respect to a set of up to 10 polygonal obstacles.

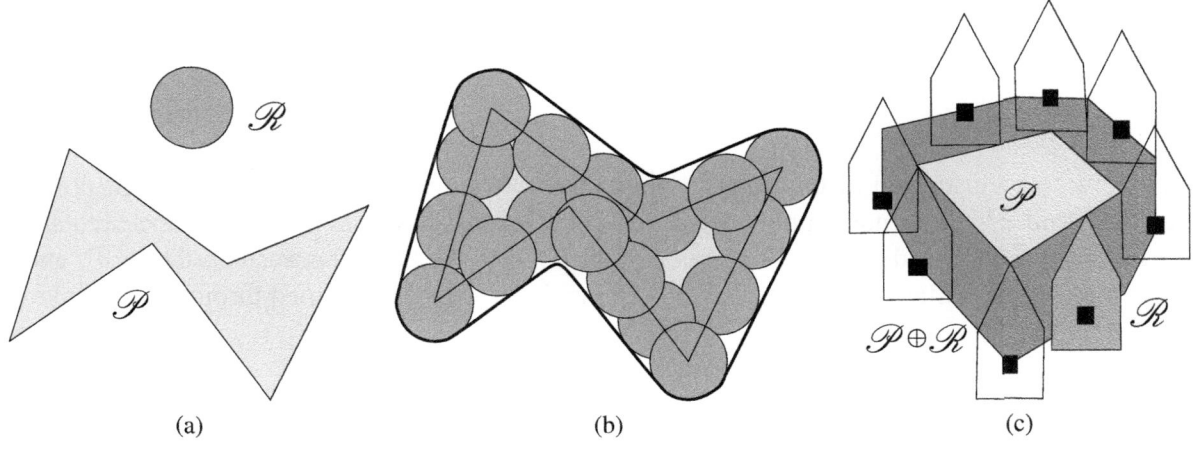

(a)　　　　　　　　　　　　　(b)　　　　　　　　　　　　　(c)

Figure 11.13: (a) The set A corresponds to the polygon $\mathscr{P}$, whereas the set B represents the disk $\mathscr{R}$. b) The resulting Minkowski sum yields the expanded polygon $\mathscr{P} \oplus \mathscr{R}$. (c) The expanded polygon $\mathscr{P} \oplus \mathscr{R}$ resulting from the application of the Minkowski sum to the polygons $\mathscr{P}$ and $\mathscr{R}$.

In Fig. 11.13 (a), the set A is represented by a polygon $\mathscr{P}$, and B is taken to be a disk $\mathscr{R}$ centered at the origin. The resulting Minkowski sum $\mathscr{P} \oplus \mathscr{R}$ geometrically expands the original polygon $\mathscr{P}$, a process that is fundamental in configuration space analysis for polygonal robots (see Fig. 11.13 (b)). It follows naturally that if the set A represents an obstacle—modeled as a polygon $\mathscr{P}$—and the set B corresponds to a polygonal robot $\mathscr{R}$, then the geometric expansion (or thickening) of the obstacle is realized through the Minkowski sum $A \oplus B$. This operation effectively enlarges the obstacle by accounting for the shape and dimensions of the robot, thereby enabling configuration-space planning (see Fig. 11.13 (c)).

The obstacle in the configuration space, denoted as $\mathscr{O}_{CS}$, for a robot $\mathscr{R}$ and an obstacle $\mathscr{P}$ from the workspace, is defined as follows:

$$\mathcal{O}_{CS} := \{(x,y) : \mathcal{R} \cap \mathcal{P} \neq \emptyset\}.$$

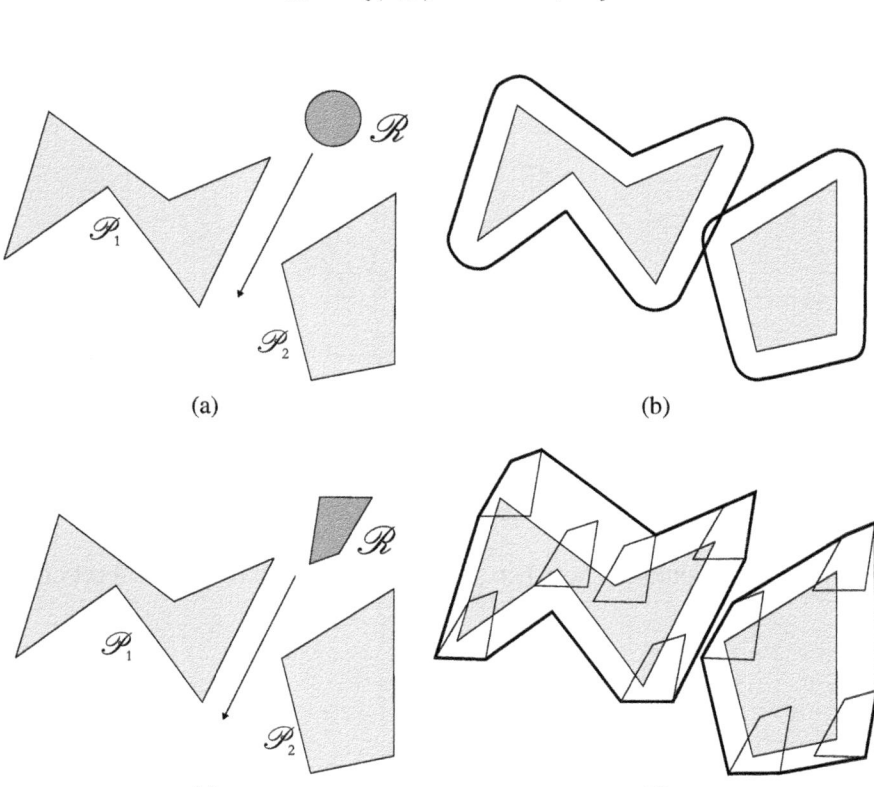

Figure 11.14: (a) Illustration of the translation of robot $\mathcal{R}$, represented as a disk, through polygonal obstacles $\mathcal{P}_1$ and $\mathcal{P}_2$. (b) A non-empty intersection of the inflated obstacles implies that the circular robot cannot pass between $\mathcal{P}_1$ and $\mathcal{P}_2$. (c) Translation of the polygonal robot $\mathcal{R}$ between obstacles $\mathcal{P}_1$ and $\mathcal{P}_2$. (d) Illustration of the inflated obstacles $\mathcal{P}_1 \oplus (-\mathcal{R})$ and $\mathcal{P}_2 \oplus (-\mathcal{R})$ obtained through the Minkowski sum.

From an intuitive perspective, the configuration space obstacle $\mathcal{O}_{CS}$ is obtained by translating (or "sweeping") the robot $\mathcal{R}$ along the boundary of the obstacle $\mathcal{P}$. In Fig. 11.14 (a), two polygonal obstacles $\mathcal{P}_1$ and $\mathcal{P}_2$ are shown in the workspace, along with a circular robot $\mathcal{R}$. A natural question arises: can the robot pass between these obstacles without collision? To answer this, one must examine whether the corresponding configuration space obstacles intersect, as illustrated in Fig. 11.14 (b). Configuration space obstacles are defined as Minkowski sums. Specifically, we examine whether the sets $\mathcal{P}_1 \oplus R$ and $\mathcal{P}_2 \oplus R$ intersect. In Fig. 11.14 (b), the boundaries of the configuration space obstacles, denoted by $\partial \mathcal{P}_1$ and $\partial \mathcal{P}_2$, clearly intersect. The intersection region is marked in gray, indicating that the robot $\mathcal{R}$ cannot pass safely between obstacles $\mathcal{P}_1$ and $\mathcal{P}_2$. In scenarios where the robot $\mathcal{R}$ is modeled as a simple polygon $\mathcal{P}$ rather than a disk, the computation of the Minkowski sum requires a modified approach (see Fig. 11.14 (c)). Specifically, the sum between a polygonal obstacle $\mathcal{P}_1$ and the polygonal robot $\mathcal{P}$ is given by $\mathcal{P}_1 \oplus (-\mathcal{P})$, where $-\mathcal{P}$ denotes the reflection of the polygon $\mathcal{P}$ with respect to a designated reference point—typically selected as the centroid of the robot's shape. Without loss of generality, assume that the polygon $\mathcal{P}$ is a triangle $\mathbb{T} \equiv \triangle ABC$, and that its centroid is positioned at the origin. The reflection $-\mathbb{T}$ is then obtained by negating the coordinates of each vertex: $-A \equiv (-x_1, -y_1)$, $-B \equiv (-x_2, -y_2)$, and $-C \equiv (-x_3, -y_3)$. This operation is equivalent to performing both vertical and horizontal flips of the original polygon: $-A = H_F(V_F(A))$, where V_F denotes reflection across the x-axis and H_F denotes reflection across the y-axis. If the centroid of polygon $\mathscr{P}$ is not located at the origin, the reflection process involves three steps:

1. Translating the polygon so that its centroid coincides with the origin;
2. Applying the reflection with respect to the origin;
3. Translating the reflected polygon back to its original position.

For example, suppose the centroid of triangle $\mathbb{T} = \triangle ABC$ is $D = (x_4, y_4) = \left(\frac{x_1+x_2+x_3}{3}, \frac{y_1+y_2+y_3}{3}\right)$. The triangle is first translated by the vector $(-x_4, -y_4)$, resulting in triangle $\mathbb{T}' = \triangle A'B'C'$. Next, the vertices are reflected to obtain $A'' = (-x'_1, -y'_1)$, $B'' = (-x'_2, -y'_2)$, and $C'' = (-x'_3, -y'_3)$. Finally, the reflected triangle $\triangle A''B''C''$ is translated by (x_4, y_4) to produce the final triangle $\triangle A'''B'''C'''$, which represents the reflection of the original triangle with respect to its centroid. Fig. 11.14 (d) demonstrates this process for a polygonal robot $\mathscr{R}$ and polygonal obstacles $\mathscr{P}_1$ and $\mathscr{P}_2$. The Minkowski sums $\mathscr{P}_1 \oplus (-\mathscr{R})$ and $\mathscr{P}_2 \oplus (-\mathscr{R})$ are computed and shown in Fig. 11.14 (d). It is evident from the figure that these expanded obstacles do not intersect, implying that the robot $\mathscr{R}$ can safely navigate between the two obstacles without collision.

> **Lemma 11.5.1** Let $\mathscr{R}$ be a planar robot that moves by translation, and let $\mathscr{P}$ be a polygonal obstacle. Then the corresponding obstacle in the configuration space $\mathscr{O}_{CS}$ is given by the Minkowski sum:
>
> $$\mathscr{O}_{CS} = \mathscr{P} \oplus (-\mathscr{R}(0,0)).$$

Proof. To demonstrate the stated equality, it is sufficient to prove both set inclusions:

$$\mathscr{O}_{CS} \subseteq \mathscr{P} \oplus (-\mathscr{R}(0,0)) \quad \text{and} \quad \mathscr{P} \oplus (-\mathscr{R}(0,0)) \subseteq \mathscr{O}_{CS}.$$

We begin by proving the first inclusion:

$$\mathscr{O}_{CS} \subseteq \mathscr{P} \oplus (-\mathscr{R}(0,0)).$$

Assume that $(x,y) \in \mathscr{O}_{CS}$. By definition of the configuration space obstacle, this implies that the robot $\mathscr{R}$, when translated so that its reference point is located at (x,y), intersects the obstacle $\mathscr{P}$. In other words,

$$\mathscr{R}(x,y) \cap \mathscr{P} \neq \emptyset.$$

Let $Q = (q_x, q_y)$ be a point of intersection, i.e., $Q \in \mathscr{R}(x,y)$ and $Q \in \mathscr{P}$. Since $Q \in \mathscr{R}(x,y)$, it follows that the corresponding point relative to the reference configuration is

$$(q_x - x, q_y - y) \in \mathscr{R}(0,0).$$

Thus, by negation, we have:

$$(-q_x + x, -q_y + y) \in -\mathscr{R}(0,0).$$

Furthermore, since $(x,y) = (q_x, q_y) + (-q_x + x, -q_y + y)$, and the first summand lies in $\mathscr{P}$, while the second lies in $-\mathscr{R}(0,0)$, we conclude that:

$$(x,y) \in \mathscr{P} \oplus (-\mathscr{R}(0,0)).$$

Since the point (x,y) was chosen arbitrarily from $\mathscr{O}_{CS}$, this proves the first inclusion. Let us now prove the converse, i.e.,

$$\mathscr{P} \oplus (-\mathscr{R}(0,0)) \subseteq \mathscr{O}_{CS}.$$

Let $(x,y) \in \mathscr{P} \oplus (-\mathscr{R}(0,0))$. Then there exist points $p \in \mathscr{P}$ and $q \in -\mathscr{R}(0,0)$ such that:

$$(x,y) = P + Q.$$

Let $P = (p_x, p_y)$ and $Q = (-p_x + x, -p_y + y)$. It follows that:

$$(p_x - x, p_y - y) \in \mathscr{R}(0,0),$$

which implies that $P \in \mathscr{R}(x,y)$ after translating $\mathscr{R}$ by vector (x,y). Since $P \in \mathscr{P}$ as well, the intersection

$$\mathscr{R}(x,y) \cap \mathscr{P} \neq \emptyset,$$

i.e., $(x,y) \in \mathscr{O}_{CS}$. As the choice of (x,y) was arbitrary, this proves the second inclusion. Having established both directions of inclusion, we conclude that holds:

$$\mathscr{O}_{CS} = \mathscr{P} \oplus (-\mathscr{R}(0,0)).$$

This completes the proof of the lemma.   ∎

The following presents an implementation of a quadratic time complexity algorithm for computing the Minkowski sum between a polygonal obstacle $\mathscr{P}$ and a polygonal robot $\mathscr{R}$, where both $\mathscr{P}$ and $\mathscr{R}$ are assumed to be arbitrary simple polygons. The core idea relies on generating a set of points by performing vector addition over all possible pairs of points $P \in \mathscr{P}$ and $Q \in \mathscr{R}$, thereby forming the set $\{P + Q \mid P \in \mathscr{P}, Q \in \mathscr{R}\}$. This set contains all potential candidates for the boundary of the resulting Minkowski sum. Once the point set is constructed, a convex hull algorithm is applied to extract the outer contour of the Minkowski sum. In this implementation, the *gift_wrapping*() function is used, which realizes the Jarvis march algorithm to compute the convex hull. When at least one of the input polygons is convex, the result serves as a good approximation of the true Minkowski sum. In the special case where both $\mathscr{P}$ and $\mathscr{R}$ are convex, the algorithm yields an exact Minkowski sum. The function `minkowski_sum`($\cdot$, $\cdot$) below implements this algorithmic procedure:

```python
from ch4_helper_functions import gift_wrapping
def minkowski_sum(obstacle: Polygon, robot: Polygon) -> Polygon:
    result_points = []
    obs_pts = obstacle.to_list()
    rob_pts = robot.to_list()
    for p in obs_pts:
        for q in rob_pts:
            result_points.append(Point2D(p[0] + q[0], p[1] + q[1]))
    return gift_wrapping(result_points)
```

The implementation of the function that reflects a polygon with respect to its centroid is given below:

```python
def reflect_polygon_about_centroid(poly: Polygon) -> Polygon:
    cx,cy=0,0; points=poly.to_list()
    for p in points:
        cx+=p[0]; cy+=p[1]
    cx/=len(points); cy/=len(points)
    reflected = [Point2D(-(p[0]-cx),-(p[1]-cy)) for p in points]
    return Polygon.from_points(reflected)
```

The following example illustrates how computing the Minkowski sum between two convex polygons $\mathscr{P}$ and $\mathscr{R}$ results in an inflated polygon.

■**Example 11.1** Compute the Minkowski sum $\mathscr{P} \oplus (-\mathscr{R}(0,0))$ where $\mathscr{P} = \{(-5,-5),(-5,5),(5,5),(5,-5)\}$ and $\mathscr{R} = \{(6,-1),(6,1),(7,1),(7,-1)\}$.

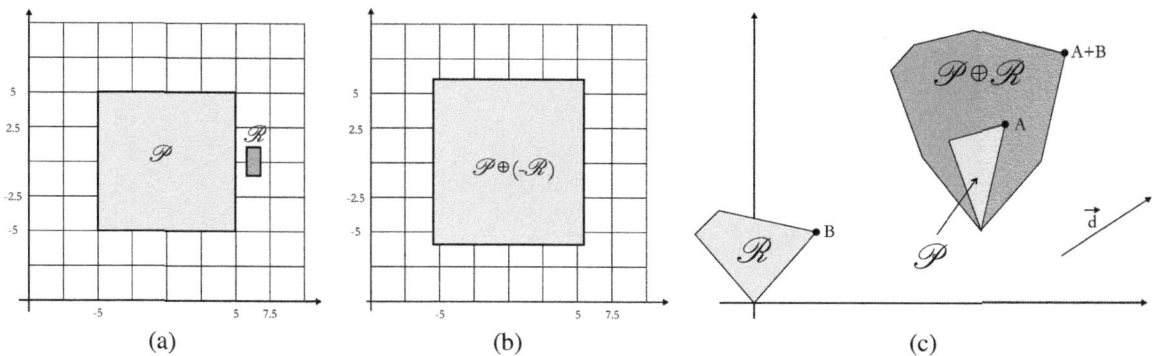

(a)   (b)   (c)

Figure 11.15: (a) Polygons $\mathscr{P}$ and $\mathscr{R}$ represented as rectangles. (b) Minkowski sum. $\mathscr{P} \oplus (-\mathscr{R}(0,0))$. (c) Extreme point composition in Minkowski sums.

Solution: The Minkowski sum of the obstacle $\mathscr{P}$ and the reflected polygonal robot $-\mathscr{R}(0,0)$, graphically illustrated in Fig. 11.15 (a), yields the following convex polygon (see Fig. 11.15 (b)):

$$\mathscr{P} \oplus (-\mathscr{R}(0,0)) = \{(-5.5,-6.0),(-5.5,-4.0),(-5.5,4.0),(-5.5,6.0),$$
$$(5.5,6.0),(5.5,4.0),(5.5,-4.0),(5.5,-6.0),$$
$$(4.5,-6.0),(-4.5,-6.0)\}.$$

This result can be obtained either analytically by direct pointwise addition or programmatically using the following code snippet:

```
1 R_reflected = reflect_polygon_about_centroid(R)
2 mink_sum_points = minkowski_sum(P, R_reflected)
```

The resulting polygon corresponds to the convex hull of all points generated by translating each vertex of the obstacle polygon $\mathscr{P}$ by every vertex of the reflected robot polygon $-\mathscr{R}(0,0)$. This convex hull effectively approximates the configuration space obstacle induced by the translational motion of the robot in the workspace.   ■

An essential geometric property of the Minkowski sum of convex polygons is the behavior of extreme points with respect to a given direction. Specifically, for two convex polygons $\mathscr{P}$ and $\mathscr{R}$ in the plane, the extreme point of their Minkowski sum $\mathscr{P} \oplus \mathscr{R}$ in the direction of an arbitrary vector $\vec{d}$ coincides with the vector sum of the extreme points of $\mathscr{P}$ and $\mathscr{R}$ in that same direction. This property is visually demonstrated in Fig. 11.15 (c), providing an intuitive basis for the structure of the resulting sum. Motivated by this geometric insight, we proceed to formalize and prove a fundamental theorem concerning the combinatorial complexity of the Minkowski sum of convex polygons.

Theorem 11.5.1 — Minkowski Sum of Convex Polygons. Let $\mathscr{P}$ and $\mathscr{R}$ be convex polygons consisting of n and m edges, respectively. Then, their Minkowski sum $\mathscr{P} \oplus \mathscr{R}$ is a convex polygon with at most $n+m$ edges. Moreover, if $\mathscr{P}$ and $\mathscr{R}$ share no pairs of parallel edges, then the resulting Minkowski sum has exactly $n+m$ edges.

Proof. Let $\mathscr{P}$ and $\mathscr{R}$ be convex polygons with n and m edges, respectively. Since both are convex, we aim to show that the Minkowski sum $\mathscr{P} \oplus \mathscr{R}$ is also convex. Consider arbitrary points $A, B \in \mathscr{P} \oplus \mathscr{R}$, and let $\lambda \in [0, 1]$ be a scalar. We must show that the convex combination $\lambda A + (1 - \lambda)B$ also belongs to $\mathscr{P} \oplus \mathscr{R}$. Since $A, B \in \mathscr{P} \oplus \mathscr{R}$, there exist points $P_1, P_2 \in P$ and $Q_1, Q_2 \in \mathscr{R}$ such that:

$$A = P_1 + Q_1, \quad B = P_2 + Q_2.$$

Then:

$$\lambda A + (1 - \lambda)B = \lambda P_1 + (1 - \lambda)P_2 + \lambda Q_1 + (1 - \lambda)Q_2.$$

Since P and $\mathscr{R}$ are convex, we have

$$\lambda P_1 + (1 - \lambda)P_2 \in P, \quad \lambda Q_1 + (1 - \lambda)Q_2 \in \mathscr{R},$$

and hence their sum belongs to $\mathscr{P} \oplus \mathscr{R}$. Therefore, $\mathscr{P} \oplus \mathscr{R}$ is convex. We now turn our attention to the combinatorial complexity of the Minkowski sum, specifically the number of edges in the resulting polygon. Given that $\mathscr{P}$ and $\mathscr{R}$ are convex polygons with at most n and m vertices, respectively, the set of extreme points of $\mathscr{P} \oplus \mathscr{R}$ arises from pairwise summation of these extreme points. Consequently, the resulting Minkowski sum polygon contains at most $n + m$ vertices and, therefore, the same number of edges. The upper hull of $n + m$ edges is achieved precisely when $\mathscr{P}$ and $\mathscr{R}$ share no pair of parallel edges. In such cases, the directional sequences of edges from both polygons are strictly distinct, preventing any merging of edge directions during the summation process. As a result, each unique edge direction contributes to a distinct edge in the final polygon, ensuring that the hull is tight. ∎

In contrast to the previously presented quadratic-time procedure, implemented in the *minkowski_sum*$(\cdot, \cdot)$ function—which exhaustively computes the Minkowski sum by evaluating all pairwise combinations of vertices from the input polygons—Algorithm 30 introduces a more computationally efficient approach. Specifically tailored for the case in which both input polygons $\mathscr{P}$ and $\mathscr{R}$ are convex, this algorithm achieves linear-time complexity by systematically exploiting the ordered nature of their edge sequences. Within the algorithm, the notation $\vec{V}_i$ denotes the radius vector of vertex V_i, and α_V refers to the angle between the radius vectors $\vec{V}_i$ and $\vec{V}_{i+1}$. This angle is computed as the difference between the angular directions α_i and α_{i+1}, where α_i represents the angle formed between $\vec{V}_i$ and the positive x-axis. This angular comparison forms the basis for determining the order in which edges from $\mathscr{P}$ and $\mathscr{R}$ are merged into the resulting Minkowski sum.

Algorithm 30: Pseudocode of the algorithm for computing the Minkowski sum of convex polygons $\mathscr{P}$ and $\mathscr{R}$.

Input : Convex polygons $\mathscr{P} = \{V_1, V_2, \ldots, V_n\}$ and $\mathscr{R} = \{W_1, W_2, \ldots, W_m\}$ are given by their vertices in clockwise order, starting from the vertex with the smallest y-coordinate; ties are resolved by selecting the vertex with the greatest x-coordinate.

Step 1: Set $i = j = 1$. Initialize the list $L \leftarrow \emptyset$: Define $V_{n+1} \leftarrow V_1$, $V_{n+2} \leftarrow V_2$, as well as $W_{m+1} \leftarrow W_1$, $W_{m+2} \leftarrow W_2$.

Step 2: While $i < n + 1$ **or** $j < m + 1$ **do:**

    i) Append the element $V_i + W_j$ to the list L.

    ii) If the angle $\alpha_V = \angle(\vec{V}_i, \vec{V}_{i+1})$ is less than the angle $\alpha_W = \angle(\vec{W}_j, \vec{W}_{j+1})$, then update $i \leftarrow i + 1$. Otherwise, check whether $\alpha_V > \alpha_W$. If so, update $j \leftarrow j + 1$; if not, update both indices: $i \leftarrow i + 1$ and $j \leftarrow j + 1$.

Step 3: Return the list L.

Output : The Minkowski sum $\mathscr{P} \oplus \mathscr{R}$.

Based on the pseudocode provided in Algorithm 30, the linear-time computation of the Minkowski sum can be implemented in a straightforward manner as follows:

```
1  def minkowski_sum_modified(P: Polygon, R: Polygon) -> Polygon:
2      P_pts = P.to_list(); R_pts = R.to_list()
3      n = len(P_pts); m = len(R_pts)
4      _,P_start=anchor_point(P_pts); _,R_start=anchor_point(R_pts) # See Chapter 4
5      P_pts = P_pts[P_start:] + P_pts[:P_start] + [P_pts[P_start]]
6      R_pts = R_pts[R_start:] + R_pts[:R_start] + [R_pts[R_start]]
7      i = j = 0; result = []
8      while i < n or j < m:
9          result.append(P_pts[i] + R_pts[j])
10         if i == n: j+=1
11         elif j == m: i+=1
12         else:
13             angle_P=(P_pts[i+1]-P_pts[i]).polar_angle()
14             angle_R=(R_pts[j+1]-R_pts[j]).polar_angle()
15             if angle_P < angle_R: i+=1
16             elif angle_P > angle_R: j+=1
17             else: i+=1; j+=1
18     return Polygon.from_points(result)
```

Based on Algorithm 30, it is straightforward to observe that the time complexity of the procedure is $\mathcal{O}(n+m)$, where n and m denote the number of vertices in the convex polygons $\mathscr{P}$ and $\mathscr{R}$, respectively. The algorithm ensures that the loop indices i and j increment monotonically and terminate as soon as they reach $n+1$ and $m+1$, respectively. This result is both efficient and elegant, yet it currently holds only in the special case when both input polygons are convex. A natural question arises: what happens when one or both of the input polygons are non-convex? Specifically, how does the time complexity of computing the Minkowski sum change in such cases? A detailed answer to this question will be provided later in this chapter. For now, we emphasize that the Minkowski sum of arbitrary (possibly non-convex) polygons can still be computed by leveraging convex decomposition techniques—such as triangulation or other polygon partitioning strategies. This approach is justified by the distributive property of the Minkowski sum over set union:

$$S_1 \oplus (S_2 \cup S_3) = (S_1 \oplus S_2) \cup (S_1 \oplus S_3),$$

where S_1, S_2, and S_3 are arbitrary sets in the plane. To formally address the complexity of computing the Minkowski sum $\mathscr{P} \oplus \mathscr{R}$ for arbitrary polygons $\mathscr{P}$ and $\mathscr{R}$, we now state and prove the following theorem.

Theorem 11.5.2 Let $\mathscr{P}$ and $\mathscr{R}$ be two arbitrary polygons in the plane, consisting of n and m vertices, respectively. Then, the time complexity of computing the Minkowski sum $\mathscr{P} \oplus \mathscr{R}$ satisfies:

   i) $\mathcal{O}(n+m)$ if both $\mathscr{P}$ and $\mathscr{R}$ are convex;
  ii) $\mathcal{O}(nm)$ if exactly one of the polygons is convex;
 iii) $\mathcal{O}(nm\log(nm))$ if both polygons are concave.

Proof. The first case (i) has already been established using a linear-time algorithm for convex polygons. We now turn our attention to cases (ii) and (iii). Without loss of generality, assume that $\mathscr{P}$ is concave, while $\mathscr{R}$ is convex polygon. A standard approach is to decompose the concave polygon $\mathscr{P}$ into a set of $n-2$ triangles $\mathbb{T}_1, \mathbb{T}_2, \cdots, \mathbb{T}_{n-2}$ via triangulation. Using the distributive property of the Minkowski sum over union, we have:

$$\mathscr{P} \oplus \mathscr{R} = \left(\bigcup_{i=1}^{n-2} \mathbb{T}_i \right) \oplus \mathscr{R} = \bigcup_{i=1}^{n-2} (\mathbb{T}_i \oplus \mathscr{R}).$$

Since each triangle $\mathbb{T}_i$ and the polygon $\mathscr{R}$ are convex, the resulting Minkowski sum $\mathbb{T}_i \oplus \mathscr{R}$ is also convex and consists of at most $m + 3$ vertices. Based on the result from case (i), each sum $\mathbb{T}_i \oplus \mathscr{R}$ can be computed in $\mathcal{O}(m)$ time. As there are $n - 2$ such triangles, the total time for computing all partial Minkowski sums is $\mathcal{O}(nm)$. Since the union of these convex polygons is linear in their total complexity, the overall time complexity remains $\mathcal{O}(nm)$. Finally, let both polygons $\mathscr{P}$ and $\mathscr{R}$ be concave. As in the previous case, we triangulate both polygons. This results in $n - 2$ triangles $\mathbb{T}_1, \cdots, \mathbb{T}_{n-2}$ for $\mathscr{P}$ and $m - 2$ triangles $\mathbb{U}_1, \cdots, \mathbb{U}_{m-2}$ for $\mathscr{R}$. Applying the distributive property twice yields:

$$\mathscr{P} \oplus \mathscr{R} = \left(\bigcup_{i=1}^{n-2} \mathbb{T}_i \right) \oplus \left(\bigcup_{j=1}^{m-2} \mathbb{U}_j \right) = \bigcup_{i=1}^{n-2} \bigcup_{j=1}^{m-2} (\mathbb{T}_i \oplus \mathbb{U}_j).$$

Each pairwise Minkowski sum $\mathbb{T}_i \oplus \mathbb{U}_j$ involves convex triangles, and since both $\mathbb{T}_i$ and $\mathbb{U}_j$ are convex, their Minkowski sum can be computed in constant time. Given that there are $(n - 2)(m - 2)$ such combinations, the total number of resulting convex components is $\mathcal{O}(nm)$. While the computation of individual Minkowski sums is straightforward, the main computational effort arises in calculating the union of these $\mathcal{O}(nm)$ convex regions. Noting that triangles represent a special subclass of rectangles, the union of triangles can be equivalently treated as a union of rectangles. Consequently, by applying the sweep line algorithm introduced in Chapter 3—which efficiently handles Boolean operations on axis-aligned rectangles—the union can be performed in $\mathcal{O}(nm\log(nm))$ time. Hence, the overall time complexity for computing the Minkowski sum in this scenario is $\mathcal{O}(nm\log(nm))$. ∎

11.6 Minkowski Sum-Based Implementation of Polygonal Robot Path Planning

In this section, we present a practical implementation that illustrates how translational motion planning for a convex polygonal robot can be effectively reduced to the motion planning of a point robot. This reduction is based on computing the Minkowski sum of each obstacle polygon with the reflection of the robot polygon about its centroid, resulting in a configuration space populated by *inflated obstacles*. As previously established, each obstacle $\mathscr{P}$ in the workspace is mapped to a configuration space obstacle $\mathscr{C}_{CS}$, defined as the Minkowski sum $\mathscr{P} \oplus (-\mathscr{R}(0,0))$. The implemented system is interactive and proceeds in several structured phases:

a. **Obstacle Definition**: The user is prompted to specify the number of obstacles in the environment. For each obstacle, the user draws a simple polygon by clicking on the canvas to define its vertices. The right mouse click is used to close each polygon and finalize the obstacle.

b. **Robot Definition**: After all obstacles are defined, the user defines the shape of the polygonal robot in the same manner. The system ensures that the robot polygon is valid (i.e., consists of at least three vertices).

c. **Start and Goal Selection**: Once the robot polygon is added, the user selects two points on the canvas—point A representing the initial configuration of the robot and point B denoting the goal configuration.

d. **Computation of the Shortest Path**: Upon clicking the *FindShortestPath* button, the following steps are executed:
   – The robot polygon is reflected about its centroid to form $-\mathscr{R}$.
   – Each obstacle polygon $\mathscr{P}$ is combined with $-\mathscr{R}$ using the Minkowski sum to yield the corresponding configuration space obstacle $\mathscr{C}_{CS}$.

- A visibility graph is constructed over all vertices of the inflated obstacles, together with points *A* and *B*.
- Dijkstra's algorithm is applied to determine the shortest collision-free path from *A* to *B*.

e. **Visualization with Robot Motion**: Finally, the computed path is interpolated into discrete steps. At each step, the original robot polygon is translated to the intermediate position, resulting in a visual trace that animates the robot's movement through the free space.

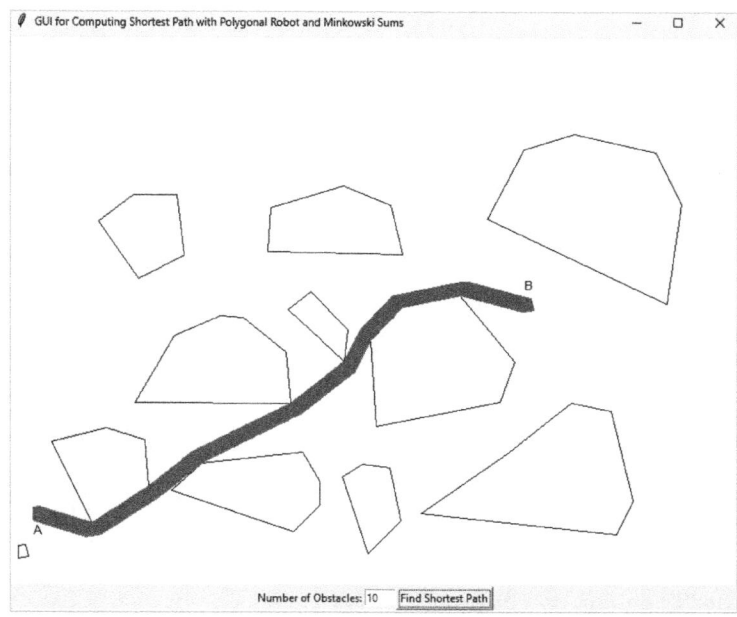

Figure 11.16: Shortest path between points *A* and *B* in the presence of polygonal obstacles via Minkowski sums.

This implementation serves as a clear and practical illustration of the configuration space methodology for motion planning. It effectively demonstrates how the Minkowski sum can be used to transform the problem of navigating a polygonal robot into a simpler pathfinding task for a point robot. The previously described procedural steps, labeled (a) through (e), are encapsulated in Listing 11.2, which represents a revised version of Listing 11.1. This updated listing includes only those code segments that differ from the original, along with the introduction of additional methods responsible for drawing polygons and visualizing the robot's trajectory. Compared to Listing 11.1, the methods *on_right_click*(·), *on_left_click*(·), and *compute_path()* have been selectively refined to support the extended functionality required for polygonal robot planning and visualization.

Listing 11.2: GUI for Computing Shortest Path with Polygonal Robot and Minkowski Sums

```
1 import tkinter as tk
2 from tkinter import messagebox
3 from geometry import Point2D, Polygon
4 from ch11_helper_functions import create_visibility_graph, dijkstra
5
6 class PolygonDrawingApp:
7     def on_left_click(self, e): # Updated Method
8         pt = Point2D(e.x, e.y)
9         if self.phase in (1, 2):
10            self.current_points.append(pt)
11            if len(self.current_points) > 1:
```

```
12              prev = self.current_points[-2]
13              self.canvas.create_line(prev[0], prev[1], pt[0], pt[1], fill='
                    black')
14          elif self.phase == 3:
15              if self.pt_A is None:
16                  self.pt_A = pt
17                  self.canvas.create_oval(pt[0]-4, pt[1]-4, pt[0]+4, pt[1]+4, fill='
                        red')
18                  self.canvas.create_text(pt[0]-4, pt[1]+10, text="A", anchor="nw",
                        font=("Arial", 10))
19              elif self.pt_B is None:
20                  self.pt_B = pt
21                  self.canvas.create_oval(pt[0]-4, pt[1]-4, pt[0]+4, pt[1]+4, fill='
                        green')
22                  self.canvas.create_text(pt[0]-4, pt[1]-30, text="B", anchor="nw",
                        font=("Arial", 10))
23
24      def on_right_click(self, event): # Updated Method
25          if len(self.current_points)<3:return # Valid poly. needs at least 3 points
26          first,last=self.current_points[0],self.current_points[-1]
27          self.canvas.create_line(last[0],last[1],first[0],first[1],fill='black')
28          polygon=Polygon.from_points(self.current_points)
29          self.current_points = []
30          if self.phase == 1:
31              self.obstacles.append(polygon); self.current_polygon_index+=1
32              if self.current_polygon_index == self.num_obstacles:
33                  self.phase=2; messagebox.showinfo("Phase Complete", "Obstacles
                        drawn. Now draw the polygonal robot.")
34          elif self.phase == 2:
35              self.robot_polygon=polygon; self.phase=3; messagebox.showinfo("
                    Robot Added", "Now select start point A and goal point B.")
36      # New Added Method
37      def draw_polygon(self, poly: Polygon, color='red', outline='red'):
38          pts = poly.to_list(); coords = []
39          for pt in pts:
40              coords.append(pt[0]); coords.append(pt[1])
41          self.canvas.create_polygon(coords, fill=color, outline=outline)
42      # New Added Method
43      def draw_robot_trace(self, path: list[int], all_points: list[Point2D]):
44          if self.robot_polygon is None or len(path)<2:return
45          r_center=self.robot_polygon.centroid(); num_steps=100 # Smooth. of trace
46          for i in range(1, len(path)):
47              p1=all_points[path[i-1]]; p2=all_points[path[i]]
48              for alpha in range(num_steps+1):
49                  t=alpha/num_steps; d_x=p1[0]*(1-t)+p2[0]*t
50                  d_y=p1[1]*(1-t)+p2[1]*t; t_vector=Point2D(d_x,d_y)-r_center
51                  moved_poly=self.robot_polygon.translate(t_vector)
52                  self.draw_polygon(moved_poly, color='red')
53      # Updated Method
54      def compute_path(self):
55          if self.phase < 3 or self.pt_A is None or self.pt_B is None:
56              messagebox.showwarning("Warning", "Please complete all steps before
                    computing path."); return
57          if not self.robot_polygon or len(self.obstacles) == 0:
58              messagebox.showerror("Error", "At least one obstacle and one robot
                    polygon are required."); return
59          all_points=[]; i_obstacles=[] # inflated obstacles
60          robot_reflected=reflect_polygon_about_centroid(self.robot_polygon)
```

```
61    for obs in self.obstacles:
62        i_obstacles.append(minkowski_sum(obs,robot_reflected))
63    for poly in i_obstacles:
64        for _ in range(poly.count):
65            all_points.append(poly.point_of_current()); poly.move_current(1)
66    all_points.append(self.pt_A); all_points.append(self.pt_B)
67    vis_graph=create_visibility_graph(all_points,i_obstacles)
68    distance,path=dijkstra(vis_graph,len(all_points)-2,len(all_points)-1)
69    self.draw_robot_trace(path, all_points)
```

Figure 11.16, generated based on the implementation provided in the listing above, illustrates the computation of the shortest path between points A and B in a workspace populated with polygonal obstacles. The computation accounts for the geometry of a convex polygonal robot by employing Minkowski sums to transform the workspace into configuration space. This transformation enables the application of point-based motion planning algorithms while preserving collision constraints inherent to the original robot shape.

11.7 Exercises

Exercise 11.1 Implement an algorithm for shortest path computation between two points, A and B, in a planar environment containing polygonal obstacles—possibly concave in nature. The algorithm should rely on triangulation as a method for decomposing concave polygons into simpler components. The computed path must avoid intersecting any obstacle regions while ensuring minimal Euclidean length.

Exercise 11.2 Consider the roadmap graph G_{road} constructed from the trapezoidal decomposition of the free space, where nodes are placed at the center of each trapezoid and on each vertical wall. Propose a modification of the graph structure such that only nodes on vertical walls are used, while preserving connectivity. Also, ensure that modification does not increase the total number of edges in the graph.

Exercise 11.3 In the implementation of the function $minkowski\_sum(\cdot, \cdot)$, the Minkowski sum of two simple polygons $\mathscr{P}_1$ and $\mathscr{P}_2$ is computed by applying the convex hull algorithm to the set of points of the form $(P_1.x + P_2.x, P_1.y + P_2.y)$, where P_1 and P_2 are the vertices of the polygons $\mathscr{P}_1$ and $\mathscr{P}_2$, respectively. Prove the correctness of this approach.

Exercise 11.4 Let $\mathscr{S}$ be a set of pairwise disjoint simple polygons in the plane, consisting of a total of n edges. Prove that, for any start and goal position in the free space, the number of segments composing the shortest path is bounded by $\mathscr{O}(n)$. Furthermore, construct an example where this bound is tight, i.e., the number of segments is $\Theta(n)$.

Exercise 11.5 Given a set of n pairwise disjoint triangles in the plane, determine the maximal number of distinct shortest paths that can exist between two fixed points located in the free space. Justify your answer in terms of asymptotic bounds.

Exercise 11.6 Let $\mathscr{S}$ be a set of pairwise disjoint polygons with a total of n edges, and let P_{start} be a fixed starting point in the free space. Describe a preprocessing strategy, computable in $\mathscr{O}(n^2 \log n)$ time, that enables efficient computation of the shortest path from P_{start} to any query point P_{goal} in $\mathcal{O}(n \log n)$ time.

Exercise 11.7 Prove that, when all obstacles are convex, the shortest path can be computed using only the common tangents between obstacle polygons, instead of all pairwise visibility edges. Justify why these tangents suffice and lead to an optimal path.

Exercise 11.8 Let $\mathscr{S}$ be a set of n pairwise disjoint circular obstacles in the plane.
- Prove that the shortest path between two non-visible points P_{start} and P_{goal} among disc-shaped obstacles must consist of circular arcs, tangents from P_{start} or P_{goal}, and common tangents between discs.
- Propose an appropriate adaptation of the visibility graph structure to support shortest path computation in the presence of disc-shaped obstacles.
- Based on this adapted visibility graph, describe an algorithm for computing the shortest path between P_{start} and P_{goal} among the discs in $\mathscr{S}$. Justify its correctness and discuss its computational complexity.

Exercise 11.9 For each of the following pairs of planar simple polygons $\mathscr{P}_1$ and $\mathscr{P}_2$, sketch the Minkowski sum $\mathscr{P}_1 \oplus \mathscr{P}_2$:
   (a) $\mathscr{P}_1$ and $\mathscr{P}_2$ are both unit discs;
   (b) $\mathscr{P}_1$ and $\mathscr{P}_2$ are both unit squares;
   (c) $\mathscr{P}_1$ is a unit disc, and $\mathscr{P}_2$ is a unit square;
   (d) $\mathscr{P}_1$ is a unit square, and $\mathscr{P}_2$ is a triangle with vertices $(0,0)$, $(-1,0)$, and $(0,-1)$.

12. AI in Computational Geometry

Computational geometry has long transcended its theoretical origins to become a foundational tool in a wide range of applied domains. While earlier chapters focused on the development and implementation of geometric algorithms, this final chapter highlights how those concepts are utilized in solving real-world problems across several scientific disciplines. The goal of this chapter is not to re-implement algorithms, but rather to showcase their role within broader computational pipelines. To achieve this, each section presents a domain of application—such as image processing, geographic information systems, or artificial intelligence—and surveys representative research problems that are inherently geometric in nature. Where appropriate, concise summaries of recent studies are provided to illustrate both the geometric foundations and the broader context of use. The organization of the chapter follows five principal domains:

- **Coverage Optimization:** exploring how geometric constraints shape sensor and camera placement, guide triangulation-based optimization strategies, and enable efficient path planning for complete spatial coverage;

- **Image Processing:** covering advanced techniques such as fractal image compression based on Quadtree decomposition, shape-based object detection using geometric primitives and probabilistic models, and morphological operations grounded in structuring element geometry and computational geometry, including their integration with deep learning frameworks and topological data analysis;

- **Geographic Information Systems:** including spatial clustering, crop-type classification, and terrain modeling via triangulations;

- **Bioinformatics:** including molecular docking and geometric representation of protein and RNA structures;

- **Artificial Intelligence:** highlighting geometric reasoning in motion planning and neural approaches for object classification.

The examples and studies presented here aim to bridge the gap between algorithmic theory and its practical relevance. For each subfield, the geometric tools employed—such as convex hulls, Voronoi diagrams, triangulations, or visibility graphs—are identified, thereby reinforcing the utility of computational geometry as a cross-cutting methodology in modern computing.

© The Author(s), under exclusive license to Springer Nature Switzerland AG 2026
A. Alihodžić, *Exploring Computational Geometry*, Texts in Computer Science,
https://doi.org/10.1007/978-3-032-06393-9_12

12.1 Coverage Optimization

Coverage optimization problems aim to determine the most effective placement of sensors, cameras, or autonomous agents to monitor, control, or explore a given spatial domain. These problems are inherently geometric, often modeled using simple or orthogonal polygons, triangulations, and visibility regions. Computational geometry provides the theoretical foundation for decomposing and covering space efficiently, while swarm intelligence and evolutionary algorithms offer powerful heuristics for solving large-scale or NP-hard variants. In this section, we highlight recent approaches that integrate classical geometric formulations with modern optimization techniques, particularly in the context of surveillance, environmental monitoring, and autonomous navigation.

12.1.1 Camera and Sensor Placement in Polygonal Environments

The problem of optimal camera and sensor placement in polygonal environments—particularly in polygons with holes—stems from the classical Art Gallery Problem and remains a central challenge in computational geometry (see Fig. 12.1).

Figure 12.1: A 3D-rendered illustration showing surveillance cameras and sensors optimally placed within a polygonal indoor environment.

The task entails determining the minimal number and optimal configuration of sensors needed to ensure complete visibility coverage, while accounting for geometric constraints such as occlusions, limited sensing range, and restricted fields of view. Recent research integrates computational geometry techniques, including visibility graphs and triangulation, with metaheuristics and deep reinforcement learning strategies to facilitate robust sensor deployment in complex, non-convex environments. These hybrid approaches have proven effective across domains such as surveillance, robotics, and smart infrastructure. In [121], the authors propose a Q-learning-based reinforcement learning framework that discretizes polygonal environments into grid structures, enabling scalable and adaptive solutions to the Art Gallery Problem. Complementarily, [40] introduces an online SAC-based reinforcement learning system for optimizing depth camera placement in indoor environments, outperforming offline baselines by reducing depth observation errors without requiring prior scene knowledge. A PSO-based method is presented in [43] for optimizing camera orientations in fixed-location networks, efficiently maximizing field-of-view coverage under occlusion and region-of-interest constraints. The study in [80] addresses multi-zone surveillance optimization by developing a multi-objective genetic algorithm grounded in NSGA-II, achieving high-quality coverage and cost efficiency in a real-world deployment. In [10], a hybrid methodology combining deterministic geometry-based strategies and swarm intelligence is applied to improve sensor coverage across intricate spatial domains. Recognizing the NP-hard nature of guarding simple concave polygons, the work in [5] introduces a comparative study between a suboptimal deterministic method and an adapted differential evolution algorithm, with the latter yielding superior results. Furthermore, [3] reformulates the placement problem as a set covering instance and solves it through a two-phase exact method using the CPLEX solver, which outperforms approximate approaches across all benchmarks. Lastly, the paper [4] compares a deterministic strategy with an adjusted bare bones fireworks algorithm, demonstrating the consistent advantage of the metaheuristic technique across more than 200 randomly generated orthogonal polygons.

12.1.2 Swarm Intelligence for Geometric Triangulation Optimization

Geometric triangulation optimization represents a core topic within computational geometry, concerned with constructing triangulations over planar point sets or polygonal domains that satisfy defined optimality criteria—most notably, the minimization of total edge length or the enhancement of triangle quality. (see Fig. 12.2).

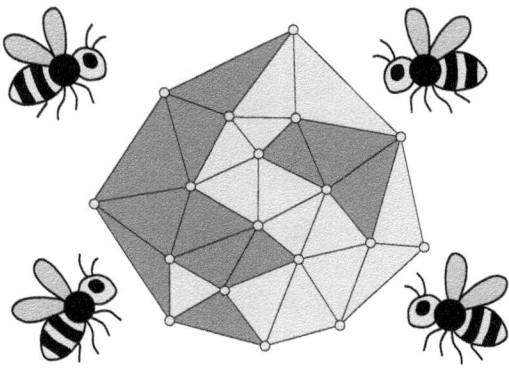

Figure 12.2: Swarm intelligence for geometric triangulation optimization. A conceptual illustration of intelligent agents collaboratively refining a triangulated geometric mesh to achieve an optimized structure.

Among such problems, the Minimum Weight Triangulation (MWT) is known to be NP-hard and thus computationally intractable for exhaustive methods as input size increases [138]. To address this challenge, heuristic and metaheuristic techniques have been widely employed. For instance, the study in [91] introduces an Ant Colony Optimization (ACO) heuristic tailored to reduce total edge length in MWT, while the work in [7] adapts the Artificial Bee Colony algorithm for the same purpose, showing superior performance compared to alternative stochastic methods and exhaustive search for smaller instances. Similarly, [8] applies the Harris Hawks Optimization (HHO) algorithm to randomly generated 2D datasets, demonstrating its robustness and consistent superiority over other nature-inspired strategies. In a related direction, the Triangulation Topology Aggregation Optimizer (TTAO), proposed in [214], leverages geometric principles of triangular topology and combines global and local aggregation strategies to effectively balance exploration and exploitation, outperforming ten contemporary algorithms across both benchmark functions and real-world engineering problems. In the domain of geometric deep learning, the paper [165] presents PointTriNet, a differentiable and scalable framework for 3D triangulation that integrates classification and proposal networks implemented via PointNet with triangle-relative encoding. This architecture enables unsupervised training and facilitates the inclusion of robust triangulation modules within broader 3D learning pipelines. Beyond MWT, Delaunay triangulation remains the most commonly applied technique in practice due to the existence of efficient algorithms with polynomial time complexity of $\Theta(n \log n)$. A comprehensive overview of Delaunay triangulation methods, including algorithmic developments, hardware-specific implementations (CPU, GPU, FPGA), and multidisciplinary applications, is provided in [54], underscoring its pivotal role across fields such as computational geometry, computer graphics, and mobile robotics.

Coverage Path Planning

Coverage path planning (CPP) refers to the process of determining optimal trajectories or deployment strategies to ensure complete or efficient monitoring of a given spatial domain [65, 201]. This class of problems plays a central role in applications such as drone-based surveillance, wireless sensor network coverage, and autonomous vehicle routing (see Fig. 12.3).

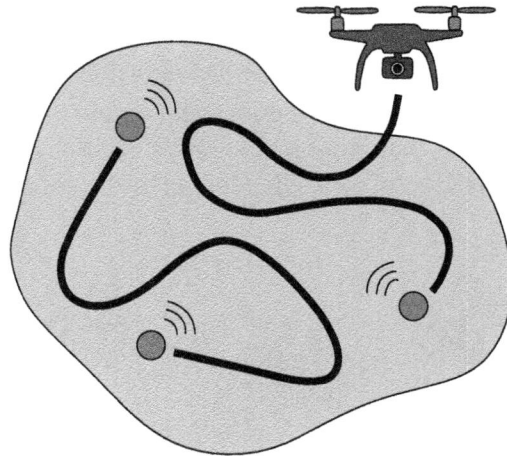

Figure 12.3: Coverage path planning in a monitored spatial domain.

Traditionally, CPP has been approached through geometric modeling and metaheuristic optimization, addressing challenges such as path generation, area decomposition, and temporal constraints. More recently, the field has witnessed a growing integration of advanced artificial intelligence techniques—including deep reinforcement learning, convolutional neural networks, and graph neural networks—which offer improved adaptability, generalization, and real-time performance in complex and dynamic environments. These hybrid methods effectively bridge computational geometry and machine learning, enabling robust solutions to CPP tasks across a wide range of application domains. Several recent studies exemplify this integration. In [25], a deep reinforcement learning framework is proposed for UAV-based CPP in complex 3D environments, incorporating power constraints, no-fly zones, and dynamic conditions. The model employs proximal policy optimization within an actor-critic architecture and is validated both in simulation and on drone hardware. Similarly, [212] introduces the GAP_SAC algorithm, which enhances path planning in dynamic spaces by integrating gated attention and prioritized experience replay, outperforming standard SAC variants. In [166], the authors propose CPPNet, a convolutional neural network that predicts edge probabilities on graph-based occupancy maps; combined with greedy search, the method enables real-time, near-optimal CPP in dynamic settings. Multi-robot coordination is addressed in [179], where a graph neural network is trained to imitate expert routing on spatial graphs, generalizing to larger environments and outperforming classical planners. In parallel, swarm intelligence remains a powerful tool for CPP. The study [6] applies an adjusted guided fireworks algorithm to the UCAV path planning problem, optimizing flight routes under fuel and safety constraints. For static drone deployment, [181] employs the Brain Storm Optimization algorithm to maximize coverage while minimizing altitude, while [182] uses the bare bones fireworks algorithm to place aerial base stations for wireless sensor networks. Finally, [9] presents a two-phase method for solving the vehicle routing problem with time windows (VRPTW), combining k-means clustering and CPLEX optimization to achieve near-optimal real-time solutions across benchmark datasets. These studies collectively demonstrate how the fusion of computational geometry, metaheuristics, and modern AI techniques can yield efficient, scalable, and adaptive solutions to coverage path planning in diverse and complex environments.

12.2 Image Processing

Image processing remains one of the most dynamic fields for the application of computational geometry. Geometric algorithms provide critical tools for object detection, edge analysis, segmentation, and compression. In this section, we explore several representative techniques, including shape-based object detection using convex structures, edge detection through gradient-based geometric operators, and morphological processing with structuring elements of defined spatial form. Additionally, we examine fractal compression methods based on quadtree decomposition, as well as emerging approaches in geometric deep learning for semantic image interpretation. These applications illustrate the deep integration of geometric reasoning in modern visual computing.

12.2.1 Fractal Compression

Fractal image compression relies on geometric decomposition of images into self-similar regions using spatial data structures such as quadtrees [61]. By identifying affine mappings between subregions, it enables compact encoding with high reconstruction fidelity (see Fig. 12.4).

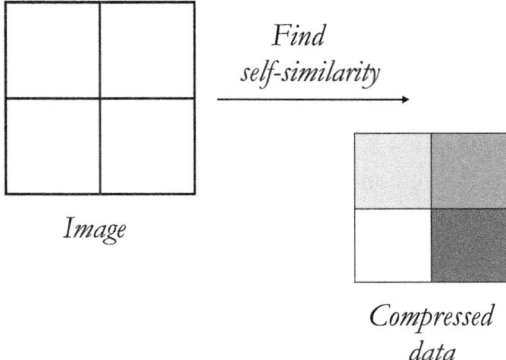

Figure 12.4: Fractal compression through recursive self-similarity.

Recent approaches [28] eliminate the need for costly block matching by applying deterministic quadtree partitioning, improving both compression speed and quality. Furthermore, fractal geometry has been applied more broadly in image analysis tasks—such as edge detection and texture modeling—highlighting its role as a unifying geometric framework in image processing [170]. A recent study further demonstrates the versatility of quadtree decomposition in a deep learning-based multiscale algorithm for coastline extraction [173]. In this approach, quadtree structures are used to hierarchically classify large-scale satellite imagery, enabling the distinction between land and sea even in low-resolution contexts. By combining scene classification networks with multiscale spatial partitioning, the method reduces confusion in boundary regions and improves classification accuracy by 6%, while simultaneously lowering the computational burden on the segmentation model. This application underscores how geometric partitioning schemes, originally designed for compression, are being adapted for high-level semantic tasks in image understanding. The paper [113] presents a block-based fractal image compression method using affine transforms, incorporating the Discrete Cosine Transform (DCT), wavelet, and Huffman techniques to capture self-similarity across image regions. To reduce encoding time, AI approaches such as reinforcement learning, neural networks are explored, addressing the main limitation of high computational cost. The paper [2] presents an image compression approach that trains feed-forward neural networks using an improved bat algorithm to optimize weight parameters. Experimental results on standard images demonstrate that the method achieves good compression ratios while maintaining acceptable image quality. In agricultural automation, the study presented in [124] employs fractal compression to reconcile image quality with transmission efficiency, using statistical loss analysis to improve encoding performance while maintaining visual fidelity. In [184], a fast fractal compression method for brain MRI images is introduced, combining Adaptive Iterated Function Systems with Deep Reinforcement Learning. The approach learns local affine transforms from data, achieving a 4× speedup and improved decoding quality. The connection between fractal image compression and the DBSCAN clustering algorithm from machine learning is explored in [92]. The study introduces an improved encoding method that utilizes DBSCAN to limit search operations to local neighborhoods, thereby substantially reducing encoding time while enabling efficient compression and decompression of color images. The paper [75] discusses the connection between k-means clustering in machine learning and fractal image coding. By classifying complex sub-blocks using k-means and restricting matching searches to local neighborhoods, the proposed method significantly accelerates encoding—achieving up to a 570× speedup—while maintaining high reconstruction quality. The study [119] introduces a hybrid fractal compression method combining CNNs and gene expression programming to accelerate encoding and improve accuracy. The approach enhances segmentation, speeds up block matching, and outperforms traditional methods in both compression ratio and quality. The paper [102] provides a comprehensive review of fractal image compression techniques, highlighting both theoretical foundations and recent advances. By examining hybrid approaches involving methods such as ICA and DBSCAN, it offers valuable insight into the evolving landscape of fractal-based image coding.

12.2.2 Shape-Based Object Detection

Shape-based object detection constitutes a fundamental task in image analysis, aiming to identify and localize objects based on their geometric configurations rather than appearance-based cues such as color or texture. Computational geometry provides a comprehensive toolbox for this purpose, including methods such as convex hulls, minimum bounding rectangles, polygonal approximations, and contour-derived shape descriptors (see Fig. 12.5).

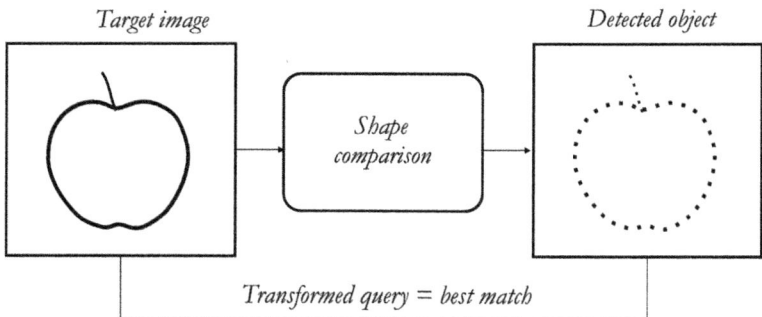

Figure 12.5: Schematic representation of shape-based object detection using geometric features for object identification and localization.

These techniques are particularly effective in scenarios where objects exhibit regular structural patterns or when edge information is more reliable than pixel-level features. Recent developments have increasingly focused on integrating geometric primitives with machine learning frameworks to improve detection robustness under noisy or low-resolution conditions. In this context, the study by Wei et al. [195] proposes a Bayesian Network-based pipeline for shape-based object recognition, which infers regions of interest through Evidence Accumulation and refines detection using spatial pyramid matching, achieving high accuracy on ETHZ and INRIA benchmarks. Complementing this, the work by Cupec et al. [48] introduces a novel approach based on aligning convex hulls from depth images with those of 3D object models using the Convex Template Instance descriptor and a three-level hypothesis evaluation strategy, yielding superior performance in cluttered scenes across three benchmark datasets. Kim and Vladimir [108] address the problem of salient object detection by combining CNN-driven shape prediction with mid- and low-level visual cues, producing refined saliency maps that surpass existing methods. Liang et al. [120] propose DeepHullNet, a deep learning framework merging Pointer Networks and Transformer models to solve convex and concave hull problems efficiently, achieving both higher accuracy and significantly reduced runtime compared to traditional algorithms. Moreover, the study [81] tackles aerial object detection by introducing a dynamic shape-adaptive sample selection method that adjusts IoU thresholds based on geometric structure, enhancing positive sample identification and outperforming state-of-the-art detectors. Finally, Jiang et al. [100] provide a comprehensive taxonomy of shape representation approaches, analyzing methods based on boundary and interior features across various domains such as image retrieval, object classification, and medical imaging. This survey outlines current research challenges and offers critical insights into the limitations and advantages of existing methodologies, guiding future developments in shape-based detection.

12.2.3 Morphological Operations and Structuring Elements Geometry

Morphological operations—such as dilation, erosion, opening, and closing—form a foundational component of image processing, acting on pixel sets via geometric transformations defined by structuring elements. These elements, typically geometric shapes like disks, lines, or polygons, determine the spatial neighborhood over which operations are performed. At a theoretical level, morphological processes are grounded in set-theoretic and geometric operations such as Minkowski sums, intersection, and translation, aligning closely with core concepts from computational geometry. Advanced applications include skeletonization, medial axis extraction, and boundary simplification, all of which rely on efficient algorithmic frameworks to interpret structural and topological information within visual data. As such, morphological processing bridges discrete image analysis and continuous geometric reasoning, enabling robust shape analysis across diverse imaging contexts (see Fig. 12.6).

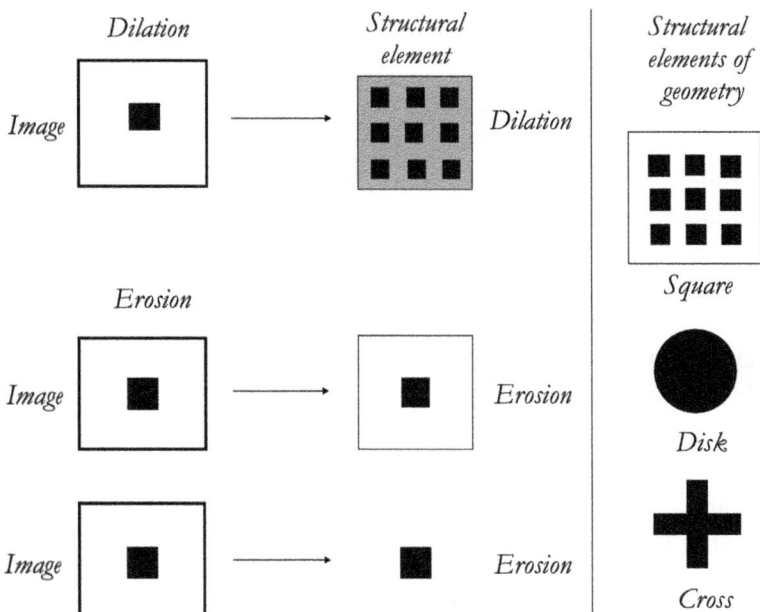

Figure 12.6: Illustration of morphological operations using structuring elements with different geometric shapes.

Recent research has demonstrated the integration of morphological operations with modern computational paradigms. The work of Franchi et al. [63] embeds morphological operators into deep learning frameworks by introducing novel nonlinear layers that complement convolutional layers, achieving high accuracy in boundary detection tasks with only 0.01% of the parameters used by standard models. A differentiable 3D skeletonization algorithm proposed in [135] preserves topological properties and supports gradient-based optimization, making it suitable for applications in medical image segmentation and registration. In another line of work, Chung et al. [44] reinterpret morphological operations through the lens of persistent homology, framing them as multiparameter filtrations. This approach supports an unsupervised image denoising method that is effective across binary, grayscale, and color modalities, matching the performance of supervised deep learning baselines. From a computational geometry perspective, morphological operations are further extended via efficient algorithms for Minkowski sums and differences. The method proposed in [49] computes the Minkowski sum of convex polytopes using face lattice representations, achieving worst-case optimal complexity and scalability for high-dimensional settings. The CVMD algorithm introduced in [17] addresses the Minkowski difference problem through contributing vertices, outperforming traditional Nef polyhedra approaches in both speed and accuracy. In applied materials science, [59] correlates 3D foam microstructure with absorption dynamics using X-ray tomography, highlighting how geometric characteristics such as pore interconnectivity and tortuosity govern functional behavior. Finally, Jiang and Bunke [96] present a geometry-driven contour extraction technique that operates on oriented feature points, yielding compact and robust contours suitable for integration with pixel-based methods. Complementarily, Hauch et al. [79] define morphological operators for directional data via depth-based vector ordering, enabling the enhancement and segmentation of complex anisotropic structures in industrial materials.

12.3 Geographic Information Systems

Geographic Information Systems (GIS) represent one of the most impactful and practical domains for the application of computational geometry. At their core, GIS platforms rely on spatial databases capable of storing and manipulating geometric primitives such as points, lines, triangles, polygons, curves and surfaces, each corresponding to real-world geographical features. Systems like PostgreSQL enhanced with the PostGIS extension provide extensive support for spatial queries, enabling the execution of geometric operations such as containment, intersection, buffering, and proximity searches directly through SQL [60, 164]. These queries operate over georeferenced data—often specified using latitude and longitude—to retrieve spatial objects that satisfy geometric or topological constraints. For instance, identifying all buildings, roads, or land parcels within a certain radius of a given coordinate on a digital map, such as Google Maps, relies on these geometric queries. PostGIS also integrates advanced computational geometry functionalities, including the construction of *Voronoi diagrams*, *Delaunay triangulations*, and *Convex Hulls*, as well as support for centroids, spatial indexing, and topological relationships (e.g., ST_Within, ST_Intersects). These operations not only enhance geometric reasoning but also support complex spatial analytics required in urban planning, environmental monitoring, and agricultural management. Furthermore, GIS analysis is increasingly complemented by artificial intelligence techniques. Crop mapping, and in particular crop-type classification, illustrates the growing synergy between machine learning, deep learning, and geometric representations of agricultural landscapes. Leveraging multispectral satellite imagery and spatial features of parcel geometries, these techniques enable accurate identification of cultivated crop types. This section explores key GIS-related applications—crop mapping, spatial clustering, polygonal map generalization, and terrain modeling—highlighting their theoretical foundations in computational geometry and their progressive integration with AI-based methodologies [215].

12.3.1 Crop Mapping

Crop mapping is a comprehensive task in agricultural monitoring that encompasses both the spatial localization and classification of crop types across geographic regions [180]. While crop-type classification focuses on identifying cultivated varieties—such as wheat, maize, or soy—from satellite or aerial imagery, crop mapping extends this objective by associating such classifications with georeferenced field boundaries, planting dates, phenological stages, and yield estimations. By leveraging spatial geometry, spectral signatures, and temporal dynamics, crop mapping supports large-scale decision-making in food security, land-use planning, and environmental sustainability. Spatial databases such as PostGIS offer robust tools for managing geometric primitives (points, lines, polygons) and executing spatial queries essential for retrieving and analyzing agricultural parcels. Computational geometry plays a central role, enabling advanced operations such as polygon generalization, spatial joins, and the use of Voronoi diagrams or Delaunay triangulations to partition and analyze heterogeneous agricultural landscapes. Recent advances in machine learning—especially convolutional and transformer-based models—have significantly enhanced classification accuracy, particularly when integrated with parcel-level geometries derived from high-resolution GIS data (see Fig. 12.7).

Crop Type Classification

Figure 12.7: Visual representation of crop mapping and crop type classification using satellite imagery and GIS, highlighting the transformation from raw aerial data to semantically labeled field segments.

Wang et al. [194] proposed Geo-CBAM-CNN, an attention-based convolutional model that incorporates geographic priors through a Convolutional Block Attention Module. Evaluated on Sentinel-2 time-series data, the model achieved an accuracy of 97.82%, outperforming traditional models in terms of spatial generalization across multiple U.S. regions. To address data scarcity in certain regions, instance-based transfer learning approaches have been explored. The study in [132] demonstrated the effectiveness of using high-confidence CDL pixels from the U.S. and multi-source satellite time series as training data. Through models like Random Forest, XGBoost, and TrAdaBoost, accuracies up to 92% were attained even with minimal target domain labeling, underscoring the cost-efficiency and transferability of such methods. Che et al. [38] introduced DSH, a deep learning framework that combines DeepLabV3+, channel self-attention, and histogram matching to enhance semantic relevance and temporal consistency in crop mapping. The model, tested across sites in the U.S., China, and France, achieved an average overall accuracy of 93.9% during peak growth phases, establishing a new standard for robustness and adaptability. Altun et al. [11] proposed a lightweight CNN tailored for parcel-level classification using Sentinel-2 time series. Their model surpassed established networks such as VGG-16, ResNet-50, and U-Net in both accuracy and computational efficiency, validating its suitability for operational-scale deployment. In efforts to reconstruct historical crop distributions, the study in [136] utilized Landsat 5 NDVI time series and pseudo-phenology curves to build multi-temporal classifiers. Random forest models trained on multi-year data yielded improved generalization and are applicable to long-term climatological and hydrological assessments. The superiority of convolutional over pixel-based methods was emphasized in [68], where the UNET model attained F1 scores of 0.77 (spatial) and 0.61 (temporal). This suggests CNNs can capture not only phenological patterns but also structural and textural cues, enabling better model transferability across regions and seasons. Furthermore, [128] validated the effectiveness of CSNet—a deep network with fine-tuned ResNet-50—achieving a classification accuracy of 91.2% on high-resolution GF-1 imagery. The fusion of spectral and vegetation features further improved classification reliability and cross-site generalization. A large-scale review conducted by [107] synthesized over 400 crop mapping studies published between 1980 and 2024. Categorizing them by sensor type (optical, radar, hybrid) and classification strategy, the review highlighted the growth of the field post-2010 and the adoption of high-resolution data, deep learning, and hybrid models. Finally, the bibliometric survey in [55] underscored the dominant role of machine learning (76%) and deep learning (24%) in agricultural mapping applications. The most frequently used algorithms—Random Forest, artificial neural networks, and Support Vector Machines (SVMs)—were applied to tasks such as crop classification, disease detection, rural infrastructure planning, and irrigation optimization, showcasing the broad utility of AI in agriculture.

12.3.2 Spatial Clustering

Spatial clustering in Geographic Information Systems (GIS) denotes the systematic grouping of georeferenced data points into coherent clusters based on both attribute similarity and spatial proximity. This analytical process underpins a wide range of applications, from delineating land use zones and soil textures to detecting environmental anomalies. Traditional clustering techniques—such as k-means (including its constrained and kernel-based variants), DBSCAN, and HDBSCAN—have proven effective in managing noisy and irregular spatial distributions. These methods remain foundational in the spatial sciences due to their interpretability and computational efficiency.

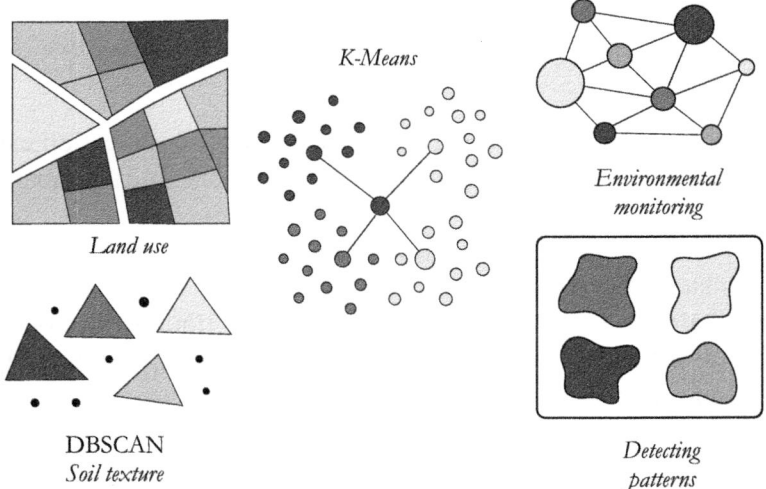

Figure 12.8: Illustration of spatial clustering in Geographic Information Systems: from traditional methods such as k-means and DBSCAN to modern AI-driven approaches using deep embedding and graph-based learning.

However, the complexity and scale of modern geospatial data increasingly necessitate the use of advanced, AI-driven methods. Emerging techniques, including deep feature embedding, graph-based representation learning, and GeoAI frameworks, enable the capture of complex spatial dependencies and the extraction of meaningful patterns from high-resolution datasets. Such advancements extend the analytical capabilities of spatial clustering, enhancing its utility in domains like environmental monitoring, urban planning, precision agriculture, and resource management. Several recent studies illustrate the evolution and diversification of spatial clustering methodologies (see Fig. 12.8). The article [220] introduces Constrained K-Means Clustering as a robust approach for digital soil texture mapping, effectively integrating a limited set of labeled data with extensive unlabeled samples. The study employs environmental variables derived from GF-2 imagery and ALOS DEM, demonstrating that the Euclidean distance metric yields superior accuracy compared to Random Forest and multi-layer perceptron (MLP) models in regions with sparse soil data. A comprehensive methodological guide is offered in [111], which systematically catalogs unsupervised and supervised machine learning techniques for spatial analysis. The study emphasizes the potential of modern spatial ML approaches for tasks such as spatial bootstrapping, cross-validation, and prediction under spatial autocorrelation and big data conditions. In the context of environmental applications, [101] presents a hybrid Kernel PCA–DBSCAN framework for assessing groundwater quality in arid zones. By employing polynomial kernels for dimensionality reduction and optimized DBSCAN parameters for anomaly detection, the model effectively identifies contamination patterns related to seawater intrusion and overuse. In the field of spatial transcriptomics, [140] proposes STMVGAE, a framework that integrates gene expression and histological image features using a multi-view variational graph autoencoder coupled with consensus clustering. This model significantly improves clustering accuracy and stability, outperforming conventional methods in spatial domain identification and downstream biological tasks. A novel clustering method for raster data is introduced in [191], which addresses the treatment of spatial outliers by employing a sliding window mechanism. This approach balances spatial integration with anomaly preservation and was validated on datasets from Beijing's Changping and Pinggu districts. Addressing computational limitations, the study [18] proposes EDBSCAN-H, an enhanced DBSCAN algorithm tailored for large satellite imagery. By incorporating histogram-based density estimation and an additional parameter (ε_2), the algorithm achieves higher clustering accuracy and reduced runtime. A more applied economic perspective is offered by [145], where AI-based clustering techniques and GIS visualization are used to analyze the spatial distribution of legal businesses. The study highlights the potential of AI-GIS integration in understanding economic agglomeration and spatial business dynamics. Finally, the review paper [33] provides a scoping synthesis of machine learning applications in urban spatial planning. By mapping prevailing research topics, data sources, and modeling approaches, the study reveals critical knowledge gaps and lays the foundation for further integration of AI techniques in spatial data science and sustainable urban governance. Collectively, these contributions underscore the transition from traditional, geometry-based clustering to hybrid, learning-driven spatial analysis frameworks capable of managing complex geographic phenomena at multiple scales.

12.3.3 Polygonal Map Generalization

Polygonal map generalization refers to the process of simplifying and abstracting polygonal features to produce cartographic representations suitable for smaller-scale maps, while preserving essential spatial topology, semantic integrity, and inter-feature relationships. As a fundamental task in automated cartography, this process typically employs computational geometry techniques such as vertex elimination, shape smoothing, and feature aggregation, ensuring multiscale consistency and contextual adaptability. Traditional rule-based and heuristic approaches have laid the foundation for polygonal generalization; however, recent developments increasingly rely on *AI-enhanced techniques*. These include *deep learning*, *explainable artificial intelligence* (XAI), and *graph-based models*, which facilitate semantic generalization by uncovering latent spatial patterns and mimicking cartographic decision-making. Zhang et al. [211] underscore persistent challenges in fully automating generalization workflows, particularly the difficulty of encoding expert cartographic knowledge into computational models. Nevertheless, advances in deep learning and the proliferation of crowdsourced geographic data offer new avenues for intelligent and scalable generalization across both visual and abstract domains (see Fig. 12.9). In this context, Fu et al. [64] demonstrate the integration of XAI into deep learning-based generalization using a ResU-Net architecture. Through visual and quantitative interpretation of the model's behavior, the study reveals a preference for boundary features over interior regions, suggesting that boundary-specific evaluation metrics yield more accurate assessments of generalization quality.

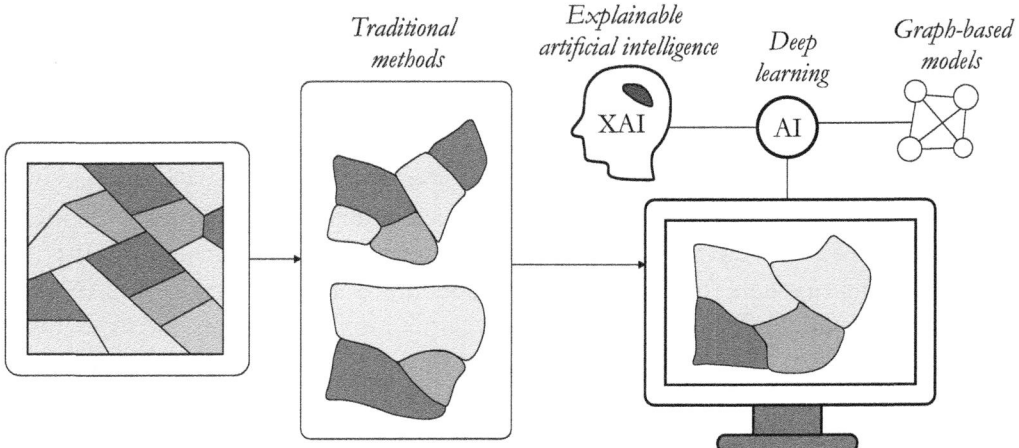

Figure 12.9: Illustration of polygonal map generalization: from detailed high-resolution land parcel polygons to simplified, semantically coherent representations suitable for smaller-scale cartographic products, integrating geometric operations and AI-assisted abstraction.

Complementary to this, the work of [67] introduces a heuristic-driven methodology for the automatic extraction and generalization of urban villages from Digital Line Graphics. By employing geometric indicators such as the modified Hausdorff distance, the method effectively identifies atypical morphologies, offering a novel solution for urban map refinement. Finally, Baig et al. [15] present a broader institutional perspective by examining the efforts of European National Mapping Agencies (NMAs) to standardize generalization practices. Their proposed dual-model framework—comprising *process-oriented* and *object-level generalization models*—has been tested on Malaysian datasets to support multiscale simplification of polygons and transportation networks, contributing to the development of centralized databases for efficient, automated map updating.

12.3.4 Terrain Modeling

Terrain Modeling involves a variety of techniques designed to digitally represent and analyze the Earth's surface through structured spatial data models, most notably Digital Elevation Models (DEMs), Triangulated Irregular Networks (TINs), and raster grids [155]. These representations form the foundation for numerous geospatial applications, including topographic mapping, hydrological modeling, geomorphological studies, infrastructure planning, and environmental simulation. Core computational operations such as surface interpolation, slope and aspect derivation, and watershed extraction enable detailed examination of terrain morphology. Fig. 12.10 illustrates the three dominant approaches used in digital terrain modeling. These spatial data structures support a variety of terrain analysis tasks in GIS, including slope estimation, watershed delineation, and topographic visualization. The study [69] proposes an efficient algorithm for 3D Delaunay triangulation that eliminates the common problem of sliver tetrahedra through topological transformations and node repositioning. The resulting method produces high-quality, adaptive meshes suitable for finite element simulations in diverse engineering contexts. New environmental demands caused by climate change and landscape degradation have driven the development of interactive tools for editing large-scale terrains. In this context, the work [88] introduces a computational landform editing tool based on 2D distance functions derived from elevation data, enabling efficient transformation of digital topographies in urban and ecological planning scenarios. Advanced GeoAI-based methods integrate deep learning techniques to automate and enhance the construction and refinement of DEMs.

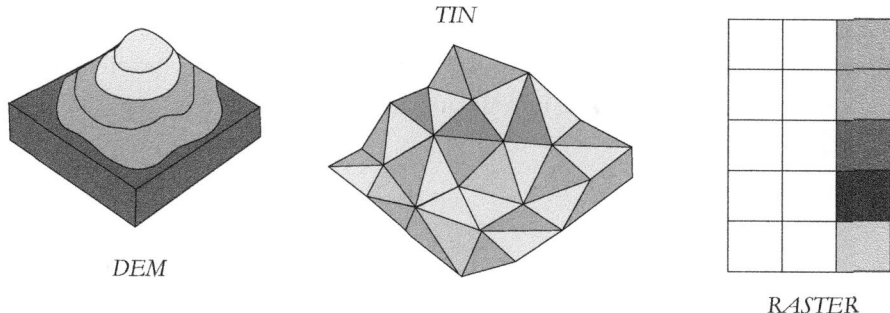

Figure 12.10: Illustration of three common terrain modeling techniques: Digital Elevation Model (DEM), Triangulated Irregular Network (TIN), and raster-based grid representation.

The fractal-based method presented in [20] reconstructs terrain from sparse elevation data while preserving both global morphology and fine local features. Its accuracy and flexibility are validated through RMSE comparisons and diverse terrain generation scenarios. Similarly, the study [99] introduces a modified super-resolution residual network (MSRResNet) for generating high-resolution DEMs in remote areas such as High Mountain Asia. By incorporating slope and curvature into the loss function, the method outperforms SRGAN and bicubic interpolation, achieving over 30% improvement in RMSE and MAE, and shows potential for both terrestrial and extraterrestrial applications. Sketch-based terrain generation is further advanced by the Terrain Diffusion Network (TDN) introduced in [85]. This framework employs multi-stage denoising and pretrained latent spaces to generate realistic terrain with fine details shaped by natural processes. The method allows for enhanced user control and high-fidelity output, validated on a NASA-derived dataset. Multispectral fusion and super-resolution enhancement are addressed in [219], where ITF-GAN is introduced—a novel algorithm that integrates implicit neural representations and Transformer-based self-attention mechanisms to enhance hyperspectral image resolution. Through guided implicit sampling during upsampling, ITF-GAN achieves superior spatial and spectral fidelity across various scaling factors. High-resolution DEM reconstruction in complex terrain is further explored in [118], which presents a Conditional GAN framework that incorporates 3D terrain features such as ridges and valleys. Tested on the Loess Plateau, the method outperforms 2D-based approaches by over 70% in elevation accuracy and offers a flexible solution for void filling and DEM refinement. A comprehensive review of terrain modeling techniques is offered in [66], categorizing existing methods into procedural, physically based, and example-driven approaches derived from scanned terrain data. The study critically evaluates these methods based on realism, variety of landforms, user control, scalability, and performance, while identifying future research directions and unresolved challenges in digital terrain modeling.

12.4 Bioinformatics

Bioinformatics is an interdisciplinary field that integrates biology, computer science, and mathematics to analyze, model, and interpret biological data. In modern bioinformatics research, computational geometry plays a critical role in modeling biomolecular structures, analyzing their spatiotemporal interactions, and optimizing biological processes at the molecular level. Geometric methods enable efficient representation of protein surfaces, spatial complementarity assessment in molecular docking, and sequence similarity analysis through spatial and topological patterns. In the remainder of this section, we focus on three specific aspects of bioinformatics where geometric approaches are particularly prominent: *Molecular Docking*, *Protein Surface Representation*, and *Sequence Alignment*.

Molecular Docking

Molecular Docking is a fundamental computational technique in structure-based drug design, aiming to predict the most favorable orientation of small molecules (ligands) when bound to the active sites of target proteins (see Fig. 12.11).

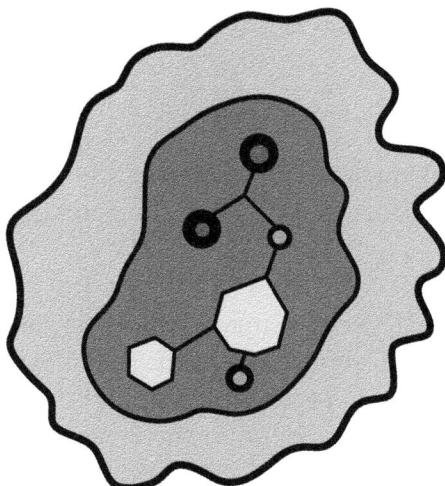

Figure 12.11: Molecular docking representation showing ligand placement within the protein binding site.

This process is deeply rooted in computational geometry, as it requires accurate assessment of spatial complementarity and binding affinities within intricate molecular environments. Traditionally, docking protocols have relied on metaheuristic optimization strategies—such as genetic algorithms (e.g., Auto-Grow), particle swarm optimization, and Lamarckian genetic algorithms (e.g., AutoDock)—to effectively explore the vast conformational space of protein-ligand interactions. In recent years, these classical approaches have been significantly enhanced by artificial intelligence (AI)-driven methods, including deep learning, reinforcement learning, and graph neural networks. These techniques have demonstrated superior performance in ligand pose prediction and scoring by leveraging data-driven representations and learning-based optimization. The study by Spiegel et al. [171] presents AutoGrow4, an open-source, modular platform that utilizes a genetic algorithm to iteratively evolve ligand structures without the need for predefined compound libraries. AutoGrow4 supports both de novo drug design and lead optimization; its application to PARP-1 successfully generated drug-like molecules with improved predicted binding affinities and binding modes comparable to FDA-approved inhibitors. Chalmers and colleagues [35] introduce *Ligand GA*, a versatile genetic algorithm framework for designing inhibitors that selectively bind to protein active sites. The algorithm incorporates a wide range of pharmacological constraints, including ADME properties, hydrogen bonding patterns, toxicity avoidance, and substructure rules, making it highly adaptable to ligand design and docking tasks. Zhou et al. [217] propose a novel docking method that integrates a multi-swarm competitive optimization algorithm with gradient descent refinement. Evaluated on the CASF-2016 benchmark (285 complexes), the approach demonstrates strong performance, particularly for ligands with high conformational flexibility, outperforming several conventional docking tools. Despite these advancements, the identification of near-native binding poses remains a central challenge. Vittorio et al. [187] highlight the limitations of traditional scoring functions, which often prioritize binding affinity at the expense of geometric accuracy. Their review introduces two novel deep learning-based pose selectors that outperform classical scoring strategies in identifying native-like conformations, underscoring the potential of deep learning (DL) methods in improving docking reliability. To further address optimization efficiency in molecular design, the JANUS algorithm [139] is introduced as a hybrid genetic algorithm inspired by parallel tempering. JANUS combines dual-population dynamics (exploration vs. exploitation) with a deep neural network for property prediction and an active learning strategy. Although it achieves state-of-the-art results across several benchmarks, the study also emphasizes the importance of incorporating synthesizability constraints into generative models. Finally, a recent review by Thomas et al. [178] surveys advances in generative molecular design that explicitly incorporate protein structure into molecule generation. These methods are categorized into distribution learning and goal-directed optimization, with further distinctions made between explicit and implicit structural conditioning. The integration of protein context into generative models is shown to significantly improve on-target binding affinity predictions. A broader overview of AI techniques applied to protein-ligand binding prediction is presented in [167], highlighting the transformative potential of machine learning across the molecular docking pipeline.

12.4.2 Protein Surface Representation

Protein Surface Representation constitutes a fundamental aspect of structural bioinformatics, focusing on the computational and mathematical modeling of the geometric and physicochemical characteristics of protein surfaces (see Fig. 12.12).

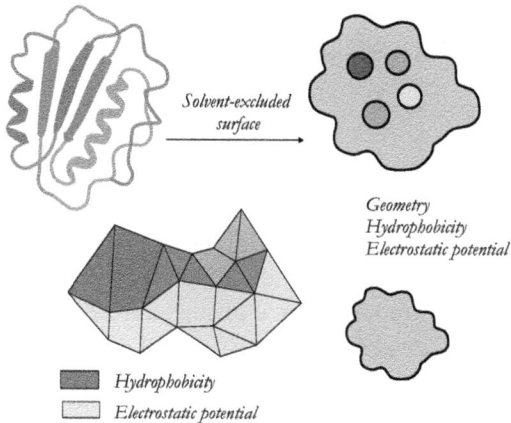

Figure 12.12: A conceptual illustration of protein surface representation, highlighting the geometric and physicochemical complexity of molecular surfaces used in binding site prediction and structural analysis.

Accurate surface representation is vital for elucidating molecular recognition mechanisms, predicting ligand binding sites, guiding molecular docking simulations, and informing rational drug design. Due to the inherent geometric complexity of protein topologies—marked by features such as grooves, cavities, and surface pockets—a range of computational geometry and computer graphics techniques have been employed to generate biologically meaningful and computationally tractable surface models [169]. Traditional approaches include solvent-accessible surface (SAS) and solvent-excluded surface (SES) models, typically computed via Connolly surface algorithms or rolling probe methods that simulate the trajectory of a water molecule across the protein's van der Waals envelope. In addition, surface triangulation, alpha shapes, and Gaussian-based smoothing techniques have been used to produce continuous, topologically consistent representations of protein surfaces. These classical methods, while effective, often depend on predefined geometric heuristics and may lack adaptability for complex or dynamic biological environments. To address such limitations, recent advances have introduced artificial intelligence (AI)-driven methodologies that enhance both the resolution and interpretability of surface representations. Geometric deep learning (GDL), graph convolutional networks (GCNs), and point cloud-based architectures facilitate end-to-end learning directly from 3D atomic coordinates while preserving spatial and chemical context. For instance, [207] proposes a method that maps 3D protein surfaces onto 2D representations using dimensionality reduction techniques, encoding geometric and biochemical features (e.g., hydrophobicity, curvature, electrostatic potential) into separate color channels. This enables rapid surface comparison through image registration techniques, with demonstrated efficacy in detecting conserved functional sites.

A systematic review presented in [14] categorizes GDL strategies for molecular applications, illustrating their capacity to process diverse data modalities (graphs, grids, surfaces, and strings) while maintaining structural symmetries. Applications span drug discovery, quantum chemistry, and reaction prediction, with the review emphasizing ongoing challenges in generalizability and interpretability. Furthermore, [198] explores the integration of protein language models—trained on large-scale 1D sequence datasets—with geometric learning frameworks, demonstrating performance gains of approximately 20% across multiple tasks such as binding affinity prediction and protein-protein interface detection. This hybrid approach effectively leverages complementary sequence-based and structure-based information. The limitations of mesh-based surface representations are addressed in [175], which introduces a deep learning model that computes molecular surfaces directly from atomic point clouds. By eliminating the need for precomputed mesh connectivity and handcrafted features, the framework achieves state-of-the-art results in predicting interaction sites and protein-protein interfaces, offering both efficiency and scalability. Complementing these developments, the study [56] provides a thorough survey of data structures employed in protein representation, highlighting their relevance to core bioinformatics tasks such as sequence alignment, motif detection, and structural comparison. Taken together, these contributions underscore the growing role of computational geometry and AI in advancing the precision and utility of protein surface modeling.

12.4.3　Sequence Alignment

Sequence alignment represents a foundational task in bioinformatics, essential for identifying functional, structural, and evolutionary relationships among biological sequences such as DNA, RNA, and proteins [72]. Traditional approaches primarily rely on dynamic programming algorithms—such as Smith–Waterman, Needleman–Wunsch, and Hirschberg—as well as heuristic methods including MAFFT, Clustal, BLAST, and Bowtie, which aim to balance alignment accuracy with computational efficiency [104]. Recent methodological advancements have introduced artificial intelligence into sequence alignment, leveraging deep learning, Transformer models, and bio-inspired heuristics to enhance scoring functions, learn alignment mappings, and accelerate computation (see Fig. 12.13).

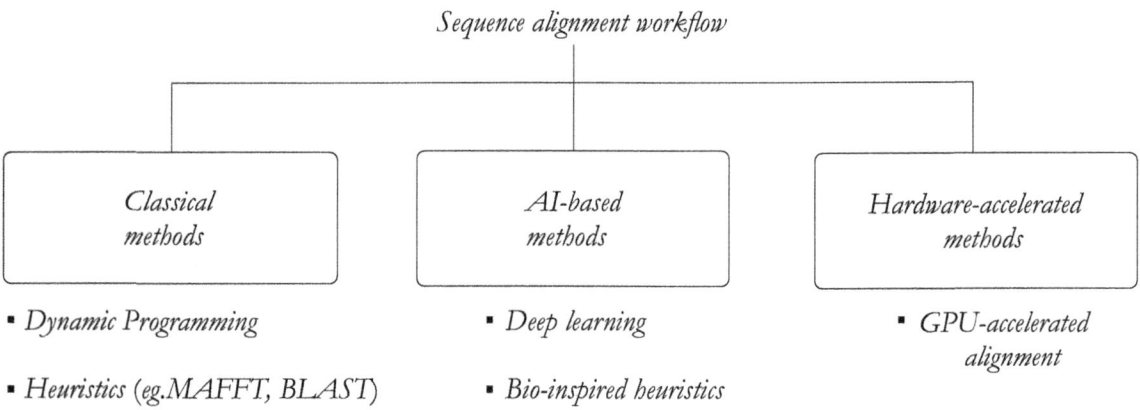

Figure 12.13: Sequence alignment workflow: from biological sequence input to alignment output, incorporating traditional and AI-driven techniques.

Notably, the Embed-Search-Align (ESA) framework [84] eliminates conventional indexing by employing Transformer-generated embeddings and contrastive learning to embed DNA reads and fragments in a shared vector space, achieving 99% accuracy on human genome alignments. Complementing this, the AnySeq/GPU library [137] utilizes warp shuffles and half-precision arithmetic to implement dynamic programming on GPUs, surpassing other GPU-based alignment libraries by up to 19.2× while attaining up to 3.8 TCUPS. Model-based and embedding-guided strategies are further explored in learnMSA2 [19], which integrates protein language model embeddings from ProtT5-XL into an extended profile

Hidden Markov Model (HMM), improving alignment accuracy by 6% over traditional amino acid-based methods. Similarly, traditional perspectives on MSA remain valuable; a comprehensive study [154] reviews foundational techniques and their applications in phylogenetics, protein structure analysis, and drug discovery. Machine learning-enhanced implementations are also gaining traction. The work in [153] proposes a multilayer perceptron-enhanced Needleman–Wunsch algorithm that achieves 99.7% alignment accuracy and over 2900 GCUPS, while maintaining compatibility with long DNA and RNA sequences. In the realm of divide-and-conquer heuristics, WMSA [196] offers improvements over MAFFT by clustering sequences and employing progressive profile–profile alignments, leading to better performance on large, conserved datasets. Hardware-accelerated approaches have also evolved significantly. TALCO [188] introduces a tiling technique for long sequence alignment that maintains constant memory usage and preserves optimality under banding constraints, with successful applications to X-Drop and WFA-Adapt algorithms. Furthermore, EdgeAlign [90] employs deep reinforcement learning and a deep Q-network to enable efficient DNA alignment on resource-constrained edge devices, such as NVIDIA Jetson Nano and Artix-7 FPGAs, offering a compact and affordable diagnostic solution through AutoML-based model compression. Literature reviews and bio-inspired perspectives are addressed in studies [41, 89]. The former analyzes the computational challenges and accuracy trade-offs in MSA, with a particular focus on multiobjective genetic algorithms. The latter provides a systematic literature review of 45 bioinspired MSA approaches published between 2010 and 2024, highlighting the dominance of genetic algorithms and memetic optimization, and emphasizing the relevance of structural evaluation metrics and benchmark datasets such as BAliBASE and SABmark.

12.5 Artificial Intelligence

Artificial Intelligence (AI) has become a transformative paradigm across scientific domains, including computational geometry, where intelligent algorithms increasingly contribute to solving complex spatial and geometric tasks. By combining principles from machine learning, optimization, and robotics, AI techniques enable adaptive reasoning in environments characterized by uncertainty, high dimensionality, and dynamic constraints. Within geometric contexts, AI facilitates advanced decision-making in navigation, planning, and classification—often surpassing traditional algorithmic solutions in terms of robustness, scalability, and generalization. This section presents selected subdomains where the intersection of AI and computational geometry is particularly pronounced: *Pathfinding and Obstacle Avoidance*, *Motion Planning*, and *Deep Learning for Geometric Object Classification*.

12.5.1 Motion Planning, Pathfinding, and Obstacle Avoidance

Autonomous navigation in complex environments fundamentally depends on the coordinated execution of three interrelated tasks: *pathfinding*, *obstacle avoidance*, and *motion planning*. Pathfinding typically addresses the computation of optimal routes within discrete representations of the environment, predominantly leveraging graph-based algorithms such as A*, Dijkstra, and their refinements (e.g., Theta*, Jump Point Search). In contrast, obstacle avoidance focuses on real-time responsiveness to dynamic or unforeseen hazards, often necessitating local and reactive strategies. Motion planning integrates both dimensions by operating in continuous configuration spaces and accounting for kinematic and dynamic constraints, thereby enabling the generation of feasible, smooth, and safe trajectories. Traditional techniques such as Rapidly-exploring Random Trees (RRT), Probabilistic Roadmaps (PRM), and Artificial Potential Fields (APF) remain prominent in high-dimensional planning, yet exhibit limitations in adaptability and robustness to environmental changes. This has catalyzed the incorporation of *AI-based approaches*, including deep reinforcement learning (e.g., DQN, PPO), attention-driven architectures, hybrid algorithms (e.g., RRT* with reinforcement learning or APF with fuzzy logic), and end-to-end neural models. Recent advancements have extended this paradigm further by introducing motion planners in curvilinear coordinate systems coupled with model predictive control (MPC), as well as leveraging *diffusion models* and multimodal sensor fusion to enhance perception and decision-making. A growing research focus is the development of real-time, energy-efficient motion planning algorithms suitable for deployment on computationally constrained platforms such as UAVs, high-DOF manipulators, and autonomous ground vehicles. The following section provides a structured overview of recent advancements that address these challenges through both traditional methods and AI-enhanced approaches. Figure 12.14 illustrates core components of this domain, including classical grid-based search, dynamic obstacle detection, trajectory generation, and hybrid control strategies driven by artificial intelligence.

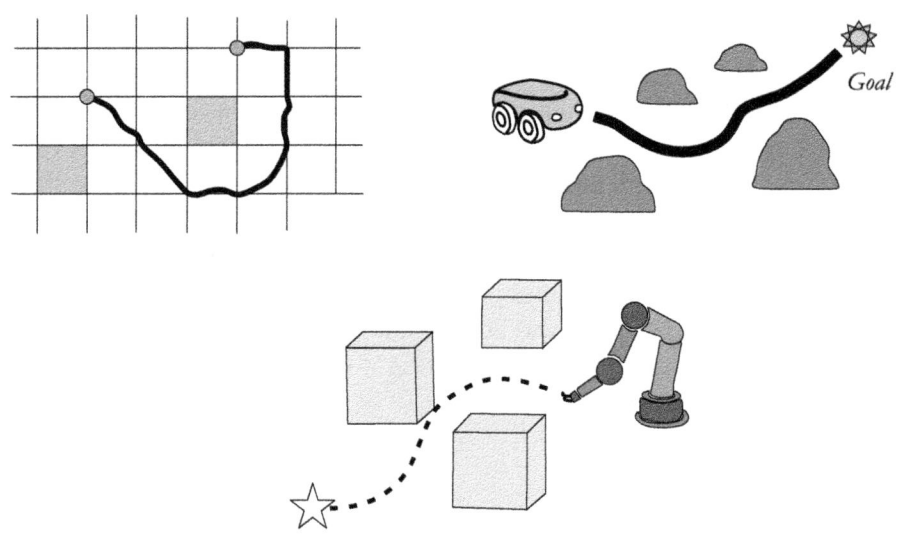

Figure 12.14: Integrated visualization of motion planning, pathfinding, and obstacle avoidance strategies in autonomous systems.

The study by Buonocore et al. [31] presents a novel obstacle avoidance path planning algorithm for hyper-redundant manipulators in virtual simulations, allowing for optimization based on customizable criteria. Its applicability is demonstrated through remote maintenance tasks executed by the HyRMan system within the DTT project. In mobile robotics, an advanced method that integrates obstacle gap characteristics into both global and local planning stages is proposed in [192]. By enhancing the traditional A* algorithm and dynamically coupling it with the Dynamic Window Approach (DWA) via geometric coordination, the approach achieves notable improvements in efficiency, reducing path length and motion time in constrained spaces. An improvement of the classical APF method is offered in [97], which mitigates the local minima problem by integrating RRT strategies into the planning of a 5-degree-of-freedom bending robot. Experimental validation confirms the method's capacity to produce smooth and operationally feasible paths. The survey Popović et al. [146] systematically reviews learning-based approaches in Adaptive Informative Path Planning (AIPP), providing a unified mathematical formulation and two taxonomies—based on learning strategies and application domains. The study outlines emerging trends and challenges, particularly regarding robotic adaptability in unknown environments. In the domain of aerial robotics, the work in [42] proposes a reinforcement learning-based navigation system for drones, utilizing a minimal set of low-cost onboard sensors. The system is validated through diverse simulated 3D scenarios, demonstrating reliable performance in real-time UAV navigation for logistics and transport applications. Enhancing sample-based planners, the study in [163] introduces a novel edge-cost function in a curvilinear planning space, minimizing path deviation while enabling obstacle avoidance. Coupled with a tailored model predictive control (MPC) framework, the approach is validated through 5 km field robotics trials, showing superior results in long-range navigation. A comprehensive overview of traditional and modern obstacle avoidance methods is presented in [105], encompassing classical algorithms (e.g.,

Bug, Dijkstra), metaheuristic approaches (e.g., genetic algorithms), and neural network-based solutions. The review emphasizes their applicability, limitations, and the increasing relevance of predictive and deep learning techniques in robotics. Finally, [200] introduces an end-to-end attention-based architecture for autonomous driving. By integrating multimodal sensor data (images, LiDAR) and employing LSTM models to adapt navigation strategies in real time, the system enhances decision-making and safety, marking a step forward in autonomous vehicle control. The survey [76] provides a systematic analysis of motion planning as a foundational capability for autonomous systems, classifying and evaluating classical, sampling-based, optimization-based, and learning-driven approaches. Particular emphasis is placed on emerging paradigms, including the integration of artificial intelligence and machine learning (AI/ML), meta-learning for task generalization, and quantum computing to address high-dimensional planning. Additionally, the review underscores critical challenges such as real-time execution under uncertainty, and the increasing importance of ethical considerations in human-robot collaboration. Complementing this, the study [218] offers a comprehensive review of motion planning frameworks for unmanned aerial vehicles (UAVs), systematically addressing three key components: environmental modeling through map representation, generation of safe and efficient paths, and trajectory optimization for energy-efficient, executable motion plans. By consolidating recent advancements and articulating open research directions, this work supports the development of more adaptable and robust autonomous UAV navigation systems.

12.5.2 Learning-Based Geometric Reconstruction

Recent developments in Artificial Intelligence (AI) have substantially reshaped geometric reconstruction paradigms, transitioning from explicit rule-based modeling to data-driven, implicit representations. Traditionally grounded in the principles of computational geometry—where algorithms are designed to process spatial data with mathematical rigor—geometric reconstruction has now evolved through integration with deep learning techniques. This synergy allows for the inference of complex 3D structures even in the presence of noise, sparsity, or occlusion, thereby extending classical geometric concepts into the data-driven domain.

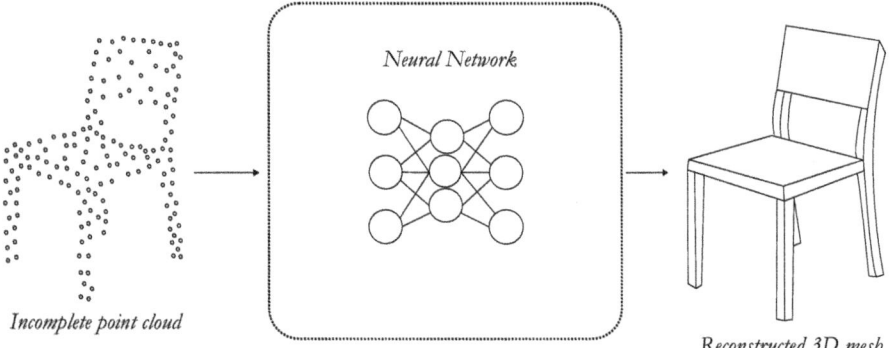

Figure 12.15: AI-based reconstruction of geometric structures from partial or noisy data using neural networks and parametric techniques.

Figure 12.15 visualizes this conceptual shift, illustrating how neural architectures and hybrid models can extract latent geometric information from partial observations. Such capabilities are crucial in a wide range of applications, including autonomous navigation, digital twin construction, robotic perception, and large-scale urban modeling, where accurate spatial representations must often be derived from incomplete or sensor-imperfect data. The method MT-NeRF [98] introduces radiance field reconstruction from RGB-D data without requiring precomputed camera poses. By utilizing multi-resolution geometric feature planes, photometric distortion loss, and a global-to-local keyframe selection strategy, it achieves high-quality, memory-efficient reconstruction with significant pose estimation improvements and computational speedup. UniSDF [190] enables the reconstruction of complex, reflective surfaces by blending camera and reflection-based color parameterizations in 3D space. A multi-resolution coarse-to-fine training framework enhances accuracy and efficiency, establishing state-of-the-art performance across standard datasets. The Parametric Gauss Reconstruction (PGR) method [122] leverages a formulation from potential theory to perform surface reconstruction without requiring surface normals or training data. It demonstrates robustness to noise, sparsity, and non-uniformity, outperforming many traditional and learning-based alternatives. A global template-matching technique [46] is proposed for reconstructing buildings from airborne LiDAR, using an industrial library of roof primitives and optimizing a smooth energy function with integrated outlier rejection via an M-estimator and L-BFGS. In the domain of materials science, a hybrid deep-learning framework [78] integrates StyleGAN-based 2D interpolation with convolutional occupancy networks to reconstruct 3D microstructures of functionally graded materials. The approach is validated on lanthanum strontium manganite (LSM), achieving high-fidelity structural recovery. A deep learning model based on voxel representation and multidimensional CNNs [213] reconstructs 3D particle morphology from 2D images across natural and synthetic datasets. High consistency in morphological descriptors validates its generalizability for particle property analysis. A three-stage pipeline [159] for indoor reconstruction combines semantic segmentation with PointNet, multiple surface reconstruction strategies (Poisson, ball-pivoting, marching cubes), and geometry simplification via edge collapse. It achieves sub-millimeter accuracy on both simple and complex geometries. A comprehensive review [58] presents a taxonomy of 3D surface reconstruction techniques—point-, mesh-, volumetric-, and implicit-based—and evaluates them based on input modalities, benchmarks, and evaluation metrics, highlighting future research directions. Another survey [189] classifies learning-based methods into binocular stereo, multiview, object-centered, and SLAM-based reconstruction, with in-depth analysis of network designs, outputs, datasets, and research challenges. The review in [209] categorizes point cloud completion strategies as point-, convolution-, GAN-, and geometry-based, offering experimental comparisons and future directions for real-world deployment in domains such as autonomous systems and smart cities. The study [186] surveys deep learning techniques for 3D object reconstruction, registration, and augmentation, analyzing benchmark architectures and noting unresolved research problems in the still-developing field of 3D deep learning. Finally, the work [32] addresses semantic scene understanding, compression, and completion of point cloud data using a novel taxonomy based on acquisition modality and network architecture, supporting more interpretable benchmarking and revealing emerging trends.

12.5.3 Geometric Object Classification Algorithms

Geometric object classification represents a core challenge in computational geometry, with critical relevance for applications including 3D scene interpretation, urban environment modeling, robotic sensing, and autonomous vehicle navigation. The task involves assigning semantic or structural categories (e.g., wall, tree, vehicle, facade) to geometric constructs, typically represented as point clouds, polygonal meshes, or volumetric grids. Classical approaches, rooted in geometric analysis, rely on manually engineered features—such as curvature, surface orientation, shape histograms, and spatial density—followed by traditional classifiers like Support Vector Machines (SVMs), Random Forests, or k-Nearest Neighbors. In contrast, contemporary strategies increasingly adopt deep learning models that process raw geometric inputs directly, eliminating the need for handcrafted descriptors. Architectures such as PointNet, 3D convolutional neural networks, and graph-based models leverage the spatial and topological properties of geometric data to learn robust classification patterns. This methodological evolution underscores a deepening integration between computational geometry and artificial intelligence, yielding powerful frameworks for object classification in high-dimensional spatial contexts. An overview of this transition from traditional geometric reasoning to AI-driven classification is illustrated in Fig. 12.16.

The paper [86] introduces FocusSA, an enhanced Set Abstraction module for 3D object detection in point clouds, addressing limitations of existing methods in capturing small or distant objects by integrating geo-

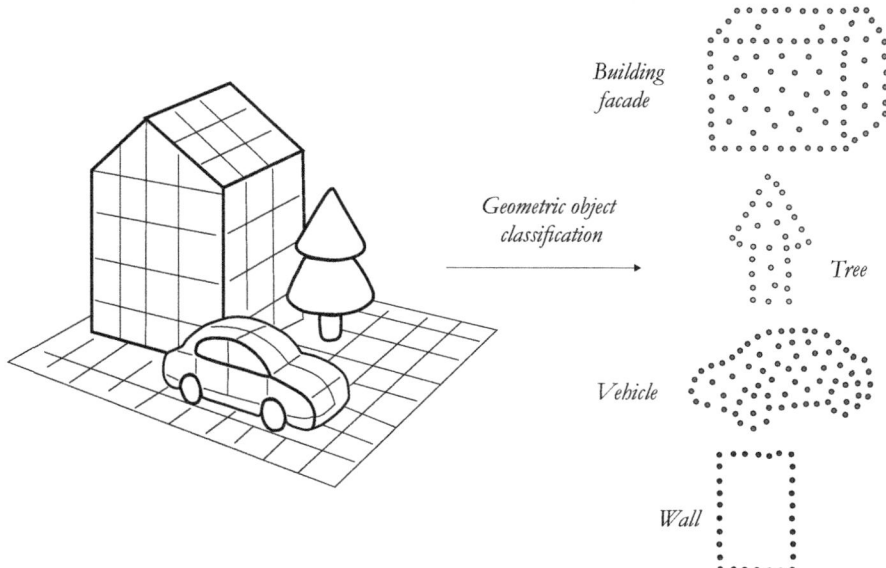

Figure 12.16: Illustration of geometric object classification: From raw 3D representations (point clouds, meshes) to semantic labels using traditional and AI-based methods.

metric and semantic awareness. Through the FocFPS and GeoFE modules, FocusSA improves contextual point selection and geometric feature representation, achieving superior accuracy on the KITTI benchmark while remaining compatible with standard architectures. The article [199] enhances the classic PointNet architecture for 3D point cloud classification by integrating transformer-based attention mechanisms, including offset-attention and cascade-attention modules. The proposed method significantly improves both classification accuracy and robustness over the original PointNet, demonstrating the effectiveness of attention-enhanced deep learning for point cloud analysis. The paper [125] introduces PointConT, a novel content-based Transformer architecture for 3D point cloud classification that addresses the limitations of local spatial attention by clustering feature-similar points and applying self-attention within those clusters. This design enables efficient long-range dependency modeling with reduced computational cost, achieving state-of-the-art 90.3% Top-1 accuracy on the challenging ScanObjectNN benchmark. The article [37] presents PointNet, a pioneering neural network architecture that directly processes raw point cloud data while preserving permutation invariance, eliminating the need for voxelization or image conversion. Despite its simplicity, PointNet achieves state-of-the-art performance in classification, segmentation, and scene parsing tasks, and is theoretically shown to be robust to input noise and perturbations. The article [152] introduces a novel classification algorithm that explicitly integrates both geometric and statistical properties of data into a unified class representation. Initial experiments on standard datasets, including noisy variants, demonstrate the algorithm's robustness and reduced sensitivity to training data compared to traditional classifiers. The study [130] proposes an integrated object classification method for BIM models that leverages expert knowledge of shape features and spatial relationships, combined with a tailored matching algorithm. The approach demonstrates high accuracy by successfully classifying complex 3D bridge objects in both misclassified CAD models and manually reconstructed point cloud models. The article [129] introduces CPCC-PES, a novel compressed point cloud classification method that leverages enhanced edge-sampling techniques based on attention mechanisms to preserve shape-defining features in the compressed domain. The method achieves over 90% Top-1 accuracy at only 0.08 bits-per-point on the ModelNet40 benchmark, outperforming state-of-the-art approaches with a 96% reduction in bitrate, and introduces BD-Top-1 Accuracy as a new evaluation metric for rate-accuracy trade-offs. The survey [205] explores recent advancements in deep learning for urban-scene point cloud semantic segmentation (USPCSS), categorizing datasets and models into road-level and urban-level applications while analyzing their architectural innovations and segmentation performance. The findings highlight the superiority of transformer-based point methods like PTv3 in complex environments, offering a clear roadmap for future research and practical deployment in urban analysis.

Bibliography

[1] Selim G. Akl and Godfried T. Toussaint. "A fast convex hull algorithm". *Information Processing Letters* 7.5 (1978), pages 219–222. ISSN: 0020-0190. DOI: 10.1016/0020-0190(78)90003-0.

[2] Adis Alihodzic. "Training feed-forward neural networks employing improved bat algorithm for digital image compression". *Large-scale scientific computing*. Volume 10665. Lecture Notes in Comput. Sci. Springer, Cham, 2018, pages 315–323. DOI: 10.1007/978-3-319-73441-5_3. URL: https://doi.org/10.1007/978-3-319-73441-5_3.

[3] Adis Alihodzic, Sead Delalic, and Damir Hasic. "An Exact Two-Phase Method For Optimal Camera Placement In Art Gallery Problem". *2020 15th Conference on Computer Science and Information Systems (FedCSIS)*. 2020, pages 215–222. DOI: 10.15439/2020F79.

[4] Adis Alihodzic, Damir Hasanspahic, Fikret Cunjalo, and Haris Smajlovic. "Adjusted Bare Bones Fireworks Algorithm to Guard Orthogonal Polygons". *Intelligent Computing*. Cham: Springer International Publishing, 2021, pages 341–356. ISBN: 978-3-030-80126-7.

[5] Adis Alihodzic, Damir Hasanspahic, Eva Tuba, and Milan Tuba. "Application of Adjusted Differential Evolution in Optimal Sensor Placement for Interior Coverage". *Proceedings of Sixth International Congress on Information and Communication Technology*. Edited by Xin-She Yang, Simon Sherratt, Nilanjan Dey, and Amit Joshi. Singapore: Springer Singapore, 2022, pages 155–163. ISBN: 978-981-16-2377-6.

[6] Adis Alihodzic, Damir Hasic, and Elmedin Selmanovic. "An Effective Guided Fireworks Algorithm for Solving UCAV Path Planning Problem". *Numerical Methods and Applications*. Edited by Geno Nikolov, Natalia Kolkovska, and Krassimir Georgiev. Cham: Springer International Publishing, 2019, pages 29–38. ISBN: 978-3-030-10692-8.

[7] Adis Alihodzic, Haris Smajlovic, Eva Tuba, Romana Capor Hrosik, and Milan Tuba. "Adjusted Artificial Bee Colony Algorithm for the Minimum Weight Triangulation". *Harmony Search and Nature Inspired Optimization Algorithms*. Edited by Neha Yadav, Anupam Yadav, Jagdish Chand Bansal, Kusum Deep, and Joong Hoon Kim. Singapore: Springer Singapore, 2019, pages 305–317. ISBN: 978-981-13-0761-4.

[8]   Adis Alihodzic, Eva Tuba, and Milan Tuba. "Adjusted Harris Hawks Optimization for the Minimum Weight Triangulation". *2023 3rd International Conference on Electrical, Computer, Communications and Mechatronics Engineering (ICECCME)*. 2023, pages 1–6. DOI: 10.1109/ICECCME57830.2023.10252267.

[9]   Adis Alihodzic, Eva Tuba, and Milan Tuba. "Two-Phase Algorithm for Solving Vehicle Routing Problem with Time Windows". *Numerical Methods and Applications*. Edited by Ivan Georgiev, Maria Datcheva, Krassimir Georgiev, and Geno Nikolov. Cham: Springer Nature Switzerland, 2023, pages 14–25. ISBN: 978-3-031-32412-3.

[10] Adis Alihodzic, Eva Tuba, and Milan Tuba. "Optimizing Camera Placement for Maximum Coverage of Simple Polygons with Holes: Deterministic Approaches and Swarm Intelligence Algorithms". *Engineering Applications of AI and Swarm Intelligence*. Edited by Xin-She Yang. Singapore: Springer Nature Singapore, 2025, pages 389–409. ISBN: 978-981-97-5979-8. DOI: 10.1007/978-981-97-5979-8_18. URL: https://doi.org/10.1007/978-981-97-5979-8_18.

[11] Muslum Altun and Mustafa Turker. "Integration of convolutional neural networks with parcel-based image analysis for crop type mapping from time-series images". *Earth Science Informatics* 18.3 (2025), pages 1–28. DOI: 10.1007/s12145-025-01819-8. URL: https://doi.org/10.1007/s12145-025-01819-8.

[12] Kenneth R. Anderson. "A reevaluation of an efficient algorithm for determining the convex hull of a finite planar set". *Information Processing Letters* 7.1 (1978), pages 53–55. ISSN: 0020-0190. DOI: 10.1016/0020-0190(78)90041-8.

[13] A.M. Andrew. "Another efficient algorithm for convex hulls in two dimensions". *Information Processing Letters* 9.5 (1979), pages 216–219. ISSN: 0020-0190. DOI: https://doi.org/10.1016/0020-0190(79)90072-3.

[14] Kenneth Atz, Francesca Grisoni, and Gisbert Schneider. "Geometric deep learning on molecular representations". *Nature Machine Intelligence* 3.12 (2021), pages 1023–1032. DOI: 10.1038/s42256-021-00418-8. URL: https://doi.org/10.1038/s42256-021-00418-8.

[15] Siddique Ullah Baig, Alias Abdul Rahman, and Edward Eric Duncan. "A Review and Conceptual Framework for Generalization of Maps". *Developments in Multidimensional Spatial Data Models*. Edited by Alias Abdul Rahman, Pawel Boguslawski, Christopher Gold, and Mohamad Nor Said. Berlin, Heidelberg: Springer Berlin Heidelberg, 2013, pages 191–206. ISBN: 978-3-642-36379-5. DOI: 10.1007/978-3-642-36379-5_12. URL: https://doi.org/10.1007/978-3-642-36379-5_12.

[16] C. Bradford Barber, David P. Dobkin, and Hannu Huhdanpaa. "The quickhull algorithm for convex hulls". *ACM Trans. Math. Softw.* 22.4 (1996), pages 469–483. ISSN: 0098-3500. DOI: 10.1145/235815.235821.

[17] Hichem Barki, Florence Denis, and Florent Dupont. "A New Algorithm for the Computation of the Minkowski Difference of Convex Polyhedra". *2010 Shape Modeling International Conference*. 2010, pages 206–210. DOI: 10.1109/SMI.2010.12.

[18] Mohammad Subhi Al-Batah, Enas Rezeg Al-Kwaldeh, Mutaz Abdel Wahed, Mazen Alzyoud, Najah Al-Shanableh, and Jayesh Soni. "Enhancement over DBSCAN Satellite Spatial Data Clustering". *JECE* 2024 (Jan. 2024). ISSN: 2090-0147. DOI: 10.1155/2024/2330624. URL: https://doi.org/10.1155/2024/2330624.

[19] Felix Becker and Mario Stanke. "learnMSA2: deep protein multiple alignments with large language and hidden Markov models". *Bioinformatics* 40.Supplement 2 (Sept. 2024), pages ii79–ii86. ISSN: 1367-4811. DOI: https://doi.org/10.1093/bioinformatics/btae381.

[20] Farès Belhadj. "Terrain modeling: a constrained fractal model". *Proceedings of the 5th International Conference on Computer Graphics, Virtual Reality, Visualisation and Interaction in Africa*. AFRIGRAPH '07. Grahamstown, South Africa: Association for Computing Machinery, 2007, pages 197–204. ISBN: 9781595939067. DOI: 10.1145/1294685.1294717. URL: https://doi.org/10.1145/1294685.1294717.

[21] Mark de Berg, Otfried Cheong, Marc van Kreveld, and Mark Overmars. *Computational Geometry: Algorithms and Applications*. 3rd. Springer Berlin, Heidelberg, 2008, page 386. ISBN: 978-3-540-77973-5.

[22] Mark de Berg, Marc van Kreveld, Mark Overmars, and Otfried Cheong Schwarzkopf. "Binary Space Partitions". *Computational Geometry: Algorithms and Applications*. Springer Berlin Heidelberg, 2000, pages 251–265. ISBN: 978-3-662-04245-8. DOI: 10.1007/978-3-662-04245-8_12.

[23] Mark de Berg and Micha Streppel. "Approximate Range Searching Using Binary Space Partitions". *FSTTCS 2004: Foundations of Software Technology and Theoretical Computer Science*. Edited by Kamal Lodaya and Meena Mahajan. Berlin, Heidelberg: Springer Berlin Heidelberg, 2005, pages 110–121. ISBN: 978-3-540-30538-5.

[24] Gino van den Bergen. *Collision Detection in Interactive 3D Environments*. CRC Press, 2003, page 308. ISBN: 978-1558608016.

[25] Julian Bialas and Mario Doller. "Coverage Path Planning for Unmanned Aerial Vehicles in Complex 3D Environments with Deep Reinforcement Learning". *2022 IEEE International Conference on Robotics and Biomimetics (ROBIO)*. 2022, pages 1080–1085. DOI: 10.1109/ROBIO55434.2022.10011936.

[26] Jiri Bittner, Jan Prikryl, and Pavel Slavik. "Exact regional visibility using line space partitioning". *Computers & Graphics* 27.4 (2003), pages 569–580. ISSN: 0097-8493. DOI: 10.1016/S0097-8493(03)00101-8.

[27] Prosenjit Bose and Godfried T. Toussaint. "Geometric and computational aspects of gravity casting". *Computer-Aided Design* 27.6 (1995), pages 455–464. DOI: 10.1016/0010-4485(95)00018-M.

[28] Aqeel M. Breesam, Yasmeen M. Hussein, and Mohammed J. Mohammed. "Fractal compression of digital image processing". *AIP Conference Proceedings* 3051.1 (Feb. 2024), page 040010. ISSN: 0094-243X. DOI: 10.1063/5.0191578.

[29] Oliver Brock, Jeff Trinkle, and Fabio Ramos. "Hybrid Motion Planning Using Minkowski Sums". *Robotics: Science and Systems IV*. 2009, pages 97–104. DOI: https://doi.org/10.7551/mitpress/8344.001.0001.

[30] Nicolas Broutin and Henning Sulzbach. "A limit field for orthogonal range searches in two-dimensional random point search trees". *Stochastic Processes and their Applications* 129.8 (2019), pages 2912–2940. ISSN: 0304-4149. DOI: https://doi.org/10.1016/j.spa.2018.08.014. URL: https://www.sciencedirect.com/science/article/pii/S030441491830454X.

[31] Sara Buonocore, Andrea Zoppoli, and Giuseppe Di Gironimo. "An obstacle avoidance path planning algorithm to simulate hyper redundant manipulators for tokamaks maintenance". *Fusion Engineering and Design* 202 (2024), page 114334. ISSN: 0920-3796. DOI: https://doi.org/10.1016/j.fusengdes.2024.114334. URL: https://www.sciencedirect.com/science/article/pii/S092037962400187X.

[32] Elena Camuffo, Daniele Mari, and Simone Milani. "Recent Advancements in Learning Algorithms for Point Clouds: An Updated Overview". *Sensors* 22.4 (2022). ISSN: 1424-8220. DOI: 10.3390/s22041357. URL: https://www.mdpi.com/1424-8220/22/4/1357.

[33] Ylenia Casali, Nazli Yonca Aydin, and Tina Comes. "Machine learning for spatial analyses in urban areas: a scoping review". *Sustainable Cities and Society* 85 (2022), page 104050. ISSN: 2210-6707. DOI: https://doi.org/10.1016/j.scs.2022.104050. URL: https://www.sciencedirect.com/science/article/pii/S2210670722003687.

[34] F. Çetin and M. O. Kulekci. "AN EXPERIMENTAL ANALYSIS OF SPATIAL INDEXING ALGORITHMS FOR REAL TIME SAFETY CRITICAL MAP APPLICATION". *ISPRS Annals of the Photogrammetry, Remote Sensing and Spatial Information Sciences* V-4-2021 (2021), pages 41–48. DOI: 10.5194/isprs-annals-V-4-2021-41-2021. URL: https://isprs-annals.copernicus.org/articles/V-4-2021/41/2021/.

[35] Gordon Chalmers. "Introducing ligand GA, a genetic algorithm molecular tool for automated protein inhibitor design". *Scientific Reports* 12.1 (2022), pages 1–20. DOI: 10.1038/s41598-022-22281-2. URL: https://doi.org/10.1038/s41598-022-22281-2.

[36] Timothy M. Chan. "Optimal Output-Sensitive Convex Hull Algorithms in Two and Three Dimensions". *Discrete & Computational Geometry* 16 (1996), pages 361–368.

[37] R. Qi Charles, Hao Su, Mo Kaichun, and Leonidas J. Guibas. "PointNet: Deep Learning on Point Sets for 3D Classification and Segmentation". *2017 IEEE Conference on Computer Vision and Pattern Recognition (CVPR)*. 2017, pages 77–85. DOI: 10.1109/CVPR.2017.16.

[38] Hongyan Che, Yaozhong Pan, Xingsheng Xia, Xiufang Zhu, Le Li, Yongsheng Huang, Xuechang Zheng, and Lingang Wang and. "A new transferable deep learning approach for crop mapping". *GIScience & Remote Sensing* 61.1 (2024), page 2395700. DOI: 10.1080/15481603.2024.2395700.

[39] Wei Chen and Zhikai Gan. "Application of Computer Triangulation Algorithm in Biomechanical Modeling". *CAIBDA 2022; 2nd International Conference on Artificial Intelligence, Big Data and Algorithms*. 2022, pages 1–4.

[40] Yichuan Chen, Manabu Tsukada, and Hiroshi Esaki. "Reinforcement Learning Based Optimal Camera Placement for Depth Observation of Indoor Scenes". *2021 IEEE International Conference on Networking, Sensing and Control (ICNSC)*. Volume 1. 2021, pages 1–6. DOI: 10.1109/ICNSC52481.2021.9702214.

[41] Biswanath Chowdhury and Gautam Garai. "A review on multiple sequence alignment from the perspective of genetic algorithm". *Genomics* 109.5 (2017), pages 419–431. ISSN: 0888-7543. DOI: https://doi.org/10.1016/j.ygeno.2017.06.007. URL: https://www.sciencedirect.com/science/article/pii/S0888754317300551.

[42] Christos Chronis, Georgios Anagnostopoulos, Elena Politi, George Dimitrakopoulos, and Iraklis Varlamis. "Dynamic Navigation in Unconstrained Environments Using Reinforcement Learning Algorithms". *IEEE Access* 11 (2023), pages 117984–118001. DOI: 10.1109/ACCESS.2023.3326435.

[43] Xu Yi-Chun, Bangjun Lei, and Emile A. Hendriks. "Camera Network Coverage Improving by Particle Swarm Optimization". *EURASIP Journal on Image and Video Processing* 2011 (2010), pages 1–10. DOI: 10.1155/2011/458283.

[44] Yu-Min Chung, Sarah Day, and Chuan-Shen Hu. "A multi-parameter persistence framework for mathematical morphology". *Scientific Reports* 12.1 (2022), pages 1–25. DOI: 10.1038/s41598-022-09464-7. URL: https://doi.org/10.1038/s41598-022-09464-7.

[45] Václav Chvátal. "A combinatorial theorem in plane geometry". *Journal of Combinatorial Theory, Series B* 18.1 (1975), pages 39–41. ISSN: 0095-8956. DOI: https://doi.org/10.1016/0095-8956(75)90061-1.

[46] Guillaume Coiffier, Justine Basselin, Nicolas Ray, and Dmitry Sokolov. "Parametric Surface Fitting on Airborne Lidar Point Clouds for Building Reconstruction". *Computer-Aided Design* 140 (2021), page 103090. ISSN: 0010-4485. DOI: https://doi.org/10.1016/j.cad.2021.103090. URL: https://www.sciencedirect.com/science/article/pii/S0010448521001019.

[47] Thomas H. Cormen, Charles E. Leiserson, Ronald L. Rivest, and Clifford Stein. *Introduction to Algorithms*. 4th. The MIT Press, 2022, page 1312. ISBN: 978-0262046305.

[48] Robert Cupec, Ivan Vidović, Damir Filko, and Petra Đurović. "Object recognition based on convex hull alignment". *Pattern Recognition* 102 (2020), page 107199. ISSN: 0031-3203. DOI: https://doi.org/10.1016/j.patcog.2020.107199. URL: https://www.sciencedirect.com/science/article/pii/S0031320320300066.

[49] Sandip Das, Subhadeep Ranjan Dev, and Sarvottamananda. "A worst-case optimal algorithm to compute the Minkowski sum of convex polytopes". *Discrete Applied Mathematics* 350 (2024), pages 44–61. ISSN: 0166-218X. DOI: https://doi.org/10.1016/j.dam.2024.02.004. URL: https://www.sciencedirect.com/science/article/pii/S0166218X24000672.

[50] Satyan L. Devadoss and Joseph O'Rourke. *Discrete and Computational Geometry*. Cambridge University Press, 2011, page 272. ISBN: 978-0691145532.

[51] Jorge Díaz, Claudio Lobos, and Nancy Hitschfeld-Kahler. "Node-Based Data Structure for Balancing Process Optimization of Quadtree Meshes". *2023 42nd IEEE International Conference of the Chilean Computer Science Society (SCCC)*. 2023, pages 1–7. DOI: 10.1109/SCCC59417.2023.10315743.

[52] Jia Duan, Yuan Yan Tang, Chu Yu Guo, Chi Fang, and Xian Chuan Hu. "Boundary expansion: An hidden surface removal method based on boundary detection for discrete points". *2013 International Conference on Wavelet Analysis and Pattern Recognition*. 2013, pages 110–114. DOI: 10.1109/ICWAPR.2013.6599301.

[53] A. Elnagar and L. Lulu. "An art gallery-based approach to autonomous robot motion planning in global environments". *2005 IEEE/RSJ International Conference on Intelligent Robots and Systems*. 2005, pages 2079–2084.

[54] Yahia S. Elshakhs, Kyriakos M. Deliparaschos, Themistoklis Charalambous, Gabriele Oliva, and Argyrios Zolotas. "A Comprehensive Survey on Delaunay Triangulation: Applications, Algorithms, and Implementations Over CPUs, GPUs, and FPGAs". *IEEE Access* 12 (2024), pages 12562–12585. DOI: 10.1109/ACCESS.2024.3354709.

[55] Ramón Espinel, Gricelda Herrera-Franco, José Luis Rivadeneira García, and Paulo Escandón-Panchana. "Artificial Intelligence in Agricultural Mapping: A Review". *Agriculture* 14.7 (2024). ISSN: 2077-0472. DOI: 10.3390/agriculture14071071. URL: https://www.mdpi.com/2077-0472/14/7/1071.

[56] Ahmed S. Fadel, Mohamed Belal, and Mostafa-sami M. Mostafa. "Protein Data Representation: A Survey". *International Journal of Computer Applications* 56.11 (2012), pages 22–27. ISSN: 0975-8887. DOI: 10.5120/8936-3075. URL: https://ijcaonline.org/archives/volume56/number11/8936-3075/.

[57] Jillian Farquhar, Nicolette Michels, and Julie Robson. "Triangulation in industrial qualitative case study research: Widening the scope". *Industrial Marketing Management* 87 (2020), pages 160–170. ISSN: 0019-8501. DOI: https://doi.org/10.1016/j.indmarman.2020.02.001.

[58] Anis Farshian, Markus Götz, Gabriele Cavallaro, Charlotte Debus, Matthias Nießner, Jón Atli Benediktsson, and Achim Streit. "Deep-Learning-Based 3-D Surface Reconstruction—A Survey". *Proceedings of the IEEE* 111.11 (2023), pages 1464–1501. DOI: 10.1109/JPROC.2023.3321433.

[59] Carlos Eloy Federico, Qiong Wu, Richard T. Olsson, and Antonio J. Capezza. "Three-dimensional (3D) morphological and liquid absorption assessment of sustainable biofoams absorbents using X-ray microtomography analysis". *Polymer Testing* 116 (2022), page 107753. ISSN: 0142-9418. DOI: https://doi.org/10.1016/j.polymertesting.2022.107753. URL: https://www.sciencedirect.com/science/article/pii/S0142941822002744.

[60] Luca Ferrari and Enrico Pirozzi. *Learn PostgreSQL. Build and Manage High-Performance Database Solutions Using PostgreSQL 16*. Birmingham, UK: Packt Publishing, 2023. ISBN: 978-1-8389-8528-8.

[61] Yuval Fisher. *Fractal Image Compression: Theory and Application*. Reprint of the 1st ed. 1995. Springer Science & Business Media, 2011. ISBN: 978-1-4612-6908-3.

[62] Steve Fisk. "A short proof of Chvátal's Watchman Theorem". *Journal of Combinatorial Theory, Series B* 24.3 (1978), page 374. DOI: https://doi.org/10.1016/0095-8956(78)90059-X.

[63] Gianni Franchi, Amin Fehri, and Angela Yao. "Deep morphological networks". *Pattern Recognition* 102 (2020), page 107246. ISSN: 0031-3203. DOI: https://doi.org/10.1016/j.patcog.2020.107246. URL: https://www.sciencedirect.com/science/article/pii/S0031320320300522.

[64] Cheng Fu, Zhiyong Zhou, Yanan Xin, and Robert Weibel and. "Reasoning cartographic knowledge in deep learning-based map generalization with explainable AI". *International Journal of Geographical Information Science* 38.10 (2024), pages 2061–2082. DOI: 10.1080/13658816.2024.2369535. eprint: https://doi.org/10.1080/13658816.2024.2369535. URL: https://doi.org/10.1080/13658816.2024.2369535.

[65] Enric Galceran and Marc Carreras. "A survey on coverage path planning for robotics". *Robotics and Autonomous Systems* 61.12 (2013), pages 1258–1276. ISSN: 0921-8890. DOI: https://doi.org/10.1016/j.robot.2013.09.004. URL: https://www.sciencedirect.com/science/article/pii/S092188901300167X.

[66] Eric Galin, Eric Guérin, Adrien Peytavie, Guillaume Cordonnier, Marie-Paule Cani, Bedrich Benes, and James Gain. "A Review of Digital Terrain Modeling". *Computer Graphics Forum* 38.2 (2019), pages 553–577. DOI: https://doi.org/10.1111/cgf.13657. eprint: https://onlinelibrary.wiley.com/doi/pdf/10.1111/cgf.13657. URL: https://onlinelibrary.wiley.com/doi/abs/10.1111/cgf.13657.

[67] Xiaorong Gao, Haowen Yan, Xiaomin Lu, Xiaolong Wang, and Rong Wang. "A Novel Approach to Urban Village Extraction and Generalization from Digital Line Graphics Using the Computational Geometric Method and the Modified Hausdorff Distance". *ISPRS International Journal of Geo-Information* 13.6 (2024). ISSN: 2220-9964. DOI: 10.3390/ijgi13060198. URL: https://www.mdpi.com/2220-9964/13/6/198.

[68] Mario Gilcher and Thomas Udelhoven. "Field Geometry and the Spatial and Temporal Generalization of Crop Classification Algorithms—A Randomized Approach to Compare Pixel Based and Convolution Based Methods". *Remote Sensing* 13.4 (2021). ISSN: 2072-4292. DOI: 10.3390/rs13040775. URL: https://www.mdpi.com/2072-4292/13/4/775.

[69] N.A. Golias and R.W. Dutton. "Delaunay triangulation and 3D adaptive mesh generation". *Finite Elements in Analysis and Design* 25.3 (1997). Adaptive Meshing, Part 2, pages 331–341. ISSN: 0168-874X. DOI: https://doi.org/10.1016/S0168-874X(96)00054-6. URL: https://www.sciencedirect.com/science/article/pii/S0168874X96000546.

[70] J. Gonzalez-Barbosa, T. Garcia-Ramirez, J. Salas, J. Hurtado-Ramos, and J. Rico-Jimenez. "Optimal camera placement for total coverage". *2009 IEEE International Conference on Robotics and Automation*. 2009, pages 844–848.

[71] Jacob E. Goodman, Joseph O'Rourke, and Csaba D. Tóth. *Handbook of Discrete and Computational Geometry*. 3rd. Chapman and Hall/CRC, 2017, page 1948. ISBN: 978-1498711395.

[72] Osamu Gotoh. "Multiple sequence alignment: Algorithms and applications". *Advances in Biophysics* 36 (1999), pages 159–206. ISSN: 0065-227X. DOI: https://doi.org/10.1016/S0065-227X(99)80007-0. URL: https://www.sciencedirect.com/science/article/pii/S0065227X99800070.

[73] Shalini Govil-Pai. *Principles of Computer Graphics*. Springer New York, 2015, page 296. ISBN: 978-0-387-95504-9.

[74] Ronald L. Graham. "An Efficient Algorithm for Determining the Convex Hull of a Finite Planar Set". *Information Processing Letters* 1.4 (1972), pages 132–133. DOI: 10.1016/0020-0190(72)90045-2.

[75] Hui Guo and Jie He. "An Improved Fractal Coding Method based on K-means Clustering". Jan. 2016. DOI: 10.2991/mmme-16.2016.67.

[76] Vivek Gurve, Smita Mahajan, and Shivali Amit Wagle. "Robot motion planning: methods, challenges, and future directions". *International Journal of Intelligent Robotics and Applications* (2025). DOI: 10.1007/s41315-025-00455-1. URL: https://doi.org/10.1007/s41315-025-00455-1.

[77] Ervin Győri, Frank Hoffmann, Klaus Kriegel, and Thomas Shermer. "Generalized guarding and partitioning for rectilinear polygons". *Computational Geometry* 6.1 (1996), pages 21–44. ISSN: 0925-7721. DOI: https://doi.org/10.1016/0925-7721(96)00014-4.

[78] Pouria Hamidpour, Alireza Araee, and Majid Baniassadi. "Transfer learning-based techniques for efficient 3D-reconstruction of functionally graded materials". *Materials & Design* 248 (2024), page 113415. ISSN: 0264-1275. DOI: https://doi.org/10.1016/j.matdes.2024.113415. URL: https://www.sciencedirect.com/science/article/pii/S0264127524007901.

[79] Konstantin Hauch and Claudia Redenbach. "Mathematical Morphology on Directional Data". *Journal of Mathematical Imaging and Vision* 66.6 (2024), pages 1019–1032. DOI: 10.1007/s10851-024-01210-0. URL: https://doi.org/10.1007/s10851-024-01210-0.

[80] Andries M. Heyns. "Optimisation of surveillance camera site locations and viewing angles using a novel multi-attribute, multi-objective genetic algorithm: A day/night anti-poaching application". *Computers, Environment and Urban Systems* 88 (2021), page 101638. ISSN: 0198-9715. DOI: https://doi.org/10.1016/j.compenvurbsys.2021.101638. URL: https://www.sciencedirect.com/science/article/pii/S0198971521000454.

[81] Nguyen Thanh Hiep, Toan Le, Quang Nguyen, Do Le Huu, Giang Huong Ngo, Dung Truong, and Khang Nguyen. "An Empirical Study of a Shape-Adaptive Approach in Aerial Object Detection". *2024 13th International Conference on Control, Automation and Information Sciences (ICCAIS)*. 2024, pages 1–6. DOI: 10.1109/ICCAIS63750.2024.10814525.

[82] Øyvind Hjelle and Morten Dæhlen. "Algorithms for Delaunay Triangulation". *Triangulations and Applications*. Springer Berlin Heidelberg, 2006, pages 73–93. ISBN: 978-3-540-33261-9. DOI: 10.1007/3-540-33261-8_4.

[83] F. Hoffmann, M. Kaufmann, and K. Kriegel. "The art gallery theorem for polygons with holes". *[1991] Proceedings 32nd Annual Symposium of Foundations of Computer Science*. 1991, pages 39–48. DOI: https://10.1109/SFCS.1991.185346.

[84] Pavan Holur, K C Enevoldsen, Shreyas Rajesh, Lajoyce Mboning, Thalia Georgiou, Louis-S Bouchard, Matteo Pellegrini, and Vwani Roychowdhury. "Embed-Search-Align: DNA sequence alignment using Transformer models". *Bioinformatics* 41.3 (Feb. 2025), pages 1–9. ISSN: 1367-4811. DOI: https://doi.org/10.1093/bioinformatics/btaf041.

[85] Zexin Hu, Kun Hu, Clinton Mo, Lei Pan, and Zhiyong Wang. "Terrain diffusion network: climatic-aware terrain generation with geological sketch guidance". *Proceedings of the Thirty-Eighth AAAI Conference on Artificial Intelligence and Thirty-Sixth Conference on Innovative Applications of Artificial Intelligence and Fourteenth Symposium on Educational Advances in Artificial Intelligence*. AAAI'24/IAAI'24/EAAI'24. AAAI Press, 2024. ISBN: 978-1-57735-887-9. DOI: 10.1609/aaai.v38i11.29150. URL: https://doi.org/10.1609/aaai.v38i11.29150.

[86] Zhe Huang, Yongcai Wang, Jie Wen, Peng Wang, and Xudong Cai. "An object detection algorithm combining semantic and geometric information of the 3D point cloud". *Advanced Engineering Informatics* 56 (2023), page 101971. ISSN: 1474-0346. DOI: https://doi.org/10.1016/j.aei.2023.101971. URL: https://www.sciencedirect.com/science/article/pii/S147403462300099X.

[87] J. Huerta, M. Chover, R. Quiros, R. Vivo, and J. Ribelles. "Binary space partitioning trees: a multiresolution approach". *Proceedings. 1997 IEEE Conference on Information Visualization (Cat. No.97TB100165)*. 1997, pages 148–154. DOI: 10.1109/IV.1997.626502.

[88] Ilmar Hurkxkens and Mathias Bernhard. "Computational Terrain Modeling with Distance Functions for Large Scale Landscape Design". en. Volume 2019. 4. Berlin: Wichmann, 2019, pages 222–230. DOI: 10.3929/ethz-b-000340536.

[89] Mohammed K. Ibrahim, Umi Kalsom Yusof, Taiseer Abdalla Elfadil Eisa, and Maged Nasser. "Bioinspired Algorithms for Multiple Sequence Alignment: A Systematic Review and Roadmap". *Applied Sciences* 14.6 (2024). ISSN: 2076-3417. DOI: https://doi.org/10.3390/app14062433. URL: https://www.mdpi.com/2076-3417/14/6/2433.

[90] Mohamed Issa, Mennahtullah Mabrouk, Bola Hosny, Abdelrahman Hazem, and Mostafa I. Soliman. "Sequence Alignment Using Deep Learning". *Deep Learning and Computer Vision: Models and Biomedical Applications: Volume 2*. Edited by Uma N. Dulhare and Essam Halim Houssein. Singapore: Springer Nature Singapore, 2025, pages 1–18.

[91] Malihe Jahani, Bahram Sadeghi Bigham, and Abbas Askari. "An Ant Colony Algorithm for the Minimum Weight Triangulation". *2010 International Conference on Computational Science and Its Applications*. 2010, pages 81–85. DOI: 10.1109/ICCSA.2010.38.

[92] Ajay James. "A New Approach to Fractal Image Compression Using DBSCAN". *International Journal of Electrical Energy* 2 (July 2014), pages 18–22. DOI: 10.12720/ijoee.2.1.18-22.

[93] O. Jansen, E. d'Humières, X. Ribeyre, S. Jequier, and V.T. Tikhonchuk. "Tree code for collision detection of large numbers of particles applied to the Breit–Wheeler process". *Journal of Computational Physics* 355 (2018), pages 582–596. ISSN: 0021-9991. DOI: https://doi.org/10.1016/j.jcp.2017.11.021. URL: https://www.sciencedirect.com/science/article/pii/S0021999117308598.

[94] Ralph E. Jarvis. *On the identification of the convex hull of a finite set of points in the plane*. Technical Report. Institute for Information Sciences, University of Chicago, 1973.

[95] Baoqing Jiang and Jingjing Han. "Improvement in the Cohen-Sutherland line segment clipping algorithm". *2013 IEEE International Conference on Granular Computing (GrC)*. 2013, pages 157–161. DOI: 10.1109/GrC.2013.6740399.

[96] Minghui Jiang, Xiaojun Qi, and Pedro J. Tejada. "A Computational-Geometry Approach to Digital Image Contour Extraction". *Transactions on Computational Science XIII*. Edited by Marina L. Gavrilova and C. J. Kenneth Tan. Berlin, Heidelberg: Springer Berlin Heidelberg, 2011, pages 13–43. ISBN: 978-3-642-22619-9. DOI: 10.1007/978-3-642-22619-9_2. URL: https://doi.org/10.1007/978-3-642-22619-9_2.

[97] Q. Jiang, K. Cai, and F. Xu. "Obstacle-avoidance path planning based on the improved artificial potential field for a 5 degrees of freedom bending robot". *Mechanical Sciences* 14.1 (2023), pages 87–97. DOI: 10.5194/ms-14-87-2023. URL: https://ms.copernicus.org/articles/14/87/2023/.

[98] Wanqi Jiang, Yafei Liu, Mujiao Ouyang, and Xiaoguo Zhang. "MT-NeRF: Neural implicit representation based on multi-resolution geometric feature planes". *Computers & Graphics* 126 (2025), page 104157. ISSN: 0097-8493. DOI: https://doi.org/10.1016/j.cag.2024.104157. URL: https://www.sciencedirect.com/science/article/pii/S0097849324002929.

[99] Yinghui Jiang, Liyang Xiong, Xiaohui Huang, Sijin Li, and Wang Shen. "Super-resolution for terrain modeling using deep learning in high mountain Asia". *International Journal of Applied Earth Observation and Geoinformation* 118 (2023), page 103296. ISSN: 1569-8432. DOI: https://doi.org/10.1016/j.jag.2023.103296. URL: https://www.sciencedirect.com/science/article/pii/S1569843223001188.

[100] Zhenghong Jiang and Chunrong Zhou. "Comprehensive Study on Shape Representation Methods for Shape-Based Object Recognition". *Journal of Optics* 53 (Aug. 2023), pages 1890–1896. DOI: 10.1007/s12596-023-01356-x.

[101] Abdulhayat M. Jibrin, Mohammad Al-Suwaiyan, Zaher Mundher Yaseen, and Sani I. Abba. "New perspective on density-based spatial clustering of applications with noise for groundwater assessment". *Journal of Hydrology* 661 (2025), page 133566. ISSN: 0022-1694. DOI: https://doi.org/10.1016/j.jhydrol.2025.133566. URL: https://www.sciencedirect.com/science/article/pii/S0022169425009047.

[102] Manish Joshi, Ambuj Kumar Agarwal, and Bhumika Gupta. "Fractal Image Compression and Its Techniques: A Review". *Soft Computing: Theories and Applications*. Edited by Kanad Ray, Tarun K. Sharma, Sanyog Rawat, R. K. Saini, and Anirban Bandyopadhyay. Singapore: Springer Singapore, 2019, pages 235–243. ISBN: 978-981-13-0589-4.

[103] Michael Kallay. "The complexity of incremental convex hull algorithms in Rd". *Information Processing Letters* 19.4 (1984), page 197. ISSN: 0020-0190. DOI: 10.1016/0020-0190(84)90084-X.

[104] Kazutaka Katoh. *Multiple Sequence Alignment*. 1st 1. Humana New York, NY, 2021, page 321. ISBN: 978-1-0716-1035-0.

[105] Kornél Katona, Husam A. Neamah, and Péter Korondi. "Obstacle Avoidance and Path Planning Methods for Autonomous Navigation of Mobile Robot". *Sensors* 24.11 (2024). ISSN: 1424-8220. DOI: 10.3390/s24113573. URL: https://www.mdpi.com/1424-8220/24/11/3573.

[106] Matthew J. Katz and Gabriel S. Roisman. "On guarding the vertices of rectilinear domains". *Computational Geometry* 39.3 (2008), pages 219–228. ISSN: 0925-7721. DOI: https://doi.org/10.1016/j.comgeo.2007.02.002.

[107] Iman Khosravi. "Advancements in crop mapping through remote sensing: A comprehensive review of concept, data sources, and procedures over four decades". *Remote Sensing Applications: Society and Environment* 38 (2025), page 101527. ISSN: 2352-9385. DOI: https://doi.org/10.1016/j.rsase.2025.101527. URL: https://www.sciencedirect.com/science/article/pii/S2352938525000801.

[108] Jongpil Kim and Vladimir Pavlovic. "A Shape-Based Approach for Salient Object Detection Using Deep Learning". Volume 9908. Oct. 2016, pages 455–470. ISBN: 978-3-319-46492-3. DOI: 10.1007/978-3-319-46493-0_28.

[109] Juyoung Kim, Seoyoung Hong, Seungchan Jeong, Seula Park, and Kiyun Yu. "SGIR-Tree: Integrating R-Tree Spatial Indexing as Subgraphs in Graph Database Management Systems". *ISPRS International Journal of Geo-Information* 13.10 (2024). ISSN: 2220-9964. DOI: 10.3390/ijgi13100346. URL: https://www.mdpi.com/2220-9964/13/10/346.

[110] Donald E. Knuth. *The Art of Computer Programming, Volume 4B: Combinatorial Algorithms*. 1st. Addison-Wesley Professional, 2022, page 736. ISBN: 978-0201038064.

[111] Katarzyna Kopczewska. "Spatial machine learning: new opportunities for regional science". *The Annals of Regional Science* 68.3 (2022), pages 714–755. DOI: 10.1007/s00168-021-01101-x. URL: https://doi.org/10.1007/s00168-021-01101-x.

[112] Erwin Kreyszig. *Advanced Engineering Mathematics*. 10th. Wiley, 2020, page 1280. ISBN: 978-1119455929.

[113] Milind Kulkarni, Sanskruti Khedkar, Sanket Kumbhar, Khushi Mohod, Shantanu Mandalpure, and Yashashri Meshram. "Fractal Image Encoding:A Comparative Study of Compression Techniques". *2024 10th International Conference on Smart Computing and Communication (ICSCC)*. 2024, pages 383–387. DOI: 10.1109/ICSCC62041.2024.10690803.

[114] D. Lee and A. Lin. "Computational complexity of art gallery problems". *IEEE Transactions on Information Theory* 32.2 (1986), pages 276–282. DOI: https://10.1109/TIT.1986.1057165.

[115] D. T. Lee and B. J. Schachter. "Two algorithms for constructing a Delaunay triangulation". *International Journal of Computer & Information Sciences* 9.3 (1980), pages 219–242. DOI: 10.1007/BF00977785.

[116] Kent D. Lee and Steve Hubbard. *Data Structures and Algorithms with Python*. Springer Cham, 2024. ISBN: 978-3-031-42208-9. DOI: https://doi.org/10.1007/978-3-031-42209-6.

[117] Shung-Shing Lee, Shi-Jinn Horng, Horng-Ren Tsai, and Shun-Shan Tsai. "Building a quadtree and its applications on a reconfigurable mesh". *Pattern Recognition* 29.9 (1996), pages 1571–1579. ISSN: 0031-3203. DOI: https://doi.org/10.1016/0031-3203(96)00003-9.

[118] Mengqi Li, Wen Dai, Guojie Wang, Bo Wang, Kai Chen, Yifei Gao, and Solomon Obiri Yeboah Amankwah. "Reconstructing high-resolution DEMs from 3D terrain features using conditional generative adversarial networks". *International Journal of Applied Earth Observation and Geoinformation* 133 (2024), page 104115. ISSN: 1569-8432. DOI: https://doi.org/10.1016/j.jag.2024.104115. URL: https://www.sciencedirect.com/science/article/pii/S1569843224004692.

[119] Wenjing Li, Qiuxia Pan, Shiaofang Liang, and Jiang Yin Jiao. "Research on fractal image compression hybrid algorithm based on convolutional neural network and gene expression programming". *Journal of Algorithms & Computational Technology* 13 (2019), page 1748302619874196. DOI: 10.1177/1748302619874196.

[120] Haojian Liang, Shaohua Wang, Song Gao, Huilai Li, Cheng Su, Hao Lu, Xueyan Zhang, Xi Chen, and Yinan Chen and. "Deephullnet: a deep learning approach for solving the convex hull and concave hull problems with transformer". *International Journal of Digital Earth* 17.1 (2024), page 2358843. DOI: 10.1080/17538947.2024.2358843.

[121] Yuan-Hsun Liao, Po-Chun Chang, and Hsiao-Hui Li. "Reinforcement Learning for Optimize Coverage in Art Gallery Problem Using Q-Learning Based in Grid World". *IEEE Access* 13 (2025), pages 52711–52724. DOI: 10.1109/ACCESS.2025.3553036.

[122] Siyou Lin, Dong Xiao, Zuoqiang Shi, and Bin Wang. "Surface Reconstruction from Point Clouds without Normals by Parametrizing the Gauss Formula". *ACM Trans. Graph.* 42.2 (Oct. 2022). ISSN: 0730-0301. DOI: 10.1145/3554730. URL: https://doi.org/10.1145/3554730.

[123] Bohong Liu and Ying Yan. "An improved fractal image coding based on the quadtree". *2010 3rd International Congress on Image and Signal Processing*. Volume 2. 2010, pages 529–532. DOI: 10.1109/CISP.2010.5647658.

[124] Shuai Liu, Zhibin Zhang, Lingyun Qi, and Ming Ma. "A fractal image encoding method based on statistical loss used in agricultural image compression". *Multimedia Tools Appl.* 75.23 (Dec. 2016), pages 15525–15536. ISSN: 1380-7501. DOI: 10.1007/s11042-014-2446-8. URL: https://doi.org/10.1007/s11042-014-2446-8.

[125] Yahui Liu, Bin Tian, Yisheng Lv, Lingxi Li, and Fei-Yue Wang. "Point Cloud Classification Using Content-Based Transformer via Clustering in Feature Space". *IEEE/CAA Journal of Automatica Sinica* 11.1 (2024), pages 231–239. DOI: 10.1109/JAS.2023.123432.

[126] Paul A. Longley, Michael F. Goodchild, David J. Maguire, and David W. Rhind. *Geographic Information Systems & Science*. 3th. John Wiley & Sons Inc, 2010, page 477. ISBN: 978-0470721445.

[127] Gian Paolo Lorenzetto, Amitava Datta, and Richard C Thomas. "A fast trapezoidation technique for planar polygons". *Computers & Graphics* 26.2 (2002), pages 281–289. ISSN: 0097-8493. DOI: https://doi.org/10.1016/S0097-8493(01)00180-7. URL: https://www.sciencedirect.com/science/article/pii/S0097849301001807.

[128] Tingyu Lu, Luhe Wan, and Lei Wang. "Fine crop classification in high resolution remote sensing based on deep learning". *Frontiers in Environmental Science* Volume 10 - 2022 (2022). ISSN: 2296-665X. DOI: 10.3389/fenvs.2022.991173. URL: https://www.frontiersin.org/journals/environmental-science/articles/10.3389/fenvs.2022.991173.

[129] Zhe Luo, Wenjing Jia, and Stuart Perry. "Compressed point cloud classification with point-based edge sampling". *EURASIP Journal on Image and Video Processing* 2024 (2024), pages 1–15. DOI: 10.1186/s13640-024-00637-0. URL: https://doi.org/10.1186/s13640-024-00637-0.

[130] Ling Ma, Rafael Sacks, Uri Kattel, and Tanya Bloch. "3D Object Classification Using Geometric Features and Pairwise Relationships". *Comput.-Aided Civ. Infrastruct. Eng.* 33.2 (Feb. 2018), pages 152–164. ISSN: 1093-9687. DOI: 10.1111/mice.12336. URL: https://doi.org/10.1111/mice.12336.

[131] Kenneth J.M. MacLean. *A Geometric Analysis of the Platonic Solids and Other Semi-Regular Polyhedra*. Loving Healing Press, 2007, page 164. ISBN: 978-1932690996.

[132] Jingjing Mai, Qisheng Feng, Shuai Fu, Ruijing Wang, Shuhui Zhang, Ruoqi Zhang, and Tiangang Liang. "Enhancing Crop Type Mapping in Data-Scarce Regions Through Transfer Learning: A Case Study of the Hexi Corridor". *Remote Sensing* 17.9 (2025). ISSN: 2072-4292. DOI: 10.3390/rs17091494. URL: https://www.mdpi.com/2072-4292/17/9/1494.

[133] Avraham Margalit and Gary D. Knott. "An algorithm for computing the union, intersection or difference of two polygons". *Computers & Graphics* 13.2 (1989), pages 167–183. ISSN: 0097-8493. DOI: 10.1016/0097-8493(89)90059-9.

[134] Steve Marschner and Peter Shirley. *Fundamentals of Computer Graphics*. 4th. A K Peters/CRC Press, 2015, page 752. ISBN: 978-1482229394.

[135] Martin J. Menten, Johannes C. Paetzold, Veronika A. Zimmer, Suprosanna Shit, Ivan Ezhov, Robbie Holland, Monika Probst, Julia A. Schnabel, and Daniel Rueckert. "A skeletonization algorithm for gradient-based optimization". *2023 IEEE/CVF International Conference on Computer Vision (ICCV)*. 2023, pages 21337–21346. DOI: 10.1109/ICCV51070.2023.01956.

[136] Henrique G. Momm, Racha ElKadiri, and Wesley Porter. "Crop-Type Classification for Long-Term Modeling: An Integrated Remote Sensing and Machine Learning Approach". *Remote Sensing* 12.3 (2020). ISSN: 2072-4292. DOI: 10.3390/rs12030449. URL: https://www.mdpi.com/2072-4292/12/3/449.

[137] André Müller, Bertil Schmidt, Richard Membarth, Roland Leißa, and Sebastian Hack. "AnySeq/GPU: a novel approach for faster sequence alignment on GPUs". *Proceedings of the 36th ACM International Conference on Supercomputing*. ICS '22. Virtual Event: Association for Computing Machinery, 2022. ISBN: 9781450392815. DOI: https://doi.org/10.1145/3524059.3532376.

[138] Wolfgang Mulzer and Günter Rote. "Minimum-weight triangulation is NP-hard". *J. ACM* 55.2 (May 2008). ISSN: 0004-5411. DOI: 10.1145/1346330.1346336. URL: https://doi.org/10.1145/1346330.1346336.

[139] AkshatKumar Nigam, Robert Pollice, and Alán Aspuru-Guzik. "Parallel tempered genetic algorithm guided by deep neural networks for inverse molecular design". *Digital Discovery* 1 (4 2022), pages 390–404. DOI: 10.1039/D2DD00003B. URL: http://dx.doi.org/10.1039/D2DD00003B.

[140] Jinyun Niu, Fangfang Zhu, Taosheng Xu, Shunfang Wang, and Wenwen Min. "Deep clustering representation of spatially resolved transcriptomics data using multi-view variational graph auto-encoders with consensus clustering". *Computational and Structural Biotechnology Journal* 23 (2024), pages 4369–4383. ISSN: 2001-0370. DOI: https://doi.org/10.1016/j.csbj.2024.11.041. URL: https://www.sciencedirect.com/science/article/pii/S2001037024004124.

[141] Joseph O'Rourke. *Art Gallery Theorems and Algorithms*. Oxford University Press, 1987, page 273.

[142] Joseph O'Rourke, Chi-Bin Chien, Thomas Olson, and David Naddor. "A new linear algorithm for intersecting convex polygons". *Computer Graphics and Image Processing* 19.4 (1982), pages 384–391. ISSN: 0146-664X. DOI: https://doi.org/10.1016/0146-664X(82)90023-5.

[143] Joseph O'Rourke. *Computational Geometry in C*. 2nd. Cambridge University Press, 1998, page 392. ISBN: 978-0521649766.

[144] PETER VAN OOSTEROM. "A modified binary space partitioning tree for geographic information systems". *International journal of geographical information systems* 4.2 (1990), pages 133–146. DOI: 10.1080/02693799008941535.

[145] Taminder Pabla, Ajmery Sultana, and Wenjun Lin. "Tracing Economic Vibrancy: AI-Driven Analysis of Geographic Clustering in Legal Businesses". *2024 IEEE/ACIS 27th International Conference on Software Engineering, Artificial Intelligence, Networking and Parallel/Distributed Computing (SNPD)*. 2024, pages 245–250. DOI: 10.1109/SNPD61259.2024.10673950.

[146] Marija Popović, Joshua Ott, Julius Rückin, and Mykel J. Kochenderfer. "Learning-based methods for adaptive informative path planning". *Robotics and Autonomous Systems* 179 (2024), page 104727. ISSN: 0921-8890. DOI: https://doi.org/10.1016/j.robot.2024.104727. URL: https://www.sciencedirect.com/science/article/pii/S0921889024001118.

[147] F. P. Preparata and S. J. Hong. "Convex hulls of finite sets of points in two and three dimensions". *Commun. ACM* 20.2 (1977), pages 87–93. ISSN: 0001-0782. DOI: 10.1145/359423.359430.

[148] Franco P. Preparata and Michael Ian Shamos. *Computational Geometry: An Introduction.* Texts and Monographs in Computer Science. New York: Springer, 1985, page 398. ISBN: 978-1-4612-7010-2.

[149] Pratama Aditya Putra, Jos Timanta Tarigan, and Elviawaty Muisa Zamzami. "Procedural 2D Dungeon Generation Using Binary Space Partition Algorithm And L-Systems". *2023 International Conference on Computer, Control, Informatics and its Applications (IC3INA)*. 2023, pages 365–369. DOI: 10.1109/IC3INA60834.2023.10285811.

[150] Liu Qiang, Huang Hao, Wang Yongmin, Liu Xu, Guo Liqian, and Huang Hao. "The KD-Tree-based nearest-neighbor search algorithm in GRID interpolation". *2012 International Conference on Image Analysis and Signal Processing*. 2012, pages 1–6. DOI: 10.1109/IASP.2012.6425061.

[151] Watanobe Y Kabir R and Naruse K. Islam MR. "Enhanced Robot Motion Block of A-Star Algorithm for Robotic Path Planning". *Sensors* 24.5 (2024), pages 1–30. DOI: https://doi.org/10.3390/s24051422.

[152] Anca Ralescu, Irene Díaz, and Luis J. Rodríguez-Muñiz. "A classification algorithm based on geometric and statistical information". *Journal of Computational and Applied Mathematics* 275 (2015), pages 335–344. ISSN: 0377-0427. DOI: https://doi.org/10.1016/j.cam.2014.07.012. URL: https://www.sciencedirect.com/science/article/pii/S0377042714003318.

[153] Amr Ezz El-Din Rashed, Hanan M. Amer, Mervat El-Seddek, and Hossam El-Din Moustafa. "Sequence Alignment Using Machine Learning-Based Needleman–Wunsch Algorithm". *IEEE Access* 9 (2021), pages 109522–109535. DOI: 10.1109/ACCESS.2021.3100408.

[154] Bharath Reddy and Richard Fields. "Multiple Sequence Alignment Algorithms in Bioinformatics". *Smart Trends in Computing and Communications*. Edited by Yu-Dong Zhang, Tomonobu Senjyu, Chakchai So-In, and Amit Joshi. Singapore: Springer Singapore, 2022, pages 89–98. ISBN: 978-981-16-4016-2.

[155] G. P. Obi Reddy. "Spatial Data Management, Analysis, and Modeling in GIS: Principles and Applications". *Geospatial Technologies in Land Resources Mapping, Monitoring and Management*. Edited by G. P. Obi Reddy and S. K. Singh. Cham: Springer International Publishing, 2018, pages 127–142. ISBN: 978-3-319-78711-4. DOI: 10.1007/978-3-319-78711-4_7. URL: https://doi.org/10.1007/978-3-319-78711-4_7.

[156] Philippe Rigaux, Michel Scholl, and Agnès Voisard. *Spatial Databases: With Application to GIS.* 1st. Morgan Kaufmann, 2001, page 410. ISBN: 978-1558605886.

[157] Fouad Sabry. *Binary Space Partitioning: Exploring Binary Space Partitioning: Foundations and Applications in Computer Vision.* Computer Vision. One Billion Knowledgeable, 2024, page 106.

[158] Sanjib Sadhu, Subhashis Hazarika, Kapil Kumar Jain, Saurav Basu, and Tanmay De. "GRP_CH Heuristic for Generating Random Simple Polygon". *Combinatorial Algorithms*. Springer Berlin Heidelberg, 2012, pages 293–302. ISBN: 978-3-642-35926-2.

[159]   Shima Sahebdivani, Hossein Arefi, and Mehdi Maboudi. "Deep Learning based Classification of Color Point Cloud for 3D Reconstruction of Interior Elements of Buildings". *2020 International Conference on Machine Vision and Image Processing (MVIP)*. 2020, pages 1–6. DOI: 10.1109/MVIP49855.2020.9116894.

[160]   Hanan Samet. "An Overview of Quadtrees, Octrees, and Related Hierarchical Data Structures". *Theoretical Foundations of Computer Graphics and CAD*. Edited by Rae A. Earnshaw. Berlin, Heidelberg: Springer Berlin Heidelberg, 1988, pages 51–68. ISBN: 978-3-642-83539-1.

[161]   Hanan Samet, Azriel Rosenfeld, Clifford A. Shaffer, and Robert E. Webber. "A geographic information system using quadtrees". *Pattern Recognition* 17.6 (1984), pages 647–656. ISSN: 0031-3203. DOI: https://doi.org/10.1016/0031-3203(84)90018-9. URL: https://www.sciencedirect.com/science/article/pii/0031320384900189.

[162]   A.D. Sands. "On generalised catalan numbers". *Discrete Mathematics* 21.2 (1978), pages 219–221. ISSN: 0012-365X. DOI: https://doi.org/10.1016/0012-365X(78)90094-8.

[163]   Jordy Sehn, Timothy D. Barfoot, and Jack Collier. "Off the Beaten Track: Laterally Weighted Motion Planning for Local Obstacle Avoidance". *IEEE Transactions on Field Robotics* 1 (2024), pages 249–275. DOI: 10.1109/TFR.2024.3492151.

[164]   Baji Shaik and Dinesh Kumar Chemuduru. *Procedural Programming with PostgreSQL PL/pgSQL*. Springer Nature, 2023. ISBN: 978-1-4842-9839. DOI: 10.1007/978-1-4842-9840-4.

[165]   Nicholas Sharp and Maks Ovsjanikov. "PointTriNet: Learned Triangulation of 3D Point Sets". *Computer Vision – ECCV 2020: 16th European Conference, Glasgow, UK, August 23–28, 2020, Proceedings, Part XXIII*. Glasgow, United Kingdom: Springer-Verlag, 2020, pages 762–778. ISBN: 978-3-030-58591-4. DOI: 10.1007/978-3-030-58592-1_45. URL: https://doi.org/10.1007/978-3-030-58592-1_45.

[166]   Zongyuan Shen, Palash Agrawal, James P. Wilson, Ryan Harvey, and Shalabh Gupta. "CPPNet: A Coverage Path Planning Network". *OCEANS 2021: San Diego – Porto*. 2021, pages 1–5. DOI: 10.23919/OCEANS44145.2021.9705671.

[167]   Jaemin Sim, Dongwoo Kim, Bomin Kim, Jieun Choi, and Juyong Lee. "Recent advances in AI-driven protein-ligand interaction predictions". *Current Opinion in Structural Biology* 92 (2025), page 103020. ISSN: 0959-440X. DOI: https://doi.org/10.1016/j.sbi.2025.103020. URL: https://www.sciencedirect.com/science/article/pii/S0959440X25000387.

[168]   Václav Skala. "A fast algorithm for line clipping by convex polyhedron in E3". *Computers & Graphics* 21.2 (1997). Graphics Hardware, pages 209–214. ISSN: 0097-8493. DOI: 10.1016/S0097-8493(96)00084-2.

[169]   Farzan Soleymani, Eric Paquet, Herna Lydia Viktor, and Wojtek Michalowski. "Structure-based protein and small molecule generation using EGNN and diffusion models: A comprehensive review". *Computational and Structural Biotechnology Journal* 23 (2024), pages 2779–2797. ISSN: 2001-0370. DOI: https://doi.org/10.1016/j.csbj.2024.06.021. URL: https://www.sciencedirect.com/science/article/pii/S2001037024002228.

[170]   Juan Song, Bangfu Wang, Qingyang Jiang, and Xiaohong Hao. "Exploring the Role of Fractal Geometry in Engineering Image Processing Based on Similarity and Symmetry: A Review". *Symmetry* 16.12 (2024). ISSN: 2073-8994. DOI: 10.3390/sym16121658. URL: https://www.mdpi.com/2073-8994/16/12/1658.

[171]   Jacob O. Spiegel and Jacob D. Durrant. "AutoGrow4: an open-source genetic algorithm for de novo drug design and lead optimization". *Journal of Cheminformatics* 12.1 (2020), pages 1–16. DOI: 10.1186/s13321-020-00429-4. URL: https://doi.org/10.1186/s13321-020-00429-4.

[172] Gilbert Strang. *Introduction to Linear Algebra*. 6th. Wellesley-Cambridge Press, 2023, page 423. ISBN: 978-1-7331466-7-8.

[173] Shuting Sun, Lin Mu, Ruyi Feng, Yifu Chen, and Wei Han. "Quadtree decomposition-based Deep learning method for multiscale coastline extraction with high-resolution remote sensing imagery". *Science of Remote Sensing* 9 (2024), page 100112. ISSN: 2666-0172. DOI: https://doi.org/10.1016/j.srs.2023.100112. URL: https://www.sciencedirect.com/science/article/pii/S2666017223000378.

[174] Ivan E. Sutherland and Gary W. Hodgman. "Reentrant polygon clipping". *Communications of the ACM* 17.1 (1974), pages 32–42. ISSN: 0001-0782. DOI: 10.1145/360767.360802.

[175] Freyr Sverrisson, Jean Feydy, Bruno E. Correia, and Michael M. Bronstein. "Fast end-to-end learning on protein surfaces". *2021 IEEE/CVF Conference on Computer Vision and Pattern Recognition (CVPR)*. 2021, pages 15267–15276. DOI: 10.1109/CVPR46437.2021.01502.

[176] Li-An Tang and T.S. Huang. "An efficient hidden-line removal method based on Z-buffer algorithm". *Proceedings of 1st International Conference on Image Processing*. Volume 1. 1994, 657–660 vol.1. DOI: 10.1109/ICIP.1994.413396.

[177] William C. Thibault and Bruce F. Naylor. "Set operations on polyhedra using binary space partitioning trees". *SIGGRAPH Comput. Graph.* 21.4 (Aug. 1987), pages 153–162. ISSN: 0097-8930. DOI: 10.1145/37402.37421.

[178] Morgan Thomas, Andreas Bender, and Chris de Graaf. "Integrating structure-based approaches in generative molecular design". *Current Opinion in Structural Biology* 79 (2023), page 102559. ISSN: 0959-440X. DOI: https://doi.org/10.1016/j.sbi.2023.102559. URL: https://www.sciencedirect.com/science/article/pii/S0959440X23000337.

[179] Ekaterina Tolstaya, James Paulos, Vijay Kumar, and Alejandro Ribeiro. "Multi-Robot Coverage and Exploration using Spatial Graph Neural Networks". *2021 IEEE/RSJ International Conference on Intelligent Robots and Systems (IROS)*. 2021, pages 8944–8950. DOI: 10.1109/IROS51168.2021.9636675.

[180] Gabriel Tseng, Ivan Zvonkov, Catherine Lilian Nakalembe, and Hannah Kerner. "CropHarvest: A global dataset for crop-type classification". *Thirty-fifth Conference on Neural Information Processing Systems Datasets and Benchmarks Track (Round 2)*. 2021. URL: https://openreview.net/forum?id=JtjzUXPEaCu.

[181] Eva Tuba, Romana Capor-Hrosik, Adis Alihodzic, and Milan Tuba. "Drone Placement for Optimal Coverage by Brain Storm Optimization Algorithm". *Hybrid Intelligent Systems*. Edited by Ajith Abraham, Pranab Kr. Muhuri, Azah Kamilah Muda, and Niketa Gandhi. Cham: Springer International Publishing, 2018, pages 167–176. ISBN: 978-3-319-76351-4.

[182] Eva Tuba, Ira Tuba, Diana Dolicanin-Djekic, Adis Alihodzic, and Milan Tuba. "Efficient drone placement for wireless sensor networks coverage by bare bones fireworks algorithm". *2018 6th International Symposium on Digital Forensic and Security (ISDFS)*. 2018, pages 1–5. DOI: 10.1109/ISDFS.2018.8355349.

[183] Kenneth Christopher Ugwoke, Nwojo Agwu Nnanna, and Saleh El-Yakub Abdullahi. "Simulation-based review of classical, heuristic, and metaheuristic path planning algorithms". *Scientific Reports* 15.1 (2025), pages 1–36. DOI: https://doi.org/10.1038/s41598-025-96614-2.

[184] Bejoy Varghese and S. Krishnakumar. "Fast Fractal Coding of MRI Images using Deep Reinforcement Learning". *International Journal of Advanced Computer Science and Applications* 12.4 (2021). DOI: 10.14569/IJACSA.2021.0120492. URL: http://dx.doi.org/10.14569/IJACSA.2021.0120492.

[185] A. Vera-López, M.A. García-Sánchez, O. Basova, and F.J. Vera-López. "A generalization of Catalan numbers". *Discrete Mathematics* 332 (2014), pages 23–39. ISSN: 0012-365X. DOI: https://doi.org/10.1016/j.disc.2014.05.017.

[186] Prasoon Kumar Vinodkumar, Dogus Karabulut, Egils Avots, Cagri Ozcinar, and Gholamreza Anbarjafari. "Deep Learning for 3D Reconstruction, Augmentation, and Registration: A Review Paper". *Entropy* 26.3 (2024). ISSN: 1099-4300. DOI: 10.3390/e26030235. URL: https://www.mdpi.com/1099-4300/26/3/235.

[187] Serena Vittorio, Filippo Lunghini, Pietro Morerio, Davide Gadioli, Sergio Orlandini, Paulo Silva, Jan Martinovic, Alessandro Pedretti, Domenico Bonanni, Alessio Del Bue, Gianluca Palermo, Giulio Vistoli, and Andrea R. Beccari. "Addressing docking pose selection with structure-based deep learning: Recent advances, challenges and opportunities". *Computational and Structural Biotechnology Journal* 23 (2024), pages 2141–2151. ISSN: 2001-0370. DOI: https://doi.org/10.1016/j.csbj.2024.05.024. URL: https://www.sciencedirect.com/science/article/pii/S2001037024001727.

[188] Sumit Walia, Cheng Ye, Arkid Bera, Dhruvi Lodhavia, and Yatish Turakhia. "TALCO: Tiling Genome Sequence Alignment Using Convergence of Traceback Pointers". *2024 IEEE International Symposium on High-Performance Computer Architecture (HPCA)*. 2024, pages 91–107. DOI: https://doi.org/10.1109/HPCA57654.2024.00044.

[189] Chuhua Wang, Md Alimoor Reza, Vibhas Vats, Yingnan Ju, Nikhil Thakurdesai, Yuchen Wang, David J. Crandall, Soon-heung Jung, and Jeongil Seo. "Deep learning-based 3D reconstruction from multiple images: A survey". *Neurocomputing* 597 (2024), page 128018. ISSN: 0925-2312. DOI: https://doi.org/10.1016/j.neucom.2024.128018. URL: https://www.sciencedirect.com/science/article/pii/S0925231224007896.

[190] Fangjinhua Wang, Marie-Julie Rakotosaona, Michael Niemeyer, Richard Szeliski, Marc Pollefeys, and Federico Tombari. "UniSDF: unifying neural representations for high-fidelity 3D reconstruction of complex scenes with reflections". *Proceedings of the 38th International Conference on Neural Information Processing Systems*. NIPS '24. Vancouver, BC, Canada: Curran Associates Inc., 2025.

[191] Haoyu Wang, Changqing Song, Jinfeng Wang, and Peichao Gao. "A raster-based spatial clustering method with robustness to spatial outliers". *Scientific Reports* 14.1 (2024), pages 1–14. DOI: 10.1038/s41598-024-53066-4. URL: https://doi.org/10.1038/s41598-024-53066-4.

[192] Hongwei Wang, Li He, Shuai Zhang, Ruoyang Bai, and Yunhang Wang. "Mobile Robot Path Planning Considering Obstacle Gap Features". *Applied Sciences* 15.11 (2025). ISSN: 2076-3417. DOI: 10.3390/app15115979. URL: https://www.mdpi.com/2076-3417/15/11/5979.

[193] Huijuan Wang, Yuan Yu, and Quanbo Yuan. "Application of Dijkstra algorithm in robot path-planning". *2011 Second International Conference on Mechanic Automation and Control Engineering*. 2011, pages 1067–1069. DOI: 10.1109/MACE.2011.5987118.

[194] Yumiao Wang, Zhou Zhang, Luwei Feng, Yuchi Ma, and Qingyun Du. "A new attention-based CNN approach for crop mapping using time series Sentinel-2 images". *Computers and Electronics in Agriculture* 184 (2021), page 106090. ISSN: 0168-1699. DOI: https://doi.org/10.1016/j.compag.2021.106090. URL: https://www.sciencedirect.com/science/article/pii/S0168169921001083.

[195] Hui Wei, Qian Yu, and Chengzhuan Yang. "Shape-based object recognition via Evidence Accumulation Inference". *Pattern Recognition Letters* 77 (2016), pages 42–49. ISSN: 0167-8655. DOI: https://doi.org/10.1016/j.patrec.2016.03.022. URL: https://www.sciencedirect.com/science/article/pii/S0167865516300265.

[196] Yanming Wei, Quan Zou, Furong Tang, and Liang Yu. "WMSA: a novel method for multiple sequence alignment of DNA sequences". *Bioinformatics* 38.22 (Sept. 2022), pages 5019–5025. ISSN: 1367-4811. DOI: https://doi.org/10.1093/bioinformatics/btac658. eprint: https://academic.oup.com/bioinformatics/article-pdf/38/22/5019/47153749/btac658.pdf.

[197] Kevin Wilson. *The Absolute Beginner's Guide to Python Programming*. Apress Berkeley, CA, 2022. ISBN: 978-1-4842-8715-6. DOI: https://doi.org/10.1007/978-1-4842-8716-3.

[198] Fang Wu, Lirong Wu, Dragomir Radev, Jinbo Xu, and Stan Z. Li. "Integration of pre-trained protein language models into geometric deep learning networks". *Communications Biology* 6.1 (2023), pages 1–8. DOI: 10.1038/s42003-023-05133-1. URL: https://doi.org/10.1038/s42003-023-05133-1.

[199] Xianfeng Wu, Xinyi Liu, Junfei Wang, Zhongyuan Lai, Jing Zhou, and Xia Liu. "Point cloud classification based on transformer". *Computers and Electrical Engineering* 104 (2022), page 108413. ISSN: 0045-7906. DOI: https://doi.org/10.1016/j.compeleceng.2022.108413. URL: https://www.sciencedirect.com/science/article/pii/S0045790622006309.

[200] Xuejin Wu, Guangming Wang, and Nachuan Shen. "Research on obstacle avoidance optimization and path planning of autonomous vehicles based on attention mechanism combined with multimodal information decision-making thoughts of robots". *Frontiers in Neurorobotics* Volume 17 - 2023 (2023). ISSN: 1662-5218. DOI: 10.3389/fnbot.2023.1269447. URL: https://www.frontiersin.org/journals/neurorobotics/articles/10.3389/fnbot.2023.1269447.

[201] Zhipeng Xi, Ying Lu, Jianjun Gui, and Xiaozhou Zhu. "Survey on UAV Coverage Path Planning and Trajectory Optimization". *Proceedings of 2021 5th Chinese Conference on Swarm Intelligence and Cooperative Control*. Edited by Zhang Ren, Mengyi Wang, and Yongzhao Hua. Singapore: Springer Nature Singapore, 2023, pages 1560–1572. ISBN: 978-981-19-3998-3.

[202] Ke Xiao. *Image Data Structures and Converting Algorithms: The Research on Raster, Vector, and Quadtree structures and Converting Algorithms between them*. LAP LAMBERT Academic Publishing, 2011. ISBN: 978-3843394734. URL: https://www.amazon.com/Image-Data-Structures-Converting-Algorithms/dp/3843394733.

[203] Chuan Xu, Beikang Wang, Zhiwei Ye, and Liye Mei. "ETQ-Matcher: Efficient Quadtree-Attention-Guided Transformer for Detector-Free Aerial–Ground Image Matching". *Remote Sensing* 17.7 (2025). ISSN: 2072-4292. DOI: 10.3390/rs17071300. URL: https://www.mdpi.com/2072-4292/17/7/1300.

[204] Tong Xu. "Recent advances in Rapidly-exploring random tree: A review". *Heliyon* 10.11 (2024), e32451. ISSN: 2405-8440. DOI: https://doi.org/10.1016/j.heliyon.2024.e32451. URL: https://www.sciencedirect.com/science/article/pii/S2405844024084822.

[205] Hailun Yan, Albert Lau, and Hongchao Fan. "Evaluating Deep Learning Advances for Point Cloud Semantic Segmentation in Urban Environments". *KN - Journal of Cartography and Geographic Information* 75.1 (2025), pages 3–23. DOI: 10.1007/s42489-025-00185-1. URL: https://doi.org/10.1007/s42489-025-00185-1.

[206] Guang Yang, Xia Wu, and Jing Zhang. "A dynamic balanced quadtree for real-time streaming data". *Knowledge-Based Systems* 263 (2023), page 110291. ISSN: 0950-7051. DOI: https://doi.org/10.1016/j.knosys.2023.110291. URL: https://www.sciencedirect.com/science/article/pii/S0950705123000412.

[207] Heng Yang, Rehman Qureshi, and Ahmet Sacan. "Protein surface representation and analysis by dimension reduction". *Proteome Science* 10.1 (2012). DOI: 10.1186/1477-5956-10-S1-S1. URL: https://doi.org/10.1186/1477-5956-10-S1-S1.

[208] Zhou Yijun, Xi Jiadong, and Luo Chen. "A Fast Bi-Directional A* Algorithm Based on Quad-Tree Decomposition and Hierarchical Map". *IEEE Access* 9 (2021), pages 102877–102885. DOI: 10.1109/ACCESS.2021.3094854.

[209] Kun Zhang, Ao Zhang, Xiaohong Wang, and Weisong Li. "Deep-learning-based point cloud completion methods: A review". *Graphical Models* 136 (2024), page 101233. ISSN: 1524-0703. DOI: https://doi.org/10.1016/j.gmod.2024.101233. URL: https://www.sciencedirect.com/science/article/pii/S1524070324000213.

[210] Liding Zhang, Kuanqi Cai, Zewei Sun, Zhenshan Bing, Chaoqun Wang, Luis Figueredo, Sami Haddadin, and Alois Knoll. "Motion planning for robotics: A review for sampling-based planners". *Biomimetic Intelligence and Robotics* 5.1 (2025), page 100207. ISSN: 2667-3797. DOI: https://doi.org/10.1016/j.birob.2024.100207. URL: https://www.sciencedirect.com/science/article/pii/S2667379724000652.

[211] Xiang Zhang, Guillaume Touya, and Martijn Meijers. "Automated Map Generalization: Emerging Techniques and New Trends (Editorial)". *Journal of Geovisualization and Spatial Analysis* 8.1 (2024), pages 1–3. DOI: 10.1007/s41651-024-00174-4. URL: https://doi.org/10.1007/s41651-024-00174-4.

[212] Zhijie Zhang, Hao Fu, Juan Yang, and Yunhan Lin. "Deep reinforcement learning for path planning of autonomous mobile robots in complicated environments". *Complex & Intelligent Systems* 11 (May 2025). DOI: 10.1007/s40747-025-01906-9.

[213] Jiangpeng Zhao, Heping Xie, Cunbao Li, and Yifei Liu. "Deep Learning-Based Reconstruction of 3D Morphology of Geomaterial Particles from Single-View 2D Images". *Materials* 17.20 (2024). ISSN: 1996-1944. DOI: 10.3390/ma17205100. URL: https://www.mdpi.com/1996-1944/17/20/5100.

[214] Shijie Zhao, Tianran Zhang, Liang Cai, and Ronghua Yang. "Triangulation topology aggregation optimizer: A novel mathematics-based meta-heuristic algorithm for continuous optimization and engineering applications". *Expert Systems with Applications* 238 (2024), page 121744. ISSN: 0957-4174. DOI: https://doi.org/10.1016/j.eswa.2023.121744. URL: https://www.sciencedirect.com/science/article/pii/S0957417423022467.

[215] Tianjie Zhao, Sheng Wang, Chaojun Ouyang, Min Chen, Chenying Liu, Jin Zhang, Long Yu, Fei Wang, Yong Xie, Jun Li, Fang Wang, Sabine Grunwald, Bryan M. Wong, Fan Zhang, Zhen Qian, Yongjun Xu, Chengqing Yu, Wei Han, Tao Sun, Zezhi Shao, Tangwen Qian, Zhao Chen, Jiangyuan Zeng, Huai Zhang, Husi Letu, Bing Zhang, Li Wang, Lei Luo, Chong Shi, Hongjun Su, Hongsheng Zhang, Shuai Yin, Ni Huang, Wei Zhao, Nan Li, Chaolei Zheng, Yang Zhou, Changping Huang, Defeng Feng, Qingsong Xu, Yan Wu, Danfeng Hong, Zhenyu Wang, Yinyi Lin, Tangtang Zhang, Prashant Kumar, Antonio Plaza, Jocelyn Chanussot, Jiabao Zhang, Jiancheng Shi, and Lizhe Wang. "Artificial intelligence for geoscience: Progress, challenges, and perspectives". *The Innovation* 5.5 (2024), page 100691. ISSN: 2666-6758. DOI: https://doi.org/10.1016/j.xinn.2024.100691. URL: https://www.sciencedirect.com/science/article/pii/S2666675824001292.

[216] Chengmin Zhou, Bingding Huang, and Pasi Fränti. "A review of motion planning algorithms for intelligent robots". *Journal of Intelligent Manufacturing* 33.2 (2022). DOI: https://doi.org/10.1007/s10845-021-01867-z.

[217] Jin Zhou, Zhangfan Yang, Ying He, Junkai Ji, Qiuzhen Lin, and Jianqiang Li. "A novel molecular docking program based on a multi-swarm competitive algorithm". *Swarm and Evolutionary Computation* 78 (2023), page 101292. ISSN: 2210-6502. DOI: https://doi.org/10.1016/j.swevo.2023.101292. URL: https://www.sciencedirect.com/science/article/pii/S2210650223000652.

[218] Yuquan Zhou, Li Yan, Yaxi Han, Hong Xie, and Yinghao Zhao. "A Survey on the Key Technologies of UAV Motion Planning". *Drones* 9.3 (2025). ISSN: 2504-446X. DOI: 10.3390/drones9030194. URL: https://www.mdpi.com/2504-446X/9/3/194.

[219] Chunyu Zhu, Tinghao Zhang, Qiong Wu, Yachao Li, and Qin Zhong. "An Implicit Transformer-based Fusion Method for Hyperspectral and Multispectral Remote Sensing Image". *International Journal of Applied Earth Observation and Geoinformation* 131 (2024), page 103955. ISSN: 1569-8432. DOI: https://doi.org/10.1016/j.jag.2024.103955. URL: https://www.sciencedirect.com/science/article/pii/S1569843224003091.

[220] Fubin Zhu, Changda Zhu, Zihan Fang, Wenhao Lu, and Jianjun Pan. "Using Constrained K-Means Clustering for Soil Texture Mapping with Limited Soil Samples". *Agronomy* 15.5 (2025). ISSN: 2073-4395. DOI: 10.3390/agronomy15051220. URL: https://www.mdpi.com/2073-4395/15/5/1220.

Index

The manufacturer's authorised representative in the EU is Springer
Nature Customer Service Centre GmbH, Europaplatz 3, 69115 Heidelberg,
Germany. If you have any concerns regarding our products, please
contact ProductSafety@springernature.com

Printed and bound by CPI Group (UK) Ltd, Croydon, CR0 4YY

03/06/2026

02126646-0001